A MODERN INTRODUCTION TO

COLLEGE MATHEMATICS

By ISRAEL H. ROSE

Associate Professor of Mathematics

University of Massachusetts

NEW YORK · JOHN WILEY & SONS, INC.

London · Chapman & Hall, Limited

A MODERN

introduction to

COLLEGE
MATHEMATICS

TO MY SON
STEVEN

It is written: "In my Father's house are many mansions."

The house of mathematics has many mansions also; and the over-all view which a writer takes of the house of mathematics plays a considerable role in determining the particular door by which he chooses to enter the rambling structure and the route he takes in touring through its various mansions.

Mathematics has been very nearly all things to all men: art, science, language, method, and tool. It has been called on the one hand "queen" and on the other, "handmaiden" of the sciences. Some have defined it as "the study of number and space," others, as "the science of drawing necessary conclusions." Some have found it the quintessence of divine order, truth, and beauty, others, "a form of low cunning."

I shall quarrel with none of these characterizations. A case may be (and in fact has been) made for each. But the point of view to which I shall subscribe in this textbook is that it is *ideas* that are fundamental in mathematics and that mathematics is best characterized, expressed, and understood in terms of its ideas.

It is important to consider the sources and uses of these ideas, and the symbols and language in which they are expressed. But even more important, and indeed absolutely necessary to a skillful manipulation of symbols and to an ability to apply mathematics well and with confidence, is an understanding of mathematical ideas themselves. In the words of Alfred North Whitehead, in *An Introduction to Mathematics:*

> The reason for this failure of the science to live up to its reputation is that its fundamental ideas are not explained to the student disentangled from the technical procedure which has been invented to facilitate their exact presentation in particular instances. Accordingly, the unfortunate learner finds himself struggling to acquire a knowledge of a mass of details which are not illuminated by any general conception.

The first two chapters of this book have therefore been devoted to a treatment of ideas that are especially pervasive in mathematics: sets; one-to-one correspondences between sets; functions, operations, and relations defined on sets; and the like.

These ideas have existed in mathematics since its very inception, but it is only comparatively recently, perhaps within the last hundred years, that they have been named, studied, and consciously used in the formulation of mathematics. It is in this sense that these ideas are "modern"; it is mainly upon this book's concern with and use of these ideas that the book bases its claim to modernity.

Until recently, among all the branches of mathematics, the reasoning processes of mathematics (that is to say the processes by which mathematics arrives at and justifies its statements) were given serious attention only in geometry. But today we recognize that all of mathematics may be formulated in the familiar logical pattern of Euclid and that a study and application of this reasoning process contributes to a clearer understanding of mathematics.

Therefore, in keeping with the modern trend, I devote attention also to the logical structure of mathematics.

Briefly, the goal sought-for in this textbook's consideration and use of these basic ideas and reasoning processes has been to arrive at a simple, modern, logically sound treatment of elementary mathematics— one in which unity and structure are visible to the naked eye.

I do not contend that a bare logical treatment alone can do justice to mathematics. Intuitive and physical arguments *and* the deductive method are inseparable partners in the development of mathematics. I have not attempted to slight one at the expense of the other, but only to put each in its proper perspective.

There is no apology, therefore, for the intuitive "free-wheeling" treatments which will be found in the text preceding and following more rigorous approaches to the same material. Furthermore, it is here freely admitted that not everything in the book has been done with rigor nor, where rigor has been attempted, has every logical "t" been crossed. It is my contention that it is not necessary to pursue these quixotic objectives in order to make the student aware of the necessity and advantages of logical structure in mathematics.

In Chapter 4, a logical structure is exhibited for the set of real numbers. The material of this chapter may very well seem strange to the student and, perhaps because of its strangeness, difficult. The chapter may seem overly concerned with things the student already "knows" too well to trouble about further. But this information is illustrative of a method (the deductive method) that is of the highest importance not only to mathematics but to all organized knowledge.   Since a great deal of the value of this chapter lies in its *exemplification* of certain ideas, it should be noted that not all of the chapter need be done in detail in order that benefit be derived from it.

The material in this book has been designed for, and for several years (in preliminary form) has been used at, the University of Massachusetts by classes of randomly chosen freshmen with a minimal background of one and one-half years of high-school algebra and one year of high-school geometry.

The following situation has had much to do with the content and organization of the book:

The advantages of a "common core" of mathematics for all students are manifest; on the other hand, the demands of the "scientific" or "technical" student are too specialized to be linked with those of the "liberal artist" for too long a time.   Furthermore, the entering freshman frequently has not made a final decision even as to the general field of his major.   It would be well to allow him at least a little more time to make up his mind and at the same time offer him that information which would be most helpful to him in coming to his decision—that is to say, offer him a considerably broader view of mathematics than most students have encountered in high school.   Finally, it happens that the foundational material which is so important for the "technical" student represents an aspect of mathematics that is interesting and valuable to the "liberal arts" student also, unquestionably more interesting and valuable, for example, than the rote calculation and manipulation with which he has for so long been afflicted.

To meet, so far as possible, the foregoing situation and arguments, the textbook has been planned so that two types of year courses, of six credit hours each, may be given from it.   In order to carry out this plan the book has been organized in the three parts described below, each constituting all or most of a semester's work.

All students may take a common course for the first semester, based upon Part 1:

Part I: Foundational material and an introduction to analytic geometry and trigonometry.

This one-semester unit represents an attempt to construct for "technical" students as firm as possible a basis for further mathematical study and at the same time to present to "liberal arts" students those aspects of mathematics which to them would be most interesting and most intellectually and culturally enriching.   It is hoped that both will gain from this semester's work a better insight into the nature and role of mathematics.

At the end of his first semester the "technical" student may elect a second semester based entirely or mainly upon Part II of the text, whereas the "liberal arts" student may elect a second semester based entirely or mainly upon Part III:

Part II: Analytic geometry and trigonometry.

This semester is designed for those who have shown some degree of competence in Part I and who desire (or who think they may at some time desire) to continue their mathematical studies after this first year's work. This study is intended to be followed by a course in the calculus.

Part III: Introductions to calculus and statistics.

Other organizations of the contents of this book to suit quarter-systems, four-credit-hour courses, etc., are possible.

In constructing a development of elementary mathematics that aims at accuracy and some degree of rigor, it is inevitable that there shall be material at too high a level, or perhaps simply too time consuming for general presentation. Nevertheless, to arrive at an account as complete as possible and to meet the needs of better students, material of this sort has been included. In the book this optional material is identified by means of fine print.

Occasionally, reference to earlier fine-print material is made in the regular text. In these instances the fine-print material may be deferred until the reference occurs.

ISRAEL H. ROSE

Amherst, Massachusetts
March, 1959

ACKNOWLEDGMENTS

My thanks and appreciation go first of all to Dr. Allen E. Andersen, head of the Mathematics Department at the University of Massachusetts, for paving the administrative way to the experimental course from which this book grew, for constant encouragement and advice in this project, and for many helpful suggestions now incorporated in the book.

I am happy to inscribe here also my great respect and affection for the wonderful students and teachers who were involved in that experimental course. Both bore with remarkably little complaint the burden of working with notes, which were, let us say, not altogether without typographical and other faults. I am most grateful for the enthusiasm they displayed and for the valuable ideas which they contributed.

I am further indebted to Mr. A. J. Ryan, manager of the University of Massachusetts Bookstore for his keen appreciation of academic problems, for his skill with red-tape scissors, and for help far beyond the line of duty in the task of reproducing and distributing the first drafts of his text; to Mrs. Bernice Martin, for her expert and intelligent typing of the manuscript; and to Jack Brin, Richard M. Kennedy, and George C. Sethares, graduate students at the University of Massachusetts, for help in working out and checking answers to problems.

Finally, thanks are due the following publishers for permission to reproduce tables and passages of appreciable length from the indicated books: The Macmillan Company, *Number, the Language of Science,* by Tobias Dantzig (1933), and *The Macmillan Tables* (1935); Simon and Schuster, Inc., *Men of Mathematics,* by E. T. Bell; J. B. Lippincott Company, *Blood Pressure,* by Damon Runyon.

I. H. R.

CONTENTS

* Fine-print (optional) sections; see Preface, p. x.

P A R T
II   ANALYTIC GEOMETRY AND TRIGONOMETRY

P A R T
III   **INTRODUCTIONS TO THE CALCULUS AND**
          PROBABILITY AND STATISTICS

LIST OF SYMBOLS AND ABBREVIATIONS

(Some, whose inclusion in this list would not
be particularly helpful, have been omitted)

Symbol or Abbreviation		See page or pages
$\Leftrightarrow$	"is equivalent to"	82
$\doteq$	"is approximately equal to"	117
d	"distance"	140
x_P, y_P	"abscissa of point P," "ordinate of point P"	148, 149
ccd	"Cartesian coordinate degree"	201
$\measuredangle(l_1, l_2)$	"the counterclockwise angle from line l_1 to line l_2"	243, 244
ccr	"Cartesian coordinate radian"	250
Σ	"summation"	435, 441
$n!$	"n factorial"	455
nPr	"the number of permutations of a set of n elements taken r at a time"	456
$\binom{n}{r}$	"the number of combinations of a set of n elements taken r at a time"	466

PART I

FOUNDATIONS AND AN INTRODUCTION TO ANALYTIC GEOMETRY AND TRIGONOMETRY

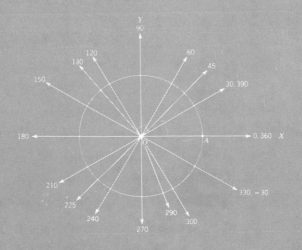

CHAPTER **I** SETS

The White Rabbit put on his spectacles. "Where shall I begin, please, your Majesty?" he asked.
"Begin at the beginning," the King said gravely . . .
LEWIS CARROLL: *Alice in Wonderland*

Here and elsewhere we shall not obtain the best insight into things until we actually see them growing from the beginning . . .
ARISTOTLE: *Politics*

1.1 INTRODUCTION

Where *is* the beginning of mathematics? The evidence at hand today seems to indicate that the earliest beings to whom the name "man" could be applied lived some 500,000 years ago, but that modern man, the creature whom anthropologists call "homo sapiens," did not make his appearance until some time between 50,000 and 25,000 years ago. To date the origin of mathematics from the birth of homo sapiens is actually to estimate only conservatively, for there are some who see, in stories like the following, evidence of a rudimentary mathematical sense even among the lower animals:

A squire was determined to shoot a crow which made its nest in the watch-tower of his estate. Repeatedly he had tried to surprise the bird, but in vain: at the approach of man the crow would leave its nest. From a distant tree it would watchfully wait until the man had left the tower and then return to its nest. One day the squire hit upon a ruse: two men entered the tower, one remained within, the other came out and went on. But the bird was not deceived: it kept away until the man within came out. The experiment was repeated on the succeeding days with two, three, then four men, yet without success. Finally, five men were sent: as before, all entered the tower, and one remained while the other four came out and went away. Here the crow lost count. Unable to distinguish between four and five it promptly returned to its nest.

3

Whether this story (which may be found on p. 3 of *Number, the Language of Science* by Tobias Dantzig) proves that the crow could count up to four is open to considerable question, as we shall soon be in a position to see. But that the crow came near to doing something at least closely related to counting is undeniable. We shall want to examine this "something" carefully, for it is both logically and historically very nearly the first, if not actually the first, of all mathematical activities.

Indeed, it is a remarkable feature of mathematics that underlying its earliest manifestations are one or two surprisingly simple concepts which over 25,000 years later still lie at the roots of and permeate and unify all of mathematics; and that is why we begin our study just here:

1.2 SETS AND ONE-TO-ONE CORRESPONDENCES

The "something" referred to above is an activity more basic than counting and is, in fact, precisely this: *The direct comparison of two collections of objects to determine whether or not they are equally numerous.*

To make clear the distinction between counting and our allegedly more basic activity, let us consider some instances of the latter. Suppose, for example, that upon entering a classroom we find each student seated in a properly restrained fashion upon only one chair which he shares with no one else. Then if all the chairs are occupied, *without counting either students or chairs*, we can conclude that there are exactly as many of one as there are of the other. Or, when we read in the Bible that "There went in two and two unto Noah into the ark, the male and the female . . .," we know that the males and the females entering into the ark were equally numerous, even though we do not know how many of each there were. And man, placing the tips of his fingers together in the well-known judicious gesture, must have recognized a certain something which the fingers of one hand had in common with the fingers of the other, long before he gave that common property the name "five."

In other words, we recognize that two collections of objects are equally numerous if it is possible to "match" or "pair off" or "associate in pairs" all the members of one collection with all the members of the other.

We pause at this point to remark that our first excursion into mathematics is immediately concerned with *collections of objects*. This preoccupation with collections of objects is profoundly characteristic of mathematics. Indeed, because they must refer to it so often in their work, mathematicians usually use the shorter term "set" in place of "collection of objects," and from now on we shall generally do the same; and we shall call the objects which constitute a set the *members* or the *elements* of the set.

Further terminology. We shall say that an element of a set *belongs to* or *is contained in* or simply *is in* the set; and that a set *contains* its elements. For example: George Washington belongs to the set of all presidents of the United States; the set of all odd whole numbers contains the number 7.

Notation. If x is an element of a set S, we write: $x \in S$ (read: x belongs to S).

Even before he could count 1, 2, 3, and so on, would it have been possible for primitive man to know whether he had as many wives as his neighbor and to record their number? The process we have been discussing would certainly have enabled him to do the first, but as a matter of fact, it would have sufficed for the second also. The oldest mathematical records which exist, some dating back more than 10,000 years, are animal bones on which marks, arranged regularly in equal groups, have been scratched. Each scratch, of course, was associated with some object. Again we have an illustration of the "matching" process, this time used actually to construct a set whose members are to be as numerous as those of a given set.

We see, then, that from earliest times the idea of a perfect matching of the members of two sets occupied an important position in the thought of man. Here we have one of the great foundational concepts of mathematics, to which mathematicians have given the name: "one-to-one correspondence." We proceed to give this idea the prominence it deserves:

> A one-to-one correspondence is said to exist between two sets when it is possible to associate the members of one set with the members of the other in such a way that each member of each set is associated with just one member of the other.

For example, it is possible for a normal person to associate the fingers of his left hand with the fingers of his right in such a way that each finger of each hand is associated with just one finger of the other. Hence we may say that these two sets of fingers are in one-to-one correspondence.

Another example: It is possible to "establish a one-to-one correspondence" between the set of letters $\{a, b, c\}$ and the set of names $\{$Tom, Dick, Harry$\}$. Here for example, is a diagram of one such association:

$$a \leftrightarrow \text{Dick}$$
$$b \leftrightarrow \text{Tom}$$
$$c \leftrightarrow \text{Harry}$$

Notation. As in the preceding example, we shall generally use braces: $\{ \ \}$, to enclose the elements of a set; "$\leftrightarrow$" is read "corresponds to," and may be read either from left to right, or from right to left.

1.3 THE NUMBER OF A SET: PART I

Now, to return to our primitive man and his wives, it is clear that by scratching a mark for each of his wives, he could establish a one-to-one correspondence between scratches and wives and thus *record* what we now call their number without actually *naming* or *counting* their number. The marks, however, might at the same time have been in one-to-one correspondence with some other set, say a collection of war-clubs. War-clubs, marks, wives, and indeed all other sets which are in one-to-one correspondence with each of these sets—what have they in common? It is an abstract property which we call the *number* of each collection.

For example, in Fig. 1.1, the abstract property which each set exhibits by virtue of the one-to-one correspondence which exists between any two of the sets is a number which has the name "three."

Fig. 1.1 Several concrete examples of the abstract idea "three."

It turns out, then, that in terms of the concept of a one-to-one correspondence, one may explain what is meant by the "number of a set."

But before we pursue this idea further, we must digress for a moment: an important word has just forced its way into our discussion, and it demands our immediate attention.

1.4 ON THE WORD "ABSTRACT"

We refer to the very much overworked adjective "abstract." It is often applied to mathematics, and entirely with justice. Mathematics *is* very much occupied with abstractions. The trouble is, however, that "abstract" is one of those words which is burdened with too many meanings.

Among them are "difficult to understand" and "having little to do with the real world"; these, unfortunately, are what most people have in mind when they apply the word to mathematics. Actually, these interpretations fall very wide of the mark. This is a most unhappy state of affairs, for a correct understanding of the word "abstract," as it is used in mathematics, is essential if we are to understand what mathematics itself is. Let us therefore try to remedy the situation.

This is a case where nothing suits the word so well as its derivation. The meaning of the pair of Latin words from which "abstract" stems is "drawn from," and *that is the principal sense* in which it is used in mathematics. To illustrate with an example:

Suppose there were to be placed before you a lump of sugar, a polar bear, an albino rabbit, a piece of uncolored chalk, a bottle of milk, the whale named Moby Dick, and (since by now you may have a headache) an aspirin tablet. That would certainly be a very oddly assorted collection, but undoubtedly you would observe a quality which they share in common, not only with each other, but with many, many other things as well. It is, of course, the quality called "whiteness."

Since we have, so to speak, isolated, or separated, or drawn from these several specific objects the general idea of whiteness, "whiteness" may properly be called an abstraction. And incidentally, any one of the particular objects from which an abstract idea is drawn is called a *concrete example* of that abstraction. Thus, a lump of sugar is a concrete example of the abstraction "whiteness." (Another illustration of the concept of abstraction may be found in Fig. 1.1.)

Although, as in the example we have just discussed, an abstraction may be closely related to a physical sense, it is well to remember the role played by the mind in the process of abstraction. As early as 500 B.C. the Greek philosopher Heraclitus remarked:

> The eyes and ears are bad witnesses for men, if the mind cannot interpret what they say.

The thought is echoed by the French novelist Proust, some 2400 years later:

> . . . their past is cluttered with innumerable snapshots that are useless because the intelligence has not "developed" them.

Indeed, there are abstractions whose connection with a physical sense is difficult to establish. "Justice," for example, being a concept derived from many specific situations, is an abstraction, but not one we can easily see, or taste, or smell, or hear, or touch. We observe, then, that the word "abstract" often carries the connotation of something which is perceived more by the mind than by the senses.

We may consider the statement that an abstraction is something removed from reality as acceptable, but only if we understand the phrase "removed from" to mean not "far away from" but "extracted from." Abstractions, although they differ in the extent to which they are evident to the physical senses, are nevertheless either derived immediately from, or else may eventually be traced to, something quite real.

An abstraction is a concentrated idea distilled from large masses of particular things. Yet, in its most useful applications, an abstraction is typical and representative of each particular concrete example; something which gets at the "heart of the matter;" something actually very close to the essential reality of the situation from which it is drawn.

Generality is, of course, an inherent characteristic of every abstraction. An abstract idea is by its very nature something which is gathered from a number of instances. Indeed, the generality of its application is often a measure of its importance. The qualities of representing the essence of a matter, of cutting through and brushing aside irrelevancies, and of generality of application are much more typical of abstractions than the purely incidental difficulties associated with their discovery and use.

1.5 THE NUMBER OF A SET: PART II

Now, finally, let us return to our primitive man and his dawning conception of "number." Somewhere, at some moment in the dim past, there must have existed a prehistoric genius who recognized the abstract property shared by:

> the set of his hands
> the set of his feet
> the set of his eyes
> the set of his ears

and in fact by all collections of objects in one-to-one correspondence with each of these sets, and who signalized his recognition by giving this quality which they shared a name corresponding to our word "two."

We are led to a second great mathematical idea, one which is related to the first. It is the idea of "the number of a set," or "the number of elements in a set," or "cardinal number." It is the type of number we use to answer the question "How many?"

A *cardinal number* describes an abstract property shared by all sets which can be put into one-to-one correspondence with a given set.

For example, the cardinal number 2 describes an abstract property shared by all sets which can be put into one-to-one correspondence with the set of names: Romeo and Juliet. The cardinal number 5 describes an abstract property exhibited by all sets which are in one-to-one correspondence with the set of toes of the writer's right foot.

▶ **EXERCISE 1**

1. List, explain the meaning of, and give original examples to illustrate the most important concepts encountered in Sections 1.1–1.5.

2. Is it possible to set up a one-to-one correspondence different from that of Section 1.2 between the sets {a, b, c} and {Tom, Dick, Harry}? If so, how many are possible in all?

3. Show that a one-to-one correspondence exists between the set of numbers {1, 2} and the set of letters {a, b}.   Write down all possible one-to-one correspondences between these sets and tell how many of these correspondences there are.

4. Name a pair of sets, each of which contains only a single element. Write down all possible one-to-one correspondences between these sets. How many of these correspondences are there?

5. Name a pair of sets in one-to-one correspondence with each other, but not with any of the sets mentioned in Problems 2, 3, and 4, above. Write down all possible one-to-one correspondences between the pair of sets you have chosen, and tell how many of these correspondences there are.

6. Name, in each of the following cases, an abstract idea drawn from the items included in that case:

(a) Sugar and saccharine.

(b) A baseball team and the Supreme Court.

(c) The sun, a full moon, and a penny.

(d) A ray of light and a taut string.

(e) "One," "two," "three," "four," "five."

(f) "Two and two make four" and "night follows day."

7. Make up a question of your own like Problem 6, above, and answer it.

8. Is every set in one-to-one correspondence with itself? Justify your answer.

9. What is the total number of one-to-one correspondences which may be established between a pair of sets, each of which contains five elements?

10. Write down a formula, or state a rule, for computing the total number of one-to-one correspondences which it is possible to establish between a pair of sets, if each set of the pair contains n elements.

1.6 THE NATURAL NUMBERS

Having mastered the concept of a one-to-one correspondence, our friend homo sapiens found himself ready to count.   To the set consisting of all the index fingers on his right hand—and to each set in one-to-one correspondence with that set—he assigned the cardinal number "1" (or something equivalent to it in his language).

We have already indicated how "2," "3," and "5" may be similarly defined. However, if we were to attempt to define each of the cardinal numbers in this way, that is by exhibiting a sample set, we would be faced with a never-ending task. The resolution of this problem (which will be found later on in the text) is beyond our present scope, but that need not delay our progress.

We shall simply assume that the student is familiar with the set of numbers he first used in counting: 1, 2, 3, . . . (the three dots are read "and so on"), and following traditional mathematical terminology, we shall call this set of numbers the set of *natural numbers*.

Later they will appear again under the name *positive integers*. Other names by which they have been known are "whole numbers" and "counting numbers."

"Natural number" and "cardinal number" are not synonymous; for although every natural number is a cardinal number, it is *not* true that every cardinal number is a natural number. In fact, zero and the natural numbers form a subset of the cardinal numbers called the *finite* cardinal numbers; there are other cardinal numbers: A cardinal number which is neither zero nor a natural number is called an *infinite* cardinal number. For example, the number of points on a line is certainly not zero, nor is it a natural number; it is an *infinite* cardinal number. Furthermore, a *set* is called finite or infinite, depending upon whether its cardinal number is finite or infinite. (We pursue the subject no further here, but refer the interested reader to George Gamow's *One, Two, Three, Infinity*, available in a pocket-book edition.)

The natural numbers are, of course, the most primitive of all numbers; yet they play an exceptionally important role in mathematics. The branch of mathematics called the "theory of numbers" is devoted entirely to a study of their properties; many other fields of mathematics may be developed, using the natural numbers as a foundation. A measure of the respect with which mathematicians regard the natural numbers may be gleaned from the following statements, made by two great nineteenth-century mathematicians. (Their terminology is different from ours, but essentially they are talking about the natural numbers):

"God made integers, all else is the work of man."
(Kronecker)

"Integral numbers are the fountainhead of all mathematics."
(Minkowski)

1.7 SUBSETS AND NULLSETS

Suppose we were offered the opportunity to choose, from among the set of people Tom, Dick, and Harry, some to go along on a picnic.

Then here are some choices of picnic-companions which we could make:

(1) Tom
(2) Dick
(3) Harry
(4) Tom and Dick
(5) Tom and Harry
(6) Dick and Harry
(7) Tom, Dick and Harry

Each of these seven sets is called a *subset* of the original set of people.

However, we have overlooked one possibility. Just as we might, feeling very friendly toward everyone, have chosen all of the people of the given set to go along with us (choice (7) above), so, in a more disagreeable mood, we might have decided to allow *none* of them to come. To take care of cases like this, mathematicians make use of the concept of a *nullset*, that is, a set which contains no elements whatever. We shall use the letter N to denote this set.

It is plausible to stipulate (and in fact, with sharper mathematical tools than we have available here at the moment it may be proved) that N is a subset of any set whatever; for given *any* set, one may choose from it exactly no elements.

We see, then, that it is reasonable to add one more subset, N, to the seven subsets above, making 8 subsets in all derivable from a set of 3 objects.

We now state the following definitions formally:

Definitions. A set A is said to be a *subset* of a set B if each element of A is also an element of B.

The *nullset* (denoted N) is the set which contains no elements.

Further terminology. If set A is a subset of set B, we also say that A *is contained in B*, or that *B contains A*; for example: the set of all English verbs is contained in the set of all English words.

Notation. If set A is contained in set B, we write: $A \subset B$ (read: "A is contained in B"), or $B \supset A$ (read: B contains A).

Relations among subsets of a set may often be clearly exhibited (see Fig. 1.2) by means of an "inclusion diagram" (sometimes termed a "Venn diagram").

The first diagram of Fig. 1.2 indicates, for example, that the set of all odd whole numbers is a subset of the set of all whole numbers; the lower indicates that the set of all two-letter English words and the set of all English verbs are subsets of the set of all English words, and that these subsets have certain elements in common, among which are the words go, is, am.

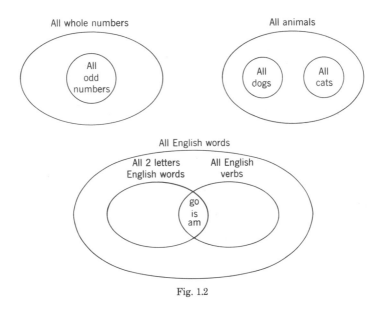

Fig. 1.2

1.8 UNION AND INTERSECTION OF SETS

Given a pair of sets A, B, we consider two very natural ways of forming a new set from them.

The first is simply to "combine" the given sets; the result is called the union of the given sets, and denoted $A \cup B$ (read: A union B or the union of A and B).

Suppose, for example, that at a certain school (in which different students never have the same first name) there is a chess team (which we shall call set A) and a checker team (which we shall call set B), and that the members of the chess team are Tom, Dick, and Harry, and of the checker team, Dick, Harry, and James. That is:

$$A = \{\text{Tom, Dick, Harry}\}$$
$$B = \{\text{Harry, Dick, James}\}$$

Then if we were to combine the two teams into one, the members of the new team would be Tom, Dick, Harry, and James. That is:

$$A \cup B = \{\text{Tom, Dick, Harry, James}\}$$

A second method of forming a new set from a given pair A, B is to choose as elements of the new set only those elements "common" to the given pair. The result is called the "intersection" of the given sets and denoted $A \cap B$ (read: A intersection B or the intersection of A and B).

Thus, if A and B are as in the preceding example:

$$A \cap B = \{\text{Dick, Harry}\}.$$

Now we make the formal definitions:

Definitions. Let A and B be sets. Then:

$A \cup B$ (read: A union B) is the set consisting of all elements which belong either to A, or to B, or to both.

$A \cap B$ (read: A intersection B) is the set consisting of all elements which belong both to A and to B.

NOTE 1. The symbols for "union" and "intersection" are sometimes, and for obvious reasons, read "cup" and "cap," respectively.

NOTE 2. "either ... or ...," as used in mathematics, does not exclude the possibility "both." That is to say, if an element is both in set A and in set B, it is considered to satisfy the condition that it be either in A or in B. As a consequence of this understanding, the definition above is redundant: the words "or to both" may be deleted.

1.9 EQUALITY OF SETS

It may seem superfluous to state the following, but it turns out to be useful to do so:

Two sets are equal (or "the same") if and only if each element of one is also an element of the other.

This principle not only supplies a handy tool for proving sets equal, but also settles certain questions which at first glance are puzzling.

To illustrate the first point, suppose A is the set of all human beings, and B is the set of all featherless, furless bipeds. Then we know that $A = B$ as soon as we know that every human being is a featherless, furless biped, and every featherless, furless biped is a human being.

(Symbolically: We may prove that set A = set B by showing that $A \subset B$ and $B \subset A$.)

To illustrate the second point, as an example of a question settled by the principle above, consider the following:

"Is the set of letters in the name ANNA, {A, N, N, A} or {A, N}?"

The answer is, it doesn't matter. Since each letter belonging to one set can be found in the other, the two sets are the same. One might as well, therefore, use the shorter designation {A, N} to represent the set of letters in the name ANNA.

In fact, it will help to avoid confusion if we agree to avoid writing down more than one symbol for a given element, or a symbol for an element more than once, in listing the elements of a set.

Note also that our principle implies that {A, N} = {N, A}, so that the order in which elements of a set are written is immaterial.

▶ **EXERCISE 2**

1. List, explain the meaning of, and give original examples to illustrate the most important concepts encountered in sections 1.6–1.8.

2. In each of the following cases, list all subsets of the given set of letters, and tell how many subsets there are in all.

  (a) $\{x\}$
  (b) $\{x, y\}$
  (c) $\{x, y, z\}$
  (d) $\{w, x, y, z\}$
  (e) N

3. (a) Suppose A is the set of letters in your first name, B the set of letters in your last name. Find $A \cup B$ and $A \cap B$.

  (b) Suppose A and B are sets which have no elements in common. Then $A \cap B = $?

  (c) Draw a pair of intersecting circles on your paper. Let A be the set of points interior to one circle, B the set of points interior to the other. Indicate, by shading, the set of points $A \cap B$.

  (d) The same as (c), but shade in $A \cup B$.

  (e) Suppose the circles of (c) do *not* intersect. What then can you say about $A \cap B$?

4. (From now on we shall use nn as an abbreviation for "natural number" or "natural numbers.")

  (a) What is meant by an *even* nn?

  (b) What is meant by an *odd* nn?

  (c) Suppose A is the set of all even nn, B the set of all odd nn, C the set of all nn. Then

$$A \cap B = ? \qquad A \cup B = ?$$

  (d) Suppose A is the set of all nn which are integer multiples of 4, B the set of all nn which are integer multiples of 6. What can you say about $A \cap B$? Can you generalize this result?

5. Restricting ourselves to the nn, i.e., considering only those divisions in which the result of dividing one nn by another nn is again a nn, every nn has either exactly one divisor, or exactly two divisors (i.e., 1 and itself), or more than two divisors. The only nn falling into the first class is 1; all those falling into the second class are called "prime nn," or for short, "primes"; all those falling into the third class are said to be "composite."

An important property of primes is that every composite nn may be expressed as the product of primes; and that the set of primes which occur in that product, and the multiplicity with which each prime occurs, are unique.

(*a*) Define: "prime."

(*b*) Write down the set of all primes less than 50.

(*c*) Express each of the composite numbers between 2 and 25 as a product of primes.

(*d*) Suppose that P represents the set of all primes, A the set of all even nn. Then $P \cap A = ?$

(*e*) Explain the reason for the restriction at the beginning of this problem.

6. Name several important subsets of the nn.

7. Is there a largest nn? Justify your answer.

8. In the following statements, A and B represent sets. Characterize each statement as true or false, and illustrate by means of an inclusion diagram.

(*a*) A is always contained in $A \cup B$.

(*b*) B is always contained in $A \cup B$.

(*c*) A always contains $A \cup B$.

(*d*) B always contains $A \cup B$.

(*e*) A is always contained in $A \cap B$.

(*f*) B is always contained in $A \cap B$.

(*g*) A always contains $A \cap B$.

(*h*) B always contains $A \cap B$.

(*i*) If $A \supset B$, then it always follows that $A \cap B = A$.

(*j*) If $A \supset B$, then it always follows that $A \cap B = B$.

(*k*) If $A \supset B$, then it always follows that $A \cup B = A$.

(*l*) If $A \supset B$, then it always follows that $A \cup B = B$.

9. Consider the sets of letters:

$$R = \{a, b\}, \quad S = \{a, b, c\}, \quad T = \{p, q\}$$

(*a*) Which of these sets are in one-to-one correspondence? Diagram a one-to-one correspondence between these sets.

(*b*) Which of these sets have the same cardinal number? Why? What is the symbol for this cardinal number?

(c)   Which of these sets is a subset of which?

(d) $R \cap S = ?$

(e) $R \cup S = ?$

10.   Find a formula for the total number of subsets which a set with n elements has. How does the concept of a nullset prove itself to be useful in this problem?

11.   What is the cardinal number of the set N? Is it a nn?

12.   Suppose a and b are the cardinal numbers of sets A and B respectively. Then with a certain condition placed on the set $A \cap B$, $a + b$ may be defined to be the cardinal number of a certain set. What is the "certain condition" and what is the "certain set?"

13.   In many situations the order in which elements of sets are written is immaterial; a committee made up of Tom and Dick, for example, is the same as a committee made up of Dick and Tom. There are other situations, however, in which order must be taken into account; for example, the name James Walter is not the same as the name Walter James.

We shall use the symbol (a, b) to represent something which we shall call "an *ordered pair* of elements a, b." In writing an ordered pair, it is, of course, our intention that an order be associated with the given elements; toward that end we define $(a, b) = (a', b')$ *if and only if* $a = a'$ and $b = b'$. With that understanding, there is no ambiguity in our calling a the *first element*, b the *second element* of the ordered pair (a, b) (cf. Section 1.9).

Note, then, that although $\{7, 11\} = \{11, 7\}$, $(7, 11)$ is *not* equal to $(11, 7)$. An example of an equality between ordered pairs which may be justified by the criterion above is: $(7, 11) = (\frac{14}{2}, 10 + 1)$.

Note further that although $\{a, a\} = \{a\}$ (see Section 1.9), the ordered pair (a, a) admits of no such contraction.

For those who would like to see an actual definition of an ordered pair—which we have, as a matter of fact, not yet given—a neat, if not immediately transparent, method of *defining* the ordered pair (a, b) is as the set $\{a, \{a, b\}\}$.

[The idea of an *ordered pair* leads quite naturally to the idea of an *ordered triple* (a, b, c), and more generally to that of an *ordered n-tuple* $(x_1, \ldots, x_n)$, where n is any nn. Ordered pairs, triples, etc., are examples of *ordered sets*.]

If S and T are sets, the *product set of S and T*, denoted $S \times T$, is defined to be the set whose members are all ordered pairs (s, t), where s is an element of S and t is an element of T.

For example, if S is the set of letters $\{a, b\}$ and T is the set of letters $\{x, y\}$, then $S \times T$ is the set of ordered pairs: $\{(a, x), (a, y), (b, x), (b, y)\}$. On the other hand, $T \times S$ is the set of ordered pairs: $\{(x, a), (y, a), (x, b), (y, b)\}$.

Now, in each of the following cases write down the members of each of the following product sets: $A \times A$, $A \times B$, $B \times A$, $B \times B$:

(a) $A = \{a, b, c\}$, $B = \{1, 2\}$.

(b) $A = \{x\}$, $B = \{y\}$.

(c) $A = \{1, 2\}$, $B = \{x\}$.

(d) $A = \{a, b, c\}$, $B = \{1, 2, 3\}$.

(e) $A = \{x, y\}$, $B = N$. (What can you say about the set $A \times B$ if A or $B = N$?)

14.   If S, T, and W are sets, how would you define the product set $S \times T \times W$? Make up an example to illustrate your definition.

15.   Suppose that a and b are the cardinal numbers of sets A and B respectively.

Then *ab* may be defined to be the cardinal number of a certain set. What is that "certain set?"

Verify that your statement is correct in a case where $a = 4$, $b = 3$.

Explain now why the "product set" $A \times B$ is so named.

16. A jukebox has two rows of buttons, one containing the letters from A to J, the other the numbers from 1 to 10. To play a selection, one button in each row must be pressed. How many selections does the jukebox offer?

Phrase your answer in the language of product sets and in the light of Problem 15 above.

17. Suppose A is a set. Then a set of subsets of A is said to be:

disjoint (or *mutually exclusive*), if no two of the subsets have an element in common;

exhaustive, if the union of the given subsets is A.

For example, if $A = \{1, 2, 3\}$, then:

(1) The set of subsets $\{1\}$, $\{2\}$ is disjoint, but not exhaustive.

(2) The set of subsets $\{1, 2\}$, $\{2, 3\}$ is exhaustive, but not disjoint.

(3) The set of subsets $\{1\}$, $\{1, 2\}$ is neither disjoint nor exhaustive.

(4) The set of subsets $\{1\}$, $\{2, 3\}$ is disjoint and exhaustive; so is the set of subsets $\{1\}$, $\{2\}$, $\{3\}$.

Construct examples like (1)–(4) above with a set of your own choosing.

18. Let $\#A$ represent the number of elements in a set A. For example, with A as in the preceding problem, $\#A = 3$.

Give an example of a case in which $\#(A \cup B) \neq (\#A) + (\#B)$, ($\neq$ is read "is unequal to"), and another in which $\#(A \cup B) = (\#A) + (\#B)$.

Under what circumstance will the last equation always hold true?

19. Suppose A and B are finite sets. What equation, involving the quantities $\#A$, $\#B$, $\#(A \cup B)$, $\#(A \cap B)$ will always hold true?

Illustrate, by means of an example and by means of a Venn diagram.

20. If A and B are sets, $A - B$ (read: A minus B) is defined to be the set of all elements of A which are not in B.

For example, if $A = \{1, 2, 3\}$, $B = \{1, 2, 4\}$, then $A - B = \{3\}$.

If B is a subset of A, then $A - B$ is called the *complement* of B in A.

If $A = B$, what is $A - B$? What if $B \supset A$?

Suppose A and B are unequal intersecting areas in a plane, neither contained in the other. Draw a diagram identifying and shading in $A - B$ and $B - A$.

Suppose A and B are unequal areas in a plane, and $A \subset B$. Draw a diagram identifying and shading in the complement of A in B.

2

FUNCTIONS,
OPERATIONS
AND RELATIONS

The bedrock is not boring.
ERIC BENTLEY: *In Search of Theater*

2.1 INTRODUCTION

Five concepts constitute the bedrock underlying this course in mathematics.   They are: *set, one-to-one correspondence, function, operation,* and *relation.*   We have encountered the first two in Chapter 1; we shall consider the remaining three in this chapter.

2.2 FUNCTIONS

The fact that we have up until now spoken always of *one-to-one* correspondences has probably already led the reader to suspect that there are other types of correspondences as well, as indeed there are.

In early times, for example, primitive man must have known very well which of the women in his community were the wives of which men.   In other words, there must have existed in his mind a "correspondence" between the set of married men and the set of married women in his community.   That correspondence associated with each married man his wives and (or) with each married woman her husbands.

In a monogamous society we are led to our old friend the one-to-one correspondence.   But in a polygamous society we encounter something

new.   Using an arrow to point from a person to his (or her) spouse, we
diagram two such cases in Fig. 2.1.

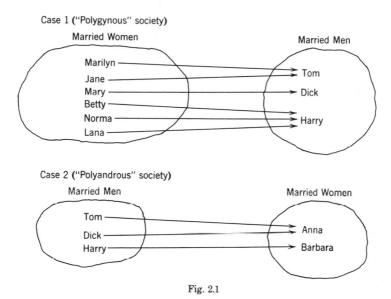

Fig. 2.1

From these situations (and with many more like them in mind) one may
abstract the concept of a *function*:

> A *function* is said to be defined when:
>   (i) A set *D* is given.
>   (ii) To each element of *D*, one and only one object is assigned.
> The set *D* is called the *domain* of the function.

With regard to functions, most of us are in a position very much like
that of Moliere's "Bourgeois Gentilhomme," who learns one day, to his
astonishment and delight, that he has been speaking "prose" all his life.
Just so with functions; whether we are aware of their existence or not, we
nevertheless deal with them all the time.   They are all about us, in situations both mathematical and unmathematical.   Simply the frequency with
which they occur in mathematical expositions justifies the stress which we
shall place upon them.

Now, as an example of a function, consider Case 2 in Fig. 2.1.   Here
we have defined a function whose domain consists of the set {Tom, Dick,
Harry}.   To Tom this function assigns Anna, etc.

At this point we introduce notation and further special vocabulary
useful in discussing functions.

First of all, we often denote a function by a single letter.   We shall, for example, use the letter *m* throughout the remainder of this section to represent the function defined in Case 2 above.

When a function *f* assigns an element *b* to an element *a*, we diagram this fact as follows:

(1) $$a \overset{f}{\to} b$$

and we say: "the function *f maps* (or *sends*) *a* to *b*."

For example, we write: Tom $\overset{m}{\to}$ Anna, etc.

Another notation which is used to express exactly the same fact as (1) above is:

(2) $$f(a) = b$$

which is read: "*f* of *a* equals (or is) *b*."

For example: *m*(Harry) = Barbara, etc.

If either (1) or (2) above is true, we say: "under the function *f*, *b* is the *image* of *a*, and *a* is a *pre-image* of *b*."

For example, we may say: "under the function *m*, Anna is the image of Dick; Dick is a pre-image of Anna; etc."

All the pre-images of a given function constitute, of course the domain of that function.   All the images of a given function constitute a set called the *range* of that function.

For example, the range of the function *m* is the set {Anna, Barbara}.

A function is called *one-one* if each element of its range has exactly one pre-image; otherwise it is called *many-one*.

For example, *m* is a many-one function, since there is an element in its range (namely Anna), which has more than one pre-image; or, reading from the diagram, the fact that two arrows point to a single element indicates that *m* is many-one.

2.3   HOW A FUNCTION MAY BE SPECIFIED

A particular function may be defined by:

(i)   telling what its domain is, and
(ii)   assigning, to each element of that domain, an object.

When we have given the information (ii) above, we say that we have described the *mapping* of the function.

We may therefore restate the opening paragraph of this section: A particular function may be defined by giving two pieces of information: its domain and its mapping.

We shall now consider two practical methods for giving the information (i) and (ii), above.

One is to list all the elements of both domain and range, and then simply to tell which element of the range is assigned to each element of the domain. This is what we have done in Cases 1 and 2 above. Often, in using this method, the elements of the domain are written in one column (or row), and the elements of the range in a parallel column (or row), with elements of the domain and their respective images placed next to each other.

This arrangement is already familiar to the student under the name of a "table of values." Here is an example:

Local Parcel Post Rates

Weight (pounds)	1	2	3	4	5	10
Cost (cents)	18	20	21	23	24	32

We shall call this method of describing a function the "tabular" method.

The tabular method has both advantages and disadvantages; the most serious of its disadvantages being that when the domain of the function contains a great many elements, tabulation becomes highly inconvenient, or even impossible. Consider, for example, the function which assigns, to each person on earth, his age. To list all the inhabitants of the earth would be a staggering project! Or consider the function which assigns to each nn, its square. A list of all nn is obviously impossible.

But these examples immediately suggest another method of specifying functions: one may *describe* the domain without actually listing all its members (as, for example, when we speak of a function whose domain is "all the inhabitants of the earth"), and one may *describe* a mapping by means of a verbal or symbolic rule (as, for example, when we assign to each person on earth, his age, or to each number x of a given domain, the number x^2). We speak, in this case, of a *descriptive* definition of domain or mapping.

(The student is reminded that if x is a number, x^2 is read "x squared" and means the product $x \cdot x$; x^3 is read "x cubed" and means the product $x \cdot x \cdot x$; etc.)

Let us examine a little more closely the symbolic rule just mentioned. Phrases like "x^2 is a function of x" occur often in elementary mathematics. Examining the phrase critically, however, we see that something is lacking. There is no mention of a domain. Therefore a function cannot have been properly defined. Actually, what the phrase does define for us symbolically is only the *mapping* of a function. We are told by the phrase to assign to each element of a yet nonexistent domain, its square.

In mathematics below the college level, omitting to specify the domain of a function rarely leads to trouble; in collegiate mathematics, however, a good deal of confusion results from carelessness in the specification of domains of functions. We shall therefore, in the sequel, attach a great deal of importance to the proper specification of functions.

In our notation, the mapping which is implied when we say "x^2 is a function of x" may be expressed by the notation: $x \to x^2$; or if we assign the name g to a function with this mapping, we may express the mapping by means of the equation: $g(x) = x^2$.

It helps, in understanding functions, to form pictures (even if only mental) something like the following: (We diagram, in Fig. 2.2, the function g whose domain consists of all nn and whose mapping is as above.)

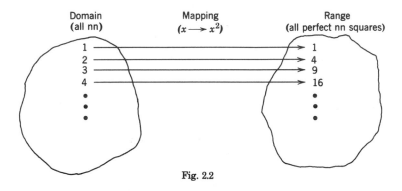

Fig. 2.2

The information imparted by the arrows in the preceding diagram may, of course, also be written: $g(1) = 1$, $g(2) = 4$, $g(3) = 9$, etc.

We see, then, that when the mapping of a function g is given by an equation like $g(x) = x^2$ this may be understood to mean that the image of any element of the domain of g may be found by mechanically substituting that element for x in the given equation. Thus:

$$\text{since } g(x) = x^2$$

$$\text{it follows that } g(7) = 7^2 = 49$$

The letter of the alphabet used in defining the mapping of a function is entirely irrelevant. "$y \to y^2$", "$a \to a^2$", "$x \to x^2$" all say the same thing; namely: "To each element of the domain, assign its square." The same, of course, is true of the alternative notation $g(x) = x^2$. The equations $g(y) = y^2$ or $g(u) = u^2$ define exactly the same mapping.

Perhaps best of all (but almost never used), would be the following equation to define this mapping: $g(\ ) = (\ )^2$.

A special type of function is given by the following example: Suppose we define h as a function whose domain is the set of all natural numbers, and whose mapping is given by: $h(u) = 7$.   Then:

$$h(1) = 7,$$

$$h(2) = 7,$$

$$h(3) = 7, \text{ etc.}$$

Figure 2.3 gives a (partial) picture of the function h.

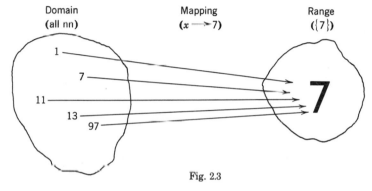

Fig. 2.3

Here the range consists of just a single element.

A function in which the range consists of exactly one element is called a *constant* function.

NOTE 1.   Still another way of saying that $f(a) = b$ is to say: "the value of the function f at a is b"; and when function f has domain D, we say also that f is "defined on" D, or on any subset of D.

Thus a function is always *defined on* elements of its domain, and the *values* of a function are always elements of its range.

NOTE 2.   The following letters are commonly used to identify functions as they arise in a single discussion: f, g, h, F, G, H, ϕ; after that the student's imagination may take over.

We shall terminate this discussion by pointing out an important application of the concept of "function:" the "man-to-man" defense in basketball, in which each man on the defending team chooses a man on the opposing team to guard.   In this situation, an inability to distinguish between a one-one and a many-one function may spell disaster for the defenders.

▶ **EXERCISE 3**

1.   What two pieces of information serve to define a particular *function*? Make up an original example of a function.

2.   What is meant by the *domain* of a function? Illustrate by means of an original example.

3.   What is meant, in speaking of functions, by an "image?" by a "pre-image?" Illustrate with an original example.

4.   What is meant by the *range* of a function? Illustrate by means of an original example.

5.   What is meant by a *one-one* function? Illustrate by means of an original example.

6.   What is meant by a *many-one* function? Illustrate by means of an original example.

7.   Name two ways in which the mapping of a function may be specified, and make up an illustrative example of each.

8.   If f is the name of a function, what is $f(x)$?

9.   What is a *constant* function? Illustrate by means of an original example.

10.   In each of the following cases, a function is defined. In each case illustrate by means of a diagram, tell what the range of the function is, what the image of the number 3 is, what the pre-images of the given numbers are, whether the function is one-one or many-one, and if the latter, why?

	NAME OF FUNCTION	DOMAIN	MAPPING	FIND PRE-IMAGES OF
(a)	f	all nn	$f(x) = 2x - 1$	11
(b)	g	all nn	$g(y) = 2y$	20
(c)	h	all nn	$h(u) = u^2 - 4u + 5$	2
(d)	F	all nn	$F(p) = p^2 - 2p + 2$	5
(e)	G	$\{1, 2, 3, 4, 5\}$	$G(a) = a$	4
(f)	H	$\{1, 2, 3\}$	$H(b) = 11$	11
(g)	ϕ	$\{3\}$	$\phi(x) = x^2 + 2x + 1$	16
(h)	q	$\{1, 2, 3\}$	$x \to x^3 - 6x^2 + 11x + 1$	7
(i)	m	$\{1, 2\}$	$m(x) = x + 1$	2
(j)	r	$\{3\}$	$r(x) = 5x + 1$	16

11.   In each of the following tabular functions, express the mapping by means of a formula for $f(x)$:

(a)		(b)		(c)		(d)		(e)		(f)		(g)		(h)		(i)	
x	$f(x)$	x	$f(x)$	x	$f(x)$	x	$f(x)$	x	$f(x)$	x	$f(x)$	x	$f(x)$	x	$f(x)$	x	$f(x)$
1	5	1	1	1	0	1	11	1	12	1	2	1	2	1	2	10	50
2	10	2	4	2	0	2	10	2	6	2	4	2	5	2	6	20	68
3	15	3	9	3	0	3	9	3	4	3	8	3	8	3	12	30	86
4	20	4	16	4	0	4	8	4	3	4	16	4	11	4	20	40	104
5	25	5	25	5	0	5	7			5	32	5	14	5	30	50	122

(*j*) Let *f* represent the tabular function "Local Parcel Post Rates" on page 21. Hint: Use the symbol ⊗ to mean $\frac{x}{2}$ if *x* is even, and $\frac{x-1}{2}$ if *x* is odd; or use the better-known symbol [*n*] to mean the largest integer (see page 45) which does not exceed *n*. In the problem utilize $\left[\frac{3x}{2}\right]$.

12. Give an example of a correspondence between two sets which might be called "many-many."

13. As commonly used, "one" and "exactly one" are not always synonymous. Explain and illustrate by means of examples.

14. Discuss relative advantages and disadvantages of the descriptive and tabular methods in the definition of particular functions.

2.4 EQUALITY OF FUNCTIONS

We have considered several methods of assigning objects to the elements of a set in order to establish a function. Of primary importance, however, is not *how* the objects are assigned, but what the final assignment is.

We shall therefore consider two functions to be the same if they have the same domain and if, given any element of that domain, each function assigns the same image to that element.

For example, suppose *f* and *g* are functions, and that the domain of each is the set of nn: {1, 2}. Suppose further that the mappings of *f* and *g* are given by: $f(x) = x^2$, $g(x) = 3x - 2$.

Then: $f(1) = 1$ $f(2) = 4$

 $g(1) = 1$ $g(2) = 4$

Therefore the functions *f* and *g* are the same, and we write: $f = g$.

2.5 SEQUENTIALLY APPLIED FUNCTIONS

Suppose *f* and *g* are functions, and that the domain of each consists of all nn. Suppose their mappings are given by: $f(x) = x^2$, $g(x) = x + 1$. Then in this situation, *f* and *g* may "operate" or "work" sequentially on any nn; that is, we may first allow g to work on a given nn, and then f to work on the result, or vice-versa.

For example: $f[g(3)] = f[4] = 16$; $g[f(3)] = g[9] = 10$

In fact, we may compute in advance the effect of either of these sequential operations on any nn x:

$$f[g(x)] = f[x + 1] = (x + 1)^2 = x^2 + 2x + 1;$$
$$g[f(x)] = g[x^2] = x^2 + 1$$

Thus, $f[g(3)] = 3^2 + 2\cdot3 + 1 = 16$; $g[f(3)] = 3^2 + 1 = 10$

agreeing with our previous results.

2.6   INVERSE FUNCTIONS

Whenever we have given a one-one function, it is possible to define another function which is called its inverse, simply by interchanging the domain and range of the given function and "reversing" its mapping. If the original function is denoted f, then its inverse is denoted f^{-1} (read: f inverse).

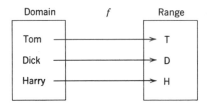

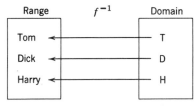

Fig. 2.4

For example, suppose f is the function whose domain is the set of names {Tom, Dick, Harry}, and whose mapping assigns to each name its initial letter.   Then in Fig. 2.4 we see a diagram of the function f, and then, derived from it, a diagram of the function f^{-1}.

Now we can see the motivation for the use of a double arrow in diagramming one-to-one correspondences: It is simply to indicate the two one-one functions, each other's inverses, which are associated with every one-to-one correspondence.

In fact, one-to-one correspondences and one-one functions are essentially the same: Whenever A and B are sets which are in one-to-one correspondence, then a one-one function exists with domain A and range B, and vice-versa.

Now we frame a formal definition for the inverse of a given one-one function f:

Let f be a one-one function with range B.
Then we define the function f^{-1} (called: the inverse of f; read: f inverse) in the following way:
(i) f^{-1} has domain B;
(ii) if b is a member of B, we define $f^{-1}(b)$ to be the unique pre-image of b under the function f.

Thus, $$f(a) = b \text{ if and only if } f^{-1}(b) = a$$

That is, $$a \xrightarrow{f} b \text{ if and only if } a \xleftarrow{f^{-1}} b$$

▶ **EXERCISE 4**

1. Which two functions of Problem 10, Exercise 3, are the same? Why?

2. Referring to Problem 10, Exercise 3, find:

    (a) $f[g(3)]$ (b) $g[f(3)]$ (c) $f[g(x)]$
    (d) $g[f(x)]$ (e) $f[g(5)]$ (f) $g[f(5)]$
    (g) $g[h(3)]$ (h) $h[g(3)]$ (i) $g[h(x)]$
    (j) $h[g(x)]$ (k) $h[g(5)]$ (l) $g[h(5)]$

3. (a) Which of the functions of Problem 10, Exercise 3, have inverses?
(b) Find the inverse of each of the functions you have named in (a) above. (We offer one solution as an illustration: f is one of the functions named that has an inverse. f^{-1} has as domain the set of all odd nn. Mapping: $f^{-1}(x) = (x + 1)/2$.)

4. (a) The most important fact about inverse functions is that when a function and its inverse are applied sequentially to an element, they leave the element unchanged.
More precisely: If b is an element of the range of a 1–1 function f, then $f[f^{-1}(b)] = b$; and if a is an element of the domain of f, then $f^{-1}[f(a)] = a$.
Show that this is so.
(b) An important function defined on a set S is the function that maps each element of S to itself. This function, which we shall denote I_S, is called the *identity function on S*. Thus, I_S has domain S, and if s is an element of S, then $I_S(s) = s$.

Suppose f is a 1–1 function with domain D and range R. Prove this sharper statement of (*a*) above:

$$ff^{-1} = I_R; f^{-1}f = I_D$$

(Hint: Use Section 2.4.)

(*c*) Show that the inverse of an inverse is the original function; i.e., show that if $g = f^{-1}$, then $g^{-1} = f$.

2.7 THE REAL NUMBERS

Up to this point, we have found a convenient source for the domains of functions to be the set of natural numbers (see, for example, Exercise 3, Problem 10). The natural numbers, however, are only part of a larger collection of numbers called *the real numbers*.

The real numbers are of overwhelming importance in mathematics: Most of the functions which we shall study will be defined on sets of real numbers; very nearly all the mathematics leading into and including calculus may be thought of as a study of the properties of real numbers.

We shall therefore, in due time, study these numbers carefully and in detail. Just now it will be our purpose simply to afford the student an intuitive grasp of what is meant by a real number.

Suppose that on a given straight line we choose two different points, labeling one 0 and the other 1:

(Note: From now on, "line" will mean "straight line," unless otherwise noted.)

Then in a "natural" sort of way, every other point on the line may be assigned a label also:

That is to say, we may think of the line segment between the points 0 and 1 as a unit of measure. In the diagram above, the point on our line a distance of one unit to the right of 1 is labeled 2; the point mid-way in distance between 0 and 1 is labeled $\frac{1}{2}$; to the left of 0 we proceed similarly, except that a minus sign is affixed to each label; and so on. If minus signs are disregarded, the label of a point represents its distance from the point 0.

The line so labeled is called a *scaled line*.

The real numbers may be thought of as those numbers that are used to label all the points of a scaled line.

It is this very concrete representation of real numbers that is responsible for the name "real." They were so named in contrast with "imaginary" numbers, which are not as easily pictured. (We shall briefly consider imaginary numbers later on.)

The edge of a ruler and a thermometer scale are examples of scaled line segments. The numbers we see printed on rulers and on thermometer scales are therefore examples of real numbers. Hence real numbers include: natural numbers and their negatives; zero; positive and negative fractions whose numerators and denominators are natural numbers; positive and negative decimals; and, as we shall see, *many other numbers besides.*

Functions defined on sets of real numbers are most often defined on a special type of set called an *interval*. Intervals themselves are of various sorts; we shall for the moment concern ourselves with just one kind of interval: the set of all real numbers between and including a given pair of real numbers.

We introduce the following notation for this type of interval: If a and b are real numbers, and a is less than b, we use the notation $\{a \mathrel{\bullet\!\!-\!\!\bullet} b\}$ to denote the set of *all* real numbers between and including a and b.

For example, in the heavily drawn line segment below, we have a pictorial representation of the interval $\{-2 \mathrel{\bullet\!\!-\!\!\bullet} 3\}$:

2.8 CARTESIAN COORDINATE PLANES

In his high-school study of "graphs" the student has already encountered a method for representing certain functions pictorially. The functional ideas which we have been discussing throw a great deal of light on the subject of graphs, and conversely, graphs help us to understand functions better.

In this section we shall therefore review, in a rough and intuitive way, the background material upon which the subject of graphs depends; in the next section graphs themselves will be considered.

We shall assume that the student already knows that we may think of a plane as a perfectly flat surface (like a table top) which extends without limit in all directions.

Suppose then that we are given a plane. On that plane we draw any pair of perpendicular straight lines, intersecting at a point which we call the "origin." Then we denote one of the lines the "X-axis," the other the "Y-axis." (See Fig. 2.5).

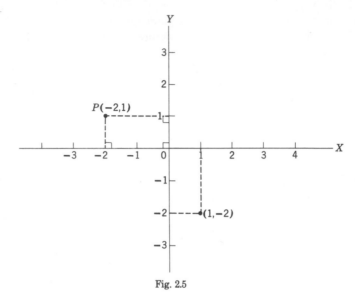

Fig. 2.5

Next let the X- and Y-axes be scaled as in the preceding section, labeling the origin with the real number "0" on each axis, and using the same unit of measure on both axes.

(Most often we draw the X-axis in a horizontal, the Y-axis in a vertical direction, with the positive real numbers labeling the right-hand part of the X-axis and the upper part of the Y-axis.)

At this point we say that we have established a *Cartesian coordinate system* on our given plane, or that the plane has been made into a *Cartesian coordinate plane.*

(The word "Cartesian" is derived from the name of the philosopher and mathematician René Descartes, who in 1637 published the first detailed study of geometry by means of a coordinate system of this sort.)

In the sequel, we shall use the letters "cc" as an abbreviation for Cartesian coordinate.

Now we put our cc system to work:

Suppose P is a point of a cc plane. Draw a line through P, perpendicular to the X-axis, and intersecting the X-axis in a point whose real-number label will be called the "x-value" or "abscissa" or "first name" of the point P. Similarly, draw a line through P, perpendicular to the Y-axis, and intersecting the Y-axis in a point whose real-number label will be called the "y-value" or "ordinate" or "last name" of the point P.

For example, the point P of Fig. 2.5 has an x-value of -2 and a y-value of 1.

The first and last names of a point are called its "coordinates," and are used to label, or identify, the point. In identifying a point by means of its coordinates, we write a pair of parentheses, within which we write the first and last names of the point, in that order, separated by a comma.

For example, the label which we assign to the point P of Fig. 2.5 is $(-2,1)$.

Note that the point $(-2,1)$ is different from the point $(1,-2)$. Pairs of real numbers that identify points of a cc plane are therefore considered to be the same only if they consist of the same real numbers *written in the same order*. Such pairs are called *ordered* pairs. (See Problem 13, Exercise 2.)

The fundamental purpose of any coordinate system on a plane is to identify points of that plane by means of ordered pairs of real numbers.

2.9 GRAPHS OF REAL-REAL FUNCTIONS

On a cc plane, every ordered pair of real numbers identifies a unique point. But we have encountered ordered pairs of real numbers before.

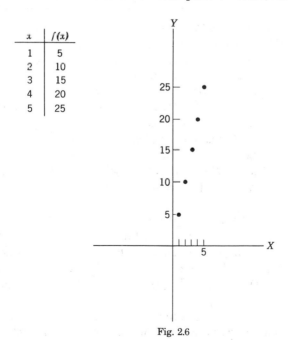

x	$f(x)$
1	5
2	10
3	15
4	20
5	25

Fig. 2.6

Look again, for example, at the function defined in Problem 11(*a*) of Exercise 3:

Here we have *five* ordered pairs of real numbers: (1,5), (2,10), etc. Each identifies a point on a coordinate plane. What is more natural, then, than to picture this function by means of the five points on a cc plane identified by these five ordered pairs? (See Fig. 2.6.)

If we do, we may always reconstruct the function from the points on the picture. The existence of the point (1,5) in the picture would tell us, for example, that 1 is in the domain of the function being described, and that under that function, 5 is the image of 1.

A collection of points, picturing a function in this way, is what we mean by the *graph* of a function. Clearly, the procedure we have illustrated above is possible only if both the domain and the range of the function being pictured contain only real numbers. We make the following definitions:

A *real-real* function is a function whose domain and range both contain only real numbers.

On a cc plane, the *graph* of a real-real function f is the set of all points (a, b), where a is in the domain of f and b is the image of a. (i.e., $b = f(a)$.)

For example, in Fig. 2.6 there is drawn the graph of the real-real function of Problem 11(*a*), Exercise 3.

Note especially that the graph consists only of the five points indicated, and not of a line passing through these points.

Real-real functions whose domains are *intervals* give rise to more substantial graphs. Consider, for example, the function g whose domain is the interval $\{-3 \bullet\!\!-\!\!\bullet 3\}$ and whose mapping is given by: $g(x) = x^2$.

For this function g, it is of course impossible to write down a complete table of values: between -3 and 3 there are more real numbers than could ever be listed. We construct, however, a partial table of values, from which at least *some* of the points on the graph of g may be obtained (Fig. 2.7).

No natural number could represent the number of points on the graph of this function g. (In other words, the number of points on the graph of g is *infinite*; see page 10.) Besides the seven points which we have "plotted" in Fig. 2.7, there are, for example, the points (.1,.01), (.2,.04), (1.1,1.21) and an infinite number of other points on the graph of g.

The student has probably been in the habit of making what is actually much more than a trivial assumption at this point: namely, that all of

x	$g(x)$
-3	9
-2	4
-1	1
0	0
1	1
2	4
3	9

Fig. 2.7

the points on the graph of a function like g "stick together" and form a smooth curve as drawn in Fig. 2.8.

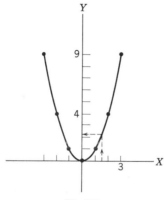

Fig. 2.8

For elementary functions *whose domains are intervals*, this assumption is usually justified. We shall therefore often follow the process familiar to the student in drawing graphs. But it should always be kept in mind that the curve which we draw in "plotting" a graph of a function is fundamentally *a set of points*. If the domain of the function contains only a natural number of elements, i.e., a *finite* number of elements, then the graph will consist of only a finite number of separated points; if the domain of the function consists of a whole interval of real numbers, then the graph will consist of an infinite number of points, which, as we have already pointed out, will, in the case of most elementary functions, form a smooth curve.

The graph of a function often brings out significant aspects of the function in a very clear and vivid way. We illustrate this remark in the case of the function g:

The real numbers which appear as x-values of points on the graph of function g constitute the domain of g, which is, of course, the interval $\{-3 \cdot\!\!-\!\!\cdot 3\}$. The domain may therefore be pictured as the shadow of the graph upon the X-axis (cast by light rays parallel to the Y-axis, as shown in Fig. 2.9).

The real numbers which appear as y-values of points on the graph form the range of the function g. This is the interval $\{0 \cdot\!\!-\!\!\cdot 9\}$. Pictorially, it is represented by the shadow of the graph upon the Y-axis (cast by light rays parallel to the X-axis, as shown in Fig. 2.9).

These "shadows" are known in mathematics as "projections." A precise definition of "projection," as it is used in plane geometry, follows:

Let l be a line, S a set of points, all in the same plane. Then the *projection* of S on l is the set of all points which are the feet of perpendiculars drawn from points of S to l.

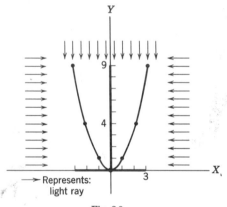

Fig. 2.9

The element 1 of the range of g is the image of both 1 and -1 in the domain of g. Hence g is a many-one function. On the graph, this appears as a situation in which we have two different points at the same height above the X-axis: $(-1,1)$ and $(1,1)$, so that it is possible for a horizontal line to cut this graph in two different points.

It is clear, in fact, that whenever it is possible for a horizontal line (i.e., a line parallel to the X-axis) to cut the graph of a function in more than one point, then the function is many-one; and when no horizontal line cuts the graph in more than one point, the function is one-one.

A graph may be thought of as simply a link between the domain and the range of a function: the link we call the *mapping*. Consider, for example, the graph of the function g. To find the image of the domain element 1.5 under this function, we may begin at the point 1.5 on the X-axis, move vertically until we encounter the graph, and then horizontally until we meet the Y-axis (Fig. 2.8). We should meet the Y-axis at the point 2.25, which is the image, under the function g, of 1.5. The immediate purpose served by the graph has been to link 1.5 with 2.25.

To serve as another illustrative example, we plot the graph of the function h whose domain is the interval $\{-1 \longmapsto 3\}$ and whose mapping is given by: $h(x) = 1 + 4x - x^2$, and we determine the range of h and whether it is one-one or many-one (Fig. 2.10).

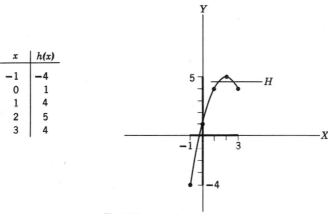

x	$h(x)$
-1	-4
0	1
1	4
2	5
3	4

Fig. 2.10

The range of h is the interval of real numbers $\{-4 \longmapsto 5\}$. The function h is many-one, since there is a horizontal line (H in Fig. 2.10) which crosses the graph more than once.

▶ EXERCISE 5

1. How may a real number be described? Name some important subsets of the set of real numbers. Give some specific examples of real numbers.

2. If a and b are real numbers, and a is less than b, what is meant by the interval $\{a \longmapsto b\}$? Draw a picture to illustrate each of the following intervals: $\{0 \longmapsto 1\}$, $\{-1 \longmapsto 1\}$, $\{2 \longmapsto 5\}$.

3. Given sets defined as follows: $A = \{2 \longmapsto 5\}$, $B = \{3 \longmapsto 7\}$, $C =$ the set of all negative real numbers, $D =$ the set of all natural numbers, $N =$ the null set. Find:

    (a) $A \cup B$ (b) $A \cap B$ (c) $A \cap C$
    (d) $A \cap D$ (e) $A \cup N$ (f) $A \cap N$
    (g) $B \cap C$ (h) $B \cap D$ (i) $B \cup N$
    (j) $B \cap N$ (k) $C \cap D$ (l) $C \cup N$
    (m) $C \cap N$ (n) $D \cup D$ (o) $D \cap D$
    (p) $N \cup N$ (q) $N \cap N$

4.   What is meant by a cc plane?   What is the purpose of establishing a cc system on a plane?

5.   On a cc plane, locate the following points: (1,1), (7,0), (0,7), (−7,0), (0,−7), (3,5), (−3,5), (3,−5), (−3,−5).

6.   Find the coordinates of (i.e., identify by means of an ordered pair of real numbers) each of the points $A, B, C, \ldots, H, O$ in Fig. 2.11.

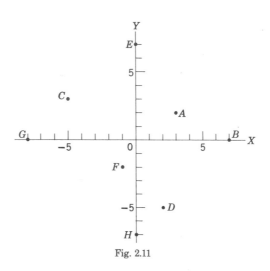

Fig. 2.11

7.   What sort of correspondence exists between all the points of a cc plane and all ordered pairs of real numbers?   Justify your answer.

8.   Define and make up an example of a real-real function.

9.   What is meant by the graph of a real-real function?   What is its purpose?

10.   How may one determine, from the graph of a function, whether the function is one-one or many-one?

11.   In Fig. 2.10, describe light rays which would cast shadows indicating the domain and the range of the function h.

12.   Draw the graph of each of the functions of Problem 10, Exercise 3. (In the first four cases a complete graph is, of course, impossible.   Why? In these cases, therefore, draw a partial graph.)

13.   Plot the graph of the function f in each of the following cases, and determine the range of f and whether f is one-one or many-one.   Also show on the graph how we may find the image of 2.5 in each case, and from the graph, estimate what that image is.

Domain	Mpg. $f(x) =$	Domain	Mpg. $f(x) =$
(a) $\{-1 \cdot\!\!-\!\!\cdot 3\}$	x^2	(b) $\{0 \cdot\!\!-\!\!\cdot 3\}$	x^2
(c) $\{-4 \cdot\!\!-\!\!\cdot 3\}$	x	(d) $\{-4 \cdot\!\!-\!\!\cdot 3\}$	$2x$
(e) $\{-4 \cdot\!\!-\!\!\cdot 3\}$	$3x$	(f) $\{-3 \cdot\!\!-\!\!\cdot 3\}$	$2x + 1$
(g) $\{-3 \cdot\!\!-\!\!\cdot 3\}$	$3x - 2$	(h) $\{-3 \cdot\!\!-\!\!\cdot 3\}$	7
(i) $\{-3 \cdot\!\!-\!\!\cdot 3\}$	0	(j) $\{-3 \cdot\!\!-\!\!\cdot 3\}$	-7
(k) $\{-3 \cdot\!\!-\!\!\cdot 3\}$	$\dfrac{x}{2}$	(l) $\{-1 \cdot\!\!-\!\!\cdot 3\}$	$x^2 - 3x + 2$
(m) $\{-3 \cdot\!\!-\!\!\cdot 3\}$	x^3	(n) $\{-3 \cdot\!\!-\!\!\cdot 3\}$	x^4
(o) $\{-3 \cdot\!\!-\!\!\cdot 3\}$	$x^2 - 2$	(p) $\{-3 \cdot\!\!-\!\!\cdot 3\}$	$2 - x^2$
(q) $\{-3 \cdot\!\!-\!\!\cdot 3\}$	$x^2 + 2$	(r) $\{2 \cdot\!\!-\!\!\cdot 12\}$	$\dfrac{12}{x}$

14. *The absolute value function.* An especially useful function is the function f which is defined as follows: The domain of f is the set of all real numbers. The mapping of f is given by the rules: If x is positive or zero, $f(x) = x$; if x is negative, $f(x) = -x$.

Thus: $f(7) = 7; f(0) = 0; f(-7) = -(-7) = 7$.

It may be seen that $f(x)$ always gives us the "numerical value" of x, that is to say, roughly speaking, the value of x disregarding the sign of x. For this reason f is known as the "absolute value" function.

There is a special symbol associated with the absolute value function: a pair of vertical lines. That is to say, with f defined as above, we write $|x|$ for $f(x)$; $|x|$ is read: the absolute value of x.

Thus, the illustrative examples above may be written:

$$|7| - 7; \quad |0| = 0; \quad |-7| = -(-7) = 7$$

and the definition of our mapping restated: If x is positive or zero $|x| = x$; if x is negative, $|x| = -x$.

Now suppose the function g has as domain the interval $\{-5 \cdot\!\!-\!\!\cdot 5\}$, and that the mapping of g is given by: $g(x) = |x|$. Draw the graph of g, determine its range, and tell whether it is one-one or many-one, and why.

15. In each of the following cases draw the graph of f and determine its range and whether it is one-one or many-one.

(a) The domain of f consists of all natural numbers between -1.5 and 10.5. The mapping of f is given by: $f(x) = 7$ if x is even, $f(x) = 11$ if x is odd.

(b) The domain of f is the interval $\{-5 \cdot\!\!-\!\!\cdot 5\}$. $f(x) = 1$ if x is positive, $f(x) = -1$ if x is negative, $f(x) = 0$ if x is zero.

(c) The domain of f is the interval $\{-5 \cdot\!\!-\!\!\cdot 5\}$. $f(x) = 5 + x$ if x is negative, $f(0) = 10$, $f(x) = 5 - x$ if x is positive.

(d) The domain of f is the interval $\{-5 \cdot\!\!-\!\!\cdot 5\}$; $f(x) = x^2 + 10x + 25$ if $x \in \{-5 \cdot\!\!-\!\!\cdot -2\}$; $f(x) = \left(\dfrac{3x}{2}\right) + 12$ if $x \in \{-2 \cdot\!\!-\!\!\cdot 0\}$; $f(x) = 12 - \left(\dfrac{3x}{2}\right)$ if $x \in \{0 \cdot\!\!-\!\!\cdot 2\}$; $f(x) = x^2 - 10x + 25$ if $x \in \{2 \cdot\!\!-\!\!\cdot 5\}$.

16.   If R represents the set of all real numbers, use the notation of product sets (see Problem 13, Exercise 2) to name a set which is in one-to-one correspondence with all the points of a cc plane.

17.   Explain why lines are said to be *one*-dimensional and planes *two*-dimensional.

18.   Suppose m is a real number.   If $f(x) = mx$ and the domain of f is an interval of real numbers, what do you think may be said about the graph of f?   How does the choice of m affect the graph?

19.   Can a vertical line cross the graph of a function more than once?   Justify your answer.

2.10   OPERATIONS

We return now, after our lengthy excursions into the realms of sets and functions, to the developing mathematics of primitive man.

Recorded history dates from the invention of writing, at about 3000 B.C. Before that is the era known as "prehistory."   Man's acquaintance with natural numbers undoubtedly antedates recorded history; and probably still well within prehistoric times, man learned also to put two and two, and other pairs of numbers, together.

That is to say: Having secured a firm grip on the natural numbers, man proceeded to do things like addition and multiplication with them.

But what exactly do we mean by "things like addition and multiplication?"   We examine the processes of addition and multiplication to see whether we can *abstract* from them a significant general concept.

Addition and multiplication have this in common: Each, given a pair of numbers, returns to us a single number.   For example, given the pair of numbers {7, 11}, addition produces the single number 18, multiplication the single number 77.

We may think in more general terms; combination is not a process which is restricted to numbers.   All sorts of things may be combined: colors, for example, or chemicals, or even routes between cities.   (A route joining New York and Chicago, for example, may be combined with a route between Chicago and San Francisco to give us a route joining New York and San Francisco.)

The abstraction we are getting at, then, may as well be one which assigns any sort of *object* to a given pair of *objects*, rather than one which necessarily assigns a *number* to a pair of *numbers*.

In the cases of addition and multiplication, and even in the combination of routes, the order in which the elements to be combined are written is immaterial.   We should like also to include division, however, in the category of "things like addition and multiplication," and in the case of division order *does* make a difference; $8 \div 2$, for example, is not the same as $2 \div 8$.

The abstraction we are getting at, therefore, will be more general if it deals with *ordered* pairs, rather than just with pairs of objects.

But now our talking about the "assignment" of objects puts us in mind of functions; we shall call the abstraction of which addition and multiplication and division are concrete examples an *operation*; and we shall define an operation as follows:

> An *operation* in a given set is a function whose domain consists of ordered pairs of elements of the given set.

> Alternative definition: An *operation* in a set S is a function whose domain is a subset of $S \times S$.

2.11 ABSTRACT PROPERTIES OF OPERATIONS

In this section we shall abstract, from operations with which we are already familiar, a number of general properties that some operations exhibit, and that others do not. For the sake of simplicity, we deal in this section only with operations defined in the natural numbers: and unless otherwise noted, we assume throughout this section that like primitive man, and like some savage tribes even today, we know of no numbers *but* the natural numbers.

Completeness. In the primitive situation to which we have restricted ourselves, what is an essential difference between $+$ and $\cdot$ on the one hand, and $-$ and $\div$ on the other? We observe that in this situation, the first two can *always* be carried through, the second two only sometimes. For example, early man could "work out" $6 - 2$, but not $2 - 6$; he was able to compute $12 \div 2$, but not $12 \div 5$.

We are led to define an abstract property of operations called *completeness*.

Roughly speaking, an operation in a set S is said to be *complete* if it works on *all* pairs of elements of S.

Remembering that an operation in a set S is a function whose domain consists of ordered pairs of elements of S, we may state our definition a bit more precisely:

> An operation in a set S is said to be *complete* if the domain of the operation consists of *all* ordered pairs of elements of S.

It follows, then, that to prove that an operation in a set S is not complete, it suffices to exhibit an ordered pair of elements of S not in the domain of the operation.   Thus, to show that when only nn are known, subtraction in the set of nn is not complete, we need only point out, for example, that $7 - 11$ does not exist, i.e., that the ordered pair $(7, 11)$ is not in the domain of the operation.

We shall find it useful to distinguish between an operation *in* a set S and an operation *on* a set S.   The former has already been defined; as to the latter, by an operation *on* a set S we shall simply mean a *complete* operation in S.

Thus, assuming nn to be the only numbers known, it would be correct to say that division is defined *in* the set of all nn, addition *on* the set of all nn.

(Note that an operation defined *on* a set S is always defined *in* S also; but an operation defined *in* a set S may or may not be defined *on* S. Thus, in the case cited in the preceding paragraph, it would be correct also to say that addition is defined *in* the set of all nn.)

Closure.   If we look ahead from the time when only nn were known to the day when fractions were invented, the operation of division in the set of nn becomes complete.   But addition and division, though now both complete, would still differ in an important respect: the result of adding one nn to another nn is always again a nn, but the result of dividing one nn by another nn is *not* always again a nn.

We are led to define an abstract property of operations called *closure*, a name which has been suggested by the fact that when an operation displays the property we have in mind, the "answers" produced by that operation always lie within the original set of definition.

Roughly speaking, an operation on a set S is said to be *closed* if the "results" of the operation are always members of S also.

More precisely:

> An operation on a set S is said to be *closed* if the range of the operation is a subset of S.

Note that our definition of closure applies only to operations defined *on* S, i.e., only to complete operations.   As it will turn out in our work, the idea involved in closure, as well as the ideas involved in other properties of operations to be discussed below, are important only for operations which are complete.   Furthermore, restricting ourselves to *complete* operations in our discussion of these properties of operations simplifies matters in a number of ways.

We therefore make completeness a prerequisite for closure, as well as for "commutativity" and "associativity," to be defined below.   If an operation is not complete, then automatically it cannot be closed, or commutative, or associative.

Commutativity.   Before we consider the property of commutativity, we shall have to say a few words about mathematical symbols.

The student is already familiar with the very useful device of using letters of the alphabet to represent numbers in making general statements about numbers, as, for example, in the well-known statement: "If a and b are real numbers, then $a(b + c) = ab + ac$."

In making general statements about operations, we find it similarly useful to have special symbols to represent operations.   We shall find just one such symbol: "∘" sufficient for our purposes here.

Now we return to commutativity.

This property of operations stems from observations such as the following:

$$2 + 3 = 3 + 2; \quad 4 + 7 = 7 + 4; \quad 2 \cdot 3 = 3 \cdot 2; \quad 4 \cdot 7 = 7 \cdot 4$$

but these statements are not true, and in fact in some situations (e.g., restricting ourselves to the nn) not even always meaningful, when $+$ and $\cdot$ are replaced by $-$ and $\div$.

We are led to the following definition:

> An operation ∘ on a set S is said to be *commutative* if, for each pair of elements a, b of S:
>
> $$a \circ b = b \circ a.$$

For example, addition on the set of nn *is* a commutative operation, since for any pair of nn a, b: $a + b = b + a$.

Associativity.   In applying the operation of addition to the numbers 1, 2, 3 in that order, one may add the first to the second, and then that sum to the third:

$$(1 + 2) + 3 = 3 + 3 = 6$$

or one may add the first to the sum of the second two:

$$1 + (2 + 3) = 1 + 5 = 6$$

Either method leads, of course, to the same result.   In general, if a, b, c are any triple of nn, we all know the following to be true:

$$a + (b + c) = (a + b) + c$$

A similar statement is true of the operation of multiplication on the set of all nn:

$$a \cdot (b \cdot c) = (a \cdot b) \cdot c$$

But similar statements are *not* true for all operations.   For example, consider the operation of division among all common fractions. The student may easily verify that $\frac{1}{2} \div (\frac{1}{3} \div \frac{1}{4})$ and $(\frac{1}{2} \div \frac{1}{3}) \div \frac{1}{4}$ are *not* equal.

We are led to the following definition. (Again, simplicity is gained by restricting ourselves somewhat: we make our definition apply only to complete, closed operations.)

A closed operation ∘ on a set S is said to be *associative* if, for each triple of elements a, b, c of S:

$$a \circ (b \circ c) = (a \circ b) \circ c$$

The reason for restricting ourselves to complete, closed operations in the preceding definition is simply this: that unless ∘ were known to be both complete and closed, $b \circ c$, for example, might not exist, or might not be a member of S. In either case, $a \circ (b \circ c)$ would not exist. In order for an operation ∘ to be associative, we should like first of all that for each triple of elements a, b, c of S, both $a \circ (b \circ c)$ and $(a \circ b) \circ c$ *exist*; the conditions that ∘ be complete and closed guarantee this existence.

We note now that it is only because $+$ is associative that we may write the expression $1 + 2 + 3$ without parentheses; for the associativity of $+$ means that either of the two reasonable interpretations, $1 + (2 + 3)$ and $(1 + 2) + 3$, of the expression $1 + 2 + 3$ leads to the same result.

In general, if ∘ is an associative operation, we *define $a \circ b \circ c$* to mean either of the equal-valued possibilities $a \circ (b \circ c)$ or $(a \circ b) \circ c$.

In the case $1 + 2 + 3 + 4$, parentheses and brackets may be inserted in many more than two ways. However, as a consequence of the associativity of $+$, it turns out that all lead to the same result. In general, when we write an expression like $a \circ b \circ c \circ d$, where ∘ is an associative operation (or a similar expression with even more than four terms) we shall mean any one of the different associations of these terms, all of which lead to the same result.

Distributivity. Distributivity is a property which involves *two* operations rather than one. Since examples of it occur relatively infrequently, we shall not define this property in general; instead we shall give one very important instance, involving the operations $+$ and $\cdot$, defined on the nn.

We all know that 5 dozen is the sum of 3 dozen and 2 dozen, and that 11 dimes is the sum of 7 dimes and 4 dimes. That is to say:

$$5 \cdot 12 = 3 \cdot 12 + 2 \cdot 12 \quad \text{and} \quad 11 \cdot 10 = 7 \cdot 10 + 4 \cdot 10$$

In other words:

$$(3 + 2) \cdot 12 = 3 \cdot 12 + 2 \cdot 12 \quad \text{and} \quad (7 + 4) \cdot 10 = 7 \cdot 10 + 4 \cdot 10$$

In fact, if a, b, c are any triple of nn, then:

$$(a + b)c = ac + bc$$

It follows, since multiplication is commutative among the nn, that if a, b, c are any triple of nn, then also:

$$c(a + b) = ca + cb$$

The last two equations are known as the *right* and *left distributive laws*, respectively. They hold true, in fact, not only for the nn, but for all real numbers.

We terminate this section with several notes on its contents:

NOTE 1. Another use for the symbol ○ is in *defining* particular operations. For example, we may define an operation ○ in the following way: ○ is defined in the set of all nn, and if x, y are nn, then:

$$x \circ y = x + 2y$$

Thus:
$$1 \circ 1 = 1 + 2 \cdot 1 = 3$$
$$1 \circ 3 = 1 + 2 \cdot 3 = 7$$
$$3 \circ 1 = 3 + 2 \cdot 1 = 5, \text{ etc.}$$

Since this operation may be carried out on all pairs of nn, it is complete. Since the operation is complete, and since the end result of the operation is always a nn, the operation is closed. The fact that $1 \circ 3$ and $3 \circ 1$ have proved to be unequal justifies our saying that this operation is not commutative. As for associativity:

$$(1 \circ 1) \circ 1 = 3 \circ 1 = 5$$
$$1 \circ (1 \circ 1) = 1 \circ 3 = 7$$

This single case proves that our operation is not associative.

As in the case of functions, the "dummy" letters used to define an operation are immaterial. $x \circ y = x + 2y$ might just as well be expressed: $u \circ v = u + 2v$, etc.

NOTE 2. What we have defined as an *operation* is sometimes called a *binary* operation to emphasize that it works on *pairs* of objects. Sometimes, however, the word "operation" is used to apply to something like a square root, which works only on one object. In that case we shall call the operation a "unary" operation.

With regard to the general properties of operations discussed above, only the terms "complete" and "closed" apply to unary operations. In fact, there is no difference between a complete unary operation defined in a set S, and a function defined on S.

NOTE 3. There is ambiguity in writing an expression like: $7 \cdot 10 + 4 \cdot 10$, as we have above. What we intend it to mean is $70 + 40$, or 110. It might, however, be taken to mean: $7 \cdot (10 + 4) \cdot 10$, or 980. To avoid this possible misinterpretation, we agree that in ambiguous situations, multiplication and division shall precede addition or subtraction.

▶ **EXERCISE 6**

1. What is an operation? Make up an original example of an operation.

2. With respect to operations, what is meant by completeness? closure? commutativity? associativity?

3. Suppose S is the set of primary colors: red, yellow, blue, and the operation o in S that of mixing colors. Is this operation complete? closed? commutative? associative? (Justify your answers.)

4. Suppose S is the set of all routes between cities in the U.S., and o is the operation of joining routes mentioned in paragraph 6 of Section 2.10. Discuss this operation as in Problem 3 above.

5. Two nn are said to have the same *parity* if both are even or if both are odd. We define an operation o in the set of nn as follows: $x \circ y = 1$ if x and y are nn of the same parity, and $x \circ y = 0$ if x and y are not of the same parity (referred to, sometimes, as being of "opposite" parity).
   Discuss this operation as in Problem 3 above.

6. Make up a chart showing, for each of the operations $+, \cdot, -, \div,$ defined in the set of nn, whether or not it is complete, closed, associative, or commutative. (Assume only nn are known; justify each entry.)

7. In each of the following cases, an operation o is defined in the set of all nn, under the assumption that only nn are known. In each case find $8 \circ 2$ and discuss the given operation with respect to general properties of operations which it does or does not exhibit, as in Note 1 of this section.

(a) $x \circ y = x + 3y$ (b) $x \circ y = 2x - y$
(c) $x \circ y = 1 + xy$ (d) $x \circ y = x + y + 1$
(e) $x \circ y = x^2 + y$ (f) $x \circ y = \sqrt{xy}$
(g) $x \circ y = x$

8. The numbers of the sum $1 + 2 + 3 + 4$ may be "associated" by finding $1 + 2$ first, then adding the result to 3, and then adding *that* result to 4; i.e.:

$$[(1 + 2) + 3] + 4 = [3 + 3] + 4 = 6 + 4 = 10$$

Indicate, by means of parentheses and brackets, four other associations of the numbers of the given sum, and show that each of them adds up to 10.

9. Suppose that a, b, c, d are members of a set on which an associative operation o is defined.
   Find all possible associations of the expression $a \circ b \circ c \circ d$ and prove that they are all equal to each other.

10. Suppose that in the preceding problem, five rather than four elements were given. How many associations would exist in that case?

11.   The same as Problem 5, except that $x \circ y = 3$ if x and y are of opposite parity.

12.   Suppose S is the set of all subsets of a given set T.   Then $\cap$ and $\cup$, as defined in Section 1.8, are actually operations in S.

Discuss the operations $\cap$ and $\cup$ in S with respect to completeness, etc.

2.12   COMMON FRACTIONS, INTEGERS AND RATIONAL NUMBERS

Long, long ago, when man knew of no numbers but the nn, the operations of subtraction and division in the set of nn were not complete.

But probably some time before 3000 B.C. the ancient peoples of Egypt and Babylonia invented *common fractions*—precisely in order to make the operation of division in the set of nn complete; that is to say, in order to make it possible, given any two nn, to divide either by the other.

This remedied one deficiency in the number system of ancient times. It is a curious fact, however, that *negative numbers*, and the number 0, which make it possible to subtract any nn from any other (i.e., which make the operation of subtraction in the set of nn complete) did not come into general use until about 1637 A.D., when Descartes used them in constructing coordinate systems (see Section 2.8).

The following formally defined sets of numbers are essentially enlargements of the set of nn which arose historically in an attempt to make complete, operations which were not complete.

The *common fractions* consist of all those numbers which may be written in the form $\frac{a}{b}$, where a and b are nn.

The *integers* consist of the nn, their negatives, and 0.

The *rational numbers* consist of the common fractions, their negatives, and 0.

(Special notice should be taken of the phrase "may be written" in the definition of a common fraction above.   Thus, so far as we are concerned, 0.23 is a common fraction; for 0.23 may be written: $\frac{23}{100}$, and both 23 and 100 are, of course, nn.   We say that 0.23 is a common fraction written in "decimal form.")

It should be easy to see now why nn are also called "positive integers"; and why common fractions are also called "positive rational numbers."

Note also that every rational number is expressible as the "ratio" of two integers (i.e., as a fraction $\frac{p}{q}$, where p, q are integers), which, indeed, accounts for the name "*rational* number."

Just as in the cases we have discussed, one may explain every enlargement which our number system has undergone, since the time when only nn were known, as following from the need or desire to make complete an operation which was not complete.

In fact, the concept of "completeness" has been introduced into our discussion of properties of operations mainly because of its importance in explaining how and why our number system has grown.

Since natural numbers, integers, common fractions and rational numbers all find their places on a scaled line, all of these numbers are also real numbers.

2.13 THE QUESTION OF DIVISION BY ZERO

What is $6 \div 3$? The answer, of course, is: 2. But why? The reason is: $3 \cdot 2 = 6$

In fact, the justification for the answer to any problem of division is always a statement involving multiplication. This is because division is *defined* in terms of multiplication: We say $a \div b = c$ only if: $a = bc$.

Now we consider the question: $1 \div 0 = ?$

Here the problem is to find a number such that 0 times that number equals 1.

But it is a fundamental property of our number system that 0 times *any* number is 0, and *not* 1. Therefore $1 \div 0$ can never be defined as a number—unless we are willing to give up the rule that 0 times any number is 0.

To give up that rule, however, would mean a serious loss in the applicability of mathematics to practical problems. For example, the area of a rectangle is the product of its length and its width. Suppose a rectangle has zero width; then no matter what its length, we should not like to assign to it an area of anything but zero.

Furthermore, this property of zero is the consequence of even more fundamental properties of numbers (as we shall demonstrate in Chapter 4), so that defining $1 \div 0$, as indeed defining $N \div 0$ for any real number N different from 0, would necessitate discarding more than one basic and useful property of numbers.

The price is too high. We therefore abandon the project of making the operation of division complete by enlarging the set upon which the operation is defined.

In dividing by zero, a case we have not yet considered is: $0 \div 0 = ?$

In dividing a nonzero number by zero, the difficulty we encountered was that of finding any answer at all; in dividing zero by zero, we find ourselves at an opposite extreme: too many answers are possible. For the problem, in the latter case, is to find a number which when multiplied by 0 will equal 0. But *any* number times 0 equals 0; *any* number, therefore, might serve as an answer to the problem: $0 \div 0 = ?$

Actually, none of the possibilities would serve any useful purpose. We therefore refrain from defining $N \div 0$ in all cases, whether N is zero or not. Thus the expression $a \div b$ will always be meaningless when $b = 0$, as will also be the fraction $\frac{a}{b}$, since $\frac{a}{b} = a \div b$.

The operation of division, then, will always fail to be complete on any set of numbers which contains zero. *Division by zero is never to be allowed.*

▶ **EXERCISE 7**

1. Define and give several examples of each, and locate each example on a scaled line:

(*a*) integer; (*b*) common fraction; (*c*) rational number.

What does the fact that each of these numbers may be located on a scaled line indicate?

2. The integers serve to make what operation in the nn complete?

3. The common fractions serve to make what operation in what set complete?

4. The rational numbers serve to make what operation in what set complete?

5. (*a*) Is 7 a rational number? Justify your answer.

(*b*) Is every integer a rational number? Justify your answer.

6. (*a*) Is 0.13 a rational number? Is 1.13 a rational number? Justify your answers.

(*b*) Define: "decimal" or "decimal fraction."

(*c*) Is every decimal a rational number? Justify your answer.

7. Draw a Venn diagram (See Section 1.7) to illustrate the inclusion relationships among the sets in each of the following cases:

(*a*) integers; nn; real numbers; rational numbers;

(*b*) rational numbers; real numbers; common fractions; positive integers.

8. The same as Problem 6, Exercise 6, except that "nn," wherever it appears in that problem is to be replaced by:

    (a) integers   (b) common fractions

    (c) rational numbers   (d) real numbers

9. An operation o is defined in the set of positive rational numbers as follows:

$$x \circ y = \frac{x + y}{2}.$$

Discuss this operation o with respect to general properties of operations which it does or does not exhibit.

2.14 RELATIONS

We return once more to primitive man and his mathematics, in order to discover the last of our great basic concepts of mathematics.

As in the case of the others, it is in very simple activities that examples of the concept may be found. Early man not only combined numbers —he compared them with each other as well; and it is likely that the first comparison was with respect to size.

We note this fact about the process of comparing two nn as to size:

Given an ordered pair of nn, the first is either greater than the second, or it is not—exactly one of the two possibilities must be true.

Now consider for a moment the concept of "being the father of," as it applies to a set of people. At first glance the concept of "being the father of" seems to have little to do with the concept of "being greater than." But observe the following fact:

Given an ordered pair of people from the given set of people, either the first is the father of the second, or he is not—exactly one of the two possibilities must be true.

Other concepts which exhibit the same sort of selectivity with respect to ordered pairs are: "being equal to," "dividing" and "being double" (among the nn); "being the brother of" and "loving" (among sets of people).

For example, given the ordered pair of nn (7, 7), one says the first is *equal* to the second; given the ordered pair of nn (7, 6), one says the first is *not equal* to the second. Given the ordered pair of nn (2, 6), one says the first *divides* the second; given the ordered pair of nn (2, 7), one says the first does *not divide* the second. Given the ordered pair of nn (4, 2), one says the first is *double* the second; given the ordered pair of nn (2, 4), one says the first is *not double* the second. Given the ordered pair (Cain, Abel), one says the first is the *brother* of the second; given the ordered pair (Cain, Adam), one says the first is *not the brother* of the second. (It is left to the student similarly to illustrate the remaining concept mentioned in the preceding paragraph.)

Each of these concepts is an example of the abstraction called a *relation*. Our preceding discussion leads to the following definition:

> A *relation R* on a set *S* is a function which associates with each ordered pair of elements of S either the word "yes" or the word "no."

If a relation R associates the word "yes" with the ordered pair (a, b), we say: $a\,R\,b$. If a relation R associates the word "no" with the ordered pair (a, b), we say: $a\,\not\!R\,b$ (read "a not R b).

For example, the relation $=$ on the set of nn maps the ordered pair $(7, 7)$ into the word "yes." We therefore say: $7 = 7$; the same relation associates the word "no" with the ordered pair $(7, 6)$. We therefore say: $7 \neq 6$ (read "7 is unequal to 6").

We append a list of names and symbols for certain important relations defined on sets of numbers. The first four are defined on the set of *all real numbers*. The last is defined on the set of *all nn*, under the assumption that only nn are known.

That is to say, if a and b are nn and we write "$a|b$" or we say "a divides b" or "b is divisible by a" or "b is a multiple of a," we shall in all these cases mean, unless otherwise noted, that there is a *natural number c* such that $b = ca$.

$>$	Greater than		$<$	Less than
$\geqslant$	Greater than or equal to		$\leqslant$	Less than or equal to
		$\mid$ Divides		

2.15 ABSTRACT PROPERTIES OF RELATIONS

I. Reflexivity. It is not too difficult to find sets of people in which everyone is in love with himself, but to find even one person who is his own father presents a real problem. Or, consider the relation $=$: Any number whatever is equal to itself; that is to say, if a is a number, then $a = a$. The analogous fact is not true, however of the relation $<$. In fact for no number a is it true that $a < a$.

We are led to the definition:

> A relation *R* on a set *A* is said to be *reflexive* if for *each a* in *A*:
> $$a\,R\,a.$$

II. Symmetry. Some relations are "reversible," and others are not. For example, if Tom is the cousin of Jerry, then it follows that Jerry is the cousin of Tom; but if Tom admires Jerry, it does not *necessarily* follow that Jerry admires Tom.

We make this definition:

> A relation R on a set A is said to be *symmetric* if *b R a always* follows from *a R b.*

III. Transitivity. Knowing that a first number is equal to a second, and the second number to a third, it is a familiar conclusion that the first number is equal to the third number. That is, there follows from the information $a = b$ and $b = c$, the conclusion $a = c$. Not all relations, however, behave in this way. For example, if John loves Mary and Mary loves James, it may be doubted that John loves James.

We make this definition:

> A relation R on a set A is said to be *transitive* if from *a R b* and *b R c, always* follows: *a R c.*

A relation which is reflexive *and* symmetric *and* transitive is called an *equivalence* or a *congruence* relation.

2.16   UNIFIED DEFINITION OF FUNCTION, OPERATION, RELATION

There is a neat way of *defining* "function," "operation," and "relation," all in terms of the concept of *ordered pair* (which itself, on page 16, was defined in terms of the concept *set*).

We shall find it convenient to begin with the concept "relation."

First of all, we note that a relation R defined on a set S may always be associated with a "favored" subset of ordered pairs in $S \times S$ (the ones to which it applies the word "yes"). For example, the relation $>$ defined on the set $\{1, 2, 3\}$ may be associated with the set of ordered pairs $\{(3, 2), (3, 1), (2, 1)\}$. It is only a step, in mathematics, from "associated with" to "defined by"; and from there, only another step to "is." We find it perfectly adequate to what we wish to do with relations to make the following definition:

Definition. A *relation R* on a set S is a subset of $S \times S$. (If a, b) belongs to the aforementioned subset of $S \times S$, we write: $a R b$; otherwise we write: $a R̸ b$.)

The point of view embodied in this definition makes it feasible to draw graphs of certain relations (which?) as well as of real-real functions. When each ordered pair in a given relation represents a point of a *cc* plane (when does this happen?) the graph of the given relation is defined to be the set of all points in a *cc* plane so represented.

For example, the graph of the relation $>$, defined on the set $\{1, 2, 3\}$ is given in Fig. 2.12.

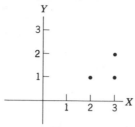

Fig. 2.12

Now we recall that in a natural way one may also associate with a *function* a set of ordered pairs; namely, those ordered pairs which may be found in the table of values of the function. The function f whose domain consists of the numbers $\{1, 2, 3\}$, and whose mapping is given by $x \to x^2$, for example, may be associated with the set of ordered pairs $\{(1, 1), (2, 4), (3, 9)\}$.

So far relations and functions seem to have a great deal in common, as indeed they do. There is a crucial distinction, however: We recall that a function may not assign two different objects to the same element. The ordered pairs $(3, 2)$, $(3, 1)$ which occur in our relation above, for example, could not occur in the case of a function (as we have defined "function"). We therefore make the following definition:

Definition. A function f is a relation with the following property: If (a, b) and (a, c) are both in the given relation, then $b = c$.

[The set of first elements occurring in the given relation is called the *domain* of f, the set of second elements the *range* of f, and if (a, b) is in the given relation, then we write: $b = f(a)$.]

Finally, the definition of "operation" which we have given above falls into place in this development without any alteration.

▶ EXERCISE 8

1. Make up an original example of a relation, and tell whether it is reflexive, symmetric or transitive; justify your statements.

2. Discuss, with respect to I, II, and III above, the relations $>$, $<$, $\geqslant$, $\leqslant$, $|$ as defined above; also the relation $=$ on all real numbers. Which are equivalence relations?

3. Discuss the following relations with respect to I, II, and III above, and identify those which are equivalence relations:

Relation	Defined on
(a) "father"	All Americans
(b) "brother"	All Americans
(c) "cousin"	All Americans
(d) "10 miles from"	All U.S. Cities
(e) "parallel"	All lines of a plane
(f) "intersects"	All lines of a plane
(g) "perpendicular"	All lines of a plane

Relation	*Defined on*
(h) "similar"	All triangles of a plane
(i) "congruent"	All triangles of a plane
(j) "contains"	All subsets of a set
(k) "differs from by an integer multiple of 5"	All integers

4.   Why are "equivalence" or "congruence" relations so named?

5.   With respect to the properties I, II, III above, every relation must fall into one of eight categories; one of these categories, for example, is: reflexive, symmetric, not transitive.

What are the other seven?

For each of these eight categories (or for as many of them as you can), give an example of a relation belonging to that category.

6.   Draw the graphs of the following relations, all defined on the set $\{1, 2, 3, 4\}$:

$$(a) >   (b) \geqslant   (c) =   (d) <   (e) \leqslant   (f) \mid$$

7.   Draw the graphs of the following relations, all defined on the interval $\{0 \longrightarrow 1\}$:

$$(a) >   (b) \geqslant   (c) =   (d) <   (e) \leqslant$$

CHAPTER 3

REASON AND IRRATIONALITY

Compared with the empirical and fragmentary knowledge which the peoples of the East had laboriously gathered together during long centuries, Greek science constitutes a veritable miracle. There the human mind for the first time conceived of the possibility of establishing a limited number of principles, and of deducing from these a number of truths which are their rigorous consequence.
ARNOLD REYMOND: *Science in Greco-Roman Antiquity*

3.1 INTRODUCTION

In what has gone before, we have been occupied with the development of ideas and vocabulary necessary to a clear and simple expression of mathematical statements. There is a question which must be settled, however, before we proceed to build mathematics upon the foundation we have laid:

What will the authority for our mathematical statements be? How shall we persuade ourselves and others of their truth? How, in other words, are they to be justified?

Consider, for example, the famous assertion of mathematics known as the "Pythagorean theorem," which states that if c is the length of the hypotenuse of a right triangle whose other sides are of lengths a and b, then $a^2 + b^2 = c^2$.

Pythagoras was a Greek who lived at about 550 B.C. The theorem which bears his name actually was known to the ancient Babylonians, probably before 2000 B.C.; but the Babylonians and the Greeks differed markedly in their attitudes toward that theorem.

Let us first consider the Babylonians. The Babylonian nations of Biblical times, together with their contemporary, ancient Egypt, share the distinction of being the earliest of civilizations contributing to our present

Western culture. The ancient Babylonians and Egyptians were busy people, with a great many practical problems to solve and a great deal of hard work to do. Their primary interest was in getting the immediate problem solved and the work at hand done.

The governments of Babylonia and Egypt were autocratic, and so indeed was their mathematics (which, incidentally, comprised a good deal of our present high-school algebra and geometry). For example, having somehow stumbled upon the Pythagorean theorem, and having observed that it seemed always to hold true when applied to specific right triangles, the Babylonians were not disposed to pursue any further the matter of its truth. Babylonians accepted the theorem on the authority of their elders and because it was "so written," persuasions which unfortunately even today carry more weight than they properly should.

But the Greek civilization which followed (dating from about 600 B.C.), fostered a leisure class of "philosophers " (i.e., "lovers of knowledge"), men who lived under a less repressive political structure than did their oriental predecessors, and who pursued their studies in an atmosphere of brave new freedom. These men asked not only "how," but also: "why?" Their deeply probing minds raised, and even *answered*, questions which occurred not at all to the Babylonians or to the Egyptians. And first among these questions was:

How shall we know that a statement is true?

It is interesting to note that the mathematics which followed from the philosophic meditations of the Greeks has turned out to be incalculably more useful in science and industry than that which we owe to the very practical-minded Egyptians and Babylonians; and that the down-to-earth Romans, expert in commerce and engineering, were able to contribute absolutely nothing to further the development of the mathematics they used.

We begin our study of the Greek contribution to the problem of how statements may be justified, or "proved," by examining several "proofs" occurring early in the development of Greek mathematics, and attributed to Pythagoras, or members of his school.

3.2 PYTHAGOREAN PROOFS: SEVERAL EXAMPLES

Many of the statements which we make about real numbers were justified by the Pythagoreans by means of line and area representations. For example, to find a general formula for $(a + b)^2$, where a and b are positive real numbers, a square whose side is of length $a + b$ units may be constructed, and subdividing lines are drawn as in Fig. 3.1.

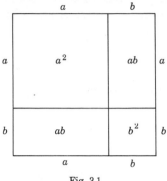

Fig. 3.1

Now the area of the square of side $a + b$ is numerically equal to $(a + b)^2$.

The areas of the four component rectangles are numerically equal to: a^2, ab, ab, b^2.

The area of the large square is equal to the sum of the areas of its four component rectangles.   Therefore:

$$(a + b)^2 = a^2 + ab + ab + b^2 = a^2 + 2ab + b^2$$

What has been demonstrated, then, is that if a and b are any positive real numbers, then $(a + b)^2 = a^2 + 2ab + b^2$.   (Actually the equation holds true if a and b are any real numbers at all, but we have not shown that.)

Many other rules which we have learned in elementary mathematics may be justified in similar fashion.   In fact, a very simple and beautiful proof of Pythagoras' famous theorem results from a slight variation of the preceding diagram:

Starting with four right triangles, each with hypotenuse of length c and arms of lengths a, b, we fit them together as in Fig. 3.2.

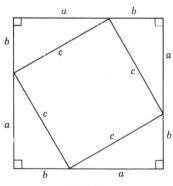

Fig. 3.2

It is not hard to see that this time we have a large square of area $(a + b)^2$ composed of a smaller square of area c^2 and four right triangles each of area $\frac{1}{2}ab$.   Therefore:

$$(a + b)^2 = c^2 + 4 \cdot \tfrac{1}{2}ab$$

or: $$a^2 + 2ab + b^2 = c^2 + 2ab$$

Now subtracting $2ab$ from both sides of the preceding equation we have:

$$a^2 + b^2 = c^2$$

which is the result we wished to arrive at.

3.3   THE IRRATIONALITY OF $\sqrt{2}$

From their predecessors, the Greeks inherited a system of numbers (the positive rational numbers) which sufficed for most practical needs, and a question of which the ancients were not even aware.   The question:

Given a unit line segment, can the length of every line segment be expressed, in terms of that unit, as a positive rational number?   In other words, do the positive rational numbers suffice for the measurement of all line segments?

The school which Pythagoras founded at Crotona in Italy was a mystic order, and the scholars who studied there observed many peculiar rules. One of them was anonymity: all discoveries were credited to their leader, Pythagoras.   We do not know, therefore, who actually made the remarkable discovery that not all line segments have rational lengths, but only that he was a Pythagorean.   The fact itself was considered a scandal.   To the mystic Pythagoreans, everything was based upon the whole numbers and the rational numbers which could be constructed from them.   Their whole philosophy seemed now to be crumbling.   They tried to hide the discovery, and legend even relates that one of their number was drowned because he disclosed the secret to outsiders.

The proof of the Pythagoreans that not all line segments are of rational length is one of the most beautiful in all of mathematics.   It goes as follows:

Consider a right triangle whose two arms are of unit length (Fig. 3.3.).

If we denote the length of the hypotenuse of this triangle by x, then by the Pythagorean theorem we have:

$$x^2 = 1^2 + 1^2 = 1 + 1 = 2$$

so that: $$x = \sqrt{2}$$

(The student is reminded that the expression $\sqrt{a}$, where a is a non-negative real number, means *the non-negative square root of a, i.e., the* *non-negative number whose square is a*; the symbol $\sqrt{}$ should, in this case, be read: the non-negative square root of).

The rest of the proof consists in showing that $\sqrt{2}$ is *irrational*, i.e., it is *not* rational, or in other words that there is no positive rational number whose square equals 2.

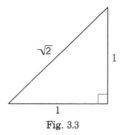

Fig. 3.3

PYTHAGOREAN PROOF OF THE IRRATIONALITY OF $\sqrt{2}$

The proof rests principally upon these definitions and assumptions:

(1)   An *even* nn is one which may be expressed in the form $2k$, where k is a nn.

(2)   Only *even* nn have squares which are even.

(3)   Every positive rational number $\dfrac{p}{q}$, where p and q are nn, may be expressed "in lowest terms," i.e., in such a way that p and q have no common divisor but 1.

(These assumptions may be proved a consequence of even more basic assumptions, but they are quite plausible themselves, and therefore a reasonable basis upon which to build our argument.)

The method of proof is the famous "reductio ad absurdum." That is, we show that the denial of what we wish to prove leads to an absurdity, so that what we wish to prove cannot be false, and must therefore be true.

Here we wish to prove that there is *not* a positive rational number whose square is 2. We therefore assume that there *is* a positive rational number whose square is 2, and show that this assumption leads to a contradiction.

By (3) above, if there is a positive rational number whose square is 2, then it may be expressed in the form $\dfrac{p}{q}$, where p and q are nn with no common divisor but 1. We have then:

$$\left(\frac{p}{q}\right)^2 = 2, \quad \text{or} \quad \frac{p^2}{q^2} = 2, \quad \text{or} \quad p^2 = 2q^2$$

By (1) above, p^2 is an even nn. Therefore, by (2), p is an even nn, i.e., $p = 2k$, where k is a nn.

Substituting this value of p in the equation $p^2 = 2q^2$ we have:

$$(2k)^2 = 2q^2, \quad \text{or} \quad 4k^2 = 2q^2, \quad \text{or} \quad 2k^2 = q^2, \quad \text{or} \quad q^2 = 2k^2$$

But just as we proved p to be even before, so we may prove q to be even now.

However, this is a contradiction; for p and q have no common divisor but 1, and so cannot both be even.

The assumption that $\sqrt{2}$ is a rational number has led to an absurd result.

Therefore $\sqrt{2}$ is irrational, Q.E.D. (quod erat demonstrandum—"which was to be proved").

The student has possibly been in the habit of replacing $\sqrt{2}$ by 1.4 or by 1.41 in certain problems. Having proved $\sqrt{2}$ to be irrational, however, we know now that neither 1.4 nor 1.41 could be equal to $\sqrt{2}$; for both 1.4 and 1.41 are *rational* numbers ($1.4 = \frac{14}{10}$; $1.41 = \frac{141}{100}$). In fact, it is easy to verify that $(1.4)^2 = 1.96$, and not 2, and similarly for 1.41.

Thus 1.4 and 1.41 are approximations to $\sqrt{2}$, in the sense that when squared they come close to being 2, the first as close as any one decimal place approximation could come, the second similarly for two decimal places.

The method which the student may recall for working out successive places of a representation for $\sqrt{2}$ can never terminate, then, for if it did, we would have $\sqrt{2}$ equal to a rational number, which we have proved to be impossible. It is therefore only an *endless* decimal which could possibly represent $\sqrt{2}$.

▶ **EXERCISE 9**

1. Define and give an example of "empirical" knowledge.

2. Prove by means of line and area representations that if a, b, c, d are real numbers (with certain restrictions) then:

(a) $a(b + c) = ab + ac$

(b) $a(b + c + d) = ab + ac + ad$

(c) $(a + b)(c + d) = ac + bc + ad + bd$

(d) $(a - b)c = ac - bc$ (e) $(a + b + c)^2 = \,?$

(f) $(a + b)(a + 2b) = \,?$ (g) $(a + b)(a - b) = \,?$

3. Show that there exist line segments of the following number of inches in length: (Hint: See Fig. 3.3).

      (a) $\sqrt{3}$ (b) $\sqrt{5}$ (c) $\sqrt{6}$ (d) $\sqrt{7}$ (e) $\sqrt{8}$ (f) $\sqrt{10}$

4. Prove that the quadrilateral in Fig. 3.2, each of whose sides has length c, is a square.

5. Prove that $\sqrt{3}$ is irrational.

3.4 REPRESENTATIONS OF REAL NUMBERS

The Greeks (as we have seen in Section 3.2) pictured numbers by means of line segments. We noted, however (in the preceding section), that not all line segments have rational lengths. The Greeks, therefore, were dealing with a more extensive set of numbers than the *positive rational numbers* familiar to the Babylonians and Egyptians. In effect they extended the number system known to man to include all *positive real numbers*, for the positive real numbers are the numbers which represent the lengths of all possible line segments.

Since they pictured numbers by means of line segments, it follows that the Greeks must have performed operations on numbers by means of geometric operations on line segments. For example, they thought of the operation of adding 2 and 3 as that of adjoining line segments of lengths 2 and 3 units to form a single line segment, 5 units in length:

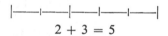

$$2 + 3 = 5$$

A second way of representing not only positive real numbers, but in fact *all* real numbers, is by means of the points of a scaled line (see Section 2.7).

Now we consider a third way of representing real numbers, quite different from the first two.

We have noted, at the end of the last section, that the well-known process for computing $\sqrt{2}$ leads to an endless decimal. This is the clue to our third method for representing real numbers: *the real numbers may be thought of as the set of all endless decimals*.

The real number $\frac{1}{4}$, for example, may be written as the endless decimal $0.25000\ldots$; the real number $\frac{1}{3}$: $0.33333\ldots$; (Both of these endless decimals are easily described, although neither, of course, can be written out completely; the first, of course, may also be written as the *terminating* decimal 0.25).

Note that the two preceding cases both had to do with *rational* real numbers, and that in each case the endless decimal expansion involved *repetition*. In the case of $\frac{1}{3}$, repetition of digits occurs right from the beginning; in the case of $\frac{1}{4}$, after the first two terms. We note further that sometimes (as in the case $\frac{7}{11} = 0.636363\ldots$) blocks of digits, rather than single digits occur repeatedly in the endless decimal expansion of a rational number.

The question arises: Does every endless decimal expansion of a rational real number repeat a pattern of one or more digits after some point?

The answer is yes. We indicate the reason for this by considering the particular rational number $\frac{8}{7}$. In dividing any nn by 7, only seven remainders are possible. Therefore, after seven or fewer steps of the division process, a remainder must be repeated, and a cycle of repetition must begin: In the case of $\frac{8}{7}$:

$$
\begin{array}{r}
1.142857 \\
\overline{\smash{\big)}\,1\ 3\ 2\ 6\ 4\ 5\ 1} \\
7\,\overline{)8.000000}
\end{array}
$$

The sequence of digits which occurs between the two remainders "1" will be repeated endlessly.

In the same way, every rational number may be expressed as an endless *repeating* decimal. But what then of those endless decimals which do not display a pattern of repeating blocks of digits? *Nonrepeating endless decimals represent all irrational real numbers.*

As a matter of fact, any repeating decimal must represent a rational number, and we may easily discover which. For example, consider the endless repeating decimal $d = 7.121212. \ldots$ We make the reasonable assumption that even among endless decimals, ordinary rules for multiplication by powers of 10, and for subtraction hold. Then:

$$100d = 712.121212\cdots$$
$$d = 7.121212\cdots$$

subtracting $\qquad\qquad 99d = 705, \qquad d = \dfrac{705}{99} = \dfrac{235}{33}$

The student may verify that this result is correct by dividing 33 into 235.

Most of the irrational real numbers (we shall call these simply the *irrational* numbers from now on) which we shall encounter are those which arise from the extraction of square roots and cube roots and so on; but there are many more irrational numbers which do not arise in this way. The most famous of these is π, which the student will recall as the number which represents the circumference of a circle whose diameter has a length of 1 unit.

That π *is* irrational was not known until 1767 A.D., however, when that fact was proved by the German mathematician, J. H. Lambert. His discovery terminated a futile search of thousands of years duration for a rational expression, like 3.14 or $\frac{22}{7}$, which would exactly equal π.

In summary: Every real number may be represented as a decimal. If the real number is rational, the decimal is terminating or repeating. If the real number is irrational, the decimal is endless and nonrepeating.

(We now have further light on why Minkowski and Kronecker (see Section 1.6) thought so highly of the natural numbers: For by using *pairs* of natural numbers, one may express all positive rational numbers; by using sequences of natural numbers (together with zero and a decimal point), one may express all positive real numbers. Add to these a minus sign, and we may express *all* real numbers. Passing over into the field of geometry, whose fundamental building block is the point, we recall that by means of a Cartesian coordinate system, every point on a plane may be identified by a pair of real numbers.)

One last word on the representation of real numbers: Actually, all methods of representation of irrational real numbers are awkward. The Greeks worked with physical lines, which is inconvenient. To add lines or endless decimals is a nuisance, and other operations are even more awkward to carry through. We therefore often simply indicate operations, as for example, when we express the sum of 2 and $\sqrt{2}$ as $2 + \sqrt{2}$.

3.5 EUCLID AND THE DEDUCTIVE METHOD

In the year 332 B.C., Alexander the Great founded the city of Alexandria in Egypt. Alexandria very soon became, and for a thousand years remained, one of the great cities of the ancient world, as well as the center of Greek cultural life. There, in about 300 B.C., the world's first university was founded; and it is believed that the first man to serve as head of its department of mathematics was the immortal Euclid.

Euclid's fame rests upon his *Elements*, a book which except for the Bible has been reproduced in more copies than any other which has ever been written. In fact, very nearly all of the high-school texts in geometry in use today are actually only revised editions of a part of Euclid's *Elements*.

It should be underlined that the mathematics in the *Elements* was, for the most part, not the original creation of Euclid, but rather an organization and summary of a great deal of the mathematics which was developed by the Greeks in the three centuries preceding the time of Euclid. It is in the selection and organization and in the method of presentation of the material at hand that the genius of Euclid lay.

The method of presentation was that of "deductive logic," a form of reasoning used so skillfully and beautifully by Euclid that his treatment has become a pattern for mathematicians to follow even up to this very day.

What is deductive logic? We have already described it as a method of reasoning or, in other words, as a method of arriving at conclusions.

It is, in fact, the method to which the Greeks were driven by the question "why?" which they asked so persistently. They soon realized, as must anyone who has ever tried to answer the questions of a curious child, that there is no end to the "whys" which may be put. Every explanation involves statements which themselves must be explained. If we are to convince someone of the truth of a particular statement, we must begin with *some* statement or statements with which he agrees, and then from that point proceed to demonstrate that the desired conclusion follows.

The same sort of thing is true of definitions. Words, for example, are defined in terms of other words. But then what do the "other words" mean? If they are to be defined, still *other* words must be utilized. For example, the word "demented" might be defined as "insane;" "insane" as "deranged;" "deranged" as "crazy";—but the process cannot go on forever without repetition, for the number of words in the English language is limited. Eventually one comes to a word which is not defined; in practical terms, one so simple that everyone agrees he knows what it means without definition.

The beginning of a deductive argument, then, must always consist of a number of words which are never defined and a number of statements which are never proved. In mathematics, these unproved statements are usually called axioms.

In the process of proceeding from statement to statement, precise rules are used: the rules of deductive logic. These very basic precepts of reasoning are used intuitively by everyone, even though they are rarely consciously expressed. One of these rules, for example, affirms that a statement cannot be both true and false; another that if a second statement follows from a first, and a third from the second, then the third statement follows from the first.

Deductive reasoning, then, is a method of arriving at conclusions by beginning with certain statements called "assumptions" or "hypotheses" or "premises" or "postulates" or "axioms," and by then applying to these statements the rules of deductive logic.

The methods of deductive logic were first systematized and expounded by Aristotle, at about 350 B.C. A classic example of this type of reasoning is his famous "syllogism":

> All men are mortal.
> Socrates is a man.
> Therefore Socrates is mortal.

Here, in the last line, is a conclusion which we feel cannot be escaped, once the two premises which precede it have been granted. It was Aristotle who gave logic the characteristic of a game governed by rules.

Every statement after the assumed statements follows from preceding statements by the rules of the game.

It is a surprising fact that the axioms of mathematics need not be "true." To the mathematician, the "truth" of the axioms is irrelevant. Beginning with axioms, he arrives at the consequences of these axioms. *If* you agree to the truth of the axioms, then deductive logic demands that you accept *also* the conclusions deduced from the axioms. But in the process of deduction, we are not in the least concerned with whether the axioms are "true" or "false."

Today, the only conclusions which mathematics stamps with its final seal of approval are those which may be arrived at deductively from sets of axioms. In that sense high-school geometry, when taught as an exercise in deductive logic, is the most mathematical of high-school courses. Algebra too, however, may be presented in the same deductive fashion, and that is what we shall soon do.

The method of deduction is not by any means the exclusive property of mathematics or even of the sciences. On July 4, 1776, a group of American patriots ratified a document which stated:

"We hold these truths to be self-evident . . .,"

and which then proceeded to deduce in masterly style the consequences of its assumptions; and on October 3, 1954, on page 1 of the *New York Times Review of the Week*, there were quoted these lines from a report of a Select Committee of the United States Senate:

> We begin with the premise that the Senate of the United States is a responsible political body. . . . From this premise, the committee advanced to its conclusion. . . .

On the other hand, although the deductive method permeates all fields of human knowledge, it is nowhere to be found in as pure a form, nor may it anywhere be seen as sharply and as clearly as in mathematics. This is one of the most powerful of all arguments in favor of the inclusion of mathematics in all college curricula. The argument fails, however, unless the course in mathematics contains clear examples of careful deductive reasoning. *The following chapter on real numbers is especially intended to serve as an example of careful deductive reasoning.*

A last word on deductive logic: There is nothing magical in it; it is not yet a final refuge for those who seek absolute truth and certainty. Even today logicians are wrestling with contradictory conclusions which seem to have been arrived at by unassailable deductive logic.

How then shall we regard this richest of all the legacies which Greece has handed down to the modern world? Simply, let us suggest, as the best method which man up to this time has devised for the purpose of persuading himself and others of the truth of statements.

3.6 INDUCTION

Another type of reasoning, and one which also plays an important role in mathematics, is *inductive* reasoning. We say that we reason inductively when we come to a general conclusion after observing a number of special instances. We consider some examples of this type of reasoning:

Every morning, for as long as I can remember, day has followed night; I am fairly certain, therefore, that tomorrow the sun will rise, just as it has risen always in the past. My reasoning in this case is inductive. That is to say, I have come to a conclusion after observing a number of occurrences of a phenomenon.

Science, with its experiments and observations, is particularly strong in the use of inductive reasoning. In genetics, for example, the conclusion that blondeness is a recessive trait is based upon nothing but the very large number of cases in which blondeness has turned out to be recessive, and the fact that in no case has blondeness turned out to be dominant. Most of our knowledge of the world around us is inductive. The "facts" that fire burns, and sugar is sweet, and even that $2 + 2 = 4$ are conclusions we have all reached inductively.

But our present interest is in mathematics. We therefore now turn our attention to the role of induction in mathematics, beginning with an example of its use:

We observe that the sum of the first two odd numbers, 1 and 3, is 4; the sum of the first three odd numbers, 1, 3, and 5, is 9; and the sum of the first four odd numbers is 16.

An alert student will note something special about these sums, namely that they are all perfect squares (i.e., squares of nn), and from this observation, and perhaps after verifying in a few more cases that his suspicion holds true, he might very well *induce* the general result: The sum of all the odd numbers up to any given odd number is always a perfect square.

Here is an indication of the reason for the importance of inductive reasoning in mathematics: It is a method for *discovering* results. But how certain are we of the truth of the statement induced?

In the example we are considering, our statement says something about *any* odd number, of which there are, of course, an infinite number. Does the fact that the statement holds true for three or four or even a hundred particular odd numbers prove that it holds true for *all* odd numbers?

The answer is *no*. A general statement may hold true in many specific cases and still not be true in all cases. We offer two examples in which this occurs.

First, consider the statement:

"All numbers are less than 1,000,000."

Many special cases of this statement happen to be true. If we check with the number 1 it is true, as it is, of course, for the number 2 and the number 3 and the number 1.7, and in fact for infinitely many numbers. But all the weight of evidence in favor of the theorem does not alter the very obvious fact that it is false, for we know very well that there *are* numbers which are *not* less than 1,000,000. Indeed, although we can never prove the truth of a statement exclusively by verifying that it is true in any subset, however numerous, of the set of all possible cases to which it applies, we can prove that a statement is false by exhibiting only *one* case in which it fails to be true.

For example, when we note that there is a number 1,000,001 which is *not* less than 1,000,000, this "counterexample" suffices to prove that the theorem in question is false. In mathematics, it is very definitely the exception which *dis*proves the rule.

The reader may perhaps consider this example to be somewhat artificial, as indeed it is. We therefore offer another example of a statement to which we might be led inductively, but which turns out to be false.

(The statement has to do with primes, and the student is therefore advised to review the definition of a prime, which will be found in Problem 5 of Exercise 2.)

Consider the result of substituting natural numbers for n in the expression: $n^2 - n + 41$. We construct a table of values:

n	1	2	3	4	5	6	7	8	9	10
$n^2 - n + 41$	41	43	47	53	61	71	83	97	113	131

There is something which may be remarked about the numbers in the second row: They are all primes. Indeed, the table may be continued for quite a way past $n = 10$, and still $n^2 - n + 41$ will be a prime. There is a tendency, on the basis of this evidence, to jump to the conclusion (i.e., to "induce") that $n^2 - n + 41$ is a formula which will yield a prime no matter *what* natural number is substituted for n.

Successive trials show, indeed, that this conclusion is true for all values of n from 1 up to 40. But alas! For $n = 41$:

$$n^2 - n + 41 = 41^2 - 41 + 41 = 41^2$$

Clearly 41^2 (i.e., 1681) is not a prime, for besides 1 and itself, 1681 has the divisor 41. The statement we have induced is false, even though it works in the first 40 of the cases to which it applies.

(Incidentally, the problem of finding a practicable formula which *will* always yield primes upon substitution of natural numbers for *n* remains one of the unsolved problems of mathematics.)

We see then that a more trustworthy method of arriving at conclusions than that of induction is necessary, and that method, of course, is the method of deduction. We emphasize once more that in mathematics the two methods go hand in hand; by induction we often discover results, but these results do not become part of the accepted body of mathematical science until they have been proved deductively.

In the sciences the inductive method is perhaps even more important than it is in mathematics; for experiments, as well as observations of phenomena which occur repeatedly under certain conditions, are methods which are basic to science in its search for general conclusions—and these, of course, are inductive methods.

Indeed, the famous "scientific method" has been defined as consisting of the following steps:

1. Experiments and/or observation of phenomena.
2. General conclusions *induced* from step 1.
3. Specific conclusions *deduced* from the general conclusions of step 2.
4. Verification of the conclusions of step 3.

Although these four steps represent an over-simplification of the very complex and varied approach known as the "scientific method," they do constitute a cycle which is typical in scientific work. One may cite, for example, the work of Newton. On the basis of many experiments and observations (perhaps even helped by the apple falling on his head, as the old, improbable story goes) he induced the very simple "law of universal gravitation," which describes how the force with which any two bodies in the universe attract each other may be computed. Together with several other laws arrived at inductively, this then enabled Newton to *deduce* many specific facts concerning the exact path of the sun and the moon and the planets in the heavens. Finally, the deduced conclusions were verified by actual astronomical observation.

The fact that induced conclusions must always be weighted with some element of uncertainty has by no means led to the abandonment of inductive reasoning in either science or mathematics. In scientific work, there is no alternative. The growth of science, in fact, is a progression from one inductive result to another, old theories discarded when new facts appear which are inconsistent with them, new theories framed to jibe with new facts.

In our day the most dramatic evidence of this is in the fall of Newtonian physics. Accepted by science because they worked in all observed cases,

Newton's laws had to be rejected when it was discovered, at the beginning of this century, that there were two places in which their conclusions did not fit all the observed facts: in the very small world of the atom and in the very large world of astronomy.

Einstein's physical theories have therefore superseded Newton's and will stand until new phenomena are discovered which contradict *their* deduced conclusions.

3.7 WHAT IS MATHEMATICS?

It is very difficult to define "mathematics" precisely. There have been many attempts to do so, but up until now no one has succeeded in framing a definition upon which all mathematicians can agree. Rather than attempt a definition, therefore, we shall content ourselves with pointing out a number of attributes especially characteristic of mathematics. The student will see in a moment why we have chosen to do so at just this point in the text.

The concepts of set, function, operation, and relation have been selected for discussion in the first two chapters not only because they are logically and historically primitive in the development of mathematics, but also because they are pervasive. They occur not only early, but often; it is extremely difficult to find a portion of mathematics in which these concepts do not play some role.

In the third chapter we spoke briefly of the principal tool used by the mathematician in working with the aforementioned concepts: the method of deductive reasoning.

We are therefore now in a position to say this about mathematics: *It is a distinctive feature of mathematics in general that it deals with functions, operations, and relations defined on sets, and that it reasons about these concepts deductively.*

But where does the raw material, that is, where do the sets, functions, operations, and relations of mathematics come from? The answer is that originally they were *abstracted* from physical situations.

The student will recall, for example, that the concept of a natural number was abstracted from concrete physical situations involving sets (see Section 1.6). The natural numbers themselves form a set, and mathematics goes on to study functions, operations, and relations defined in this set. Both the world of experience and the developing mathematics continually suggest new sets, and new functions, operations and relations to study.

This should enable the student to understand that the widespread idea that mathematics is a completed body of knowledge, in which nothing very much now remains to be done, is grossly inaccurate. Today, for example, although more mathematics journals exist than ever before, their editors are still finding it difficult to print all the new mathematics which is being created.

Another misconception we should like to correct is that *all* of the ideas of mathematics are suggested by physical experience. Often it is only the creative imagination of the mathematician which leads him into new paths, and it is only later, if ever, that the practical world finds a use for mathematics of this sort. A case in point would be the invention of negative numbers. Between the time of the Egyptians of 3000 B.C. and the 17th century, many isolated mathematicians conceived of the idea of negative numbers, and some even worked out the rules for their addition and multiplication with which we are now all familiar. It was not until Descartes showed that they had a simple, reasonable, and *useful* interpretation on a scaled line, however, that their use became general.

Concerning mathematics up to and including calculus, we may say a bit more: this mathematics concerns itself especially with two sets abstracted from physical experience, the set of all real numbers and the set of all points in space. High school algebra, for the most part, studies the real number system; geometry may be regarded as the study of sets of points; trigonometry is an off-shoot of geometry.

Since we shall make use of the real numbers in our study of geometry and trigonometry, in what follows we shall consider the real number system first.

▶ **EXERCISE 10**

1. Name two ways in which all real numbers may be represented, and one more in which all positive real numbers may be represented.

2. Express the following rational numbers as repeating endless decimals:

$$(a)\ \frac{1}{6} \quad (b)\ \frac{9}{11} \quad (c)\ \frac{1}{25} \quad (d)\ \frac{1}{13} \quad (e)\ \frac{1}{8}$$

3. Express the following repeating decimals as rational numbers in lowest terms:

    (a) $0.2222\cdots$ (b) $0.450000\cdots$ (c) $1.242424\cdots$

    (d) $0.123123123\cdots$ (e) $0.037037\cdots$ (f) $0.123454545\cdots$

4. Having answered Problem 3 of Exercise 9, what do we know about the numbers $\sqrt{3}$, $\sqrt{5}$, $\sqrt{6}$, $\sqrt{7}$, $\sqrt{8}$, and $\sqrt{10}$?

5. Devise a physical experiment to produce a straight line segment of length π inches. What does the existence of this line segment tell us about the number π?

6. It may be proved that if n is any natural number which is not a perfect square, then $\sqrt{n}$ is irrational. Therefore we know that $\sqrt{2}$, $\sqrt{3}$, $\sqrt{5}$ are each irrational.

Justify each of the following statements in *two* ways.

·(a) $\sqrt{2} \neq 1.41$ (b) $\sqrt{3} \neq 1.73$ (c) $\sqrt{5} \neq 2.24$

7. What is *deductive* logic? Illustrate by means of an original example.

8. What is *inductive* reasoning? Illustrate by means of an original example.

9. Describe two outstanding Greek contributions to mathematics, giving associated names and approximate dates.

10. If a number belongs to a class, indicate by a check mark:

	Natural Number	Positive Integer	Negative Integer	Rational Number	Positive Rational Number	Negative Rational Number	Irrational Number	Real Number
0.77								
$\sqrt{3}$								
2								
$-\frac{3}{4}$								
-1.7								
4π								
0								
$\sqrt{4}$								
7								
$\frac{7}{11}$								
$-\frac{7}{11}$								

CHAPTER 4

THE REAL NUMBER SYSTEM

> *Athenodorus told me, the very first day of his tutorship, that he proposed to teach me not facts which I could pick up anywhere for myself, but the proper presentation of facts.*
>
> ROBERT GRAVES: *I Claudius*

4.1 INTRODUCTION

We are committed in this course to the thesis that mathematics may best be described and understood in terms of the concepts of sets, functions, operations, and relations, and that the final justification for any mathematical statement must be deductive in nature. That is to say, if a question is asked as to *why* some mathematical statement holds (if one were to ask, for example: "Why does $2 + 2 = 4$?") the answer must always be either that the statement is an assumption, or that it follows from certain assumptions by the methods of deductive logic.

For obvious reasons, the plan of presenting mathematics deductively is called the "Euclidean program." To some degree, the student has seen this program at work in his study of high-school geometry. In this chapter we shall apply the Euclidean program to the development of the real number system. The study of the properties of the real number system includes all of the subject matter of elementary school arithmetic and most of the content of high-school algebra; and based directly upon the real number system are, among other branches of mathematics, analytic geometry and calculus.

We now present a set of axioms which characterize the real numbers. The student will recognize all but the last as statements which we have already remarked to be reasonable and plausible, and in fact, as statements which we would like to hold true for real numbers. From these few assumptions, *all* the properties of real numbers follow.

As a matter of convenience, we shall separate the axioms into three sets, which we shall deal with in separate sections. The first six will be called the "field" axioms (since mathematicians call any set of objects satisfying these axioms a *field*); the next three because they deal with the concept of order, are called "order" axioms; the last we have called the "axiom of Dedekind" (since it derives from the work of the great German mathematician, Richard Dedekind, 1831–1916).

4.2 REAL NUMBERS CHARACTERIZED

(In the sequel, the symbols $=$, $<$, $+$ and $\cdot$ are read "equals," "less than," "plus," and "times," respectively.)

We shall assume that *the real number system* is a set (the members of which are called *real* numbers) in which there exist two relations, $=$ and $<$, and two operations, $+$ and $\cdot$, satisfying ten axioms.

The ten axioms are written out below as six "field" axioms (Section 4.3), three "order" axioms (Section 4.14), and the "Axiom of Dedekind" (Section 4.15).

NOTE: We shall often write ab or $a(b)$ or $(a)b$ or $(a)(b)$ for $a \cdot b$.

4.3 THE SIX FIELD AXIOMS

Axiom F1. $=$ is an equivalence relation (see Section 2.15).

Axiom F2. $+$ and $\cdot$ are each complete, closed, commutative, and associative operations (see Section 2.11).

Axiom F3. (*a*) ("sum substitution") In any sum of real numbers, equals may be substituted for equals without altering the value of the sum.

(*b*) ("product substitution") In any product of real numbers, equals may be substituted for equals without altering the value of the product.

More precisely: If a, b, x, y are real numbers such that $a = x$ and $b = y$, then:

$$a + b = a + y \qquad ab = ay$$
$$a + b = x + b \qquad ab = xb$$
$$a + b = x + y \qquad ab = xy$$

Axiom F4. ("left distributive law") If F, S, T are real numbers, then:

$$F(S + T) = FS + FT$$

Axiom F5. There are unequal real numbers, 0 and 1 (read "zero" and "one," respectively), which have the property that if a is any real number, then:

$$\text{("zero-axiom")}: \quad a + 0 = a$$

$$\text{("one-axiom")}: \quad a \cdot 1 = a$$

Axiom F6. If a is any real number, then there is a real number $\bar{a}$ (read: a bar) such that:

$$\text{("negative axiom")}: \quad a + \bar{a} = 0$$

and if a is any *nonzero* real number, then there is a real number a' (read: a prime) such that:

$$\text{("reciprocal axiom")}: \quad aa' = 1$$

NOTES ON THE FIELD AXIOMS:

Axiom F3 is sometimes referred to as the "well-definedness" axiom for addition and multiplication, since the axiom guarantees, essentially, that the sum or product of two real numbers is not altered when different names are used for the same number. Addition, for example, would certainly deserve to be considered badly defined if $\frac{2}{3} + 1$ turned out to be unequal to $\frac{4}{6} + 1$.

The student will recognize Axiom F3 as a more precisely stated form of the "equals plus equals" and "equals times equals" axioms of high-school mathematics.

The word "law" in Axiom F4 has no special significance; its use is only a matter of custom.

In Axiom F6, the number we have denoted $\bar{a}$ is that which the student already knows as $-a$, or "minus a," or the "negative of a"; and a' denotes the number already familiar to the student as $\frac{1}{a}$ or $1/a$, or the "reciprocal of a." The reason for the stipulation $a \neq 0$ in the second part of Axiom F6 is, of course, that we have seen that it is unreasonable to ask for an answer to the problem: $1/0 = ?$. The reason for the change from the usual notation for negatives and reciprocals is to emphasize the similarities between them, and to avoid the confusion which results from the use of the symbol " $-$ " to indicate both the *sign* of a number and the *operation* of subtraction.

4.4   SEVERAL THEOREMS AND THEIR PROOFS

In our deductive processes we shall borrow from the vocabulary and usage of high-school geometry. For example, relatively important statements following from our axioms will be called "theorems." In "proving" theorems, that is in demonstrating that a theorem actually *is* the consequence of our axioms, we shall for some time follow a familiar pattern: statements will appear in one column, and the reason which justifies each statement will be placed to its right in a parallel column.

It is important to note that only the following are acceptable as entries in the "Reason" column:

1. The hypothesis of the theorem to be proved.
2. An axiom.
3. A definition.
4. A previously proved result.

The following are explanations or comments on 1–4 above:

1. *The hypothesis of the theorem to be proved.*

Every theorem is made up of statements which may be written in the form: "If . . ., then . . ."   For example, the theorem:

"The base angles of an isosceles triangle are equal" may be written: "If a triangle is isosceles, then its base angles are equal."

When an assertion is written in the "If . . ., then . . ." form, the statement following "If" (and preceding "then") is called the *hypothesis*, and the statement following "then" is called the *conclusion* of the assertion.

2. *An axiom.*

To the Greeks an axiom was a "self-evident truth"; but with the passage of time, mathematicians have become more modest in their claims. Experience (especially the discovery of "non-Euclidean geometry" in the early nineteenth century) has taught that that which seems self-evident is not always even true; and in fact that it is very difficult, if not impossible, to be sure about the absolute truth of *any* statement.

Mathematicians today, therefore, do *not* claim that the axioms of mathematics are truths, whether self-evident or otherwise.   The axioms are simply statements, mathematicians now say, from which other statements will be made to follow by the rules of deductive logic.   *If* one accepts the axioms as "true," and *if* one accepts the rules of deductive logic, then one is constrained to accept the logical consequences of the axioms as "true."

3. *A definition.*

A deductive treatment of a branch of mathematics begins, as we have already pointed out, with a number of unproved statements (called "axioms") and a number of undefined terms.   After that all new terms which are introduced must be defined in terms of the undefined terms and/or in terms of previously defined terms.

For example, in our axiomatic development of real numbers, $=$, $<$, $+$, and $\cdot$ are undefined, or as they are sometimes called, "primitive" terms. Although the axioms say things *about* these terms, we actually never tell what the terms themselves mean.

However $>$ ("greater than") will be a *defined* term, and in fact will be defined in terms of the undefined term $<$; and "positive" will be a defined term, defined in terms of the previously defined term $>$; etc. (See Section 4.14).

Definitions in mathematics are framed with two things in mind: First of all, we attempt to make a definition agree with intuitive feelings about the thing being defined. Euclid, for example, followed this requirement when he defined a point as "that which has no parts." But secondly, we attempt to make the definition fruitful, in the sense that the definition lends itself to proving statements about the thing defined. Euclid's definition of a point fails utterly in this second respect, for not even once do we find Euclid making use of the definition in proving the theorems which follow it.

Since, in fact, only definitions and axioms and previously proved statements about a mathematical term may be used in proving assertions about that term, these are the resources the student should look to in trying to prove such assertions. Physical intuition or the imagination may help greatly in indicating the right path to follow, but in the final write-up of a proof, the raw material must come from one of the four sources listed above.

A word concerning the arbitrariness of mathematical definitions is appropriate here. It is typical of the English language that many of its words have a multiplicity of meanings. In mathematics, where we seek for precision of thought and statement, we prefer that one defined term, insofar as is practicable, have only one clearly defined meaning. Different authors make different choices among a number of meanings, and as a consequence, the student will find that many texts apparently disagree with each other, and with dictionaries, as to the meaning of certain terms.

This, however, should not disturb the student. For him, it is simply a matter of understanding what the author is saying in the light of the *author's* definitions. In this text, for example, we have arbitrarily chosen a definition of "angle" (see page 144) that happens to coincide with the definition of some texts, that happens to be different from that of most texts, and that agrees with very few dictionaries. After that definition has been given, "angle" throughout the rest of *this* text will mean nothing more nor less than what that definition states.

Furthermore, the definition agreed upon is what the mathematician seeks when he asks: "What is . . .?" In ordinary usage, for example, when one is asked: "What is a camel?" there is an inclination to tell as much as possible about that animal, in an attempt to conjure up in the questioner's mind an image as nearly as possible like that in the mind of the person answering the question. But when a mathematician asks: "What is an angle?" he does not want in response a mass of descriptive detail or an enumeration of properties or attributes or characteristics; he wants only to know the *definition* you have agreed upon for an angle —only that and nothing more.

4. *A previously proved result.*

The student may assume that any statement which occurs as a problem to be proved in the exercises which follow, may actually be proved, and may therefore be used in the proof of any statement in the text which follows that problem.

The construction of proofs is one of the more difficult of mathematical activities; in fact, the ability to construct proofs, together with a knack for discovering mathematical statements worth attempting to prove, may generally be considered to be two distinguishing characteristics of the "mathematical mind."

Not everyone, therefore, should be expected to be able to construct any but fairly simple proofs. The reader of this text, however, should in any case be able to follow (i.e., to understand) proofs once they are constructed, since following a proof is in the main only a question of seeing that each step is properly justified.

We now proceed to state and prove our first theorem on real numbers.

Theorem RI. (right distributive law) If F, S, T are real numbers, then:
$$(F + S)T = FT + ST$$

PROOF

Statements		*Reasons*
1. F and S are real numbers	1.	Hyp.
2. $F + S$ exists	2.	Completeness of $+$
3. $F + S$ is a real number	3.	Closure of $+$
4. T is a real number	4.	Hyp.
5. $(F + S)T = T(F + S)$	5.	Commutativity of $\cdot$
6. $T(F + S) = TF + TS$	6.	Left dist. law
7. $\therefore (F + S)T = TF + TS$	7.	Transitivity of $=$ (Steps 5, 6)
8. $TF = FT$, $TS = ST$	8.	Commutativity of $\cdot$
9. $\therefore TF + TS = FT + ST$	9.	Sum sub.
10. $\therefore (F + S)T = FT + ST$	10.	Transitivity of $=$ (Steps 7, 9)

A mathematical proof is said to be more or less "rigorous," depending upon the extent to which necessary steps are included and justified.   The preceding proof, for example, would be considered to be fairly rigorous.

But exceedingly rigorous proofs often have the disadvantage of being long and tedious; even worse, major ideas tend to be lost in a maze of minor steps.   It is customary, therefore, to omit "obvious" statements in proofs.   As an example of a proof which is acceptable, although less rigorous than our first, we offer another proof of Theorem R1:

NOTE 1:   From now on the headings *Statements* and *Reasons* will be understood, but not written in our proofs.

NOTE 2:   " $= TF + TS$" in step 2 below is to be understood as following the expression directly above it; i.e., step 2, as it stands, is an abbreviation for: $T(F + S) = TF + TS$.

ALTERNATE PROOF OF THEOREM R1

1.	$(F + S)T = T(F + S)$	1.	Comm. of $\cdot$
2.	$= TF + TS$	2.	LDL
3.	$= FT + ST$	3.	Comm. of $\cdot$
4.	$\therefore (F + S)T = FT + ST$	4.	Tr. of $=$ (more than once)

In further illustration of the process of deductive proof, here is another theorem and its proof:

Theorem R2.   If a is any real number, $0 + a = a$.

PROOF

1.	$0 + a = a + 0$	1.	Comm. of $+$
2.	$a + 0 = a$	2.	Zero axiom
3.	$\therefore 0 + a = a$	3.	Tr. of $=$

4.5 PROPERTIES OF EQUALITY

In this section we shall state, and from our axioms prove, certain useful properties of the relation of equality among the real numbers.

Theorem R3.   ("Things equal to the same thing are equal to each other.")   If a, b, x are real numbers such that $a = x$ and $b = x$, then $a = b$.

PROOF

1.	$a = x, b = x$	1.	Hyp.
2.	$x = b$	2.	Sym. of $=$
3.	$\therefore a = b$	3.	Tr. of $=$

NOTE: From now on, spaces to be filled in by the student will appear in proofs.

Theorem R4. ("Things equal to equal things are equal to each other.") If a, b, x, y are real numbers such that $a = x$ and $b = y$ and $x = y$, then $a = b$.

PROOF

1.	$a = x, x = y$	1.	
2.	$\therefore a = y$	2.	
3.	$b = y$	3.	
4.	$\therefore a = b$	4.	Th. R3

The usefulness of our results on equality is augmented when we note that because of the symmetric property of equality, any equation may be read either from left to right or from right to left. Therefore, in what follows, we shall for example read "$a = b$" as either "a equals b" or "b equals a," whichever suits our convenience.

► **EXERCISE 11**

1. Prove: If a is any real number, then $1 \cdot a = a$.
2. Prove: If a is any real number, then $\bar{a} + a = 0$.
3. Prove: If a is any nonzero real number, then $a' a = 1$.
4. Definition: $a^2 = a \cdot a$.
   Prove: If $a = b$, then $a^2 = b^2$.
5. Definition: $a^3 = a^2 \cdot a$.
   Prove: If $a = b$, then $a^3 = b^3$.
6. (a) Can a theorem be proved without making use of the hypothesis of the theorem?
   (b) How do you explain the fact that the hypothesis of Theorem R2 has not been used in the proof of Theorem R2 above?
7. A "sharpened" statement of Theorem R1 is: If F, S, T are real numbers, then the following exist and are real numbers: $F + S$, $(F + S)T$, FT, ST, and $FT + ST$; furthermore, $(F + S)T = FT + ST$.
   Indicate respects in which the proof of Theorem R1 given in the text is not perfectly rigorous. Construct a proof of Theorem R1 which is more rigorous, using the sharper statement of that theorem given above.

NOTE: To facilitate writing out the proofs which follow, we shall combine several statements of this section as follows:

Zero Law: The zero axiom and Theorem R2.
One Law: The one axiom and Problem 1 above.
Negative Law: The negative axiom and Problem 2 above.
Reciprocal Law: The reciprocal axiom and Problem 3 above.

4.6 CANCELLATION LAWS

In this section we shall justify certain cancellations which may be effected on both sides of certain equations.

We begin with a "lemma," that is to say with a statement of relatively minor importance whose chief purpose is to aid in the proof of the theorem which follows it.

Lemma. If k and x are real numbers, then $(k + x) + \bar{x} = k$.

PROOF

1. $(k + x) + \bar{x} = k + (x + \bar{x})$ 1.
2. $= k + 0$ 2.
3. $= k$ 3.
4. $\therefore (k + x) + \bar{x} = k$ 4.

Theorem R5. If a, b, x are real numbers and $a + x = b + x$, then $a = b$.

PROOF

1. $a + x = b + x$ 1.
2. $\therefore (a + x) + \bar{x} = (b + x) + \bar{x}$ 2.   Sum sub.
3. $(a + x) + \bar{x} = a$ 3.
        $(b + x) + \bar{x} = b$
4. $\therefore$ $a = b$ 4.

Corollary. If a, b, x are real numbers and $x + a = x + b$, then $a = b$.

PROOF

1. $x + a = x + b$ 1.
2. $x + a = a + x$ and $x + b = b + x$ 2.
3. $\therefore a + x = b + x$ 3.
4. $\therefore$ $a = b$ 4.

Theorem R6. If a, b, x, y are real numbers such that $a + x = b + y$ and $x = y$, then $a = b$.

PROOF

1. $x = y$ 1.
2. $\therefore a + x = a + y$ 2.
3. $a + x = b + y$ 3.
4. $\therefore a + y = b + y$ 4.
5. $\therefore$ $a = b$ 5.

NOTE: Further cancellation theorems, having to do with both addition and multiplication, will be included in the exercise which follows.

▶ **EXERCISE 12**

1. Prove: If a, b, x, y are real numbers such that $a + x = b + y$ and $a = b$, then $x = y$.

2. Prove: If k and x are real numbers and $x \neq 0$, then $(kx)x' = k$.

3. Prove: If a, b, x are real numbers such that $ax = bx$ and $x \neq 0$, then $a = b$.

4. Prove: If a, b, x are real numbers such that $xa = xb$ and $x \neq 0$, then $a = b$.

5. Prove: If a, b, x, y are real numbers such that $ax = by$ and $x = y \neq 0$, then $a = b$.

6. Prove: If a, b, x, y are real numbers such that $ax = by$ and $a = b \neq 0$, then $x = y$.

7. Prove: If a and b are real numbers and $a + b = 0$, then $a = \bar{b}$ and $b = \bar{a}$.

8. Prove: $\bar{0} = 0$.

9. Prove: If a and b are real numbers and $ab = 1$, then $a = b'$ and $b = a'$.

10. Prove: $1' = 1$.

11. Prove: If a and b are real numbers and $a = b$, then $\bar{a} = \bar{b}$.

12. Prove: If a and b are nonzero real numbers and $a = b$, then $a' = b'$.

13. When $\bar{a}$ is called "*the* negative of a" there is an implication that only one negative of a could possibly exist. (In fact, although this is not *always* true, in mathematics we generally understand that an object to which we apply the word "the" is unique; otherwise we tend to use "a" rather than "the.")

The defining property of $\bar{a}$ is that when it is added to a the result is 0. To prove that $\bar{a}$ *is* unique, and therefore that we are justified in calling $\bar{a}$ *the* negative of a, show that if real numbers r and s both have the defining property of $\bar{a}$, then necessarily: $r = s$.

14. (Uniqueness of "0") Prove that only the real number 0 has its defining property.

15. (Uniqueness of "1") Prove that only the real number 1 has its defining property.

16. Show that we are justified in referring to a' as *the* reciprocal of a, where a is any nonzero real number.

17. Prove: If a is a real number, then $\bar{\bar{a}} = a$. (i.e., $-(-a) = a$)

18. Prove: If a is a real number and $a \neq 0$, then $a'' = a$. $\left(\text{i.e., } 1/\frac{1}{a} = a\right)$

19. Prove: If a and b are real numbers, then $\overline{a + b} = \bar{a} + \bar{b}$. (i.e., $-(a + b) = (-a) + (-b)$)

20. Prove: If a and b are nonzero real numbers, then $(ab)' = a'b'$. Also: State this result in another way.

21. Prove: $\bar{1} \neq 0$.

NOTE: We shall refer to Theorem R5 and its Corollary, and to Theorem R6, and to Problem 1 above as "the cancellation laws for addition."

We shall refer to Problems 3, 4, 5, 6 above as "the cancellation laws for multiplication."

4.7 MULTIPLICATION BY ZERO

We all "know" that the result of multiplying any real number by 0 is 0, and that the product of two real numbers cannot be 0 unless at least one of them is 0.

In this section we shall demonstrate that these important properties are consequences of the assumptions we have made about real numbers.

Theorem R7.   If a is any real number, $a \cdot 0 = 0$.

PROOF

(The idea in this proof is to arrive at the statement: $a \cdot 0 + a \cdot 0 = 0 + a \cdot 0$, from which, by the cancellation theorem R5, the desired result follows.)

1.	$a \cdot 0 + a \cdot 0 = a \cdot (0 + 0)$	1.
2.	$= a \cdot 0$	2.
3.	$= 0 + a \cdot 0$	3.
4.	$\therefore a \cdot 0 + a \cdot 0 = 0 + a \cdot 0$	4.
5.	$\therefore \qquad a \cdot 0 = 0.$	5.

Corollary.   If a is any real number, then $0 \cdot a = 0$.

(The proof of this corollary is left as an exercise for the student.)

Theorem R7 and its Corollary may be combined into a statement that we shall refer to as the "multiplicative property of zero" (MPZ).

MPZ Theorem.   If a and b are real numbers, and if either $a = 0$ or $b = 0$, then $ab = 0$.

NOTE.   The words "either . . . or . . ." as used in mathematics connote "at least one and possibly both." Thus "either $a = 0$ or $b = 0$" does not exclude the possibility that *both* a and b are 0 (cf. Note 2, page 13).

We digress for a moment, to consider a relevant question of logic:

A "converse" of a given statement (as we shall understand it in this text) may be arrived at by interchanging all or part of the hypothesis and the conclusion of the given statement. For example, the statement: "If x *is normal*, and x *is a man*, then x *has two eyes*" has the converses:

(1)   If x is normal, and x has two eyes, then x is a man.   (Interchanging second hypothesis and conclusion)

(2)   If x has two eyes and x is a man, then x is normal.   (Interchanging first hypothesis and conclusion)

(3)   If x has two eyes, then x is normal and x is a man.   (Interchanging all of hypothesis and conclusion)

These illustrations show (how?) that a converse of a true statement need not necessarily be true.

A very important converse of the MPZ theorem *is* true, however, as we proceed to prove:

Theorem R8. If a and b are real numbers, and if $ab = 0$, then either $a = 0$ or $b = 0$.

PROOF

We shall prove this theorem by means of the "indirect method," that is, we shall show that the assumption that the theorem is false leads to a contradiction.

If the theorem is false, then there must exist real numbers a and b such that $ab = 0$, but neither a nor b is equal to zero. We shall assume that such numbers exist, and show that this leads to the situation: $b \neq 0$, $b = 0$. Since a statement cannot be both true and not true, this result is a contradiction. The statement $b \neq 0$ is part of our assumption. Therefore, as soon as we have arrived at the statement $b = 0$, we shall know that our theorem cannot be false, and must therefore be true.

1. $a \neq 0, b \neq 0, ab = 0$	1. Hyp.
2. $\therefore a'$ and b' exist	2. Rec. axiom
3. $a'(ab) = a' \cdot 0$	3.
4. $= 0$	4.
5. $\therefore a'(ab) = 0$	5.
6. $a'(ab) = (a'a)b$	6.
7. $= 1 \cdot b$	7.
8. $= b$	8.
9. $\therefore a'(ab) = b$	9.
10. $\therefore \quad b = 0$	10.

4.8 LOGICAL INTERLUDE

In this section we consider certain notation and vocabulary common in logic and useful in mathematics.

If P and Q are statements, the statement: "If P, then Q" is often expressed in other ways. For example, the following are synonymous statements:

(1) If P, then Q.
(2) P implies Q.
(3) From P follows Q.
(4) P is a *sufficient* condition for Q.
(5) Q is a *necessary* condition for P.

The symbol $\Rightarrow$ (read from left to right) or $\Leftarrow$ (read from right to left) is used to mean "implies." For example, the MPZ theorem may be written:

If a and b are real numbers, then:

$$a = 0 \text{ or } b = 0 \Rightarrow ab = 0$$

The preceding line is read: "$a = 0$ or $b = 0$ implies $ab = 0$." This statement may also be expressed in the following ways:

If $a = 0$ or b $= 0$, then $ab = 0$.

From $a = 0$ or $b = 0$, follows $ab = 0$.

$a = 0$ or $b = 0$ is a *sufficient* condition for $ab = 0$ (i.e., in order for ab to equal 0, it is *sufficient* that $a = 0$ or $b = 0$).

$ab = 0$ is a *necessary* condition for $a = 0$ or $b = 0$ (i.e., if $a = 0$ or $b = 0$ is true, then *necessarily* $ab = 0$ is true also).

When we have statements P and Q such that each implies the other (i.e., such that if either is true, then the other is true), we say and write:

(1) P if and only if Q.
(2) $P \Leftrightarrow Q$ (read: P is equivalent to Q; means: $P \Rightarrow Q$ and $Q \Rightarrow P$.)
(3) P is a necessary and sufficient condition for Q.

Thus, the MPZ Theorem and Theorem R8 may be combined into the statement:

If a and b are real numbers, then:

$$a = 0 \text{ or } b = 0 \Leftrightarrow ab = 0$$

4.9   THE SIGN LAWS IN MULTIPLICATION

Why is the product of a negative number and a positive number a negative number? And why is it that two negatives, when multiplied together, yield a positive result?

The first statement may be made to seem plausible by means of an intuitive argument. For example: -3 may be thought of in connection with a *loss* of 3 objects; $2 \cdot (-3)$, then, would be associated with two losses of 3 objects, or a loss of 6 objects, or -6.

The other rules for the multiplication of signed numbers may be justified intuitively also, but by arguments not all as plausible as the preceding.

However, the point of this chapter is that as mathematicians, we no longer look to intuitive arguments for the final justification of mathematical statements. At this stage, only a deductive proof based upon our assumptions will convince us; and when we have shown that the rules for the multiplication of signed numbers follow logically from our assumptions about real numbers, then we shall be able to say to anyone who accepts our axioms about the real numbers, that he must accept these rules also. We proceed, then, to deduce the rules in question.

Lemma. If a and b are real numbers, then:

$$\text{(i)} \quad ab + a\bar{b} = 0$$
$$\text{(ii)} \quad \bar{a}b + ab = 0$$
$$\text{(iii)} \quad \bar{a}b + \bar{a}\bar{b} = 0$$

PROOF OF (i)

1.	$ab + a\bar{b} = a(b + \bar{b})$	1.
2.	$= a \cdot 0$	2.
3.	$= 0$	3.
4.	$\therefore ab + a\bar{b} = 0$	4.

(The proofs of (ii) and (iii) are left as exercises for the student.)

Theorem R9. If a and b are real numbers, then:

$$\text{(i)} \quad a\bar{b} = \overline{ab}$$
$$\text{(ii)} \quad \bar{a}b = \overline{ab}$$
$$\text{(iii)} \quad \bar{a}\bar{b} = ab$$

PROOF OF (i)

1.	$ab + a\bar{b} = 0$	1. Lemma; (i)
2.	$ab + \overline{ab} = 0$	2. Neg law
3.	$\therefore ab + a\bar{b} = ab + \overline{ab}$	3.
4.	$\therefore \quad a\bar{b} = \overline{ab}$	4.

PROOF OF (ii)

1.	$\bar{a}b + ab = 0$	1.
2.	$\overline{ab} + ab = 0$	2.
3.		3.
4.		4.

PROOF OF (iii)

1.		1.
2.	$\bar{a}b + ab = 0$	2.
3.		3.
4.		4.

In more familiar notation, the conclusion of Theorem R9 is:

$$\text{(i)} \quad a \cdot (-b) = -(ab)$$
$$\text{(ii)} \quad (-a) \cdot b = -(ab)$$
$$\text{(iii)} \quad (-a) \cdot (-b) = ab$$

4.10 THE OPERATION OF SUBTRACTION AMONG THE REAL NUMBERS

In *subtracting* 2 from 5, we seek a number which when added to 2 will equal 5. There is such a number, namely 3, and in fact there is no other real number which will do the trick.

Although we have not yet formally defined what we mean by subtraction, the following theorem will eventually enable us to say that any real number may be subtracted from any real number, and that the result of a subtraction is unique.

Theorem R10. If a and b are real numbers, then there is one and only one real number d such that $d + a = b$, and that real number d is equal to $b + \bar{a}$.

This theorem actually has two parts. We shall first prove that there *is* a real number d such that $d + a = b$ (the so-called "existence" part of the theorem), and then we shall prove that there is *only one* such number (the "uniqueness" part of the theorem).

In the existence proof, we shall show that if $d = b + \bar{a}$, then the requirement of the theorem is satisfied.

In the uniqueness proof, we shall assume that both $d + a = b$ and $e + a = b$, and then show that necessarily: $d = e$.

PROOF (EXISTENCE)

1.	$d = b + \bar{a}$	1. Hyp.
2.	$\therefore d + a = (b + \bar{a}) + a$	2.
3.	$= b + (\bar{a} + a)$	3.
4.	$= b + 0$	4.
5.	$= b$	5.
6.	$\therefore d + a = b$	6.

PROOF (UNIQUENESS)

1.	$d + a = b, e + a = b$	1.
2.	$\therefore d + a = e + a$	2.
3.	$\therefore \quad d = e$	3.

We are now able to *define* the operation of subtraction among the real numbers, the symbol for which is, of course, "$-$."

Definition R1. If a and b are real numbers, we define: $b - a = d$, where d is the unique real number such that $d + a = b$; i.e., $b - a = b + \bar{a}$.

It follows that among the real numbers every subtraction may be justified by means of an addition; to prove, for example, that $5 - 3 = 2$, it is sufficient to demonstate that $2 + 3 = 5$.

▶ **EXERCISE 13**

1. Prove the corollary to Theorem R7.

2. Prove parts (ii) and (iii) of the lemma preceding Theorem R9.

3. Prove: If k is any real number, then:
$$\bar{1} \cdot k = \bar{k}; \quad k \cdot \bar{1} = \bar{k}; \quad \bar{1} \cdot \bar{k} = k; \quad \bar{k} \cdot \bar{1} = k$$
Also: State these results in another way.

4. Subtraction and addition among the real numbers are called "inverse" operations because each undoes the work of the other, in the sense that if a and b are real numbers, adding a to b and then subtracting a (or vice-versa) leaves b unchanged. More precisely:

(i) $(b + a) - a = b$ (ii) $(b - a) + a = b$

Prove (i) and (ii) above. [Hint: Resort to the definition of subtraction above: $b - a = b + \bar{a}$; hence $(b + a) - a = (b + a) + \bar{a}$.]

5. Prove if a, b, c are real numbers then: $a(b - c) = ab - ac$.

6. Prove: If a, b are real numbers, then: $\overline{a - b} = b - a$; $\overline{a + b} = -a - b$; $\overline{-a - b} = a + b$. (Hint: Use Def. R1 and Problems 17, 19 of Ex. 12.)

Also: State these results entirely in the more familiar notation.

7. (Well-definedness of subtraction, or subtraction substitution.)

Prove: If a, b, x, y are real numbers such that $x = y$ and $a = b$, then $x - a = y - b$. (Hint: Use Def. R1 and Problem 11, Ex. 12.)

What well-known high-school axiom corresponds to this result?

4.11 THE OPERATION OF DIVISION AMONG THE REAL NUMBERS

In the problem $6 \div 3 = ?$ we seek a number which when multiplied by 3 will equal 6. That number, of course, is 2, and there is no other real number which will do the trick.

In fact, so long as the divisor is not zero, division is always possible among the real numbers, and that, in effect, is what the following theorem guarantees:

Theorem R11. If a and b are real numbers, and $a \neq 0$, then there is one and only one real number r such that $ra = b$; and that real number r is equal to ba'.

As in the preceding case, the proof of this theorem is made up of an existence proof and a uniqueness proof. In the existence proof, we show that if $r = ba'$, then the requirement of the theorem is satisfied. In the uniqueness proof we assume that both $xa = b$ and $ya = b$, and then show that necessarily $x = y$.

(The rest of this proof is left as an exercise for the student.)

We are now able to *define* the operation of division, the symbol for which is " $\div$ "; but note that $b \div a$ may also be written b/a and $\dfrac{b}{a}$.

Definition R2. If a and b are real numbers and $a \neq 0$, we define $b \div a = r$, where r is the unique real number such that $ra = b$; i.e., $b \div a = b/a = \dfrac{b}{a} = ba'$.

In other words, among the real numbers every division may be justified by means of a multiplication. To prove, for example, that $6 \div 3 = 2$, it is sufficient to show that $3 \neq 0$ and that $2 \cdot 3 = 6$.

▶ EXERCISE 14

1. Prove Theorem R11.

2. Prove: If k is a nonzero real number then:

$$\frac{1}{k} = k'; \quad \frac{k}{k} = 1; \quad \frac{k}{1} = k; \quad \frac{0}{k} = 0$$

(Note: the first equation says that $1/k$ is the reciprocal of k.)

3. Prove: If a, b are real numbers and $b \neq 0$ then:

$$\left(\frac{a}{b}\right)b = a; \quad b\left(\frac{a}{b}\right) = a; \quad \frac{ab}{b} = a; \quad \frac{ba}{b} = a$$

4. If a, b, c, d are real numbers such that $b \neq 0$ and $d \neq 0$, then:

$$\frac{a}{b} \cdot \frac{c}{d} = \frac{ac}{bd}$$

(*Hint*: The left side of the equation is equal to $ab'cd'$; then use comm. law of mult., Problem 20, Exercise 12, etc.)

5. Prove: If a, $b \neq 0$, $k \neq 0$ are real numbers, then:

$$\frac{ak}{bk} = \frac{a}{b}; \quad \frac{ka}{kb} = \frac{a}{b}$$

(*Hint*: Use Problems 4 and 2 above.)

6. (Well-definedness of division, or division substitution.)

Prove: If a, b, x, y are real numbers such that $a \neq 0$, $b \neq 0$, $x = y$ and $a = b$, then: $x/a = y/b$. (*Hint*: Use Def. R2 and Problem 12, Exercise 12.) What well-known high-school axiom corresponds to this result?

7. Prove: If a and b are nonzero real numbers, then $\left(\dfrac{a}{b}\right)\left(\dfrac{b}{a}\right) = 1$.

(As a corollary, in the light of Problem 9 of Exercise 12, it follows that $\left(\dfrac{a}{b}\right)' = \dfrac{b}{a}$ and $\left(\dfrac{b}{a}\right)' = \dfrac{a}{b}$, i.e., that $\dfrac{a}{b}$ and $\dfrac{b}{a}$ are each other's reciprocals.)

8. Prove: If $r, a \neq 0, b \neq 0$ are real numbers, then $r \div \dfrac{a}{b} = r \cdot \dfrac{b}{a}$

9. Prove: If $a, b, k \neq 0$ are real numbers, then:

$$\frac{a+b}{k} = \frac{a}{k} + \frac{b}{k} \text{ and } \frac{a-b}{k} = \frac{a}{k} - \frac{b}{k}$$

10. Prove: $\dfrac{-1}{-1} = 1; \quad \dfrac{-1}{1} = -1; \quad \dfrac{1}{-1} = -1.$

(*Hint*: First of all, note Problem 21, Exercise 12.)

11. Prove: If r is a real number and $r \neq 0$, then $-r \neq 0$. (*Hint*: Use the "indirect method.")

12. Prove: If r is a real number and $r \neq 0$, then $(-r)' = -(r')$; state this result without using the "prime" notation.

13. Prove: If a and $b \neq 0$ are real numbers, then:

$$\frac{-a}{-b} = \frac{a}{b}; \quad \frac{-a}{b} = -\frac{a}{b}; \quad \frac{a}{-b} = -\frac{a}{b}$$

14. Prove that if a and b and $\dfrac{a}{b}$ are real numbers and $\dfrac{a}{b} = 0$, then $b \neq 0$ and $a = 0$.

15. For what real numbers x is it true that $\dfrac{x-7}{x-7} = 1$? Why?

16. For what real numbers x is it true that $\dfrac{(x-7)(x-11)}{(x-7)(x-13)} = \dfrac{x-11}{x-13}$? Why?

17. If $a, b, x \neq 0, y \neq 0$ are real numbers, prove that $\dfrac{a}{x} = \dfrac{b}{y}$ if and only if $ay = bx$.

4.12 ELEMENTARY ARITHMETIC

What is more certain than that "two and two make four"? As far as we as mathematicians are concerned, however, no matter how obvious the statement about real numbers, its acceptability must rest finally on whether it can be made to follow from our real number axioms by the methods of deductive logic.

In this section we shall prove that $2 + 2 = 4$, and show how other results of elementary arithmetic are consequences of the real number axioms we have stated so far, that is to say of the "field" axioms.

Before we can prove anything about "2," however, we must *define* what we mean by "2" in terms of the real number concepts already at hand. We note that there is an axiom which presents us with "1," and another which gives us the operation " + ". A natural definition for the other natural numbers is then:

Definition R3. $2 = 1 + 1$
$3 = 2 + 1$
$4 = 3 + 1$, etc.

Theorem R12. $2 + 2 = 4.$

PROOF

1. $2 + 2 = 2 + (1 + 1)$ 1.
2. $= (2 + 1) + 1$ 2.
3. $= 3 + 1$ 3.
4. $= 4$ 4.
5.   5.

Corollary. $4 - 2 = 2.$

PROOF

1. $2 + 2 = 4$ 1. Th. R12
2. $\therefore 4 - 2 = 2$ 2. Def. of " $-$ "

Theorem R13. $2 \cdot 2 = 4.$

PROOF

1. $2 \cdot 2 = 2(1 + 1)$ 1.
2. $= 2 \cdot 1 + 2 \cdot 1$ 2.
3. $= 2 + 2$ 3.
4. $= 4$ 4.
5.   5.

▶ **EXERCISE 15**

1.   Prove each of the following statements:

(i) $2 + 3 = 5$ (v) $2 + 6 = 8$ (ix) $6 - 4 = 2$
(ii) $2 + 4 = 6$ (vi) $2 \cdot 3 \ = 6$ (x) $6 - 3 = 3$
(iii) $3 + 3 = 6$ (vii) $2 \cdot 4 \ = 8$ (xi) $7 - 4 = 3$
(iv) $3 + 4 = 7$ (viii) $5 - 3 = 2$ (xii) $8 - 6 = 2$

2.   If x is a real number, prove that:

(i) $2x + 3x = 5x$ (iii) $x + x = 2x$
(ii) $7x - 4x = 3x$ (iv) $x - x = 0$

4.13   FACTORS AND PRODUCTS

Precisely what do we mean when we say that $x^2 - 4$ "factors" into $(x - 2)(x + 2)$?

What we mean is this: that *if x is any real number*, then $x^2 - 4 = (x - 2)(x + 2)$. It is very important to note that the italicized phrase, whether expressed or simply understood, is an essential part of the statement.

For example, suppose x is the real number 30. Then our statement says: $30^2 - 2^2 = (30 - 2)(30 + 2)$, or (reading from right to left): $28 \cdot 32 = 900 - 4 = 896$. The student may verify by ordinary multiplication that this result is correct. (As a matter of fact, this and similar "factorizations" may be used to reduce the difficulty of working out certain arithmetic problems mentally.)

In Section 3.2, we saw how Pythagoras justified certain simple factorizations. In this section we shall prove similar formulas, but this time more precisely, for now we have the clearly stated field axioms upon which to base our proofs.

The simplest of these formulas is already known to the student as the "common factor" type of factorization. This is only a simple generalization of the distributive laws:

Theorem R14. If a, b, c, k are real numbers, then:

(i) $ka + kb = k(a + b)$ (i') $ak + bk = (a + b)k$
(ii) $ka + kb + kc = k(a + b + c)$ (ii') $ak + bk + ck = (a + b + c)k$

(and so on)

PROOF

(i):   1. $k(a + b) = ka + kb$ 1.
      2. $\therefore ka + kb = k(a + b)$ 2.
(i'): (Proof left as an exercise for the student.)
(ii):   1. $k(a + b + c) = k[(a + b) + c]$ 1.   Def. (see page 42)
      2. $= k(a + b) + kc$ 2.
      3. $= (ka + kb) + kc$ 3.
      4. $= ka + kb + kc$ 4.
      5.   5.

(and so on)

Theorem R15. If a, b, c, d are real numbers, then:

$$(a + b)(c + d) = ac + bc + ad + bd$$

NOTE. It is important in the following proof (as in the preceding) to realize that $a + b$ is a symbol for a single real number, just as $2 + 3$ is a symbol for the single real number 5.

We may therefore treat $a + b$ as a single real number, and this has been done in the following proof, in an application of the left distributive law. That law states that if F, S, T are real numbers (we have used these letters to suggest "first," "second" and "third" respectively) then $F(S + T) = FS + FT$. In the proof which follows, the "first" real number is $\underline{a + b}$, the "second" is $\underline{c}$, and the "third" is $\underline{d}$. Hence:

$$\underline{(a + b)} \, \underline{(c} + \underline{d)} = \underline{(a + b)}\underline{c} + \underline{(a + b)}\underline{d}$$

PROOF

1. a and b are real numbers   1.
2. $\therefore$ $a + b$ exists and is a real number   2.
3. c and d are real numbers   3.
4. $\therefore (a + b)(c + d) = (a + b)c + (a + b)d$ 4.
5. $\qquad\qquad = (ac + bc) + (ad + bd)$ 5.
6. $\qquad\qquad = ac + bc + ad + bd$ 6.
7.   7.

The word "FOIL" may be used as a mnemonic device for remembering a scheme of multiplication equivalent to that of the preceding theorem. That is, in finding the product of two sums, one may multiply together the First terms in each sum, then the Outer terms, then the Inner terms, and then the Last terms, and the sum of these four products is the required result.

For example, if x is a real number, then: $(x + 2)(x + 3) = x^2 + 3x + 2x + 6 = x^2 + 5x + 6$. (We have, of course, written $3x$ rather than the $x3$ which the theorem would require, but that is permissible because of the commutativity of multiplication.)

Theorem R16.   If a and b are real numbers, then $(a + b)(a - b) = a^2 - b^2$.

PROOF

1. $(a + b)(a - b) = (a + b)(a + \bar{b})$ 1.
2. $\qquad\qquad = a^2 + ba + a\bar{b} + b\bar{b}$ 2.
3. $\qquad\qquad = a^2 + ab + \overline{ab} + \overline{b^2}$ 3.
4. $\qquad\qquad = a^2 + 0 + \overline{b^2}$ 4.
5. $\qquad\qquad = a^2 + \overline{b^2}$ 5.
6. $\qquad\qquad = a^2 - b^2$ 6.
7.   7.

▶ **EXERCISE 16**

1. Show how the following products may easily be worked out mentally:

(a) $19 \cdot 21$ (b) $17 \cdot 23$ (c) $29 \cdot 31$

2. Prove (i') and (ii') of Theorem R14.

3. Prove and illustrate each by means of an example: If F, S are real numbers then:

(a) $(F + S)^2 = F^2 + 2FS + S^2$
(b) $(F - S)^2 = F^2 - 2FS + S^2$
(c) $(F + S)(F^2 - FS + S^2) = F^3 + S^3$
(d) $(F - S)(F^2 + FS + S^2) = F^3 - S^3$
(e) $(F + S)^3 = F^3 + 3F^2S + 3FS^2 + S^3$
(f) $(F - S)^3 = ?$

4. Prove: If x is a real number, then:

(a) $(x - 1)(x + 1) = x^2 - 1$
(b) $(x - 2)(x + 2) = x^2 - 4$
(c) $(2)(3x) = 6x$
(d) $(2x)(3x) = 6x^2$
(e) $(2x - 3)(2x - 2) = ?$

4.14 THE AXIOMS OF INEQUALITY

We now present three axioms which characterize the relation $<$ on the set of all real numbers. They are known as the "axioms of inequality" or the "order axioms."

Axiom O1. $<$ is a transitive relation.

Axiom O2. ("Trichotomy" axiom). If a and b are real numbers, then one and only one of the following three statements is true:

(i) $a < b$ (ii) $a = b$ (iii) $b < a$

Axiom O3. If a, b, k are real numbers and: $a < b$
then: $a + k < b + k$
and if furthermore $0 < k$, then: $ak < bk$

Definition R4. The relation $>$ (greater than) is defined on the set of real numbers in terms of the relation $<$ as follows:

If a and b are real numbers, then we say: $a > b$
if and only if: $b < a$

As a consequence of Definition R4, the statement "$a < b$" may be read either forward ("*a* is less than *b*") or backward ("*b* is greater than *a*"). Furthermore, it is easily proved that the relation $>$ is transitive also, and we may now restate Axiom 02 in the more symmetric form:

Axiom 02. If *a* and *b* are real numbers, then one and only one of the following three statements is true:

(i) $a < b$ (ii) $a = b$ (iii) $a > b$

Definition R5. A real number *k* is said to be *positive* if $k > 0$, and *negative* if $k < 0$.

NOTE now that the condition "$0 < k$" in Axiom 03 may be read "*k* is positive."

Now we are ready to prove a theorem involving the substitution of equals for equals in an inequality:

Theorem R17. If *a*, *b*, *x* are real numbers such that $a < b$ and $x = a$, then: $x < b$.

PROOF

By the trichotomy axiom, $x < b$ must follow if $x = b$ and $x > b$ can both be proved impossible.

We therefore consider two cases.

In the first case we assume $x = b$ and show that this leads to the result $a = b$, which is impossible, since by the trichotomy axiom $a = b$ and $a < b$ cannot both be true.

In the second case we assume $x > b$ and arrive at the result $x > a$, which again is impossible. (Why?)

(The rest of the proof of Theorem R17 is left as an exercise for the student.)

There are two relations which are closely related to those we have been discussing:

Definition R6. The relations $\leqslant$ ("less than or equal to") and $\geqslant$ ("greater than or equal to") are defined on the real numbers as follows:

If *a* and *b* are real numbers, we say $a \leqslant b$ if $a < b$ or $a = b$;
and: we say $a \geqslant b$ if $a > b$ or $a = b$

We shall call the four relations $<$, $>$, $\leqslant$, $\geqslant$ the *inequality relations*. It is now possible to prove:

Theorem R18. (i)   All the inequality relations are transitive.

(ii)   Any real number may be added to (or subtracted from) both sides of an inequality without altering the inequality relation.

(iii)   Both sides of an inequality may be multiplied (or divided) by the same *positive* real number without altering the inequality relation.

(iv)   Equals may be substituted for equals in any inequality.

(Although (i)–(iv) of Theorem R18 are a little loosely stated, it is assumed that the student will be able to translate them into more precise statements. The proof of Theorem R18 is not difficult, but since it involves so many separate statements it is tedious, and will therefore be omitted here.)

Our next theorem has to do with the effect of changing the signs of both sides of an inequality:

Theorem R19. If a and b are real numbers, then:

$$\text{(i)} \quad a > b \Rightarrow \bar{a} < \bar{b}$$
$$\text{(ii)} \quad a < b \Rightarrow \bar{a} > \bar{b}$$

PROOF

(i):
1. $a > b$ 1.
2. $\bar{b} + \bar{a} + a > b + \bar{b} + \bar{a}$ 2.
3. $\bar{b} + 0 > 0 + \bar{a}$ 3.
4. $\bar{b} > \bar{a}$ 4.

(ii)   (Proof left as exercise for student.)

Corollary. If a is a real number, then:

$$\text{(i)} \quad a \text{ is positive} \Rightarrow \bar{a} \text{ is negative}$$
$$\text{(ii)} \quad a \text{ is negative} \Rightarrow \bar{a} \text{ is positive}$$

(Proof of corollary left as exercise for student.)

The comment which follows Theorem R18 applies to the following theorem also:

Theorem R20. Changing the sign of both sides of an inequality relation reverses the sign of inequality.

With the help of Theorem R19, we can now establish the order relation between 1 and 0, and then we go on to establish a few other order relations:

Theorem R21. $1 > 0$.

PROOF

By the trichotomy axiom, $1 > 0$ will follow if we can show $1 = 0$ and $1 < 0$ to be impossible. The first, $1 = 0$, is immediately impossible, however, since Axiom F5 specifically states that 1 and 0 are unequal.

We therefore assume: $1 < 0$ and arrive at the conclusion: $1 > 0$; but, by the trichotomy axiom, the situation $1 < 0$ *and* $1 > 0$ is impossible.

1. $1 < 0$ 1.
2. $\therefore$ $\bar{1} > 0$ 2.
3. $\therefore$ $\bar{1} \cdot \bar{1} > \bar{1} \cdot 0$ 3.
4. $\bar{1} \cdot \bar{1} = 1$ 4.
5. $\bar{1} \cdot 0 = 0$ 5.
6. $\therefore$ $1 > 0$ 6.

Corollary. $\bar{1} < 0$. (i.e., $-1 < 0$.)

(The proof of the corollary above is left as an exercise for the student.)

Theorem R22.　$2 > 1$

PROOF

1. $\qquad 1 > 0$	1.
2. $\therefore 1 + 1 > 1 + 0$	2.
3. $\qquad 1 + 1 = 2$	3.
4. $\qquad 1 + 0 = 1$	4.
5. $\therefore \qquad 2 > 1$	5.

Corollary.　$2 > 0$

(The proof of the corollary above is left as an exercise for the student.)

Theorems R21 and R22, and the corollary to Theorem R22 show that the natural numbers 1 and 2 are both positive, and set up an order relation between 1 and 2.　Similarly, it may be shown that all the natural numbers are positive, and an order relation may be established between any pair of natural numbers.

We note that since $2 > 1$, it is permissible to write: $1 < 2$, $2 \geqslant 1$, $1 \leqslant 2$; in fact, it is also correct to write: $1 \leqslant 1$, $1 \geqslant 1$, $2 \leqslant 2$, $2 \geqslant 2$.

We now consider several theorems which are useful in working with inequalities:

Theorem R23.　"Like" inequalities may be added.

(This theorem has many cases.　For illustrative purposes, we shall prove only one: If a, b, x, y are real numbers such that:

$a < x$

and:　$b < y$

then:　$a + b < x + y$)

PROOF

1. $\qquad a < x,$	$b < y$	1.
2. $\therefore a + b < x + b,$	$x + b < x + y$	2.
3. $\therefore a + b < x + y$		3.

Theorem R24.　Among *positive* real numbers, like inequalities may be multiplied.

We prove only this case: If a, b, x, y are positive real numbers such that:

$a < x$

and:　$b < y$

then:　$ab < xy$

PROOF

1. $\qquad a < x$	$b < y$	1.
2. $\therefore ab < xb,$	$xb < xy$	2.
3. $\therefore ab < xy$		3.

Theorem R25. Multiplying both sides of an inequality by a negative real number reverses the sign of the inequality.

We prove this case: If a, b, c are real numbers such that $a < b$ and $c < 0$, then $ac > bc$.

PROOF

1.	$a < b, c < 0$	1.
2.	$\therefore -c > 0$	2.
3.	$\therefore (a)(-c) < (b)(-c)$	3.
4.	i.e., $-ac < -bc$	4.
5.	$\therefore -(-ac) > -(-bc)$	5.
6.	i.e., $ac > bc$	6.

Theorem R26.　(i)　If a is a positive real number, then so is $1/a$.

(ii)　If a is a negative real number, then so is $1/a$.

PROOF OF (i)

By the trichotomy axiom, it will follow that $1/a$ is positive if we can show that $1/a$ cannot be zero or negative.

We therefore consider two cases:

Case 1. We assume that $1/a = 0$ and show that this leads to the conclusion $1 = 0$; but this is impossible, by Axiom F5.

Case 2. We assume that $1/a < 0$ and show that this leads to the conclusion $1 < 0$; but this is impossible, since we have proved $1 > 0$ (Theorem R21), and the trichotomy axiom does not permit both statements to be true.

Case 1.	1.	$\dfrac{1}{a} = 0$	1.
	2.	$\therefore 1 = 0$	2.　Problem 14, Exercise 14
Case 2.	1.	$\dfrac{1}{a} < 0, a > 0$	1.
	2.	$\therefore a \cdot \dfrac{1}{a} < a \cdot 0$	2.
	3.	$a \cdot \dfrac{1}{a} = 1$	3.　Problem ?, Exercise 14
	4.	$a \cdot 0 = 0$	4.
	5.		5.

[The proof of (ii) is left as an exercise for the student.]

We are now in a position to define exactly what we mean by "betweenness" among the real numbers:

Definition R7. If a, b, c are real numbers, then b is said to be *between* a and c (or between c and a) if:

$a \leqslant b$ and $b \leqslant c$ (written: $a \leqslant b \leqslant c$)

or if: $a \geqslant b$ and $b \geqslant c$ (written: $a \geqslant b \geqslant c$).

Thus, the real numbers between 2 and 4 include, according to our definition, 2 and 3 and 3.7 and 4, and of course many other real numbers.

EXERCISE 17

1. Complete the proof of, or prove:

(a) Theorem R17

(b)   Theorem R19, (ii)   (c)   Corollary, Theorem R19
(d)   Corollary, Theorem R21   (e)   Corollary, Theorem R22
(f)   Theorem R26, (ii)

2.   Prove: (a) $3 > 2$ (b) $4 > 2$ (c) $2 \neq 0$
             (d) $3 \neq 0$ (e) $4 \neq 0$

3.   Prove:

(a) $4 \div 2 = 2$.   (*Hint*: This may be proved as a corollary to Theorem R13; compare Theorem R12 and its corollary, and make use of the definition of division.)

(b) $6 \div 3 = 2$ (c) $8 \div 4 = 2$
(d) $2' \cdot \bar{4} = \bar{2}$ (restate this result)   (e) $\frac{1}{2} = \frac{3}{6}$
(f) $\frac{1}{3} = \frac{2}{6}$ (g) $\frac{1}{2} + \frac{1}{3} = \frac{5}{6}$

4.   Prove:

(a)   If a, p are real numbers and p is positive, then $a + p > a$.
(b)   If a, n are real numbers, and n is negative, then $a + n < a$.
(c)   If a is a positive real number, then $a < 1 \Rightarrow a^2 < a$.
(d)   If a is a positive real number, then $a > 1 \Rightarrow a^2 > a$.
(e)   If a and b are positive real numbers, then:

$$a < b \Rightarrow \frac{1}{a} > \frac{1}{b}$$

(In fact, among positive real numbers, taking the reciprocal of both sides of any inequality reverses the sign of inequality.)

5.   State more precisely and prove:

(a)   The sum of a pair of positive real numbers is positive.
(b)   The sum of a pair of negative real numbers is negative.
(c)   The product of a pair of positive real numbers is positive.
(d)   The product of a pair of negative real numbers is positive.
(e)   The product of a pair of real numbers of opposite sign is negative.
(f)   The square of a real number is never negative. (i.e., always what?)
(g)   The product of a pair of non-negative real numbers is non-negative.

6. Make and prove statements concerning quotients analogous to 5 (c), (d), (e) above.

7. Prove: If a and b are real numbers, then:

(i) $ab > 0 \Leftrightarrow a > 0$ and $b > 0$, or $a < 0$ and $b < 0$.

(ii) $ab < 0 \Leftrightarrow a > 0$ and $b < 0$, or $a < 0$ and $b > 0$.

8. (a) Following Problems 4, 5, Exercise 11, how would you define a^n in terms of a^{n-1}, where a is a real number and n a natural number?

(b) Prove: If a and b are real numbers and n is a natural number, then:

$$a = b \Rightarrow a^n = b^n$$

(Hint: The process of Problems 4, 5, Exercise 11, may be continued indefinitely.)

(c) Prove: If a and b are positive real numbers and n is a natural number, then:

$$a < b \Rightarrow a^n < b^n$$

(Hint: Multiply both sides of $a < b$ first by a and then by b and then conclude: $a^2 < b^2$; then derive $a^3 < b^3$ in somewhat similar fashion; the process may be continued indefinitely.)

(d) Prove: If a and b are positive real numbers and n is a natural number, then:

$$a^n = b^n \Rightarrow a = b$$

(Hint: By the trichotomy axiom, one of the following three must be true: $a = b$, $a < b$, $a > b$; prove each of the latter two impossible in this situation.)

(e) Prove: If a and b are positive real numbers and n is a natural number, then:

$$a^n > b^n \Rightarrow a > b$$

(f) Prove: If r is a real number and n is a natural number, then:

$$r > 0 \Rightarrow r^n > 0$$

9. Assuming x and k are real numbers and k is positive, prove:

(a) $x^2 < k^2$ if and only if $-k < x < k$.

(b) $x^2 > k^2$ if and only if $x > k$ or $x < -k$.

10. Prove that if a and b are real numbers and $a < b$, then:

$$a < \frac{a + b}{2} < b$$

11. Prove that if a and b are real numbers such that $a \leqslant b$ and $b \leqslant a$, then $a = b$.

12. State more precisely and prove a case of Theorem R18 not proved in the text.

13. In this problem we re-introduce the absolute value function, whose definition is given in Problem 14 of Exercise 5.

The following important and useful properties of absolute value may be proved, assuming that a and b are real numbers:

(1) $|a| \geqslant 0$

(2) $a = 0 \Leftrightarrow |a| = 0$

(3) $a \neq 0 \Leftrightarrow |a| > 0$

(4) $|a|^2 = a^2$

(5) $|a| = |-a|$

(6) $a \leqslant |a|$

(7) $a \geqslant - |a|$

(8) $|a|\,|b| = |ab|$

(9) $-b < a < b \Leftrightarrow |a| < b$

(10) $|a + b| \leqslant |a| + |b|$

(11) $|a| - |b| \leqslant |a - b|$

(12)   If $b \neq 0$, then $\left|\dfrac{a}{b}\right| = \dfrac{|a|}{|b|}$

(13) $|a - b| = a - b$ or $b - a$, whichever is non-negative.

We shall find it convenient to utilize less formal proofs, as we go on, as illustrated by the following.

The student may answer the questions which occur below, and supply the proofs, or parts of proofs which have been omitted:

PROOFS

(1): *Case* 1. $a \geqslant 0$.   Then $|a| = a$ (why?).   Hence (substituting equals for equals in an inequality), $|a| \geqslant 0$, Q.E.D.

Case 2. $a < 0$.   Then $|a| = -a$ (why?).   Also, $-a > 0$ (why?).   Hence $|a| > 0$ (why?) and therefore $|a| \geqslant 0$ (why?), Q.E.D.

(2)   ($\Rightarrow$): If $a = 0$, then $a \geqslant 0$, and $|a| = a$ (why?), Q.E.D.

($\Leftarrow$): We use the indirect method.

Suppose $a \neq 0$, then $a < 0$ or $a > 0$ (why?).   If $a < 0$, then $|a| = -a > 0$ (why?) which together with the hypothesis $|a| = 0$ contradicts what axiom?   Similarly, $a > 0$ leads to a contradiction (show this).   Therefore $a \neq 0$ is false, i.e., $a = 0$ is true, Q.E.D.

(3)   This can be proved as a corollary to (1) and (2) above.

(4)   Hint: $|a| = \pm a$.

(5)   Hint: Consider cases as in (1) above.

(8)   Hint: Consider four cases: $a \geqslant 0, b \geqslant 0$; $a \geqslant 0, b < 0$; $a < 0, b \geqslant 0$; $a < 0$ $b < 0$.

(9)   This theorem has a nice geometric interpretation.   On a scaled line, $|a|$ may be thought of as the distance from the point labeled a to the origin:

Hint for Proof: Consider cases for proof of $\Rightarrow$, and use (6), (7) for proof of $\Leftarrow$.

(10)   Hint: By (9), it will be sufficient to prove:

$$-(|a| + |b|) \leqslant a + b \leqslant |a| + |b|$$

(11)   Hint: Restate (10): If x and y are real numbers, then $|x + y| \leqslant |x| + |y|$. Then let $x = a - b$, $y = b$.

4.15   THE AXIOM OF DEDEKIND

First of all, we introduce several definitions.

Definition.   Suppose A and B are non-null sets of real numbers such that the following is true:

$$a \in A, b \in B \Rightarrow a < b$$

(i.e., such that whenever a is an element of A and b is an element of B, then $a < b$). Then we shall call the ordered pair of sets (A, B) a *tandem pair*.

Examples of tandem pairs (A, B): (It will help to picture these sets on a scaled line.)

(1) $A =$ the set of all negative real numbers.
     $B =$ the set of all positive real numbers.
(2) $A = \{2 \longrightarrow 4\}$
     $B = \{6 \longrightarrow 7\}$
(3) $A = \{1, 2, 3\}$
     $B = \{7, 11\}$
(4) $A =$ the set of all positive rational numbers whose squares are less than 2.
     $B =$ the set of all positive rational numbers whose squares are greater than 2.

Definition. A real number x is said to be *between* the sets A, B of a tandem pair (A, B) if the following is true:

$$a \in A, \; B \in B \Rightarrow a \leqslant x \leqslant b$$

(i.e. ?)

Examples of real numbers between the sets of a tandem pair:

(1) In example (1) above, 0 is between A and B.
(2) In example (2) above, $\sqrt{23}$ is between A and B.
(3) In example (3) above, 3 is between A and B.
(4) In example (4) above, $\sqrt{2}$ is between A and B.

We have introduced the notions above first of all in order to make it possible to describe, in simple terms, a deep-lying deficiency of the rational number system—one which, for example, makes the rational numbers unsuitable for the development of the very important branch of mathematics known as calculus.

The deficiency to which we refer is the following: There exist tandem pairs of sets of rational numbers with no rational number whatever between them.

This is intuitively evident in example (4) above. For between all positive rational numbers whose squares are less than 2 and all positive rational numbers whose squares are greater than 2, one would expect to find only a number whose square is equal to 2. But we have proved (see Section 3.3) that *no* rational number has a square equal to 2.

We feel, however, that such a gap between tandem sets could not exist in the real number system.   The real number: $\sqrt{2}$, for example, repairs the gap in the preceding example.   Again, thinking pictorially of a pair of tandem sets as they appear on a scaled line, we feel that between a pair of tandem sets of real numbers there must always be at least one point, i.e., at least one real number.

We are led, therefore, to include the following in our set of axioms characterizing real numbers:

Axiom of Dedekind.   Between the sets of every tandem pair of sets of real numbers, there is at least one real number.

We shall now put the axiom of Dedekind to work in the proof of the following important theorem:

Theorem.   There is a unique positive real number whose square is 2.

PROOF: Let A be the set of all positive real numbers whose squares are less than 2, B the set of all positive real numbers whose squares are greater than 2.

It is left to the student to verify that the ordered pair (A, B) is a tandem pair.

At this point we introduce a lemma:

Lemma 1.   There is a unique real number between the sets A, B defined above.

PROOF OF LEMMA 1: We know that there is a real number between A and B by the axiom of Dedekind.

To show that it is unique, we suppose that there are two different real numbers between A and B, and arrive at a contradiction.

By the trichotomy axiom, one of these real numbers (call it u) must be less than the other (call it v).

Let $x = (u + v)/2$ and $y = (x + v)/2$. Then by Problem 10, Exercise 17,

$$u < x < y < v$$

Now if a and b are (respectively) any elements of A and B whatever, we have, since u and v are between A and B:

$$a \leqslant u < x < y < v \leqslant b$$

This means that x and y are positive real numbers which are members of neither A nor B; i.e., we have that x^2 is neither less than nor greater than 2, and y^2 is neither less than nor greater than 2.

Hence, by the axiom of trichotomy, $x^2 = 2$ and $y^2 = 2$, from which follows: $x^2 = y^2$. But then: $x = y$ [by Problem 8 (d) of Exercise 17].

We now have: $x = y$ and $x < y$, which, in the light of the trichotomy axiom, is a contradictory situation.

This completes the proof of Lemma 1.

We now introduce a second lemma:

Lemma 2. If $a \in A$, then $\dfrac{2}{a} \in B$, and if $b \in B$, then $\dfrac{2}{b} \in A$.

PROOF OF LEMMA 2. Suppose $a \in A$. Then $a^2 < 2$ (why?). Hence $\dfrac{2}{a^2} > 1$, (why?) from which follows: $\dfrac{4}{a^2} > 2$ (why?), i.e. $\left(\dfrac{2}{a}\right)^2 > 2$, i.e., $\dfrac{2}{a} \in B$.

The proof of the other part of the lemma is similar, and is left as an exercise for the student.

Now we are ready to complete the proof of the theorem.

Let p be that unique real number between sets A and B whose existence is guaranteed by Lemma 1. Clearly p is positive, for since A is non-null, we know that there exists a positive real number q in A, and by the definition of p, $p \geqslant q$. Since $q > 0$, it follows that $p > 0$, i.e., p is positive.

Now suppose that a is any element of A and b any element of B. Then by Lemma 2, $\dfrac{2}{b} \in A$ and $\dfrac{2}{a} \in B$. Therefore, since p is between the sets A and B:

$$\frac{2}{b} \leqslant p \leqslant \frac{2}{a}$$

and dividing through by 2:

$$\frac{1}{b} \leqslant \frac{p}{2} \leqslant \frac{1}{a}$$

Hence [by Problem 4(e) of Exercise 17]:

$$b \geqslant \frac{2}{p} \geqslant a$$

i.e.:

$$a \leqslant \frac{2}{p} \leqslant b$$

Thus, $2/p$ is also between the sets A and B. Therefore, by Lemma 1, $p = 2/p$, i.e., $p^2 = 2$.

We have now shown that there is a positive real number whose square is 2. That this positive real number is unique follows from Problem 8(d) of Exercise 17; and the proof of our theorem is now complete.

EXERCISE

1. Supply suggested details and answer questions posed in Section 4.15.

2. Prove the following:

Theorem. If r is a positive real number, then there exists a unique positive real number p such that $p^2 = r$.

Hints:

(1) Follow, but with appropriate changes, the proof of the theorem of Section 4.15.

(2) How should A and B be defined now?

(3) To prove A and B non-null, consider the cases $r = 1, r < 1, r > 1$. Problems 4(c), (d) of Exercise 17 will be found useful.

The unique positive real number whose square is the positive real number r is, of course, denoted $\sqrt{r}$.

3. Prove the following:

Theorem. If r is a positive real number, then there exists a unique positive real number p such that $p^3 = r$.

Hints:

(1) Follow, but with appropriate changes, the proof of the theorem of Problem 2, above.

(2) How should A and B be defined now?

(3) In proving A and B non-null, the following lemma will be found useful:

Lemma. If r is a positive real number such that $r < 1$, then $r^3 < r$ and $1^3 > r$; and if r is a positive real number such that $r > 1$, then $1^3 < r$ and $r^3 > r$.

(4) As an analog of Lemma 2, prove the following:

Lemma. If $a \in A$, then $\sqrt{\dfrac{r}{a}} \in B$, and if $b \in B$, then $\sqrt{\dfrac{r}{b}} \in A$.

The process illustrated by the preceding two theorems may be continued, and in fact we may prove that for *any* given natural number n, if r is a positive real number, then there is a unique positive real number p such that $p^n = r$; and this unique positive real number p is, of course, denoted $\sqrt[n]{r}$.

In the case $n = 4$, the preceding lemma is changed to: Lemma: If $a \in A$, then $\sqrt[3]{\dfrac{r}{a}} \in B$, etc.; and so on for $n \geqslant 5$.

4. Prove: Zero is the only real number whose nth power is zero (assuming n to be a natural number).

Hence we define: $\sqrt[n]{0} = 0$.

4.16 THE NATURAL NUMBERS DEFINED

We now consider a definition of the natural numbers within the logical framework of the real number system.

Two very important characteristics of the set of natural numbers are that it contains 1 and that it is closed under the operation of adding 1 to each member of the set. But there are other sets which exhibit this property: Adding 1 to any real number, for example, yields again a real number; adding 1 to any integer produces once more an integer; and 1 belongs to both of these sets.

We therefore make a preliminary definition.

Definition. An *inductive set* S is a set of real numbers with the properties:

(i) $1 \in S$

(ii) $s \in S \Rightarrow s + 1 \in S$

Examples, then, of inductive sets are the set of all real numbers, the set of all integers and the set of all natural numbers.

We feel, however, that the natural numbers are in a sense the *smallest* of all inductive sets. The sense in which we mean "smallest" here is that *every* inductive set must contain at least the natural numbers as a subset. For by (i), an inductive set S must include the number 1. And by (ii), the fact that 1 belongs to S implies that $1 + 1$, or 2 belongs to S; and again by (ii), since 2 belongs to S, it follows that $2 + 1$, or 3 belongs to S; and so on. And the numbers 1, 2, 3, ... are, of course, those which we think of as the natural numbers.

Since we feel that the natural numbers are precisely those which are "common" to all inductive sets, we are led to the following definition (see Section 1.8).

Definition. The set of *natural numbers* is the intersection of all inductive sets of real numbers.

Since the intersection of sets is always contained within each of the original sets, there follows immediately:

Corollary. Every inductive set contains all the natural numbers.

4.17 THE PRINCIPLE OF MATHEMATICAL INDUCTION

A row of dominoes may be toppled by knocking down only the first, if the dominoes are close enough together; and one may be sure of being able to reach *any* rung of an upright ladder, knowing that the first rung is within reach, and that one can span the distance from any rung to the next.

These examples illustrate the intuitive background of the so-called "Principle of Mathematical Induction":

Principle of Mathematical Induction: A set S contains all the natural numbers if S satisfies the following two conditions:

(i) $1 \in S$

(ii) $s \in S \Rightarrow s + 1 \in S$

This principle, in fact, is nothing more than a restatement of the preceding corollary.

The Principle of Mathematical Induction finds its use in proving theorems about natural numbers. It is especially useful in rigorizing proofs of the "and so on" type. In Section 4.14, for example, beginning with Theorem R21, we proved that the numbers 1 and 2 are positive, and we stated that "similarly" one may prove that all the other natural numbers are positive. But now, as an example of the application of the Principle of Mathematical Induction we rigorously prove this:

Theorem. All the natural numbers are positive.

PROOF: Let S be the set of all *positive* natural numbers. We wish to show that actually *all* the natural numbers belong to S. By the Principle of Mathematical Induction, our goal will be achieved as soon as we have proved (i) and (ii) above.

Proof of (i): That 1 is positive has been proved in Section 4.14, Theorem R21. Therefore $1 \in S$, Q.E.D.

Proof of (ii): Suppose $s \in S$. Then s is positive; i.e., $s > 0$. Adding 1 to both sides of this inequality: $s + 1 > 1$. But as we have just noted, $1 > 0$. Therefore (why?) $s + 1 > 0$; therefore (why?) $s + 1 \in S$, Q.E.D.

One may also prove by mathematical induction that 1 is the "least" natural number:

Theorem. If n is any natural number, then $1 \leqslant n$. (The proof of this theorem is left as an exercise for the student.)

We see another application of the principle of mathematical induction in the proof of the following theorem:

Theorem. If n is any natural number, then $n < 2^n$.

PROOF: Let S be the set of natural numbers for which this theorem is true. We wish to show that *all* natural numbers belong to S. We shall show this by proving (i) and (ii) of the Principle of Mathematical Induction.

Proof of (i): For $n = 1$, the theorem states: $1 < 2$, which *is* true (how do we know that?)

Proof of (ii): Suppose $s \in S$. Then:

(1) $$s < 2^s \qquad \text{(why?)}$$

We wish to show that there follows now that $s + 1 \in S$, i.e., $s + 1 < 2^{s+1}$. But from (1) we have:

(2) $$2s < 2^{s+1} \qquad \text{(why?)}$$

Our desired result would now follow if we knew that $s + 1 \leqslant 2s$ (why?); but $s + 1 \leqslant 2s$ is equivalent to $1 \leqslant s$, which *is* true, by the preceding theorem.

The proof of the theorem is now complete.

A classical application of the method of mathematical induction is to problems involving summation of sets of numbers:

Theorem. The sum of the first n odd natural numbers is n^2; i.e.:

(3) $$1 + 3 + \cdots + (2n - 3) + (2n - 1) = n^2$$

PROOF: Let S be the set of all natural numbers n for which (3) is true. We prove the theorem by proving (i) and (ii) of the principle of mathematical induction.

Proof of (i): For $n = 1$, the theorem states: $1 = 1$, which is true (why?). (Note that the sum of the elements of a set which contains only one element is defined to be simply that element.)

Proof of (ii): Suppose $s \in S$. Then:

(4) $$1 + 3 + \cdots + (2s - 3) + (2s - 1) = s^2$$

We wish to show that $s + 1 \in S$, i.e., that

$1 + 3 + \cdots + [2(s + 1) - 3] + [2(s + 1) - 1] = (s + 1)^2$, or in other words that $1 + 3 + \cdots + (2s - 1) + (2s + 1) = (s + 1)^2$. But from (4):

$$1 + 3 + \cdots + (2s - 1) + (2s + 1) = s^2 + (2s + 1) = (s + 1)^2, \text{ Q.E.D.}$$

REMARK. The name "mathematical induction" is a historical misnomer; proof by mathematical induction is actually a *deductive* proof. In fact, many results which are discovered inductively, are then proved deductively by means of mathematical induction. A case in point is the statement that the sum of the first n odd numbers is n^2 which we approached inductively in Section 3.6, and which we proved deductively, by means of mathematical induction, in this section.

EXERCISE

1. Give several examples of inductive sets different from those mentioned in the text.

2. Answer the questions posed in Section 4.17.

3. Prove the theorem: If n is any natural number, then $1 \leqslant n$.

4. Prove that if n is any natural number, then:

(a) $n + 1 \leqslant 2^n$

(b) $n^2 < 4^n$

(*Hint:* First prove, not by induction, but by inequality properties: *Lemma:* If n is any natural number, then $2n + 1 \leqslant 3n^2$.)

(c) $n^2 < 3^n$.

5. Prove that if n is any natural number, then:

(a) $1 + 2 + \cdots + n = \dfrac{n(n + 1)}{2}$

(b) $1^2 + 2^2 + \cdots + n^2 = \dfrac{n(n + 1)(2n + 1)}{6}$

(c) $1^3 + 2^3 + \cdots + n^3 = \dfrac{n^2(n + 1)^2}{4}$

5 ALGEBRAIC EQUATIONS AND INEQUALITIES

Mathematics is the science of the connection of magnitudes. Magnitude is anything which can be put equal or unequal to another thing.

HERMANN GRASSMANN: *A Textbook in Arithmetic*

5.1 INTRODUCTION

Like other definitions of mathematics, the above definition of the great midnineteenth century German mathematician Grassmann is open to attack. Yet, it says, in a sense, that mathematics is the science of *relations*; and although it may be debated that the science (or art) of mathematics exactly coincides with all that can be said about relations, few mathematicians would deny that relations play an especially important role in mathematics.

In particular, the relation of "equality" and, even more specifically, the general problem of solving "equations" have been the sources of a great deal of mathematics.

In this chapter we first consider the problem of solving certain equations, and then of solving certain "inequalities," both of types that occur most often in practical applications of mathematics.

We shall depart in our presentation, however, from the coldly formal and relentlessly logical style emphasized in the preceding chapter. For mathematics has great variety in its aspects, and in order to develop a feeling for what the subject is like, and what it is all about, more than one of the many sides of mathematics must be seen.

The deductive presentation of the last chapter indicates something of an ideal toward which all mathematics bends. But that ideal is the end result of a long process of mathematical creation involving intuition and imagination and often a great deal of interplay with physical situations and practical problems.   To neglect the deductive or the intuitive sides of mathematics, or the give-and-take between mathematics and its applications, is to arrive at an incomplete and distorted picture of mathematics.

But there are still other aspects of mathematics that should not be overlooked: it has to do with people and it has a history.   Not only does mathematics serve humanity; it is indeed created by human beings also, and not in a vacuum nor in an ivory tower, but in societies and civilizations which leave their indelible impressions on the mathematicians and on the mathematics of their times, and which throughout the breadth of their cultures—in science, in art, in philosophy, in literature, and even in music and in poetry—reflect the converse influence of mathematics.

We shall therefore attempt, in this chapter, to present something of the human and historical side of mathematics; and, together with material which for the sake of complete clarity has been formulated in rigorous, deductive fashion, there will also be included some material justified here only by intuition.

That which has to do with people and history lends itself to being told as a story; and nowhere in mathematics, nor probably even in all the annals of science, is there a better story to be found than that which has to do with the apparently mundane subject of algebraic equations.

5.2   THE STORY OF THE ALGEBRAIC EQUATION IN ONE UNKNOWN

Some four thousand years ago, in the Biblical times of Abraham, Isaac, and Jacob, there flourished the two earliest of Western civilizations: the Egyptian, on the banks of the Nile in Northern Africa, and the Babylonian, between the Tigris and Euphrates Rivers—legendary site of both the Garden of Eden and the Arabian Nights' adventures—in Western Asia.

Many records of these nations have come down to us; the Babylonians' on durable baked clay tablets, and the Egyptians' on a paper-like material called "papyrus," preserved by the dry Egyptian climate.   The records show remarkable progress in many fields, but at the moment our interest is in mathematics, and in particular in the algebraic equation.   We note particularly, therefore, this translation of a line from an ancient Egyptian papyrus:

"A quantity whose fourth part is added to it becomes 15 . . ."

There is a problem implied here, of course, namely to find the quantity. In modern notation, we would say the problem is to solve the equation:

$$x + \frac{x}{4} = 15$$

The Egyptians did not, of course, write the problem in this way. Nevertheless, they were able not only to state but also to solve the problem in verbal terms. But it is interesting that there has not yet been found anything very much more complicated than this in the records that have been discovered so far of the work done by Egyptians on algebraic equations.

We may say, then, that the ancient Egyptians knew how to solve the simple type of algebraic equation that we call the "linear" or "first-degree" equation in one "unknown."

On the other hand, the Babylonians seem to have been much further advanced in the field of algebraic equations. They could solve "quadratic" or "second-degree" equations in one unknown like:

$$x^2 - 3x + 2 = 0$$

For example, here is a problem taken from a tablet of about the time of King Hammurabi that leads to such an equation (Hammurabi, c. 1800 B.C., is famous as the king whose name is affixed to recorded history's first codified body of law):

"Two bur is the area; the length exceeded the width by 126 gar. What are the length and width?"

A rectangle may be assumed to be the figure to which the problem refers. In order to solve the problem, it is necessary to know further that a "bur" is the area of a rectangle whose length is 60 "gar" and whose width is 30 "gar."

(The solution of this problem is left as an exercise for the reader.)

Now, before we can go on with our story, we shall find it necessary to define with greater precision some of the terms we have been using.

First of all, we introduce the following nomenclature:

The equation $ax + b = 0$ is called a *general algebraic equation of the first degree in x.*

Particular first degree equations in x may be derived from this general equation by substituting numbers for a and b, with the stipulation that the number 0 shall *never* be substituted for a; having made such a substitution, we say that we have an equation in the "form" $ax + b = 0$. Furthermore, any equation which may be transformed into this form by certain operations on equations with which we are familiar (and which we shall presently discuss) is also called an equation of the first degree in x.

For example, by adding -5 to both its sides, the equation $4x - 3 = 5$

is transformed into $4x - 8 = 0$, which may be derived from the general equation $ax + b = 0$ by the substitution: $a = 4$, $b = -8$. Therefore $4x - 3 = 5$ is an equation of the first degree in x.

Similarly, the equation $ax^2 + bx + c = 0$ is called a *general algebraic equation of the second degree in* x.

Particular second degree equations in x may be derived from this general equation by substituting numbers for a, b, and c, but again we stipulate: $a \neq 0$. As in the preceding case, equations that may by certain legal methods be transformed into the form $ax^2 + bx + c = 0$ are also called equations of the second degree in x.

For example, the equation $x^2 - 3x + 2 = 0$ is already in the form $ax^2 + bx + c = 0$, for it may be derived from the general equation by the substitution: $a = 1$, $b = -3$, $c = 2$. 'Therefore $x^2 - 3x + 2 = 0$ is an equation of the second degree in x.

Similar remarks hold for the following general algebraic equations:

"cubic" or "third
degree":

$$ax^3 + bx^2 + cx + d = 0 \qquad (a \neq 0)$$

"quartic" or "fourth
degree":

$$ax^4 + bx^3 + cx^2 + dx + e = 0 \qquad (a \neq 0)$$

"quintic" or "fifth
degree":

$$ax^5 + bx^4 + cx^3 + dx^2 + ex + f = 0 \quad (a \neq 0)$$

etc.

In the equations above, a, b, c, etc., are called the "coefficients" of their respective equations.

From now on, unless otherwise noted, we shall use the term "algebraic equation" to mean an algebraic equation of any degree in x or in y or in any other single "unknown," such that all of its coefficients are real numbers.

Now we consider the general problem of solving algebraic equations by means of formulas.

The linear equation is very easy to dispose of. The same method that enables us to solve particular linear equations enables us to solve the general equation $ax + b = 0$ also. The solution, of course, is: $x = -b/a$. This last may be considered as a formula which once and for all gives the solution to any linear equation, once its coefficients a and b are known. For example, by this formula, the solution to $4x - 8 = 0$ would be:

$$x = \frac{-(-8)}{4} = \frac{8}{4} = 2$$

The student will recall that there is a formula also for the solution of quadratic equations in terms of their coefficients, the famous "quadratic formula":

$$x = \frac{-b \pm \sqrt{b^2 - 4ac}}{2a}$$

For example, applying this formula to the solution of the equation:

$$x^2 - 3x + 2 = 0$$

the general equation: $ax^2 + bx + c = 0$ may be transformed into our particular case by the replacements: $a = 1$, $b = -3$, $c = 2$. Therefore, by the quadratic formula:

$$x = \frac{-(-3) \pm \sqrt{(-3)^2 - 4 \cdot 1 \cdot 2}}{2 \cdot 1} = \frac{3 \pm \sqrt{9 - 8}}{2} = \frac{3 \pm 1}{2} = 2 \text{ or } 1$$

The student may now easily verify that the numbers 1 and 2 are both solutions of the equation $x^2 - 3x + 2 = 0$, and, using the quadratic formula, he should now be able to solve the Babylonian problem above. As a matter of fact, the quadratic formula, not of course in modern notation, but in terms of indicated steps of procedure was known to the Babylonians of 4000 years ago!

At this point we begin to recognize the outlines of a very general problem: Formulas exist which in terms of the operations of addition, subtraction, multiplication, division and the extraction of roots, all working on the coefficients of the equations, enable us to solve any linear or quadratic equation in a finite number of steps. Do similar formulas exist for the solution of cubics and quartics, and in fact for algebraic equations of any degree whatever?

Since the linear and quadratic formulas were already known as early as 2000 B.C., it comes as something of a surprise to learn that a cubic formula was not discovered until about 1535 A.D. During the 3500 years or so that separated these discoveries, there flourished the glorious civilization of Greece, with its incomparable array of magnificent minds, as well as Indian and Arabic civilizations of considerable intellectual accomplishment. Many brilliant mathematicians must have tried and failed to find the elusive formula. But it was not until Renaissance times, almost half a century after Columbus discovered America, that the problem was solved.

The times were turbulent and the actors in the drama not in the highest degree scrupulous. Versions of how the solution was attained, therefore, differ somewhat. One which is generally accepted is incorporated into the following account.

In histories of medicine we learn that Jerome Cardan of Italy, who lived during that period of brilliant cultural achievement in Europe known as the Renaissance, was one of the leading physicians of the early sixteenth century. It was the era of such universal geniuses as Michelangelo,

Cellini, and Leonardo da Vinci, so that we are not overly surprised to learn that Cardan's reputation as a mathematician was greater even than his reputation in medicine. Indeed, the formula for the solution of cubic equations, with which we are at the moment concerned, appears in many present-day mathematics texts under the name "Cardan's formula." But Cardan did *not* discover the formula, nor did he even claim to have done so!

Actually it was Tartaglia (whose name was not Tartaglia) who discovered "Cardan's formula."

In Italian, *tartaglia* means "stammerer." In the year 1512, politically dismembered Italy found itself torn by bloody wars. The disorderly period left its lifelong mark on a twelve-year-old boy called Nicolo Fontana, when a soldier, in the massacre of the inhabitants of the town of Brescia, succeeded only in gashing the child's mouth with his sword. The injury impeded his speech, and Nicolo became known as "Tartaglia."

Poverty-stricken Tartaglia enjoyed no education but that which he gave himself. Too poor to afford paper, he pursued his studies in cemeteries, writing on tombstones with pieces of charcoal. And one day he found the answer to a riddle which had evaded solution for almost four thousand years! He found a method for solving *any* cubic equation.

Learning of the discovery, the great Cardan persuaded Tartaglia to reveal it to him, but under a strict oath of secrecy.

The reason for the oath of secrecy? It was due to the fact that the tradition of a free exchange of ideas among scholars, which has existed for so long in modern times (and which only recently, because of international tensions, has suffered a reversal) did not exist at the time of the Renaissance. Learning, in those days, was a highly competitive field of endeavor. Indeed, the reputation and hence the very livelihood of Renaissance mathematicians might depend upon their performance in public contests of mathematical skill. These contests often took the form of an exchange of problems, each mathematician attempting to confound his opponent. Popular among the posers of Tartaglia's day were one particular cubic equation or another which the proposer had already managed to solve by some special method. A general formula solving *any* cubic equation would be a valuable commodity to a mathematician who engaged in these contests; good reason, certainly, for keeping such a formula secret.

But when Cardan published a monumental treatise on mathematics in 1545, Tartaglia's formula, credited to Tartaglia, but nevertheless no longer secret, was included; that publication accounts for the name "Cardan's formula," which, as we have noted, persists up to this very day.

The student may now be curious to see this famous formula. It is, as one might guess, considerably more complicated than the quadratic formula. Even worse, it often presents comparatively simple solutions in a form in which square roots of negative numbers—then considered to be totally fantastic—are inextricably involved. Nevertheless, to satisfy the student's curiosity at least partially, we give below a streamlined version of how the formula operates to give one root of the cubic equation whose general form we have given above.

Beginning with the given values of the coefficients a, b, c, d, we compute successively:

$$p = \frac{3ac - b^2}{3a^2}, \quad q = \frac{2b^3 - 9abc + 27a^2d}{27a^3}, \quad r = \sqrt{q^2 + \frac{4p^3}{27}}$$

$$s = \sqrt[3]{\frac{r - q}{2}}, \quad t = \sqrt[3]{\frac{r + q}{2}}$$

Now a solution of our cubic equation will be: $x = s - t - (b/3)$.

For example, consider the equation $4x^3 - 3x + 1 = 0$. Here $a = 4$, $b = 0$, $c = -3$, $d = 1$. Then $p = -3/4$, $q = 1/4$, $r = 0$, $s = -1/2$, $t = 1/2$, and finally $x = -1$, all of which the student should verify, as well as the fact that $x = -1$ is a root of the given equation.

With the cubic equation conquered, mathematicians naturally turned their attention to the problem of finding a similar formula for the solution of quartic equations. Here success came relatively quickly. Only five years or so after Tartaglia found a cubic formula, a pupil of Cardan's named Ferrari found and gave his name to a quartic formula.

We pause for a moment to remark upon the dramatic lives of Renaissance scholars. We have encountered three great names among the sixteenth-century mathematicians: Ferrari, Tartaglia, and Cardan. Ferrari was poisoned by his sister; of Tartaglia's life we have already spoken; and as to Cardan—he was an immoderate gambler, a man of furious temper who cut off his son's ears in a fit of rage, who spent time in prison, whose son was hanged for murder, and who himself committed suicide in order to make his own prophecy of the date of his death come true.

But to get on with our story: Ferrari's formula, though even more complicated than Tartaglia's, amounts to nothing more than a clever trick which reduces the solution of a quartic to a problem involving the solution of a cubic. Nothing would be gained by considering Ferrari's formula here, and for that very good reason we omit it.

If the reader begins to grow weary of a seemingly endless progression of equations and their solutions, we have at this point a word of reassurance. The next case, that of the quintic equation, is the most interesting of all, and for a reason soon to be revealed, the last which we shall want to discuss.

As time goes on the Renaissance fades into history and century follows century, but still the quintic equation remains an "enigma wrapped in a mystery." Giants of mathematics live and die; seventeenth century England produces Newton and eighteenth century Germany, Gauss, two who rank among the very greatest mathematicians of all time. But still the quintic resists every attack, and the inductive suspicion begins to grow that the search for a formula which solves the quintic and which involves nothing more complicated than radicals (i.e., square roots, cube roots, etc.) is a search for something which does not exist.

To another Italian physician, Paolo Ruffini, belongs the honor of being the first to prove that no such formula exists for equations of degree higher than 4. He first attempted to prove that fact in 1799, but it was not until 1813 that he completed his proof. Eleven years later, in 1824, another completely independent proof was constructed by the Norwegian Niels Henrik Abel. Only 22 when he wrote this paper, only 27 when he died of poverty and tuberculosis, Abel is one of the immortals of mathematics.

But in the work which they did on equations, Ruffini and Abel are both eclipsed by the incomparable genius of Evariste Galois, who was killed in a duel at the age of *twenty*! The story loses nothing from an investigation of the cause of his death: "*Cherchez la femme!*" He died, in his own words: "the victim of an infamous coquette."

When Galois was born, in 1811, Napoleon was emperor of France; but still fresh in the minds of the French nation was the memory of the Revolution of 1789 and the brief period afterward when France had been a republic. Throughout Galois' short life France remained a monarchy, but in the face of continual republican opposition. Galois threw himself heart and soul into the most extreme faction of the republicans. The details of the duel in which he died are lost to us, but despite the evidence of his quoted statement, it is likely that the primary reason for the challenge was not romantic, but political, in nature. In and out of jail, he was a thorn in the flesh of the monarchists. A duel would seem to have been a convenient device for putting him out of the way, and a coquettish woman may well have served the purpose of arranging a situation of "honor."

What do we have of Galois' work? Only several manuscripts and the contents of a letter written to a friend on the eve of his death. Here is what two present-day mathematicians have to say about Galois:

> This letter, if judged by the novelty and profundity of ideas it contains, is perhaps the most substantial piece of writing in the whole literature of mankind.
>
> Hermann Weyl: *Symmetry*

> All night . . . he had spent the fleeting hours feverishly dashing off his scientific last will and testament, writing against time to glean a few of the

great things in his teeming mind before the death which he foresaw could overtake him. Time after time he broke off to scribble in the margin "I have not time; I have not time," and passed on to the next frantically scrawled outline. What he wrote in those desperate last hours before the dawn will keep generations of mathematicians busy for hundreds of years. He had found, once and for all, the true solution of a riddle which had tormented mathematicians for centuries: under what conditions can an equation be solved? But this was only one thing of many. In this great work, Galois used the theory of groups with brilliant success. Galois was indeed one of the great pioneers in this abstract theory, today of fundamental importance in all mathematics. . . .

He was buried in the common ditch of the South Cemetery, so that today there remains no trace of the grave of Evariste Galois. His enduring monument is his collected works. They fill sixty pages.

E. T. Bell: *Men of Mathematics*

Often the question is raised as to who was the greatest mathematician who ever lived. It is a difficult question to answer; usually the three greatest are named (Archimedes, Gauss, and Newton), rather than just one. But it is not unlikely that if Galois had lived only a few years longer, his name would have served to answer the question unequivocally. Certainly no mathematician has ever done more before he was twenty-one.

▶ EXERCISE 18

1. Suppose f and g are functions and we are given the equation: $f(x) = g(x)$. Explain verbally and by means of symbols exactly what is meant when we say: "The number r is a solution (or 'root') of the equation $f(x) = g(x)$."

2. Solve the Egyptian problem of this section.

3. Solve the Babylonian problem of this section.

4. What is the reason for the stipulation "$a \neq 0$" in our definitions of algebraic equations of various degrees?

5. An artistic tradition, which it has been said goes back to Greek times, claims that a rectangle is most pleasing to the eye when it has the following property:

If two squares are constructed with the length and width respectively of the given rectangle as sides, then the difference between the areas of the two squares will be equal to the area of the given rectangle. (This is the so-called "golden rectangle.")

Assuming that a golden rectangle has width 1 unit and length x units, where $x > 1$, express its defining property as a quadratic equation in x and solve for x. Obtain a rational approximation to your answer by using the approximation 2.2 for $\sqrt{5}$. Examine several actual rectangles to see how close they come to being golden rectangles (i.e., find the ratio between their length and width and compare with your solution for x).

6.   With the aid of formulas, solve for x, and where feasible, verify that your solutions are correct:

(a) $2x - 14 = 0$ (b) $x - 7 = 7 - x$
(c) $x^2 - 1 = x$ (d) $6x^2 - 13x + 6 = 0$
(e) $2x^2 + 3x - 2 = 0$ (f) $2x^2 + 3x + 2 = 0$
(g) $x^2 - 1 = 0$ (h) $x^2 = 0$
(i) $x^2 + x = 0$ (j) $a^2x^2 - 5ax + 4 = 0$
(k) $x^2 + x + 1 = 0$ (l) $x^2 + (p^2 + 1)x + 1 = 0$
(m) $x^3 + 3x^2 + 3x + 1 = 0$ (n) $x^3 + 3x^2 + 9x + 5 = 0$
(o) $x^3 - 6x^2 - 4 = 0$ (p) $x^3 + 63x = 316$
(q) $x^3 - 9x + 8 = 0$ (r) $x^3 - 63x = 162$

7.   Find, by trial, integer solutions of equations (q) and (r) above.

5.3   AN APPROXIMATION METHOD FOR SOLVING EQUATIONS

In practical applications of mathematics, whenever a real number is sought which is to be the solution, or "root" of an equation, it is almost always a *rational* real root which is desired, or a decimal approximation to a real root, correct to a certain number of decimal places.

Thus, the exact solutions of the equation $x^2 = 2$ are $x = \pm \sqrt{2}$. Approximate solutions, correct to one decimal place: $x = \pm 1.4$; to two decimal places: $x = \pm 1.41$; to three decimal places: $x = \pm 1.414$; etc.

As we have seen, beginning with cubic equations, formula methods for solving algebraic equations are generally impracticable, or even impossible. A great deal of work has been done, therefore, on the problem of finding roots of equations approximately, since approximate solutions are, after all, all that are usually needed in practical applications.

There is one *highly intuitive*, very simple, versatile and effective method for attacking this problem which goes all the way back to the Babylonians. It is the method called "linear interpolation."

An example of this method turned up when the writer talked to a printer. The printer had listed prices per page for 100 copies and for 200 copies of a certain booklet.   The following dialogue ensued:

"What would the price for 150 copies be?"

"Why that would be just half-way between the price for 100 copies and the price for 200 copies."

"And for 175 copies?"

"That would be 3/4 of the way between the price for 100 copies and the price for 200 copies."

From which the writer induced, and then verified, that the printer used the method of linear interpolation to compute the cost of printing any number of copies which fell between two actually listed in his schedule of prices.

Let us examine the method more closely:

In the case of 150 copies, the situation may be diagrammed as follows:

NUMBER OF COPIES   **PRICE PER PAGE (in dollars)**

The numbers beside the brackets show the "way between," i.e., the difference between the indicated entries. We say that the number 150 is 50/100, or 1/2 of the way between the numbers 100 and 200. To find a number in the right-hand column corresponding to 150 on the left, we find 1/2 of the way between 1.22 and 1.60, that is (1/2)(0.38), or 0.19, and proceed that much farther than 1.22, to arrive at the result 1.41.

When 150 copies of the booklet are printed, the price per page is therefore $1.41.

In the case of 175 copies:

NUMBER OF COPIES   **PRICE PER PAGE (in dollars)**

```
             ┌──────100                1.22┐
          75 │                             │
   100  │    └─ 175                    ?    │  0.38
        │                                  │
        └──────200                    1.60┘
```

The fractional "way between" in this case is 75/100 or 0.75, and our result in this case is 1.22 + (0.75)(0.38) dollars, or (to the next higher cent) $1.51 as the price per page when 175 copies are printed.

In general, the process of interpolation involves a "table of values" (i.e., a function) as follows: (all entries are real numbers)

a	a'
b	$? = b'$
c	c'

We are given real numbers a' and c' corresponding to a and c respectively; b is a real number between a and c; the problem is to find a real number b' to correspond with b.

Generalizing the procedure we have followed above, the method of linear interpolation is to form the fraction f:

$$f = \frac{b - a}{c - a}$$

and then to assume: $b' = a' + f \cdot (c' - a')$
Solving the last equation for f:

$$f = \frac{b' - a'}{c' - a'}$$

In other words, this method of choosing b' causes b' to be the same fractional way between a' and c' that b is between a and c. In most functional tables, b' will not, of course, behave in just this way. But when a and c are relatively close to each other, this method usually gives fairly accurate results.

We now apply the method of linear interpolation to the problem of finding an approximation to $\sqrt{2}$. Actually, what we seek here is a positive real number x such that $x^2 = 2$. We therefore form a table of values:

x	x^2
1	1
?	2 1 3
2	4

Further progress now depends on the following intuitively plausible theorem. (The proof of this theorem is omitted, since it requires a more thorough investigation of real-number and function theory than we have time for in this course.)

Theorem. Suppose $f(x) = k$ is an algebraic equation, and suppose that a and c are real numbers such that: $f(a) < k, f(c) > k$.
Then the equation $f(x) = k$ has at least one real root b between a and c.

In the preceding example, $x^2 = 2$ may be thought of as the algebraic equation $f(x) = k$, and 1 and 2 play the role of a and c respectively. Since $f(1) = 1 < 2$ and $f(2) = 4 > 2$, the theorem assures us that there is a real root of the equation $x^2 = 2$ between 1 and 2.

Now the method of linear interpolation offers as a first approximation to $\sqrt{2}$, $1 + (1/3)$, or approximately 1.3. But squaring 1.3 results in only 1.69, which falls considerably short of the goal of 2. Trying 0.1 more: $(1.4)^2 = 1.96$, which still falls short of 2, but this time not by very much.

APPROXIMATION METHOD FOR SOLVING EQUATIONS 117

And when we square the next natural candidate, 1.5, the result is 2.25, and we have gone right past 2.

However, now we are sure (because of the theorem above) that $\sqrt{2}$ is between 1.4 and 1.5, and we interpolate again:

x	x^2
1.4	1.96
0.1 ?	2.00 0.04 0.29
1.5	2.25

Our next approximation to $\sqrt{2}$ is: $1.4 + (4/29)(0.1)$, or $1.4 + 0.01$, or 1.41. (We advance only one decimal place at a time.) Squaring, we find: $(1.41)^2 = 1.9881$ and $(1.42)^2 = 2.0164$.

Now we know (again by the theorem above) that $\sqrt{2}$ is between 1.41 and 1.42, and at this point we may say that correct to one decimal place, $\sqrt{2}$ is approximately 1.4.

But as a matter of fact, to be able to say that a correct one decimal-place approximation to $\sqrt{2}$ is 1.4, it is only necessary to know that $\sqrt{2}$ is between 1.4 and 1.45. Therefore, if all that we require is a correct one-decimal place approximation to $\sqrt{2}$, we may proceed as follows.

Having determined that $\sqrt{2}$ lies between 1.4 and 1.5, we would see what happens when we square 1.45: $(1.45)^2 = 2.1025$, which is greater than 2. Therefore $\sqrt{2}$ lies between 1.4 and 1.45, which means that correct to one decimal place $\sqrt{2} \doteq 1.4$. (We use the symbol $\doteq$ to mean "approximately equals.")

Note that in approximating $\sqrt{2}$, our second interpolation required less adjustment than our first; this, of course, is due to the fact that in the second interpolation, the tabular gaps are smaller.

As a final illustrative example of the use of interpolation in approximating a real root of an algebraic equation, we apply the method to the equation:

$$x^3 - 2x - 1 = 0$$

First of all, we simply guess at an integer value of x, say $x = 1$, and substitute on the left-hand side of the equation, to arrive at the result: -2. Trying the next larger integer value $x = 2$, the left hand side of the equation becomes 3. Described tabularly:

x	$x^3 - 2x - 1$
1	-2
?	0
2	3

Since 0 lies between -2 and 3, we know that there is a root of this equation between 1 and 2. Interpolation now offers 1.4 as a possible approximation to this root. Substituting 1.4 for x on the left side of our equation, the result is -1.056, which is not too close to our desired result of 0; but we know now that there must be a root between 1.4 and 2 (why?).

Our next attempt, therefore, is: $x = 1.5$. The result of substitution in this case is -0.625, and now we know that there is a root between 1.5 and 2; the next candidate is $x = 1.6$, whose substitution leads to -0.104. We are now, of course, aiming at a value of x whose substitution will lead to a *non*-negative result, and we seem to be getting there, but we have not yet quite made the grade.

But when we try $x = 1.7$, the result is 0.513. Now we know that there is a root between 1.6 and 1.7, and we are ready for another interpolation:

x	$x^3 - 2x - 1$
1.6	-0.104
?	$0 \qquad \left(x \doteq 1.6 + \dfrac{104}{617}(0.1) \doteq 1.62\right)$
1.7	0.513

The result of substituting 1.62 for x on the left-hand side of our equation is approximately 0.0115 (which we note is quite close to being the desired result 0). Therefore we now know that a root lies between 1.6 and 1.62 (why?); we also know that correct to one decimal place, a root of this equation is 1.6.

In finding further decimal places, a next step would be to try the value 1.61 for x. It will be left to the student to continue with the goal of finding a root of the given equation correct to *two* decimal places.

The work involved in the preceding example is admittedly burdensome and tedious. Devices for lightening the task are therefore welcome. Much of the mechanical labor involved has in recent times been taken over by computing machines, we are happy to report. Furthermore, greater theoretical understanding of the properties of equations is very helpful, and is therefore the subject of study in more advanced courses in mathematics.

NOTE: It is assumed that the student is familiar with the "rounding-off" process by which a decimal is replaced by one with fewer decimal places. We round off, for example, 1.23, when we require the best possible one-decimal place approximation, to 1.2; and with the same requirement we round off 2.351 to 2.4, since 2.351 is between 2.3 and 2.4, but nearer 2.4.

But what shall we do with a number like 2.45, when we seek a one-decimal place approximation? The number 2.45 is exactly mid-way between 2.4 and 2.5. In such cases, mainly for the sake of uniformity, we agree always to choose that possibility which makes the last digit an *even* digit. Thus we shall round off 2.45 to 2.4, and 2.35 to 2.4 also.

▶ **EXERCISE 19**

1. Carry the process of approximating $\sqrt{2}$ one place further than the text does, to arrive at an approximation correct to two decimal places.

2. By linear interpolation, find approximations to the following numbers correct to one decimal place:

(a)	$\sqrt{3}$	(b)	$\sqrt{5}$	(c)	$\sqrt{6}$	(d)	$\sqrt{7}$
(e)	$\sqrt{8}$	(f)	$\sqrt{10}$	(g)	$\sqrt[3]{2}$	(h)	$\sqrt[3]{3}$
(i)	$\sqrt[3]{4}$	(j)	$\sqrt[3]{5}$	(k)	$\sqrt[3]{6}$	(l)	$\sqrt[3]{7}$
(m)	$\sqrt[4]{17}$	(n)	$(1.1)^{1.1}$	(o)	$56/7.5$	(p)	$\sqrt{110.5}$

3. Carry the process begun in the text to the point of finding a root of the equation $x^3 - 2x - 1 = 0$ correct to two decimal places.

4. Approximate a root of the equation $x^3 - x - 3 = 0$ correct to one decimal place.
What does Cardan's formula offer as a root of this equation?

5. Apply Cardan's formula to the cubic equation of Problem 3 above.

6 Find a root of the equation of Problem 4 above, correct to two decimal places.

7. Find a root of the equation $x^4 = 2$: (a) correct to one decimal place; (b) correct to two decimal places.

8. Find a root of the equation $x^3 - x = 2$: (a) correct to one decimal place; (b) correct to two decimal places.

9. Find a root of the equation $x^3 + x - 3 = 0$: (a) correct to one decimal place; (b) correct to two decimal places.

10. Given the equation $x^3 - 4x^2 + 3x + 1 = 0$:
(a) Find a root correct to one decimal place.
(b) Find another root correct to one decimal place.
(c) Find a third root correct to one decimal place.
(d) Find the root of (a) correct to two decimal places.
(e) Find the root of (b) correct to two decimal places.
(f) Find the root of (c) correct to two decimal places.

5.4 COMPLEX NUMBERS

It is, of course, well-known that if a real number is either positive or negative, then its square is positive; and if a real number is 0, then its square is 0. The square of a real number, then, is *never* negative.

As a consequence, so long as only real numbers are known, there will be some real numbers whose square roots do not exist; namely, the negative real numbers.

The deficiency is a serious one. It means, among other things, that so long as it exists, some algebraic equations, as for example the equation $x^2 = -7$, can have no solutions.

Just as it occurred historically that the system of natural numbers was enlarged to become the system of common fractions, in order to make the operation of division complete—and just as the number system has after that been extended again and again in order to make various other operations complete—so we now extend the real number system in order to make the operation $\sqrt{}$ complete. The larger system of numbers that results is called the *complex number system*.

The student will be relieved to learn that so far as this course is concerned, complex numbers represent finally the culmination of our long process of extending number systems. Further extensions exist, but they belong to the realm of advanced scientific work, and furthermore they lack one or another of the important attributes of the complex number system. For these reasons the complex number system is at present *the* number system of science.

One of the basic deficiencies of the real number system is that it lacks a square root of -1. Very well; let us repair this defect by inventing a new number "i" which shall have the defining property:

$$i^2 = -1$$

so that "i" will be a square root of -1. This is not as daring as it may seem; it is very much like what is done when the number -1 is invented with the defining property that it shall be a number whose addition to 1 yields 0.

Now we "adjoin" i to our real number system. But this involves more than just the inclusion of one more number in our system. Among other things, we wish to be able to multiply i by any real number, and we wish to be able to add any real number to the result.

In other words, if a and b are any real numbers, we would like a number $a + bi$ to exist.

The process of extending the real number system to a larger system, having the useful "field" properties (see Section 4.3) and containing a square root of -1, is a complicated one; here we shall only state the final result:

The set of real numbers may be enlarged, and the relation $=$ and the operations $+$ and $\cdot$ may be extended to apply to the enlarged set, to arrive at a *field* (whose elements are called "complex numbers") which contains not only the field of real numbers, but also an element i such that $i^2 = -1$. Furthermore, every complex number is uniquely expressible in the form $a + bi$, where a and b are real numbers.

Examples of complex numbers are: $2 + 3i$, $3 + i$, $\sqrt{7} + \pi i$, $7i$, 7, $\sqrt{7}$, 0.

We classify complex numbers $a + bi$ as: real (if $b = 0$); imaginary (if $b \neq 0$); pure imaginary (if $a = 0$, $b \neq 0$).

Examples of operations on complex numbers:

$$(2 + 3i) + (3 + i) = 5 + 4i$$
$$(2 + 3i)(3 + i) = 6 + 11i + 3i^2 = 6 + 11i - 3 = 3 + 11i$$
$$(2 + 3i) \div (3 + i) - \frac{2 + 3i}{3 + i} - \frac{2 + 3i}{3 + i} \cdot \frac{3 - i}{3 - i} = \frac{9 + 7i}{10} = \frac{9}{10} + \frac{7}{10}i$$

Note that in carrying out the division, we have used the trick of multiplying numerator and denominator by the "conjugate" of the denominator. (If a and b are real numbers, the *conjugate* of $a + bi$ is defined to be $a - bi$.)

Note also that in carrying out these operations, liberal use of such field axioms as distributivity, associativity, etc., has been made, and also we have used such field definitions and theorems as Definition R2 and Problem 5 of Exercise 14. This is an example of the economy of the abstract approach. The definitions we have made and the theorems we have proved for the *field* of real numbers apply immediately to any field, without any further work; for if the complex numbers satisfy the six field axioms, as they do (replacing "real number" in these axioms by "complex number"), they must satisfy the consequences of these axioms also.

Our treatment of complex numbers has been deliberately brief, since we shall find very little use for them in this course. Our reason for considering complex numbers at all, however, is that reference to them is necessary in discussing the possibility of solving algebraic equations with real coefficients, as well as other questions which arise in an attempt to solve such equations.

For example, one of the most important properties of the complex number system is that which is given in the so-called "fundamental theorem of algebra," first proved (in his doctoral dissertation) by the German mathematician Carl Friedrich Gauss (1777–1855).

Fundamental Theorem of Algebra. Every algebraic equation whose coefficients are complex numbers has a solution which is a complex number.

(The proof of this theorem is omitted, since it requires a great deal of mathematics not yet at our disposal.)

Real numbers are, of course, special cases of complex numbers. Hence algebraic equations whose coefficients are real numbers are included among algebraic equations whose coefficients are complex numbers. Thus by the fundamental theorem of algebra, we can always be sure that an algebraic equation with real coefficients will have a complex root, even if it has no real roots. It is essentially for this reason that it is more natural to work with the larger set of complex numbers when we seek roots of an algebraic equation with real coefficients, rather than with the restricted set of real numbers.

As we have remarked, the complex numbers form a field; that is to say they satisfy all of our six field axioms, and therefore it follows that *they satisfy the consequences of these axioms also.* But it is easy to show that the complex numbers cannot be ordered; i.e., it is impossible to introduce a relation < among the complex numbers which satisfies the three order postulates.

For we have shown that it is a consequence of these postulates that the square of any number is never negative (Problem 5(f), Exercise 17). Among the complex numbers, there is, however, a number whose square is negative, namely i (see corollary to Theorem R21). Therefore the postulates of order could not apply to the complex numbers.

As a consequence, when dealing with *inequality* relations, we shall restrict ourselves to the real number system.

We remark, finally, that the names "imaginary" and "real" as they apply to numbers reflect only early attitudes toward these numbers. In the light of their definition in terms of simpler numbers and their practical applications, "imaginary" numbers are just as real as "real" numbers.

5.5 THE UNARY OPERATION $\sqrt{\ }$

Up until now we have dealt informally with the unary operation $\sqrt{\ }$ (see Section 2.11, Note 2, and Section 3.3), and later on (page 101, Problems 2 and 4) we precisely defined the unary operation $\sqrt{\ }$ on the set of all non-negative real numbers.

We have seen that a number may have more than one square root. For example, 9 has the square roots 3 and -3. The expression $\sqrt{9}$ is intended to represent just one of these square roots, namely 3. In general, since the symbol $\sqrt{}$ will always indicate just one among possibly several square roots, we shall be careful from now on to read this symbol as "the *principal* square root of."

Now that we have complex numbers at our disposal, we are prepared to extend the domain of the unary operation $\sqrt{}$ to include *all* real numbers.

Problems 2 and 4, page 101, guarantee that given any non-negative real number r, there is a unique non-negative real number whose square is r. This makes possible the following definition:

Definition A. If r is a non-negative real number, $\sqrt{r}$ is defined to be the unique non-negative real number whose square is r.

Directly from this definition, it follows that if r is a non-negative real number, then:

$$(1) \qquad\qquad (\sqrt{r})^2 = r$$

There is still left to us, now, the task of defining $\sqrt{-p}$, where p is any positive real number.

What we seek is a number whose square is $-p$. But a fairly obvious choice for such a number is $i\sqrt{p}$. For:

$$(i\sqrt{p})^2 = (i\sqrt{p})(i\sqrt{p}) = (i)^2(\sqrt{p})^2 = (-1)(p) = -p$$

Therefore we make the:

Definition B. If $-p$ is a negative real number, $\sqrt{-p}$ is defined to equal $i\sqrt{p}$.

Directly from this definition, there follows that if $-p$ is a negative real number, then:

$$(2) \qquad\qquad (\sqrt{-p})^2 = -p$$

Thus, from (1) and (2) above, we have the following important fact:

(i) If r is any real number, then $(\sqrt{r})^2 = r$.

It is necessary to distinguish carefully between $(\sqrt{r})^2$ and $\sqrt{r^2}$, where r is a real number; for example, suppose $r = -2$. Then by (i) above:

$$(\sqrt{-2})^2 = -2$$

But:

$$\sqrt{(-2)^2} = \sqrt{4} = 2$$

And we see that $\sqrt{r^2}$ is not always r! However, using the notation of absolute value (see Exercise 5, Problem 14), we can state the situation precisely:

(ii) If r is any real number, then $\sqrt{r^2} = |r|$.

PROOF OF (ii): By Problem 5(f) of Exercise 17, r^2 is a non-negative real number. Therefore, Definition A, above, applies, and to prove (ii) we need merely show that $|r|$ is a non-negative real number and that its square is r^2. But $|r|$ is non-negative by the definition of absolute value; and since always $|r| = \pm r$, it follows that $(|r|)^2 = r^2$.

A third important property of the unary operation $\sqrt{}$ follows:

(iii) If r, s are any non-negative real numbers, then $\sqrt{r} \cdot \sqrt{s} = \sqrt{rs}$.

PROOF OF (iii): First of all, by the rules we have proved for the multiplication of signed numbers, if r and s are non-negative real numbers, then rs is a non-negative real number. Now to prove that a given real number is $\sqrt{rs}$, our definition of $\sqrt{}$ requires us to show that the given real number is non-negative, and that its square is rs.

But we know (again by our definition of $\sqrt{}$) that $\sqrt{r}$ and $\sqrt{s}$ are non-negative. Therefore, by our laws for the multiplication of signed numbers, $\sqrt{r} \cdot \sqrt{s}$ is non-negative.

Furthermore: $(\sqrt{r} \cdot \sqrt{s})^2 = (\sqrt{r} \cdot \sqrt{s})(\sqrt{r} \cdot \sqrt{s}) = (\sqrt{r})^2(\sqrt{s})^2 = rs$.

Therefore both conditions for $\sqrt{r} \cdot \sqrt{s}$ to be the principal square root of rs have been satisfied, so that the theorem is proved.

Note. Actually, the preceding theorem enables us to simplify the product of $\sqrt{r}$ and $\sqrt{s}$ even when r, or s, or both are negative. For example:

$$\sqrt{2} \cdot \sqrt{-3} = \sqrt{2} \cdot i \cdot \sqrt{3} = i\sqrt{6}$$

Illustrative Example I.   Express each of the following complex numbers in the form $a + bi$, where a and b are real:

(a) 7

(b) 2i

(c) $\sqrt{-3}$

(d) $\dfrac{1 + \sqrt{-3}}{2}$

(e) $(3 + 2i)(3 - 2i)$

(f) $\dfrac{1 + i}{1 - i}$

Solution.

(a) $7 = 7 + 0i$ $(a = 7, b = 0)$

(b) $2i = 0 + 2i$ $(a = 0, b = 2)$

(c) $\sqrt{-3} = i\sqrt{3}$ (by Definition B above)

$\qquad = 0 + \sqrt{3}\,i$ $(a = 0, b = \sqrt{3})$

(d) $\dfrac{1 + \sqrt{-3}}{2} = \dfrac{1 + i\sqrt{3}}{2} = \dfrac{1}{2} + \dfrac{\sqrt{3}}{2}i$ $\left(a = \dfrac{1}{2}, b = \dfrac{\sqrt{3}}{2}\right)$

(e) $(3 + 2i)(3 - 2i) = 9 - 4i^2 = 9 + 4 = 13 = 13 + 0i$

$\qquad (a = 13, b = 0)$

(f) $\dfrac{1 + i}{1 - i} = \dfrac{1 + i}{1 - i} \cdot \dfrac{1 + i}{1 + i} = \dfrac{1 + 2i + i^2}{1 - i^2} = \dfrac{1 + 2i - 1}{1 + 1} = \dfrac{2i}{2}$

$\qquad = i = 0 + 1i$ $(a = 0, b = 1)$

Illustrative Example 2. Classify the complex numbers (*a*)–(*f*) of Illustrative Example 1 according to type.

SOLUTION. Real: (*a*), (*e*), since $b = 0$ in these cases.
Imaginary: (*b*), (*c*), (*d*), (*f*), since $b \neq 0$ in these cases.
Pure imaginary: (*b*), (*c*), (*f*), since $a = 0$, $b \neq 0$ in these cases.

Illustrative Example 3. Solve the equation: $x + yi = 2 + 3i$, under the condition that x and y must be real.

SOLUTION. The *unique* expressibility of a complex number in the form $a + bi$, where a and b are real, means that the only solution of the given equation is $x = 2$, $y = 3$.

▶ **EXERCISE 20**

1. Express in the form $a + bi$, where a and b are real numbers, each of the following complex numbers, and tell what type of complex number each is:

(*a*)   0

(*b*)   1

(*c*)   2i

(*d*)   2

(*e*) $(2 - 3i)^2$

(*f*) $(2 - 3i)(2 + 3i)$

(*g*) $(2 - 3i) + (2 + 3i)$

(*h*) $(3 - 4i)(3 + 4i)$

(*i*) $(3 - 4i) + (3 + 4i)$

(*j*) $(2 + 3i)(3 + 4i)$

(*k*) $(2 + 3i) - (3 + 4i)$

(*l*) $(7 + 11i) - (7 - 11i)$

(*m*) $\dfrac{1 + 5i}{2}$

(*n*) $\dfrac{1 - i}{1 + i}$

(*o*) $\dfrac{2 + 4i}{3 + 2i}$

2. (*a*)   What can always be said about the sum and product of conjugate complex numbers?

(*b*)   Prove the statement you have made in answer to (*a*) above.

(*c*)   What type of reasoning led to your statement made in answer to (*a*)? Explain.

(*d*)   What type of reasoning did you use in part (*b*) above? Explain.

3. Where is the flaw in reasoning in the following paradox?

(1) $\sqrt{-1} \cdot \sqrt{-1} = \sqrt{(-1)(-1)} = \sqrt{1} = 1$

(2) $\sqrt{-1} \cdot \sqrt{-1} = i \cdot i = i^2 = -1$

(3) $\therefore 1 = -1$!

4. In what sense do the complex numbers "complete" the set of all real numbers? That is to say, what is it which is not always possible within the set of all real numbers before the set of all complex numbers is known, but which becomes possible once the set of all complex numbers is available?

5.   In Exercise 18, Problem 6, express the roots of equations (a)–(i) and (k) in the form $a + bi$, where a and b are real, and tell what type of complex number each root is.

6.   Given: $\sqrt{2} \doteq 1.41$, $\sqrt{3} \doteq 1.73$, $\sqrt{5} \doteq 2.24$, find approximations to the following. (Note that results should not be given to a greater degree of accuracy than given information.)

(a) $\sqrt{6}$ (b) $\sqrt{8}$ (c) $\sqrt{10}$ (d) $\sqrt{12}$

(e) $\sqrt{15}$ (f) $\sqrt{18}$ (g) $\sqrt{20}$ (h) $\sqrt{24}$

7.   Simplify the following, given that x is a real number

(a) $\sqrt{x^2 + 2x + 1}$. Solution: $\sqrt{x^2 + 2x + 1} = \sqrt{(x + 1)^2} = |x + 1|$, by (ii) above.

(b) $\sqrt{x^2}$ (c) $\sqrt{4x^2}$

(d) $\sqrt{(-3)^2}$ (e) $(\sqrt{-3})^2$

(f) $\sqrt{x^2 - 2x + 1}$ (g) $\sqrt{x^2 - 6x + 9}$

(h) $\sqrt{x^2 + 4x + 4}$ (i) $\sqrt{6x - x^2 - 9}$

8.   Illustrate by means of a Venn diagram, the inclusion relationships among the following sets: complex numbers; integers; natural numbers; rational numbers; real numbers.

5.6   ON THE SOLUTION OF EQUATIONS: THE "CANDIDATE" POINT OF VIEW

In this section we shall consider a very general approach to the problem of solving equations.

Throughout this section we shall assume that we are dealing with *complex numbers*. That is to say, throughout this section "number" will mean *complex number*, and "root" or "solution" of an equation will refer to *a root or solution among the complex numbers*.

We apply the point of view we have in mind to the solution of the equation:

$$2x + 4 = 0$$

In solving this equation, we may reason as follows:

Let us suppose for the moment that there *is* a solution of this equation, i.e., that there is a number x such that $2x + 4 = 0$.

Then adding -4 to both sides of this equation, it must be true (why?) that $2x = -4$.

And now, dividing both sides of the preceding equation by 2, it must be true (why?) that $x = -2$.

Our conclusion, then, is that *if* there is a number x such that $2x + 4 = 0$, then there is only one such, and it is -2.   In other words, we have shown that the only *possibility* for a solution is -2, but we have not proved that this possibility actually *is* a solution.   That, however, is easily done; for substituting -2 for x in the given equation:

$$2(-2) + 4 = -4 + 4 = 0$$

This is a true statement; and since a solution of the equation $2x + 4 = 0$ is simply a number which yields a true statement when substituted for x in the equation, it follows that -2 *is* a solution of the given equation.

Now, by way of contrast, consider the equation:

$$x + 1 = x + 2$$

Here ordinary methods lead to no solution; for subtracting x from both sides, we arrive at: $1 = 2$.   This is a very peculiar statement, and in any case suggests no solution for x.

Let us attempt, then, something out of the ordinary: We multiply both sides by $x - 1$.   Then:

$$x^2 - 1 = x^2 + x - 2$$
$$x = 1.$$

But substituting $x = 1$ in the original equation leads to: $1 + 1 = 1 + 2$, or $2 = 3$, which is of course not true; hence 1 is *not* a solution of the given equation.

With regard to this paradoxical situation, the facts are actually these:

First of all, *if* there were a number x such that $x + 1 = x + 2$, *then* by subtracting x from both sides, we would be able to conclude that $1 = 2$. Since this conclusion is absurd (i.e., contradictory; see Theorem R22 and trichotomy axiom), our hypothesis, which states that there is such a number x, must be false.   A correct conclusion, then, is this: The equation $x + 1 = x + 2$ has no solution.

Secondly, we point out that our work in deriving the result $x = 1$ directly above is perfectly valid, but again, it is based upon the assumption that the equation $x + 1 = x + 2$ has a solution.   What we have shown is that *if* the given equation has a solution, *then* a solution is $x = 1$.   But actually the equation has no solution, and the *possibility* $x = 1$ must be discarded.

Now we turn our attention to the solution of quadratic equations in x; we consider, in particular, the equation:

$$x^2 - 3x + 2 = 0$$

Again, we suppose to begin with that there *is* a number x such that $x^2 - 3x + 2 = 0$.   But we can show that if x is any real number, then $x^2 - 3x + 2 = (x - 1)(x - 2)$. Since numbers equal to the same number are equal to each other, it follows that:

$$(x - 1)(x - 2) = 0$$

Now (by Theorem R8 of Section 4.7) if the product of the numbers $x - 1$ and $x - 2$ is 0, then:

$$x - 1 = 0 \quad \text{or} \quad x - 2 = 0$$

Furthermore, if $x - 1 = 0$, then $x = 1$; and if $x - 2 = 0$, then $x = 2$.

We conclude, then, that *if* the equation $x^2 - 3x + 2 = 0$ has a solution, that solution must be 1 or 2. Our process of reasoning has not yet justified our saying that either of these numbers *is* a solution of the given equation, but only that there are *no other* solutions possible; our method, so to speak, has given us the only possible "candidates" for the position of solution to the given equation, but the candidates have not yet been elected—we must substitute into the original equation to see which, if any, of the possible solutions are actual solutions:

Substituting 1 for x: $\quad 1^2 - 3 \cdot 1 + 2 = 1 - 3 + 2 = 0$

Substituting 2 for x: $\quad 2^2 - 3 \cdot 2 + 2 = 4 - 6 + 2 = 0$

Both candidates have been elected; now we may say that the roots of the given equation are $x = 1$ and $x = 2$.

Finally, we consider a third equation, one involving a square root:

$$x + \sqrt{x} = 6$$

Remember that throughout this section, complex roots are what we seek; but in this case we must further restrict ourselves to *real* complex numbers, since the symbol $\sqrt{}$ has been defined only for real numbers.

Our reasoning in solving the above equation might go as follows:

If x is a real number such that $x + \sqrt{x} = 6$

$$\text{then:} \quad \sqrt{x} = 6 - x$$

$$\text{and squaring both sides:} \quad x = 36 - 12x + x^2$$

Working with this quadratic equation as in the preceding case, we conclude that the only possible candidates for a solution to the given equation are $x = 4$ and $x = 9$. Now let us see whether either, or both, or neither are solutions.

Checking 4: $\quad 4 + \sqrt{4} = 4 + 2 = 6$

Checking 9: $\quad 9 + \sqrt{9} = 9 + 3 = 12 \neq 6.$ (Remember that $\sqrt{9}$ means: non-negative square root of 9!)

Our final conclusion, then, is that $x = 4$ is the only solution of the equation $x + \sqrt{x} = 6$.

(Values like $x = 9$ in the preceding case, which are suggested by certain methods of solving equations, but which turn out *not* to be roots, are unfortunately sometimes called "extraneous roots." It has been said of the Holy Roman Empire that it was neither holy, nor Roman, nor an empire. It may be remarked that extraneous roots are roots in the same sense that the Holy Roman Empire was an empire.)

5.7 QUADRATIC EQUATIONS

One of the techniques to which we shall have to resort especially often in the mathematics which follows is that of solving quadratic equations. The student will therefore find it greatly to his advantage to make sure that he is competent in this technique. Toward this end, we shall review certain methods, commonly presented in high-school algebra, for the solution of quadratic equations.

We note that as a last resort, the quadratic formula may be used to solve *any* quadratic equation in one unknown. In this section we shall be concerned, however, with methods which, when they are applicable, are simpler than the formula method.

Illustrative Example 1. Solve: $3 - 2x = x^2$.

SOLUTION: We add -3 and $2x$ to both sides and reverse the equality to arrive at an equation in "standard" form (see definition of quadratic equation, Section 5.2):

$$x^2 + 2x - 3 = 0$$

Factoring: $(x + 3)(x - 1) = 0$

By Theorem R8: $x + 3 = 0$ or $x - 1 - 0$

Therefore: $x = -3$ or $x = 1$

From what we have said so far, it would appear that all we can say at this point is that -3 and 1 are the only *candidates* for solutions to the given equation.

In the particular case of algebraic equations, however, it can easily be seen (and will be even more evident after reading the next section) that candidates for roots arrived at by the method of factoring, and by the use of Theorem R8, will always be successful candidates.

In such a case, if we check to see that our candidates satisfy the given equation, it need only be to make sure that we have not made an error in the process of solution.

The student may verify that no error has been made in this case, by substituting -3 and 1 for x in the given equation, and arriving at true statements.

Illustrative Example 2. Solve: $4x^2 = 8x$.

SOLUTION: The temptation to divide both sides by $4x$ to arrive at: $x = 2$, should be avoided. For although 2 actually *is* a root, there happens to be another root, which has been lost in this process.

When solving equations, avoid, if possible, multiplying or dividing by anything but nonzero numbers.

In this case, there is no harm in dividing both sides by the number 4:

$$x^2 = 2x$$

But then, in order to take advantage of Theorem R8, we add $-2x$ to both sides, to arrive at:

$$x^2 - 2x = 0$$

Factoring: $$x(x - 2) = 0$$

Therefore: $x = 0$ and $x = 2$ are the solutions.

Illustrative Example 3.   Solve: $x^2 - 2x = 8$.

SOLUTION: Here the trap to be avoided is to imagine that since the equation may be written: $x(x - 2) = 1 \cdot 8$, that equating the factors: $x = 1, x - 2 = 8$ will yield solutions.   It is easy to verify that neither 1 nor 10 are solutions of the given equation, and indeed there is no reason why they should be.   *The method of factoring, and the use of Theorem R8 require that one side of the equation be 0.*

We therefore proceed in this fashion:

$$x^2 - 2x - 8 = 0$$
$$(x - 4)(x + 2) = 0$$
$$x = 4 \text{ and } x = -2 \text{ are the solutions.}$$

▶ **EXERCISE 21**

1.   Solve, without using formulas:

(a) $x^2 - 4 = 0$ (b) $x^2 - x = 0$
(c) $x^2 - x = 6$ (d) $4x^2 - 9 = 0$
(e) $4x^2 \div 9x = 0$ (f) $4x^2 - 9x = -5$
(g) $x^2 - 5x + 6 = 0$ (h) $5x = 6x^2 + 1$
(i) $5x + 2 = 1 - 6x^2$ (j) $6x^2 + 5x = 6$
(k) $x^2 = 0$ (l) $x^2 = 2x$
(m) $x^3 = 0$ (n) $x^2 - 2 = (x - 1)(x + 1)$
(o) $x^4 - 12x^2 + 27 = 0$.   (p) $x^3 - x^2 - x + 1 = 0$

2.   Solve:

(a) $x - \sqrt{x} = 2$ (b) $x + \sqrt{x - 2} = 8$
(c) $3x + \sqrt{1 + x} = 7$ (d) $9x - 3\sqrt{x} = 2$
(e) $1 + x = 2\sqrt{x}$ (f) $1 + x = \sqrt{2x}$
(g) $\sqrt{x} + \sqrt{4x} = 2$ (h) $\sqrt{x} + \sqrt{2x} = \sqrt{3x}$
(i) $\sqrt{x^2} = -1$ (j) $(\sqrt{x})^2 = -1$
(k) $\sqrt{x + 6} + \sqrt{x - 6} = 10$ (l) $2\sqrt{x} + \sqrt{10 + 4x} = 5$

3.   Prove (rigorously) that if x is a complex number such that $2x + 4 = 0$, then $x = -2$.

5.8 ON THE SOLUTION OF EQUATIONS AND IN-EQUALITIES: THE "EQUIVALENCE" POINT OF VIEW

We return to the equation: $2x + 4 = 0$.

In our preceding treatment, we derived from this equation, by adding -4 to both sides, the equation: $2x = -4$; and we may say the following about the relation between these equations:

If x is a complex number such that $2x + 4 = 0$, then $2x = -4$. That is to say, any complex number which satisfies ("which is a root of") the equation $2x + 4 = 0$ must also satisfy the equation $2x = -4$.

But now suppose a complex number satisfies the *second* of these two equations, namely: $2x = -4$. Then by adding 4 to both sides, we would have: $2x + 4 = 0$. In other words, any complex number which satisfies the equation $2x = -4$ must also satisfy the equation $2x + 4 = 0$.

We have shown that any complex number which satisfies *either* of these two equations satisfies the other. Thus, to solve one, we may, if we wish, solve the other. In practice, in our particular case, we now forget about the equation $2x + 4 = 0$ and make our new problem that of solving the equation $2x = -4$.

In general, we make the following definitions:

Definition. Two equations are called *equivalent* if any complex number which satisfies one also satisfies the other.

Definition. Two inequalities are called *equivalent* if any real number which satisfies one also satisfies the other.

(As usual, in dealing with inequalities, we restrict ourselves to the set of real numbers rather than to the set of *all* complex numbers, since the relations $<$, $>$, etc., are not defined for any but *real* complex numbers; see page 122.)

Now if, in solving an equation (or an inequality) we proceed from our first step to our final solution by a sequence of *equivalent* equations (or inequalities), then there can be no "extraneous" numbers creeping in; our results *must* be solutions.

To analyze all the circumstances under which derived equations or inequalities would be equivalent to the original would be tedious. We shall, however, consider several of the most useful of these. The student will recognize them as the processes used most often in the solution of equations.

First of all, we may add to (hence of course also subtract from) both sides of an equation any complex number, and the result will be an equivalent equation. The reason for this was brought out in our examination of the relation between the equations $2x + 4 = 0$ and $2x = -4$.

An analogous statement may be made about inequalities. For example (by Theorem R18, page 92), the inequality $2x + 4 > 0$ may be shown to be equivalent to $2x > -4$.

The statements made in the following two tables may be similarly justified.

I
SOME PROCESSES WHICH TRANSFORM EQUATIONS INTO EQUIVALENT EQUATIONS

(i)   Adding to (or subtracting from) both sides, equal complex numbers.

(ii)   Multiplying (or dividing) both sides by equal *nonzero* complex numbers.

(iii)   Substitution of equals for equals (see below).

(iv)   "Transposition." [That is, the equation $a(x) + b(x) = c(x)$ is equivalent to $a(x) = c(x) - b(x)$.]

II
SOME PROCESSES WHICH TRANSFORM INEQUALITIES INTO EQUIVALENT INEQUALITIES

(*a*)   Adding to (or subtracting from) both sides, equal real numbers.

(*b*)   Multiplying (or dividing) both sides by equal *positive* real numbers.

(*c*)   Multiplying (or dividing) both sides by equal negative real numbers, *and at the same time reversing the sign of inequality*.

(*d*)   Substitution of equals for equals (see below).

(*e*)   "Transposition." (In I (iv) above, replace $=$ by any one of the inequality relations.)

A word as to (iii) and (*d*) above:

By "substitution of equals for equals" we mean first of all, that in both equalities and inequalities a number may be replaced by an equal number. One may, for example, replace 4/2 by 2; or, if a and b are real numbers, one may replace $(a - b)(a + b)$ by $a^2 - b^2$; both replacements would transform a given equation or inequality only into an equivalent equation or inequality.

Secondly, suppose f and g are equal functions; in the case of equations, both with domain *all* complex numbers; in the case of inequalities both with domain *all* real numbers. Then, in solving for $x, f(x)$ may be replaced by $g(x)$, and the result will be an equivalent equation or inequality. For example, in solving the equation $x^2 - 3x + 2 = 0$, one may replace

$x^2 - 3x + 2$ by $(x - 1)(x - 2)$ to arrive at the equivalent equation: $(x - 1)(x - 2) = 0$.

REMARK. This last paragraph may be sharpened, but we shall find no need to frame a more general statement here. Note that the substitution of 0 for $1/x - 1/x$ does not fall within our set of allowable substitutions, for $1/x - 1/x$ is defined neither for all real, nor for all complex numbers. Why not?

We shall now prove a lemma, and use it, together with the principles of I above, to derive the formula for the solution of a quadratic equation.

Lemma. The equation $[f(x)]^2 = [g(x)]^2$ is equivalent to the pair of equations: $f(x) = \pm g(x)$.

PROOF: We must prove: (a): that if a number p is a root of $[f(x)]^2 = [g(x)]^2$, then p is a root of $f(x) = \pm g(x)$; and (b): conversely.

PROOF OF (a). We are given that p is a complex number such that: $[f(p)]^2 = [g(p)]^2$. Then $[f(p)]^2 - [g(p)]^2 = 0$, so that $[f(p) - g(p)][f(p) + g(p)] = 0$. Therefore (by Theorem R8), $f(p) - g(p) = 0$ or $f(p) + g(p) = 0$, i.e., $f(p) = g(p)$ or $f(p) = -g(p)$. But this means that p is a root of $f(x) = g(x)$ or of $f(x) = -g(x)$, Q.E.D.

PROOF OF (b). We are given that p is a complex number such that: $f(p) = g(p)$ or $f(p) = -g(p)$. By the axiom of "product substitution," and in the second case by the law of signs for multiplication, $[f(p)]^2 = [g(p)]^2$. But this means that p is a root of $[f(x)]^2 = [g(x)]^2$, Q.E.D.

The derivation of the quadratic formula utilizes a trick called "completing the square," which is useful in a number of other applications also:

Suppose we wish to add a real number to the expression $x^2 + 6x$ so that the resulting expression shall be a "perfect square"; that is to say, suppose we wish to replace the question marks in the following equation by numbers so that the resulting statement will be true for any number x:

$$x^2 + 6x + \ ? = (x + \ ?)^2$$

But if x and a are any real numbers:

$$x^2 + 2ax + a^2 = (x + a)^2$$

Comparing equations, we see that we seek a value of a such that $2a = 6$, i.e., such that $a = 6/2 = 3$. In that case, a^2 must be 9. And indeed, letting $a = 3$ in the preceding equation:

$$x^2 + 6x + 9 = (x + 3)^2$$

so that the addition of $(6/2)^2$ to $x^2 + 6x$ transforms the expression into a perfect square.

In general, it is easily verified that:

$$x^2 + kx + \left(\frac{k}{2}\right)^2 = \left(x + \frac{k}{2}\right)^2$$

so that adding to $x^2 + kx$ the expression $(k/2)^2$ will always result in a perfect square.

Now we derive the quadratic formula by successively transforming the original equation

$$ax^2 + bx + c = 0$$

(where a, b, c are real numbers and $a \neq 0$) into equivalent equations. The student is expected to fill in one of the numbers (i)–(iv) of I above, or the preceding lemma, to the right of each of the following equations, as a reason for that equation being equivalent to its predecessor.

1. $x^2 + \dfrac{b}{a}x + \dfrac{c}{a} = 0$ 1.

2. $x^2 + \dfrac{b}{a}x = -\dfrac{c}{a}$ 2.

3. $x^2 + \dfrac{b}{a}x + \left(\dfrac{b}{2a}\right)^2 = \left(\dfrac{b}{2a}\right)^2 - \dfrac{c}{a}$ 3.

4. $\left(x + \dfrac{b}{2a}\right)^2 = \dfrac{b^2 - 4ac}{4a^2}$ 4.

5. $\left(x + \dfrac{b}{2a}\right)^2 = \left(\dfrac{\sqrt{b^2 - 4ac}}{2a}\right)^2$ 5.

6. $x + \dfrac{b}{2a} = \pm\dfrac{\sqrt{b^2 - 4ac}}{2a}$ 6.

7. $x = -\dfrac{b}{2a} \pm \dfrac{\sqrt{b^2 - 4ac}}{2a}$ 7.

8. $x = \dfrac{-b \pm \sqrt{b^2 - 4ac}}{2a}$ 8.

Now we turn our attention to the solution of an *in*equality; in particular, the inequality: $2x - 4 < 10$. The student is asked to justify each of the following steps by a number chosen from II above, and written in the appropriate place:

1. $2x < 14$ 1.
2. $x < 7$ 2.

As another illustrative example, we solve: $4 - 2x < 11$:

1. $-2x < 7$ 1.
2. $2x > -7$ 2.
3. $x > -3.5$ 3.

Finally, we solve the "simultaneous" inequalities: $6 \leqslant 4 - 2x < 16$ (read "$4 - 2x$ is greater than or equal to 6 and less than 16"):

1. $2 \leqslant -2x < 12$ 1.
2. $-2 \geqslant 2x > -12$ 2.
3. $-1 \geqslant x > -6$ 3.

Our result means that a real number will satisfy the given conditions if and only if it lies between -1 and -6 and is unequal to -6; i.e., if and only if it belongs to an interval which we denote $\{-1 \cdot\!-\!\cdot 6\}$ (cf. page 29).

Before leaving this subject, we note several processes that are useful in solving equations, but that do *not* always lead to equivalent equations.

We have encountered such processes already: In Section 5.6, for example, multiplying both sides of the equation $x + 1 = x + 2$ by $x - 1$ led to an equation of which 1 is a root, although 1 is not a root of the original equation.

Later on in Section 5.6, we squared both sides of the equation $\sqrt{x} = 6 - x$ to arrive at an equation of which 9 is a root, although it is not a root of the original equation.

We concluded, then, that multiplication by anything other than nonzero numbers, and squaring both sides of an equation, are processes which may lead to a new equation which is not equivalent to the original.

▶ **EXERCISE 22**

1. Solve the following inequalities:

(a) $2x + 3 > 5$ (b) $3x + 2 < 5$
(c) $3 - 2x \leqslant 5 + 3x$ (d) $1 \leqslant 2x + 3 < 1$
(e) $-5 \leqslant 3 - 2x < 5$ (f) $-2 \leqslant -x < 3$
(g) $1 < 2 - x < -1$ (h) $1 \leqslant 5 - x \leqslant 1$
(i) $7 \leqslant 4 - 3x < 10$ (j) $8 < 4 - 4x \leqslant 16$

2. Solve the following inequalities; draw diagrams to illustrate intervals of solution.
(a) $x^2 < 4$. Solution: By Problem 9 of Exercise 17, the solution is: $-2 < x < 2$.
(b) $x^2 < 9$ (c) $x^2 > 9$
(d) $x^2 > 5$ (e) $x^2 < 5$
(f) $x^2 > 0$ (g) $x^2 < 0$
(h) $x^2 - 4x + 1 < 0$. Solution: This is equivalent to: $x^2 - 4x < -1$; then complete the square by adding 4 to both sides: $x^2 - 4x + 4 < 3$. Thus: $(x - 2)^2 < 3$. By Problem 9 of Exercise 17: $-\sqrt{3} < x - 2 < \sqrt{3}$; finally: $2 - \sqrt{3} < x < 2 + \sqrt{3}$.
(i) $x^2 + 2x < 3$ (j) $x^2 < 2x$
(k) $x^2 + 3x - 4 < 0$ (l) $x^2 + 2x > 3$
(m) $x^2 > 2x$ (n) $x^2 + 3x - 4 > 0$
(o) $2x^2 + 3x - 2 < 0$ (p) $x^2 + 1 > 0$
(q) $x^2 + 1 < 0$

3. Solve the following equations or inequalities:
(a) $|x + 1| = 5$. Solution: From the definition of absolute value (Problem 14, Exercise 5), this equation is equivalent to: $x + 1 = \pm 5$. Therefore our solution is $x = 4$ or -6.
(b) $|2x + 3| = 7$ (c) $|2x - 3| = 7$
(d) $|3 - 2x| = 7$
(e) $|x + 1| < 5$. Hint: By Problem 13, part (9), of Exercise 17, this inequality is equivalent to: $-5 < x + 1 < 5$.

(*f*) $|x + 1| > 5$ (*g*) $|x + 1| \leqslant 5$

(*h*) $|x^2 - 4| < .1$ (Find endpoints of interval of solution correct to two decimal places)

4. Show by means of an example that *division* of both sides of an equation by something other than a number may lead to an equation not equivalent to the original.

5. Is the equation $\sqrt{x^2 + 1} = 5$ equivalent to the equation $x^2 + 1 = 25$? Justify your answer.

How about the equations $\sqrt{x^2 + y^2} = 5$ and $x^2 + y^2 = 25$?

6. Are equivalences of equations and inequalities equivalence relationships? (Cf. Section 2.15.) Justify your answer.

6 INTRODUCTION TO ANALYTIC GEOMETRY

. . . I believed that I could borrow all that was best both in Geometrical Analysis and in Algebra, and correct all the defects of the one by help of the other.

RENE DESCARTES: *Discourse on Method*

6.1 MATHEMATICAL MODELS AND EUCLIDEAN GEOMETRY

Mathematics has been called both queen and handmaiden of the sciences. With respect to the humbler role we put this question:

Just how is it that mathematics goes about serving not only the sciences, but also engineering and business, and in fact almost all fields of practical endeavor?

The secret lies in the "mathematical model."

A mathematical model is simply a set of assumptions, that is to say, of axioms, which characterize some practical situation in terms of mathematical ideas. The importance of mathematical models lies in the following fact: To the extent to which the axioms accurately describe the original situation, the logical consequences of the axioms will be true of that situation also.

Certainly one of the finest mathematical models ever constructed is Euclidean geometry. What Euclid did, actually, was to look at the world of objects of countless shapes and sizes all about him, and with hundreds of facts about this world (the work of three centuries of brilliant predecessors) before him, to construct a superb mathematical model to fit this world and these facts. He set down just ten marvelously well-chosen axioms, from which followed not only all known geometrical facts, but also many new and physically verifiable but previously unsuspected statements.

The Babylonians, for example, came upon the Pythagorean theorem as a consequence of their having made a great many actual measurements of the sides of a great many right triangles. But evidence is not conclusive that their experimental methods ever led them even to so simple a geometric fact as the formula for the area of a general triangle; and evidence is conclusive that a number of the geometric facts which they *induced* were actually incorrect. Euclid's axioms, of course, point the way not only to the formula for the area of any triangle, but to countless other geometric facts undreamed of by the Babylonians. For by retaining only that which could be proved deductively, Euclid not only assured himself of the correctness of his statements, but also laid the proper foundation for a continually deeper penetration into geometry.

The discovery of new facts, then, and the verification or disproval of hypothesized statements, without the extended time and trouble and expense of relatively clumsy experimental methods, constitute the main advantages of a mathematical model. (See Fig. 6.1.)

These advantages are dramatically illustrated in the case of another famous mathematical model: Newton's formulation of the laws governing the motion of everything in the universe. The facts about the position of heavenly bodies at given times, for example, which had by actual observation been laboriously computed over a period of many centuries, followed easily from Newton's axioms and could be discovered with no instrument but pencil and paper. And the *new* discoveries to which Newton's model gave rise revolutionized science and industry in Newton's day (about 1670) and continue to be fruitful even today.

But it must be confessed that neither Newton nor Euclid created perfect models. Although the results of *both* theories check very well with observation in most every-day applications, *neither* leads to verifiable results in certain astronomical situations involving very great distances, and in certain atomic situations involving very small distances. Today, therefore, Newton's model has been supplanted by Einstein's, and Euclidean by so-called "non-Euclidean" geometry. However, because of their greater simplicity and because they are quite as accurate as necessary for ordinary applications, the models of Euclid and Newton continue to be useful.

There is another deficiency which must be noted in Euclid's set of axioms. Although his formulation was an amazing accomplishment for Euclid's time, in the more than 2000 years which have elapsed since then, a number of slips have been discovered in his proofs. These slips are, however, not really serious, for they can be mended simply by setting down several axioms which Euclid overlooked.

"Ah know yore arithmetic book says watermelons, Luke...but why don't you
try figgerin' it with a pencil first?"

Fig. 6.1

An axiom which is especially useful in patching up Euclid's treatment
is one which is suggested by the work of the contemporary French
mathematician Maurice Fréchet, and which, in our formulation, will be
called the "distance axiom." The distance axiom will enable us to
utilize, in our study of geometry, the considerable knowledge we already
have at hand about the real numbers.   With the entrance of real numbers

into geometry we shall find ourselves able to relate algebra to geometry. The duet which these two play is an especially characteristic aspect of that part of geometry (which we shall soon define and study) called "analytic geometry."

6.2 THE DISTANCE AXIOM

The measurement of distance between points is one of the most common and one of the most important applications of mathematics to the world around us.

Examining this activity with the idea of extracting its mathematical essentials we note:

(*a*) When we measure the distance between two points, we actually *assign* a *real number* to the given pair of points.   When we measure distance in miles, for example, we assign the real number 7 to the ordered pair of Massachusetts towns: (Amherst, Northampton).

The word "assign" suggests to us that there is a *function* involved in this situation.   We shall call it a "distance function," and it will be one which assigns real numbers to *ordered pairs* of points, i.e., a "function of two variables."

In the case of the distance function it is intuitively evident (and we shall actually prove) that the order of the points is immaterial; the distance, for example, from Amherst to Northampton is the same as the distance from Northampton to Amherst.

In general, however, we should like to allow order to make a difference in some functions of two variables.   For example, consider the function f which assigns to each ordered pair (x, y) of natural numbers the rational number x/y. Then: $f(1, 2) = 1/2$, $f(2, 1) = 2$; and we see that here ordered pairs are indispensable.

It is in order to make the distance function a special case of the general concept of a function of two variables, that we utilize *ordered* pairs in our description of distance.

If P and Q are points, we shall call the distance function we are discussing "d," and we shall read the symbol $d(P, Q)$ as "the distance from P to Q," or, more briefly: "d of P, Q."

Now we note two more commonplace properties of the physical concept of distance:

(*b*) The distance between two points is 0 if and only if the two points are identical. ·

(*c*) The distance traversed in going from one point to another by way of a third is always greater than or equal to the distance traversed in going directly from the first to the second (see Fig. 6.2).

We are led to make the following assumption about the points of a plane:

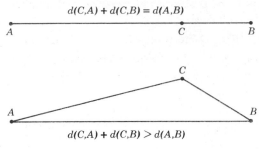

Fig. 6.2

Distance Axiom. If S is a plane, then there is a function d, called a distance function, such that:

(i) The domain of d consists of all ordered pairs of points of S.

(ii) The range of d consists of real numbers.

(iii) If A, B are points of S, then $d(A, B) = 0$ if and only if $A = B$.

(iv) If A, B, C are points of S, then $d(C, A) + d(C, B) \geqslant d(A, B)$.

It should be noted that (iv) above does not require that the points A, B, C be three different points. So far as the axiom is concerned, any two, or all three, may be the same.

Note also that the distance axiom does not assume the existence of a *unique* distance function. In actual practice we measure distance between points using many different units. If we measured in inches, for example, our distance function would assign a number to the pair (Amherst, Northampton) much different from the number 7 which the distance function based on the mile unit assigns. The development of our theory, however, requires only that we assume the existence of at least one distance function, which we have named d.

From here on we shall follow the general practice of present-day mathematicians in writing less formal proofs than most of those that we wrote, for example, in the chapter on real numbers. In the less formal type of proof, gaps are left and reasons often omitted, the tacit assumption being that the reader will be able to supply whatever is missing.

Furthermore, the relation of equality being as universally useful as it is, mathematicians generally assume common properties of equality in all axiom systems without bothering to state them explicitly. We shall therefore feel perfectly free, for example, to substitute different symbols for the same point for each other in any distance function, and in other situations also, even though we have not explicitly stated axioms which permit us to do so.

We expect, of course, the distance between two points to be the same regardless of which point we start from; we also expect the distance between points to be always a *non-negative* real number.   Both of these expectations are fulfilled:

Theorem G1.   If P, Q are points of plane S, then $d(P, Q) = d(Q, P)$.

PROOF: In (iv) above, let A, B, C be Q, P, P, respectively.   Then:

$$d(P, Q) + d(P, P) \geqslant d(Q, P)$$

or (since by (iii), $d(P, P) = 0$):

$$d(P, Q) \geqslant d(Q, P)$$

Now we use (iv) again, but this time we let the points A, B, C be P, Q, Q, respectively. It will follow that:

$$d(Q, P) \geqslant d(P, Q)$$

Finally (by Problem 11, page 97):

$$d(P, Q) = d(Q, P).$$

Corollary.   If P, Q, R are points of plane S, then:

$$d(P, Q) + d(Q, R) \geqslant d(P, R)$$

PROOF: In (iv) above, let A, B, C be P, R, Q, respectively.   It is left to the student to complete the proof.

NOTE.   This corollary may be considered as simply a neater expression of (iv) above.

Theorem G2.   The distance between points of plane S is never negative.

PROOF: Let P, Q be points of S.   By the trichotomy axiom, it will be sufficient to prove: $d(P, Q) \geqslant 0$.

This may be done by letting A, B, C (in (iv) above) be Q, Q, P, respectively. It is left to the student to comylete the proof.

6.3   BETWEEN-NESS AND THE BASIC LINEAR FIGURES OF GEOMETRY

Under what circumstances does it happen that $d(P, Q) + d(Q, R) = d(P, R)$?   It seems natural that this should happen when the points P, Q, R lie on a straight line, with Q between P and R.   This leads us, first of all, to make the following definition:

Definition G1.   If points P, Q, R are points of plane S, Q is said to be *between P and R* if:

$$d(P, Q) + d(Q, R) = d(P, R)$$

Corollary.   If point Q is between points P and R, then Q is between R and P also.

PROOF.   Left as exercise.

Now we are ready to define a number of basic "linear" figures of geometry.   (We shall find it convenient to use the notation ABC to mean "B is between A and C.")

Definition G2. Let A and B be different points of the plane S. Then we define:

(*a*) *Line segment AB*: the set of all points P such that APB.

(*b*) *Straight line AB*: the set of all points P such that PAB or APB or ABP.

(*c*) *Ray AB*: the set of all points P such that APB or ABP. (A is called the *vertex* or *pole* of ray AB.)

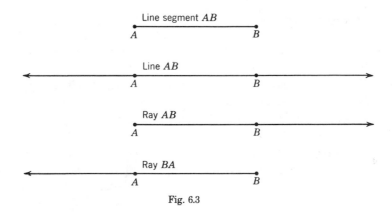

Fig. 6.3

NOTE. Unless otherwise noted, "line" means "straight line"; a ray is also called a "half-line"; we say a point "lies on" a line or a line "passes through" a point when the line (which is a *set* of points) contains the point in question; and we say points are "collinear" when we mean that they lie on the same line.

We note that the following two theorems may now be proved rigorously. The first, of course, is a famous *axiom* in Euclid's development, and is sometimes expressed as: "Two points determine a line." We omit the proofs of these theorems (and of Theorem G5 which follows) because it is not our purpose in this text to go deeply into elementary geometry, but only to indicate the beginning of a correct path. The theorems themselves are intuitively evident.

Theorem G3. Given points $A \neq B$, there is one and only one line which contains them, and that line may be denoted line AB.

Theorem G4. Given points $O \neq P$, there is one and only one ray with vertex O which contains P, and that ray may be denoted ray OP.

Angles may be defined as sets of points also; in fact an angle may be thought of as the set of all points contained in two rays that have a common vertex. (With respect to the notation below, see Section 1.8; see also the remarks on definitions beginning on page 73.)

Definition G3. Angle AOB. If OA and OB are rays, then angle AOB (written ⦡AOB) is the set of points: (ray OA)∪(ray OB).

We now state another intuitively plausible axiom. The axiom guarantees that on any ray, there is a unique point at any given distance from the ray's vertex.

Ray Axiom. If OA is a ray, and r is a non-negative real number, then there is one and only one point P on ray OA such that $d(O, P) = r$.

▶ **EXERCISE 23**

1. In the first sentence of the fourth paragraph of Section 6.1, what is meant by: "mathematical ideas"?

2. What can you say about the permanence of Einstein's theory?

3. Indicate two different points A and B on your paper, and then a point P such that PAB, a point Q such that AQB, and a point R such that ABR.

4. Boston (B), Chicago (C), Los Angeles (L), and Pike's Peak (P) lie approximately on a straight line. Using our between-ness notation and the indicated initials, write down a between-ness relation exhibited by each triple of cities that may be chosen from the four above.

5. Suppose we identify each point on the edge of a 12″ ruler by the real number that is printed next to that point (or that would be printed there if ink and space sufficed). Then:

(a) $d(2, 5) = $?

(b) $d(5, 2) = $?

(c) Can you give a general formula for $d(x, y)$, where x and y are numbers identifying points on the ruler's edge?

6. Draw a ray OP, and on ray OP (using the "inch" as a unit of measure) find:

(a) a point A such that $d(O, A) = 1$

(b) a point B such that $d(O, B) = 2$

(c) a point C such that $d(O, C) = \frac{1}{2}$

(d) a point D such that $d(O, D) = \sqrt{2}$

(e) a point E such that $d(O, E) \doteq \pi$

Which axiom guarantees that in each of cases (a)–(d) there will be one and only one point which satisfies the requirement?

7. Express in words, and prove each of the following, assuming that A and B are points of a plane:

(a) AAA; (b) ABB; (c) AAB; (d) If ABA, then $A = B$.

8. Prove: Line AB contains points A and B; ray OP contains points O and P.

9.   Prove: If P, A, B are three different points of S, then not more than one of the following can be true: PAB, APB, ABP.

10.   Fill in further details in the proof of Theorem G1 and complete the proofs of its corollary and of Theorem G2.

11.   Suppose A, B, C are three noncollinear points.   How would you define triangle ABC as a set of points?

6.4   DISTANCE BETWEEN POINTS ON A SCALED LINE

We shall be concerned, in this section, with a "scaled line" (see Section 2.7), i.e., a line whose points have been put into one-to-one correspondence with all the real numbers in a "natural" way.

The X-axis of a coordinate system is such a line, and we shall suppose, for the moment, that our scaled line is an X-axis.

We shall find it convenient to use the symbol x_P (read "x sub P") to represent the real number labeling the point P on the X-axis.   For example, if P is a point on the X-axis three units to the left of the origin, we would say:

$$x_P = -3$$

Now suppose that P and Q are points such that $x_P = 2$ and $x_Q = 7$:

Then it looks as though: $d(P, Q) = 5 = 7 - 2 = x_Q - x_P$.
On the other hand, if $x_P = 7$ and $x_Q = 2$:

Then it seems as though: $d(P, Q) = 5 = 7 - 2 = x_P - x_Q$.
Finally, suppose $x_P = 2$ and $x_Q = -7$:

Then apparently: $d(P, Q) = 9 = 2 - (-7) = x_P - x_Q$.
We are led to induce that whenever P and Q are points on an X-axis, then $d(P, Q)$ is either $x_P - x_Q$ or $x_Q - x_P$, whichever is non-negative.

Or, to put it a bit differently, $d(P, Q)$ seems always to be the "numerical" or "absolute value" of $x_P - x_Q$; i.e., $d(P, Q) = |x_P - x_Q|$ (see (13), page 98).

Our induced result happens to be true, and we state it below as Theorem G6.

We shall devote the rest of this section to a clarification of the meaning of a "natural scale" on a line, and a rigorous proof of Theorem G6.

Roughly speaking, a "natural scale" on a line is a labeling of the points of the line by means of real numbers in such a way that *distances* between points is given by *differences* between labels.

A more precise treatment of this idea follows.

A consequence of the axioms we have stated so far is that every point on a line separates the line into two rays which overlap only in the given point:

We state this fact as a theorem, whose proof we omit.

Theorem G5. If O is a point on line l, then there exists a unique pair of rays with vertex O, union l, and intersection O. (Each of these rays, with its vertex deleted, is called a "side" of the given point on the given line.)

Now we can show deductively that every line actually can be scaled in the "natural" way discussed in Section 2.7.

Suppose we have given a line l separated into two sides by a point O, as above. We shall call one of these sides the "positive" side, and the other the "negative" side, simply to distinguish between the two. (It does not matter, for our theory, which we call which. In most applications, however, if l is "horizontal" we call the right-hand side positive, and if l is "vertical" we call the upper side positive.)

Now suppose P is a point of l on the positive side of O:

Then since the sides of O (by definition) do not contain O, $P \neq O$. It follows therefore (from the distance axiom and Theorem G2) that $d(O, P)$ is a positive real number, which we denote x_P:

If P is a point of l on the positive side of O: $x_P = d(O, P)$

By the ray axiom, there is one and only one point on the positive side of l whose distance from O is the real number x_P, so that the real number x_P may be used to *label* P; and in effect this labeling establishes a one-to-one correspondence between all the points on the positive side, and all the positive real numbers.

On the other hand, for a point P on the negative side, we make the following definition of x_P:

If P is a point of l on the negative side of O: $x_P = -d(O, P)$

One may now prove (the proof will be left as an exercise) that if P is any point on a scaled line X, then:

(1) $$d(O, P) = |x_P|$$

This supplies a graphic way of thinking of the absolute value of a real number: the absolute value of a real number on a scaled line is its distance from the origin.

Now, finally, we are ready to state and prove:

Theorem G6.   If P and Q are points on a scaled line X, then: $d(P, Q) = |x_P - x_Q|$.

PROOF: Suppose O is the origin of the scaled line X. We consider several cases.

Case 1. $P = O$. Then:

$$d(P, Q) = d(O, Q) = |x_Q|, \text{ by (1) above.}$$

On the other hand:

$|x_P - x_Q| = |x_O - x_Q| = |0 - x_Q| = |-x_Q| = |x_Q|$, by Problem 13, part (5), of Exercise 17.

Therefore $d(P, Q) = |x_P - x_Q|$, Q.E.D.

Case 2. $Q = O$. (Proof left as exercise.)

Case 3. $P = Q$. (Proof left as exercise.)

Case 4. $P \neq O, Q \neq O, P \neq Q, P$ *and* Q *are on the same side of* O.

Then $Q \in$ ray OP, so that either OQP or OPQ. Therefore $d(O, Q) + d(Q, P) = d(O, P)$, or $d(O, P) + d(P, Q) = d(O, Q)$; i.e., $d(P, Q) = \pm [d(O, P) - d(O, Q)]$.

Now since P and Q are on the same side of O, either $d(O, P) = x_P$ and $d(O, Q) = x_Q$, or $d(O, P) = -x_P$ and $d(O, Q) = -x_Q$.

Therefore $d(O, P) - d(O, Q) = x_P - x_Q$ or $-x_P - (-x_Q)$.

Therefore $d(P, Q) = \pm [\pm (x_P - x_Q)] = \pm (x_P - x_Q)$, whichever is positive.

But $|x_P - x_Q| = \pm (x_P - x_Q)$, whichever is positive.

Therefore $d(P, Q) = |x_P - x_Q|$, Q.E.D.

Case 5. $P \neq O, Q \neq O, P \neq Q, P,$ *and* Q *are on different sides of* O.

By Theorem G3, line X must be the same as line OP. Therefore $Q \in$ line OP, and QOP or OQP or OPQ must be true. However, only QOP is consistent with the hypothesis that P and Q are on different sides of O. Therefore, in this case: QOP.

The rest of the proof is left as an exercise.

6.5 THE FIRST BASIC FACT OF PLANE ANALYTIC GEOMETRY

In Section 2.8 we saw how a "coordinate system" set up in a plane might be useful in the pictorial representation of real-real functions. *That part of geometry which has to do with coordinate systems is called "analytic geometry."*

All of plane analytic geometry (in fact all of plane Euclidean geometry) may be made to follow from just two theorems of plane Euclidean geometry. For that reason, we shall call these two theorems the two basic facts of plane analytic geometry.

First Basic Fact of Plane Analytic Geometry. There is a one-to-one correspondence between the following sets:

(i)   All points of a given plane.

(ii) All ordered pairs of real numbers.

Because of this first basic fact, each point of a plane may be labeled with (or "identified" by) a unique ordered pair of real numbers in such a way that each ordered pair of real numbers is the label of a unique point of the plane. We have already encountered such a labeling in Section 2.8, when we first considered the "Cartesian coordinate plane."

Now we shall show how this first basic fact of analytic geometry may be *proved* as a theorem of Euclidean geometry. We shall need to use certain results of Euclidean geometry with which we assume the student is, or has been, familiar, and certain other results which may be justified in a very careful development of Euclidean geometry, but which are generally omitted in high school courses.

First of all, we suppose that we are given a plane, and we assume that there exists on that plane a pair of perpendicular straight lines intersecting in a point O, called the "origin."

We call one of these lines (it does not matter which) the "X-axis" and the other the "Y-axis." (In practice, the X-axis is usually drawn "horizontally" and the Y-axis "vertically," but this is only a matter of convenience and tradition and has no mathematical significance.)

Each of these lines may be scaled as in the preceding section, so that each point P on the X-axis is labeled with a real number which we denote x_P, each point P on the Y-axis is labeled with a real number which we denote y_P, and the origin is labeled with the real number 0 on both axes.

Now suppose P is *any* point on our given plane. Then there exists a unique line through P perpendicular to the X-axis, and intersecting it in a unique point whose unique real number label we denote by x_P, *whether P is on the X-axis or not*; and there exists a unique line through P perpendicular to the Y-axis, and intersecting it in a unique point whose unique real number label we denote by y_P *whether P is on the Y-axis or not*. (See Fig. 6.4).

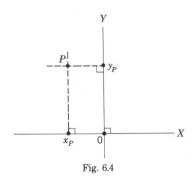

Fig. 6.4

Thus, with each point P of our plane we may associate a unique ordered pair of real numbers (x_P, y_P), called the "coordinates" of P (relative to the given X- and Y-axes).

Now suppose we are given any ordered pair of real numbers (a, b). We show that there is a unique point on our plane with coordinates (a, b).

We know, since the X-axis is a scaled line, that there is a unique point A on the X-axis such that $x_A = a$, and similarly a unique point B on the Y-axis such that $y_B = b$. There exists, furthermore, a unique pair of lines through A and B, perpendicular to the X- and Y-axis respectively, and intersecting in a unique point P. (See Fig. 6.5).

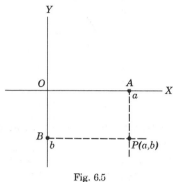

Fig. 6.5

Clearly, the coordinates of P are (a, b). Furthermore, any point in our plane with coordinates (a, b) would have to be the unique intersection of the unique perpendiculars we have drawn through the unique points A, B. Therefore there can be no other point in our plane with coordinates (a, b).

This completes the proof of the first basic fact of analytic geometry.

The student is reminded that a plane which has been subjected to the constructions of the preceding proof is called a *Cartesian coordinate plane* (cc plane), and we say that we have established a *Cartesian coordinate system* in that plane. Furthermore, if P is a point on a cc plane, x_P is called the "x-value," or "abscissa" of P, y_P the "y-value" or "ordinate" of P.

6.6 THE SECOND BASIC FACT OF PLANE ANALYTIC GEOMETRY

The second basic fact of plane analytic geometry has to do with the distance between points. We shall therefore first consider two specific problems that will enable us to induce a general formula for the distance between a pair of points.

Problem 1. What is the distance between the points $(2, 3)$ and $(7, 11)$? (See Fig. 6.6).

Intuitively, starting at the point $(2, 3)$, which is 2 units to the right of Y-axis, we must move 5 units to the right to be as far to the right as the

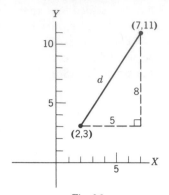

Fig. 6.6

point (7, 11); in the same way, the difference in heights between the two points is clearly $11 - 3$ or 8.

A right triangle may thus be formed in which d, the distance we seek, is the hypotenuse, and 5 and 8 are the shorter sides. Then by the Pythagorean theorem:

$$d^2 = 5^2 + 8^2 = 89, \text{ and } d = \sqrt{89}$$

Generalizing, suppose we replace these points by P and Q with co-ordinates (x_P, y_P) and (x_Q, y_Q), respectively (see Fig. 6.7).

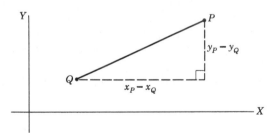

Fig. 6.7

Then what we have done in Problem 1 would amount to using the following general formula for the distance between P and Q:

$$d(P, Q) = \sqrt{(x_P - x_Q)^2 + (y_P - y_Q)^2}$$

But would this formula continue to hold true in all possible positions of P and Q? Let us examine another case:

Problem 2. What is the distance between the points $P(-4, 5)$ and $Q(1, -7)$? (See Fig. 6.8).

In this case, P being 4 units to the left of the Y-axis and Q being 1 unit to the right, the horizontal distance between P and Q is 5 units. Similarly

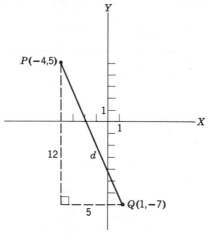

Fig. 6.8

the vertical distance between P and Q is 12 units. Therefore $d^2 = 5^2 + 12^2 = 169$, and in this case $d = 13$.

According to the formula we are testing:

$$
\begin{aligned}
d(P, Q) &= \sqrt{(x_P - x_Q)^2 + (y_P - y_Q)^2} \\
&= \sqrt{(-4 - 1)^2 + (5 - (-7))^2} \\
&= \sqrt{(-5)^2 + (12)^2} \\
&= \sqrt{25 + 144} \\
&= \sqrt{169} \\
&= 13
\end{aligned}
$$

We are now inclined to believe that the formula may be true in all cases, and this is what we proceed to prove.

Second Basic Fact of Plane Analytic Geometry. If P, Q are points of a cc plane, then:

$$d(P, Q) = \sqrt{(x_P - x_Q)^2 + (y_P - y_Q)^2}$$

(We shall find it convenient to refer to a line in a cc plane which is parallel to the X-axis (i.e., perpendicular to the Y-axis) as a "horizontal" line; similarly, we shall call a line in a cc plane which is parallel to the Y-axis (i.e., perpendicular to the X-axis) a "vertical" line.)

In proving our second basic fact of plane analytic geometry, we shall make use of several lemmas.

Lemma 1. If $P \neq Q$ are points on a cc plane, then line PQ is horizontal if and only if $y_P = y_Q$. (See Fig. 6.9).

PROOF: First, suppose line PQ is horizontal. Then line PQ is perpendicular to the

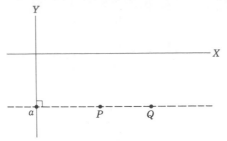

Fig. 6.9

Y-axis and intersects the Y-axis in a point with a real number label a. By definition of y_P and y_Q, then, it follows that $y_P = a$ and $y_Q = a$, i.e., $y_P = y_Q$, Q.E.D.

Conversely, suppose $y_P = y_Q$. Denote the real number which both y_P and y_Q are equal to by: "a." Then P and Q both lie on a line l which is perpendicular to the Y-axis and which passes through the point on the Y-axis labeled a. Since two different points on a line determine that line, line $l =$ line PQ. Therefore line PQ is horizontal, Q.E.D.

Lemma 2.   If $P \neq Q$ are points on a cc plane, then line PQ is vertical if and only if: $x_P = x_Q$.

PROOF: Similar to the proof of Lemma 1.

Lemma 3.   If line PQ is horizontal, then: (see Fig. 6.10)

$$d(P, Q) = |x_P - x_Q|$$

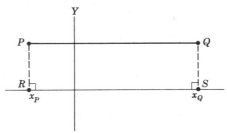

Fig. 6.10

PROOF: Call the points in which vertical lines through P and Q intersect the X-axis "R" and "S" respectively. Then $x_R = x_P$, $x_S = x_Q$, and by Theorem G6 (page 146):

$$d(R, S) = |x_R - x_S| = |x_P - x_Q|$$

We now consider two cases, namely $y_P = 0$ and $y_P \neq 0$. If $y_P = 0$, then $P = R$ and $Q = S$, so that:

$$d(P, Q) = d(R, S) = |x_P - x_Q|, \text{ Q.E.D.}$$

If $y_P \neq 0$, then $PQSR$ is a rectangle, whose opposite sides must be equal in length. Therefore in this case also:

$$d(P, Q) = d(R, S) = |x_P - x_Q|$$

completing the proof of the lemma.

Lemma 4.   If line PQ is vertical, then:

$$d(P, Q) = |y_P - y_Q|$$

PROOF: Similar to the proof of Lemma 3.

Now we are ready for the proof of the second basic fact of plane analytic geometry. Given the points P, Q we may distinguish the following cases:

Case 1. $x_P = x_Q, y_P = y_Q$

Case 2. $x_P = x_Q, y_P \neq y_Q$

Case 3. $x_P \neq x_Q, y_P = y_Q$

Case 4. $x_P \neq x_Q, y_P \neq y_Q$

PROOF OF CASE 1: In this case $P = Q$.

  Therefore (by the distance axiom): $d(P, Q) = 0$.

  Furthermore: $\sqrt{(x_P - x_Q)^2 + (y_P - y_Q)^2} = 0$.

  Therefore $d(P, Q) = \sqrt{(x_P - x_Q)^2 + (y_P - y_Q)^2}$, Q.E.D.

PROOF OF CASE 2: In this case, by Lemma 2, line PQ is vertical.

  Therefore, by Lemma 4, $d(P, Q) = |y_P - y_Q|$.

  Furthermore, $\sqrt{(x_P - x_Q)^2 + (y_P - y_Q)^2} = \sqrt{(y_P - y_Q)^2} = |y_P - y_Q|$.

Therefore, $d(P, Q) = \sqrt{(x_P - x_Q)^2 + (y_P - y_Q)^2}$, Q.E.D.

PROOF OF CASE 3: Similar to that of Case 2.

PROOF OF CASE 4: (See Fig. 6.11).

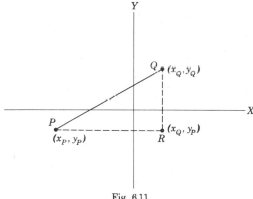

Fig. 6.11

Let R represent the point with coordinates (x_Q, y_P).   Then by Lemmas 1 and 2, PR and QR are horizontal and vertical lines, respectively, so that $\angle PRQ$ must be a right angle, and hence $\triangle PRQ$ a right triangle.

By the Pythagorean theorem it follows that:

$$d(P, Q) = \sqrt{[d(P, R)]^2 + [d(R, Q)]^2}$$

But by Lemmas 3 and 4:

$$d(P, R) = |x_P - x_Q|$$
$$d(R, Q) = |y_P - y_Q|$$

Substituting in the preceding equation for $d(P, Q)$:

$d(P, Q) = \sqrt{(|x_P - x_Q|)^2 + (|y_P - y_Q|)^2} = \sqrt{(x_P - x_Q)^2 + (y_P - y_Q)^2}$, Q.E.D.
[See (4), page 97.]

NOTE. The Pythagorean theorem is often referred to as the most important theorem of plane geometry. We see here, finally, the reason for its importance. The Pythagorean theorem is crucial in developing the formula for the distance between two points, and it is, as a matter of fact, the last of a sequence of theorems necessary to prove the two basic facts of analytic geometry.

As we have mentioned before, with the identification of points by means of ordered pairs of real numbers, and with this distance formula at hand, all of Euclidean plane geometry may be developed.

Illustrative Example. Find, by the easiest formula which applies, the distance between each of the following pairs of points:

$$
\begin{aligned}
&(a) \quad P = (2, 3), \quad Q = (2, 3) \\
&(b) \quad P = (2, 3), \quad Q = (2, -4) \\
&(c) \quad P = (2, 3), \quad Q = (-5, 3) \\
&(d) \quad P = (2, 3), \quad Q = (6, -1)
\end{aligned}
$$

SOLUTION: (a) Since $P = Q$, $d(P, Q) = 0$

(b) Since $x_P = x_Q$, line PQ is vertical, and

$$d(P, Q) = |y_P - y_Q| = |3 - (-4)| = 7$$

(c) Since $y_P = y_Q$, line PQ is horizontal, and

$$d(P, Q) = |x_P - x_Q| = |2 - (-5)| = 7$$

(d) Here line PQ is neither horizontal nor vertical, so we use the formula:

$$d(P, Q) = \sqrt{(x_P - x_Q)^2 + (y_P - y_Q)^2} = \sqrt{16 + 16} = \sqrt{32} = 4\sqrt{2}$$

▶ **EXERCISE 24**

1. In each of the following cases, sketch the given points on a cc plane and find, by the easiest formula which applies, the distance between them.

(a) $(-2, 1)$ and $(2, -3)$ (b) $(-2, 1)$ and $(6, 5)$
(c) $(6, 5)$ and $(2, -3)$ (d) $(0, 0)$ and $(3, 4)$
(e) $(0, 0)$ and $(4, 3)$ (f) $(1, 2)$ and $(1, 7)$
(g) $(2, 1)$ and $(7, 1)$ (h) $(7, 7)$ and $(7, 7)$
(i) $(1, -2)$ and $(1, 7)$ (j) $(-3, 5)$ and $(-4, 5)$
(k) $(0, 0)$ and $(0, 5)$ (l) $(0, 0)$ and $(5, 0)$
(m) $(0, 0)$ and $(-5, 0)$ (n) $(1, -2)$ and $(\sqrt{1^2}, \sqrt{(-2)^2})$

2. If $P \neq Q$ are points, the *length* of the line segment PQ is defined to be $d(P, Q)$.

In each of the following cases draw and find the length of line segment PQ:

(a) $P(1, 2)$, $Q(3, 4)$ (b) $P(-1, 2)$, $Q(3, -4)$
(c) $P(3, -3)$, $Q(-2, 10)$ (d) $P(-3, 2)$, $Q(2, -10)$

3. In each of the following cases, draw the triangle PQR, determine whether it is isosceles, equilateral, right, or none of these and find the perimeter of $\triangle PQR$. (*Hint*: The converse of the Pythagorean theorem is true.)

(a) $P(0, 0)$, $Q(1, 7)$, $R(5, 5)$
(b) $P(10, -4)$, $Q(4, 4)$, $R(-11, 4)$
(c) $P(3, 9)$, $Q(0, 3)$, $R(12, -3)$
(d) $P(0, -2)$, $Q(-1, 6)$, $R(4, 5)$
(e) $P(0, 6)$, $Q(0, -4)$, $R(5\sqrt{3}, 1)$

4. If a point P of a cc plane does not lie on the Y-axis, then there are two possibilities for the sign of x_P: $x_P > 0$ or $x_P < 0$; and if P does not lie on the X-axis, then there are two possibilities for the sign of y_P: $y_P > 0$ or $y_P < 0$.

Thus, for a nonaxial point P, one of the following four possibilities must hold true:

$$\text{I.} \quad x_P > 0, \ y_P > 0$$
$$\text{II.} \quad x_P < 0, \ y_P > 0$$
$$\text{III.} \quad x_P < 0, \ y_P < 0$$
$$\text{IV.} \quad x_P > 0, \ y_P < 0$$

All points P such that I is true are said to constitute the *first quadrant* (abbreviated QI) of the cc plane; etc.

Draw a cc plane and label each quadrant appropriately; note that the quadrants follow each other in "counter-clockwise" succession.

For each point mentioned in Problem 1 above, name the quadrant, if any, in which the point falls.

5. Suppose the point (x, y) is at a distance of 5 units from the point $(1, 2)$.

(a) What equality, involving the real numbers x and y, must hold true?
(b) What equality, involving no radical, must hold true?

6. Suppose the point (x, y) is at a distance of 5 units from the origin; answer (a) and (b) of Problem 5 above.

7. Suppose the point (x, y) is at a distance of r units from the origin; answer (a) and (b) of Problem 5 above.

8. Suppose the point (x, y) is at a distance of r units from the point (h, k); answer (a) and (b) of Problem 5 above.

9. Prove that if P is any point on a scaled line X, then $d(O, P) = |x_P|$.

10. Prove Cases 2 and 3 of Theorem G6.
11. Complete the proof of Case 5 of Theorem G6.
12. Prove Lemma 2 above.
13. Prove Lemma 4 above.

14. Suppose P is a point in a cc plane, and that a line through P is perpendicular to the X-axis at point Q.

Prove: (a) If $y_P \geqslant 0$, then $y_P = d(P, Q)$
(b) If $y_P < 0$, then $y_P = -d(P, Q)$
(c) If $x_P \geqslant 0$, then $x_P = d(O, Q)$
(d) If $x_P < 0$, then $x_P = -d(O, Q)$

15. Prove Case 3 of the second basic fact of plane analytic geometry.

16. Suppose $(a, 0) \neq (b, 0)$ are points, and (x, y) is a point equidistant from $(a, 0)$ and $(b, 0)$.

$$\text{Prove:} \quad x = \frac{a + b}{2}$$

17. *Directed distance between points on a scaled line.* If X is a scaled line, we define a directed distance function $\vec{d}$ on all ordered pairs of points of X as follows: $\vec{d}(A, B) = x_B - x_A$. We denote $\vec{d}(A, B)$ more concisely by $\overrightarrow{AB}$.

For the ordinary distance function, $AB + BC = AC$ if and only if ABC. The most important fact about the *directed* distance function is that if A, B, C are *any* points on a scaled line: $\overrightarrow{AB} + \overrightarrow{BC} = \overrightarrow{AC}$.

Prove this fact.

Prove also: $\overrightarrow{AB} = 0 \Leftrightarrow A = B$.

Prove that the alternate distance function $\overleftarrow{d}$ such that $\overleftarrow{d}(A, B) = x_A - x_B$ has analogous properties.

(The existence of these two functions is what is meant when we speak of the existence of two "directions" on a line.)

Prove that if r is any real number (except -1), and if $A \neq B$ are two points on a scaled line X, there is one and only one point C that "divides line segment AC in the directed ratio r," i.e., one and only one point C on line X such that $\overrightarrow{AC}/\overrightarrow{CB} = r$.

What can you say about C if $r = 0$? If $r > 0$? If $-1 < r < 0$? If $r < -1$? C may turn out to be any point of line X except which?

6.7 LINEAR INTERPOLATION

The problem of finding a number some fraction of the way between two numbers has its geometric counterpart in the problem of finding a point some fraction of the way between two points. One such important problem in geometry, for example, is the problem of finding a point *half*-way between two points, or in other words, the problem of finding the midpoint of a line segment.

Indeed, the two problems are closely related. In this section we shall see what that relation is, and why the process of interpolation discussed in Section 5.2 is called *linear* interpolation.

We attack the general problem by considering a specific case: We seek a point C, $\frac{1}{3}$ of the way between the points $A(2, 1)$ and $B(11, 7)$ on the line segment AB. (See Fig. 6.12).

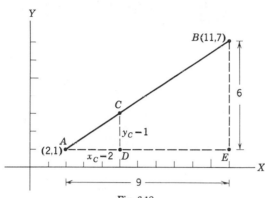

Fig. 6.12

That is, we want C to be a point on line segment AB such that: $d(A, C) = \frac{1}{3} \cdot d(A, B)$.

(We use the abbreviation "AC," etc., below, to represent: $d(A, C)$; etc.)

By drawing lines parallel to the axes as in the figure, we have $\triangle ACD \sim \triangle ABE$, from which follows:

$$\frac{x_C - 2}{9} = \frac{AC}{AB} = \frac{1}{3} \text{ and } \frac{y_C - 1}{6} = \frac{AC}{AB} = \frac{1}{3}$$

so that:

$$x_C - 2 = \tfrac{1}{3} \cdot 9 \qquad\qquad y_C - 1 = \tfrac{1}{3} \cdot 6$$
$$x_C = 2 + \tfrac{1}{3} \cdot 9 \qquad\qquad y_C = 1 + \tfrac{1}{3} \cdot 6$$
$$x_C = 5 \qquad\qquad\qquad y_C = 3$$

$$C = (5, 3)$$

Now we check this result: $d(A, C) = \sqrt{13}$; $d(C, B) = \sqrt{52} = 2\sqrt{13}$; $d(A, B) = \sqrt{117} = 3\sqrt{13}$.

Since $d(A, C) + d(C, B) = d(A, B)$, C *does* lie on line segment AB; and $d(A, C) = \frac{1}{3} \cdot d(A, B)$, as required.

More generally, if A and B are any points on a coordinate plane, the steps we have gone through would seem to point to the following formula for the coordinates of a point C, $\frac{1}{3}$ of the way from A to B on line segment AB:

$$x_C = x_A + \tfrac{1}{3}(x_B - x_A), \qquad y_C = y_A + \tfrac{1}{3}(y_B - y_A)$$

But these (see Section 5.2) are exactly the formulas used in interpolating $\frac{1}{3}$ of the way between x_A and x_B in the first case, and y_A and y_B in the second!

Now what we have been doing up to this point in this section has been rough and intuitive, but designed to lead to a clear statement which would then be carefully proved.

The statement and proof follow. It will be noticed that the theorem which follows involves a situation a little more general than that of placing a point on a line segment, namely that of placing a point on a *ray*. The more general theorem is, of course, more useful, and can be proved with very little extra effort.

Interpolation Theorem. Let $A \neq B$ be points in a coordinate plane and let r be any non-negative real number.

Then there is a unique point C on ray AB such that $d(A, C) = r \cdot d(A, B)$, and the coordinates of C are:

$$x_C = x_A + r \cdot (x_B - x_A)$$
$$y_C = y_A + r \cdot (y_B - y_A)$$

PROOF: The existence and uniqueness of point C follow from the ray axiom.

Now we shall prove that the point $C(x_C, y_C)$ with coordinates as given above satisfies the requirements of the theorem. First of all we compute:

$$\begin{aligned} d(A, C) &= \sqrt{(x_C - x_A)^2 + (y_C - y_A)^2} \\ &= \sqrt{r^2 \cdot (x_B - x_A)^2 + r^2 \cdot (y_B - y_A)^2} \\ &= r \cdot \sqrt{(x_B - x_A)^2 + (y_B - y_A)^2} \\ &= r \cdot d(A, B) \end{aligned}$$

This proves part of the theorem. We must still prove that point C lies on ray AB. To do so we compute several distances:

$$d(C, B) = \sqrt{(x_B - x_C)^2 + (y_B - y_C)^2}$$

$$\begin{aligned} \text{But } x_B - x_C &= x_B - [x_A + r \cdot (x_B - x_A)] \\ &= (x_B - x_A) - r \cdot (x_B - x_A) \\ &= (x_B - x_A)(1 - r) \\ &= (1 - r)(x_B - x_A); \text{ and similarly} \end{aligned}$$

$$y_B - y_C = (1 - r)(y_B - y_A)$$

Therefore,

$$\begin{aligned} d(C, B) &= \sqrt{(1 - r)^2(x_B - x_A)^2 + (1 - r)^2(y_B - y_A)^2} \\ &= \sqrt{(1 - r)^2} \ \sqrt{(x_B - x_A)^2 + (y_B - y_A)^2} \\ &= \sqrt{(1 - r)^2} \cdot d(A, B) \end{aligned}$$

Now we distinguish two cases, according as $r \leqslant 1$ or $r > 1$.

Case 1. $r \leqslant 1$. Then adding $-r$ to both sides, $1 - r \geqslant 0$. Since $\sqrt{N^2} = N$ if N is non-negative, $\sqrt{(1 - r)^2} = 1 - r$ in this case. Therefore

$$\begin{aligned} d(C, B) &= (1 - r) \cdot d(A, B) \\ &= d(A, B) - r \cdot d(A, B) \\ &= d(A, B) - d(A, C) \end{aligned}$$

$$d(A, C) + d(C, B) = d(A, B)$$

Therefore ACB, so that C lies on ray AB, Q.E.D.

(In fact, in this case C lies on segment AB.)

Case 2. $r > 1$. Then $r - 1 > 0$. Since $(1 - r)^2 = (r - 1)^2$, $\sqrt{(1 - r)^2}$ $= \sqrt{(r - 1)^2} = r - 1$. In this case, then, $d(C, B) = (r - 1) \cdot d(A, B) = r \cdot d(A, B) - d(A, B) = d(A, C) - d(A, B)$, or:

$$d(A, B) + d(B, C) = d(A, C)$$

Therefore ABC, so that C lies on ray AB in this case also, and the proof of the interpolation theorem is complete.

NOTE: When as in Case 1, point C lies *between* A and B, that is, when $r < 1$, then the process of finding C is called *interpolation*.

When, as in Case 2, point C lies on the so-called *extension of segment AB through B*, that is when $r > 1$, then the process of finding C is called *extrapolation*.

Finally, we see the reason for the adjective "linear" in the process of linear interpolation: The method applies exactly to a function f if all functional pairs $[a, f(a)]$, when plotted, are collinear. For most elementary functions, a *small* section of graph approximates a straight line. Therefore, in such cases, we can say this: The method applies when tabular values are close together, and the closer the values between which interpolation takes place, the better the method applies.

We now work out a typical example:

Problem. Find a point C, $\frac{2}{3}$ of the way between $A(-2, 5)$ and $B(7, 11)$, on the line segment AB.

SOLUTION. Using the formulas of the Interpolation Theorem (i.e., interpolating $\frac{2}{3}$ of the way between the given x- and y-values):

$$x_C = -2 + \tfrac{2}{3}(7 - (-2)) = 4$$
$$y_C = 5 + \tfrac{2}{3}(11 - 5) = 9$$

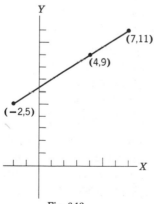

Fig. 6.13

▶ **EXERCISE 25**

1. Find a point half way between $(-3, 2)$ and $(7, -4)$ on the line determined by them. Locate these three points on a cc plane.

2. Using the value $r = 1/2$, show that the coordinates of the midpoint of a line segment are the averages of the coordinates of the endpoints of the line segment. More precisely, show that the mid-point of line segment AB is

$$\left(\frac{x_A + x_B}{2}, \frac{y_A + y_B}{2}\right)$$

3. Do Problem 1 by means of the formula of Problem 2.

4. Find the midpoint and points of trisection of the line segments whose endpoints are as follows, and sketch:

(a) $(2, 5), (8, 11)$ (b) $(2, -7), (-3, 3)$
(c) $(3, -2), (-1, -6)$ (d) $(5, 9), (-3, 9)$
(e) $(-4, -5), (-2, -2)$ (f) $(-3, 4), (5, 8)$

5. Sketch triangle ABC: $A(-5, 5)$, $B(3, 8)$, $C(1, -2)$, and:

(a) Find the lengths of the sides of triangle ABC.
(b) Find the midpoints of the sides of triangle ABC, and locate them on the sides of triangle ABC.
(c) Find the lengths of the medians of triangle ABC.

6. Suppose $A = (3, -4)$. Find B if line segment AB has:

(a) Midpoint $(0, 0)$
(b) Midpoint $(2, -1)$
(c) Midpoint $(1, -2)$
(d) Midpoint $(3, 0)$
(e) Midpoint $(0, 3)$
(f) Point of trisection nearest A: $(0, 0)$
(g) Point of trisection nearest B: $(0, 0)$
(h) Point of trisection nearest A: $(2, -1)$
(i) Point of trisection nearest B: $(2, -1)$

7. Given points $A(-2, 3)$, $B(1, -3)$:

(a) Find a point C on ray AB such that $AC/AB = 2$.
(b) Find a point C on ray BA such that $BC/BA = 2$.
(c) Find a point C on line segment AB dividing it in the ratio $1 : 2$ (i.e., such that $AC/CB = \frac{1}{2}$). (See Fig. 6.14).

Hint: It is easy to show that if C is a point on segment AB, then $AC/CB = \frac{1}{2}$ is equivalent to $AC/AB = 1/(2 + 1) = \frac{1}{3}$.

For $\dfrac{AC}{CB} = \dfrac{1}{2}$ is equivalent to:

$$2AC = CB = AB - AC$$
$$3AC = AB$$
$$\frac{AC}{AB} = \frac{1}{3}$$

Fig. 6.14

(d) Find two points C on line AB such that $AC/AB = 3$.

8. Given points $P(-2, 4)$ and $Q(3, -1)$, find two points M on ray PQ "dividing" segment PQ in the ratio $3 : 2$.

9. Find formulas for the points of trisection of a line segment AB on a cc plane.

10. Suppose $A = (-2, 1)$ and $B = (4, 5)$. Find a point C such that: $\overrightarrow{AC}/\overrightarrow{CB} =$ (cf. Problem 17, Exercise 24):

$\quad\quad\quad$ (a) 1 $\quad$ (b) 2 $\quad$ (c) $-\frac{1}{4}$ $\quad$ (d) -2

6.8 EQUATIONS AND GRAPHS

In Section 2.9 we learned what is meant by the graph of a function. In this section we consider something which is very closely related to that concept, namely the graph of an equation.

The type of equation we have in mind is, roughly speaking, one which involves one or two "unknowns." Examples of simple equations of this type are: $x + y = 10$, $x^2 + y^2 = 2x$, $8 = 2y$.

We say a point of a coordinate plane *satisfies* an equation in the unknowns x or y or both, if the result of substituting the x- and y-values of that point for x and y in the equation is a true statement.

Thus the points $(1, 9)$, $(2, 8)$, $(3, 7)$ all satisfy the equation $x + y = 10$, but $(7, 11)$ does not, since $7 + 11 \neq 10$; and the points $(1, 4)$, $(2, 4)$, $(3, 4)$, $(\pi, 4)$, $(\sqrt{2}, 4)$ all satisfy the equation $8 = 2y$, but $(7, 11)$ again does not since $8 \neq 2 \cdot 11$.

Now we are ready to define both the graph of an equation and the equation of a graph.

Definition. Suppose G is a set of points in a coordinate plane and E is an equation, and furthermore that:

(i)   Every point of G satisfies E.

(ii)   No other point of the coordinate plane satisfies E; *or*, what comes to the same thing: Every point of the coordinate plane which satisfies E lies in G.

Then we say that *G is the graph of E* and that *E is the equation of G*.

In sketching the graph of an equation, we form a table of values as in the case of functions, but headed x, y rather than x, $f(x)$. The construction of a table of values is facilitated if it is possible to solve the given equation for y or x. If we are able to solve for y, then generally we may assign values to x and from our solution find the corresponding values of y; if we have solved for x the process is reversed.

After the table of values has been constructed, the remarks on drawing graphs in Section 2.9 apply here also.

Example.   Sketch the graph of: $2x + 3y = 12$.

SOLUTION.   We first solve for y: $3y = 12 - 2x$.
$$y = \frac{12 - 2x}{3}$$

(For the rest, see Fig. 6.15.)

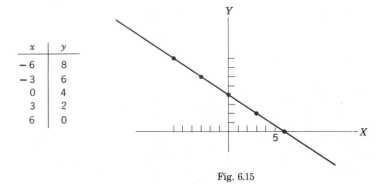

x	y
-6	8
-3	6
0	4
3	2
6	0

Fig. 6.15

Note that as in the case of graphs of functions (cf. Problem 12 of Exercise 5), physical limitations sometimes prevent our sketching a complete graph.   In the preceding case for example, the graph of $2x + 3y = 12$ is actually a straight line extending forever both upward to the left and downward to the right.   Since it is impossible, of course, to draw a graph of unlimited extent upon a sheet of paper, we satisfy ourselves in such cases with an attempt to draw as much of the graph as is necessary to bring out its characteristic behavior.

Note also that in solving a given equation for x or y, or in making other transformations on the given equation, we attempt simply to change it into an *equivalent* equation.   Since equivalent equations are always satisfied by the same values of x and y, the graphs of both the original and the new equations will be the same.

▶ **EXERCISE 26**

Sketch the graphs of the following equations:

1. $y = x$
2. $x + y = 0$
3. $x + y = 5$
4. $x + y = 10$
5. $2x - 3y + 6 = 0$
6. $y = x^2$
7. $x + y^2 = 0$
8. $x - 2y + 7 = 0$
9. $x^2 + y^2 = 25$
10. $x = 4$
11. $y = -2$
12. $x + 4 = 0$
13. $2y - 7 = 0$
14. $x^2 + y^2 = 0$
15. $y = |x|$
16. $x = |y|$
17. $|x| = |y|$
18. $|x| + |y| = 5$
19. $|x| - |y| = 5$
20. $y = \sqrt{25 - x^2}$
21. $y = -\sqrt{25 - x^2}$

6.9   THE EQUATION OF A STRAIGHT LINE

A straight line is one of the most important of all the sets of points which we encounter in geometry. Our goal in this section will be to find an equation for a given straight line AB in a cc plane. What we shall seek, then, is an equation which is satisfied by each point of line AB, and by no other points in our cc plane.

We shall find it convenient to consider vertical lines and non-vertical lines separately.

Case I. **AB is a vertical line.** (See Fig. 6.16.)

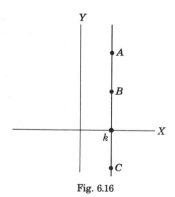

Fig. 6.16

PART I

(We show that every point of line AB satisfies a certain equation E.)

Line AB, being perpendicular to the X-axis, intersects it in a point whose real number label we denote by k.

Then $x_A = k$ and $x_B = k$, and in fact if C is *any* point on line AB, $x_C = k$.

That is to say, every point on line AB satisfies the equation $x = k$, or its equivalent:

$$\text{(E)} \quad x = x_A$$

PART II

(We show that every point of our cc plane which satisfies equation E lies on line AB.)

Suppose D is a point satisfying equation (E), i.e., $x_D = x_A = k$. Then D lies on a line perpendicular to the X-axis at the point labeled k, i.e., on the line AB.

Now in the light of Parts I and II above, we are justified in saying:

> The equation of a vertical line AB is:
>
> $$x = x_A$$

Case 2.   AB is a nonvertical line.   Here we shall induce an equation for line AB from one sort of situation, and then prove deductively that the induced equation is actually correct for all cases.

Suppose that A and B are points, and that C is a point on line AB, as in Figure 6.17.

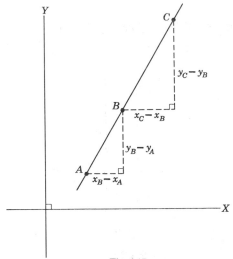

Fig. 6.17

Then from the similar triangles in Figure 6.17, we may read the following proportion:

$$\frac{y_C - y_B}{x_C - x_B} = \frac{y_B - y_A}{x_B - x_A}$$

For simplicity, let m represent the real number $(y_B - y_A)/(x_B - x_A)$. Then:

$$\frac{y_C - y_B}{x_C - x_B} = m$$

so that

$$y_C - y_B = m(x_C - x_B)$$

which is to say that the point C satisfies the equation:

$$y - y_B = m(x - x_B)$$

Here, then, is an equation arrived at by considering a diagram in which C is above points A and B on line AB. We shall now show that this equation is satisfied by each point C on line AB no matter where C happens to be situated relative to A and B. In fact we shall prove the following even more comprehensive statement:

The equation of a non-vertical line AB is:

(1) $y - y_B = m\ (x - x_B)$, where $m = \dfrac{y_B - y_A}{x_B - x_A}$

(NOTE. Equation (1) above is called the "point-slope" form of the equation of a line for a reason which will become apparent in Section 6.10.)

PROOF:

PART I

[We show that every point on line AB satisfies (1).]

Suppose C is *any* point on line AB. Then C is either on ray AB or on ray BA. We therefore consider two subcases:

Case 2a. C is on ray AB.

Let r denote the non-negative real number: $\dfrac{d(A, C)}{d(A, B)}$. Then $d(A, C) = r \cdot d(A, B)$, and by the interpolation theorem:

$$x_C = x_A + r \cdot (x_B - x_A)$$
$$y_C = y_A + r \cdot (y_B - y_A)$$

We wish to show that C satisfies (1); that is, we wish to show that $y_C - y_B = m(x_C - x_B)$. But

$y_C - y_B = y_A + r \cdot (y_B - y_A) - y_B = (y_A - y_B) + r \cdot (y_B - y_A) = (y_A - y_B)(1 - r)$

And:

$$m(x_C - x_B) = \left(\frac{y_B - y_A}{x_B - x_A}\right)[x_A + r \cdot (x_B - x_A) - x_B]$$

$$= \left(\frac{y_A - y_B}{x_A - x_B}\right)(x_A - x_B)(1 - r) = (y_A - y_B)(1 - r)$$

Therefore $y_C - y_B = m(x_C - x_B)$, Q.E.D.

Case 2b.   C is on ray BA.

In this case we let r represent the real number $\dfrac{d(B, C)}{d(B, A)}$.   Then $d(B, C) = r \cdot d(B, A)$,

and by the interpolation theorem:

$$x_C = x_B + r \cdot (x_A - x_B)$$
$$y_C = y_B + r \cdot (y_A - y_B)$$

It is now left to the reader to verify that C satisfies (1) in this case also.

PART II

[We show that every point of our cc plane which satisfies equation (1) lies on line AB.]
   Suppose D is a point which satisfies (1).   Then:

(2)

$$y_D - y_B = \left(\frac{y_B - y_A}{x_B - x_A}\right)(x_D - x_B) = \left(\frac{y_A - y_B}{x_A - x_B}\right)(x_D - x_B) = (y_A - y_B)\left(\frac{x_D - x_B}{x_A - x_B}\right)$$

Let $s = (x_D - x_B)/(x_A - x_B)$, so that:

(3) $$x_D = x_B + s(x_A - x_B)$$

and (2) may now be written:

(4) $$y_D = y_B + s(y_A - y_B)$$

If $s \geqslant 0$, then D is on ray BA (hence on line AB), by the interpolation theorem.
   There remains only to consider the possibility $s < 0$, in which case we shall prove
that D must be on ray AB:
   From (3) and (4):

(5) $$x_D - x_A = x_B - x_A + s(x_A - x_B) = (1 - s)(x_B - x_A)$$
(6) $$y_D - y_A = y_B - y_A + s(y_A - y_B) = (1 - s)(y_B - y_A)$$

Therefore:

(7) $$x_D = x_A + (1 - s)(x_B - x_A)$$
(8) $$y_D = y_A + (1 - s)(y_B - y_A)$$

Now if $s < 0$, it follows that $-s > 0$, from which: $1 - s > 1 > 0$.   Hence $1 - s > 0$.
Therefore, by the interpolation theorem, it follows that in this case D lies on ray AB,
hence on line AB, Q.E.D.
   Now in the light of Parts I and II above, we are finally justified in making the boxed
statement on p. 165.

Illustrative Example 1.   Find the equation of the line which passes
through the points $(-3, 1)$ and $(7, 11)$.

SOLUTION.   Note that since $\dfrac{y_A - y_B}{x_A - x_B} = \dfrac{y_B - y_A}{x_B - x_A}$, we may compute m
by thinking of *either* of the given points as A, and the other as B, whichever
seems to be more convenient:

$$m = \frac{11 - 1}{7 - (-3)} = \frac{10}{10} = 1$$

Now, having computed m, we may choose *either* of the given points as
B in the formula:

$$y - y_B = m(x - x_B)$$

For example, suppose we let $B = (-3, 1)$. Then the required equation is:

$$y - 1 = 1 \, (x - (-3))$$
or
$$y - 1 = x + 3$$
or
$$y = x + 4$$

It is easy now to verify that each of the given points satisfies the equation $y = x + 4$.

Illustrative Example 2. Find the equation of the line which passes through the points $(1, 11)$ and $(7, 11)$.

SOLUTION. Since the y-values of the given points are equal, the required line is horizontal, and (by analogy with Case 1 above) has an equation of the form $y = y_A$.

In this problem the required equation is clearly: $y = 11$.

This problem may also be done, but not as neatly, by the method of Illustrative Example 1 above.

NOTE. The equation of a graph may, of course, be given in equivalent forms. Thus, in Illustrative Example 1, $x - y + 4 = 0$ would be perfectly acceptable as a solution, as would $y - 11 = 0$ in Illustrative Example 2.

▶ **EXERCISE 27**

1. Find the equation of a line through each of the following pairs of points. In each case:

(i) Verify that the given points satisfy the equation of the line.
(ii) Sketch the given points and the line on a cc plane.
(iii) On the line, locate a point P different from the given points, and verify that P satisfies the equation of the line.
(iv) If possible, find (algebraically) a point Q satisfying the equation of the line such that $y_Q = 1$, and verify that Q lies on the line.

(a) $(2, 3), (7, 11)$　　(b) $(0, 0), (5, 5)$　　(c) $(0, 0), (-5, -5)$
(d) $(-1, 2), (5, -3)$　　(e) $(2, 4), (-3, -7)$　(f) $(2, -4), (-2, -4)$
(g) $(1, -3), (-7, 2)$　　(h) $(0, 4), (4, 0)$　　(i) $(3, 4), (2, 5)$
(j) $(7, 1), (3, -3)$　　(k) $(2, 2), (2, 2)$　　(l) $(-4, 2), (-4, 2)$

2. Complete the proof of Case 2b, p. 166.

6.10　THE SLOPE OF A NONVERTICAL STRAIGHT LINE

The number $m = (y_B - y_A)/(x_B - x_A)$, defined in deriving the equation of a nonvertical line AB, is an important and interesting one, and we shall consider it further in this section. It is called the *slope* of line AB.

First of all this question arises: The same line may be determined by many different pairs of points. Will different pairs of points on a line lead to different values of its slope?

Figure 6.18 throws some light on the problem:

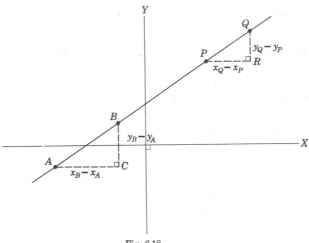

Fig. 6.18

Now here is our question again: If $A \neq B$ and $P \neq Q$ are pairs of points on a nonvertical line l in a coordinate plane, will the value of the slope of l as determined by A and B be the same as that determined by P and Q?

In other words, will $\dfrac{y_B - y_A}{x_B - x_A} = \dfrac{y_Q - y_P}{x_Q - x_P}$?

The evidence of our diagram is that the preceding equation will be true; for the triangles ABC and PQR are similar and the preceding equation seems to follow from the proportionality of corresponding sides.

But we do not yet have a *proof* of this fact, for the vertical distance we have labeled $y_B - y_A$, for example, might in some relative positions of A and B be $y_A - y_B$, and similarly for the other sides we have labeled. It happens, however, that in all positions of A, B, P, Q on any nonvertical line the preceding equation is true, and this is easily proved:

Theorem. If $A \neq B$ and $P \neq Q$ are points on a nonvertical line l in a cc plane, then:

$$\frac{y_B - y_A}{x_B - x_A} = \frac{y_Q - y_P}{x_Q - x_P}$$

PROOF.   As we have shown, the equation of l (i.e., of line AB) is:

$$(1) \quad y - y_B = m(x - x_B)$$

where $\qquad$ (2) $\qquad m = \dfrac{y_B - y_A}{x_B - x_A}$

Since P, Q lie on line AB, they satisfy (1).

Therefore: $\qquad$ (3) $\quad y_Q - y_B = m(x_Q - x_B)$

$\qquad\qquad\qquad$ (4) $\quad y_P - y_B = m(x_P - x_B)$

Subtracting: $\qquad$ (5) $\quad y_Q - y_P = m(x_Q - x_P)$

Now since line l is nonvertical, it follows that $x_P \neq x_Q$, i.e., that $x_Q - x_P \neq 0$. Therefore we may divide both sides of equation (5) by $x_Q - x_P$:

$$\frac{y_Q - y_P}{x_Q - x_P} = m = \frac{y_B - y_A}{x_B - x_A}, \quad \text{Q.E.D.}$$

As a consequence of this theorem, we may now formally define "slope" as follows:

Let $P \neq Q$ be any pair of points on a nonvertical line l in a cc plane. Then the unique real number:

$$m = \frac{y_Q - y_P}{x_Q - x_P}$$

is called the *slope* of line l.

Figure 6.19 will help to bring out the significance of the number which is called the *slope* of a line.

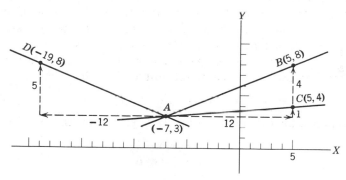

Fig. 6.19

Note that by our formula for slope, the slopes of lines AB, AC and AD, are $5/12$, $1/12$, and $-5/12$, respectively.

In each case, the numbers $x_Q - x_P$ and $y_Q - y_P$ which occur in the formula for slope may be pictured graphically by dotted rays as in the figure. One may think, for example, of traveling from A to D by a journey of 12 units to the left (-12), followed by a journey of 5 units up ($+5$). The slope of line AD will then be the "rise" divided by the "run," i.e., $-5/12$.

Now observe that the slope of line AC (1/12) is a much smaller positive number than the slope of line AB (5/12). This reflects the fact that line AC is not as steep as line AB. A horizontal journey of 12 units causes a rise of 5 units in the case of line AB, but in the case of line AC, a rise of only 1 unit.

We note further that lines AB and AD have slopes which are equal in numerical value, indicating that the two lines have the same steepness; and finally the fact that the first slope is positive and the second negative tells us that the first line slants upward to the right and the second upward to the left.

We see now the reason for calling m the *slope* of a line. The *slope* of a line is a number m which determines its *direction* and *steepness*:

> A line with positive slope slants upward to the right.
> A line with negative slope slants upward to the left.
> A line with zero slope is horizontal.
> The larger the absolute value of the slope, the steeper the line.
> A vertical line has no slope.

We now have at hand a second method of determining a line, namely by giving *one* point on the line and its direction (i.e., its slope). Thus, to draw the line through $P(-7, 3)$ with slope 5/12, one may proceed from P 12 units to the right and then 5 up to arrive at point Q, and the required line is PQ; to draw the line through P with slope $-5/12$, one may proceed from P 12 units to the *left* and then 5 up (or 12 units to the right and then 5 down) to arrive at a point S, and the required line is PS.

Furthermore, given a point on a line and the slope of a line, the equation of that line may be determined by substitution into the form:

$$y - y_B = m(x - x_B)$$

For example, the equation of a line through (2, 3) with slope 5 is:

$$y - 3 = 5(x - 2)$$
$$y - 3 = 5x - 10$$
$$y = 5x - 7$$

This last equation is in the form $y = ax + b$, where a and b are real numbers; in the preceding equation $y = 5x - 7$, $a = 5$ happens to be the slope of the given line. Will the graph of every equation in the form $y = ax + b$ be a straight line whose slope is a?

The answer is *yes*. For, first of all, it is easy to verify that the point $(0, b)$ is on the graph of the equation: $y = ax + b$. Now suppose we work out the equation of the straight line with slope a which passes through $(0, b)$:

$$y - b = a(x - 0)$$
$$y - b = ax$$
$$y = ax + b$$

Therefore $y = ax + b$ is the equation of a straight line with slope a through the point $(0, b)$; but by definition (see page 161) this is the same thing as saying that the graph of the equation $y = ax + b$ is a straight line with slope a through the point $(0, b)$.

In view of this last result, we may substitute m for a in the equation $y = ax + b$. Furthermore, since $(0, b)$ is on the Y-axis and on the graph of $y = ax + b$, we call the point $(0, b)$ (and also the alternate label "b" of that point) the Y-*intercept* of the graph of $y = ax + b$.

We summarize:

> The graph of the equation $y = mx + b$, where m and b are real numbers, is a straight line with slope m and Y-intercept b.

It follows that the graph of any equation equivalent to $Ax + By + C = 0$, where A, B, C are real numbers and A, B are not *both* zero, is a straight line. For if $B \neq 0$, we may solve for y and arrive at an equation equivalent to the original, but of the form $y = mx + b$ whose graph is a nonvertical straight line. If $B = 0$, then $A \neq 0$, and our original equation is equivalent to an equation in the form $x = k$ whose graph is a vertical straight line.

Conversely, every straight line in a coordinate plane has an equation of the form $Ax + By + C = 0$, where A, B, C are real numbers and A, B are not both zero; for if a line is vertical it has an equation of the form $x = k$, or $x - k = 0$. This is in the form $Ax + By + C = 0$ with $A = 1$, $B = 0, C = -k$. If a line is nonvertical, it has an equation of the form $y = mx + b$, or $mx - y + b = 0$. This is in the form $Ax + By + C = 0$ with $A = m, B = -1, C = b$.

The preceding two paragraphs indicate why equations in the form $Ax + By + C = 0$ are called *linear* equations.

Illustrative Examples:

(1) The equation $2x - 3y = 15$ is equivalent to $y = \frac{2}{3}x - 5$. In the latter form we see immediately that the line which is the graph of either of these equations has slope $\frac{2}{3}$ and Y-intercept -5. We may draw the line, then, by passing it through the point -5 on the Y-axis and forcing it to have slope $\frac{2}{3}$ as in Fig. 6.20.

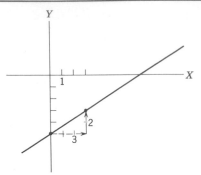

Fig. 6.20

(2)   The line whose equation is $y = -\frac{2}{3}x - 5$ may be drawn as in Fig. 6.21.

(3)   The equation $2x + 4 = 0$ is equivalent to $x = -2$. The graph of $2x + 4 = 0$ is therefore a vertical straight line whose X-intercept is -2. This line has no slope.

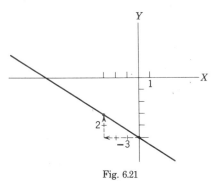

Fig. 6.21

▶ **EXERCISE 28**

1.   How does the formula $m = (y_Q - y_P)/(x_Q - x_P)$ fail when mis-applied to vertical lines?

2.   Plot the graphs of the following equations either by the two point method or by the slope and Y-intercept method.

(a) $3x + 5y = 30$	(b) $2x - y = 7$
(c) $y = -x$	(d) $4x - 2y - 12 = 0$
(e) $y = x\sqrt{3} - 3$	(f) $x\sqrt{5} + y\sqrt{4} = 1$
(g) $2x + y = 7$	(h) $14x + 7y = 49$
(i) $2x + y = 11$	(j) $y - 7 = 0$
(k) $x + y = 5$	(l) $x - 5 = 0$

3.   Find the slope and Y-intercept of each of the lines in Problem 2.

4. Find the equations of each of the following lines:

(a) With slope 3 and Y-intercept 6.

(b) With slope $-\frac{1}{2}$ and through the point $(0, 3)$.

(c) With slope $\frac{2}{3}$ and through the point $(6, 0)$.

(d) With slope $\frac{1}{4}$ and through the point $(5, -7)$.

(e) With slope k and through the point (a, b), where a, b, k are real numbers.

(f) Through the points $(1, 7)$ and $(5, 6)$.

(g) Through the points $(-7, 4)$ and $(2, -6)$.

(h) Through the points $(0, 3)$ and $(4, 0)$.

5. (a) Show that a line with X-intercept 7 and Y-intercept 11 has the equation: $\frac{x}{7} + \frac{y}{11} = 1$.

(b) Prove that if $a \neq 0$ and $b \neq 0$ are the X- and Y-intercepts respectively of a line, then the equation of the line is: $x/a + y/b = 1$. (This is called the "intercept form" of the equation of a line.)

(c) Use the intercept form to solve Problem 4(h) above.

6. Prove that a line is horizontal if and only if its slope is zero.

7. A more precise way of saying that a nonvertical line l slants upward to the right is: If P, Q are points on l such that $x_Q > x_P$, then $y_Q > y_P$.
Prove that a nonvertical line l slants upward to the right if and only if its slope is positive.

8. Make up and answer a question analogous to Problem 7 above, having to do with a line slanting upward to the left.

6.11 PARALLELISM OF LINES

Since the slope of a line determines its "direction," it seems reasonable to suppose that lines with equal slopes should have the same direction and should therefore be parallel; and by the same token that nonvertical parallel lines should have equal slopes. We prove that this is so.

Theorem. Nonvertical lines in a cc plane are parallel if and only if their slopes are equal.

PROOF:

Part I ("if"). Suppose we have given two nonvertical lines with the same slope. We wish to prove that the lines are parallel. We use the indirect method, supposing the lines are *not* parallel, and arriving at a contradiction.

Two lines in a plane are defined to be parallel either if they are identical, or if they are different and do not intersect. The only alternative to the parallelism of our given lines, then, is that they are *different* and intersect in at least one point.

But if our two lines have the same slope and a point in common, they have the same equation (in the "point-slope" form), and are therefore *identical*, which contradicts the statement above that the lines are different.

Part II ("*only if*"). Here we use the well-known statement of Euclidean plane geometry that through a given point one and only one line can be drawn parallel to a given line.

In this part of the theorem we assume that we have given parallel nonvertical lines u, v in a cc plane and we prove that u and v have the same slope.

Let P be any point on line u. Then we have shown (see Illustrative Example (1) of Section 6.10) how to construct a line w through P with the same slope as line v. By Part I above, $w \parallel v$. By hypothesis, $u \parallel v$. Since only one line can be drawn through P parallel to v, it follows that $u = w$. Since w has the same slope as v, it follows that u has the same slope as v, Q.E.D.

6.12   INTERSECTION OF LINES IN A PLANE

So far as the intersection of two lines in a plane is concerned, we may distinguish these cases:

(1)   The lines intersect in no points in which case the lines are parallel and different.

(2)   The lines intersect in exactly one point.

(3)   The lines intersect in more than one point, in which case the lines are identical, hence parallel.

Now in drawing the graphs of a pair of linear equations, any one of (1), (2), (3) above may occur.

But to find the points of intersection of lines, and in fact of any pair of graphs, we shall generally prefer an algebraic approach. A point will lie on several graphs if and only if the point (i.e., its coordinates) satisfies the equation of each of these graphs. To find points of intersection of graphs, therefore, we solve the equations of the graphs "simultaneously;" i.e., we find ordered pairs of real numbers which satisfy these equations.

We note that in solving pairs of *linear* equations simultaneously, we proceed by the method of equivalent (pairs of) equations. (This method, in fact, will apply to most of the pairs of simultaneous equations which we shall encounter in this course.)

The three cases we have listed above, and methods of solving pairs of simultaneous linear equations will be illustrated in examples below.

Illustrative Example 1.   Solve the equations $2x + 3y = 6$ and $y = -(2x/3) + 2$ simultaneously.

SOLUTION.   Substituting $-(2x/3) + 2$ for y in the first equation:

$$2x + 3\left(-\frac{2x}{3} + 2\right) = 6$$
$$2x - 2x + 6 = 6$$
$$6 = 6$$

Apparently we have gotten nowhere! The result $6 = 6$ is true, but indicates no solution. Actually, our work shows that no matter what real number x is, if y is then determined by the second equation, then the first equation will be satisfied.

The reason for this peculiarity may be seen if we take a closer look at the equation $y = -(2x/3) + 2$. It is equivalent to $3y = -2x + 6$, or $2x + 3y = 6$.

In other words, the two equations are equivalent. Any pair of values of x and y which satisfies one satisfies the other.

It is hardly necessary to verify that in this case the graphs of the given equations are identical lines, and that there are an infinite number of simultaneous solutions of these equations.

Illustrative Example 2. Solve the equations $2x + 3y = 6$ and $4x + 6y = 7$ simultaneously.

SOLUTION. Doubling the first: $\quad 4x + 6y = 12$
Writing the second: $\quad 4x + 6y = 7$
and subtracting: $\qquad\qquad 0 = 5$

we have an even *more* peculiar result!

Actually, what we have shown in this case is that if there were a simultaneous solution to the given equations, then 0 would equal 5. But the conclusion is impossible; therefore there can be no simultaneous solution to these two equations, hence no point satisfying both.

The straight lines which are the graphs of these equations must therefore be parallel, but not identical, which facts the student may verify by drawing the graphs of these equations.

Illustrative Example 3. Solve the equations $3x + 2y = 1$ and $5x - 3y = 8$ simultaneously.

SOLUTION: Multiplying the first by 3: $\quad 9x + 6y = 3$
and the second by 2: $\quad 10x - 6y = 16$
and adding: $\qquad\qquad\qquad 19x = 19$
$\qquad\qquad\qquad\qquad x = 1$

Substituting $x = 1$ in the first: $\qquad 3 + 2y = 1$
$\qquad\qquad\qquad\qquad 2y = -2$
$\qquad\qquad\qquad\qquad y = -1$

(Alternatively, y might have been found by multiplying the first equation by 5, the second by -3, and adding.)

In this case, then, there is a unique solution: $x = 1$, $y = -1$. In other words, the lines whose equations are $3x + 2y = 1$ and $5x - 3y = 8$ meet in one and only one point: $(1, -1)$. This, again, may be checked by the student graphically.

6.13 PERPENDICULARITY OF LINES

In this section we shall derive a simple test for perpendicularity of lines in a cc plane.

Suppose u and v are perpendicular lines with slopes m, n, respectively, and that u intersects v at the point $P\ (a, b)$.   (See Fig. 6.22).

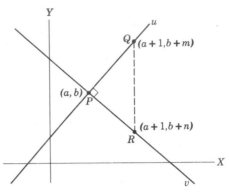

Fig. 6.22

It is easy to see that the point $Q\ (a + 1, b + m)$ is on u; for the slope of line PQ is $\dfrac{b + m - b}{a + 1 - a} = m$, so that line PQ has the slope m and the point P in common with line u.   Since a line is determined by one of its points and its slope, line $PQ =$ line u.   Therefore Q lies on line u.

Similarly, the point $R(a + 1, b + n)$ is on line v.

Since we are given that $u \perp v$, we have:

(1) $\triangle PQR$ is a right triangle with $PQ \perp QR$.   This is equivalent to:

(2) $(PQ^2) + (PR)^2 = (QR)^2$.   This is equivalent to:

(3) $(\sqrt{1 + m^2})^2 + (\sqrt{1 + n^2})^2 = (\sqrt{0^2 + (m - n)^2})^2$. This is equivalent to:

(4) $1 + m^2 + 1 + n^2 = (m - n)^2$.   This is equivalent to:

(5) $2 + m^2 + n^2 = m^2 - 2mn + n^2$.   This is equivalent to:

(6) $mn = -1$.

Thus, if two nonvertical lines are perpendicular, the product of their slopes must be -1.

Now we prove a converse of this statement:

Suppose u and v are lines with slopes m, n respectively and that $mn = -1$. We prove that $u \perp v$.

First of all we note that $m \neq n$; for since $mn = -1$, if $m = n$, we have $m^2 = -1$.   This is impossible, since the square of no real number is -1.

Since $m \neq n$, u and v are not parallel, and therefore must intersect in a point $P\ (a, b)$.   We now define Q and R exactly as above.

We are assuming (6) above.   But (6) is equivalent to (1) above.   Hence $PQ \perp QR$, i.e., $u \perp v$, Q.E.D.

In summary:

> Two nonvertical lines in a cc plane are perpendicular if and only if
> the product of their slopes is -1.

Note that $mn = -1$ is equivalent to $m = -\dfrac{1}{n}$ or $n = -\dfrac{1}{m}.$ Thus we
may also say: Two nonvertical lines in a cc plane are perpendicular if and
only if the slope of one is the *negative reciprocal* of the slope of the other.

▶ **EXERCISE 29**

1. In each of the following cases, prove that the given lines (i.e., the
lines whose equations are given) are parallel, and draw the lines on a cc
plane:

(a) $y = 2x + 1$; $y = 2x - 5$
(b) $2x + 3y = 6$; $2x + 3y = 12$
(c) $x + 2y = 3$; $2x + 4y = 7$
(d) $x - 2y = 7$; $2y - x = 7$
(e) $y = x - 1$; $x - y = 1$
(f) $x = 2$; $x = -3$
(g) $y = 0$; $y = 5$

2. In each of the following cases prove that lines u and v are parallel,
and illustrate on a cc plane:

(a) u: $y = 3x - 2$; v passes through (2, 4), (4, 10).
(b) u passes through $(-1, 4), (3, -2)$; v passes through (3, 2), (1, 5).
(c) u is perpendicular to: $x + 7 = 0$; v passes through (1, 2), (5, 2).

3. Find the intersection of each of the following pairs of lines, and then
draw the lines on a cc plane:

(a) $3x + 4y = 6$; $x - y = 9$
(b) $2x + y = 13$; $3x - 2y - 6$
(c) $2x + y = 8$; $6x + 3y = 20$
(d) $3x - y = 7$; $39x - 13y - 91$
(e) $2x + 3y - 6$; $3x - 5y + 10 - 0$

4. In each of the following cases, prove that lines u and v are perpendicular, and draw the lines on a cc plane:

(a) u: $y = 2x + 3$; v: $x + 2y = 6$
(b) u: $y = 3x + 3$; v passes through (3, 4), (6, 3).
(c) u passes through $(2, -3), (3, -2)$; v passes through (7, 11), (12, 6).
(d) u: $2x + 3y = 6$; v: $3x - 2y = 6$
(e) u: $x = 3$; v: $y = -2$
(f) u: $x = 0$; v: $y = 0$

5. Find the equation of, and draw, each of the following lines:

(a) A line through $(3, 7)$ parallel to $2x - 3y = 13$.

(b) A line through $(3, 7)$ perpendicular to $2x - 3y = 13$.

(c) A line through $(1, 2)$ parallel to $x - 7 = 0$.

(d) A line through $(1, 2)$ perpendicular to $x - 7 = 0$.

(e) A line through $(1, 2)$ parallel to $y - 7 = 0$.

(f) A line through $(1, 2)$ perpendicular to $y - 7 = 0$.

(g) A line through $(1, 2)$ parallel to $x + y = 7$.

(h) A line through $(1, 2)$ perpendicular to $x + y = 7$.

6. Draw the quadrilateral with vertices $(-1, 3)$, $(4, 5)$, $(8, 2)$, $(3, 0)$ on a cc plane, and prove that it is a parallelogram.

7. Draw the quadrilateral with vertices $(6, -2)$, $(4, 4)$, $(-5, 1)$, $(-3, -5)$ on a cc plane and prove that it is a rectangle.

8. Given the points $(0, 0)$ and $(a, 0)$, find two other points such that the four form the vertices of a square.

What about the existence and uniqueness of the solution to this problem?

9. Given the points $(0, 0)$, $(a, 0)$, $(0, b)$, find another point such that the four form the vertices of a rectangle.

What about the existence and uniqueness of the solution to this problem?

10. Given the points $(0, 0)$, $(a, 0)$, (b, c), find another point such that the four form the vertices of a parallelogram.

What about the existence and uniqueness of the solution to this problem?

11. Given that $D \neq 0$, $E \neq 0$, prove that the lines:
$$Ax + By + C = 0$$
$$Dx + Ey + F = 0$$
are parallel if and only if: $A/D = B/E$.

12. Given that $D \neq 0$, $E \neq 0$, $F \neq 0$, prove that the lines:
$$Ax + By + C = 0$$
$$Dx + Ey + F = 0$$
are identical if and only if: $A/D = B/E = C/F$.

13. Prove that the lines:
$$Ax + By + C = 0$$
$$Bx - Ay + D = 0$$
are perpendicular.

Hint: Consider the three cases: (1) $A = 0$, $B \neq 0$. (2) $A \neq 0$, $B = 0$. (3) $A \neq 0$, $B \neq 0$.

6.14 DISTANCE FROM A POINT TO A LINE

In this section we shall consider the problem of finding the distance from a point in a cc plane to a *line* in that plane; that is to say, given a point P and a line l in a cc plane, we shall seek $d(P, Q)$, where the point Q lies on l, and where the perpendicular to l at

Q passes through P. It is this distance $d(P, Q)$ which we define to be the distance from P to l, and which we denote $d(P, l)$. (See Fig. 6.23).

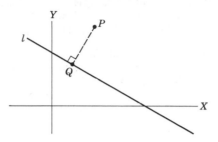

Fig. 6.23

Suppose the equation of l is $Ax + By + C = 0$. Then since Q lies on l:

(1) $Ax_Q + By_Q + C = 0$

Now consider the line l' whose equation is: $Bx - Ay = Bx_P - Ay_P$. By Problem 13 of Exercise 29, $l' \perp l$. Furthermore, (x_P, y_P) clearly satisfies the equation of l'. Hence P lies on l'.

In other words, l' is a line through P and perpendicular to l. Therefore Q lies on l' and must satisfy its equation:

(2) $Bx_Q - Ay_Q = Bx_P - Ay_P$

The distance we seek is:

(3) $d(P, l) = \sqrt{(x_P - x_Q)^2 + (y_P - y_Q)^2}$

Essentially, all we need to do now is to solve (1) and (2) for x_Q and y_Q and substitute into (3). However, a "change of variable" will make the computation easier:

Let $u = x_P - x_Q$, $v = y_P - y_Q$; then the distance we seek becomes:

(4) $d(P, l) = \sqrt{u^2 + v^2}$

Equation (2) becomes:

(5) $Bu - Av = 0$

And since $x_Q = x_P - u$, $y_Q = y_P - v$, equation (1) becomes:

(6) $Au + Bv = Ax_P + By_P + C$

Now we need only solve (5) and (6) for u and v and substitute into (4). But a trick way of achieving our end is to square and add (5) and (6):

(7) $(A^2 + B^2)(u^2 + v^2) = (Ax_P + By_P + C)^2$

So that:

(8) $u^2 + v^2 = \dfrac{(Ax_P + By_P + C)^2}{A^2 + B^2}$

Therefore:

(9) $d(P, l) = \sqrt{\dfrac{(Ax_P + By_P + C)^2}{A^2 + B^2}} = \dfrac{|Ax_P + By_P + C|}{\sqrt{A^2 + B^2}}$

We summarize:

In a cc plane, if P is a point and l is a line whose equation is $Ax + By + C = 0$, then:

$$d(P, l) = \frac{|Ax_P + By_P + C|}{\sqrt{A^2 + B^2}}$$

---

180   **INTRODUCTION TO ANALYTIC GEOMETRY**

Illustrative Example. Find the distance from the point $(7, 11)$ to the line $2x - 3y = 5$.
SOLUTION: We first write the equation of the given line in the form $Ax + By + C = 0$:
$2x - 3y - 5 = 0$. Then the required distance is:

$$\frac{|2 \cdot 7 - 3 \cdot 11 - 5|}{\sqrt{2^2 + (-3)^2}} = \frac{|-24|}{\sqrt{13}} = \frac{24}{\sqrt{13}}$$

EXERCISE

1. In each of the following cases, find the distance from the given point to the given line, and illustrate with a diagram:

(a) $(2, 3), 3x + 4y = 5$ (b) $(7, 11), y = x + 5$
(c) $(-1, 2), x = y + 5$ (d) $(2, 2), x + y = 4$
(e) $(-2, -3), 5x + 12y + 60 = 0$ (f) $(2, 2), x + y = 0$
(g) $(7, 11), y = 5$ (h) $(7, 11), x = 5$
(i) $(u, v), y = -p$ (j) $(0, 0), Ax + By + C = 0$
(k) $(a, a), y = 0$

2. (a) Find the length of the altitude AA' of triangle ABC, if triangle ABC is as in Problem 5 of Exercise 25.

(b) Find the area of the triangle ABC above, using the formula:

$$\text{Area} = \tfrac{1}{2}(AA')(BC)$$

(c) Find the area of triangle ABC above by inscribing it in a rectangle with sides parallel to the X- and Y-axes, and computing the areas of the rectangle and several right triangles.

3. We define a point P in a cc plane to be *above* a nonvertical line l if a vertical line through P intersects l in a point Q such that $y_P > y_Q$; and similarly we define *below*.

Prove that if l has the equation $Ax + By + C = 0$, where $B > 0$, then P is above l if and only if $Ax_P + By_P + C > 0$; and P is below l if and only if $Ax_P + By_P + C < 0$.

4. We define the *directed* distance $\bar{d}(P, l)$ from a point P in a cc plane to a nonvertical line whose equation is $Ax + By + C = 0$, where $B > 0$, as follows:

$$\bar{d}(P, l) = \frac{Ax_P + By_P + C}{\sqrt{A^2 + B^2}}$$

Prove that $\bar{d}(P, l)$ has the same numerical value as $d(P, l)$, but $\bar{d}(P, l)$ is positive when P is above l and negative when P is below l.

5. The graph of an inequality in x and y is defined to be the set of all points (a, b) in a cc plane which make the inequality a true statement when a and b are substituted for x and y, respectively, in the inequality (cf. Section 2.16, graphs of relations).

Thus $(7, 11)$ is a point in the graph of $y > x$, but $(11, 7)$ is not.

(a) What is the graph of $y - x > 0$? (*Hint:* $(y_P - x_P)/\sqrt{2} = \bar{d}(P, l)$; $\bar{d}(P, l) > 0$ $\Leftrightarrow$ P is above l.)

(b) What is the graph of $y - x < 0$?
(c) What is the graph of $2x - y + 1 > 0$?
(d) What is the graph of $y > 0$?
(e) What is the graph of $x > 7$?

6.15 WHY ANALYTIC GEOMETRY?

The creation of a new field of knowledge is almost always the work not of one man, but of many. A germ of analytic geometry, for example, may be found in the system of locating a point on the earth's surface by means of its latitude and longitude, a system which goes all the way back to the time of the Greeks; and between the time of the Greeks and the time of the man of whom we are about to speak, many men created mathematics that we now would call part of analytic geometry.

Generally, however, it is the name of the great French philosopher and mathematician, René Descartes, that we associate with analytic geometry. This is due mainly to the fact that he published the first treatise on the subject; which treatise, it is very much worth noting, occurred as an appendix to a philosophical work called: *A Discourse on the Method of Rightly Conducting the Reason and Seeking Truth in the Sciences.*

The *Discourse on Method* was published in 1637, during a period of history which has been called the "Age of Reason." Descartes was one of the pioneers in this movement to understand and master nature by the power of reason, and his analytic geometry may be regarded as a magnificent demonstration of the extent to which man's reason may be aided by proper methods.

For it must be confessed that there are aspects of Euclidean geometry that trouble the mind. They disturbed the great Descartes as much as they perplex present-day high-school students. Euclidean geometry he described as "greatly fatiguing the imagination"; and on the subject of deductive logic, he said that it is "of avail rather in the communication of what we already know . . . than in the investigation of the unknown."

Let us, for example, consider this problem of Euclidean geometry:

Problem I. Prove that the line joining the midpoints of two non-parallel sides of a trapezoid is parallel to the bases of the trapezoid and equal to half their sum in length. (See Fig. 6.24).

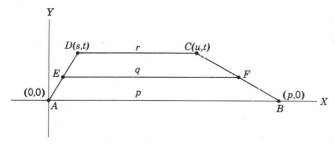

Fig. 6.24

Referring to the diagram, if E and F are the midpoints of nonparallel sides AD, BC of trapezoid $ABCD$, we are to prove that $EF \parallel AB$; and if p, q, r are the lengths of segments AB, EF, CD, respectively, that $q = (p + r)/2$.

This is a challenging problem of high-school geometry. The approach there is to draw lines that will enable us eventually to prove the desired conclusion. But what lines shall we draw? The brilliant student of mathematics often knows "intuitively" what the right steps are; but even for great mathematicians, intuition has its limitations.

The approach of analytic geometry to problems such as these leaves much less to the imagination. One simply draws a coordinate system in some convenient position and then labels important points in the figure; after that the rest of the proof is fairly "cut and dried." We illustrate by proving the statement of the preceding problem analytically.

First of all, let an X- and a Y-axis be drawn with A as the origin and B on the positive side of the X-axis.

Then clearly A may be labeled $(0, 0)$ and $B(p, 0)$. Since points C and D are on a line parallel to the X-axis, they must have the same Y-values. We may therefore label $D: (s, t)$ and $C: (u, t)$.

By the midpoint formula (Problem 2, Exercise 25), we have:

$$E = \left(\frac{s}{2}, \frac{t}{2}\right) \qquad F = \left(\frac{p+u}{2}, \frac{t}{2}\right)$$

Half the problem is disposed of immediately, for since $y_E = y_F$, EF is parallel to the X-axis, i.e., to the line AB, as required.

The other part is almost as easy. Since EF is parallel to the X-axis, $q = d(E, F) = x_F - x_E = (p + u - s)/2$.

Similarly, $r = d(C, D) = u - s$. Therefore:

$$q = \frac{p + u - s}{2} = \frac{p + r}{2}, \quad \text{Q.E.D}$$

One advantage of analytic geometry, then, is that it offers us a specific *method* for penetrating into geometrical problems. Prior to its development the geometer was often forced, as is the present day high-school student, to grope and stumble about in search of an appropriate starting point for attacking a specific geometrical problem.

It is worth remarking again upon the extent to which this method leans upon the real number system. Actually, as in the problem we worked out, analytic geometry always substitutes real-number problems for geometry problems, thus allowing us to bring to bear upon the problems of geometry the powerful algebraic machinery already developed in the study of real numbers. For this reason, analytic geometry is often described as a combination of algebra and geometry, or a treatment of geometry by algebraic methods. To be more specific, it is a treatment of geometry in which real numbers and algebraic equations play a dominant role.

A second very important application (and one which Descartes himself investigated in the form of studies on mechanically drawn curves) is to problems of what we may call "compound motion."

Here is an example of one such problem.

Problem 2. Suppose that while H. G. Wells' "Invisible Man" walks straight down a street at a rate of 3 feet per second, a fly alights upon his back and proceeds to crawl straight upward at a rate of 6 inches per second.

To a startled spectator, along what path would the fly seem to be crawling?

SOLUTION. We construct the following *mathematical model*: Let the point at which the fly alights be the origin of a coordinate system whose positive X-axis is a ray along which the invisible man moves towards increasing x-values.

Then when t seconds have elapsed, the invisible man has moved $3t$ feet along the X-axis, and the fly $\frac{1}{2}t$ feet upward, as in Fig. 6.25.

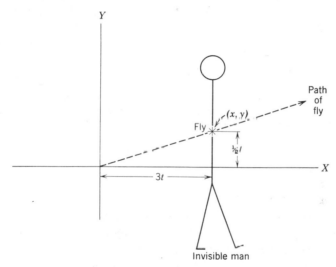

Fig. 6.25

The point (x, y) reached by the fly t seconds after it alights is such that $x = 3t$, $y = \frac{1}{2}t$. But no matter what real number t is, if these equations hold true, then $y = (1/2)(x/3) = x/6$.

The points which the fly passes in its trip therefore satisfy the equation $y = x/6$. But as we have seen, this is the equation of a straight line, and clearly it passes through the origin and has a slope of $\frac{1}{6}$.

To a spectator, then, the fly would seem to be climbing in space along a straight line which rises with a slope of $\frac{1}{6}$.

In similar fashion the scientist is enabled to predict the path taken by the earth and the sun and the planets and comets in the heavens, of satellites both real and man-made, of electrons in an atom and of projectiles fired from stationary or moving vehicles; and these are only a few of the countless important instances of compound motion which occur all about us.

Finally, analytic geometry opened up a whole new world of mathematical curves, and even offered means for the study of their properties; for now any equation in x and y, when graphed, might lead to a curve with interesting physical attributes.   Until the invention of analytic geometry, only a relatively few curves had been discovered and studied, and these, like the circle, were mainly curves drawn by mechanical instruments.

The hundreds of new curves that arose from the graphing of equations were at first studied purely out of intellectual curiosity by Descartes and his contemporaries and successors.   But as happens so often, the results of these purely mathematical investigations have finally found countless practical applications.

NOTE.   In order not to obscure the main points in the proof of Problem 1 of this section, we have swept a bit of mathematical dust under the carpet.   We have assumed, for example that the length of line segment EF is $x_F - x_E$.   This assumption is valid only if we are sure that $x_F > x_E$.

The trouble lies first of all in the fact that we have not defined "trapezoid" precisely. Since a careful treatment of this question would lead us rather far afield, we shall not undertake to make our proof completely rigorous here.

▶ **EXERCISE 30**

1.   Prove analytically:

(*a*)   The diagonals of a rectangle are equal in length.

(*b*)   The diagonals of a rectangle bisect each other (i.e., the midpoint of one diagonal is identical with the midpoint of the other).

(*c*)   The diagonals of a parallelogram bisect each other.

(*d*)   A converse of (*c*).

(*e*)   The diagonals of a rhombus are perpendicular to each other and bisect each other.

(*f*)   A converse of (*e*).

(*g*)   A line segment joining the midpoints of two sides of a triangle is parallel to the third side and is half its length.

(*h*)   The midpoint of the hypotenuse of a right triangle is equidistant from the three vertices of the triangle.

(*i*)   A converse of (*h*).

(*j*)   The sum of the squares of the sides (i.e., of the lengths of the sides) of a parallelogram is equal to the sum of the squares of its diagonals.

(*k*)   The midpoints of the sides of any plane quadrilateral are the vertices of a parallelogram.   (The theorem, in fact, is true of *any* quadrilateral.   Non-analytic proof?)

(*l*)   The point of intersection of lines joining the midpoints of opposite sides of a quadrilateral bisects the line segment joining the midpoints of the diagonals of the quadrilateral.

(*m*)   The diagonals of an isosceles trapezoid are equal.

(*n*)   A converse of (*m*).

(*o*)   The altitudes of a triangle are concurrent (i.e., intersect in a point). *Hint*: Find the equations of the three altitudes.   Solve a pair simultaneously to find their point of intersection H.   Then show that H satisfies the third equation also.

(*p*)   The perpendicular bisectors of the sides of a triangle intersect in a point O which is equidistant from its vertices (i.e., is the center of the circumscribed circle of the triangle).

(*q*)   The medians of a triangle intersect in a point M which trisects each median.

(*r*)   Point M trisects line segment OH (M, O, H as above).

2.   As an ancient black automobile drives down a straight road at 20 miles per hour on a pitch-dark night, a firefly alights, and scurries straight up the straight back of the car at a speed of 5 miles per hour.

Describe the appearance of the path of the firefly to a stationary onlooker.

3.   An airplane heads eastward at a speed of 200 miles per hour; at the same time a gale blows the plane northward at a speed of 50 miles per hour.   Describe the actual path and speed (i.e., the distance it traverses in one hour) of the airplane, as it appears to a ground observer.

4.   Answer Problem 3 if the plane is headed in the first named direction, the wind in the second:

(*a*)	eastward, southward.	(*b*)	westward, southward.
(*c*)	westward, northward.	(*d*)	northward, eastward.
(*e*)	northward, westward.	(*f*)	southward, eastward.
(*g*)	southward, westward.	(*h*)	eastward, eastward.
(*i*)	eastward, westward.		

5.   While a plane is headed eastward at 300 miles per hour, it drops a bomb. Describe the path of the bomb.

Hint: The bomb's motion, like that of the fly in our illustrative example, may be regarded as a combination of two motions.   The bomb moves *forward* at a speed of 300 miles per hour.   The bomb *drops* a distance of $16t^2$ feet in t seconds.   (This, according to laws of physics, is approximately the distance any heavy body falls in air in t seconds.)

6. Plot the graphs of the following equations:

(a) $y = x$ (b) $y = x^2$ (c) $y = x^3$

(d) $y = x^4$ (e) $y^2 = x$ (f) $y^3 = x$

(g) $y^4 = x$ (h) $y^2 = x^2$ (i) $y^2 = x^3$

(j) $y^3 = x^2$ (k) $y^2 = x^4$ (l) $\sqrt{x} + \sqrt{y} = 5$

7

INTRODUCTION TO
TRIGONOMETRY

The science of trigonometry arose from that of the relations of the angles of a right-angled triangle, to the ratios between the sides and hypotenuse of the triangle. Then, under the influence of the newly discovered mathematical science of the analysis of functions, it broadened out into the study of the simple abstract periodic functions which these ratios exemplify.

The birth of modern physics depended upon the application of the abstract idea of periodicity to a variety of concrete instances.

ALFRED NORTH WHITEHEAD: *Science and the Modern World*

7.1 MEASURING THE INACCESSIBLE

Thanks to the labors of archaeologists, mathematical historians today have at their disposal an abundance of Babylonian clay tablets and Egyptian papyrus rolls that tell a great deal about the mathematics of our early cultural ancestors. But nowhere among all of these records is there to be found the name of even one creator of mathematics. It is not until the time of the Greek civilization, which followed that of the Babylonians and the Egyptians, that history finally records the name of a mathematician.

Thales, a Greek philosopher who lived at about 600 B.C., famed as one of the "seven wise men of antiquity," was the first mathematician whose name is known to us. His reputation is secured by much more than the chronological primacy of his name, however. For to him has been attributed the deductive method of proof that became the hallmark of Greek mathematics, and which is an integral characteristic of mathematics to this very day.

A particular mathematical skill for which Thales was greatly admired in his day is one which has been called "shadow-reckoning." Once, while traveling in Egypt, Thales applied this method to finding the height of a pyramid, *without directly measuring its height.*

Several accounts exist as to exactly how he accomplished this. One of the procedures described is simplicity itself: He waited for an hour of the day when the shadow cast by his vertical staff was exactly as long as the staff. At that moment, he measured the distance from the center of the base of the pyramid to the tip of the pyramid's shadow, which length he assumed to be the same as the height of the pyramid.

But although it is easier to measure a shadow on the ground than to clamber up the side of a pyramid, this first method of Thales may rather obviously be made even more practicable. It is a nuisance to have to wait all day for just the precise moment when height and shadow are equal, and in fact it is unnecessary.

For one may suppose that at *any* time of day, whatever the ratio that exists between a staff's height and the staff's shadow, that ratio exists also between the pyramid's height and the pyramid's shadow (measured from the center of the base of the pyramid). More precisely, if S and T represent the staff's height and the length of its shadow, respectively, and P and Q represent the pyramid's height and the length of its shadow, respectively, then: $S/T = P/Q$ (see Fig. 7.1).

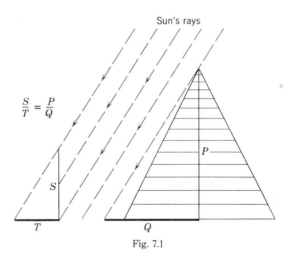

Fig. 7.1

Since S, T, and Q are easily measured, the value of P may easily be determined by solving the above equation. (Actually, this second method has been attributed to Thales also.)

Processes like these led to the theory of similar triangles. We shall review the principal statements of Euclidean geometry with respect to similar triangles as soon as we have discussed some relevant questions of angle measurement.

With respect to angle measurement and triangles, we shall assume (without proof) the following:

(i) One may associate with each angle (see Definition G3, page 144) a real number in the interval $\{0 \cdot\!\!-\!\!\cdot 180\}$, called the number of "degrees" in that angle. In this association, if the number r corresponds to the angle ABC, we write: $\angle ABC = r°$.

We translate r' (read: r minutes) as $(r/60)°$ (i.e., $r' = (r/60)°$), and r'' (read: r seconds) as $(r/60)'$.

It follows that $60' = 1°$ and $60'' = 1'$.

Note that although angles of a number of degrees outside the range $\{0 \cdot\!\!-\!\!\cdot 180\}$ are considered in other developments of mathematics, in this text, to make the correspondence between angles and numbers simpler, the number of degrees in an angle will never be a number outside of the set $\{0 \cdot\!\!-\!\!\cdot 180\}$.

An angle is said to be *acute* if its degree measure is in the interval $\{0 \cdot\!\!-\!\!\cdot 90\}$, but is not 0 or 90; *right*, if its degree measure is 90; *obtuse*, if its degree measure is in the interval $\{90 \cdot\!\!-\!\!\cdot 180\}$, but is not 90 or 180; *straight*, if its degree measure is 180.

A 180° angle is a straight line. (What is a 0° angle?)

(ii) Two angles are congruent if and only if their degree measures are equal. When we write $\angle A = \angle B$, we mean that angles A and B are congruent, i.e., that their degree measures are equal.

Further statements about angle measurement will be postponed until we need them.

Now with respect to the similarity of triangles: (see Fig. 7.2).

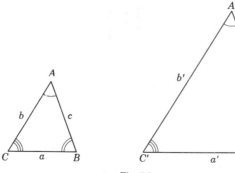

Fig. 7.2

Definition. Two triangles are said to be *similar* if they may be labeled $\triangle ABC$ and $\triangle A'B'C'$ in such a way that:

(i) $\angle A = \angle A'$, $\angle B = \angle B'$, $\angle C = \angle C'$

(ii) $\dfrac{a}{a'} = \dfrac{b}{b'} = \dfrac{c}{c'}$

(where a is the length of side BC, etc.).

Theorem. ($aa = aa$).   Two triangles are similar if two angles of one are respectively equal to two angles of the other.

In solving Thales' problem, we actually work with a *mathematical model* of the situation, consisting of two right triangles.   Assuming that the sun's rays are parallel straight lines, the angles made by these rays at the bases of both triangles will be the same.   The triangles are therefore similar ($aa = aa$), and the equation $P/Q = S/T$ may therefore be eventually justified as a consequence of the axioms of plane geometry.

The theory of similar triangles leads directly into the study known as "trigonometry."   The word "trigonometry" means literally "triangle measurement," and although the subject has now far outstripped its origins, it is the triangle measurement aspect of trigonometry that we will consider first.

Utilizing angle measurements, we shall now find it possible to introduce even another labor-saving device into Thales' problem.

Suppose, for example, that the situation was as in Fig. 7.3.

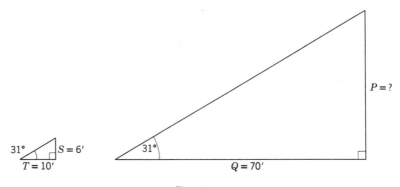

Fig. 7.3

Then $P/70 = 6/10$, or $P/70 = 0.6$, or $P = 42$ (feet).

Now suppose Thales encountered another pyramid in his travels, at a time when the sun's rays happened again to form a 31° angle with the ground (Fig. 7.4).

Then, unless he had discarded the results of his first measurements, it would be quite unnecessary for Thales to measure the length of a staff and its shadow again.   In fact, having previously computed that $S/T = 0.6$, he could now say (Fig. 7.4)

$P/Q = 0.6$,   or $P/90 = 0.6$ or $P = 54$ (feet)

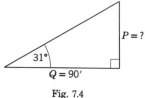

Fig. 7.4

It would thus seem to be sensible to keep a record of the ratio S/T for various angles made by the sun's rays at the base of a right triangle. More generally and more precisely:

Suppose ABC is a right triangle with right angle at C and suppose that a, b, c are the lengths of the sides opposite angles A, B, C respectively, as in Fig. 7.5.

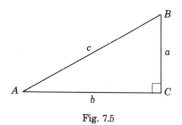

Fig. 7.5

(Unless otherwise noted, we shall always keep to this notation for right triangles.)

Now suppose we choose a value for angle A, say 31°, and after constructing a right triangle ABC with $\angle A = 31°$, we measure the lengths a, b and compute the ratio a/b. *Then for all other right triangles ABC with $\angle A = 31°$, the ratio a/b will be the same as for our original triangle;* for any right triangle ABC with $\angle A = 31°$ must be similar to our original right triangle ABC (why?), so that ratios between corresponding sides must be equal.

Associated with the angle 31°, therefore, is a unique and useful ratio, the ratio a/b as computed above. A table of the values of a/b for different angles may be prepared in advance and used, for example, to find the heights of objects inaccessible to convenient direct measurement.

But the word *associate* immediately puts us in mind of functions. In fact, the process outlined above defines a function for us, the so-called *tangent* function. There are practical situations in which ratios between sides other than a and b are useful, and these lead to other "trigonometric" functions. We now define in formal terms the following trigonometric functions:

Definition.   The degree measure (restricted) *sine, cosine, tangent,* and *cotangent* functions are defined as follows:

The domain of each of the four functions consists of all the real numbers between, but not including, 0 and 90.

The mappings for all four functions are based upon the following construction: Let p be any real number such that $0 < p < 90$.   Then there are many right triangles ABC with $\angle A = p°$, but in all of them the ratios a/c, b/c, a/b, and b/a are the same.   Choose, therefore, *any* such right triangle ABC.   The mappings are now defined (and abbreviated) as follows:

$$\sin p° = \frac{a}{c}; \quad \cos p° = \frac{b}{c}; \quad \tan p° = \frac{a}{b}; \quad \cot p° = \frac{b}{a}$$

read: sin of p degrees equals a/c, etc.

NOTES ON THE ABOVE DEFINITION:

(1)   There are other units besides degrees for the measurement of angles; to indicate that we have in mind the *degree* measure definition above, we write: $\sin p° = a/c$, etc., rather than just $\sin p = a/c$, etc.

It should be understood, however, that when we write $\sin p° = a/c$, we mean simply that the degree-sine function we have in mind assigns the real number a/c to the real number p:

$$p \rightarrow \frac{a}{c}$$

(2)   Eventually we shall enlarge the domain of these functions so as to contain (with relatively few exceptions) *all* real numbers; that is why we have applied the adjective "restricted" to the functions defined in this section; and in time we shall introduce two more trigonometric functions, called the *secant* and *cosecant*, to take care of the ratios c/a and c/b.

(3)   If we have in mind a particular acute angle of a right triangle, the side opposite that angle is often denoted "opposite," the longest side "hypotenuse" and the remaining side of the triangle "adjacent," as in Fig. 7.6.

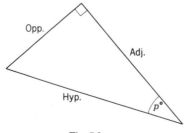

Fig. 7.6

If the angle in question is one of $p°$, then the preceding definitions amount to:

$$\sin p° = \frac{\text{opp.}}{\text{hyp.}}; \quad \cos p° = \frac{\text{adj.}}{\text{hyp.}}; \quad \tan p° = \frac{\text{opp.}}{\text{adj.}}; \quad \cot p° = \frac{\text{adj.}}{\text{opp.}}$$

where the abbreviations opp., adj., hyp. stand for the real numbers equal to the indicated lengths. (The mnemonic device "SOHCAHTOA" is useful in recalling the first three definitions: "*S*ine involves *O*pposite over *H*ypotenuse, etc.")

Tables of values for these trigonometric functions have, of course, been computed (although not, as might be imagined, by actual measurement; actually, results of the branch of mathematics known as "calculus" are used in the computation). We shall utilize trigonometric tables (see pages 496–500) in solving problems like Thales' pyramid problem, and also in other problems of indirect measurement.

As with previous tables of values, we shall find the method of linear interpolation extremely useful.

Here are several illustrative examples:

Illustrative Example I. The angle between a horizontal ray drawn from a man's eye to a flagpole, and a ray drawn from his eye to the top of the flagpole (the so-called "angle of elevation") is 73°. If the man stands 38 feet from the flagpole, how much higher than the man's eye is the top of the flagpole? What is the distance from the man's eye to the top of the flagpole?

SOLUTION. First of all, we construct a mathematical model (Fig. 7.7— E represents the man's eye, F the top of the flagpole—note that no attempt has been made to draw the figure to scale).

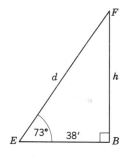

Fig. 7.7

Then we have: $\qquad\qquad \tan 73° = \dfrac{h}{38}$

or, from the tables: $3.2709 = \dfrac{h}{38}$

So that: $h = 124.2942$

Since our results cannot be more accurate than our given information, we state, as our answer: The height of the flagpole above the man's eye is approximately 124 feet.

(Actually 3.2709 is not exactly the tangent of 73°, but only the best possible four-decimal place approximation to tan 73°. We shall conform to general practice in using the symbol = often to represent only approximate, rather than exact, equality. In most cases it is clear which meaning of the equal sign is intended.)

Now, to find d: $\cos 73° = \dfrac{38}{d}$

$$.2924 = \dfrac{38}{d}$$

$$d = \dfrac{38}{.2924} = 130 \text{ ft}$$

Illustrative Example 2. Suppose that in the preceding example, $\angle E$ had been $73° \, 12'$. Then we would have approximated tan $73° \, 12'$ by linear interpolation:

$$\tan 73° \, 12' = 3.3052 + 0.2(.0350) = 3.3122$$

Similarly for cos $73° \, 12'$; but note that in the case of "co-functions" tabular differences are *negative*, since for these functions tabular values decrease as the angle increases:

$$\cos 73° \, 12' = .2896 - 0.2(.0028) = .2890$$

Illustrative Example 3. A man stands at a distance of 130 ft from a building whose height (above the man's eye) is 120 ft. At the man's eye, what is the angle of elevation of the top of the building?

SOLUTION.   (See Fig. 7.8.)

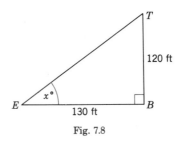

Fig. 7.8

Here we chose to work with the tangent function, since the sides *opposite* and *adjacent* to the angle in question are involved:

$$\tan \angle E = \frac{120}{130} = .9231$$

Examining the tables, we find that $\angle E$ must lie between $42° 40'$ and $42° 50'$. Once more we interpolate:

$$\angle E = 42° 40' + \left[\frac{.9231 - .9217}{.9271 - .9217}\right] (10')$$

$$= 42° 40' + \left[\frac{14}{54}\right] (10')$$

$$= 42° 40' + \left[\frac{70}{27}\right]'$$

$$= 42° 40' + 3'$$

$$= 42° 43'$$

▶ **EXERCISE 31**

1. Using a protractor and a centimeter ruler, construct a right triangle ABC in which $\angle A = 35°$ and side $AB = 5$ cms. Then measure the lengths in centimeters of sides BC and AC and compute: sin, cos, tan, and cot $35°$. Compare your results with the values given in the tables.

2. Using the procedure of Problem 1, find (and compare with tabular values) sin, cos, tan, and cot of the following number of degrees:

(a) 10   (b) 80   (c) 20   (d) 70   (e) 30
(f) 60   (g) 40   (h) 50   (i) 45

3. Induce a general law from the results of Problem 2.

4. What is the range of each of the following functions, as defined in this section: sine, cosine, tangent, cotangent? Tell whether each is one-one or many-one.

5. In each of the following problems, E represents a man's eye, F the top of a flagpole, B a point on the flagpole such that line EB is horizontal. Find, in each case, whichever of the following are not given: EB, BF, EF, $\angle E$, $\angle F$. (Recall that the sum of the degree measures of the acute angles of a right triangle is $90°$.)

(a) $\angle E = 77°$ $EB = 23'$ (b) $\angle E = 22° 10'$ $EB = 214'$
(c) $\angle E = 22° 13'$ $EB = 214'$ (d) $\angle E = 68° 15'$ $EB = 78'$
(e) $\angle E = 37° 19'$ $BF = 98'$ (f) $\angle E = 81° 11'$ $BF = 61'$
(g) $\angle E = 49° 17'$ $BF = 48'$ (h) $\angle E = 51° 16'$ $BF = 59'$
(i) $EB = 18'$ $BF = 56'$ (j) $EB = 18'$ $BF = 54'$
(k) $EB = 125'$ $BF = 30'$ (l) $EB = 100'$ $BF = 100'$

6.   A ladder 10 ft long leans against a building and makes an angle of 36° 14′ with the ground.   How high above the ground is the top of the ladder?

7.   The width of a river is indirectly measured in the following way: Point *C* is marked on one bank and point *A* is sighted directly across the river from *C*.   A distance of 100 ft is paced from *C* to a point *B* directly up the river bank.   Then point *A* is sighted from *B* and ∡ *CBA*, measured by means of a surveyor's "transit," is found to be 87° 17′.

How wide is the river?

8.   How many degrees are there in each acute angle of a "3, 4, 5" right triangle?

9.   If an inclined road rises 10 ft for every 100 ft of horizontal distance that it traverses, at what angle does the road rise?

10.   A telephone pole is supported by a wire which runs from a point 32 ft up the pole to a point 17 ft from the base of the pole.   How long is the wire, and what angles does it make with pole and ground?

11.   From the top of a cliff whose height is 212 ft, the "angle of depression" of a boat in the sea below (i.e., the angle made by a horizontal ray from the top of the cliff and a ray from the top of the cliff to the boat) is 8° 18′.

How far is the boat from the shore, and how far (as the crow flies) from the cliff top?

12.   If a building 100 ft tall casts a shadow whose length is 123 ft, what is the angle of elevation of the sun?   (*Hint:* To find the angle in question, it is better to use the cotangent rather than the tangent function. Why?)

13.   A hill stands 5000 ft from a sheer cliff.   From the top of the hill, the angles of elevation and depression of the top and foot of the cliff are 51° 12′ and 8° 11′, respectively.   How high is the hill?   How high is the cliff?

14.   From an altitude of 3000 ft directly above a town *P*, an airplane sights town *Q*, and, collinear with towns *P* and *Q*, town *R*.   The angles of depression of towns *Q* and *R* from the airplane are 70° and 40°, respectively.

How far apart are towns *Q* and *R*   (*a*) if *PQR*?   (*b*) if *QPR*?

15.   The following method has been suggested for finding the radius of the earth:

Climb to the top *T* of Mont Blanc, which is almost exactly 3 miles high. Sight the farthest point *F* on the horizon, and measure the angle which that line of sight makes with a vertical line (i.e., with a line passing through

T and the center O of the earth). Suppose that angle turns out to be equal to $87°\ 46'$.

The line TF will be tangent to the earth's surface, so that triangle OTF will be a right triangle. If r represents the radius of the earth, then $OF = r$ and $OT = r + 3$.

Draw a diagram; write an equation involving r; solve for r to find an approximate value for the radius of the earth.

7.2   TWO WELL-KNOWN TRIANGLES

The computation of trigonometric functions of angles is generally a tedious business. In the case of the angles 30°, 60°, and 45°, however, the results in question follow rather easily from the properties of two well-known right triangles.

One of them is the so-called 30-60-90 triangle; we shall arrive at this triangle in the following way:

First we construct an equilateral triangle, each of whose sides is (for a reason of convenience which will be apparent in a moment) 2 units long. Then we draw a median (i.e., a line from a vertex to the midpoint of the opposite side) as in Fig. 7.9.

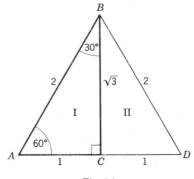

Fig. 7.9

It is clear that $\triangle\,\text{I} \cong \triangle\,\text{II}$ (why?), and therefore that $\angle\ ABC = \angle\ DBC$ and that $\angle\ ACB = \angle\ DCB$ (why?). Furthermore, since $\triangle\ ABD$ is equilateral, it must also be equiangular, so that the angles of $\triangle\ ABD$, in particular $\angle\ ABD$ and $\angle\ BAD$, must each equal 60°. Therefore $\angle\ ABC = 30°$ (why?) and also $\angle\ ACB = 90°$ (why?). We now turn our attention to $\triangle\ ABC$.

Since $\triangle\ ABC$ is a right triangle, it is easy to show, by means of the Pythagorean theorem, that the length of BC is $\sqrt{3}$ units.

Since all 30-60-90 triangles must be similar (why?) the ratios between pairs of sides in the above triangle must be the same as the corresponding ratios in *any* 30-60-90 triangle.   The following statement summarizes the situation:

In any 30-60-90 *triangle, the side opposite the* 30° *angle is half the hypotenuse, and the side opposite the* 60° *angle is half the hypotenuse times* $\sqrt{3}$.

The student will be asked in an exercise to make use of the above triangle in computing trigonometric functions of 30° and 60°.

The other well-known right triangle which we now consider is the isosceles right triangle.   Our choice for such a triangle is one in which each "leg" (or "arm") is 1 unit in length (Fig. 7.10).

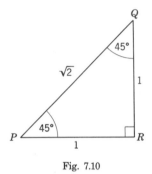

Fig. 7.10

Then again by the Pythagorean theorem: $PQ = \sqrt{2}$.

Furthermore, $\measuredangle\, P = \measuredangle\, Q$ (why?), so that $\measuredangle\, P = 45°$ and $\measuredangle\, Q = 45°$ (why?).

As in the preceding case, a general statement may be made:

In every isosceles right triangle (i.e., in every 45-45-90 triangle), the hypotenuse is $\sqrt{2}$ *times each leg.*

The student will be asked in an exercise to make use of the above triangle in computing trigonometric functions of 45°.

▶ **EXERCISE 32**

1.   Answer the "whys" in Section 7.2.

2.   Justify the statements above that $BC = \sqrt{3}$ and that $PQ = \sqrt{2}$.

3.   Using $\triangle\, ABC$ and $\triangle\, PQR$, above, find sin, cos, tan, and cot of 30°, 45°, and 60°, first exactly, and then with values correct to three decimal places.   (Use $\sqrt{2} = 1.414$, $\sqrt{3} = 1.732$.)

7.3   RAY LABELING

Imagine (see Fig. 7.11) a cc plane, and, in that cc plane, all possible rays with vertex at 0.

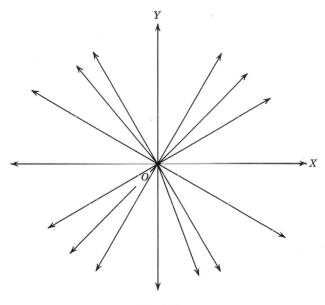

Fig. 7.11

Then just as there is a "natural" way of labeling the points of a line with all the real numbers (once we have chosen a unit length), so there is a "natural" way of labeling these rays with all the real numbers (once we have chosen a unit *angle*).

We shall treat the labeling of the rays of a plane with common vertex intuitively in this section, and somewhat more carefully in the next chapter.

The angle unit we choose to deal with at this point is that which is familiar to the student as the *degree*.

The natural labeling we have in mind may be described as follows. First of all, in Fig. 7.11, draw a circle with center 0, and let A represent the intersection of this circle with the positive X-axis (see Fig. 7.12).

Now suppose we begin a journey around this circle at A, and proceed in a counter-clockwise direction (i.e., opposite to the way the hands of a clock rotate). Since we begin on the positive X-axis, we label this ray with the real number 0. After we proceed around the circle a little way, we meet a ray which makes a 30° angle with the positive X-axis. We label *that* ray with the real number 30; and so on, until we encounter the

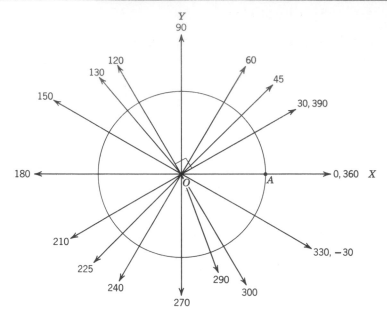

Fig. 7.12

positive Y-axis, which makes a 90° angle with the positive X-axis, and which we therefore label 90.

But we do not stop at this point. Continuing past 90, we reach a ray which makes a 30° angle with the ray labeled 90; we therefore label the new ray 120. Intuitively, one may imagine that the ray labeled 90 has reached its position by beginning at the 0 position and rotating through 90° in a counter-clockwise direction, while the ray labeled 120 may have reached its position by beginning at the 90 position and rotating 30° further in a counter-clockwise direction.

And so on; the negative X-axis makes a 90° angle with the positive Y-axis and is therefore labeled 180; and as we continue our journey around the circle (being careful, in order to avoid confusion, to advance not more than 90° at a time), the negative Y-axis acquires the label 270, and the positive X-axis *another* label, namely 360.

Here, then, is an important difference between the natural methods of ray labeling and labeling points on a scaled line: The correspondence that we have set up between all the points of a line and all the real numbers is a one-to-one correspondence. The correspondence that we are setting up between all rays of a plane with common vertex and all the real numbers is *not* one-to-one. In fact, as we shall see, each ray will have many, many real number labels.

Having reached the X-axis again, we do not pause in our circuit, but continue traveling around the circle in the same direction. Now when we reach the ray which makes a 30° angle with the 360 ray, we label that ray 360 + 30, or 390. And we continue the process, on, and on, and on.

A final effect is that a ray that is labeled r will also be labeled $r + 360$, $r + 720$, etc.

But so far we have applied only the non-negative real numbers as labels to our rays.

Negative labels for rays are introduced simply by imagining a *clockwise* circuit of our circle, beginning at A. This time when we reach a ray which makes a 30° angle with the 0 ray, we label it -30, etc.

Note that the ray already labeled 330 now acquires the additional label -30. In fact, it now becomes true that if r is a label for a ray, so is $r - 360$, $r - 720$, etc.

The labeling system is now complete: Each real number labels one of our rays; each ray has many real number labels, one of them being a number r such that $0 \leqslant r < 360$, the others consisting of all numbers of the form $r + k \cdot 360$, where k is an integer.

It is interesting to note a further analogy between the natural labelings of lines and rays. On a scaled line, *distances* between points are measured by *differences* between real number labels. On a system of rays labeled as above, *angles* between rays are measured by *differences* between real number labels. For example, the angle formed by rays labeled 120 and 30 is $(120 - 30)°$, or 90° (see Fig. 7.12).

Starting with a Cartesian coordinate system with origin O in a plane, we shall say, when we have labeled all the rays with vertex O in that plane in the natural way we have been describing, that we have a Cartesian coordinate-degree system (ccd system) in that plane.

Now we suppose that we have a ccd system in a plane, and we draw a circle of radius 2 with center O in that plane, as in Fig. 7.13.

As before, we call the point of intersection of the circle with the positive X-axis, A. Clearly, the coordinates of A are $(2, 0)$. But suppose B represents the point of intersection of this circle and the 30 ray. What are the coordinates of B?

The question is easily answered. Let the foot of a perpendicular from B to the X-axis be called B' (see Fig. 7.13). Then OBB' is a 30-60-90 triangle, with hypotenuse $OB = 2$, so that $OB' = \sqrt{3}$ and $BB' = 1$. Therefore $B = (\sqrt{3}, 1)$.

From the symmetry of Fig. 7.13, we may immediately label three other points in the figure that are points of intersection of rays with vertex O and our circle.

The concept of a ccd system will now make it possible for us to define

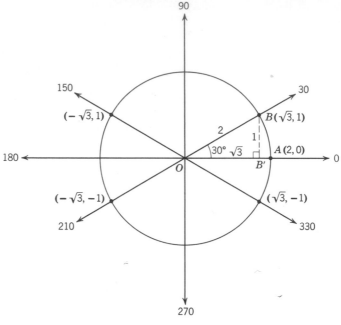

Fig. 7.13

the exceptionally important *extended* trigonometric functions. (The points of intersection we have just been discussing will play a role in our further work also.)

▶ EXERCISE 33

1. Draw (to scale) a ccd system, drawing and labeling only those rays whose labels are non-negative integer multiples of 30 and 45 that are less than 360. On that ccd system draw a circle with center O and radius 2. Label (with its coordinates) the point of intersection of each of the rays with the circle.

2. The same as Problem 1 above, but draw a "unit" circle, i.e., a circle of radius 1.

3. Excluding the point O, which rays of a ccd system fall into QI? QII? QIII? QIV? (See Problem 4 of Exercise 24.)

4. Using a protractor, draw a ccd system, and in that system draw and label the rays with the following labels: 20, 140, 195, 320, −20, −140, −195, −320, 400, −400, 720, −720, 1080, −1080.

5. If r is a real number, what fact is always true about rays labeled r and $−r$ in a ccd system? about rays labeled $90 + r$ and $90 − r$? about rays labeled r and $180 + r$? about rays labeled r and $360 + r$?

6. In each of the following cases, draw the rays whose labels in a ccd system are given, and find the number of degrees in the angle formed by the given rays.

Hint: The difference between ray labels measures the angle made by two rays in a ccd system, but by (*i*), page 189, that difference must be a number in the interval {0 ⸱—⸱ 180}. If the difference between given labels does not fall in that range, one may alter the labels so that they do. For example, rays labeled 40 and 240 may alternatively be labeled 400 and 240, respectively, and therefore they make an angle of (400 − 240)° or 160° with each other.

(a)	70, 0	(b)	120, 180	(c)	135, 180
(d)	150, 180	(e)	180, 180	(f)	210, 180
(g)	225, 180	(h)	240, 180	(i)	270, 180
(j)	270, 0	(k)	300, 0	(l)	315, 0
(m)	330, 0	(n)	360, 0	(o)	−30, 0
(p)	−45, 0	(q)	−60, 0	(r)	−90, 0
(s)	500, 0	(t)	−500, 0	(u)	700, 0
(v)	−700, 0	(w)	30, 70	(x)	30, 100
(y)	30, 200	(z)	30, 300		

7. Suppose OA is the ray labeled 30 in a ccd system.

(a) What number, subtracted from each original label, would produce a new ccd system in which ray OA is labeled 0?

(b) The rays whose labels are 0, ?, ?, ? constitute the $+X$, ?, ?, ? axes respectively of our original ccd system. Label each of these rays in the new ccd system produced in part (a) above. Illustrate by means of a diagram.

(c) The rays whose labels in the new ccd system are 0, ?, ?, ? constitute the $+X$, ?, ?, ? axes respectively of the new ccd system. What were the labels for each of these rays in the old system? Illustrate by means of a diagram.

8. Suppose that in a ccd system rays OA and OB are labeled a and b, respectively.

(a) How may we arrive at a ccd system in which ray OA is labeled 0?

(b) In the new ccd system of part (a) above, what is a label for ray OB?

9. Suppose that in a ccd system, ray OA with label a makes an acute angle of degree measure a' with either the $+X$- or the $-X$-axis. Then $a'°$ is called the *reference angle* for a. (Use will be made of this concept in Section 8.2.)

In each of the following cases draw a diagram and find and indicate the reference angle for the given number of degrees.

(a)	120	(b)	135	(c)	150	(d)	170
(e)	210	(f)	225	(g)	240	(h)	280
(i)	300	(j)	315	(k)	330	(l)	350
(m)	36,030	(n)	700	(o)	−700	(p)	400

7.4 THE EXTENDED SINE, COSINE, TANGENT, AND COTANGENT FUNCTIONS

We have seen that the practical problem of determining the distance between two points, when that distance is not conveniently accessible to direct measurement, often leads to a mathematical model involving a right triangle. The mathematical formulation of this problem requires us to compute the length of one side of a right triangle when certain information about that triangle is given. In solving this mathematical problem, we found it convenient to define certain "trigonometric" functions and to utilize tables of values of these functions.

At this point we draw attention to the fact that our manner of definition of the mappings of these trigonometric functions forced upon us, in each case, a domain which consisted *only* of the real numbers between (but excluding) 0 and 90.

In this section we shall see that it is possible to "extend" the domains of the sine, cosine, tangent, and cotangent functions in a natural way, so that in each case the new domain (with minor exceptions) includes *all* the real numbers.

The trigonometric functions with restricted domain which we defined originally find their use mainly in the computation of parts of right triangles, and in this way they play an important role in engineering, surveying, navigation, and other fields. Of far greater scientific importance, however, are the extended trigonometric functions we are about to study. Their value to science stems from a remarkable property (called "periodicity") that they display. We shall discuss the property of periodicity and the reasons for its importance in later sections.

The motivation for the definitions we shall make for the extended trigonometric functions lies in the following theorem:

Theorem. Suppose we are given a real number p such that $0 < p < 90$, and a ccd system with origin O. (See Fig. 7.14).

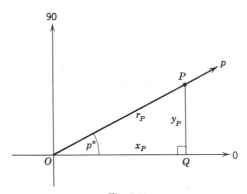

Fig. 7.14

Suppose further that OP is the ray with label p in the given system, and that $r_P = d(O, P)$.

Then:

$$\sin p = \frac{y_P}{r_P}$$

$$\cos p = \frac{x_P}{r_P}$$

$$\tan p = \frac{y_P}{x_P}$$

$$\cot p = \frac{x_P}{y_P}$$

We shall not prove this theorem rigorously, but merely indicate how the proof goes:

A perpendicular from P to the X-axis must intersect the X-axis at a point Q on the positive side of the X-axis. The triangle OPQ is a right triangle, and $\angle POQ = p°$. Furthermore, $d(O, Q) = x_P$, $d(P, Q) = y_P$, and by definition, $d(O, P) = r_P$.

Now, by our original definitions of the trigonometric functions, the conclusion of the theorem follows.

The preceding theorem suggests the following definitions of the *extended* sine, cosine, tangent, and cotangent functions:

Definition of Extended (Degree-System) Trigonometric Functions

(In each of the following definitions, p represents any real number in the domain of the given function, OP the ray labeled p in a ccd system and $r_P = d(O, P)$.)

Sine function: Domain: All real numbers.

Mapping: $p \to \dfrac{y_P}{r_P}$. $\left(\text{Usually written } \sin p° = \dfrac{y_P}{r_P}\right)$

Cosine function: Domain: All real numbers.

Mapping: $p \to \dfrac{x_P}{r_P}$. $\left(\text{Usually written } \cos p° = \dfrac{x_P}{r_P}\right)$

Tangent function: Domain: All real numbers, except those equal to $k \cdot 90$, where k is any odd integer.

Mapping: $p \to \dfrac{y_P}{x_P}$. $\left(\text{Usually written } \tan p° = \dfrac{y_P}{x_P}\right)$

Cotangent function: Domain: All real numbers, except those equal to $k \cdot 90$, where k is any even integer.

Mapping: $p \to \dfrac{x_P}{y_P}$. $\left(\text{Usually written } \cot p° = \dfrac{x_P}{y_P}\right)$

(These definitions may be proved to be "well-defined," in the sense that they are independent of the particular ccd system we chose to work with, and the particular point P we choose to determine ray OP; the proof of this statement is omitted here.)

From Fig. 7.13 we may now compute the values of a number of trigonometric functions.

For example, suppose we wish to find sin 0°.

Then we locate the ray labeled 0 in that figure, and on that ray, any point $P \neq O$. Since $(2, 0)$ is a convenient point $\neq O$ on that ray, we let $P = (2, 0)$.

Then in this case: $x_P = 2, y_P = 0, r_P = 2$.

Therefore $\sin 0° = \dfrac{y_P}{r_P} = \dfrac{0}{2} = 0$.

At the same time we may easily compute:

$$\cos 0° = \frac{x_P}{r_P} = \frac{2}{2} = 1, \text{ and } \tan 0° = \frac{y_P}{x_P} = \frac{0}{2} = 0$$

Cot 0° does not exist, since 0 is not in the domain of the cotangent function (0 is an even multiple of 90). (If we were to overlook this fact, and attempt to compute cot 0° by the formula $\dfrac{x_P}{y_P}$, what difficulty would arise?)

Or, suppose we wish to compute trigonometric functions of 150°. Again referring to Fig. 7.13, we locate the ray labeled 150, and on that ray the convenient point: $P = (-\sqrt{3}, 1)$. Here, then, $x_P = -\sqrt{3}$, $y_P = 1, r_P = 2$, so that:

$$\sin 150° = \frac{1}{2}, \cos 150° = -\frac{\sqrt{3}}{2}, \tan 150° = -\frac{1}{\sqrt{3}}, \cot 150° = -\sqrt{3}$$

If a decimal approximation to tan 150° is desired, we may write:

$$\tan 150° = -\frac{1}{\sqrt{3}} = -\frac{1}{\sqrt{3}} \cdot \frac{\sqrt{3}}{\sqrt{3}} = -\frac{\sqrt{3}}{3} = -\frac{1.732}{3} = -0.577$$

It is to be noted that where our restricted and extended definitions overlap, i.e., for angles between (but not including) 0° and 90°, they agree with each other. For example, whether we compute sin 30° by the restricted or the extended definition, the result in either case will be $\frac{1}{2}$.

From now on, unless otherwise noted, when we speak of a sine, cosine, tangent, or cotangent function, it is the *extended* definition of the function that we shall have in mind.

▶ **EXERCISE 34**

1. Fill in the blanks in the following table with exact values:

	0°	30°	45°	60°	90°	120°	135°	150°	180°	210°	225°	240°	270°	300°	330°	360°
sin																
cos																
tan																
cot																

2. Make a table as in Problem 1 above, but fill in with decimal values, correct to three decimal places. (Use $\sqrt{2} = 1.414$, $\sqrt{3} = 1.732$.)

3. Find:

(a) sin 390°. (*Hint:* 390 and 390 − 360, or 30, label the same ray; therefore sin 390° = sin 30° = ?)

(b) sin (−900°). (*Hint:* −900 and −900 + 3·360, or 180, label the same ray; therefore sin (−900°) = sin 180° = ?)

(c) sin 405°   (d) sin 420°   (e) sin 450°
(f) sin 540°   (g) sin 630°   (h) sin 720°
(i) sin (−30°)   (j) sin (−45°)   (k) sin (−90°)
(l) sin (−180°)   (m) sin (−270°)   (n) sin (−360°)
(o) cos 36000°   (p) tan 18060°   (q) cos 1500°
(r) tan (−1500°)   (s) cos (−30°)   (t) cos (−45°)

4. Draw the graph of the function sin x over the interval $0 \leqslant x \leqslant 360$ (i.e., over the interval {0 •—• 360}). (*Hint:* Use the results of Problem 2 above, and use unequal scales on X- and Y-axes to make up for the disparity in size between values in the domain and values in the range; for example, one inch might be used to represent 1 on the Y-axis, 360 on the X.

5. Draw the graphs of the following functions over the interval $0 \leqslant x \leqslant 360$:

            (a) cos x   (b) tan x   (c) cot x

6. Use the results of Problems 2 and 4 above to draw the graph of the function sin x over the interval $-360 \leqslant x \leqslant 720$.

7. What is the range of each of the following extended functions? Tell whether each is one-one or many-one.

        (a) sine   (b) cosine   (c) tangent   (d) cotangent

7.5 INCLINATION AND SLOPE: $m = \tan \theta$

As a corollary to our definition of the extended tangent function, we derive an interesting alternative characterization of the slope of a line (see page 169).

We approach the situation by studying a special case, in somewhat intuitive fashion.

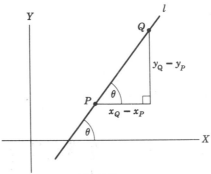

Fig. 7.15

Suppose that P and Q are points on a nonvertical line l, situated as in Fig. 7.15. Suppose further that the slope of line l is m. Then we know, from our formula for slope (see page 169), that:

$$(1) \qquad m = \frac{y_Q - y_P}{x_Q - x_P}$$

The quantities $y_Q - y_P$ and $x_Q - x_P$ which occur in the formula for m have interpretations in Fig. 7.15; for since P is x_P units to the right of the Y-axis, and Q is x_Q units to the right of the Y-axis, a line segment beginning at P and extending as far to the right as Q must have length $x_Q - x_P$. Similarly, a line segment beginning at Q (whose height above the X-axis is y_Q) and descending to the level of P (whose height above the Y-axis is y_P) must have length $y_Q - y_P$.

Now consider the angles we have labeled θ in Fig. 7.15. (Why are they equal?) From the right triangle in which θ is an acute angle we have:

$$(2) \qquad \tan \theta = \frac{y_Q - y_P}{x_Q - x_P}$$

and from Eqs. (1) and (2) there follows:

$$m = \tan \theta$$

The angle θ is known as the *inclination* of line l. Knowing the inclination of a line, the formula $m = \tan \theta$ enables us to find its slope. The converse is true also; but before we go further, it will be necessary for us to define "inclination" somewhat more precisely and generally, and to establish that the formula $m = \tan \theta$ is true more generally than our figure or derivation indicates.

We proceed, then, to a more general and a more precise treatment.

Definition. Suppose a nonhorizontal line l in a ccd system intersects the X-axis in a point P (Fig. 7.16).

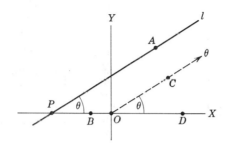

Fig. 7.16

Then it may be proved (although we do not do so here) that the points of l with non-negative ordinates form a ray PA, and the points on the X-axis with abscissas $\geq x_P$ form a ray PB.

Suppose now that $\angle APB = \theta^\circ$. Then $0^\circ < \theta^\circ < 180^\circ$ (see page 189), and we define θ° (or its equivalent in any other unit of measure) to be the *inclination* of l.

If l is a *horizontal* line in a cc plane, we simply define its inclination to be 0°.

It follows (why?) that we may think of the inclination of a nonhorizontal line as the angle between 0° and 180° made by the "upper" part of the line and the "right-hand side" of *any* horizontal line.

The main theorem concerning the inclination of a line follows:

Theorem. Suppose that l is a line in a ccd system with slope m and inclination θ. Then $m = \tan \theta$.

PROOF: *Case 1.* *l is horizontal.* Then $\theta = 0^\circ$ and $m = 0$ (see page 170), so that $m = \tan \theta$, Q.E.D.

Case 2. *l is nonhorizontal.* In the given ccd system locate the ray OC with label θ (see Fig. 7.16).

Then if D is any point on the positive side of the X-axis, $\angle COD = \theta^\circ$ (why?) so that line OC is parallel to line l (why?)

Now the slope of line OC is

$$\frac{y_C - y_O}{x_C - x_O} = \frac{y_C}{x_C}$$

But since $l \parallel$ line OC, the slope of l is equal to the slope of line OC (see Section 6.11).

Therefore $m = y_C/x_C$. And by the definition of the tangent function, $\tan \theta = \dfrac{y_C}{x_C}$.

Therefore $m = \tan \theta$, Q.E.D.

▶ **EXERCISE 35**

1.   Using a straightedge and protractor, draw the lines that pass through the following points and have the indicated inclinations; also, find the slope and write the equation of each line.

(a) $(1, 2), 45°$ (b) $(3, 4), 135°$
(c) $(-1, 2), 0°$ (d) $(2, -1), 90°$
(e) $(-5, 7), 30°$ (f) $(7, -5), 60°$
(g) $(4, 2), 120°$ (h) $(2, 4), 150°$

2.   Draw and find the inclination of each of these lines:

(a) $x + y = 5$ (b) $x - y = 5$
(c) $y = 7$ (d) $x = 7$
(e) $2x + 5y = 10$ (f) $2x - 5y = 10$
(g) $5x + 2y = 10$ (h) $5x - 2y = 10$

7.6 PERIODIC FUNCTIONS

The graph of the function $\sin x$, in the interval $\{0 \mathbin{\cdot\!\!-\!\!\cdot} 360\}$ is sketched in Fig. 7.17.

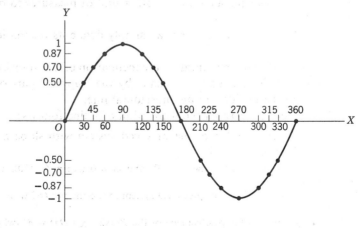

Fig. 7.17

The complete graph of the sine function is related to this **partial graph** in the following way:

Suppose we were to move 30 units to the right of the 360 mark on the
X-axis. Then, clearly, the height reached by the graph of sin x at this
point, that is, at the point $x = 390$, is the same as the height reached by
the same graph at $x = 30$; for sin 390° = sin 30°. In fact, it is true for
any real number r, that r and $r + 360$ and $r - 360$ all determine the same
ray on a ccd system, and therefore that sin r = sin $(r + 360)$
= sin $(r - 360)$.

Thus, the pattern of y-values exhibited by the graph of sin x between
$x = 0$ and $x = 360$ will be exactly repeated between $x = 360$ and $x = 720$,
and also between $x = -360$ and $x = 0$ (see Fig. 7.18).

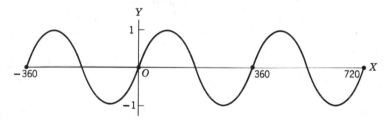

Fig. 7.18

The same process of reasoning may be repeated again and again; the
whole graph of sin x is an endless repetition of that part of the graph
which appears over *any* interval of length 360 on the X-axis. Usually
we think, however, of the sine graph as being generated by a repetition
of the fundamental pattern of Fig. 7.17.

A number of important properties of the sine function are evident from
its graph, and may be rigorously proved:

(1) The maximum value achieved by the function sin x is 1, and this
value is achieved only when $x = 90 + k \cdot 360$, where k is any integer.

(2) The minimum value achieved by the function sin x is -1, and this
value is achieved only when $x = 270 + k \cdot 360$, where k is any integer.

(3) The value 0 is achieved by the function sin x only when $x = k \cdot 180$,
where k is any integer.

(4) The range of the sine function is the interval of real numbers
$\{-1 \cdots 1\}$. Therefore, for any real number x, it is always true that
$-1 \leqslant \sin x \leqslant 1$.

(5) If the interval $\{0 \cdots 360\}$ is divided into quarters, then the graph
of sin x may be described as follows: In the first quarter the graph rises
in a smooth curve from the axis to its maximum value; in the second
quarter it falls from its maximum point back to the axis; in the third
quarter it falls from the axis to its minimum point; in the last quarter it

rises from its minimum point to the axis; and these four sections of the curve are all congruent.

If "quarter points" continue to be marked everywhere on the X-axis, that is if we consider the values $x = k \cdot 90$, where k is any integer, then the successive y-values assumed at these x-values run as follows: ("max" and "min" are abbreviations for "maximum" and "minimum" respectively):

$$0, \text{max}, 0, \text{min}, 0, \text{max}, 0, \text{min}, \text{etc.}$$

But the most important property of the sine function which is evidenced by its graph is that which is known as "periodicity."

By this time we have all but discussed the property of periodicity, short of defining it formally. Roughly speaking, "periodicity" has to do with phenomena which occur over and over again, at equally spaced intervals. The moon, for example, waxes and wanes in just this way. The waves of the sea rise up and down repeatedly. A pendulum swings back and forth continually. Business has its periodic ups and downs, and the seasons come and go in predictable pattern.

But until we encounter the trigonometric functions in our study of mathematics, there is no function that displays this property of periodicity, and we are therefore severely limited in describing periodic phenomena mathematically. When we come to consider trigonometric functions, however, even in their definitions we observe that they repeat the same functional values over and over again, at equally spaced intervals; and in the graphs of the trigonometric functions the property of periodicity is even more vividly evident.

Now, before we continue our discussion, we shall frame a precise definition of periodicity.

Let us consider the sine function. It has the property that if 360 is added to or subtracted from any real number, the sine of that number remains unchanged. That is, if x is any real number:

$$\sin (x - 360) = \sin x = \sin (x + 360)$$

But 360 is not the only number that will do this trick. For example, if x is any real number:

$$\sin (x - 720) = \sin x = \sin (x + 720)$$

We are led to make the following definition:

Definition. A function f with real domain is said to be *periodic* with *periodic number k* if the following is true:

  (i) k is a positive real number.
  (ii) Whenever x is in the domain of f, then so are $x - k$ and $x + k$.
  (iii) $f(x) = f(x + k)$.

In the case of the sine function, the periodic number 360 seems to play a special role: it seems to be the *smallest* of the periodic numbers of the sine function. We are led, thus, to make this definition:

Definition. If p is the smallest of the periodic numbers of a function f, then p is called the *period* of the function f.

In certain applications it is also found convenient to include constant functions, with domain all real numbers, among the periodic functions and to define the period of such a constant function to be 0.

Now we shall prove that 360 really is the period of the degree-sine function.

Theorem. The period of the (degree) sine function is 360.

PROOF: It follows directly from the definition of the sine function, and from the fact that if x is any real number, then x and $x + 360$ label the same ray in a ccd system, that 360 is a periodic number for the sine function.

What remains to be proved, then, is that 360 is the *smallest* of the periodic numbers of the sine function. We shall prove that this is so by demonstrating that the assumption that there is a smaller one leads to a contradiction.

Suppose k is a periodic number of the sine function which is less than 360. Then $0 < k < 360$.

By the definition of a periodic number, $\sin (0 + k) = \sin 0$; i.e., $\sin k = 0$. But there is only one real number k such that $0 < k < 360$ and $\sin k = 0$: $k = 180$.

Again by the definition of a periodic number, $\sin (90 + k) = \sin 90$. But since $k = 180$, we have $\sin 270 = \sin 90$, or $-1 = 1$. This contradiction proves the theorem.

In many practical applications, it is desirable to have a function similar to $\sin x$, whose maximum and minimum values are, however, not necessarily 1 and -1 respectively, and whose period is not necessarily 360.

Functions whose mappings are given by a formula $a \sin bx$, where a and b are nonzero real numbers, afford the desired flexibility with respect to extreme values and period. We may, and shall, take the domain of such a function to be the set of all real numbers, unless otherwise noted.

Illustrative Example. Plot the graph of the function $3 \sin 2x$ over the interval $\{0 \longrightarrow 360\}$.

SOLUTION. We construct a table of values:

x (degrees)	0	45	90	135	180	225	270	315	360
3 sin 2x	0	3	0	-3	0	3	0	-3	0

and plot the graph in Fig. 7.19.

Note on the computation of the table of values above:

When $x = 0°$, $3 \sin 2x = 3 \sin (2 \cdot 0)° = 3 \sin 0° = 3 \cdot 0 = 0$;
When $x = 135°$, $3 \sin 2x = 3 \sin (2 \cdot 135)° = 3 \sin 270° = 3 \cdot (-1)$
$= -3$; etc.

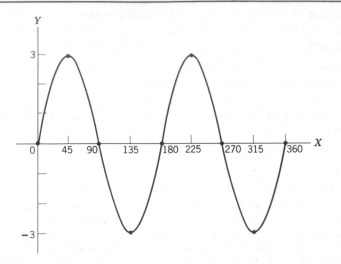

Fig. 7.19

In this example, the period of the function seems to be 180; that is to say, the graph of the function 3 sin 2x seems to repeat its fundamental pattern every 180°. This is reasonable, for when x "runs through" the values 0 · · · 180, 2x runs through the values 0 · · · 360, and sin 2x therefore through one "cycle."

(A rigorous proof of the fact that the function 3 sin 2x has a period of 180 is left as an optional exercise.)

The maximum value assumed by a function of the form $a \sin bx$, where a and b are real numbers, is called the *amplitude* of this function.

In the case of the function 3 sin 2x, the amplitude, or maximum value is 3. For when $x = 45°$, $3 \sin 2x = 3 \sin 90° = 3·1 = 3$, so that 3 is a value of the function 3 sin 2x; furthermore, for any value of x, $\sin 2x \leqslant 1$, so that $3 \sin 2x \leqslant 3$, i.e., 3 sin 2x never assumes a value greater than 3. Thus 3 actually is the amplitude of the function 3 sin 2x.

▶ **EXERCISE 36**

1. Plot the graph of each of the following functions over the interval {0 ⌐—⌐ 360}. In each case, tell what the period and amplitude of the function are.

(a) $2 \sin 3x$	(b) $\sin 2x$	(c) $2 \sin 2x$
(d) $\sin 3x$	(e) $2 \sin 3x$	(f) $3 \sin 4x$
(g) $5 \sin \dfrac{x}{2}$	(h) $-2 \sin 3x$	(i) $2 \sin (-3x)$
(j) $-2 \sin (-3x)$		

2.   From their graphs (see Problem 5, Exercise 34), what would seem to be the periods of the functions $\cos x$, $\tan x$, and $\cot x$?

In each case, prove that your answer is correct.

3.   Prove that the period of the function $g(x) = 3 \sin 2x$ is 180. *Hint:* Since the domain of $g(x)$ consists of all real numbers, all that need be shown is: (i) that if x is any real number, then $g(x + 180) = g(x)$, and (ii) that 180 is the *smallest* periodic number of the function $g(x)$.

7.7   APPLICATIONS OF THE SINE FUNCTION

It is clear that since trigonometric functions have values that occur over and over again, these functions may be used to describe, at least roughly, natural phenomena that occur over and over again.

But it turns out that in many cases, the description of periodic phenomena by means of trigonometric functions is actually not rough, but quite precise; and it is this fact that explains the great importance we attach to the periodic property of trigonometric functions.

By way of illustration, we consider the phenomenon of musical sound.

In general, a sound owes its existence to the fact that something, the plucked string of a banjo, for example, or the wing of a zooming fly, has set a surrounding mass of air into *vibration*. When the pulsating air reaches an auditor, his eardrum is set into vibration also; and if that vibration falls within a certain range (not too fast, and not too slow) then it is transmitted to the brain as the sensation of sound.

A vibrating string and the eardrum which it excites to vibration both follow similar patterns: They move from a normal position to an extreme in one direction, back to normal, from there to an extreme in an opposite direction, and finally back to normal—after which the "cycle" is repeated over and over again.

But this is very much like the pattern of ordinates of the sine function's graph: 0, max, 0, min, etc.   It would seem, then, that the sine function describes the behavior of a vibrating body at least approximately.   The fact of the matter is that the description happens to be quite exact.

Suppose, for example, that we set the end of a tuning fork to vibrating vertically and that we plot the position of one moving endpoint on the fork, above and below a normal position at times x beginning with $x = 0$.   Then it is a consequence of the laws of physics that the resulting graph is *exactly* the graph of $a \sin bx$ (for some choice of real numbers a and b and neglecting the weakening of the vibration with the passage of time).

All musical tones have properties known as loudness, pitch, and quality.

The first two are well-known; the last is the property that enables us to distinguish between two notes of the same pitch and loudness, played on different instruments.

A tuning fork, when struck, emits what is known as a "pure tone." The loudness of the tone is related to the force with which it is struck, and the force determines the maximum distance that the vibrating end of the fork moves from its original position. As a consequence, the amplitude of the graph generated by the tuning fork is related to the loudness of the sound produced by the tuning fork: The louder the sound, the greater the amplitude of the graph.

The pitch of the tone produced by a tuning fork is related to the rapidity of its regular vibrations: The faster the vibration, the higher the pitch. But the faster the vibration, the shorter the time interval necessary for the completion of one cycle of vibration—hence the smaller the *period* of the graph generated by the tuning fork.

Now all sounds are simply combinations of pure tones. Along with every pure tone (called a "fundamental" or first "partial") musical instruments produce "overtones" (also called second, etc., "partials" or "harmonics"), which are tones with periods which are $\frac{1}{2}$ the period, $\frac{1}{3}$ the period, $\frac{1}{4}$ the period, etc., of the fundamental. Different instruments are constructed so as to emphasize certain overtones and dampen others. It is the fundamental tone that determines the pitch of the note we hear; it is the arrangement of overtones that gives a note played on a particular instrument its characteristic quality.

In Fig. 7.20, we see a graph of a violin tone, together with the graphs of four pure tones whose combination produces a close approximation to the illustrated violin tone.

With the coordinate axes appropriately scaled, the functions whose graphs appear in Fig. 7.20 are:

First partial: $f_1(x) = 10 \sin x.$
Second partial: $f_2(x) = 5 \sin 2x.$
Third partial: $f_3(x) = 2 \sin 3x.$
Fourth partial: $f_4(x) = 2 \sin 5x.$
Composite tone (approximately): $f(x) = f_1(x) + f_2(x) + f_3(x) + f_4(x).$

We shall now consider the problem of drawing the graph of a function which, like $f(x)$ above, is the sum of functions of the form $a \sin bx$.

But first, we shall present a short-cut method for drawing the graph of a function of the form $a \sin bx$, where a and b are positive real numbers.

The method is contained in statement (5) below; statements (1)–(5) below are consequences of (1)–(5) on page 211.

Assuming a and b to be positive real numbers, then:

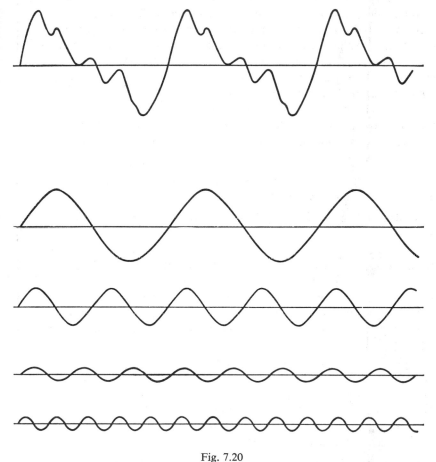

Fig. 7.20

(From D. Blackwood and W. Kelly, *General Physics—A Textbook for Colleges*, 2nd Ed., John Wiley and Sons, N.Y.)

(1) The maximum value assumed by the function $a \sin bx$ is a, and this value is achieved only when $bx = 90 + k \cdot 360$, i.e., when $x = 90/b + k \cdot (360/b)$, where k is any integer.

(2) The minimum value achieved by the function $a \sin bx$ is $-a$, and this value is achieved only when $x = 270/b + k \cdot (360/b)$, where k is any integer.

(3) The value 0 is achieved by the function $a \sin bx$ only when $x = k \cdot (180/b)$, where k is any integer.

(4) The range of the function $a \sin bx$ is the interval of real numbers $\{-a \cdot\!\!-\!\!\cdot a\}$.

(5)   If the interval $\{0 \,\cdot\!\!-\!\!\cdot\, (360/b)\}$ is divided into quarters, then the graph of the function $a \sin bx$ may be described as follows:

In the first quarter the graph rises in a smooth curve from the axis to its maximum value; in the second quarter it falls from its maximum point back to the axis; in the third quarter it falls from the axis to its minimum point; in the last quarter it rises from its minimum point to the axis; and these four sections of the curve are all congruent.

If "quarter points" continue to be marked everywhere on the X-axis, that is if we consider the values $x = k \cdot (90/b)$, where k is any integer, then the successive y-values assumed at these x-values run as follows:

$$0, \text{ max}, 0, \text{ min}, 0, \text{ max}, 0, \text{ min}, \text{ etc.}$$

Furthermore, as may be induced from Problem 1, Exercise 36, $a \sin bx$ has amplitude a and period $360/b$.

Illustrative Example I.   Sketch one period of the graph of the function $3 \sin 2x$.

SOLUTION.   In this case $a = 3$, $b = 2$, so that the amplitude of the required graph is 3 and the period is 360/2, or 180.   We divide the interval $\{0 \,\cdot\!\!-\!\!\cdot\, 180\}$ into quarters by the quarter points, 0, 45, etc., and proceed as in (5) above.   The graph is part of that drawn in Fig. 7.19.

Now, we return to the problem of drawing the graph of a sum of functions of the form $a \sin bx$.   A convenient way of accomplishing this is as follows:

First, draw the graphs of each of the functions $a \sin bx$ on the same set of axes; then, at convenient points along the X-axis, add the ordinates of the "component" graphs geometrically to form ordinates of the graph of $f(x)$, and thus locate points on the graph of $f(x)$.   A curve drawn through the points located on the graph of $f(x)$ will, of course, be the graph we seek.

The method is illustrated below:

Illustrative Example 2.   Sketch the graph of $f(x) = 3 \sin 2x + \sin x$.

SOLUTION.   We first sketch the graphs of $3 \sin 2x$ and $\sin x$ on the same set of axes, over the interval $\{0 \,\cdot\!\!-\!\!\cdot\, 360\}$ (why that interval?).

Then we add ordinates (taking *sign* into account) as shown in Fig. 7.21. One period of the graph of $f(x)$ is illustrated.

We note finally that similar combinations of sine functions give precise descriptions and are of the greatest importance in the following cases also:

(1)   *Alternating electric current.*   The electric current we are accustomed to using reverses its direction 120 times a second in the wires through which it passes.   It describes, during each second, 60 cycles of the following type: In each 1/60 of a second it begins at zero strength, builds up to a maximum strength in one direction, falls to zero, builds up to a maximum in the opposite direction, and falls back to zero strength again.

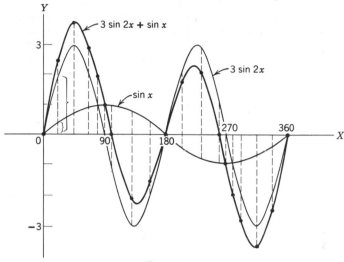

Fig. 7.21

(2) *Light.* The various colors that we recognize are described by "electromagnetic" waves of varying *periods.*

(3) *Radio waves.* Our radios are calibrated to different *frequencies*, i.e., to different numbers of vibrations per second of radio waves. These frequencies are of course related to the *periods* of the waves: the larger the frequency, the smaller the period.

▶ **EXERCISE 37**

1. Draw one period of the graph of each of the following functions:

(*a*) $\sin x + \sin 2x$ (*b*) $2 \sin 2x + \sin x$
(*c*) $2 \sin x + \sin 3x$ (*d*) $\sin 2x + \sin 3x$
(*e*) $2 \sin 2x + \sin 3x$ (*f*) $3 \sin 2x + 2 \sin 3x$
(*g*) $4 \sin x - \sin 4x$ (*h*) $\sin x + \sin 2x + \sin 3x$

2. In Problem 1 above, discuss the relative loudness and pitch of the component and composite tones described by the functions in each case.

3. The following news item appeared in the *Springfield Republican* on September 18, 1955:

SOUND FIGHTS SOUND AND CREATES SILENCE

NEW YORK.—*Chemical Engineering* magazine reports that the newest concept in the war against noise is fighting sound with sound. A machine has been developed that determines the frequency and character of an existing sound wave, then sends out its own sound of the same frequency but opposite phase. Interference results and the waves cancel each other, giving a localized cone of silence.

Write down two functions representing pure tones that "cancel each other" when combined. Draw their graphs and show how the addition of ordinates leads to a graph representing complete silence.

P ART II ▶

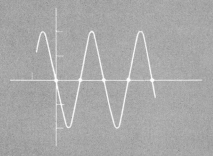

ANALYTIC
GEOMETRY
AND
TRIGONOMETRY

8

TRIGONOMETRY
CONTINUED

8.1 THE SECANT AND COSECANT FUNCTIONS

To round out the set of functions defined in Section 7.4, we introduce two new functions. The following is to be appended to the definitions of page 205:

Secant function: Domain: All real numbers except those equal to $k \cdot 90$, where k is any odd integer.

Mapping: $p \,\rangle\, \dfrac{r_P}{x_P}$ $\left(\text{Usually written: } \sec p° - \dfrac{r_P}{x_P}. \right)$

Cosecant function: Domain: All real numbers except those equal to $k \cdot 90$, where k is any even integer.

Mapping: $p \to \dfrac{r_P}{y_P}.$ $\left(\text{Usually written: } \csc p° = \dfrac{r_P}{y_P}. \right)$

From now on, unless otherwise noted, when we use the term "trigonometric function" we shall mean one of the six functions: sine, cosine, tangent, cotangent, secant, cosecant.

8.2 REFERENCE ANGLES

In this section we shall develop a short-cut method for finding trigonometric functions of a number of degrees not an integer multiple of 90.

For example, suppose we seek $\sin 150°$, $\cos 150°$, etc. The definition of these functions leads us to locate a ray labeled 150 on a ccd system, and on that ray to determine a point $P \neq O$. (See Fig. 8.1).

Suppose we choose a point P on the 150-ray such that $d(O, P) = 2$,

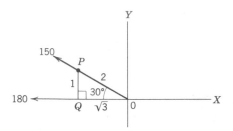

Fig. 8.1

and suppose we let Q be the foot of a perpendicular from P to the X-axis. Then since ray OQ is labeled 180 and ray OP is labeled 150, it follows that $\angle\, QOP = (180 - 150)° = 30°$.

Thus triangle OPQ is a 30–60–90 triangle, and therefore $d(P, Q) = 1$ and $d(O, Q) = \sqrt{3}$.

It follows that $x_P = -\sqrt{3}, y_P = 1$.

Now, from the definition of the trigonometric functions:

$$\sin 150° = \frac{y_P}{r_P} = \frac{1}{2};\ \cos 150° = \frac{x_P}{r_P} = -\frac{\sqrt{3}}{2};\ \text{etc.}$$

And utilizing right triangle OPQ:

$$\sin 30° = \frac{1}{2};\ \cos 30° = \frac{\sqrt{3}}{2};\ \text{etc.}$$

Corresponding trigonometric functions of 150° and 30° seem to differ, if at all, only in sign. This idea is made more precise in the theorem which follows.

Theorem. Let p be any real number, not an integer multiple of 90, and let f be any trigonometric function.

Suppose that OP is the ray labeled p in a ccd system, and that ray OP makes with one side of the X-axis an acute angle whose degree measure is p'. Then:

$$f(p) = \pm f(p')$$

(Figure 8.2 illustrates just one case, and is intended to be only suggestive. The statements of the proof hold for all possible cases and for all possible illustrative diagrams.)

PROOF. Let Q be the foot of a perpendicular from P to the X-axis. Then $\angle\, QOP = p'°$.

We know (see Problem 14, Exercise 24) that $y_P = \pm\, d(P, Q)$ and $x_P = \pm d(O, Q)$. Now

$$\sin p = \frac{y_P}{r_P} = \pm \frac{d(P, Q)}{d(O, P)}$$

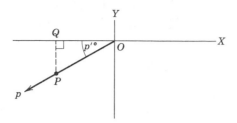

Fig. 8.2

But utilizing triangle OQP:

$$\sin p' = \frac{d(P, Q)}{d(O, P)}$$

Therefore $\sin p = \pm \sin p'$; which proves our theorem in case f is the sine function.

The other five cases of the proof are left as an exercise.

The angle p' of the preceding theorem is called the *reference* angle for p (see Problem 9, Exercise 33).

Note that the reference angle for p is always an *acute angle* made by a ray labeled p with a side of the X-axis. Thus, if $p = 150°$, for example, then $p' = 30°$, and the reference angle for $210°$ is $30°$ also.

Suppose now that we wish to find $\sin 160°$. The reference angle for $160°$ is $20°$ (Fig. 8.3). Hence, by the preceding theorem, $\sin 160° = \pm \sin 20°$. We may now find the (approximate) value of $\sin 20°$ in our tables, but still we have not quite solved the problem, since we have not yet determined which of the signs, $+$ or $-$, is the correct one.

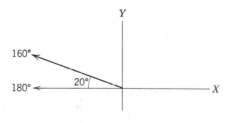

Fig. 8.3

Our short-cut method will be complete as soon as we know how to resolve the ambiguity in sign in the preceding theorem. But that is easily done:

Suppose that OP is a ray labeled p, and that P falls in QI (see Problem 4, Exercise 24). Then $x_P > 0$, $y_P > 0$, $r_P > 0$. Therefore each trigonometric function of p is the ratio of positive real numbers, and hence each is a positive real number.

If P falls in QII, then $x_P < 0, y_P > 0, r_P > 0$. Therefore $\sin p$ $= y_P/r_P > 0$, etc. It will be left to the student to complete the following table:

	QI	QII	QIII	QIV
sin	+	+		
cos	+			
tan	+			

Now let us return to the problem of finding $\sin 160°$. We know already that $\sin 160° = \pm \sin 20°$. It is clear (from a diagram, or more precisely because $90 < 160 < 180$—see Problem 3, Exercise 33) that the ray labeled 160 in a ccd system falls in QII. Therefore (from the chart above) we know that $\sin 160°$ is positive. Therefore $\sin 160° = \sin 20°$. Finally, from a trigonometric table: $\sin 160° = 0.3420$.

Furthermore, again from the chart, $\cos 160°$ is negative and $\tan 160°$ is negative. Therefore $\cos 160° = -\cos 20° = -0.9397$ and $\tan 160° = -\tan 20° = -0.3640$.

The following examples show how this short-cut method may be applied to other cases.

Illustrative Example 1. To find $\tan 700°$, we first use the fact that adding or subtracting 360° any whole number of times to 700° results in a label that identifies the same ray as 700°. Therefore: $\tan 700° = \tan (700-360)° = \tan 340° = -\tan 20° = -0.3640$.

Illustrative Example 2. To find $\tan (-600°)$:

$\tan (-600°) = \tan (-600 + 720)° = \tan 120° = -\tan 60° = -\sqrt{3}$

NOTE. The following table will be found useful enough to be worth memorizing. The task of memorization may be made rather easy by means of the mnemonic device given below the table:

	0°	30°	45°	60°	90°	180°	270°
sin	0	$\frac{1}{2}$	$\frac{1}{2}\sqrt{2}$	$\frac{1}{2}\sqrt{3}$	1	0	-1
cos	1	$\frac{1}{2}\sqrt{3}$	$\frac{1}{2}\sqrt{2}$	$\frac{1}{2}$	0	-1	0
tan	0	$\dfrac{1}{\sqrt{3}}$	1	$\sqrt{3}$		0	

Mnemonic device: It will be noted that up to 180°, the "sin" row of the table consists of: $\frac{1}{2}\sqrt{0}$, $\frac{1}{2}\sqrt{1}$, $\frac{1}{2}\sqrt{2}$, $\frac{1}{2}\sqrt{3}$, $\frac{1}{2}\sqrt{4}$. The "cos" row (up to 180°) is the "sin" row written in reverse order: and the "tan" row, throughout the table, is the result of dividing the "sin" row terms by their corresponding "cos" row terms.

This leaves only four entries to be memorized.

▶ **EXERCISE 38**

1. Complete the proof of the theorem of the preceding section.

2. Complete the first table in the preceding section.

3. Find, by the most convenient method which applies in each case, the sine, cosine, tangent and cotangent of each of the following number of degrees:

(a)	120	(b)	330	(c)	135	(d)	315	(e)	150
(f)	210	(g)	300	(h)	240	(i)	225	(j)	130
(k)	340	(l)	145	(m)	310	(n)	160	(o)	200
(p)	700	(q)	800	(r)	900	(s)	1000	(t)	2000
(u)	−700	(v)	−800	(w)	−900	(x)	−1000	(y)	−2000

8.3 NEW FUNCTIONS FROM OLD

One may derive new functions from given functions in various simple ways. For example, suppose we are given the sine and cosine functions, each, of course, having as domain the set of all real numbers. Then we may define a new function g as follows:

The mapping of g is given by the formula: $g(x) = (\sin x) \cdot (\cos x)$. With this mapping, we may choose, in fact, any set of real numbers as domain. Unless otherwise noted, when functions are combined to arrive at new functions, we shall always choose the largest possible set as domain of the new function. In the case of the aforementioned g, therefore, we choose as domain the set of *all* real numbers, since for *each* real number x, $(\sin x) \cdot (\cos x)$ is "defined," i.e., exists.

But now consider the case of a function h whose mapping is to be given by the formula $h(x) = \sin x / \cos x$. The value $h(x)$ is defined only if $\cos x$ is not 0. We therefore take as domain of the function h all real numbers except those which are odd integer multiples of 90° (see the definition of the cosine function, page 205).

8.4 IDENTITIES

Consider the equations:

(1) $2x + 1 = 7$

(2) $(x + 1)(x - 1) = x^2 - 1$

(3) $\dfrac{x - 7}{x - 7} = \dfrac{x - 11}{x - 11}$

They differ in important respects: (1) is satisfied only if $x = 3$; (2) is satisfied if x is equal to any complex number; (3) is satisfied if x is any complex number except 7 or 11, i.e., if x is any complex number for which both sides of the equation are defined.

An equation like (2) or (3) which is true for all numbers for which both sides are defined is called an *identity*. An equation like (1) which is not true for all values for which both sides are defined is called a conditional equation.

A central problem of algebra is : Given a conditional equation, i.e., one which is not true for all values of the unknown, to find what values it is true for, i.e., to solve the equation.

Identities are of great help in solving conditional equations. The identity (2) above, for example, enables us to transform the equation $x^2 - 1 = 0$ into the equivalent equation $(x + 1)(x - 1) = 0$, which is then easily solved.

Identities involving trigonometric functions are abundant, useful and interesting, and we therefore proceed to consider them.

8.5 FUNDAMENTAL TRIGONOMETRIC IDENTITIES

If p is a real number, then, as a matter of definition:

(1) $$\sin p = \frac{y_P}{r_P}$$

(2) $$\cos p = \frac{x_P}{r_P}$$

where OP is a ray labeled p in a ccd system.

Now if $x_P \neq 0$ (i.e., if p is not an odd multiple of 90), then we may divide equation (1) by (2) to arrive at:

(3) $$\frac{\sin p}{\cos p} = \frac{y_P}{x_P}$$

But we recall that (again when p is not an odd multiple of 90):

(4) $$\tan p = \frac{y_P}{x_P}$$

We have shown that when the expressions $(\sin p)/(\cos p)$ and $\tan p$ are both defined, then they are equal.

The following equation is therefore an identity:

(5)
$$\tan p = \frac{\sin p}{\cos p}$$

Similarly, one may prove the identity:

(6)
$$\cot p = \frac{\cos p}{\sin p}$$

And the identities:

(7)
$$\sin p \csc p = 1$$
$$\cos p \sec p = 1$$
$$\tan p \cot p = 1$$

From the preceding three identities one may derive the identities in "reciprocal" form:

(8)
$$\sin p = \frac{1}{\csc p} \qquad \cos p = \frac{1}{\sec p} \qquad \tan p = \frac{1}{\cot p}$$
$$\csc p = \frac{1}{\sin p} \qquad \sec p = \frac{1}{\cos p} \qquad \cot p = \frac{1}{\tan p}$$

We return now to (1), (2) above. Squaring and adding:

$$\sin^2 p + \cos^2 p = \frac{x_P^2 + y_P^2}{r_P^2}$$

(Note that we use the abbreviation $\sin^2 p$ to represent $(\sin p)^2$.)

But we recall that $r_P = d(O, P)$; $O = (0, 0)$ and $P = (x_P, y_P)$, so that by the formula for the distance between two points:

$$r_P = \sqrt{x_P^2 + y_P^2}$$

from which follows

$$r_P^2 = x_P^2 + y_P^2$$

and therefore

$$\sin^2 p + \cos^2 p = \frac{r_P^2}{r_P^2} = 1$$

We have arrived at the especially important identity:

(9)
$$\sin^2 p + \cos^2 p = 1$$

Note that both sides of this identity are defined and equal for *all* real numbers p.

If $\cos p \neq 0$ (i.e., if p is not an odd multiple of 90), then we may divide both sides of (9) by $\cos^2 p$ to arrive at the identity:

$$\frac{\sin^2 p}{\cos^2 p} + 1 = \frac{1}{\cos^2 p}$$

or, using (5) and (8):

(10)
$$1 + \tan^2 p = \sec^2 p$$

And dividing both sides of (9) by $\sin^2 p$ leads to the identity:

(11)
$$1 + \cot^2 p = \csc^2 p$$

The fundamental trigonometric identities above enable us to express any one of the trigonometric functions in terms of any one of the others. For example, from (9) we derive:

(12) $\sin p = \pm \sqrt{1 - \cos^2 p}$

(13) $\cos p = \pm \sqrt{1 - \sin^2 p}$

We now consider several illustrative examples involving trigonometric identities.

Illustrative Example I.   Prove the identity:

(I) $\sec A \csc A = \tan A + \cot A$

SOLUTION.   One approach to the proof of identities, when many functions are involved, is to express the given functions in terms of fewer functions.   In this case, suppose we express each of the given trigonometric functions in terms of the sine and cosine functions.   We work in parallel columns, with each side of (I):

$\sec A \csc A$	$\tan A + \cot A$
$= \dfrac{1}{\cos A} \cdot \dfrac{1}{\sin A}$	$= \dfrac{\sin A}{\cos A} + \dfrac{\cos A}{\sin A}$
$= \dfrac{1}{\cos A \sin A}$	$= \dfrac{\sin^2 A + \cos^2 A}{\cos A \sin A}$
	$= \dfrac{1}{\cos A \sin A}$

Now, since we have proved that both sides of (I) are equal to the same expression, we are tempted to say that they are therefore equal to each other, and that we have therefore proved what we set out to prove.

We have indeed, except for an annoying detail. We have not considered the values of A for which the given expressions and those which we substituted are meaningful.

This aspect of the proof of a trigonometric identity rarely leads to trouble, and may therefore usually be omitted. The careful student, however, will want to be prepared to investigate this question.

In (I), for example, we note: sec A and tan A are defined if and only if A is a real number of degrees not an odd multiple of 90; csc A and cot A are defined if and only if A is a real number of degrees not an even multiple of 90.

Both sides of (I) are therefore defined if and only if A is a real number of degrees not an integer multiple of 90.

Each of the substitutions made in the parallel colums above is valid if A is such a number.

Therefore sec A csc A and tan A cot A are equal whenever both are defined, and the equation sec A csc A = tan A + cot A is an identity.

Illustrative Example 2. Prove that the following equation is an identity:

(II) $\quad \dfrac{1 - \sin x}{\cos x} = \dfrac{\cos x}{1 + \sin x}$

SOLUTION. Equation (II) is equivalent to:

(III) $\quad \dfrac{1 - \sin x}{\cos x} - \dfrac{\cos x}{1 + \sin x} - 0$

We turn our attention to a proof that (III) is an identity:

$$\dfrac{1 - \sin x}{\cos x} - \dfrac{\cos x}{1 + \sin x} \qquad\qquad 0$$

$$= \dfrac{1 - \sin^2 x - \cos^2 x}{\cos x\,(1 + \sin x)}$$

$$= \dfrac{1 - (\sin^2 x + \cos^2 x)}{\cos x\,(1 + \sin x)}$$

$$= \dfrac{0}{\cos x\,(1 + \sin x)}$$

$$= 0$$

Thus, (III), and therefore (II), is an identity.

In what follows, we shall find it unnecessary to return to the definitions of the trigonometric functions in proving equations to be identities. As in the illustrative examples, we shall find it necessary to use only the fundamental identities (5)–(11) in our proofs.

▶ **EXERCISE 39**

1. Express each of the trigonometric functions in terms of the sine function. (For example, $\tan x = \dfrac{\sin x}{\cos x} = \pm \dfrac{\sin x}{\sqrt{1 - \sin^2 x}}$.)

2. Express each of the trigonometric functions in terms of the cosine function.

3. Express each of the following in simpler form:

    (a) $\sin^2 x \csc x$ (b) $\dfrac{\tan x}{\sec x}$

    (c) $\tan A \cos A$ (d) $1 + \dfrac{1}{\cot^2 \theta}$

    (e) $\cos^2 y \, (\tan^2 y + 1)$ (f) $\sin^2 x + \dfrac{\cos x}{\sec x}$

    (g) $\dfrac{1}{\tan p} + \dfrac{1}{\cot p}$ (h) $\dfrac{\sin x}{\cos x} + \dfrac{\cos x}{\sin x}$

    (i) $\sqrt{1 + \cot^2 x}$ (j) $\sqrt{\sec^2 y - 1}$

4. Prove that each of the following equations is an identity.

    (a) $\dfrac{\tan x}{\sin x} = \sec x$

    (b) $\sin x + \cot x \cos x = \csc x$

    (c) $\cot x \sec^2 x - \tan x = \cot x$

    (d) $\dfrac{\sec x}{\csc x} = \tan x$

    (e) $\dfrac{\sin x + \tan x}{1 + \cos x} = \tan x$

    (f) $\sec^2 x \, (1 - \sin^2 x) = 1$

    (g) $\dfrac{1 + \cot x}{1 + \tan x} = \cot x$

    (h) $\dfrac{\sec x - 1}{\tan x} = \dfrac{\tan x}{\sec x + 1}$

    (i) $\dfrac{\csc x + 1}{\cot x} = \dfrac{\cot x}{\csc x - 1}$

    (j) $\dfrac{1}{1 - \sin x} + \dfrac{1}{1 + \sin x} = 2 \sec^2 x$

    (k) $\dfrac{1 + \tan^2 \phi}{\csc^2 \phi} = \tan^2 \phi$

(*l*) $\tan^2 p + \cot^2 p = \sec^2 p \csc^2 p - 2$

(*m*) $(\tan x - 1)^2 = \sec^2 x - 2\tan x$

(*n*) $\sin^4 A - \cos^4 A = \sin^2 A - \cos^2 A$

(*o*) $\sin x \tan x = \sec x - \cos x$

(*p*) $\dfrac{\cot^2 p}{\csc^2 p + 4\csc p - 5} = \dfrac{1 + \sin p}{1 + 5\sin p}$

(*q*) $\dfrac{1 + \cot^2 x}{\cot x} = \sec x \csc x$

(*r*) $\dfrac{\tan x}{1 + \tan^2 x} = \sin x \cos x$

5.   In each of 4(*a*)–(*r*) above, determine the values for which both sides of the given equation are defined and equal.

6.   (*a*)   A calculus textbook offers as an answer to a problem: $1 - 2\sin^2 x$; a student arrives at the answer: $2\cos^2 x - 1$. Are these answers essentially the same?

(*b*)   What if the respective answers were $\sin x$ and $\dfrac{1}{\csc x}$?

7.   Since the square of a real number is never negative (see Problem 5(*f*) of Exercise 17), we know that for each real number x, $\cos^2 x \geqslant 0$. But then, substituting for $\cos^2 x$ its equal, $1 - \sin^2 x$, we have $1 - \sin^2 x \geqslant 0$, and from this: $\sin^2 x \leqslant 1$; and now (see Problem 9(*a*) of Exercise 17), we may conclude: $-1 \leqslant \sin x \leqslant 1$. Thus we see that the values of the sine function always fall between -1 and 1.

Similarly, show: $-1 \leqslant \cos x \leqslant 1$; $\sec x \geqslant 1$ or $\sec x \leqslant -1$; $\csc x \geqslant 1$ or $\csc x \leqslant -1$.

Show that the range of the tangent function is the set of all real numbers, and likewise for the cotangent function.

Show also: $|\sec x| > |\tan x|$ and $|\csc x| > |\cot x|$, whenever the functions in question are defined.

Note: It will be instructive to check the statements above with the graphs of the respective functions. See Problem 5, Exercise 34, and Problem 8, below.

8.   Draw the graphs of the secant and cosecant function over one period of each. *Hint:* Derive these graphs from the graphs of $\sin x$ and $\cos x$ and from the identities:

$\sec x = \dfrac{1}{\cos x}$, $\csc x = \dfrac{1}{\sin x}$.

8.6   GIVEN ONE TRIGONOMETRIC FUNCTION OF p, TO FIND ANOTHER

Suppose that we are given that $\sin p = -\frac{3}{5}$, and asked to find $\tan p$. Then we might proceed as follows:

$$\tan p = \frac{\sin p}{\cos p} = \frac{\sin p}{\pm\sqrt{1 - \sin^2 p}} = \frac{-\frac{3}{5}}{\pm\sqrt{1 - \frac{9}{25}}} = \frac{-\frac{3}{5}}{\pm\frac{4}{5}} = \pm\frac{3}{4}$$

We see then that two answers to this problem are possible. Since the given value of sin p is negative, we know (see chart, page 226) that p falls in QIII or QIV. If p is required to be in QIII, then (by the same chart) tan $p = \frac{3}{4}$. If p is to be in QIV, then tan $p = -\frac{3}{4}$.

Thus the fundamental identities may be used to compute possible values for one trigonometric function of a real number, given another.

Another method, however, may be used to arrive at the answer to a problem of this sort without the burden of recalling and using identities. The problem we have just solved may, for example, be worked in this way.

Suppose we consider the reference angle p' for p (see section 7.6). Then sin $p' = \frac{3}{5}$. This may be illustrated as in Fig. 8.4.

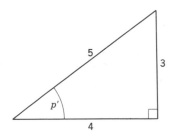

Fig. 8.4

(By the Pythagorean theorem, the third side of the triangle of Fig. 8.4 is 4.)

Therefore: tan $p' = \frac{3}{4}$.

Therefore: (see Theorem, page 224) tan $p = \pm\frac{3}{4}$.

Now, if a ray OP in a ccd system is labeled p, we know that tan $p = y_P/x_P$. Therefore, if P is any one of the points:

$$(4, 3), \ (-4, 3), \ (-4, -3), \ (4, -3),$$

then tan $p = \pm\frac{3}{4}$.

However, our problem requires that p fall in QIII or QIV. Therefore the first two of the four possibilities above must be discarded.

Either $p = p_1$ or $p = p_2$, where p_1, p_2 are labels of rays OP_1, OP_2 respectively (Fig. 8.5) will satisfy the condition: sin $p = -\frac{3}{5}$.

The labels of no other rays will satisfy the condition sin $p = -\frac{3}{5}$.

In fact, the following theorem may be proved.

Theorem. Suppose p and v are real numbers such that sin $p = v \neq \pm 1$ (or cos $p = v \neq 0$ or tan $p = v$).

Then in a ccd system there exist exactly two rays with label p such that sin $p = v$ (or cos $p = v$ or tan $p = v$).

PROOF: We consider only the case sin $p = v \neq \pm 1$, leaving the other two cases as exercises.

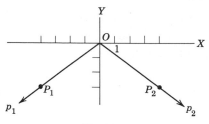

Fig. 8.5

Let OP be a ray with label p, where P has been chosen so that $d(O, P) = 1$; it follows that $x_p^2 + y_p^2 = 1$.

Now $\sin p = v$ is equivalent to $y_P/r_P = y_P/1 = v$, i.e., $y_P = v$. And since $x_p^2 + y_p^2 = 1$, if $y_P = v$, then $x_P = \pm\sqrt{1 - v^2}$.

Thus, if $\sin p = v$, then P must be either the point P_1: $(\sqrt{1 - v^2}, v)$ or P_2: $(-\sqrt{1 - v^2}, v)$; and if P is either of these points, then $\sin p = v$.

If $v \neq \pm 1$, then $P_1 \neq P_2$, so that rays OP_1, OP_2 must be two different rays (see ray axiom, page 144).

The rays OP_1, OP_2 of Fig. 8.5 may also be determined from the information $\sin p = -\frac{3}{5}$ in the following simple way:

Since $\sin p = y_P/r_P$, we seek points P such that $y_P/r_P = -\frac{3}{5}$. Clearly points P such that $r_P = 5$, $y_P = -3$ will satisfy this condition. But points P such that $r_P = 5$ lie on a circle of radius 5 with center at the origin; and points such that $y_P = -3$ lie on the horizontal line whose equation is $y = -3$. The points P which we seek are then the intersection of this circle and this line. (See Fig. 8.6).

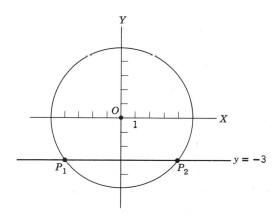

Fig. 8.6

▶ **EXERCISE 40**

1. In each of the following cases draw two rays which may be labeled p, and find all trigonometric functions of p associated with that ray which falls in the quadrant of lower number.

$\quad$ (a) $\quad \sin p = -0.6$ $\qquad$ (b) $\quad \cos p = -0.8$

$\quad$ (c) $\quad \tan p = \frac{3}{4}$ $\qquad\qquad$ (d) $\quad \cot p = -1$

$\quad$ (e) $\quad \sec p = 2$ $\qquad\qquad$ (f) $\quad \csc p = -2$

2. Illustrate with a diagram and find all trigonometric functions of p, given:

$\quad$ (a) $\quad \sin p = \frac{1}{2}, p$ in QI $\qquad$ (b) $\quad \cos p = \frac{1}{2}, p$ in QIV

$\quad$ (c) $\quad \tan p = 1, p$ in QIII $\qquad$ (d) $\quad \cot p = 2, p$ in QIII

$\quad$ (e) $\quad \sec p = \frac{5}{4}, p$ in QIV $\qquad$ (f) $\quad \csc p = \frac{5}{3}, p$ in QII

$\quad$ (g) $\quad \sin p = -\frac{1}{2}, \cos p < 0$ $\qquad$ (h) $\quad \cos p = -\frac{1}{2}, \sin p > 0$

$\quad$ (i) $\quad \tan p = -1, \cos p < 0$ $\qquad$ (j) $\quad \cot p = -2, \sec p > 0$

$\quad$ (k) $\quad \sec p = -\frac{5}{4}, \sin p > 0$ $\qquad$ (l) $\quad \csc p = -\frac{5}{3}, \cos p > 0$

3. What can you say about a ray labeled p if:

$\quad$ (a) $\quad \tan p$ does not exist? $\qquad$ (b) $\quad \cos p = 0$?

$\quad$ (c) $\quad \sin p = 1$? $\qquad\qquad$ (d) $\quad \sin p = -1$?

4. Complete the proof of the theorem of Section 8.6.

5. Given that $\sin p = -\frac{3}{5} = -0.6000$ one might attempt to find $\tan p$ by using a sine table to find p, and then a tangent table to find $\tan p$.
What objections are there to this procedure?

8.7 ADDITIVE AND NON-ADDITIVE FUNCTIONS

Brown and Jones are partners in a firm called "Brown and Jones." We point out that although one may find the combined *weight* of Mr. Brown and Mr. Jones by adding the weight of Brown and the weight of Jones, it is very unlikely that one could find the *telephone number* of "Brown and Jones" by adding the individual telephone numbers of Mr. Brown and Mr. Jones.

In other words, some functions are "additive," others not. We make the following definition:

A real-real function is said to be *additive* if the following is true: Whenever x, y and $x + y$ are in the domain of f:
$$f(x + y) = f(x) + f(y)$$

It is a distinctive property of the "doubling" and "tripling" functions (and in fact of all functions of the form $f(x) = kx$, with domain all real numbers, k a real number) that they are additive.   That is to say, if x and y are real numbers:

$$2 \cdot (x + y) = 2 \cdot x + 2 \cdot y$$
$$3 \cdot (x + y) = 3 \cdot x + 3 \cdot y$$
$$k \cdot (x + y) = k \cdot x + k \cdot y$$

It is a distinctive error of beginning students in mathematics to imagine that *all* functions are additive, especially the "square" and "square root" functions.   But we may easily show by examples that in general:

$$(x + y)^2 \neq x^2 + y^2$$
$$\sqrt{x + y} \neq \sqrt{x} + \sqrt{y}$$

Now, how about the trigonometric functions?   Is it true for all real numbers x, y, for example, that $\sin (x + y)$ is equal to $\sin x + \sin y$? Suppose we put the matter to a test, letting $x = 45°$, $y = 45°$.   Then:

$$\sin (x + y) = \sin 90° = 1; \sin x = \sin y = \frac{\sqrt{2}}{2}; \sin x + \sin y = \sqrt{2}.$$

In this case, then, $\sin (x + y) \neq \sin x + \sin y$.

That is to say, the sine function is *not* additive.   In the same way it is easy to show that none of the trigonometric functions are additive.   However, simple formulas do exist for $\sin (x + y)$ etc., and we now proceed to derive them.   We shall find it convenient to begin with the expression $\cos (F - S)$.

8.8   SINE AND COSINE FORMULAS

First we shall prove several lemmas:

Lemma 1.   In a ccd system, let point A lie on a ray labeled θ, and suppose $d(O, A) = a$.   Then point A has the coordinates $(a \cos \theta, a \sin \theta)$.

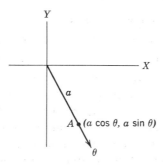

Fig. 8.7

PROOF. If $A \neq O$, then $\cos \theta = x_A/a$ and $\sin \theta = y_A/a$ (by the definition of the trigonometric functions); it follows that $x_A = a \cos \theta, y_A = a \sin \theta$, Q.E.D.

If $A = O$, then $x_A = 0$, $y_A = 0$, $a = 0$, so that we have $x_A = a \cos \theta$, $y_A = a \sin \theta$, Q.E.D.

Lemma 2. In a ccd system, let rays OP, OQ be labeled F, S respectively, and suppose $d(O, P) = p$, $d(O, Q) = q$, $d(P, Q) = r$. Then $r^2 = p^2 + q^2 - 2pq \,(\cos F \cos S + \sin F \sin S)$.

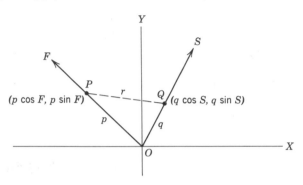

Fig. 8.8

PROOF. By Lemma 1 above, the coordinates of P and Q are: $(p \cos F, p \sin F)$ and $(q \cos S, q \sin S)$, respectively. Therefore:

$$r = \sqrt{(p \cos F - q \cos S)^2 + (p \sin F - q \sin S)^2}$$

and:
$$r^2 = p^2 \cos^2 F - 2pq \cos F \cos S + q^2 \cos^2 S + p^2 \sin^2 F$$
$$\qquad\qquad\qquad\qquad\quad - 2pq \sin F \sin S + q^2 \sin^2 S$$
$$= p^2 \,(\cos^2 F + \sin^2 F) + q^2 \,(\cos^2 S + \sin^2 S)$$
$$\qquad\qquad\qquad\qquad - 2pq \,(\cos F \cos S + \sin F \sin S)$$
$$= p^2 + q^2 - 2pq \,(\cos F \cos S + \sin F \sin S), \text{ Q.E.D.}$$

And now we prove a theorem:

Theorem. If F, S are real numbers, then:

$$\cos (F - S) = \cos F \cos S + \sin F \sin S$$

PROOF. With the notation of the preceding lemma, we have:

(1) $r^2 = p^2 + q^2 - 2pq \,(\cos F \cos S + \sin F \sin S)$

Now it is a property of ccd systems (see Problems 7, 8 of Exercise 33) that subtracting a real number k from each ray-label of a ccd system produces a new ccd system in which rays acquire new labels—unless k happens to be zero. (Subtracting a positive real number k from each label corresponds to the intuitive notion of rotating the original ccd system in a counter-clockwise direction through $k°$.)

In the situation of this theorem, for example, suppose we subtract the real number S from each ray label (Fig. 8.9).

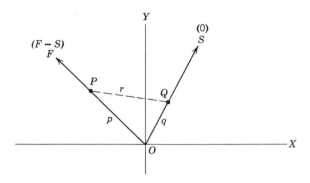

Fig. 8.9

Then we arrive at a new ccd system in which ray OQ is labeled 0 and ray OP is labeled $F - S$.

But the preceding lemma applies to the new ccd system as well as to the old. Therefore:

(2) $r^2 = p^2 + q^2 - 2pq \,[\cos (F - S) \cos 0 + \sin (F - S) \sin 0]$
$= p^2 + q^2 - 2pq \cos (F - S)$

From (1) and (2):

$p^2 + q^2 - 2pq \cos (F - S) = p^2 + q^2 - 2pq\,(\cos F \cos S + \sin F \sin S)$

From which follows:

(I) $\boxed{\cos (F - S) = \cos F \cos S + \sin F \sin S}$ Q.E.D.

Now we derive several simple consequences of the preceding formula. If p is a real number and

(i) $F = 0$, $S = p$, then from (I): (II) $\boxed{\cos (-p) = \cos p}$

(ii) $F = 90$, $S = p$, then from (I): (III) $\boxed{\cos (90 - p) = \sin p}$

(iii) $F = 90$, $S = 90 - p$, then from (I): (IV) $\boxed{\sin (90 - p) = \cos p}$

(iv) $F = p$, $S = -90$, then from (I): $\cos (90 + p) = -\sin p$

If p is a real number, then $-p$ is a real number also. Therefore (III) must hold if we replace p by $-p$. Hence: $\cos (90 + p) = \sin (-p)$. This, together with the preceding equation gives us:

(V) $\boxed{\sin (-p) = -\sin p}$

Now, if F, S are any real numbers we may write:

$$\cos (F + S) = \cos [F - (-S)]$$
$$= \cos F \cos (-S) + \sin F \sin (-S)$$
$$= \cos F \cos S - \sin F \sin S$$

Therefore: (VI) $\boxed{\cos (F + S) = \cos F \cos S - \sin F \sin S}$

Also: $\sin (F + S) = \cos [90 - (F + S)]$
$$= \cos [(90 - F) - S]$$
$$= \cos (90 - F) \cos S + \sin (90 - F) \sin S$$
$$= \sin F \cos S + \cos F \sin S$$

Therefore: (VII) $\boxed{\sin (F + S) = \sin F \cos S + \cos F \sin S}$

Again: $\sin (F - S) = \sin [F + (-S)]$
$$= \sin F \cos (-S) + \cos F \sin (-S)$$
$$= \sin F \cos S - \cos F \sin S$$

Therefore: (VIII) $\boxed{\sin (F - S) = \sin F \cos S - \cos F \sin S}$

Note to student: Formulas (I)–(VIII) above should be memorized.

▶ **EXERCISE 41**

1. Find all six trigonometric functions of:

(a) $75°$ [*Hint:* $\sin 75° = \sin (30° + 45°)$].
(b) $15°$; (c) $105°$; (d) $165°$.
2. Prove that for all real numbers x: $\sin 2x = 2 \sin x \cos x$.
3. Prove that for all real numbers x: $\cos 2x = \cos^2 x - \sin^2 x$.
4. Prove the identities: (a) $\cos 2x = 2 \cos^2 x - 1$
(b) $\cos 2x = 1 - 2 \sin^2 x$.

5. Simplify each of the following expressions:

(a) $\sin (x + 180)$	(b) $\sin (180 - x)$	(c) $\sin (x - 180)$
(d) $\cos (x + 180)$	(e) $\cos (180 - x)$	(f) $\cos (x - 180)$
(g) $\sin (90 + x)$	(h) $\cos (x - 90)$	(i) $\sin (270 - x)$
(j) $\sin (x - 270)$	(k) $\sin (x + 270)$	(l) $\cos (270 - x)$

(m) $\cos (x - 270)$ (n) $\cos (x + 270)$ (o) $\sqrt{2} \sin (x + 45)$
(p) $\sqrt{2} \sin (x - 45)$ (q) $\sqrt{2} \cos (x + 45)$ (r) $\sqrt{2} \cos (x - 45)$

6. Prove the following identities:

(a) $\sin (60 + x) + \cos (30 + x) = \sqrt{3} \cos x$
(b) $\sin (60 + x) = \sin (120 - x)$
(c) $\sin (x + 20) \cos 20 - \cos (x + 20) \sin 20 = \sin x$
(d) $\cos (60 + x) \cos x + \sin (60 + x) \sin x = \frac{1}{2}$
(e) $\dfrac{\sin 3x}{\sin x} - \dfrac{\cos 3x}{\cos x} = 2.$

7. Evaluate:

(a) $\sin 75 \cos 45 - \cos 75 \sin 45$
(b) $\sin 75 \cos 45 + \cos 75 \sin 45$
(c) $\cos 75 \cos 45 + \sin 75 \sin 45$
(d) $\cos 75 \cos 45 - \sin 75 \sin 45$
(e) $4 \sin 15 \cos 15$
(f) $\cos^2 60 + \sin^2 60$
(g) $\cos^2 60 - \sin^2 60$

8. Prove the identities:

(a) $\sin (x + y) + \sin (x - y) = 2 \sin x \cos y$
(b) $\sin (x + y) - \sin (x - y) = 2 \cos x \sin y$
(c) $\cos (x + y) + \cos (x - y) = 2 \cos x \cos y$
(d) $\cos (x + y) - \cos (x - y) = -2 \sin x \sin y$

9. Suppose p and q are real numbers. Then $x = (p + q)/2$ and $y = (p - q)/2$ are real numbers also. Substitute in Problem 8(a) above to derive the identity (a), and complete identities (b), (c), (d):

(a) $\sin p + \sin q = 2 \sin \dfrac{p + q}{2} \cos \dfrac{p - q}{2}$
(b) $\sin p - \sin q =$
(c) $\cos p + \cos q =$
(d) $\cos p - \cos q =$

10. Prove that if p, q, r are the degree measures of the angles of a triangle, then:

(a) $\sin p = \sin (q + r)$
(b) $\cos p + \cos (q + r) = 0$
(c) $\tan p + \tan (q + r) = 0$

8.9 TANGENT FORMULAS

If we divide both sides of formula (VII), p. 240, by $\cos F \cos S$ we have the identity:

$$\frac{\sin (F + S)}{\cos F \cos S} = \frac{\sin F \cos S}{\cos F \cos S} + \frac{\cos F \sin S}{\cos F \cos S}, \text{ or:}$$

(1) $\dfrac{\sin (F + S)}{\cos F \cos S} = \tan F + \tan S$

Similarly, from formula (VI) above:

(2) $\dfrac{\cos (F + S)}{\cos F \cos S} = 1 - \tan F \tan S$

Dividing (1) by (2):

(IX)
$$\tan (F + S) = \frac{\tan F + \tan S}{1 - \tan F \tan S}$$

Similarly, one may prove the following identity:

(X)
$$\tan (F - S) = \frac{\tan F - \tan S}{1 + \tan F \tan S}$$

The identities (IX) and (X) above are not useful when F or S is 90, for then their right sides are not defined. We therefore derive separately formulas for $\tan (90 + p)$, $\tan (90 - p)$ and $\tan (p - 90)$:

(The derivation of a formula for $\tan (90 + p)$ will be left as an exercise.)

Dividing (IV) by (III):   (XI)
$$\tan (90 - p) = \cot p$$

Dividing (V) by (II):   (XII)
$$\tan (-p) = -\tan p$$

Therefore $\tan (p - 90) = \tan [-(90 - p)] = -\tan (90 - p) = -\cot p$, so that:

(XIII)
$$\tan (p - 90) = -\cot p$$

Formulas (I)–(XII) should be memorized; the task may be facilitated by separating these formulas into the following natural groups: (I), (VI)–(X); (II), (V), (XII); (III), (IV), (XI).

It should be noted that formulas (I)–(XIII) are identities, and therefore not necessarily true for all real values of F, S, p.

In fact, only the sine and cosine formulas above are true for all real values of F, S, p. In each of the tangent formulas, certain values of p must be excluded.

▶ **EXERCISE 42**

1. Derive formulas for:

(a) $\tan 2x$ (b) $\tan (180 + x)$ (c) $\tan (180 - x)$
(d) $\tan (x - 180)$ (e) $\tan (45 + x)$ (f) $\tan (45 - x)$
                 (g) $\tan (90 + p)$

2. Derive a set of cotangent formulas by taking the reciprocals of the tangent formulas.

3. Derive Formula (X).

4. Evaluate:

(a) $\dfrac{\tan 20° + \tan 25°}{1 - \tan 20° \tan 25°}$ (b) $\dfrac{\tan 155° - \tan 20°}{1 + \tan 155° \tan 20°}$

5. Prove the following identities:

(a) $\tan (45 + x) \tan (45 - x) = 1$ (b) $\dfrac{\cos (270 - x)}{\tan (180 + x)} = -\cos x$

6. Given that $\sin p = \frac{3}{5}$, p in QII, $\cos q = \frac{3}{5}$, q in QIV, find all the trigonometric functions of:

(a) p (see Section 8.6)   (b) q
(c) $p + q$ (d) $p - q$

7. Given that $\tan p = \frac{3}{4}$, p in QIII, $\cos q = \frac{5}{13}$, q in QIV, find all trigonometric functions of:

(a) $p + q$ (b) $p - q$

8. Prove: $\tan 18° + \tan 27° + \tan 18° \tan 27° = 1$.

9. Prove: If A, B, C are the degree measures of the angles of a triangle, then:

$$\tan A + \tan B + \tan C = \tan A \tan B \tan C$$

8.10 ANGLE BETWEEN LINES

Suppose two nonvertical, nonperpendicular lines in a ccd system meet in exactly one point P. (See Fig. 8.10.).

Since this amounts to assuming that the given lines are not parallel, their inclinations must be unequal. Let l_1 be the line with lesser inclination $\theta_1°$, and l_2 the line with greater inclination $\theta_2°$.

In the given ccd system, locate rays OR, OS labeled θ_1, θ_2, respectively, and let $\theta°$ represent the degree measure of $\angle ROS$.

Then $\theta°$ is said to be the measure of the *counterclockwise angle from* l_1 *to* l_2 and $(180 - \theta)°$ is said to be the measure of the *counterclockwise angle from* l_2 *to* l_1. Intuitively, $\theta°$ and $(180 - \theta)°$ measure the rotations necessary to bring one line into coincidence with the other, in the required direction of rotation.

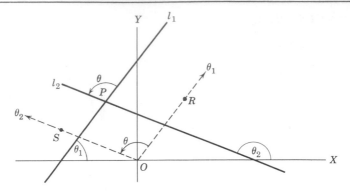

Fig. 8.10

Now it may be seen (cf. Problem 6, Exercise 33) that the inclinations of lines OR and OS are $\theta°_1$ and $\theta°_2$, respectively, and that $\angle ROS = \theta°$ $= (\theta_2 - \theta_1)°$. Therefore line $OR \parallel$ line l_1 and line $OS \parallel$ line l_2. Therefore lines l_1 and l_2 form an angle of $\theta°$ also (why?).

Note further that if m_1, m_2 represent the slopes of l_1, l_2 respectively, then $m_1 = \tan \theta_1$, $m_2 = \tan \theta_2$ (see Section 7.5).

Since we have assumed that l_1, l_2 are nonvertical and nonperpendicular, we know that θ_1, θ_2 and θ are each $\neq 90$. Therefore the tangent of each of these angles and also the slopes of lines l_1 and l_2 exist. Therefore we may write:

$$\tan \theta = \tan (\theta_2 - \theta_1) = \frac{\tan \theta_2 - \tan \theta_1}{1 + \tan \theta_2 \tan \theta_1} = \frac{m_2 - m_1}{1 + m_2 m_1}$$

Let us denote the counterclockwise angle from a line a to a line b by $\angle (a, b)$.

Then we have shown above:

(1) If $\theta_1 < \theta_2$, then $\tan \angle (l_1, l_2) = \dfrac{m_2 - m_1}{1 + m_2 m_1}$

There follows from (1):

(2) If $\theta_2 < \theta_1$, then $\tan \angle (l_2, l_1) = \dfrac{m_1 - m_2}{1 + m_1 m_2}$

But now suppose $\theta_2 < \theta_1$, and we seek $\tan \angle (l_1, l_2)$. Then:

$$\tan \angle (l_1, l_2) = \tan [180 - \angle (l_2, l_1)] = \frac{\tan 180 - \tan \angle (l_2, l_1)}{1 + \tan 180 \tan \angle (l_1, l_2)}$$

$$= -\tan \angle (l_2, l_1)$$

$$= -\left(\frac{m_1 - m_2}{1 + m_1 m_2}\right)$$

$$= \frac{m_2 - m_1}{1 + m_2 m_1}$$

We see then, that whether $\theta_1 < \theta_2$ or $\theta_2 < \theta_1$, the formula of (1) above holds for tan $\measuredangle$ (l_1, l_2).

This leaves only the case $\theta_1 = \theta_2$ to consider; i.e., the case in which $l_1 \parallel l_2$. In the case of parallel lines l_1, l_2 we simply define $\measuredangle$ $(l_1, l_2) = 0°$. In that case the formula of (1) above for tan $\measuredangle$ (l_1, l_2) continues to be valid, for if $l_1 \parallel l_2$, then $m_1 = m_2$; the formula then says that tan $0° = 0$, which is of course true.

Thus, the formula of (1) above turns out to hold for *any* nonvertical, nonperpendicular lines l_1, l_2.

We summarize:

Let l_1, l_2 be nonperpendicular lines of slopes m_1, m_2 respectively. Let the counterclockwise angle from l_1 to l_2 be denoted: $\measuredangle$ (l_1, l_2).

Then:

$$\tan \measuredangle \ (l_1, l_2) = \frac{m_2 - m_1}{1 + m_2 m_1}$$

▶ **EXERCISE 43**

1. Draw each of the following pairs of lines, and in each case find the counterclockwise angle from the first to the second:

(a) $y = x + 3$, $y = 2x$ (b) $y = 2x + 3$, $y = x$

(c) $x + y - 5$, $x - 2y - 4$ (d) $x + y = 5$, $x - y = 5$

(e) $x + y = 5$, $x + y = 7$ (f) $y = 2x + 3$, $x = 5$

2. In each of the cases of Problem 3 of Exercise 24, the vertices of a triangle are given. In each case, find the angles of the given triangle.

3. *Prove:* There exists no equilateral triangle in a cc plane all of whose vertices have only rational coordinates.

8.11 DOUBLE AND HALF-ANGLE FORMULAS

The following identities (whose proofs have been left to the student as exercises) are known as the *double angle* formulas:

(XIV)	$\sin 2x = 2 \sin x \cos x$	(XVI)	$\cos 2x = \cos^2 x - \sin^2 x$
(XV)	$\tan 2x = \dfrac{2 \tan x}{1 - \tan^2 x}$	(XVII)	$\cos 2x = 1 - 2 \sin^2 x$
		(XVIII)	$\cos 2x = 2 \cos^2 x - 1$

From the formulas for cos $2x$, the useful *half-angle* formulas may be derived:

The equation $\cos 2x = 1 - 2 \sin^2 x$ is equivalent to:

$$(1) \qquad\qquad \sin^2 x = \frac{1 - \cos 2x}{2}$$

an identity in which both sides are defined when x is *any* real number. If θ is a real number, then so is $\theta/2$. Letting $x = \theta/2$ in (1):

$$(\text{XIX}) \qquad \boxed{\; \sin^2 \frac{\theta}{2} = \frac{1 - \cos \theta}{2} \;}$$

Similarly:

$$(\text{XX}) \qquad \boxed{\; \cos^2 \frac{\theta}{2} = \frac{1 + \cos \theta}{2} \;}$$

Dividing (XIX) by (XX):

$$(\text{XXI}) \qquad \boxed{\; \tan^2 \frac{\theta}{2} = \frac{1 - \cos \theta}{1 + \cos \theta} \;}$$

▶ **EXERCISE 44**

1. Find:

(a) $\sin 22° \, 30'$ (*Hint:* In (XIX), let $\theta = 45°$.)

(b) $\cos 22° \, 30'$

(c) $\tan 22° \, 30'$

2. Prove the identities:

(a) $\sin 3x = 3 \sin x - 4 \sin^3 x$. [*Hint:* $\sin 3x = \sin (2x + x)$.]

(b) $\cos 3x = \cos^3 x - 3 \sin^2 x \cos x$

(c) $\sin 2x = \dfrac{2 \tan x}{1 + \tan^2 x}$

(d) $\sin^2 2x \cos^2 2x = \dfrac{1}{8} (1 - \cos 8x)$

(e) $\cot \theta - \tan \theta = 2 \cot 2\theta$

(f) $\sec 2x = \dfrac{1}{2 \cos^2 x - 1}$

(g) $1 - \sin 2x = (\sin x - \cos x)^2$

(h) $\csc 2\theta + \cot 2\theta = \cot \theta$

(*i*) $\sin \theta = 2 \sin \dfrac{\theta}{2} \cos \dfrac{\theta}{2}$ (*Hint:* use formula for sin 2*x*.)

(*j*) $1 + \cos \theta = 2 \cos^2 \dfrac{\theta}{2}$

(*k*) $\tan \dfrac{\theta}{2} = \dfrac{\sin \theta}{1 + \cos \theta}$ [*Hint:* use (*i*) and (*j*).]

(*l*) $\tan \dfrac{\theta}{2} = \dfrac{1 - \cos \theta}{\sin \theta}$

3. Find formulas for:

(*a*) sin 4*x*, in terms of functions of *x*.

(*b*) cos 4*x*, in terms of functions of *x*.

4. Use the half-angle formulas to find sin 15, cos 15, tan 15. Show that the results are equivalent to those obtained in Problem 1(b), Exercise 41.

5. Find all the trigonometric functions of 2*x* and *x*/2 if:

(*a*) sec $x = \frac{12}{5}$ and *x* is acute.

(*b*) csc $x = \frac{4}{3}$ and *x* is obtuse. (*Hint:* $90 < x < 180$; Therefore: $45 < x/2 < 90$; i.e., *x*/2 is in QI.)

(*c*) tan *x* = 1 and *x* is in QIII.

(*d*) cos *x* = −0.4, sin *x* > 0.

(*e*) sin $x = -\frac{1}{3}$, cos *x* > 0.

(*f*) cot *x* = 2, sin *x* < 0.

6. Prove that in △ *ABC*:

$$\sin A + \sin B + \sin C = 4 \cos \frac{A}{2} \cos \frac{B}{2} \cos \frac{C}{2}$$

8.12 RADIAN MEASURE

Suppose we divide a circle into 360 congruent arcs. Then a central angle of that circle, subtending one of those arcs, would serve as an example of an angle of 1°.

But note that the number 360 is quite arbitrary. Its use stems historically from the Babylonians, whose utilization of multiples of 60 in counting lives on today not only in our degree system of angle measurement, but also in our measurement of time. One reason for the persistence of this ancient system of angle measurement is that the number 360 displays the advantageous property of being divisible by many different integers.

There is, however, another more natural unit for angle measurement which for many purposes turns out to be more convenient than the degree unit. It is called the *radian* unit. In the study of calculus, for example, formulas involving trigonometric functions are generally more simply expressed in terms of radian measure than in terms of degree measure.

The idea of radian measure goes back to the intuitive idea which seeks to measure the size of an angle by the size of the "opening" between the sides of the angle.

We shall make this idea precise, assuming that we know what is meant by the arc of a circle subtended by a central angle, and also that we know what is meant by the length of that arc.

Definition. Given an angle with vertex O, draw a circle with center O and radius 1. Then the length of the arc which the given angle subtends from that "unit" circle is called the *radian* measure of the given angle.

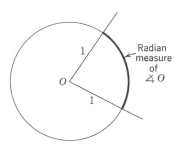

Fig. 8.11

Now that we have two units of angle measure at our disposal, we shall have to be careful to distinguish between them. From this point on, we shall use the degree symbol to indicate degree measure, and either the word "radian" or no symbol at all to indicate radian measure. That is to say, if $\measuredangle ABC$ has the degree measure a we shall write: $\measuredangle ABC = a°$; if $\measuredangle ABC$ has radian measure b we shall write: $\measuredangle ABC = b$ radians or simply $\measuredangle ABC = b$.

Since the circumference of a circle of radius r is equal to $2\pi r$, it follows that the circumference of a unit circle is 2π. Supposing that $\measuredangle AOB$ is a straight angle, i.e., that $\measuredangle AOB = 180°$, $\measuredangle AOB$ subtends an arc equal to half the circumference in a unit circle with center O. Therefore $\measuredangle AOB = \pi$ radians. We therefore write:

(1)
$$\boxed{\pi \text{ radians } = 180°}$$

(meaning that an angle of radian measure π will have degree measure 180, and vice-versa).

Now we shall further assume that the arc subtended by a central angle in a circle is proportional to the degree measure of that central angle. One interpretation of this statement is that if the degree measure of one central angle is k times that of another, then the length of the arc which the first central angle subtends from a circle is k times that which the second subtends from the same circle. (See Fig. 8.12).

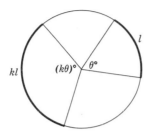

Fig. 8.12

It follows that equation (1) above may be multiplied (hence divided) by properly restricted real numbers to arrive at further equivalences between radians and degrees:

Dividing (1) by 2: $\qquad \frac{\pi}{2}$ radians $= 90°$

Dividing (1) by 3: $\qquad \frac{\pi}{3}$ radians $= 60°$

Dividing (1) by π: $\qquad 1$ radian $= \left(\frac{180}{\pi}\right)°$

Dividing (1) by 180: $\qquad 1° = \left(\frac{\pi}{180}\right)$ radians

Illustrative Example 1. To the nearest degree, how many degrees are there in an angle of 1 radian?

SOLUTION. $\qquad \pi$ radians $= 180°$

$$\therefore 1 \text{ radian} = \left(\frac{180}{\pi}\right)° \doteq \left(\frac{180}{3.14}\right)°$$

$$1 \text{ radian} = 57°, \text{ to the nearest degree}$$

Illustrative Example 2. Convert $150°$ to radian measure.

SOLUTION. $\qquad 180° = \pi$ radians

$$\therefore 30° = \frac{\pi}{6} \text{ radians}$$

$$\therefore 150° = \frac{5\pi}{6} \text{ radians}$$

Illustrative Example 3. Convert $75°$ to radian measure.

SOLUTION. $\qquad 180° = \pi$ radians

$$\therefore \quad 1° = \frac{\pi}{180} \text{ radians}$$

$$\therefore \quad 75° = \frac{75\pi}{180} \text{ radians} = \frac{5\pi}{12} \text{ radians}$$

Illustrative Example 4. Convert $\frac{3\pi}{4}$ radians to degree measure.

SOLUTION. π radians $= 180°$

$$\therefore \frac{3}{4} \cdot \pi \text{ radians} = \frac{3}{4} \cdot 180° = 135°$$

Now we may pursue a development of the theory of angles in terms of radian measure entirely analogous to that which we pursued in terms of degree measure.   For example, we may state:

With every angle, there is associated a real number r, called the number of *radians* in that angle, such that $0 \leqslant r \leqslant \pi$.

Furthermore, just as we arrived intuitively at the concept of a Cartesian-coordinate degree system (see Section 7.3), we may arrive at the concept of a Cartesian-coordinate radian (ccr) system.   In fact, since $a° = a \cdot (\pi/180)$ radians, it is only necessary to multiply each ray label in a ccd system by $\pi/180$ to arrive at a ccr system (Fig. 8.13).

It is important to note that in a ccr system, it continues to be true that angles are measured by label differences; that is to say, in a ccr system, if

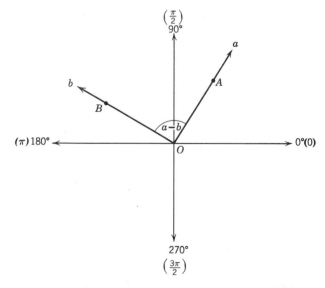

Fig. 8.13

ray OA is labeled a and ray OB is labeled b, and $0 \leqslant a - b \leqslant \pi$, then $\measuredangle AOB = (a - b)$ radians (Fig. 8.13).

With a ccr system at hand, we may now define *radian* measure trigonometric functions, just as we defined degree measure trigonometric functions (see Sections 7.4 and 8.1); we simply substitute the word "radian" for the word "degree" in these definitions. Again, in most cases, we distinguish between degree functions and radian functions by using the symbol $^\circ$ when and only when we have the degree function in mind. Thus: $\sin 30^\circ = 0.5$; $\sin \pi = \sin 180^\circ = 0$; $\sin 1^\circ = 0.0175$; $\sin 1 = 0.84$.

Finally we note that the trigonometric identities which we have proved in the preceding sections and the methods of Section 8.6 hold for radian as well as for degree functions. Incidentally, the trigonometric identities constitute one case in which we do not imply by the omission of the degree symbol that we are restricting ourselves to radian measure. The reason for this is, of course, that the identities happen to be valid in both systems of measure; for example, $\sin^2 x + \cos^2 x = 1$ is true for all real values of x, whether x is measured in terms of degrees or radians.

▶ **EXERCISE 45**

1. (a) Find the best approximation to one radian in terms of degrees, minutes, and an integer number of seconds (use $\pi = 3.14159$).

(b) Find an approximation, correct to six decimal places, for the value of one degree in terms of radians.

2. Express the following number of degrees exactly in terms of radians:

(a)	30°	(b)	45°	(c)	60°
(d)	15°	(e)	10°	(f)	20°
(g)	40°	(h)	50°	(i)	70°
(j)	100°	(k)	120°	(l)	135°
(m)	150°	(n)	180°	(o)	210°
(p)	225°	(q)	240°	(r)	270°
(s)	300°	(t)	315°	(u)	330°
(v)	360°	(w)	36,000°	(x)	700°
(y)	−700°				

3. Convert the following number of radians to degrees:

(a)	π	(b)	$\dfrac{\pi}{2}$	(c)	$\dfrac{\pi}{3}$
(d)	$\dfrac{2\pi}{3}$	(e)	$\dfrac{\pi}{4}$	(f)	2π
(g)	$\dfrac{3\pi}{4}$	(h)	$\dfrac{\pi}{5}$	(i)	$\dfrac{2\pi}{5}$

(j) $\dfrac{3\pi}{5}$ (k) 3π (l) $\dfrac{4\pi}{5}$

(m) $\dfrac{\pi}{6}$ (n) $\dfrac{5\pi}{6}$ (o) $\dfrac{\pi}{8}$

(p) 4π (q) $\dfrac{3\pi}{8}$ (r) $\dfrac{5\pi}{8}$

(s) $\dfrac{7\pi}{8}$ (t) $\dfrac{9\pi}{8}$ (u) 0.1π

(v) 0.3π (w) 0.5π (x) 0.7π

(y) 0.9π

4.   Express in terms of degrees, correct to the nearest minute, the following number of radians:

(a) 1 (b) 2 (c) 3

(d) 4 (e) 5 (f) 0.1

(g) 0.2 (h) 0.3 (i) 0.4

(j) 0.5

5.   Express the following in terms of radians, correct to six decimal places:

(a) $1'$ (b) $1''$

6.   The arc which a central angle subtends in a circle is proportional to the radius of the circle; more precisely: If a central angle subtends an arc of length a in a circle of radius r, then a central angle of equal measure will subtend an arc of length ka in a circle of radius kr.   (Fig. 8.14.)

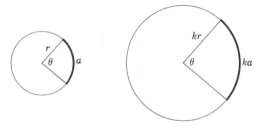

Fig. 8.14

Since a central angle of θ radians subtends an arc of length θ in a circle of radius 1, it follows that a central angle of θ radians subtends an arc of length $r\theta$ in a circle of radius r.   If we denote the length of this subtended arc by s, we have the formula:

$$s = r\theta$$

for the length of arc subtended by a central angle of θ radians in a circle of radius r.   (Fig. 8.15).

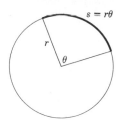

Fig. 8.15

In each of the following cases, find whichever of s, r, θ is not given, and illustrate with a diagram drawn approximately to scale.

(a) $r = 1.5''$, $\theta = 1$ (b) $r = 2''$, $\theta = \pi$

(c) $r = 2''$, $\theta = 60°$ (d) $s = 4''$, $\theta = 120°$

(e) $r = 2$ cms, $s = 1$ cm   (f) $r = 1.5$ cms, $\theta = 80°$

(g) $s = 5$ cms, $\theta = 135°$ (h) $r = 1$ cm, $s = 1''$

7. (a) Two flywheels with centers 10 ft apart have radii of 1 ft and 6 ft, respectively. How long is the (untwisted) belt which runs around the two?

(b) Solve problem (a) for a belt with one twist in it.

8. Find the "angular speed" in terms of radians per second of:

(a) the second hand of a clock

(b) the minute hand of a clock

(c) the hour hand of a clock.

9. If a ray OA rotates about O through θ radians in a unit of time, then the point A travels a distance of $(OA) \cdot \theta$ in that unit of time.

Therefore, the linear speed of point A is equal to the angular speed of ray OA multiplied by the radius OA of the circle along which A travels. Thus if v, w represent these linear and angular speeds, respectively, and $r = d(O, A)$, then $v = rw$.

(a) The second hand of a clock is 3 in. long (measured from the center of the clock to the tip of the second hand). What is the linear speed of the tip of the second hand?

(b) The minute hand of a clock is 3 in. long (measured as above). What is the linear speed of the tip of the minute hand?

(c) The hour hand of a clock is 2-in. long (measured as above). What is the linear speed of the tip of the hour hand?

(d) An old oaken bucket hangs 15 ft. down a well, attached to a rope wound round a windlass of radius 3 in. If the crank of the windlass is turned at a rate of 1 revolution per second, how long does it take to raise the bucket to the top of the well?

(e) How fast would a merry-go-round have to rotate (in revolutions per minute) in order for a person 2 ft. from its center to be moving at a linear speed of 5 miles per hour? At what linear speed would a person 12 feet from the center then be moving?

8.13 TRIGONOMETRIC EQUATIONS

Illustrative Example I. Solve the equation:

(1) $\sin 2x = -\frac{1}{2}$

SOLUTION. Trigonometric equations supply another exception to the general rule that the omission of the degree symbol implies a restriction to radian measure. In fact, we will solve (1) in terms of both degrees and radians.

The notation p' will again be used to represent the reference angle for a real number p. Then no matter what the unit of angle measure, (1) above is equivalent (see Section 8.2) to:

(2) $\sin (2x)' = \frac{1}{2}$ and $2x$ is in QIII or QIV.

(For if f is a trigonometric function and p any real number we always have $f(p') = |f(p)|$; and if $\sin p$ is negative, p must be in QIII or QIV.)

But now (2) is equivalent to:

(3) $(2x)' = 30°$ and $2x = 210° + k\cdot 360°$ or $330° + k\cdot 360°$

where k is any integer. (Fig. 8.16)

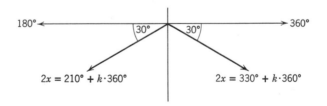

$$180° \longleftarrow \qquad 30° \quad 30° \qquad \longrightarrow 360°$$

$$2x = 210° + k\cdot 360° \qquad\qquad 2x = 330° + k\cdot 360°$$

Fig. 8.16

(The values 210° and 330° were arrived at by inserting the reference angle 30° into the proper quadrants.)

By the theorem of Section 8.6, there are no other possible values for $2x$.

In what follows we shall leave it to the student to supply the phrase "where k is any integer," where it is necessary.

Now our final solution in terms of degrees follows from (3); we shall write this solution in the form:

$$x = \{105°, 165°\} + k \cdot 180°$$

Actually, then, we have two infinite sets of solutions.

Now we verify that our solutions are correct:

$$\sin 2\,(105° + k \cdot 180°) = \sin\,(210° + k \cdot 360°) = \sin 210° = -\sin 30° = -\tfrac{1}{2}$$
$$\sin 2\,(165° + k \cdot 180°) = \sin\,(330° + k \cdot 360°) = \sin 330° = -\sin 30° = -\tfrac{1}{2}$$

Finally, we solve (1) in terms of radians.

Returning to (3), we convert to radians and arrive at:

(4) $(2x)' = \dfrac{\pi}{6}$ and $2x = \pi + \dfrac{\pi}{6} + k \cdot 2\pi$, or $2\pi - \dfrac{\pi}{6} + k \cdot 2\pi$

Solution in terms of radians: $$x = \left\{\frac{7\pi}{12}, \frac{11\pi}{12}\right\} + k\pi$$

(Alternatively, one may simply convert the solution above in degrees directly into radians.)

Illustrative Example 2.   Solve: $2 \cos 3x + 1 = 0$.

SOLUTION.   We proceed as above, but omit explanatory statements.

$$2 \cos 3x + 1 = 0$$
$$2 \cos 3x = -1$$
$$\cos 3x = -\tfrac{1}{2}$$

Therefore: $\cos\,(3x)' = \tfrac{1}{2}$ and $3x$ falls in QII or QIII.

Therefore: $(3x)' = 60°$ and $3x = 120° + k \cdot 360°$ or $240° + k \cdot 360°$

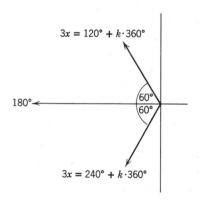

Fig. 8.17

Solution: $$x = \{40°, 80°\} + k \cdot 120°$$

In terms of radians:

$$(3x)' = \pi/3 \text{ and } 3x = \pi - \pi/3 + k \cdot 2\pi \text{ or } \pi + \pi/3 + k \cdot 2\pi$$

Solution in radians:

$$x = \left\{\frac{2\pi}{9}, \frac{4\pi}{9}\right\} + \frac{2k\pi}{3}$$

Illustrative Example 2a.   In the preceding example, what are the solutions that lie between 0° and 360°?

SOLUTION.   Letting $k = 0, 1, 2$ in our general solution in terms of degrees will produce all possible solutions between 0° and 360°: $x = 40°$, 80°, 160°, 200°, 280°, 320°.

Illustrative Example 3.   Solve: $3 - \cos^2 x = 3 \sin x$.

SOLUTION.   Since for all real numbers x, $\cos^2 x = 1 - \sin^2 x$, we may replace $\cos^2 x$ by $1 - \sin^2 x$ in the given equation, and arrive at an equivalent equation that involves only *one* trigonometric function:

$$\sin^2 x - 3 \sin x + 2 = 0$$

This last equation may be regarded as a quadratic equation in $\sin x$, and one may therefore attempt to arrive at a solution by the method of factoring:

$$(\sin x - 2)(\sin x - 1) = 0$$
$$\sin x = 2 \text{ or } 1$$

There is no real number x such that $\sin x = 2$.   In fact, for all real numbers x, $-1 \leqslant \sin x \leqslant 1$.

Sin $x = 1$ if and only if x labels the ray OP which falls along the positive Y-axis of a cc system.   Therefore:

Solution in degrees:

$$x = 90° + k \cdot 360°$$

Solution in radians:

$$x = \frac{\pi}{2} + k \cdot 2\pi$$

Illustrative Example 4.   Solve: $\sin x + \cos x = 1$.

SOLUTION.   The given equation is equivalent to:

$$\sin x = 1 - \cos x$$

Squaring: $\sin^2 x = 1 - 2 \cos x + \cos^2 x$

(But having squared an equation, the result may not be an equivalent equation.   Therefore our final roots *must* be checked to see which are actually roots of the original equation.)

Continuing:
$$1 - \cos^2 x = 1 - 2\cos x + \cos^2 x$$
$$2\cos^2 x - 2\cos x = 0$$
$$\cos^2 x - \cos x = 0$$
$$(\cos x)(\cos x - 1) = 0$$
$$\cos x = 0 \text{ or } 1$$
$$x = \{0°, 90°, 270°\} + k \cdot 360°$$

Of these values, all but $270° + k \cdot 360°$ check in the original equation. Therefore:

Solution in degrees:

$$\boxed{x = \{0°, 90°\} + k \cdot 360°}$$

(Note that the solution $x = 0° + k \cdot 360°$ may be written simply: $x = k \cdot 360°$.)
  Similarly:

Solution in radians:

$$\boxed{x = \left\{0, \frac{\pi}{2}\right\} + k \cdot 2\pi}$$

(This equation may also be solved by squaring the original and making use of the identity $\sin^2 x + \cos^2 x = 1$ and the formula for $\sin 2x$; it is suggested that the student work through this alternative method also.)

Illustrative Example 5.   Solve: $\sin x = \cos x$
SOLUTION.   Dividing by $\cos x$: $\tan x = 1$.
(NOTE.   The last is a step that *may* lead to a nonequivalent equation. In this case, however, it may be shown that the two equations *are* equivalent.   For: If x is a real number such that $\sin x = \cos x$, then $\cos x$ cannot be zero, since if $\cos x = 0$ then $\sin x = \pm 1$, and $\sin x \neq \cos x$; therefore we may divide by $\cos x$ and arrive at $\tan x = 1$.   On the other hand, if $\tan x = 1$, then again $\cos x \neq 0$, so that $\tan x = (\sin x)/(\cos x) = 1$. from which follows $\sin x = \cos x$.)

Solution in degrees:

$$\boxed{x = \{45°, 225°\} + k \cdot 360°}$$

Solution in radians:

$$\boxed{x = \left\{\frac{\pi}{4}, \frac{5\pi}{4}\right\} + 2k\pi}$$

Illustrative Example 6.   Solve: $\sin 2x = \sin x$
SOLUTION. $$2\sin x \cos x = \sin x$$
$$2\sin x \cos x - \sin x = 0$$
$$(\sin x)(2\cos x - 1) = 0$$
$$\sin x = 0, \cos x = \tfrac{1}{2}$$

Solution in degrees:
$$x = \{0°, 60°, 180°, 300°\} + k \cdot 360°$$

Solution in radians:
$$x = \left\{0, \frac{\pi}{3}\,\pi, \frac{5\pi}{3}\right\} + 2k\pi$$

(Note that dividing through by $\sin x$ in the equation $2 \sin x \cos x = \sin x$ would have led to an incomplete solution.)

▶ **EXERCISE 46**

Solve the following equations:

1. $2 \sin x = 1$
2. $\tan x = -1$
3. $2 \cos 3x = 1$
4. $\sin 2x = 0$
5. $2 \sin^2 x = 3$
6. $2 \sin^2 2x = 3$
7. $\tan 2x = 1$
8. $\tan 3x = -1$
9. $2 \cos 2x = -1$
10. $2 \cos^2 x = 3$
11. $2 \cos^2 2x = 3$
12. $\sin^2 x + 2 \sin x - 3 = 0$
13. $\sin^2 x - 2 \cos x + 2 = 0$
14. $\sin^2 x + \sin x = 0$
15. $2 \sin^2 x + \sin x = 0$
16. $\sin x + \cos x = 0$
17. $2 \sin x + \cos x = 2$
18. $\sin x + \cos x = 2$
19. $\cos 2x = \cos x$
20. $\cos 2x = \sin x$
21. $\sin 2x = \sin^2 x$
22. $2 \sin^2 x = 1 + \cos x$
23. $\sin x = \tan (\frac{1}{2}) x$
24. $2 \cos^2 x - 3 \sin x = 3$
25. $2 \cos 2x - \cot 2x = 0$
26. $\sin^2 x - \cos^2 x = 0$
27. $2 \sin^2 x + 3 \cos x = 0$
28. $\cos x = 1 - \sin^2 x$
29. $2 \cos^2 x + 3 \sin x = 0$
30. $\tan 2x - 2 \cos x = 0$
31. $\sin 3x + \sin x = 0$
32. $\cos 3x - \cos x = 0$

8.14 TRIGONOMETRIC GRAPHS

Consider the function: $f(x) = 3 \sin (\pi x + \pi)$.

Since the sine of any number cannot exceed 1, $f(x)$ cannot exceed 3. Are there values of x for which $f(x) = 3$? The question is answered by solving the equation:

$$3 \sin (\pi x + \pi) = 3, \text{ i.e., } \sin (\pi x + \pi) = 1$$

This equation has the solution: $\pi x + \pi = \dfrac{\pi}{2} + k \cdot 2\pi$

$$x + 1 = \tfrac{1}{2} + 2k$$
$$x = 2k - \tfrac{1}{2}$$

where k may be any integer.

Thus $3 \sin (\pi x + \pi)$ attains a maximum value of 3 when $x = -\frac{1}{2}, 1\frac{1}{2}, 3\frac{1}{2}, \ldots$

Similarly, we observe that $3 \sin (\pi x + \pi)$ attains a minimum value of -3 when: $\pi x + \pi = \dfrac{3\pi}{2} + k \cdot 2\pi,$

i.e., when: $$x + 1 = \frac{3}{2} + 2k$$

i.e., when: $$x = 2k + \frac{1}{2}$$

for example, when $x = \frac{1}{2}, 2\frac{1}{2}, 4\frac{1}{2}, \ldots$

Finally, $3 \sin (\pi x + \pi) = 0$ when $\pi x + \pi = k\pi$, i.e., when $x = k - 1$; for example, when $x = -1, 0, 1, \ldots$

We use this information to draw (part of) the graph of the function $3 \sin (\pi x + \pi)$ (Fig. 8.18).

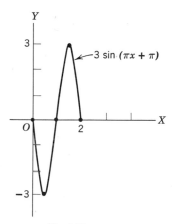

Fig. 8.18

Note that in drawing graphs of trigonometric functions using radian measure, it is customary to use the same scale on both axes.

In general, the graph of $a \sin (bx + c)$, where $a \neq 0$, $b \neq 0$, c are real numbers, resembles the graph we have drawn above. In fact the following may be proved:

If $a \neq 0$, $b \neq 0$, c are real numbers, then the graph of $a \sin (bx + c)$ is periodic with period $\left| \dfrac{2\pi}{b} \right|$ and maximum and minimum values $|a|$, $-|a|$ respectively. The pattern 0, max, 0, min, 0, max, 0 min, $\ldots$ is displayed by the graph at quarter-period intervals on the X-axis.

A method of drawing graphs of functions of the form $a \sin (bx + c)$, then, is to find the values of x at which the function attains its maximum, and then to use the information of the preceding paragraph in drawing the graph.

Illustrative Example 1. Draw the graph of the function: $-2 \sin (\pi - \pi x)$.

SOLUTION. The given function attains a maximum value of 2 when:

$$-2 \sin (\pi - \pi x) = 2$$
$$\sin (\pi - \pi x) = -1$$
$$\pi - \pi x = \frac{3\pi}{2} + k \cdot 2\pi$$
$$1 - x = \frac{3}{2} + 2k$$
$$-\frac{1}{2} - 2k = x$$

Here, in order to avoid values of x far out on the negative X-axis, we let $k = 0, -1, -2$.

Then the given function attains a maximum of 2 at $x = -\frac{1}{2}, 1\frac{1}{2}, 3\frac{1}{2}$.

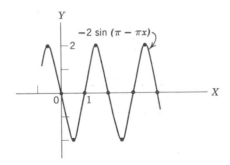

Fig. 8.19

Bisecting the interval between maxima gives us a point at which a minimum of -2 occurs; and bisecting the intervals between maxima and minima gives us points at which 0-ordinates occur.

The period of this graph is $\left|\dfrac{2\pi}{-\pi}\right|$, or 2. With this information, the graph may be extended left or right as far as we please.

Note: By the *amplitude* of a function of the form $a \sin (bx + c)$ (and of its graph), is meant the maximum value $|a|$ of the function.

▶ **EXERCISE 47**

1. Draw the graphs of the following functions:

(a)　$\sin \pi x$　　　　　　　　　　(b)　$2 \sin \pi x$

(c) $3 \sin 2\pi x$
(d) $2 \sin \frac{\pi}{2} x$

(e) $4 \sin \left(2\pi x + \frac{\pi}{2}\right)$
(f) $3 \sin \left(\frac{\pi}{2} - 2\pi x\right)$

(g) $-2 \sin (\pi x + \pi)$
(h) $-3 \sin \left(\frac{\pi}{2} - 2\pi x\right)$

(i) $-2 \sin \left(\frac{\pi}{2} x - \frac{\pi}{2}\right)$

2.   Draw the graphs of the following functions:

(a) $\sin x$
(b) $\sin (-x)$
(c) $2 \sin (2x + 1)$
(d) $3 \sin (2x + \pi)$
(e) $-\sin (\pi - x)$
(f) $\tan x$
(g) $\cot x$
(h) $\sec x$
(i) $\csc x$

3.   Graphs of equations of the form $a \cos (bx + c)$ may be handled by converting the cosine to a sine function, using the easily proved identity: $\cos \theta = \sin (\theta + \pi/2)$.

For example, $\cos x = \sin (x + \pi/2)$; to draw the graph of $\cos x$, we simply draw the graph of $\sin (x + \pi/2)$.

Or alternatively, one may follow a method analogous to that by which we graphed sine functions, using principally the fact that $\cos \theta$ attains a maximum value of 1 when $\theta = 2k\pi$.

Draw the graphs of the following functions:

(a) $\cos x$
(b) $2 \cos \pi x$

(c) $3 \cos \left(\pi x - \frac{\pi}{2}\right)$
(d) $-3 \cos \left(\pi x - \frac{\pi}{2}\right)$

(e) $-2 \cos \frac{\pi}{2} x$
(f) $2 \cos \left(\frac{\pi}{2} - x\right)$

(g) $-2 \cos \left(\frac{\pi}{2} - \pi x\right)$
(h) $-2 \cos \pi x$

(i) $2 \cos (-\pi x)$

4.   Draw the graphs of the following functions by the "addition of ordinates" method (see Section 7.7, Illustrative Example 2).

(a) $\sin \pi x + \sin 2\pi x$
(b) $\sin x + 2 \sin x$
(c) $2 \sin \pi x - \sin 2\pi x$
(d) $\sin x + \cos x$

(e) $\sin \pi x + \cos \pi x$
(f) $3 \sin \frac{\pi}{2} x + 4 \cos \frac{\pi}{2} x$

(g) $\sin \pi x - \cos \pi x$
(h) $\sin x - \cos x$

8.15   INVERSE TRIGONOMETRIC FUNCTIONS

This section is to a large extent based upon Section 2.6 and should therefore be preceded by a study of that section.

For simplicity we shall assume in this section that all trigonometric functions discussed are *radian* measure functions. It should be understood, however, that statements may be made in terms of degree measure that are analogous to those we make in terms of radian measure. For example, in the table which follows, the entry $\left\{ -\dfrac{\pi}{2} \cdot\!\!-\!\!\cdot \dfrac{\pi}{2} \right\}$ would be replaced by $\{-90° \cdot\!\!-\!\!\cdot 90°\}$ if the degree measure trigonometric functions were under consideration.

Since the trigonometric functions with which we are now dealing (i.e., the *extended* trigonometric functions) are not one-one (how is that evident?), it follows that they do not have inverses. However, by restricting their domains, the trigonometric functions may be transformed into functions which *are* one-one. We shall consider one such natural restriction for each of the six trigonometric functions.

First of all, let us examine the graph of the sine function (Fig. 8.20).

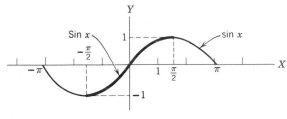

Fig. 8.20

Clearly, if we consider only that part of the graph between $x = -\pi/2$ and $x = \pi/2$, then no horizontal line crosses this part more than once, and we may thus reduce the sine function to a one-one function *without sacrificing any of the original range*. Actually, what we have done is to choose, from among the many pre-images that the sine function assigns to each element of its range, just one pre-image that is to lie in the interval $\left\{ -\dfrac{\pi}{2} \cdot\!\!-\!\!\cdot \dfrac{\pi}{2} \right\}$.

We shall call the restriction of the sine function to the domain $\left\{ -\dfrac{\pi}{2} \cdot\!\!-\!\!\cdot \dfrac{\pi}{2} \right\}$ the "principal" sine function, which we denote: Sine (note the capital "S"). The darker portion of the graph of Fig. 8.20 is the graph of the principal sine function.

Since the principal sine function *is* one-one, it has an inverse. We denote the inverse of the Sine function: Arcsine, read as spelled, or as "inverse sine," or as "the principal number whose sine is."

For example:

$$\frac{\pi}{2} \xrightarrow{\text{Sine}} 1$$

$$1 \xrightarrow{\text{Arcsine}} \frac{\pi}{2}$$

That is to say, the statement Sin $\pi/2 = 1$ is equivalent to the statement Arcsin $1 = \pi/2$; one way in which the preceding equation may be read is: "the principal number whose sine is 1 is $\pi/2$."

The other trigonometric functions may be similarly treated. A summary of results follows:

(*Note:* We make use of the following notation:

(i) $\{a - b\}$ denotes the interval $\{a \cdot\!\!-\!\!\cdot b\}$ with a and b excluded.

(ii) If A and B are sets, $A - B$ denotes the set of elements of A with elements of B excluded; i.e., the set of all elements of A which are not in B (cf. Problem 20 of Exercise 2).

(iii) $R^\#$ denotes the set of all real numbers.)

Function	Domain	Range
Sin	$\left\{-\frac{\pi}{2} \cdot\!\!-\!\!\cdot \frac{\pi}{2}\right\}$	$\{-1 \cdot\!\!-\!\!\cdot 1\}$
Arcsin	$\{-1 \cdot\!\!-\!\!\cdot 1\}$	$\left\{-\frac{\pi}{2} \cdot\!\!-\!\!\cdot \frac{\pi}{2}\right\}$
Cos	$\{0 \cdot\!\!-\!\!\cdot \pi\}$	$\{-1 \cdot\!\!-\!\!\cdot 1\}$
Arccos	$\{-1 \cdot\!\!-\!\!\cdot 1\}$	$\{0 \cdot\!\!-\!\!\cdot \pi\}$
Tan	$\left\{-\frac{\pi}{2} - \frac{\pi}{2}\right\}$	$R^\#$
Arctan	$R^\#$	$\left\{-\frac{\pi}{2} - \frac{\pi}{2}\right\}$
Cot	$\{0 - \pi\}$	$R^\#$
Arccot	$R^\#$	$\{0 - \pi\}$
Sec	$\{0 \cdot\!\!-\!\!\cdot \pi\} - \left\{\frac{\pi}{2}\right\}$	$R^\# - \{-1 - 1\}$
Arcsec	$R^\# - \{-1 - 1\}$	$\{0 \cdot\!\!-\!\!\cdot \pi\} - \left\{\frac{\pi}{2}\right\}$
Csc	$\left\{-\frac{\pi}{2} \cdot\!\!-\!\!\cdot \frac{\pi}{2}\right\} - \{0\}$	$R^\# - \{-1 - 1\}$
Arccsc	$R^\# - \{-1 - 1\}$	$\left\{-\frac{\pi}{2} \cdot\!\!-\!\!\cdot \frac{\pi}{2}\right\} - \{0\}$

If (a, b) is a point on the graph of a function, then clearly (b, a) is a point on the graph of its inverse. By reversing the coordinates of points on the graph of a function, one may therefore arrive at points on the graph of its inverse.

Thus, for example, since $(-\pi/2, -1)$, $(0, 0)$ and $(\pi/2, 1)$ are points on the graph of the Sine function, it follows that $(-1, -\pi/2)$, $(0, 0)$ and $(1, \pi/2)$ are points on the graph of the Arcsine function.

In fact, it may be proved that if $a \neq b$ are real numbers, then the line whose equation is $y = x$ is the perpendicular bisector of the line segment joining the points (a, b) and (b, a) (Fig. 8.21); and of course, if $a = b$, the point (a, b) is identical with the point (b, a) and lies on the line whose equation is $y = x$.

The graph of an inverse function may therefore always be derived by "reflecting" the graph of the given function in the line $y = x$.

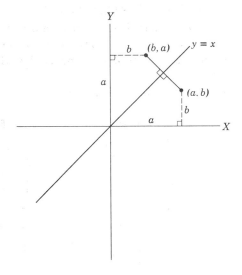

Fig. 8.21

Illustrative Example 1. Find Arctan (-1).

SOLUTION. We seek a number p such that $\tan p = -1$ and $-\pi/2 < p < \pi/2$ (see table above); $p = -\pi/4$ is the only such number. Therefore Arctan $(-1) = -\pi/4$ (see Fig. 8.22).

Note that one may also write: Arctan $(-1) = -45°$.

Illustrative Example 2. Solve: $\sin x = .3$.

SOLUTION. Without going so far as to approximate answers by the use of trigonometric tables, one may express the solutions of this equation as:

$$x = \{\text{Arcsin } 0.3, \ \pi - \text{Arcsin } 0.3\} + k \cdot 2\pi$$

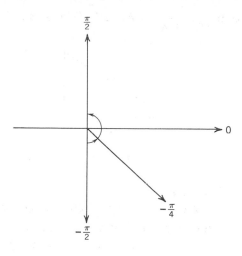

$\dfrac{\pi}{2}$

0

$-\dfrac{\pi}{4}$

$-\dfrac{\pi}{2}$

Fig. 8.22

Illustrative Example 3.   Prove: Arctan 2 + Arctan 3 = 135°.

SOLUTION.   To find, using tables, numbers whose tangents are 2 and 3, and to show then that these numbers have a sum of 135°, would not constitute a valid proof of our statement; for the tables give only approximate values.

A valid proof follows:

Let p = Arctan 2, q = Arctan 3.   Then tan p = 2, tan q = 3, $-\pi/2 <$ $p, q < \pi/2$.

But, in fact, we can narrow the range of possible values for p and q; for since tan $p > 0$ and tan $q > 0$, p and q cannot fall in the interval $\left\{ -\dfrac{\pi}{2} \longrightarrow 0 \right\}$.   Therefore $0 < p < \dfrac{\pi}{2}$, $0 < q < \dfrac{\pi}{2}$.

Now we seek $p + q$, knowing $0 < p + q < \pi$.

But tan $(p + q) = \dfrac{\tan p + \tan q}{1 - \tan p \tan q} = \dfrac{2 + 3}{1 - 6} = -1.$

Therefore $p + q = 135°$.

Therefore Arctan 2 + Arctan 3 = 135°.

Illustrative Example 4.   Sketch the graph of the function:
$$f(x) = 3 \cos x + 4 \sin x.$$

SOLUTION.   The graph may be drawn by the "addition of ordinates" method, but there is a better method which applies to all functions of the form $r \cos (vx + w) + s \sin (vx + w)$, where $r \neq 0$, $s \neq 0$, $v \neq 0$, w are real numbers:

Let $p = \text{Arcsin} \dfrac{3}{\sqrt{3^2 + 4^2}} = \text{Arcsin} \dfrac{3}{5}$ (Fig. 8.23).

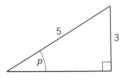

Fig. 8.23

Then $\sin p = 3/5$ and $\cos p = 4/5$.

Therefore $3 = 5 \sin p$, $4 = 5 \cos p$.   Substituting in the given function:

$$f(x) = 5 \sin p \cos x + 5 \cos p \sin x$$
$$= 5 (\sin p \cos x + \cos p \sin x)$$
$$= 5 \sin (p + x)$$
$$= 5 \sin (x + p)$$

The given function may therefore be written in the form $a \sin (bx + c)$, a form whose graph is familiar to us (see Section 8.14).

In this case, $f(x)$ has a maximum value of 5, which it attains when $x + p = (\pi/2) + k \cdot 2\pi$, i.e., when $x = (\pi/2) - p + k \cdot 2\pi$.

Since $\sin p = .6000$, we find, from the tables, that $p = 37°$, approximately; or, in terms of radians, $p = \dfrac{37 \cdot \pi}{180}$, or $p = 0.2\pi$, approximately.

Maxima occur, therefore, when $x = 0.5\pi - 0.2\pi + k \cdot 2\pi = 0.3\pi + k \cdot 2\pi$; in particular when $x = 0.3\pi, 2.3\pi$; i.e., when $x = 0.9, 7.2$, approximately.

The period of $5 \sin (x + p)$ is clearly $2\pi/1$, or 6.3, approximately.   It is helpful to note that when $x = 0, f(x) = 3 \cos 0 + 4 \sin 0 = 3$.   The graph is drawn in Fig. 8.24.

Illustrative Example 5. $\sin \text{Arccos} \left(-\tfrac{4}{5}\right) = ?$

SOLUTION.   Let $\text{Arccos} \left(-\tfrac{4}{5}\right) = \theta$.   Then $\cos \theta = -\tfrac{4}{5}$, θ is in QII (see table, p. 263), and our problem requires us to find $\sin \theta$.   The process is given in Section 8.6; the solution: $\sin \text{Arccos} \left(-\tfrac{4}{5}\right) = \sin \theta = \tfrac{3}{5}$.

Illustrative Example 6. $\text{Arctan} (\sin \pi) = ?$

SOLUTION. $\text{Arctan} (\sin \pi) = \text{Arctan} \, 0 = 0$.

Note: The notation "arcsin x," etc. (note the small "a"), is used in some texts to represent any one, or perhaps the set of all of the preimages of x under the sine function. We shall not use this notation at all in this text.

Another related notation that is sometimes used is $\sin^{-1} x$ for Arcsin x, etc.   We shall not use this notation, in order to avoid possible confusion between inverse and reciprocal functions $\left(\sin^{-1} x \text{ might be confused with } \dfrac{1}{\sin x}\right)$.

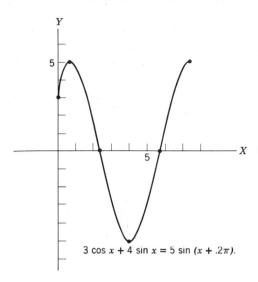

$$3 \cos x + 4 \sin x = 5 \sin (x + .2\pi).$$

Fig. 8.24

▶ **EXERCISE 48**

1. Sketch the graphs of:
(a) Cos x; Arccos x (b) Tan x; Arctan x (c) Cot x; Arccot x
(d) Sec x; Arcsec x (e) Csc x; Arccsc x

2. Find, if possible

(a) Arcsin $\frac{1}{2}$ (b) Arcsin $\left(-\frac{1}{2}\right)$ (c) Arccos $\frac{1}{2}$

(d) Arccos $\left(-\frac{1}{2}\right)$ (e) Arctan 1   (f) Arctan (-1)

(g) Arcsin $\frac{\sqrt{3}}{2}$ (h) Arcsin $\left(-\frac{\sqrt{3}}{2}\right)$ (i) Arccos $\left(\frac{\sqrt{3}}{2}\right)$

(j) Arccos $\left(-\frac{\sqrt{3}}{2}\right)$ (k) Arcsin $\frac{\sqrt{2}}{2}$ (l) Arccos $\left(-\frac{1}{\sqrt{2}}\right)$

(m) Arcsin 1   (n) Arcsin (-1) (o) Arccos 1
(p) Arccos (-1) (q) Arcsin 0   (r) Arccos 0
(s) Arctan 0   (t) Arccot 0   (u) Arcsec (-2)

3. Using inverse trigonometric functions, express all solutions of the following equations:

(a) $\sin x = 0.1$ (b) $\sin x = -0.1$ (c) $\cos x = 0.1$
(d) $\cos x = -0.1$ (e) $\tan x = 0.1$ (f) $\tan x = -0.1$

4. (a) Prove: $\operatorname{Arctan}\left(-\frac{1}{5}\right) - \operatorname{Arctan}\left(-\frac{3}{2}\right) = \frac{\pi}{4}.$

(b) Find: $\sin(\operatorname{Arccos}\frac{1}{2} + \operatorname{Arcsin}\frac{1}{7}).$

(c) Suppose $\triangle ABC$ is a right triangle, with $AC = 2$, $\angle C = 90°$, $BC = 6$, and D is a point on side BC such that $DC = 1$. Express $\angle BAD$ as the difference between two "Arctans"; find $\tan \angle BAD$; find $\angle BAD$.

(d) Suppose $\triangle ABC$ is a right triangle, D a point on side BC such that $DC = d$. Express $\angle BAD$ in terms of a, b, d.

5. Sketch the graphs of the following functions:

(a) $3 \cos x - 4 \sin x$

(b) $\sin x + \cos x$

(c) $\sin x - \cos x$

(d) $\sin 2x + \cos 2x$

6. The following equations may be solved by transposing and squaring, or by applying the device of Illustrative Example 4 above. Try both methods.

(a) $\sin x + \cos x = 1$

(b) $6 \cos x + 8 \sin x = 5$

(c) $\sin x - \cos x = 1$

7. Find:

(a) $\sin \operatorname{Arccos} \frac{4}{5}$

(b) $\cos \operatorname{Arcsin} \frac{4}{5}$

(c) $\cos \operatorname{Arcsin} \left(-\frac{4}{5}\right)$

(d) $\operatorname{Arcsin}\left(\sin \frac{\pi}{6}\right)$

(e) $\operatorname{Arcsin}\left(\sin \frac{5\pi}{6}\right)$

(f) $\sin \operatorname{Arcsin}(0.7)$

(g) $\cos \operatorname{Arccos}(0.7)$

(h) $\cot \operatorname{Arctan} 2$

(i) $\operatorname{Arctan}(\cot 40°)$

(j) $\operatorname{Arcsin}(0.1) + \operatorname{Arccos}(0.1)$

(k) $\operatorname{Arctan}(0.1) + \operatorname{Arccot}(0.1)$

(l) $\operatorname{Arccot}(-0.1) - \operatorname{Arctan}(-0.1)$

(m) $\sin \operatorname{Arctan}(-1)$

(n) $\operatorname{Arctan}\left(\sin \frac{\pi}{2}\right)$

8. Prove that if $a \neq b$ are real numbers, then the line whose equation is $y = x$ is the perpendicular bisector of the line segment joining the points (a, b), (b, a).

8.16 ON THE SOLUTION OF TRIANGLES

In section 7.1 we learned how to "solve" a right triangle; that is to say, given certain parts of a right triangle we learned how to find the lengths of the sides and the measures of the angles which were not given. In the next two sections we shall develop methods for solving *any* triangle.

But first of all, what sort of information about a triangle will be sufficient to enable us to solve it? A clue to the answer to this question is given by well-known congruence theorems of geometry:

Theorem. Two triangles are congruent if:

(*a*) A side and two angles of one are respectively equal to a side and two angles of the other. (*saa* = *saa* or *asa* = *asa*).

(*b*) The three sides of one are respectively equal to the three sides of the other. (*sss* = *sss*)

(*c*) Two sides and an included angle of one are respectively equal to two sides and an included angle of the other. (*sas* = *sas*)

Suppose now that we are given three sides of a triangle; as, for example, suppose we are told that in a certain triangle the sides are of lengths 4 ft, 5 ft, and 6 ft.

Then by (*b*) of the preceding theorem, any two such triangles would have to be congruent; corresponding angles of two such triangles would therefore have to be equal. In all such triangles the number of degrees in the angle opposite the 4 ft side would thus have to be the same and similarly for the other two angles.

The information "*sss*" therefore determines the measures of the respective angles of a triangle *uniquely*.

Note. This is not to say that if we are given *any* three lengths, a triangle exists with sides of these lengths. For example, it is impossible to have a triangle whose sides are 4 ft, 5 ft, and 10 ft in length. (Why?) What we *are* saying is that *if* it is possible to have a triangle with sides of three given lengths, *then* the measures of the respective angles of that triangle are uniquely determined.

8.17 THE LAW OF SINES (SOLUTION OF CASES *asa*, *saa*)

The law of sines, which we are about to develop, may be used to solve a triangle when a side and any two angles of that triangle are given.

Suppose *ABC* is a triangle, and that the foot *D* of a perpendicular from *A* to *BC* falls between *B* and *C* and is not either *B* or *C*: (Fig. 8.25).

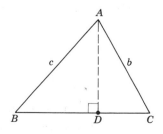

Fig. 8.25

Then: (1) $\sin B = \dfrac{AD}{c}$

                          (2) $\sin C = \dfrac{AD}{b}$

dividing (1) by (2):   (3) $\dfrac{\sin B}{\sin C} = \dfrac{b}{c}$

Although this is only one of the cases that may occur, so far as the position of D on line BC is concerned, the results (1) and (2), and hence the result (3), turn out to be true for *any* triangle ABC. A proof that this is so follows.

We shall require the following property of angles which we append to the list on page 189:

(iii)   Suppose $\measuredangle POR = \theta°$. Then there is a ccd system with origin O in which ray OR is labeled 0 and ray OP is labeled θ.

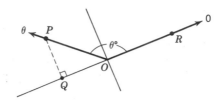

Fig. 8.26

We now prove the following lemma.

Lemma.   Given $\measuredangle POR = \theta°$, let Q be the foot of a perpendicular from P to line OR (Fig. 8.26). Then $\sin \theta° = PQ/OP$.

PROOF: By (iii) above, there is a ccd system with origin O in which ray OR is labeled 0 and ray OP is labeled θ.

By the definition of the sine function:

(a) $\sin \theta° = \dfrac{y_P}{r_P}$

Now θ is the degree measure of an angle. Therefore [see (i), page 189] $0 \leqslant \theta \leqslant 180$. Hence (see Problem 3, Exercise 33) P falls in QI or QII or on the X-axis. Therefore $y_P \geqslant 0$, so that (see Problem 14, Exercise 24) $y_P = PQ$.

Furthermore, $r_P = OP$.

Therefore, substituting in (a) above, we have:

$$\sin \theta° = \frac{PQ}{OP}, \text{ Q.E.D.}$$

Now for *any* triangle ABC, (1) and (2), above, follow immediately from the lemma, and hence (3), which follows from (1) and (2), is true for any triangle ABC.

Since any pair of sides of a triangle and their opposite vertices may be labeled b, c, B, C respectively, the following may be stated:

Law of Sines

In a triangle, the ratio between any pair of sides is equal to the ratio between the sines of their opposite angles.

In other words: If $\angle U$ is opposite side u and $\angle V$ is opposite side v in a triangle, then:

$$\frac{u}{v} = \frac{\sin U}{\sin V}$$

Illustrative Example:

Suppose that in triangle ABC we have given: $a = 10$, $B = 40° 40'$, $C = 10° 30'$. Then:

$$B + C = 50° 70' = 51° 10'$$
$$\therefore A = 179° 60'$$
$$\underline{-51° 10'}$$
$$A = \overline{128° 50'}$$
$$\frac{b}{a} = \frac{\sin B}{\sin A} \cdot \frac{b}{10} = \frac{\sin 40° 40'}{\sin 128° 50'} = \frac{\sin 40° 40'}{\sin 51° 10'}$$
$$b = \frac{10 \sin 40° 40'}{\sin 51° 10'} = \frac{(10)\,(0.6517)}{(0.7790)} = 8.366; \text{ similarly } c$$

may be computed.

As a corollary to the law of sines, a useful formula for the area of a triangle may be derived.

It is a result of geometry that the area of triangle ABC is $\frac{1}{2}ah$, where h is the length of the altitude AD of triangle ABC, and a is the length of the side opposite A.

But it follows from the preceding lemma that $h = c \sin B$. Therefore:

$$\text{Area of triangle } ABC = \tfrac{1}{2}ac \sin B$$

Or in other words:

If u, v are sides of a triangle and I is their included angle, then the area of the triangle is:

$$\tfrac{1}{2}uv \sin I$$

▶ **EXERCISE 49**

1. Complete the solution of triangle ABC in the illustrative example above.

2. Solve the following triangles and find their areas.

(a) $A = 30°$, $B = 45°$, $c = 10$
(b) $B = 45°$, $C = 60°$, $b = 10$
(c) $A = 120°$, $C = 45°$, $a = 10$
(d) $A = 47°$, $B = 74°$, $a = 125$
(e) $A = 19° \ 12'$, $B = 108° \ 44'$, $b = 213$
(f) $B = 67° \ 21'$, $C = 106° \ 47'$, $a = 123$

3. Observation posts are established at points A and B on a beach, 1000 yards apart. A boat is sighted at point C, and angles CAB and CBA are measured and found to be $63° \ 14'$ and $46° \ 18'$, respectively. How far is the boat from each observation post? from the shore?

4. The shadow of a pyramid is found to be 400 ft longer when the angle of elevation of the sun is $31°$ than when it is $61°$. Find the distances from the top of the pyramid to the tips of these shadows, and find the height of the pyramid.

5. When the angle of elevation of the sun is $44°$, a vertical pole, on a hill which is inclined at $10°$, casts a shadow down the slope whose length is 80 ft. Find the length of the pole.

6. Suppose we are asked to solve a triangle in which $a = 1$, $b = \sqrt{2}$, $B = 45°$. Then applying the law of sines:

$$\sin A = \frac{a \cdot \sin B}{b} = \frac{1}{2}$$

Therefore: $\qquad\qquad\qquad A = 30° \ or \ A = 150°$

But $A = 150°$ is not possible, since then $A + B > 180°$. Therefore we have the unique solution:

$$A = 30°, \ C = 105°, \ c = \frac{a \sin C}{\sin A} = (2)(0.9659) = 1.9318$$

It is possible, however, to have no solution, one solution or two solutions for a triangle when given two sides and an angle opposite one. For this reason, the situation in which we have given "*ssa*" is called the "ambiguous case."

Determine all solutions in the following cases and draw accurate diagrams to illustrate:

(a) $C = 30°$, $b = 10$, $c = 3$ $\qquad$ (b) $C = 30°$, $b = 10$, $c = 5$
(c) $C = 30°$, $b = 10$, $c = 7$ $\qquad$ (d) $C = 30°$, $b = 10$, $c = 12$

7. Given C, b, c, state general circumstances under which zero, one or two solutions will exist for triangle ABC.

8. A freshman-mathematics student watching a boat race from the shore of a river notes the following facts with respect to one of the crews:

It is nearer to him now than it was when it started the race.
It has travelled 4280 feet since starting.
The starting point was 6240 feet from the student.
The angle made by rays from the student to the initial and present position of the crew is $36° \ 39'$.

How far apart are the student and the crew at the present time?

8.18 THE LAW OF COSINES (SOLUTION OF CASES *sas*, *sss*).

Theorem. (Law of Cosines). Suppose that in $\triangle\,UVW$, sides of lengths u, v, w are opposite vertices U, V, W, respectively. Then $v^2 = u^2 + w^2 - 2\,uw\cos V$.

PROOF. Suppose $\measuredangle\,V = \theta$ (degrees or radians). By (iii) of Section 8.17, there exists a ccd (or a ccr) system with origin V in which ray VU is labeled 0 and ray VW is labeled θ (Fig. 8.27).

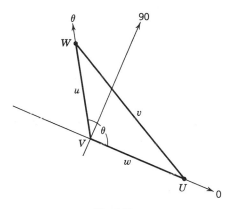

Fig. 8.27

Now (by Lemma 1 of Section 8.8), points W and U have the coordinates $(u\cos\theta,\ u\sin\theta)$ and $(w, 0)$, respectively.

Therefore: $v = \sqrt{(u\cos\theta - w)^2 + (u\sin\theta)^2}$
and:
$$v^2 = u^2\cos^2\theta - 2uw\cos\theta + w^2 + u^2\sin^2\theta$$
$$= u^2\,(\sin^2\theta + \cos^2\theta) + w^2 - 2uw\cos\theta$$
$$= u^2 + w^2 - 2uw\cos\theta$$
$$= u^2 + w^2 - 2uw\cos V,\ \text{Q.E.D.}$$

Law of Cosines

In any triangle, the square of any given side is equal to the sum of the squares of the other two sides, minus twice the product of the other two sides with the cosine of the angle opposite the given side.

Illustrative Example. Suppose we are given that in triangle ABC, $a = 8$, $c = 5$ and $\measuredangle\,B = 60°$.

Then from the law of cosines: $b^2 = 8^2 + 5^2 - 2\cdot 8\cdot 5\ \cos\ 60° = 49$.
Therefore: $b = 7$.

Now we know all three sides of triangle ABC. The following procedure is therefore that which applies in the case *sss* also:

Again from the law of cosines: $a^2 = b^2 + c^2 - 2bc \cos A$.

Therefore:

$$\cos A = \frac{b^2 + c^2 - a^2}{2bc} = \frac{49 + 25 - 64}{2 \cdot 7 \cdot 5} = \frac{1}{7} = 0.1429$$

Therefore:

$$A = 81° 47'$$

Similarly, we may find $\angle C$.

The correctness of our solution may be checked by adding to the given value of B the computed values of A and C. Ideally, of course, the sum should be 180°.

8.19 VECTORS

Suppose an object were to be moved 3 ft to the right of an original position, and then 4 ft forward. These "displacements" of the object might be pictured as in Fig. 8.28.

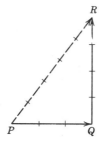

Fig. 8.28

The arrow PQ represents the first displacement; the arrow QR the second. The arrow PR represents a single displacement whose final effect on the object moved would be the same as the combined effect of the other two displacements.

That is to say, starting at P, a single movement of 5 ft in the direction PR will attain the same final position as a movement of 3 ft to the right followed by a movement of 4 ft forward.

For this reason, the displacement represented by the arrow PR is called the *resultant* of the *component* displacements represented by the arrows PQ and QR.

It will be noted that a displacement (from *any* point) may be described by telling these two facts about it:

(*a*)   the *amount* of the displacement (in terms of some unit of distance).

(*b*)   the direction of the displacement.

Concepts whose description may be given in terms of an amount and a direction are called *vector* concepts, or more usually, "vector quantities." Arrows are particularly suited to the representation of vector quantities; for we may indicate the amount of the vector quantity by the length of the arrow (having chosen a suitable scale) and we may indicate the direction of the vector quantity by the direction of the arrow—just as we have done in the case of the vector quantity of displacement.

Such arrows are called *vectors*.

Vector quantities are especially important in the field of physics. *Velocity*, for example, since it is defined to be the displacement which occurs in some unit of time (e.g., 30 miles northward per hour), is a vector concept.   It turns out that *acceleration* and *force* are vector quantities also.

Quite apart from their immediate practical applications, vectors have shown themselves to be useful in the development of many purely mathematical theories.   There is therefore a well-developed abstract formulation of the concept of a vector, which characterizes vectors axiomatically, just, for example, as we defined the real numbers axiomatically in Chapter 4.

Our treatment here, however, will be informal both from the physical and mathematical points of view.

We will assume, for example, that vectors may always be "added" (i.e., the resultant of vectors may always be obtained) as in the case of displacements.   That is to say, if the "tail" of a second vector coincides with the "point" of a first, then the resultant of the two is an arrow drawn from the tail of the first to the point of the second, as in Fig. 8.28.

This idea may be generalized to apply to the addition of more than two vectors (Fig. 8.29).

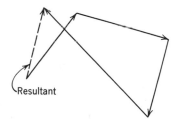

Fig. 8.29

In solving vector problems, the law of cosines is often useful.

Illustrative Example I. A man walks 5 miles E and then 8 miles S 30° W (i.e., in the direction of a ray lying between rays pointing south and west, and making a 30° angle with the ray pointing south). How far is he from his starting point, and in what direction (Fig. 8.30)?

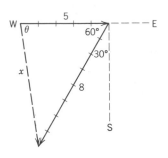

Fig. 8.30

SOLUTION. $x^2 = 25 + 64 - 2 \cdot 5 \cdot 8 \cos 60° = 49$
Therefore: $x = 7$.
$$8^2 = 5^2 + 7^2 - 2 \cdot 5 \cdot 7 \cos \theta$$
Therefore: $\cos \theta = 0.1429$
$$\theta = 81° \, 47'$$

The man is 7 miles from his starting point, in the direction E 81° 47′ S.

Illustrative Example 2. An airplane flying directly south at a speed of 200 miles per hour encounters a wind blowing N 60° E at a speed of 75 miles per hour (Fig. 8.31).

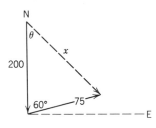

Fig. 8.31

In what direction will the plane actually fly after it meets the wind (assuming no controls in the plane are changed) and at what speed?

SOLUTION. $x^2 = 75^2 + 200^2 - 2 \cdot 75 \cdot 200 \cos 60° = 30625$
Therefore: $x = 175$.
$$75^2 = 175^2 + 200^2 - 2 \cdot 200 \cdot 175 \cos \theta$$

Therefore: $\cos\theta = \frac{13}{14} = 0.9286$

$$\theta = 21°\,47'$$

The plane (although still headed south) will proceed in the direction S 21° 47′ E at a speed of 175 miles per hour.

Illustrative Example 3. Three ropes are knotted together (at point A in Fig. 8.32). Two make an angle of 60° with each other, and are being tugged separately by two boys exerting forces of 60 pounds and 100 pounds, respectively. The third is being tugged by their father. What force, in what direction, must Dad exert if he is not to lose the tug-of-war?

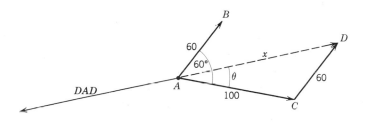

Fig. 8.32

SOLUTION. First we find the resultant of the two given forces. To add them, one arrow may be shifted, *without changing either its magnitude or its direction*, until its tail coincides with the point of the other.

That is to say (referring to Fig. 8.32), if AB and AC are arrows representing the two given forces, we draw an arrow CD in the same direction and of the same length as AB.

AD is then the required resultant; since $AB \parallel CD$, $\angle ACD = 120°$. We now have: $x^2 = 60^2 + 100^2 - 2 \cdot 60 \cdot 100 \cdot (-\frac{1}{2}) = 19600$.

Therefore: $x = 140$.

Furthermore: $60^2 = 100^2 + 140^2 - 2 \cdot 100 \cdot 140 \cos\theta$.

Therefore: $\cos\theta = \frac{13}{14} = 0.9286$.

$$\theta = 21°\,47'$$

Now we see that the force exerted by the boys is equivalent to a single force of 140 pounds exerted between the component forces at an angle of 21° 47′ with the rope AC.

The father, to hold his own, must therefore exert a force of 140 pounds in a direction opposite to that of the resultant AD.

▶ **EXERCISE 50**

1. Complete the solution of the illustrative example of Section 8.18.
2. Solve the following triangles:

(a) $a = 8, c = 15, B = 60°$ (b) $a = 3, b = 8, C = 60°$
(c) $b = 16, c = 55, A = 60°$ (d) $a = 5, b = 6, c = 7$
(e) $a = 4, b = 5, c = 6$ (f) $a = 5, b = 4, c = 3$

3. An airplane headed S 50° E at a speed of 182 miles per hour is being blown off its course by a wind blowing in the direction S 70° W at a speed of 80 mph.

How fast, and in what direction, does the airplane travel?

4. Solve illustrative example 3 of this section, assuming that $\angle BAC$ is 120° and that the forces exerted by the boys are 80 and 105 pounds.

5. A force of 48 pounds in the direction N 10° E and a force of 13 pounds in the direction S 70° W are applied to a body.

Find the resultant of these forces.

6. Find the lengths of the diagonals of a parallelogram in which two sides are 6 in. and 4 in. long, and one angle is equal to 75°.

7. A toy boat that has a speed of 3 miles per hour in still water is headed in the direction N 45° E on a stream that flows from north to south. If the boat opposes a current of 2 miles per hour, in what direction does it proceed? If the stream is 10 yards wide, how long does the boat take to cross the stream?

8. Two ropes, both tied at one end to the same point, are pulled with forces F_1 and F_2 pounds respectively. The ropes make an angle of θ with each other, and the resultant of the applied forces is R pounds.

In each of the following cases, find whichever of F_1, F_2, R and θ is not given.

(a) $F_1 = 2, F_2 = 3, \theta = 35°$ (b) $F_1 = 3, F_2 = 6, \theta = 40°$
(c) $F_1 = 4, R = 5, \theta = 100°$ (d) $F_1 = 4, R = 3, \theta = 100°$
(e) $F_1 = 3, F_2 = 4, R = 5$ (f) $F_1 = 3, F_2 = 4, R = 2$
(g) $F_1 = 2, F_2 = 3, R = 5$ (h) $F_1 = 2, F_2 = 3, R = 1$
(i) $F_1 = 2, F_2 = 2, \theta = 60°$ (j) $F_1 = 2, F_2 = 2, \theta = 120°$
(k) $F_1 = 2, R = 2, \theta = 100°$ (l) $F_1 = 2, R = 0$

9. Derive the theorem of Section 8.18 as a corollary of Lemma 2 of Section 8.8.

10. Prove that in any triangle ABC, the following is true: $a \cos B + b \cos A = c$. [*Hint:* use the law of cosines.]

9.1 INTRODUCTION

Wherever functions and equations are important, which is to say almost everywhere in the realm of contemporary knowledge, the question of graphical representation of these functions and equations is also likely to be important.

We shall therefore devote this chapter to a further study of graphs.

A review of Sections 2.9 and 6.8 will be found to be helpful at this point.

9.2 POLYNOMIAL FUNCTIONS (OF ONE VARIABLE)

If we were asked to specify a mapping to be used in defining a real-real function f, we might suggest that the mapping be given by the equation: $f(x) = x$; or it might perhaps occur to us to specify the mapping by setting $f(x)$ equal to any one of the following instead:

$$0; 7; x + 1; 2x; 1 - x; x^2 + 3x - 2; x^3$$

Functions like these are called *polynomial* functions. The simplest functions that may be graphed belong to the class of polynomial functions. We shall therefore consider the graphs of polynomial functions before we consider other graphs in this chapter; but first a better definition is required:

Definition. A *polynomial function of one real variable* is a real-real function p whose mapping may be given by setting $p(x)$ equal to one of the following:

(i) 0

(ii) a

(iii) $ax + b$
(iv) $ax^2 + bx + c$
(v) $ax^3 + bx^2 + cx + d$
       etc.,

where $a, b, c \cdots$ are real numbers and $a \neq 0$.

$0, a, ax, b, ax^2, bx, c, ax^3, \cdots$ are called the *terms* of their respective polynomial functions.

$0, a, b, c, \cdots$ are called the *coefficients* of their respective polynomial functions; also, a is called the *coefficient* of x in the term ax, b the *coefficient* of x^2 in the term bx^2, etc.

Except for terms with coefficient 0, every term of a polynomial function has assigned to it a number called its *degree* in the following way: If k is a nonzero real number, then the degree of a term k is 0; of a term kx, 1; of a term kx^n, n.

Except for case (i) above, every polynomial function also has a degree assigned to it. The *degree* of a polynomial function is the highest degree which any of its terms exhibits. Thus, since $a \neq 0$ in cases (i)–(v), etc., above, the degree of the polynomial function p in cases (ii), (iii), (iv), (v), etc., would be 0, 1, 2, 3, etc., respectively.

Polynomial functions of type (i) or (ii) above are called *constant* polynomial functions (cf. page 23); those of degrees 1, 2, 3, 4, 5 are called *linear*, *quadratic*, *cubic*, *quartic*, and *quintic* polynomial functions, respectively.

Examples of polynomial functions p of one real variable. (In all of these examples we take the domain of p to be the set of all real numbers.)

(*a*) $p(x) = 0$ (falls under (i) above).
(*b*) $p(x) = 7$ (falls under (ii) above).
(*c*) $p(x) = 2x + 3$ (falls under (iii) above).
(*d*) $p(x) = x^2$ (falls under (iv) above, for this mapping *may* be given by: $p(x) = 1x^2 + 0x + 0$).

In the sequel, unless otherwise noted, we shall assume that the domain of each polynomial function of one real variable that we shall consider is "maximal," i.e., is the set of *all* real numbers.

It is worth noting that one may consider polynomial functions with coefficients other than real numbers. Polynomial functions whose coefficients are complex numbers, for example, are important in mathematics. In this text however, unless otherwise noted, all polynomial functions will be assumed to have only real coefficients.

No degree has been assigned to 0, since no useful purpose would be served by doing so. For nonzero polynomials, for example, it may be proved that the degree of a product is equal to the sum of the degrees of the factors. This theorem would not hold if the polynomial 0 were included, no matter what degree were assigned to 0.

Note that our definition of the degree of a polynomial function p of one real variable assumes that the mapping of p cannot be expressed by more than *one* of the forms (i)–(v), etc., above, with $a \neq 0$; otherwise this degree would not be "well-defined." The uniqueness we have assumed can be proved, although we do not do so here.

Examples:

(*a*) $p(x) = 3x^2 + 4x + 5$ defines a polynomial function of degree 2, i.e., a quadratic function, with coefficients 3, 4, 5; 3 is said to be the coefficient of x^2, 4 the coefficient of x; (5 is sometimes called the "constant" term).

In the sequel we shall often follow the general practice of referring to an expression such as $3x^2 + 4x + 5$ as a polynomial function, or even as just a polynomial, when what we have in mind is the function p whose domain is the set of all real numbers, or some specified subset of that set, and whose mapping is given by the equation $p(x) = 3x^2 + 4x + 5$.

(*b*) $2v - 7$, since it may be expressed as $2v + (-7)$, is a polynomial ("in v," we say) of the first degree, i.e., a linear polynomial; 2 is the coefficient of v, and -7 is the constant term of this polynomial.

(*c*) 11 is a zero-degree, i.e., a constant polynomial. (We have in mind, of course, the function p whose domain consists of the set of all real numbers, and whose mapping is given by the equation $p(x) = 11$.)

(*d*) 0 is a constant polynomial also, but one to which no degree is assigned.

(*e*) $y - y^3$ is a cubic (i.e., a third-degree) polynomial in y, since $y - y^3 = (-1)y^3 + 0y^2 + 1y + 0$. (This equality is an *identity*, i.e., the two sides are defined and equal for all real numbers, y.)

A polynomial expressed in one of the forms (i)–(v), etc., above will be said to be in *standard form*.

9.3 THE GRAPH OF A POLYNOMIAL $p(x)$

In Section 6.10 we showed that the graph of an equation in the form $y = mx + b$, with m and b any real numbers, is a nonvertical straight line with slope m. If $m = 0$, the equation reduces to $y = b$, whose graph is a straight line with slope $m = 0$, i.e., a "horizontal" straight line.

But from the definitions of graphs of functions and equations, the graph of an equation $y = f(x)$ is the same as the graph of the function $f(x)$.

We may therefore say that the graph of a function $mx + b$, where m and b are any real numbers, is always a straight line.

A constant polynomial function, i.e., one of degree 0, falls into the pattern $mx + b$, with $m = 0$. Therefore, in a cc plane, the graph of a constant polynomial is always a horizontal straight line.

For example, the graph in a cc plane of the polynomial 2, i.e., of the polynomial function $p(x) = 2$, i.e., of the equation $y = 2$, is a line parallel to the X-axis with y-intercept 2.

A linear polynomial function, i.e., one of degree 1, falls into the pattern $mx + b$ with $m \neq 0$. Therefore, the graph in a cc plane of a first degree polynomial in x is always a straight line that is neither horizontal nor vertical.

For example, the straight line which is the graph of the polynomial $2x + 3$ is easily drawn, either by the "slope-intercept" method ($m = 2$, $b = 3$) or by locating points $(0, 3)$, $(4, 11)$, for example, on that line (cf. Section 6.10).

So far as the graphs of quadratic and higher degree functions are concerned, we shall now make several definitions and statements, most of which, although they will be given roughly and intuitively and without proof, will nevertheless turn out to be helpful in drawing these graphs.

(i)   A point on a graph that is higher than any "nearby" point is called a *maximum* point; a point on a graph that is lower than any nearby point is called a *minimum* point; an *extremum* is either a maximum or a minimum point.

The graph of a polynomial $p(x)$ of degree n has at most $n - 1$ extrema. Furthermore, the exact number of extrema differs from $n - 1$ by an even number. (See Fig. 9.1)

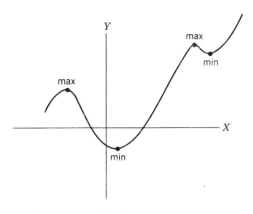

Fig. 9.1

(ii)   The graph of a polynomial $p(x)$ is always "continuous"; that is to say there are no "breaks" in the graph. Graphs of polynomials are also free of sharp points.

(The statements made in (i) and (ii) above are made more precisely and proved in courses in mathematics which go under such names as "calculus" and "functions of a real variable.")

(iii) The term of highest degree in a polynomial $p(x)$ eventually "dominates" the polynomial. For example, in the polynomial $p(x)$ $= 2x^4 - 7x^3 - x^2 - 2$, the term of highest degree is $2x^4$. For sufficiently large positive x, $2x^4$ will be very large positively, enough to outweigh the negative effect of the other terms. Therefore, in this case, after we have gone sufficiently far to the right, the graph simply continually rises. We say that on the right the graph eventually only rises. On the left, it is again the term of highest degree, examined this time for large *negative* values of x, which determines the behavior of $p(x)$. In the case above, since $2x^4$ is positive regardless of the sign of x, the graph eventually only rises as we move to the left also.

The graph of $-2x^4 + 6x^2 - 7$, however, will eventually only fall on both its left and right; the graph of $x^3 - 999$ will eventually rise on the right and fall on the left; and the graph of $-2x^3 + 999$ will fall on the right and rise on the left.

(iv) Consider the polynomial: $p(x) = x^4 + x^2$. It happens that $(2, 20)$ is a point of the graph of $p(x)$. It follows, without further computation, that $(-2, 20)$ is a point of this graph also. For since only even exponents occur in $p(x)$, $p(-2)$ must have the same value as $p(2)$.

Thus, whenever (a, b) is a point on the graph of $x^4 + x^2$, then so is $(-a, b)$.

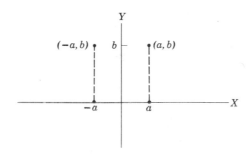

Fig. 9.2

But if the Y-axis were a mirror, the points (a, b) and $(-a, b)$ would be each other's images (Fig. 9.2). For this reason, the points (a, b) and $(-a, b)$ are said to be *symmetric with respect to the Y-axis*. And when it is true that for each point (a, b) on a graph, $(-a, b)$ is on the graph also, then we say that the graph is symmetric to the Y-axis. What we

have remarked, then, is that the graph of $x^4 + x^2$ is symmetric to the
Y-axis.   And in fact:

*The graph of a polynomial $p(x)$ is symmetric to Y-axis if and only if all
the terms of $p(x)$ are of even degree.*

(Note that a nonzero constant term is of even degree, for it is of degree
0, and 0 is an even number.)

On the other hand, suppose all the terms of a polynomial $p(x)$ are of
odd degree, as for example in the case $p(x) = x^3 + x$.   We note that
$(1, 2)$ and $(-1, -2)$ are points of the graph of $x^3 + x$, and in fact it may
be shown that whenever (a, b) is a point of the graph of $x^3 + x$, then so
is $(-a, -b)$.

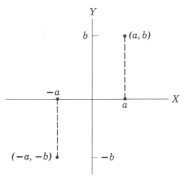

Fig. 9.3

Points (a, b), $(-a, -b)$ are said to be *symmetric with respect to the
origin* (Fig. 9.3).   And when it is true that for each point (a, b) on a
graph, $(-a, -b)$ is on the graph also, then we say that the graph is
symmetric to the origin.   Thus the graph of $x^3 + x$ is symmetric to the
origin and in fact:

*The graph of a polynomial $p(x)$ is symmetric to the origin if and only if all
the terms of $p(x)$ are of odd degree.*

(v)   The points in which a graph intersects the X-axis and Y-axis are
called the x- and *y-intercepts*, respectively, of the graph.

Given an equation in x and y, the x-intercepts of its graph are the
x-values of the points of the graph for which $y = 0$, and, correspondingly,
the y-intercepts are the y-values of the points of the graph for which $x = 0$.

Given a polynomial $p(x)$, the graph of $p(x)$ is, of course, the same as
that of the equation $y = p(x)$; here the x-intercepts are therefore simply
the roots of the equation: $p(x) = 0$.

The graph of a polynomial $p(x)$ will always have just one y-intercept,
whose ordinate will be: $y = p(0)$.

Illustrative Example 1. We sketch the graph G of: $p(x) = x^3 - 8x$.

We note that: G has either 2 or 0 extrema.

On the right, G eventually only rises.

On the left, G eventually only falls.

G is symmetric to the origin.

x-intercepts occur when $x^3 - 8x = 0$.

The solution of this equation is: $x(x^2 - 8) = 0$; $x = 0$, $\pm 2\sqrt{2}$; or $x = 0$, ± 2.8, approximately.

The unique y-intercept is $y = p(0)$, or $y = 0$.

Since G is symmetric to the origin and since we already have $p(0)$, only the functional values for x positive had actually to be computed in working out the following table of values:

x	-3	-2	-1	0	1	2	3
$p(x)$	-3	8	7	0	-7	-8	3

Using this information, we sketch the graph of $x^3 - 8x$ (Fig. 9.4).

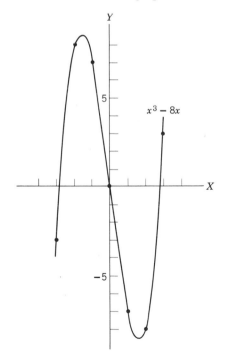

$x^3 - 8x$

Fig. 9.4

Illustrative Example 2. We sketch the graph G of: $p(x) = x^3 - x + 2$.
We note that: G has either 2 or 0 extrema.

G rises as we go far to the right and falls as we go far to the left.

G is symmetric to neither the Y-axis nor to the origin.

x-intercepts are not easily computed, but we note from the table of values below that one exists between $x = -2$ and $x = -1$ (see the theorem on page 116).

y-intercept: $y = p(0) = 2$.

Table of values:

x	-2	-1	0	1	2
$p(x)$	-4	2	2	2	8

The graph of $x^3 - x + 2$ is drawn in Fig. 9.5.

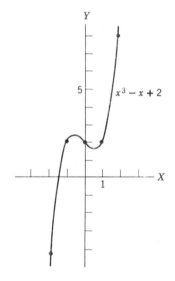

Fig. 9.5

▶ EXERCISE 51

1. Write out standard forms for quartic and quintic polynomials in x.

2. In each of the following cases state the degree (if any) and the type of the polynomial function given, and discuss and sketch its graph.

(a) 0   (b) 7

(c) $-\pi$ (d) x

(e) x^2

(f) x^3

(g) x^4

(h) $2x$

(i) $1 - x$

(j) $2x^2$

(k) $-2x^2$

(l) $-x^3$

(m) $-x^4$

(n) $x^2 - x + 5$

(o) $-x^2 + 2x + 1$

(p) $x^3 - x^2 - 5$

(q) $(x - 1)(x + 4)$

(r) $x^2(x - 3)$

(s) $-x^3 + x^2 + x + 1$

(t) $(x - 2)(x + 1)(x + 3)$

(u) $x^3 - x^2 - x + 1$

(v) $x^3 - x^2 + x - 1$

(w) $x^4 - x^2$

(x) $x - x^4$

3. A single standard form for polynomials which includes the forms 0, a, $ax + b$, $ax^2 + bx + c$, etc., as special cases is the following:

$a_0 x^n + a_1 x^{n-1} + \cdots + a_{n-1} x + a_n$, where n is a non-negative integer.

For $n = 0$, this form is understood to represent simply $a_0 x^0$, or a_0. For $n = 1$: $a_0 x + a_1$; for $n = 2$: $a_0 x^2 + a_1 x + a_2$; etc.

Write down what this form represents for $n = 3$ and $n = 4$.

In the case of each of the polynomials of Problem 2 above, identify n and $a_0, \cdots, a_n$, so that this new form expresses the given polynomial.

4. Frame general definitions of symmetry with respect to lines and points; i.e., given points P, P' and line l, under what circumstance will points P, P' be said to be symmetric with respect to line l? And given points P, P' and O, under what circumstances will points P, P' be said to be symmetric with respect to point O?

Suppose (p, q) is a point in a cc plane. What point is symmetric to (p, q) with respect to the line:

(a) $y = x$?

(b) $x = k$ (k any real number)?

(c) $x = p$?

(d) $y = -x$?

(e) $y = mx + b$?

5. Why have we not discussed the symmetry of graphs of functions with respect to the X-axis?

9.4 RATIONAL FUNCTIONS (OF ONE VARIABLE)

Roughly speaking, a rational function is the "ratio" of polynomial functions. More precisely:

Definition. A *rational function of one variable* is a real-real function r whose mapping may be given by:

$$r(x) = \frac{p(x)}{q(x)}$$

where p and q are polynomial functions.

[$r(x)$ is said to be *in lowest terms* if $p(x)$ and $q(x)$ have no common factor.]

For example, setting $r(x)$ equal to $\dfrac{x + 1}{x - 1}$ or $\dfrac{1}{x}$ or $\dfrac{x^2 + 1}{x^2 - 1}$, and naming a set of real numbers to be the domain of r, would define a rational function r for us.

In the sequel, unless otherwise noted, we shall assume that the domain of each rational function which we shall discuss is "maximal;" i.e., that if $r(x)$ is as above, then the domain of r consists of all real numbers except those that are roots of the equation $q(x) = 0$.

Also we shall refer, for example, to the rational function $1/x$, when what we have in mind is the function r whose domain consists of all real numbers except 0, and whose mapping is given by: $r(x) = 1/x$.

Similarly, we observe that we assume the domain of the rational function $\dfrac{x + 1}{x - 1}$ to be the set of all real numbers except 1, and of the rational function $\dfrac{x^2 + 1}{x^2 - 1}$ all real numbers except 1 and -1.

Note that every polynomial function is also a rational function; for the polynomial function $p(x)$ is identical with the rational function $p(x)/1$.

9.5   THE GRAPH OF A RATIONAL FUNCTION $r(x)$

We shall now examine the graph of the very simple rational function: $1/x$.

According to our agreement concerning the domain of rational functions, the domain of the function $1/x$ consists of all real numbers except 0.

We construct a table of values:

x	-4	-3	-2	-1	$-\frac{1}{2}$	$-\frac{1}{3}$	$-\frac{1}{4}$	0	$\frac{1}{4}$	$\frac{1}{3}$	$\frac{1}{2}$	1	2	3	4
$1/x$	$-\frac{1}{4}$	$-\frac{1}{3}$	$-\frac{1}{2}$	-1	-2	-3	-4		4	3	2	1	$\frac{1}{2}$	$\frac{1}{3}$	$\frac{1}{4}$

and we plot the indicated points, and through these points we draw a graph (Fig. 9.6).

Two facts are suggested by the graph, and may be verified upon examining the function $1/x$:

(i)   As x becomes large (either positively or negatively) the function $1/x$ approaches more and more nearly the value 0; but it never attains this value.

(ii)   As x approaches the value 0 (either positively or negatively) the function $1/x$ becomes larger and larger (either positively or negatively).

In case (i) we may say that as x becomes large our graph approaches, but never reaches, the straight line whose equation is $y = 0$.   In case (ii) we may say that as x approaches 0 our graph approaches the vertical straight line whose equation is $x = 0$.

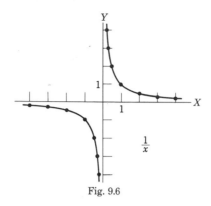

Fig. 9.6

In both cases, the straight lines approached by our graph are called *asymptotes* for the graph. Roughly speaking, an asymptote for a graph is a straight line that is approached (but not reached) by a graph as x or y become very large. A bit more precisely:

(*a*) *Nonvertical asymptote:* Suppose G is the graph of a function $f(x) = a(x) + b(x)$, and the straight line l is the graph of the function $a(x)$.

Then l is said to be an asymptote for G if $b(x)$ approaches (but never equals) 0 as x becomes large either positively or negatively (Fig. 9.7).

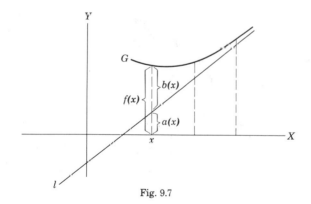

Fig. 9.7

For example, consider the function: $f(x) = x + (1/x)$. Clearly, $b(x) = 1/x$ approaches, but never equals, 0 as x becomes large either positively or negatively. The graph of the function $a(x) = x$ is a straight line, which is therefore approached by the graph of $x + (1/x)$ as we move far out on both the left and the right sides of our cc plane.

(We shall further consider the function $x + (1/x)$ below.)

(b)   Vertical asymptote: Suppose G is the graph of a function $f(x)$ and the vertical line l is the graph of the equation $x = k$.

Then l is said to be an asymptote for G if $f(x)$ becomes unboundedly larger and larger (positively or negatively) as x approaches the value k, either from the left, or from the right, or both (Fig. 9.8).

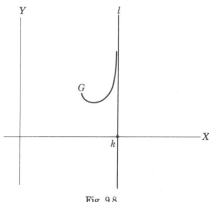

Fig. 9.8

If $f(x)$ is a rational function in lowest terms, $f(x)$ will become unboundedly large whenever its denominator approaches 0.

For example, the rational function $\dfrac{x - 10}{x - 2}$ becomes unboundedly large as x approaches 2, for as x approaches 2 the numerator and denominator of the function in question approach -8 and 0, respectively.   Therefore the line whose equation is $x = 2$ is an asymptote for the graph of the function $\dfrac{x - 10}{x - 2}$.

In fact, *if a rational function* $\dfrac{p(x)}{q(x)}$ *is in lowest terms, then whenever k is a root of $q(x) = 0$, $x = k$ will be the equation of a vertical asymptote for the graph of* $\dfrac{p(x)}{q(x)}$.

So far as symmetry, in the case of rational functions, is concerned, considerations similar to those which obtained in the case of polynomials lead to the following rules:

If $r(x) = \dfrac{p(x)}{q(x)}$ *is a rational function in lowest terms, then the graph G of $r(x)$ is symmetric to:*

(i)   *The Y-axis, if and only if, $p(x)$ and $q(x)$, in standard form, both involve only terms of even degree.*

(ii) *The origin, if and only if, $p(x)$ and $q(x)$, in standard form, are such that one involves only terms of even degree and the other only terms of odd degree.*

Illustrative Example 1.   We discuss and draw the graph G of the rational function: $r(x) = \dfrac{x^2 + 1}{x}$.

Domain: All real numbers except $x = 0$.

Intercepts: x: none; for $r(x) = 0$ if and only if the numerator
$x^2 + 1 = 0$, and $x^2 + 1 = 0$ has no real roots.
  y: none; for $r(0)$ is not defined.

Symmetry: with respect to the origin.

Asymptotes: (*a*)   nonvertical: We may write:

$$r(x) = \frac{x^2 + 1}{x} = \frac{x^2}{x} + \frac{1}{x} = x + \frac{1}{x}$$

As we have already noted above, the graph of the function x is an asymptote for G, approached both on the right and left by G.

(*b*)   vertical: 0 is an immediate root of the equation $x = 0$ which results from setting $q(x)$ equal to 0 in this case.   Therefore the vertical line whose equation is $x = 0$, i.e., the Y-axis, is an asymptote for G.

Now, with the help of the above information, and the following table of values, we sketch the graph of G (Fig. 9.9).

x	-2	-1	$-\frac{1}{2}$	0	$\frac{1}{2}$	1	2
$r(x)$	-2.5	-2	-2.5		2.5	2	2.5

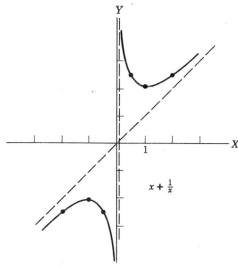

$$x + \frac{1}{x}$$

Fig. 9.9

Illustrative Example 2.   We discuss and draw the graph G of the function $r(x) = \dfrac{x^2 - 3x}{x^2 - 4}$.

Domain: All real numbers except $x = \pm 2$.

Intercepts: x-intercepts: we solve: $x^2 - 3x = 0$; $x(x - 3) = 0$; $x = 0, 3$.
    y-intercept: $r(0) = 0$.

Symmetry: G is symmetric to neither the y-axis nor the origin.

Asymptotes: (a)   Nonvertical.   By long division: $r(x) = 1 + \dfrac{4 - 3x}{x^2 - 4}$.

As x becomes large, $\dfrac{4 - 3x}{x^2 - 4}$ approaches but never equals zero.   Therefore the line that is the graph of the function 1 is an asymptote for G.

(b)   Vertical.   The roots of $x^2 - 4 = 0$ are $x = \pm 2$.   Therefore the vertical lines with equations $x = \pm 2$ are asymptotes for G.

Table of values:

x	-3	-2	-1	0	1	2	3
$r(x)$	3.6		$-\frac{4}{3}$	0	$\frac{2}{3}$		0

Graph of G (Fig. 9.10).

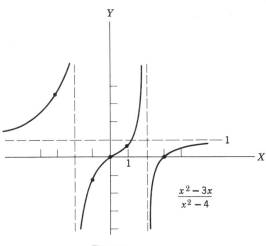

Fig. 9.10

▶ **EXERCISE 52**

1.   Discuss and sketch the graphs of the rational functions:

(a) $\dfrac{12}{x}$ (b) $-\dfrac{12}{x}$ (c) $\dfrac{k}{x}$ (k a real no.)

(d) $\dfrac{36}{x^2}$ (e) $\dfrac{1}{x^2-1}$ (f) $\dfrac{x}{x^2-1}$

(g) $\dfrac{x^2}{x^2-1}$ (h) $\dfrac{x^3}{x^2-1}$ (i) $\dfrac{1}{x^2+1}$

(j) $\dfrac{x}{x^2+1}$ (k) $\dfrac{x^2}{x^2+1}$ (l) $\dfrac{x^3}{x^2+1}$

(m) $\dfrac{x^3+1}{x}$ (n) $\dfrac{x-1}{x^2-2x-3}$ (o) $\dfrac{x^2+x-2}{2x^2+1}$

(p) $\dfrac{x^2-1}{x}$ (q) $\dfrac{x-1}{x+1}$ (r) $\dfrac{x+3}{x^2-1}$

(s) $\dfrac{x^2-1}{x^2}$ (t) $\dfrac{3x^2-2}{x}$ (u) $\dfrac{x^2+4}{x+2}$

(v) $\dfrac{x^2+4}{x-2}$ (w) $\dfrac{2x+1}{x^2-2x-3}$ (x) $\dfrac{x^2-4}{x-2}$

2. Discuss and sketch the graphs of the following equations. [*Hint:* Our discussion of rational functions applies, with the roles of x and y everywhere interchanged.]

(a) $x = \dfrac{y}{y^2+1}$ (b) $x = \dfrac{y}{y^2-1}$ (c) $x = \dfrac{y^2}{4y^2-1}$

(d) $x = \dfrac{1}{y^3}$ (e) $x = \dfrac{1}{y^3+y}$ (f) $x = \dfrac{1}{y^4+y^2}$

3. To apply more generally, our tests for symmetry of graphs may be stated as follows:

The graph of a real-real function f is symmetric to the Y-axis if and only if: Whenever x is in the domain of f, then so is $-x$, and $f(-x) = f(x)$.

The graph of a real-real function f is symmetric to the origin if and only if: Whenever x is in the domain of f, then so is $-x$, and $f(-x) = -f(x)$.

Apply these tests to the graphs of the following functions:

(a) $\sin x$ (b) $\cos x$ (c) $\tan x$

(d) $x \sin x$ (e) $x \cos x$ (f) $x \tan x$

(g) $x + \sin x$ (h) $x + \cos x$ (i) $x + \tan x$

9.6 THE GRAPH OF A POLYNOMIAL EQUATION IN TWO REAL VARIABLES

The expression $x^2 + y$ may be used to define a function f which maps ordered pairs of real numbers into real numbers by specifying the mapping of f in the following way: $f(x, y) = x^2 + y$. This function f maps the ordered pair $(1, 2)$, for example, into the real number 3, and the ordered pair $(2, 1)$ into the real number 5.

We shall call a function whose domain consists of ordered pairs of real numbers a *function of two real variables.*

The simplest functions of two real variables are *polynomial* functions of two real variables. After several preliminary definitions, we shall define this class of functions.

Definition. A *monomial function of two real variables* is a function m whose mapping may be given by:

$$m(x, y) = kx^r y^s$$

where k is any real number and r, s are any non-negative integers.

k is called the *coefficient* of $x^r y^s$. If $k \neq 0$, the *degree* of m is defined to be $r + s$. (Following the usual practice, we understand the symbols x^0 and y^0 each to mean the real number 1 in the above context.)

Two monomials are said to be *like* or *alike* if they are identical, or if they differ only in their coefficients. For example, $2x^2 y$ and $-2x^2 y$ are like monomials.

Now suppose $m_1, \cdots m_n$ are nonzero monomial functions of two real variables, no two of which are alike. Then we define a *polynomial* function p of two real variables to be either a monomial function or a function whose mapping may be given by:

$$p(x, y) = m_1(x, y) + \cdots + m_n(x, y);$$

$m_1(x, y), \cdots, m_n(x, y)$ are called the *terms* of $p(x, y)$.

In the sequel we shall assume, unless otherwise noted, that the domain of each polynomial function of two variables that we shall consider is maximal, i.e., that it is the set of *all* ordered pairs of real numbers.

We shall follow the practice of referring to an expression such as $3x^2 y^4$ as a monomial function or even as just a "monomial" when what we have in mind, in the case of $3x^2 y^4$, for example, is a monomial function m whose mapping is given by $m(x, y) = 3x^2 y^4$; and similarly for "polynomials."

Examples. 7, $2x$, $3y$, $x^2 y$ are monomials of degrees 0, 1, 1, 3, respectively "in x and y"; 7, $2x$, $7 + 2x$, and $2x + x^2 y + 3y$ are polynomials in x and y.

Note that neither x nor y need necessarily appear in the expression of a polynomial in x and y; note further, however, that although neither x nor y appears in the polynomial 7, this polynomial may be written so that they do appear: namely, in the form $7x^0 y^0$.

Now we define a *polynomial equation* to be one in which two polynomials are set equal. That is to say, if f and g are polynomials in two variables, the equation $f(x, y) = g(x, y)$ is said to be a polynomial equation in two variables.

The equations whose graphs we shall consider in this section are polynomial equations in x and y in which it is practicable to solve for x in terms of y, or for y in terms of x, or both.

Illustrative Example I. We discuss and sketch the graph of the equation: $x^2y + y - 1 = 0$.

It is easy to solve for y, arriving at the equivalent equation:

$$y = \frac{1}{x^2 + 1}$$

Now the graph of the equation $y = \frac{1}{x^2 + 1}$ is the same as the graph of the rational function $\frac{1}{x^2 + 1}$, and we may proceed as before to find the graph of this function [cf. Exercise 52, Problem 1 (i)].

However, some of the information which we seek with respect to the graph may be derived more easily directly from the original equation:

Intercepts. x-intercepts may be found by letting $y = 0$ in the given equation and solving for x; y-intercepts may be found by letting $x = 0$ and solving for y.

In the case $x^2y + y - 1 = 0$, letting $y = 0$ leads to the impossibility: $-1 = 0$; therefore the graph of $x^2y + y - 1 = 0$ has no x-intercept. Letting $x = 0$ leads to the y-intercept: $y = 1$.

Symmetry. The following rule applies to polynomial equations E in x and y.

(1) The graph of E is symmetric to the Y-axis if x appears in E only with even exponents.

(2) The graph of E is symmetric to the X-axis if y appears in E only with even exponents.

(3) The graph of E is symmetric to the origin if all the terms of E are of even degree, or all the terms of E are of odd degree.

In the case $x^2y + y - 1 = 0$, the graph, by these rules, may be seen to be symmetric to the Y-axis. (The terms of this equation are of degrees 3, 1, 0, respectively.)

We shall find it useful also to consider values of x or y that must be excluded because they lead to imaginary values of x or y, which cannot, of course, be plotted on a cc plane. Such values often arise when a solution for x or y involves an even root.

For example, solving the given equation for x:

$$x^2y = 1 - y$$

$$x = \pm \sqrt{\frac{1 - y}{y}}$$

Now any value of y such that $(1 - y)/y$ is negative must be excluded. But $(1 - y)/y$ is negative if:

(i) $1 - y < 0$ and $y > 0$, or
(ii) $1 - y > 0$ and $y < 0$.

(i) is equivalent to $y > 1$ and $y > 0$, which in turn says no more than $y > 1$ (for if $y > 1$, then certainly $y > 0$).

Similarly, (ii) is equivalent to $y < 0$.

Therefore all values of y such that $y > 1$ or $y < 0$ must be excluded, and the graph must be drawn in the unstriped region in Fig. 9.11.

(*Note:* The value $y = 0$ must also be excluded (why?), but we shall usually not bother to mention such single points in our discussion of excluded values, since their existence, if they exist in the examples we shall do, will generally be obvious.)

Since y approaches 0 as x becomes large positively or negatively, the line whose equation is $y = 0$, i.e., the X-axis, is an asymptote for the graph we seek.

The above information and the following table now enable us to sketch the graph (Fig. 9.11).

x	-3	-2	-1	0	1	2	3
y	0.1	0.2	0.5	1	0.5	0.2	0.1

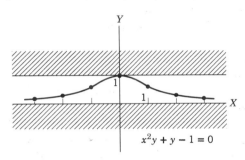

$$x^2y + y - 1 = 0$$

Fig. 9.11

Illustrative Example 2. We discuss and sketch the graph of the equation: $x^2y^2 - 2x + 1 = 0$.

Intercepts. x: Letting $y = 0$, $-2x + 1 = 0$, $x = \frac{1}{2}$.

y: Letting $x = 0$, $1 = 0$; impossible; no y-intercept.

Symmetry. With respect to X-axis, for y appears only with even exponents.

Further discussion is facilitated by solving the given equation for x and y. To solve for y we proceed as follows:

$$x^2y^2 = 2x - 1$$

$$y^2 = \frac{2x - 1}{x^2}$$

$$y = \pm \sqrt{\frac{2x - 1}{x^2}} = \pm \frac{\sqrt{2x - 1}}{x}$$

To solve for x, we make use of the quadratic formula ($a = y^2$, $b = -2$, $c = 1$):

$$x = \frac{-b \pm \sqrt{b^2 - 4ac}}{2a} = \frac{2 \pm \sqrt{4 - 4y^2}}{2y^2} = \frac{2 \pm 2\sqrt{1 - y^2}}{2y^2}$$

$$= \frac{1 \pm \sqrt{1 - y^2}}{y^2}$$

(Note that the solution for x is not quite equivalent to the given equation; the point $(\frac{1}{2}, 0)$ satisfies the given equation, but not the solution for x.)

Since we are not dealing with *rational* functions in this example, our preceding discussion of asymptotes will not apply here. A modification, however, will apply:

Asymptotes. Examining our solution for y, we see that as x becomes large positively (why positively?), y approaches 0. (For example, when $x = 50$, $y = \pm \dfrac{\sqrt{99}}{50} \doteq \dfrac{1}{5}$; as x increases, it "overpowers" $\sqrt{2x - 1}$.)

Therefore the line whose equation is $y = 0$, i.e., the X-axis, is an asymptote for the graph.

Excluded values. From the solution for x, values of y such that $1 - y^2 < 0$ must be excluded.

But $1 - y^2 < 0$ is equivalent to $y^2 > 1$, which is true if and only if $y > 1$ or $y < -1$ (see Problem 9 (*b*), Exercise 17).

Similarly we must exclude: $2x - 1 < 0$, i.e., $2x < 1$, i.e., $x < \frac{1}{2}$.

The graph must therefore be drawn in the unstriped region in Fig. 8.44.

Using the information above and the following table of values, we sketch the graph (Fig. 9.12).

x	$\frac{1}{2}$	1	5	13
y	0	± 1	± 0.6	± 0.4

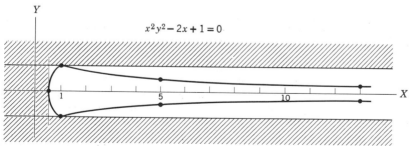

$$x^2y^2 - 2x + 1 = 0$$

Fig. 9.12

▶ **EXERCISE 53**

1. Discuss and draw the graphs of the following equations:

(a) $x + y + xy = 2$ (b) $x + y = xy$

(c) $y^2 - x^2 = x$ (d) $x = x^2y^2 + 1$

(e) $y^2 = x^3$ (f) $y^2(4 - x) = x^3$

(g) $x^2y + 4y - 8 = 0$ (h) $y^2 = \dfrac{x}{x - 2}$

(i) $y^2 = \dfrac{x^2}{4 - x^2}$ (j) $y^3 = x^2$

(k) $x^2y - 2x^2 - 16y = 0$ (l) $x^3 - x^2y + y = 0$

(m) $x^3 + 4x^2 + xy^2 - 4y^2 = 0$ (n) $y^2 = x^2(x - 2)$ [Note the "isolated" point $(0, 0)$]

(o) $y^2 = x(x - 2)^2$ (p) $\sqrt{x} + \sqrt{y} = 1$

(q) $\sqrt[3]{x} + \sqrt[3]{y} = 1$ (r) $\sqrt[3]{x^2} + \sqrt[3]{y^2} = 1$

(s) $y^2 = x(x - 2)(x + 2)$ [*Hint:* to determine excluded values of x, examine the sign of $x(x - 2)(x + 2)$ in the intervals $x < -2$, $-2 < x < 0$, $0 < x < 2$, $x > 2$]

2. Assuming that a is a positive real number, discuss and sketch the graphs of the following equations. Use a scale on the X- and Y-axes in which the points $0, \pm a, \pm 2a$, etc., are marked, rather than the points $0, \pm 1, \pm 2$, etc.

(a) $y = \dfrac{1}{a^2} x^3$ (Cubical Parabola)

(b) $y^2 = \dfrac{1}{a} x^3$ (Semicubical Parabola)

(c) $x^2y = 4a^2(2a - y)$ (Witch of Agnesi)

(d) $y^2(2a - x) = x^3$ (Cissoid of Diocles)

(e) $\sqrt{x} + \sqrt{y} = \sqrt{a}$ (Parabola)

(f) $\sqrt[3]{x^2} + \sqrt[3]{y^2} = \sqrt[3]{a^2}$ (Four-Cusped Hypocycloid)

(g) $y^2 = \dfrac{x^2(a + x)}{a - x}$ (Strophoid)

3. The tests for symmetry given in the preceding section may be generalized as follows:

Suppose E is an equation in x and y which has a graph G. Then:

(i) G is symmetric to the Y-axis if and only if the replacement of x by $-x$ in the equation E leads to an equivalent equation.

(ii) G is symmetric to the X-axis if and only if the replacement of y by $-y$ in the equation E leads to an equivalent equation.

(iii) G is symmetric to the origin if and only if the replacement of x by $-x$ and y by $-y$ in the equation E leads to an equivalent equation.

The proof of (i): Suppose $f(x, y) = g(x, y)$ is the given equation E, and suppose the equation $E' : f(-x, y) = g(-x, y)$, is equivalent to E.

Then if the point (a, b) satisfies one of these equations, it must satisfy the other. Thus, if (a, b) is a point of the graph G of the equation E, we have both $f(a, b) = g(a, b)$ and $f(-a, b) = g(-a, b)$. But the latter equation tells us that $(-a, b)$ satisfies E. Thus, whenever (a, b) is a point of G, so is $(-a, b)$, so that G is symmetric to the Y-axis.

Conversely, suppose G is symmetric to the Y-axis, and suppose (a, b) satisfies E. Then (a, b) is a point of G; since G is symmetric to the Y-axis, $(-a, b)$ must be a point of G also. Thus $(-a, b)$ satisfies E, i.e., $f(-a, b) = g(-a, b)$. But this means that (a, b) satisfies E'.

On the other hand (still assuming G to be symmetric to the Y-axis), if (a, b) satisfies E', we have $f(-a, b) = g(-a, b)$, so that $(-a, b)$ satisfies E. Hence $(-a, b)$ is a point of G. Since G is symmetric to the Y-axis, (a, b) must now be a point of G also, so that (a, b) must satisfy E.

Thus E and E' are equivalent. Both parts of (i) have now been proved.

(*a*)   Prove (ii) and (iii).

(*b*)   Discuss the symmetry of the graphs of the following equations with respect to the X-axis, the Y-axis, and the origin:

$$y^2 = \sin x; \; x^2 = \cos y; \; \sin x = \sin y; \; \sin x = \cos y$$

10 GRAPHS OF SECOND DEGREE EQUATIONS

10.1 INTRODUCTION

Every polynomial equation $p(x, y) = q(x, y)$ is equivalent to an equation $p(x, y) - q(x, y) = 0$, i.e., to a polynomial equation $f(x, y) = 0$. There will be no loss in generality, therefore, if we restrict ourselves in some of our statements to polynomial equations in the form $f(x, y) = 0$; and similarly, of course, for polynomials in a number of variables other than two.

We have defined the degree of a monomial in two variables, but not the degree of a polynomial, or of a polynomial equation in two variables. We do so now. Actually, the following definition applies to polynomials in any number of variables.

Definition. The *degree* of a polynomial is the maximum degree which any of its terms exhibits.

The *degree* of a polynomial equation $f(x, y) = 0$ is the degree of the polynomial f.

Examples. The terms of the polynomial in two variables: $1 + x + 2y - x^2y + 7x^3y^5$ are of degrees 0, 1, 1, 3, 8, respectively. Therefore $1 + x + 2y - x^2y + 7x^3y^5$ is a polynomial of degree 8 "in the variables x and y."

Therefore $1 + x + 2y - x^2y + 7x^3y^5 = 0$ is a polynomial equation "in x and y" of degree 8.

A polynomial equation in x and y of degree 1 would contain at least one term of degree 1 and might contain a term of degree 0. The following is a standard form for all polynomial equations of degree 1 in x and y:

$$Ax + By + C = 0$$

where A, B, C are real numbers and A, B are not *both* 0.

A polynomial equation in x and y of degree 2 would contain at least one term of degree 2, and possibly other terms of lesser degree. The following is a standard form for all polynomial equations of degree 2 in x and y:

$$Ax^2 + Bxy + Cy^2 + Dx + Ey + F = 0$$

where $A, \cdots, F$ are real numbers and A, B, C are not *all* 0.

We have already studied the graphs that may arise from a first degree equation (see Section 6.9), and in fact we may say this: *The graph of an equation is a straight line if and only if the equation is equivalent to a first-degree equation.*

Now we are ready to make a two-pronged advance. From the algebraic point of view, knowing all about the graph of a *first-degree equation*, the next step would be to consider the graphs that may arise from a *second-degree equation*. From the geometric point of view, knowing all about the equation of a *straight line*, it would be natural to go on to consider the equation of the next most familiar curve, the *circle*.

As a matter of fact, the two approaches complement each other nicely; for it turns out that every circle has an equation of the second degree. The converse is not true, however. Not all second-degree equations have graphs that are circles. Indeed, we shall make our main goal in this chapter: the determination of all graphs that may arise from a second-degree equation.

10.2 THE CIRCLE

In this text, when we speak of a circle C of radius r and center Q, we mean the set of all points in a given plane whose distance from Q is r, where r is a non-negative real number.

Suppose C is a circle of radius r and center Q in a cc plane (Fig. 10.1).

We seek the equation of C. That is to say, we seek an equation in x and y which is satisfied by each point of C, and by no other points in the given cc plane.

Suppose (a, b) is a point of C, and (h, k) is the center Q of C. Then by our definition of C, the distance from (a, b) to (h, k) must be r. That is:

$$\sqrt{(a - h)^2 + (b - k)^2} = r$$

so that:

$$(a - h)^2 + (b - k)^2 = r^2$$

In other words, each point of C satisfies the equation:

(1)
$$(x - h)^2 + (y - k)^2 = r^2$$

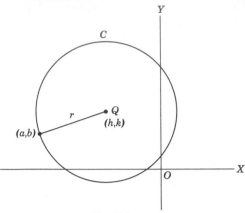

Fig. 10.1

But before we can say that the equation (1) is the equation of C, we must show that *no other* points of the given cc plane satisfy (1), i.e., each point of the cc plane that satisfies (1) must be on C.

Suppose, then, that $A = (u, v)$ satisfies (1).   Then:

$$(u - h)^2 + (v - k)^2 = r^2$$

We note that since r is the radius of a given circle, r must be a non-negative real number.   Therefore $\sqrt{r^2} = r$.   Therefore:

$$\sqrt{(u - h)^2 + (v - k)^2} = \sqrt{r^2} = r$$

i.e., $d(A, Q) = r$.   But this means that A must be on C.   We have proved:

> The equation of a circle C with centre (h, k) and radius r is:
>
> $$(x - h)^2 + (y - k)^2 = r^2$$

As a corollary, we note that the equation of a circle with center at the origin and radius r is:

$$x^2 + y^2 = r^2$$

Thus, the equation of a circle of radius 5 with center at the origin is: $x^2 + y^2 = 25$.   The equation of a circle of radius 5 with center at $(-2, 3)$ is:

$$(x + 2)^2 + (y - 3)^2 = 25$$

This last equation may be transformed into an equivalent equation of somewhat different appearance by "squaring out" and simplifying:

$$x^2 + 4x + 4 + y^2 - 6y + 9 = 25$$
$$x^2 + y^2 + 4x - 6y - 12 = 0$$

which the student will note is a second-degree equation in x and y.

In general, it is easily seen that every equation $(x - h)^2 + (y - k)^2 = r^2$ is equivalent to a second-degree equation in x and y, in fact one in which the coefficients of x^2 and y^2 are each 1, and in which there is no xy term.

We may prove, as a matter of fact, that the following is true:

> ● Using the notation of page 301, suppose that in a given second degree equation we have $A = C$ and $B = 0$.
> Then one of the following must be true:
>
> (i) The graph of the given equation contains no points whatever.
> (ii) The graph of the given equation is a circle.

The method illustrated in the following example leads to a general proof of the statement above.

Consider the equation:

(2) $$4x^2 + 4y^2 - 4x + 12y - 15 = 0$$

We first divide both sides by 4:

$$x^2 + y^2 - x + 3y - \tfrac{15}{4} = 0$$

Then we collect x terms together, y terms together, and bring the constant term to the right:

$$(x^2 - x \qquad) + (y^2 + 3y \qquad) = \tfrac{15}{4}$$

The space we have left within each parenthesis is for "completing the square" (see page 133). Also, to arrive at an equivalent equation, we add the same quantities to *both* sides of our equation:

$$[x^2 - x + (\tfrac{1}{2})^2] + [y^2 + 3y + (\tfrac{3}{2})^2] = \tfrac{15}{4} + \tfrac{1}{4} + \tfrac{9}{4}$$

which is equivalent to:

(3) $$(x - \tfrac{1}{2})^2 + (y + \tfrac{3}{2})^2 = \tfrac{25}{4}$$

Comparing this with the general equation of a circle:

$$(x - h)^2 + (y - k)^2 = r^2$$

we see that the values $h = \tfrac{1}{2}$, $k = -\tfrac{3}{2}$, $r = \tfrac{5}{2}$ will make the general equation coincide with (3). The graph of (3), and hence of the equivalent equation (2), is therefore a circle with center $(\tfrac{1}{2}, -\tfrac{3}{2})$ and radius $\tfrac{5}{2}$ (Fig. 10.2).

If we had arrived, let us say, at the equation $(x - \tfrac{1}{2})^2 + (y + \tfrac{3}{2})^2 = 0$, our circle would have had center $(\tfrac{1}{2}, -\tfrac{3}{2})$ and radius 0; i.e., our graph would have consisted of the single *point* $(\tfrac{1}{2}, -\tfrac{3}{2})$; and if we had arrived at the equation $(x - \tfrac{1}{2})^2 + (y + \tfrac{3}{2})^2 = -1$, our graph would have been a *null graph*, i.e., a graph containing no points whatever—for a sum of squares of real numbers must be non-negative, and can never, therefore, equal -1.

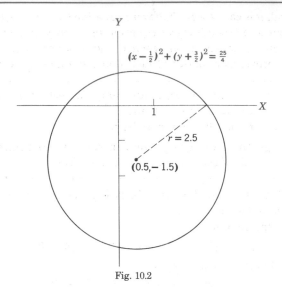

Fig. 10.2

▶ **EXERCISE 54**

1. Write the equations of and draw the circles whose centers and radii are respectively:

(a) $(1, 2)$; 3   (b) $(-1, 2)$; 3   (c) $(1, -2)$; 3
(d) $(-1, -2)$; 3   (e) $(3, 4)$; 5   (f) $(-3, 4)$; 5
(g) $(3, -4)$; 5   (h) $(-3, -4)$; 5   (i) $(0, 0)$; 7
(j) $(3, 4)$; 0   (k) $(0, 0)$; 0   (l) $(5, 5)$; 5

2. Draw the graph (if it exists) of each of the following equations:

(a) $x^2 + y^2 = 9$ (b) $x^2 + y^2 = 16$
(c) $x^2 + y^2 = 0$ (d) $x^2 + y^2 = 10$
(e) $y = \pm \sqrt{25 - x^2}$ (f) $x = \pm \sqrt{36 - y^2}$
(g) $y = \sqrt{25 - x^2}$ (h) $y = -\sqrt{25 - x^2}$
(i) $x = \sqrt{25 - y^2}$ (j) $x = -\sqrt{25 - y^2}$
(k) $(x - 2)^2 + (y - 3)^2 = 25$ (l) $(x - 2)^2 + (y + 3)^2 = 36$
(m) $(x + 2)^2 + (y - 3)^2 = 16$ (n) $(x + 2)^2 + (y + 3)^2 = 20$
(o) $x^2 + y^2 - 2x + 10y + 1 = 0$
(p) $x^2 + y^2 + 6x - 12y + 20 = 0$
(q) $x^2 + y^2 = 8x + 8y$ (r) $x^2 + y^2 = 20x - 75$
(s) $x^2 + y^2 + 7x + 3y - 10 = 0$
(t) $4x^2 + 4y^2 + 28y + 13 = 0$
(u) $4x^2 + 4y^2 - 60x - 20y + 225 = 0$
(v) $y = -5 \pm \sqrt{24 + 2x - x^2}$ (w) $y = -5 + \sqrt{24 + 2x - x^2}$

(x) $\quad y = -5 - \sqrt{24 + 2x - x^2}$ $\quad$ (y) $\quad x = 1 + \sqrt{-y^2 - 10y}$

(z) $\quad x = 1 - \sqrt{-y^2 - 10y}$ $\quad$ (z') $\quad x^2 + y^2 + 1 = 0$

3. (a) Write a standard form for a third-degree equation in two variables, x and y.

(b) How would you define the degree of a monomial $kx^r y^s z^t$ in three variables, assuming $k \neq 0$ is a real number?

(c) Write a standard form for a first degree equation in three variables, x, y, and z.

(d) Write a standard form for a second-degree equation in three variables, x, y, and z.

4. Prove the boxed statement of page 303, determining the condition under which a graph exists, and the center and radius of the circular graph, when it exists.

[*Hint:* Use the method of completing the square in the equation: $Ax^2 + Ay^2 + Dx + Ey + F = 0$, where $A \neq 0$.]

10.3 CIRCLES SATISFYING CERTAIN CONDITIONS

A classical problem of geometry is to circumscribe a circle about a triangle, i.e., to find a circle passing through three given points.

We solve a problem of this sort analytically.

Illustrative Example I. (a) We find the equation of a circle passing through the points $(4, 1)$, $(1, 2)$, $(-2, -7)$.

We know that every circle has an equation of the form $x^2 + y^2 + Dx + Ey + F = 0$. It is a question, then, of determining the particular values of D, E, F which will lead to a circle passing through the given points.

However, the given points will lie on the graph of a given equation if and only if they satisfy the equation. Therefore, our problem is equivalent to that of solving the following sets of equations:

$$4^2 + 1^2 + D \cdot 4 + E \cdot 1 + F = 0$$
$$1^2 + 2^2 + D \cdot 1 + E \cdot 2 + F = 0$$
$$(-2)^2 + (-7)^2 + D(-2) + E(-7) + F = 0$$

or:

(1) $\qquad 4D + E + F + 17 = 0$

(2) $\qquad D + 2E + F + 5 = 0$

(3) $\qquad -2D - 7E + F + 53 = 0$

But these simultaneous equations are particularly easy to solve, since F may be eliminated by two subtractions:

(1) – (2): $\qquad 3D - E + 12 = 0$

(2) – (3): $\qquad 3D + 9E - 48 = 0$

Taking the difference of these two equations:

$$10E - 60 = 0, \quad E = 6$$

Substituting in (1) – (2): $D = -2$

Substituting in (1): $F = -15$

Therefore the required equation is: $x^2 + y^2 - 2x + 6y - 15 = 0$.

(*b*)   Suppose we were asked to find the center and radius of a circle passing through the three points given in (*a*) above.

We might proceed first as in part (*a*); then, having found the equation of the required circle as above, we might find its center and radius by the process of completing the square.   (It turns out that this circle has center $(1, -3)$ and radius 5.)

(Alternatively, we might have begun with the other general equation for a circle: $(x - h)^2 + (y - k)^2 = r^2$, in which (h, k) represents the center and r the radius of the circle.   This method, however, involves a little more work than the first.)

There are many other cases in which one wishes to determine a circle satisfying certain conditions.   In all such problems it should be kept in mind that one or the other of two general equations for the circle may be utilized.   It is important also to remember the following general principle:

Requiring that a point lie on a given graph is equivalent to requiring that the point satisfy the equation of the given graph.

Illustrative Example 2.   We find a circle that is tangent to the X-axis and that passes through the points $(3, 1)$, $(4, 2)$.

First of all we note that if a circle has center (h, k) and radius r, then tangency to the X-axis is equivalent to the condition: $k = \pm r$ (Fig. 10.3).

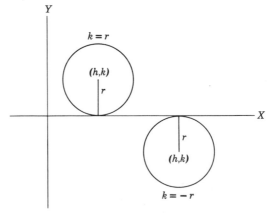

Fig. 10.3

It would seem, then, that the form $(x - h)^2 + (y - k)^2 = r^2$ is best suited to this problem.   We have:

(1) $(4 - h)^2 + (2 - k)^2 = r^2$

(2) $(3 - h)^2 + (1 - k)^2 = r^2$

(3) $r = \pm k$

From which follows:

(1) – (2): $10 - 2h - 2k = 0$

(4) $h = 5 - k$

Substituting (3) and (4) in (2):

$$(3 - 5 + k)^2 + (1 - k)^2 = k^2$$
$$(k - 2)^2 + (1 - k)^2 = k^2$$
$$k^2 - 6k + 5 = 0$$
$$(k - 1)(k - 5) = 0$$

So that: $k = 1, h = 4, r = 1$; or $k = 5, h = 0, r = 5$.   (Remember that r must be non-negative.)

We see now that there are *two* solutions to the problem.   One circle has center (4, 1) and radius 1.   The other has center (0, 5) and radius 5. It is, of course, now easy to write the equations of these circles, and to draw their graphs (Fig. 10.4).

A notable advantage of the analytic method is evident here: Its use

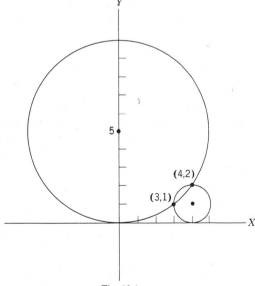

Fig. 10.4

greatly diminishes the likelihood that some of the possible solutions of a problem will be overlooked.

▶ **EXERCISE 55**

1.   In each of the following cases find the equation of a circle that passes through the given triple of points.   In each case, find the center and radius of the circle and plot the given points and the required circle.

(*a*)   (0, 0), (0, 4), (6, 0)   (*b*)   (0, 0), (8, 0), (4, 8)
(*c*)   (4, 2), (5, 1), (2, −2)   (*d*)   (5, 6), (4, −1), (2, −3)
(*e*)   (6, −2), (4, 2), (1, −7)   (*f*)   (4, 1), (3, 3), (8, 0)
(*g*)   (1, 5), (3, 1), (−2, 2)   (*h*)   (2, 4), (−2, 3), (4, −1)
(*i*)   (1, 2), (3, 5), (5, 8)   (what's the trouble?)

2.   In each of the following cases find the equation of a circle which satisfies the given conditions.   In each case, illustrate graphically:

(*a*)   center (−2, 1); passes through (4, 5).
(*b*)   center (2, −3); tangent to the *X*-axis.
(*c*)   center (2, −3); tangent to the *Y*-axis.
(*d*)   center (2, −3); passes through the origin.
(*e*)   center at the origin; tangent to $3x + 4y = 12$. [*Hint:* see Section 6.14.]
(*f*)   center at (7, 11); tangent to $x = y$.

3.   In each of the following cases find (algebraically; why?) the points of intersection of the graphs of the given equations, and plot the graphs:

(*a*) $3x - y = 5, x^2 + y^2 = 5$
(*b*) $x + y = 7, x^2 + y^2 = 25$
(*c*) $x^2 + y^2 = 11, x^2 + y^2 - 2x - 8 = 0$
(*d*) $x^2 + y^2 + 3x - 2y - 4 = 0, x^2 + y^2 - 2x - y - 6 = 0$

4.   A circle passes through the origin if and only if the point (0, 0) satisfies its equation.   If we write the equation of a circle in the form: $x^2 + y^2 + Dx + Ey + F = 0$, then that circle will pass through the origin if and only if: $0^2 + 0^2 + D \cdot 0 + E \cdot 0 + F = 0$, i.e., if and only if $F = 0$.

Therefore the equation $x^2 + y^2 + Dx + Ey = 0$ is called a "general equation" for a circle that passes through the origin.   (We also speak of the set of all circles which may arise from this equation as the "family" of circles with equation $x^2 + y^2 + Dx + Ey = 0$.)

Write a general equation for

(*a*)   A circle passing through the origin (in terms of *h, k*).
(*b*)   A circle tangent to the *X*-axis.

(c) A circle tangent to the Y-axis.

(d) A circle with center on the X-axis.

(e) A circle with center on the Y-axis.

(f) A circle tangent to the X-axis at 0.

(g) A circle tangent to the Y-axis at 0.

(h) A circle tangent to both the X-axis and the Y-axis.

5. Suppose (a, b) is a point on a circle with center at the origin and radius $r > 0$. Prove that the equation of a tangent line to the circle at the point (a, b) is $ax + by = r^2$.

10.4 THE ELLIPSE

Throughout high-school geometry, and in this course also, the curves we have studied in detail have been only the straight line and the circle. Now, finally, we shall devote attention to several others of the countless interesting and important curves that occur in nature and science.

In this section, we shall study a curve that may very easily be drawn. All that is necessary is a string fastened at two points F_1, F_2 on a sheet of paper (Fig. 10.5).

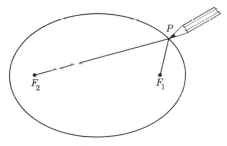

Fig. 10.5

Suppose we draw the string taut with a pencil point, and keeping the string taut, move the pencil so as to trace a curve, first on one side of the line F_1F_2, and then on the other.

Then the resulting curve is called an *ellipse*.

Each of the points F_1, F_2 is called a *focus* (plural: "foci") of the ellipse.

It is traditional to denote the length of string between the foci by $2a$, and the distance between the foci by $2c$. (This choice of notation is for reasons of convenience which will soon become evident.) The ellipse may then be regarded as the set of all points (also called the "locus" of all points) P in the given plane such that $PF_1 + PF_2 = 2a$. We now make the following precise definition:

> Let $a > c \geqslant 0$ be real numbers, and F_1, F_2 points in a given plane such that $d(F_1, F_2) = 2c$.
>
> Then the set of all points P in the given plane such that $PF_1 + PF_2 = 2a$ is called an *ellipse*, with *foci* F_1, F_2.

If $c = 0$, then $d(F_1, F_2) = 0$, so that $F_1 = F_2$. Physically, this would correspond to a situation in which both ends of our string are tied to the same point, so that our pencil would be constrained to trace a circle. Later on we shall prove mathematically that if $c = 0$, then our ellipse is a circle.

We proceed to study the ellipse *analytically*. Our first step will be to choose a convenient pair of coordinate axes, and then we shall derive a general equation for the ellipse.

If $F_1 \neq F_2$, the line $F_1 F_2$ is a natural choice for the X-axis. If $F_1 = F_2$, any line through F_1 may be chosen to be the X-axis, but in both cases we make F_1 fall on the non-negative side of the X-axis (Fig. 10.6).

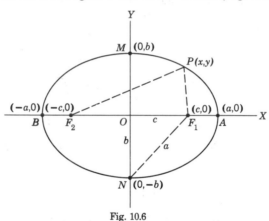

Fig. 10.6

If $F_1 \neq F_2$, let O be the midpoint of line segment $F_1 F_2$. If $F_1 = F_2$, let $O = F_1$. In either case, O is called the *center* of the ellipse.

And now it is natural to take a line perpendicular to the X-axis at O as Y-axis.

It follows that $OF_1 = OF_2 = c$, so that the coordinates of F_1, F_2 are $(c, 0)$, $(-c, 0)$ respectively.

Now suppose $P = (x, y)$ is any point on our ellipse. Then by our definition of "ellipse":

(1) $PF_1 + PF_2 = 2a$

From (1) we may successively derive the following equations (omitted steps are to be supplied by the student):

(2) $\sqrt{(x - c)^2 + y^2} + \sqrt{(x + c)^2 + y^2} = 2a$

(3) $\sqrt{(x + c)^2 + y^2} = 2a - \sqrt{(x - c)^2 + y^2}$

(4) $(x + c)^2 + y^2 = 4a^2 - 4a\sqrt{(x - c)^2 + y^2} + (x - c)^2 + y^2$

(5) $a\sqrt{(x - c)^2 + y^2} = a^2 - cx$

(6) $a^2x^2 + a^2c^2 + a^2y^2 = a^4 + c^2x^2$

(7) $x^2(a^2 - c^2) + a^2y^2 = a^2(a^2 - c^2)$

But note that $a > c \geqslant 0$. Thus neither a^2 nor $a^2 - c^2$ nor $a^2(a^2 - c^2)$ can be zero, so that we may divide both sides of (7) by $a^2(a^2 - c^2)$:

(8) $\dfrac{x^2}{a^2} + \dfrac{y^2}{a^2 - c^2} = 1$

Since $a^2 > c^2$, $a^2 - c^2$ is a positive real number, so that there exists a positive real number $\sqrt{a^2 - c^2}$, which we denote by b. Hence $b^2 = a^2 - c^2$, and equation (8) may be written in the more attractive form:

(9) $\dfrac{x^2}{a^2} + \dfrac{y^2}{b^2} = 1$

What we have shown, then, is that if (x, y) is a point on our ellipse, then equation (9) holds true.

To prove that (9) *is* the equation of our ellipse, we must now show conversely that if equation (9) holds true, then $P = (x, y)$ is a point of our ellipse. We proceed to do so:

Assuming (9) to be true, we shall first prove that $a - (cx/a) > 0$ and $a + (cx/a) > 0$, which we shall need in order to prove that $P = (x, y)$ lies on our ellipse.

Since the square of any real number is non-negative, we have that $y^2/b^2 \geqslant 0$. Therefore $-y^2/b^2 \leqslant 0$. Therefore $1 - (y^2/b^2) \leqslant 1$. But from (9), $x^2/a^2 = 1 - (y^2/b^2)$. Therefore $x^2/a^2 \leqslant 1$, from which follows: $-1 \leqslant x/a \leqslant 1$ [see Problem 9(a), Exercise 17].

Since $x/a \leqslant 1$, we have: $cx/a \leqslant c$; and since $c < u$, we have $cx/a < u$, from which we have $a - (cx/a) > 0$, Q.E.D.

It is left to the student to prove that $a + (cx/a) > 0$ also.

Now from (9), since $b^2 = a^2 - c^2$, we have:

(10) $\dfrac{x^2}{a^2} + \dfrac{y^2}{a^2 - c^2} = 1$

(11) $(a^2 - c^2)\dfrac{x^2}{a^2} + y^2 = a^2 - c^2$

(12) $x^2 - \dfrac{c^2x^2}{a^2} + y^2 = a^2 - c^2$

(13) $a^2 + \dfrac{c^2x^2}{a^2} = x^2 + y^2 + c^2$

Now we compute:

$$PF_1 = \sqrt{(x - c)^2 + y^2}$$
$$= \sqrt{x^2 + y^2 + c^2 - 2cx}$$
$$= \sqrt{a^2 + \dfrac{c^2x^2}{a^2} - 2cx} \quad \text{(by (13) above)}$$
$$= \sqrt{a^2 - 2cx + \dfrac{c^2x^2}{a^2}}$$

$$= \sqrt{\left(a - \frac{cx}{a}\right)^2}$$

$$= a - \frac{cx}{a} \left(\text{since } a - \frac{cx}{a} > 0\right)$$

It is left to the student to show similarly that: $PF_2 = a + \frac{cx}{a}$.

Finally: $PF_1 + PF_2 = a + (cx/a) + a - (cx/a) = 2a$, so that P *does* lie on our ellipse.

The proof that (9) is the equation of our ellipse is now complete.

Now we discuss the graph of equation $\dfrac{x^2}{a^2} + \dfrac{y^2}{b^2} = 1$.

First of all we solve for x and y:

$$\frac{x^2}{a^2} = 1 - \frac{y^2}{b^2} = \frac{b^2 - y^2}{b^2}$$

$$x^2 = \frac{a^2}{b^2}(b^2 - y^2)$$

$$x = \pm\frac{a}{b}\sqrt{b^2 - y^2}$$

Similarly: $y = \pm\dfrac{b}{a}\sqrt{a^2 - x^2}$

Intercepts. x: $\pm a$; y: $\pm b$

Symmetry.   With respect to X-axis, Y-axis, and origin.

Excluded values. $b^2 - y^2 < 0$, i.e., $y^2 > b^2$, i.e., $y > b$ and $y < -b$; similarly $x > a$ and $x < -a$ must be excluded.

The graph, of course, is that of Fig. 10.6.

Note that since we have defined b so that $b^2 = a^2 - c^2$, it follows that c may be computed, once we know a and b.   Note further that if $c = 0$, then $b^2 = a^2$, and the equation of our ellipse becomes $x^2 + y^2 = a^2$; i.e., if $c = 0$, then our ellipse is a circle of radius a.

In summary:

If a, b are real numbers such that $a \geqslant b > 0$, then:

$$\frac{x^2}{a^2} + \frac{y^2}{b^2} = 1$$

is the equation of an ellipse with x-intercepts $\pm a$, y-intercepts $\pm b$, and foci $(\pm c, 0)$, where $a^2 = b^2 + c^2$.

If we had interchanged our choices of X- and Y-axes, the effect would have been simply to interchange the roles of x and y, so that the following statement may be made (see Fig. 10.7):

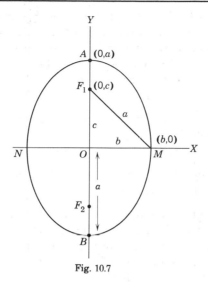

Fig. 10.7

If a, b are real numbers such that $a \geqslant b > 0$, then:

$$\frac{y^2}{a^2} + \frac{x^2}{b^2} = 1$$

is the equation of an ellipse with x-intercepts $\pm b$, y-intercepts $\pm a$, and foci $(0, \pm c)$, where $a^2 = b^2 + c^2$.

If $F_1 \neq F_2$, the points A, B in which line F_1F_2 intersects the ellipse are called the *vertices* of the ellipse. The line segment AB joining the vertices of the ellipse is called the *major axis* of the ellipse. The line segments OA and OB are called *semi-major axes* of the ellipse. The points M, N in which the perpendicular bisector of line segment F_1F_2 intersects the ellipse are the endpoints of the *minor axis* of the ellipse. The line segments OM and ON are called *semi-minor axes* of the ellipse. Clearly:

The major and minor axes of an ellipse are of lengths $2a$ and $2b$ respectively; the semi-major and semi-minor axes of an ellipse are of lengths a and b, respectively.

Note that the line segment joining the end of a minor axis to a focus, e.g., line segment MF_1 has the length a also; for

$$MF_1 = \sqrt{(0 - c)^2 + (b - 0)^2} = \sqrt{b^2 + c^2} = \sqrt{a^2} = a$$

That this is true may also be seen from the facts that since M is on the perpendicular bisector of line segment F_1F_2: $MF_1 = MF_2$; and since M is on the ellipse: $MF_1 + MF_2 = 2a$. Therefore $MF_1 + MF_1 = 2a$, $2(MF_1) = 2a$, $MF_1 = a$.

Thus we see that the foci of an ellipse lie on the major axis at a distance a from an end of the minor axis, so that the foci of an ellipse may easily be located with a compass, once the axes have been drawn.

Note that either of the equations of the ellipses described in the boxes above is equivalent to an equation of the form:

$$Ax^2 + Cy^2 + F = 0$$

where A and C are of like sign and F is of opposite sign. Conversely, any equation in this form may easily be shown to be equivalent to one of the two equations given above for an ellipse.

Illustrative Example 1. We plot the graph G of the equation:

$$144 - 16x^2 - 9y^2 = 0.$$

By the paragraph preceding this example, G is an ellipse with center at the origin and axes along the coordinate axes.

Letting $x = 0$, the y-intercepts of G are: ± 4.

Letting $y = 0$, the x-intercepts of G are: ± 3.

The graph G is drawn in Fig. 10.8.

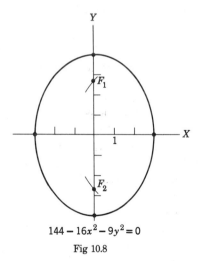

$$144 - 16x^2 - 9y^2 = 0$$

Fig 10.8

The foci must be on the major axis at a distance of $c = \sqrt{a^2 - b^2} = \sqrt{7}$ from the center of the ellipse. They are more easily located, however, by opening compasses to a radius of 4, and with center $(3, 0)$ swinging arcs which intersect the major axis at the foci.

Illustrative Example 2. We find the equation of an ellipse that passes through the points $(1, -4)$, $(3, 2)$:

Actually, there *may* be many ellipses that satisfy this condition, for there are ellipses (not yet considered) in a coordinate plane, whose axes and centers are not the coordinate axes and the origin respectively.

We shall attempt, however, to find an ellipse of the type we *have* considered which passes through the given points. We begin, therefore, with a form equation for such an ellipse:

$$Ax^2 + Cy^2 + F = 0$$

and try to find values of A and C of like sign which result in an equation satisfied by the given points. We must therefore solve:

(1)
$$A + 16C + F = 0$$
$$9A + 4C + F = 0$$

Subtracting: $8A - 12C = 0$, or $A = \frac{3}{2}C$ is an equation that we wish to satisfy. Clearly $C = 2$, $A = 3$ are convenient values that do the trick, and referring back to the first of the equations (1), $F = -A - 16C = -35$ is consistent with these values as a solution of (1).

Substituting back in our form equation: $3x^2 + 2y^2 - 35 = 0$ is the equation of an ellipse, is satisfied by our given points, and is therefore a solution of the problem.

10.5 THE ECCENTRICITY OF AN ELLIPSE

The real number $e = c/a$, called the *eccentricity* of the ellipse we have defined, is often used to tell something about the shape of the ellipse.

First of all, since $c \geqslant 0$ and $a > 0$, it follows that $c/a \geqslant 0$; and since $a > c$, it follows that $c/a < 1$.

Thus, if e is the eccentricity of an ellipse, $0 \leqslant e < 1$.

Now we consider extreme values of e.

At one extreme, suppose $e = 0$. Then $c/a = 0$, i.e., $c = 0$, and our ellipse is a circle.

If e is close to 0, we may expect the ellipse to be almost circular in shape. That this is true may be seen by dividing the equation $b^2 = a^2 - c^2$ by a^2:

$$\frac{b^2}{a^2} = 1 - \frac{c^2}{a^2} = 1 - e^2$$

If $e \doteq 0$, then $\frac{b^2}{a^2} \doteq 1$, $\frac{b}{a} \doteq 1$; the ratio of major and minor axes is close to 1; i.e., the ellipse comes close to being a circle.

If e is close to 1, the equations above indicate that b/a is close to 0, i.e., b is small compared with a. Thus an ellipse for which e is close to 1 would look more like a cigar than a circle.

▶ **EXERCISE 56**

1. Sketch the graphs of the following equations, locating foci and computing eccentricities:

(a) $25x^2 + 9y^2 = 225$ (b) $9x^2 + 25y^2 = 225$
(c) $4x^2 + y^2 = 16$ (d) $16x^2 + 25y^2 = 400$
(e) $x^2 + 4y^2 = 4$ (f) $25x^2 + 16y^2 = 400$
(g) $x^2 + 2y^2 = 2$ (h) $x^2 + y^2 = 25$

2. Find the equation of an ellipse passing through the points:

(a) $(3, 4)$, $(5, 2)$ (b) $(4, 1)$, $(3, 2)$
(c) $(4, 3)$, $(3, 4)$ (d) $(0, 7)$, $(11, 0)$
(e) $(3, 4)$, $(2, 3)$ (what's the trouble?)

3. Find the equations of two ellipses each with major axis 8 and minor axis 4, and plot.

4. Find the equations of two ellipses each with major axis 10 and eccentricity 0.5, and plot.

5. Find the equation of an ellipse with minor axis 8 and foci at $(\pm 3, 0)$, and plot.

6. Find the eccentricity of an ellipse whose major axis is twice as long as its minor axis.

7. Find the eccentricity of an ellipse in which F_1F_2M is an equilateral triangle, where M is an end of a minor axis.

8. An ellipse is to be drawn within a $6'' \times 8''$ rectangle, with vertices and ends of minor axes at midpoints of opposite sides. Where should the foci be placed, and what length of string should be used in drawing the ellipse?

9. Suppose a line through a focus F of an ellipse and perpendicular to its major axis meets the ellipse in points P, Q. Then line segment PQ is called the *latus rectum* of the ellipse.

(a) What is the length of a latus rectum of an ellipse?
(b) Show how knowing the fact of (a) is helpful in drawing an ellipse.

10. In the proof that every point that satisfies the equation $\dfrac{x^2}{a^2} + \dfrac{y^2}{b^2} = 1$ lies on a certain ellipse, complete the proof of those portions that were left to the student to prove.

11. The possibility $a = c$, though physically feasible, was rejected in our definition of an ellipse, since the admission of this extreme possibility would have forced inelegant exceptions upon us in our later discussions of the ellipse and certain related curves.

But suppose we had allowed the possibility $a = c$ in our definition of an ellipse. What would an ellipse in which $a = c$ turn out to be? (Consider two cases: $c = 0$; $c > 0$.)

10.6 THE HYPERBOLA

A variation upon the definition of an ellipse suggests itself: Suppose that instead of seeking all points in a plane the *sum* of whose distances from two fixed points is constant, we seek all points in a plane the *difference* of whose distances from two fixed points is constant. Then the resulting locus is called a *hyperbola*. More precisely (see Fig. 10.9):

> Let $c > a > 0$ be real numbers and F_1, F_2 points in a given plane such that $d(F_1, F_2) = 2c$.
>
> Then the set of all points P in the given plane such that $PF_1 - PF_2 = \pm 2a$ is called a *hyperbola* with *foci* F_1, F_2.

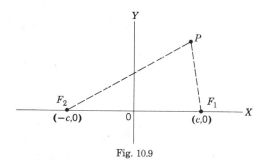

Fig. 10.9

Coordinate axes may be chosen exactly as in the case of the ellipse, so that if $P - (x, y)$ is a point of our hyperbola:

(1) $$\sqrt{(x - c)^2 + y^2} - \sqrt{(x + c)^2 + y^2} = \pm 2a$$

By means of steps similar to those we followed in deriving the equation of an ellipse, it may be proved that equation (1) is equivalent to:

(2) $$\frac{x^2}{a^2} - \frac{y^2}{c^2 - a^2} = 1$$

Since $c > a$, we have that $c^2 > a^2$, so that the number $\sqrt{c^2 - a^2}$ is a real number, which we denote by b, i.e., $b - \sqrt{c^2 - a^2}$; hence $b^2 = c^2 - a^2$, $a^2 + b^2 = c^2$. Equation (2) is then equivalent to:

(3) $$\frac{x^2}{a^2} - \frac{y^2}{b^2} = 1$$

(Note that the relationship among a, b, c is not the same for the hyperbola as it is for the ellipse.)

Now we analyze the graph of the equation (3); first we solve for x and y:

$$x = \pm \frac{a}{b} \sqrt{y^2 + b^2} \qquad y = \pm \frac{b}{a} \sqrt{x^2 - a^2}$$

Intercepts. x: $\pm a$; y: none.

Symmetry.   With respect to X-axis, Y-axis, and origin.

Excluded values.   From the solution for y, we see that there is no graph for $x^2 - a^2 < 0$, i.e., for $-a < x < a$. The solution for x reveals that no value of y need be excluded.

Asymptotes.   The straight lines whose equations are $y = \pm(b/a)x$ are asymptotes for our graph.

PROOF: Because the hyperbola and the union of the lines $y = \pm(b/a)x$ are symmetric with respect to both coordinate axes, it will be sufficient to restrict our proof to the first quadrant.

We must show, then, that $(b/a)x - (b/a)\sqrt{x^2 - a^2}$ approaches, but does not reach 0 as x becomes large. We "rationalize the numerator:"

$$\frac{b}{a}x - \frac{b}{a}\sqrt{x^2 - a^2} = \frac{b}{a}(x - \sqrt{x^2 - a^2})$$

$$= \frac{b}{a}(x - \sqrt{x^2 - a^2})\left(\frac{x + \sqrt{x^2 - a^2}}{x + \sqrt{x^2 - a^2}}\right)$$

$$= \frac{b}{a} \cdot \frac{x^2 - x^2 + a^2}{x + \sqrt{x^2 - a^2}}$$

$$= \frac{ab}{x + \sqrt{x^2 - a^2}}$$

And now it is clear that as x becomes large positively, $\dfrac{ab}{x + \sqrt{x^2 - a^2}}$ approaches, but never reaches 0.

To draw the asymptotes of this hyperbola, it is convenient first to draw an "asymptote box" whose vertices are $(\pm a, \pm b)$; the asymptotes are then simply the extended diagonals of this box (Fig. 10.10).

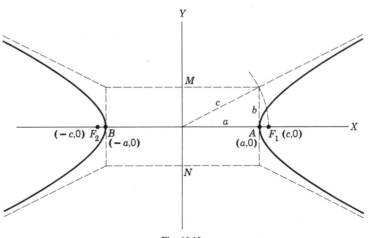

Fig. 10.10

In summary:

If a, b are positive real numbers, then:

$$\frac{x^2}{a^2} - \frac{y^2}{b^2} = 1$$

is the equation of a hyperbola with x-intercepts $\pm a$, no y-intercepts, asymptote box with vertices $(\pm a, \pm b)$, and foci $(\pm c, 0)$, where $c^2 = a^2 + b^2$.

Interchanging our choices of X-axis and Y-axis leads to the following statement:

If a, b are positive real numbers, then:

$$\frac{y^2}{a^2} - \frac{x^2}{b^2} = 1$$

is the equation of a hyperbola with y-intercepts $\pm a$, no x-intercepts, asymptote box with vertices $(\pm b, \pm a)$, and foci $(0, \pm c)$, where $c^2 = a^2 + b^2$.

The points A, B in which line $F_1 F_2$ intersects the hyperbola are called the *vertices* of the hyperbola. The midpoint O of line segment $F_1 F_2$ is called the *center* of the hyperbola. The line segment AB is called the *transverse* axis, the line segments OA, OB *semi-transverse* axes of the hyperbola. (A *conjugate* axis, of length $2b$, perpendicular to line $F_1 F_2$ and bisected by O, is sometimes defined, but we shall find no use for it here.)

Clearly the transverse axis is of length $2a$, and the semi-transverse axes each of length a.

Note that a semidiagonal of an asymptote box has the length $\sqrt{a^2 + b^2} = \sqrt{c^2} = c$. The foci of a hyperbola may therefore be located by swinging an arc with center O, which passes through a vertex of the asymptote box, until it intersects the extended transverse axis in two places.

Note further that either of the equations of the hyperbolas described in the boxes above is equivalent to an equation of the form:

$$Ax^2 + Cy^2 + F = 0$$

where A and C are of opposite sign and $F \neq 0$. Conversely, any equation in this form is equivalent to one of the two equations given above for a hyperbola.

Illustrative Example. We plot the graph G of the equation: $9y^2 - 16x^2 + 144 = 0$. By our last paragraph, G is a hyperbola.

Letting $x = 0$, we find no y-intercept, but letting $y = 0$, we find x-intercepts of ± 3. Therefore $a = 3$, and the vertices of the hyperbola are $(\pm 3, 0)$.

Now we put the equation of G in "standard" form by dividing through by 144:

$$16x^2 - 9y^2 = 144$$

$$\frac{x^2}{9} - \frac{y^2}{16} = 1$$

Comparing this with equation (3), page 317, we see again that $a = 3$, but now also that $b = 4$. Furthermore, since $c^2 = a^2 + b^2$, $c = 5$.

Thus the foci are at $(\pm 5, 0)$.

Now we draw asymptote box, asymptotes, and finally the hyperbola (Fig. 10.11).

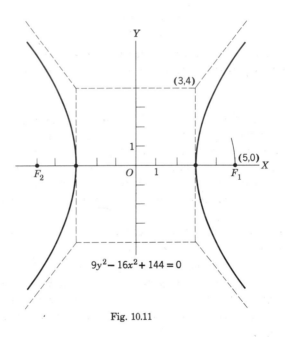

Fig. 10.11

Note that the hyperbola is tangent to the asymptote box at the vertices of the hyperbola.

10.7 THE ECCENTRICITY OF A HYPERBOLA

Just as for the ellipse, in the case of the hyperbola we again define the real number $e = c/a$ to be *eccentricity* of the curve. In the case of the ellipse we found that always: $0 \leqslant e < 1$; in the case of the hyperbola, since $0 < a < c$, we see that always: $e > 1$.

Here also the eccentricity tells us something about the shape of the curve, as we discover by examining extreme values of e.

At one extreme, suppose e is close to 1. We examine the curve $\frac{x^2}{a^2} - \frac{y^2}{b^2} = 1$, with asymptotes $y = \pm \frac{b}{a} x$.

Since $c^2 = a^2 + b^2$, we have $\left(\frac{c}{a}\right)^2 = 1 + \left(\frac{b}{a}\right)^2$, i.e., $e^2 = 1 + \left(\frac{b}{a}\right)^2$. If $e \doteq 1$, then $\frac{b}{a} \doteq 0$, i.e., the slopes of the asymptote lines are numerically small; the hyperbola is pinched between lines which make a comparatively small angle with the transverse axis.

At the other extreme, suppose e is a very large number. Then from the equation $e^2 - 1 = \left(\frac{b}{a}\right)^2$, we see that $\frac{b}{a}$ must be a very large number also. Thus, the slopes of the asymptote lines are large numerically; i.e., the asymptotes rise very steeply, and are close to being vertical. The hyperbola, approaching almost vertical lines, appears, near its center, almost like a pair of parallel lines.

10.8 RECTANGULAR HYPERBOLAS

A hyperbola whose asymptotes are perpendicular to each other is called a *rectangular* (i.e., a "right-angled") hyperbola.

Since the diagonals of a rectangle are perpendicular if and only if the rectangle is a square, a hyperbola is rectangular if and only if $a = b$. For this reason a rectangular hyperbola is also called an *equilateral* hyperbola.

Now we investigate a case in which the equation of a rectangular hyperbola assumes a particularly simple form.

Suppose we choose as foci the points (a, a), $(-a, -a)$ where $a > 0$. Then $2c = d(F_1, F_2) = 2a\sqrt{2}$. Therefore $c = a\sqrt{2}$. Since $c^2 = a^2 + b^2$, it follows that $a = b$. This hyperbola will therefore be rectangular.

Furthermore, a point (x, y) will be on this hyperbola if and only if:

$$\sqrt{(x - a)^2 + (y - a)^2} - \sqrt{(x + a)^2 + (y + a)^2} = \pm 2a$$

We may proceed to derive an equivalent equation as before; in this case the final form turns out to be simply:

$$xy = \frac{a^2}{2}$$

If we had chosen as foci the points $(a, -a)$, $(-a, a)$, the equation of the hyperbola would have turned out to be:

$$xy = \frac{-a^2}{2}$$

We conclude: Let k be any nonzero real number.   Then:

$$xy = k$$

is the equation of a rectangular hyperbola.

It is easily seen that the asymptotes of the hyperbola whose equation is $xy = k$ are simply the coordinate axes.

▶ **EXERCISE 57**

1.   Identify by name and plot the graphs of the following equations; in each case, find the foci and compute the eccentricity; if asymptotes exist, find them.

(a) $9x^2 - 16y^2 = 144$ (b) $9x^2 + 16y^2 = 144$
(c) $16y^2 - 9x^2 = 144$ (d) $16x^2 - 25y^2 = 400$
(e) $4x^2 + y^2 = 64$ (f) $4x^2 - y^2 = 64$
(g) $y^2 - 4x^2 = 64$ (h) $x^2 - 4y^2 = 64$
(i) $25x^2 - 9y^2 = 225$ (j) $9x^2 - 25y^2 = 225$
(k) $4x^2 - y^2 = 16$ (l) $x^2 - 4y^2 = 4$
(m) $x^2 - y^2 = 25$ (n) $y^2 - x^2 = 25$
(o) $xy = 18$ (p) $xy = -18$
(q) $xy = 32$ (r) $xy = -32$
(s) $xy + 4 = 0$ (t) $xy - 4 = 0$

2.   Find the equation of a hyperbola passing through each of the following pairs of points:

(a) $(3, 4)$, $(1, 2)$ (b) $(2, 4)$, $(3, 5)$
(c) $(2, 3)$, $(3, 2)$ (d) $(1, 1)$, $(2, 2)$

3.   Find the equations and plot the graphs of hyperbolas satisfying the following conditions:

(a)   Transverse axis $= 8$; $d(F_1, F_2) = 10$.
(b)   Transverse axis $= 6$; $e = \frac{5}{3}$.
(c)   Asymptotes: $y = \pm 3x$; transverse axis $= 4$.
(d)   Foci: $(\pm 13, 0)$; passes through $(13, 28.8)$.
(e)   Vertices $(\pm 5, 0)$; passes through $(6, 2)$.

4.   Suppose a line through a focus of a hyperbola is perpendicular to the line F_1F_2, and intersects the hyperbola in points L, R.   Then line segment LR is called a *latus rectum* of the hyperbola.

Prove that a semi-latus rectum is of length b^2/a, and show how this fact is useful in drawing the hyperbola.

5.   Suppose a, b, c are real numbers such that $c > a > 0$ and $b = \sqrt{c^2 - a^2}$.

Prove that the equation of a hyperbola with foci at $(\pm c, 0)$, such that the difference of the distances from any point on the hyperbola to the foci is $\pm 2a$, is $(x^2/a^2) - (y^2/b^2) = 1$.

6. Suppose $xy = k$ is the equation of a hyperbola H.

(a) If $k > 0$, where, in terms of k, are the vertices of H?

(b) If $k < 0$, where, in terms of k, are the vertices of H?

(c) What is the eccentricity of H?

10.9 THE PARABOLA

In a first course in plane geometry one learns that the locus of points equidistant from *two distinct points A, B* is the perpendicular bisector of line segment AB; and the locus of points equidistant from *two distinct intersecting lines* is the pair of bisectors of the angles formed by these lines.

But what would be the locus of points in a plane equidistant from a given line and a given point not on the line? It turns out to be something quite different from a straight line:

> In a given plane, let d be a line and F a point not on d. Then the set of points in the given plane equidistant from F and d is called a *parabola* with focus F and *directrix d*.

Now we proceed to study the parabola analytically. First of all, of course, we choose a pair of coordinate axes. We elect to utilize a line through F perpendicular to line d at point D as Y-axis; and because it turns out that it makes our final result especially simple, we use the perpendicular bisector of line segment FD as X-axis. (See Fig. 10.12.)

Note that the midpoint of line segment FD is equidistant from focus

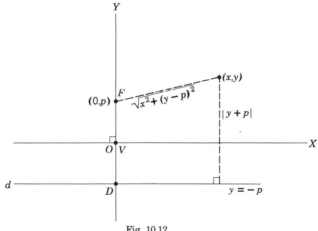

Fig. 10.12

and directrix. Therefore this midpoint is a point of the parabola, called its *vertex V*. As we have chosen our coordinate axes, $V = (0, 0)$.

Let $F = (0, p)$; then the equation of line d is $y = -p$.

Now suppose (x, y) is a point of our coordinate plane. Then (see Section 6.17) the distance from (x, y) to d is $\dfrac{|y + p|}{\sqrt{0^2 + 1^2}} = |y + p|$.

Furthermore, the distance from (x, y) to F is: $\sqrt{x^2 + (y - p)^2}$.

Therefore (x, y) is on our parabola if and only if:

$$|y + p| = \sqrt{x^2 + (y - p)^2}$$

We successively transform the preceding equation into the following equations, each equivalent to the preceding equation:

$$(y + p)^2 = x^2 + (y - p)^2$$
$$4py = x^2$$
$$y = \frac{1}{4p} x^2$$

If we let $a = 1/4p$, then $p = 1/4a$, and we conclude:

> If $a \neq 0$, then $y = ax^2$ is the equation of a parabola with focus $(0, 1/4a)$, vertex $(0, 0)$, and directrix $y = -1/4a$.

As before, we may interchange the roles of x and y to arrive at the statement:

> If $a \neq 0$, then $x = ay^2$ is the equation of a parabola with focus $(1/4a, 0)$, vertex $(0, 0)$, and directrix $x = -1/4a$.

The line FV is called the *axis* of the parabola.

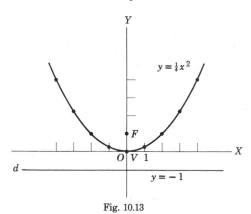

Fig. 10.13

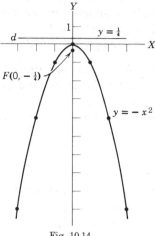

Fig. 10.14

Note that the graph of $y = ax^2$ is symmetric to the Y-axis, and if a is positive then y is never negative, whereas if a is negative, then y is never positive; and analogously for the graph of $x = ay^2$.

Illustrative Example 1. We discuss and draw the graph of: $y = \frac{1}{4}x^2$.

The graph is a parabola, symmetric to the Y-axis; y is never negative; $V = (0, 0)$; $F = (0, 1)$; directrix: $y = -1$.

We then determine a few actual points on the graph. In fact, it is usually easy to sketch the graph of a parabola simply from a well chosen table of values. The graph is drawn in Fig. 10.13.

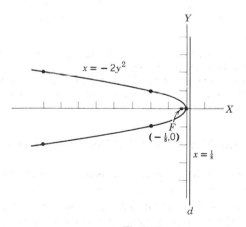

Fig 10.15

Illustrative Example 2. We discuss and draw the graph of $y = -x^2$.
The graph is a parabola, symmetric to the Y-axis; y is never positive; $V = (0, 0)$, $F = (0, -\frac{1}{4})$, directrix: $y = \frac{1}{4}$.
Utilizing a few points on the graph, it is drawn in Fig. 10.14.

Illustrative Example 3. We discuss and draw the graph of: $x = -2y^2$.
The graph must be a parabola, symmetric to the X-axis; x is never positive; $V = (0, 0)$, $F = (-\frac{1}{8}, 0)$, directrix: $x = \frac{1}{8}$.
Utilizing a few points on the graph, it is drawn in Fig. 10.15.

▶ **EXERCISE 58**

1.   Discuss and plot the graphs of the following equations:

(a) $y = x^2$ (b) $y = 4x^2$ (c) $x = y^2$
(d) $x = -y^2$ (e) $y = 3x^2$ (f) $x = 3y^2$
(g) $y = -3x^2$ (h) $x = -3y^2$ (i) $16y = x^2$
(j) $16x - y^2 = 0$ (k) $16x + y^2 = 0$ (l) $16y + x^2 = 0$

2.   In each of the following cases write the equation of and plot the graph of a parabola satisfying the given condition or conditions:

(a) $F = (3, 0)$, $V = (0, 0)$ (b) $F = (0, 3)$, $V = (0, 0)$
(c) $F = (-3, 0)$, $V = (0, 0)$ (d) $F = (0, -3)$, $V = (0, 0)$
(e) Passes through $(7, 11)$ (f) $F = (4, 0)$, directrix: $x = 2$.
(g) $F = (0, 2)$, $V = (0, 4)$.

3.   Find (algebraically) the points of intersection of each pair of curves and draw the curves:

(a) $y = x^2$, $x = y^2$ (b) $y = 4x^2$, $x + 2y^2 = 0$.
(c) $y = x^2$, $y = x$ (d) $y = x^2$, $4x^2 + 9y^2 = 36$
(e) $y = x^2$, $x + y = 6$

4.   A line segment through the focus of a parabola, perpendicular to line FD and terminated by the parabola is called its *latus rectum*.
Prove that the latus rectum of the parabola whose equation is $y^2 = 4px$ is of length $|4p|$; prove the same fact for the parabola whose equation is $x^2 = 4py$.

10.10   TRANSLATION OF COORDINATE AXES

On a Cartesian coordinate plane, consider the mutually perpendicular lines, intersecting at (h, k), whose equations are: $x = h, y = k$ (Fig. 10.16).
Let $\bar{O}$ represent (h, k). Then we may use the perpendicular lines $x = h$, $y = k$ as the axes of a new cc system with new origin $\bar{O}$. In particular, the points on the line $y = k$ whose abscissas are $\geqslant h$ constitute

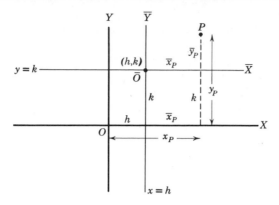

Fig. 10.16

a ray that we shall designate as the new non-negative X-axis, and the points on the line $x = h$ with ordinates $\geqslant k$ constitute a ray that we shall designate as the new non-negative Y-axis.

When this has been done, we say that we have *translated* the old axes into the new position. (A translation, in the physical sense, is a motion that leaves directions of rays unchanged.)

Now given any point in our plane, it may be labeled either in the new or in the original system. In this section a "bar" will generally be used to distinguish between the two. Thus if P is a point in our plane, in the original cc system $P = (x_P, y_P)$; in the new system, $P = (\bar{x}_P, \bar{y}_P)$.

We seek a relation between the coordinates of a point in the new and in the original systems.

From Fig. 10.16, it appears that if P is a point on our plane, then:

(1)
$$\boxed{\begin{aligned} \bar{x}_P &= x_P - h \\ \bar{y}_P &= y_P - k \end{aligned}}$$

Although we have derived the equations (1) above only by examining a diagram, and although the diagram represents only one special case, it may be proved rigorously that the equations (1) hold for any point P in our plane.

A rigorous proof of the validity of (1) may be made in this fashion:
Suppose a line through P perpendicular to the new X-axis meets it in point Q.

CASE 1. Q is on the non-negative side of the new X-axis. Then $\bar{x}_P = d(\bar{O}, Q)$ and $x_Q \geqslant h = x_{\bar{O}}$.

By Lemma 3, page 152, $d(\bar{O}, Q) = |x_Q - x_{\bar{O}}|$. But if $x_Q \geqslant x_{\bar{O}}$, then $x_Q - x_{\bar{O}} \geqslant 0$, so that $|x_Q - x_{\bar{O}}| = x_Q - x_{\bar{O}}$. Finally, since line PQ is parallel to the original Y-axis, $x_P = x_Q$.

We now have:

$$\bar{x}_P = d(\bar{O}, Q) = |x_Q - x_{\bar{O}}| = x_Q - x_{\bar{O}} = x_P - x_{\bar{O}} = x_P - h$$

which completes part of the proof.

The rest of the proof is left as an optional exercise.

The equations (1), above, are called "equations of translation."

Now we consider an application of the equations of translation. Suppose that in a cc plane C is a circle whose center is $\bar{O} = (h, k)$ and whose radius is r, and suppose we translate the axes so that the new origin is $\bar{O}$ (Fig. 10.17).

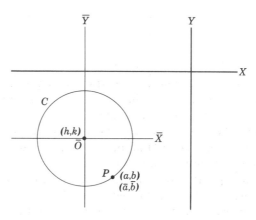

Fig. 10.17

Now if P is a point of our coordinate plane whose coordinates in the original system are (a, b) and in the new system $(\bar{a}, \bar{b})$, we must have, by (1):

$$\bar{a} = a - h, \quad \bar{b} = b - k$$

Furthermore, since C, in the new system, is a circle with radius r and center at the origin, the equation of C, in the new system is:

$$\bar{x}^2 + \bar{y}^2 = r^2$$

Hence point P belongs to circle C if and only if:

$$\bar{a}^2 + \bar{b}^2 = r^2$$

i.e., if and only if:

$$(a - h)^2 + (b - k)^2 = r^2$$

i.e., if and only if the original coordinates of P satisfy the equation:

(2) $$(x - h)^2 + (y - k)^2 = r^2$$

That is to say, (2) is the equation of C in the original coordinate system. Of course, we know this already (see Section 10.2). But now we generalize the method by which we have just derived equation (2), and then apply it to new situations.

> Suppose X and Y are the axes and $\bar{O} = (h, k)$ a point of a cc plane, and suppose we translate the axes to arrive at a new set, $\bar{X}, \bar{Y}$ with origin $\bar{O}$.
>
> Suppose E and $\bar{E}$ are the equations in the original and new systems, respectively, of a graph G.
>
> Then given $\bar{E}$, we may arrive at E by replacing (in $\bar{E}$) $\bar{x}$ by $x - h$ and $\bar{y}$ by $y - k$.

(The proof of this statement is exactly as in the special case of the circle we have just considered, and we therefore omit it.)

Illustrative Example I.   Find the equation of a parabola with vertex $(3, 7)$ and focus $(3, 4)$ (Fig. 10.18).

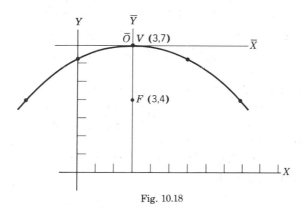

Fig. 10.18

SOLUTION:

We translate the axes to the new origin $\bar{O} = (3, 7)$, so that here $h - 3$, $k = 7$.

In the new system: $F = (0, -3) = (0, 1/4a)$.   Therefore $a = -\frac{1}{12}$.

Hence the equation of the parabola, in the new system, is: $\bar{y} = -\frac{1}{12}\bar{x}^2$.

Therefore the equation of the parabola, in the original system, is: $y - 7 = -\frac{1}{12}(x - 3)^2$.

Just as we generalized the equation of a circle from center at O to center at (h, k) by means of the equations of translation, so we may arrive at the following conclusions also:

(i)   The equation of an ellipse with center (h, k) and axes parallel to the coordinate axes is:

either: $\qquad \dfrac{(x - h)^2}{a^2} + \dfrac{(y - k)^2}{b^2} = 1$ (major axis $\parallel$ X-axis)

or: $\qquad \dfrac{(y - k)^2}{a^2} + \dfrac{(x - h)^2}{b^2} = 1$ (major axis $\parallel$ Y-axis)

where $2a$ = major axis, $2b$ = minor axis of ellipse.

(ii) The equation of a hyperbola with center (h, k) and axes parallel to the coordinate axes is:

either: $\qquad \dfrac{(x - h)^2}{a^2} - \dfrac{(y - k)^2}{b^2} = 1$ (transverse axis $\parallel$ X-axis)

or: $\qquad \dfrac{(y - k)^2}{a^2} - \dfrac{(x - h)^2}{b^2} = 1$ (transverse axis $\parallel$ Y-axis)

where $2a$ = transverse axis of hyperbola.

(iii) The equation of a parabola with vertex (h, k) and axis parallel to a coordinate axis is:

either: $\qquad x - h = a(y - k)^2, (a \neq 0,$ axis $\parallel$ X-axis)
or: $\qquad y - k = a(x - h)^2, (a \neq 0,$ axis $\parallel$ Y-axis)

Illustrative Example 2. Plot the graph of the equation:

(1) $\qquad\qquad 16x^2 - 9y^2 - 64x - 54y - 161 = 0$

SOLUTION:

We use the method of "completing the square":

(2) $\qquad\qquad (16x^2 - 64x\ \ ) - (9y^2 + 54y\ \ ) = 161$
(3) $\qquad\qquad 16(x^2 - 4x\ \ ) - 9(y^2 + 6y\ \ ) = 161$
(4) $\qquad 16(x^2 - 4x + 4) - 9(y^2 + 6y + 9) = 161 + 64 - 81$
(5) $\qquad\qquad 16(x - 2)^2 - 9(y + 3)^2 = 144$

Now dividing both sides by 144:

(6) $\qquad\qquad \dfrac{(x - 2)^2}{9} - \dfrac{(y + 3)^2}{16} = 1$

If we translate the coordinate axes so that the point $(2, -3)$ becomes the new origin, equation (6) becomes:

(7) $\qquad\qquad \dfrac{\bar{x}^2}{9} - \dfrac{\bar{y}^2}{16} = 1$

We have already drawn the *hyperbola* which is the graph of this equation. (See Illustrative Example, Section 10.6.)

The required graph is simply the graph of equation (7), drawn with respect to the *new* coordinate system (Fig. 10.19).

Illustrative Example 3. Plot the graph of the equation:

$$x^2 - 6x + 12y - 75 = 0$$

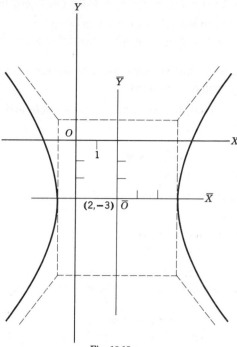

Fig. 10.19

SOLUTION:
$$x^2 - 6x = -12y + 75$$
$$x^2 - 6x + 9 = -12y + 75 + 9$$
$$(x - 3)^2 = -12y + 84$$
$$(x - 3)^2 = -12(y - 7)$$
$$y - 7 = -\tfrac{1}{12}(x - 3)^2$$

In a translated system with origin (3, 7), the equation of the required graph would be:

$$\bar{y} = -\tfrac{1}{12}\bar{x}^2$$

This equation has been encountered in Illustrative Example 1, and its graph drawn in Fig. 10.18.

10.11 THE GRAPH OF A SECOND-DEGREE EQUATION WITH *xy* TERM MISSING

We are not quite ready to settle completely the question of what graphs may arise from a second-degree equation, but we are ready to take the major step toward that goal. We shall now consider the equation:

(1) $Ax^2 + Cy^2 + Dx + Ey + F = 0$ (A, C not both 0)

i.e., the general second-degree equation in x and y with $B = 0$, and we shall determine all the graphs which may arise from equations of the form (1).

First of all we note that we have already encountered the following as graphs of second-degree equations:

1. An *ellipse* (which may or may not be a *circle with nonzero radius*).
2. A *hyperbola*.
3. A *parabola*.
4. A single *point*.   (See page 303.)
5. A *null graph*.   (See page 303.)

We show now that we may add to this list:

6. A single *line*.
7. A pair of $\neq$ *intersecting lines*.
8. A pair of $\neq$ *parallel lines*.

For example, consider the second-degree equation $x^2 = 0$. This is equivalent to the equation $x = 0$, whose graph is the Y-axis, namely a *line*.

Next consider the second-degree equation: $y^2 - x^2 = 0$. This is equivalent to: $(y + x)(y - x) = 0$, which is satisfied if $y + x = 0$, or if $y - x = 0$, and not otherwise.   The points which satisfy $y + x = 0$ constitute one straight line, and the points which satisfy $y - x = 0$ constitute another, and the two straight lines intersect at $(0, 0)$.   The graph of $y^2 - x^2 = 0$ is the *union* of the graphs of $y + x = 0$ and $y - x = 0$, i.e., a pair of $\neq$ *intersecting lines*.

Similarly, the graph of the second-degree equation $x^2 = 4x$ is the pair of $\neq$ *parallel lines* whose equations are $x = 0$, $x = 4$ (since $x^2 = 4x$ is equivalent to $x^2 - 4x = 0$, $x(x - 4) = 0$).

And now we prove that *no other* graphs may arise from the equation (1) above.

Since A and C cannot both be 0, one of three cases must occur, and we shall consider each in turn.

CASE 1. $A \neq 0, C \neq 0$.

In this case, just as we have done in particular cases, we may [unless the equation is already in the simpler form (2) below] complete the square in (1) and translate to new axes to arrive at an equation in the simpler form:

(2) $A\bar{x}^2 + C\bar{y}^2 = K$

Throughout the rest of Case 1 we shall restrict ourselves to the new coordinate system, with which understanding we may omit the "bars" and write equation (2) as:

(3) $Ax^2 + Cy^2 = K$

Now we consider subcases:

CASE 1a. *A* and *C* are of like sign.

Then if *K* is of sign opposite to *A* and *C*, our graph is *null*. For otherwise (3) would yield a non-negative number equal to a negative number.

If $K = 0$, we note that only one point (0, 0) fails to make the left side of equation (3) $\neq 0$. The graph consists of a single *point*.

If *K* is of the same sign as *A* and *C*, we have noted (see page 314) that the graph of (3) is an *ellipse*. (If further, $A = C$, the graph will be a *circle of nonzero radius*.)

CASE 1b. *A* and *C* are of opposite sign.

Then if $K \neq 0$, we have noted (see page 319) that the graph of (3) is a *hyperbola*.

Suppose, then, that $K = 0$. The equation whose graph we seek becomes:

$$(4) \qquad Ax^2 + Cy^2 = 0$$

which is equivalent to:

$$(5) \qquad y^2 + \frac{A}{C}x^2 = 0$$

Since *A* and *C* are of opposite sign, the real number $-A/C$ is positive, so that there exists a real number $m = \sqrt{-A/C}$; hence $m^2 = -A/C$, $-m^2 = A/C$.

Therefore (5) is equivalent to:

$$(6) \qquad y^2 - m^2 x^2 = 0$$

which in turn is equivalent to:

$$(7) \qquad (y + mx)(y - mx) = 0$$

The graph of (7) is a pair of $\neq$ *intersecting lines*.

CASE 2. $A \neq 0$, $C = 0$.

Then (1) is equivalent to:

$$(8) \qquad Ax^2 + Dx + Ey + F = 0$$

and unless (8) is already in the simpler form (9) below, we may complete the square and translate, to arrive at the equation:

$$(9) \qquad A\bar{x}^2 + E\bar{y} + R = 0$$

If $E = 0$, (9) is equivalent to an equation $\bar{x}^2 = K$, whose graph will be *null*, a *line*, or a pair of $\neq$ *parallel lines*, depending upon whether $K < 0$, $= 0$, or > 0, respectively.

If $E \neq 0$, then (9) is equivalent to the equation $\bar{y} + R/E = -(A/E)\bar{x}^2$, whose graph [see (iii) above] is a *parabola*

CASE 3. $A = 0$, $C \neq 0$.

The situation here is simply that of Case 2, with the roles of *x* and *y* interchanged. Therefore no new types of graphs will occur in this case.

And now we have shown that the eight graphs listed above are the only graphs that may arise from a second-degree equation in *x* and *y* with the *xy* term missing.

We are familiar with at least one type of second-degree equation in which the *xy* term is *not* missing, namely the equation $xy = k$, where $k \neq 0$. We know the graph of this equation to be a hyperbola, with transverse axis *not* parallel to a coordinate axis.

Actually, we shall prove in Section 10.13 that *the graph of any second-degree equation in x and y, even one whose xy term is not missing, must be one of the eight graphs listed above*. It will turn out that the effect of an xy term (i.e., $B \neq 0$) in our second-degree equation is to produce a graph whose axes of symmetry are generally not parallel to either coordinate axis, as is illustrated in the case of the equation $xy = k$.

A by-product of the analysis of this section is the following set of criteria:

The graph of a second-degree equation with xy term missing can be:

(a) A circle of nonzero radius only if $A = C$.
(b) An ellipse only if A and C are of like sign.
(c) A hyperbola only if A and C are of opposite sign.
(d) A parabola only if A or C is 0 (i.e., if x^2 or y^2 is missing).

It must be borne in mind, however, that even if these conditions hold, the graphs 4–8 listed above may occur also.

We say that the conditions given above are *necessary*, but not sufficient for the graph to turn out as stated (see Section 4.8).

▶ **EXERCISE 59**

1. Identify, sketch, and find the foci of the graphs of each of the following equations:

(a) $x^2 + 4y^2 - 2x + 16y + 13 = 0$
(b) $16x^2 - 9y^2 + 64x + 72y - 224 = 0$
(c) $2x^2 + 2y^2 - 4x + 8y + 5 = 0$
(d) $y = x^2 - 3x + 4$
(e) $9x^2 - 16y^2 - 18x - 64y - 199 = 0$
(f) $x = 2y^2 - 3y + 1$
(g) $16x^2 - 9y^2 + 90y - 81 = 0$
(h) $y^2 + 2x + 6y = 5$
(i) $4x^2 - 20x + 24y + 61 = 0$
(j) $9x^2 - 16y^2 + 18x + 64y + 89 = 0$
(k) $x^2 - 4x - 4y = 0$
(l) $9x^2 + 25y^2 - 108x - 250y + 724 = 0$
(m) $4x^2 - 9y^2 - 8x - 36y = 176$
(n) $x^2 - 4x + 3y = 7$
(o) $y = -x^2 - x + 6$
(p) $x = y^2 - 9$
(q) $y = x^2 - 9$

2. Write the equation of the parabola with vertex at the point $(-4, 0)$ which passes through the ends of the major axis of the ellipse:

$$9x^2 + 4y^2 = 36$$

3. What is the equation of the ellipse with center at $(2, 1)$, the end of an axis at $(0, 1)$, and passing through $(3, 4)$?

4. Find the equation of an ellipse or a hyperbola with foci $(1, 8)$ and $(1, -2)$ and vertices $(1, 7)$ and $(1, -1)$.

5. Find the equation of the hyperbola that has one vertex at $(1, 9)$, the corresponding focus at $(1, 7)$ and eccentricity equal to 2.

6. Find the equation of a parabola with focus $(1, -7)$ and directrix $y = 3$.

7. Find the equation of an ellipse that has one focus at $(2, -1)$ and an end of one axis at $(-1, 3)$.

8. A point moves in a plane so as to stay equidistant from the line $x = 4$ and the point $(7, 3)$. Find an equation satisfied by all points of its path.

9. Find the equation of the locus of all points the sum of whose distances from the points $(-2, 3)$ and $(4, 3)$ is 10.

10. What is the locus of all points the difference of whose distances from the points $(-2, 3)$ and $(4, 3)$ is 10?

11. Draw, or identify as null, each of the following graphs:

(a) $xy = 0$ (b) $x^2 - 2x + 1 = 0$
(c) $x^2 = -4$ (d) $x^2 = 4x$
(e) $x^2 + y^2 = 2y - 1$ (f) $y^2 = 4x^2$
(g) $xy + x + y + 1 = 0$ (h) $x^3 - 9x = 0$
(i) $9x^2 + 16y^2 = 0$ (j) $9x^2 - 16y^2 = 0$
(k) $x^2 + y^2 = 2y - 2$ (l) $x^2 - 2xy + y^2 = 0$

12. We have found the loci of points which move in a plane so that in one case the sum, in another the difference of their distances from two fixed points is kept constant. What about keeping the *ratio* of these distances constant? That is, suppose $F_1 \neq F_2$ are points in a plane, and $a \geq 0$ is a real number. Find an equation in an appropriate cc system for the locus of all points P in the given plane such that $PF_1/PF_2 = a$.

Show then that if $a = 1$, the locus is a straight line, the perpendicular bisector of line segment F_1F_2; and if $a \neq 1$, the locus is a *circle* (called the "circle of Apollonius").

10.12 ROTATION OF COORDINATE AXES

Suppose we are given a ccd (or a ccr) system in a plane. Then (although we shall not prove this fact) given any real number, θ, we may arrive at a *new* ccd (or ccr) system in the same plane simply by subtracting θ from each of the labels in the original system (see Problems 7, 8, Exercise 33).

We shall now assume that we have an original ccd or ccr system, and also a new system derived by subtracting the real number θ from each of the labels in the original system (Fig. 10.20).

We say that the new system has been derived from the old by "rotating through the angle θ;" i.e., "rotating through the angle θ" means subtracting θ from each ray label, so that the ray originally labeled θ becomes the 0-ray.

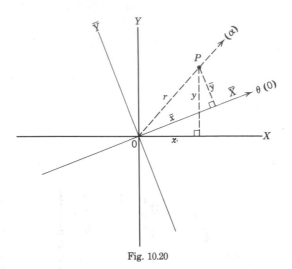

Fig. 10.20

Now suppose we have a point P in our plane with coordinates (x, y) in the original system and coordinates $(\bar{x}, \bar{y})$ in the new system.

We seek relations among $x, y, \bar{x}, \bar{y}$.

Let $OP = r$, and suppose that ray OP is labeled α in the new system; then in the old system ray OP must have been labeled $\alpha + \theta$. From Lemma 1, page 237 we now have:

$$x = r \cos (\alpha + \theta) \qquad \bar{x} = r \cos \alpha$$
$$y = r \sin (\alpha + \theta) \qquad \bar{y} = r \sin \alpha$$

Therefore:

$$x = r \cos \alpha \cos \theta - r \sin \alpha \sin \theta = \bar{x} \cos \theta - \bar{y} \sin \theta$$
$$y = r \sin \alpha \cos \theta + r \cos \alpha \sin \theta = \bar{y} \cos \theta + \bar{x} \sin \theta$$

(1)

$$x = \bar{x} \cos \theta - \bar{y} \sin \theta$$
$$y = \bar{x} \sin \theta + \bar{y} \cos \theta$$

The equations (1) above are called "equations of rotation."

As in the case of translation, the following may be proved.

> Suppose we are given an original ccd (or ccr) system and a new system derived from the old by rotating through θ degrees (or radians).
>
> Suppose E and $\bar{E}$ are the equations in the original and new systems, respectively, of a graph G.
>
> Then given E, we may arrive at $\bar{E}$ by replacing (in E) x by $\bar{x} \cos \theta - \bar{y} \sin \theta$ and y by $\bar{x} \sin \theta + \bar{y} \cos \theta$.

Illustrative Example. Given the equation $xy = x^2 + y^2$ of a graph G, find the equation of G in a new cc system derived from the old by rotating the coordinate axes through $45°$.

SOLUTION: We have: $x = \dfrac{\bar{x}}{\sqrt{2}} - \dfrac{\bar{y}}{\sqrt{2}} = \dfrac{1}{\sqrt{2}}(\bar{x} - \bar{y})$

$$y = \dfrac{\bar{x}}{\sqrt{2}} + \dfrac{\bar{y}}{\sqrt{2}} = \dfrac{1}{\sqrt{2}}(\bar{x} + \bar{y})$$

The equation of G in the new system is therefore:

$$\frac{1}{\sqrt{2}}(\bar{x} - \bar{y}) \cdot \frac{1}{\sqrt{2}}(\bar{x} + \bar{y}) = \left[\frac{1}{\sqrt{2}}(\bar{x} - \bar{y})\right]^2 + \left[\frac{1}{\sqrt{2}}(\bar{x} + \bar{y})\right]^2$$

which reduces to:

$$\bar{x}^2 + 3\bar{y}^2 = 0$$

which is satisfied only if $\bar{x} = 0$, $\bar{y} = 0$. Therefore the graph G consists only of a single point, the origin of both coordinate systems.

10.13   THE GRAPH OF THE GENERAL SECOND DEGREE EQUATION IN x AND y

We shall attempt, by rotating coordinate axes, to "eliminate" the xy term from the equation:

(1) $Ax^2 + Bxy + Cy^2 + Dx + Ey + F = 0$ (A, B, C not all 0)

Suppose we rotate the axes through θ (the number θ not yet determined).   Then the new equation of the graph of (1) above will be:

$A(\bar{x}\cos\theta - \bar{y}\sin\theta)^2 + B(\bar{x}\cos\theta - \bar{y}\sin\theta)(\bar{x}\sin\theta + \bar{y}\cos\theta) +$
      $C(\bar{x}\sin\theta + \bar{y}\cos\theta)^2 + D(\bar{x}\cos\theta - \bar{y}\sin\theta) + E(\bar{x}\sin\theta + \bar{y}\cos\theta) + F = 0$

Collecting terms, this equation may be written in the form:

(2) $\bar{A}\bar{x}^2 + \bar{B}\bar{x}\bar{y} + \bar{C}\bar{y}^2 + \bar{D}\bar{x} + \bar{E}\bar{y} + F = 0$

The coefficient of $\bar{x}\bar{y}$ in (2), as derived from the equation which precedes it, is:

$\bar{B} = -2A\sin\theta\cos\theta + B(\cos^2\theta - \sin^2\theta) + 2C\sin\theta\cos\theta$

or

(3) $\bar{B} = (C - A)\sin 2\theta + B\cos 2\theta$

If $A = C$, then the coefficient $\bar{B}$ will be 0 if $\theta = 45°$.   If $A \neq C$, we solve:

(4) $(C - A)\sin 2\theta + B\cos 2\theta = 0$

$$\frac{\sin 2\theta}{\cos 2\theta} = -\frac{B}{C - A} = \frac{B}{A - C}$$

$$\tan 2\theta = \frac{B}{A - C}$$

Since it is always possible to find a value of θ which will satisfy this last equation, it will in all cases be possible to find a value of θ which makes $\bar{B} = 0$.

We see then, that by rotating the coordinate axes, it is always possible to transform a second-degree equation into an equation of degree ≤ 2, with the xy term eliminated. (Actually, we shall show in an exercise that the new equation is also of degree 2.)

Therefore the graphs which any second-degree equation in x and y may give rise to are exactly 1–8 *of page* 332, *in "oblique" position if the given equation contains an xy term.*

In the illustrative example of the preceding section, $A = C$.   It was for this reason that we elected to rotate the axes through $45°$ in that example.

Illustrative Example. Draw the graph of the equation:

$$288x^2 + 168xy + 337y^2 = 3600$$

SOLUTION: Since $A \neq C$, we let:

$$\tan 2\theta = \frac{B}{A - C} = \frac{168}{288 - 337} = -\frac{24}{7}$$

We choose 2θ in QII. Then $\cos 2\theta = -\frac{7}{25}$, θ is in QI, $\sin \theta = \sqrt{\frac{1 - \cos 2\theta}{2}}$

$$= \sqrt{\frac{1 + \frac{7}{25}}{2}} = \frac{4}{5};\ \text{therefore } \cos \theta = \frac{3}{5}.\ \text{(See Fig. 10.21)}$$

Fig. 10.21

Now we substitute into the original equation:

$$x = \frac{3}{5}\bar{x} - \frac{4}{5}\bar{y} = \frac{1}{5}(3\bar{x} - 4\bar{y})$$

$$y = \frac{4}{5}\bar{x} + \frac{3}{5}\bar{y} = \frac{1}{5}(4\bar{x} + 3\bar{y})$$

arriving at:

$$288\left[\frac{1}{5}(3\bar{x} - 4\bar{y})\right]^2 + 168 \cdot \frac{1}{5}(3\bar{x} - 4\bar{y}) \cdot \frac{1}{5}(4\bar{x} + 3\bar{y}) + 337\left[\frac{1}{5}(4\bar{x} + 3\bar{y})\right]^2 = 3600$$

$$288(3\bar{x} - 4\bar{y})^2 + 168(3\bar{x} - 4\bar{y})(4\bar{x} + 3\bar{y}) + 377(4\bar{x} + 3\bar{y})^2 = 25 \cdot 3600$$

$$10,000\ \bar{x}^2 + 5625\ \bar{y}^2 = 25 \cdot 3600$$

$$\frac{\bar{x}^2}{9} + \frac{\bar{y}^2}{16} = 1$$

The graph is therefore an ellipse, which we now plot (Fig. 10.22).

EXERCISE

1. Identify, and if it is not null, draw the graph of:

(a) $xy = 12$ (Also, find the equation we arrive at when we eliminate the xy term in this example.)

(b) $xy - 2x - 4y + 6 = 0$ (It is easily seen that this graph has asymptotes. Therefore the graph must be a —? Find the resulting equation when we eliminate the xy term in this example also.)

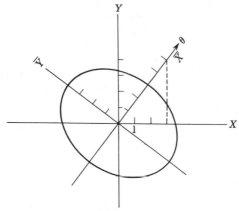

Fig. 10.22

(c) $y^2 + 3xy - 3x^2 - 4 = 0$
(d) $2x^2 + y^2 - 3xy + 2x - y = 0$
(e) $x^2 + xy + y^2 = 1$
(f) $5y^2 + 4xy + 8x^2 - 9 = 0$
(g) $3y^2 - 10xy + 3x^2 + 32 = 0$
(h) $\sqrt{x} + \sqrt{y} = 1$ [*Hint:* Consider excluded values; then show that the graph is a part of a parabola by squaring the given equation, isolating the radical which appears, squaring again.]
(i) $x^2 - 2xy + 2y^2 = 0$
(j) $x^2 - 2xy + 2y^2 + 2 = 0$

2.   Referring to equations (1) and (2) of Section 10.13, we found, in (3), $\bar{B}$ in terms of coefficients of (1).

(a)   Similarly, find $\bar{A}, \bar{C}$.

(b)   Show that under any rotation of the coordinate axes, $A + C$ is "invariant;" i.e., $\bar{A} + \bar{C} = A + C$.

(c)   Show also that under any rotation of the coordinate axes the "discriminant" $B^2 - 4AC$ of equation (1) is invariant.

(d)   Show, as follows, that equation (2) actually is of the second degree: Suppose, to the contrary, that $\bar{A} = \bar{B} = \bar{C} = 0$. Then from (b), (c) above, $A + C = B^2 - 4AC = 0$. Deduce from this the contradiction that $A = B = C = 0$.

(e)   Prove: A necessary (but not a sufficient) condition for the graph of equation (1) to be:

  (i)   An ellipse is: $B^2 - 4AC < 0$.

  (ii)   A parabola is: $B^2 - 4AC = 0$.

  (iii)   A hyperbola is: $B^2 - 4AC > 0$. [*Hint:* See (b)–(d), page 334; assume that by rotating axes, (1) has been transformed into (2), with $\bar{B} = 0$. Then by (c) above, $B^2 - 4AC = -4\bar{A}\bar{C}$; now complete the proof.]

  (iv)   Prove that (1) is the equation of a circle of nonzero radius only if $A = C$ and $B = 0$.

3.   Suppose that in an original ccd system a point $P = (x, y)$, and that in a new system derived from the original by rotating through an angle θ, $P = (\bar{x}, \bar{y})$. Derive

the equations of rotation:

$$\bar{x} = x \cos \theta + y \sin \theta$$
$$\bar{y} = - x \sin \theta + y \cos \theta$$

in the following ways:

(a)   Solve the simultaneous equations (1), page 336, for $\bar{x}$ and $\bar{y}$.

(b)   Follow the method by which the equations (1), page 336, were derived, but use α to denote a label in the *original* system for a ray on which P lies.

(c)   In the equations (1), page 336, reverse the roles of (x, y) and $(\bar{x}, \bar{y})$; that is to say, think of $(\bar{x}, \bar{y})$ as the original coordinates of P, and (x, y) as the new coordinates of P, in a system derived from the original by rotating the axes through an angle $-\theta$.

10.14   THE CONIC SECTIONS

We have seen (page 332) that the following are the only non-null sets of points that may occur as graphs of second-degree equations:

1.   A noncircular ellipse.
2.   A hyperbola.
3.   A parabola.
4.   A circle of nonzero radius.
5.   A circle of zero radius (i.e., a point).
6.   A line.
7.   A pair of $\neq$ intersecting lines.
8.   A pair of $\neq$ parallel lines.

It is a remarkable fact that these point-sets, besides being related *algebraically* in that they constitute all possible non-null graphs of second-degree equations, are also related *geometrically* in this way: they represent all possible cross sections of the simplest types of cones and cylinders.

In order to clarify our last statement we shall first define certain terms.

Definition.   Let B be a curve in a plane, V a point not in the given plane. Then the set of points which is the union of all lines VQ, where Q is a point of B, is called a *cone* with vertex V and base B. (Fig.10.23)

Each line VQ is called an *element* of the cone.

The union of the rays VQ, is called a *nappe* of the cone. V and all the points of the cone not on the first nappe constitute another *nappe* of the cone.

If B is a circle of nonzero radius, the cone is called a *circular cone.*

If B is a circle of nonzero radius and center O, and if line VO is perpendicular to the plane of B, then the cone is called a *right circular cone.*

Definition.   Let B be a set of points in a plane, and let L be a set of parallel lines not lying in the plane of B, such that each line of L passes through a point of B and each point of B lies on a line of L.   Then the

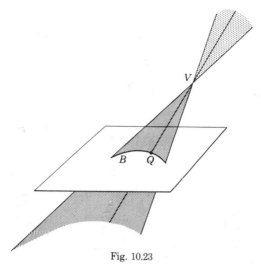

Fig. 10.23

set of points which is the union of all lines in L is called a *cylinder* with base B.

Each line in L is called an *element* of the cylinder.

If B is a circle of nonzero radius, the cylinder is called a *circular* cylinder.

If B is a circle of nonzero radius, and the lines of L are perpendicular to the plane of B, the cylinder is called a *right circular cylinder*.

Definition. A (planar) *cross section* of a set of points S is the intersection (see page 13) of a plane and S.

Now as a matter of fact, of the graphs 1–8 above, all but the last are cross sections of a right circular cone, and the last is a cross section of a right circular cylinder.

For it may be proved (although we do not do so here) that:

A noncircular ellipse is the cross section that results when a plane intersects all the elements of a right circular cone on only one nappe.

A hyperbola is the cross section that results when a plane intersects both nappes of a right circular cone, but does not pass through its vertex.

A parabola is the cross section that results when a plane that is parallel to an element intersects only one nappe of the cone. (See Fig. 10.24)

It is left to the student to show how the other second-degree graphs may be derived as cross sections of right circular cones or cylinders.

The noncircular, nontrivial "conic sections," i.e., the ellipse, the parabola, and the hyperbola, have a long and interesting history and many practical applications. They were known and studied by the Greeks, who discovered them some 2500 years ago, in the course of attempting to solve the "Three Famous Problems of Antiquity." First studied purely out of

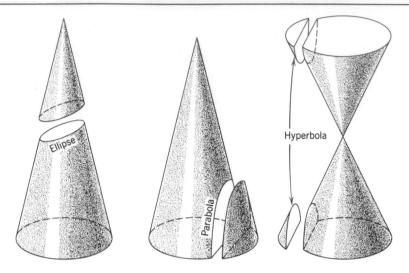

Fig. 10.24

intellectual curiosity, the conic sections turned out later, as happens so often in mathematics, to be of the greatest practical importance. For it was discovered (empirically) by Johann Kepler, early in the seventeenth century, that the path of the earth and the other planets about the sun is an *ellipse*, with the sun at one focus; some seventy years later Isaac Newton proved this fact deductively, as a consequence of his law of gravitation.

Indeed, it has since turned out that not only ellipses, but parabolas and hyperbolas also, are paths that are traced by heavenly bodies.

The question of the path or "trajectory" of a "projectile," i.e., an object thrown like a baseball or fired like a bullet, is of the greatest importance, especially militarily. The parabola has turned out to be important in this connection since (neglecting relatively minor factors such as air-resistance) the trajectory of a projectile is parabolic. (See Problem 5, Exercise 30.)

The ellipse and parabola display interesting focal properties that have been put to practical use. In the case of the ellipse, all rays emanating at one focus, and reflected from the ellipse, will be reflected through the other focus. This explains the phenomenon of the "whispering gallery," in which a whisper emanating from one point may be heard clearly at a distant point, but not at intermediate points.

In the case of the parabola, rays emanating from its focus and reflected from the parabola become rays parallel to its axis, so that these rays form a powerful, unscattered beam (Fig. 10.25). The principle finds application in automobile headlights and aircraft beacons.

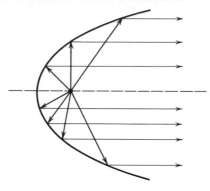

Fig. 10.25

Conversely, rays parallel to an axis are reflected through the focus of a parabola. Solar furnaces make use of this fact. (See, in this connection, the derivation of the word "focus.")

(Proofs of these focal properties may be made using differential calculus.)

Engineers employ conic sections in the building of bridges for example; in this connection it is interesting to note that when a bridge is uniformly loaded, the cable by which it is suspended assumes the form of a parabola.

Finally, we mention that innumerable formulas in varied fields are of the second degree and have graphs, therefore, which are of the type we have been discussing. The curve the economist calls "the demand curve in the case of unitary elasticity," for example, is simply the hyperbola whose equation is $PQ = k$, where P is the price of an item, Q the quantity demanded at price P, and k is a real number.

▶ EXERCISE 60

1. What condition on a cutting plane will guarantee that its intersection with a right circular cone will be a circle of nonzero radius? A point? A line? A pair of intersecting lines?

Which of the point-sets 1–8 of page 340 are cross sections of a right circular cylinder, and how is each produced by a cutting plane?

2. *Focus-directrix definition of certain conic sections.* The definitions we have given for the ellipse and the hyperbola are closely related to each other, but our definition of the parabola is of a different type. An approach that results in a more unified set of definitions is to define these curves as particular conic sections, but then our analytic treatment is made more difficult. A third type of definition, generalizing our definition of the parabola, will be considered in this problem.

The definition we have in mind stems from the following theorem:

Theorem. Let F be a point, l a line not containing F, and e a positive real number.

Let G be the locus of points P (in the plane determined by F and l) the ratio of whose distances to F and l (in that order) is e.

Then:

(a) If $e = 1$, G is a parabola with focus F and directrix l.

(b) If $e < 1$, G is a noncircular ellipse with focus F and eccentricity e.

(c) If $e > 1$, G is a hyperbola with focus F and eccentricity e.

PROOF: The proof of (a) is almost immediate. *Why?* For the rest: (Fig. 10.26)

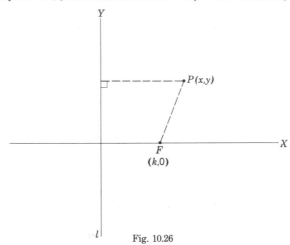

Fig. 10.26

Use l as Y-axis, a line through $F \perp l$ as X-axis, and suppose $F = (k, 0)$, $k > 0$. Then (x, y) is a point of G if and only if:

$$\frac{\sqrt{(x - k)^2 + y^2}}{|x|} = e$$

From this derive the equivalent equation:

$$(1 - e^2)x^2 + y^2 - 2kx + k^2 = 0$$

from which show that if $e < 1$, G is an ellipse, and if $e > 1$, G is a hyperbola. Then complete the square and arrive at:

(1)
$$\frac{\left(x - \dfrac{k}{1 - e^2}\right)^2}{\dfrac{k^2 e^2}{(1 - e^2)^2}} + \frac{y^2}{\dfrac{k^2 e^2}{1 - e^2}} = 1$$

If $e < 1$, (1) is the equation of an ellipse in which:

$$a^2 = \frac{k^2 e^2}{(1 - e^2)^2}, \quad b^2 = \frac{k^2 e^2}{1 - e^2}$$

Show now that $c^2 = a^2 - b^2 = k^2 e^4/(1 - e^2)^2$.

(The fact that $a^2 - b^2$ is positive proves that we have identified a^2 and b^2 correctly in equation (1) above.)

Hence $\dfrac{c}{a} = \dfrac{ke^2/(1 - e^2)}{ke/(1 - e^2)} = e$. Thus, the eccentricity of G is e, as was to be proved.

Finally, the foci of equation (1) lie at $\left(\dfrac{k}{1 - e^2} \pm c, 0\right)$. *Show that one of these points is F.*

This completes the proof of (b) above.

To complete the proof of (c), we write (1) in the form:

$$(2) \qquad \frac{\left[x - \dfrac{k}{(1 - e^2)}\right]^2}{k^2 e^2/(1 - e^2)^2} - \frac{y^2}{k^2 e^2/(e^2 - 1)} = 1$$

Then since we are now assuming $e > 1$, (2) is the equation of a hyperbola with $a^2 = ?,\ b^2 = ?,\ c^2 = ?$

The rest of the proof of (c) is left to the student to carry through.

Now, finally, if the theorem above is to supply a definition of the parabola, the noncircular ellipse, and the hyperbola, we must show that *every one* of these curves may be defined as in the theorem.

In the case of the parabola the old and new definitions are trivially equivalent.

In the case of a noncircular ellipse:

Suppose axes have been established so that the equation of the given ellipse is:

$$(3) \qquad \frac{x^2}{a^2} + \frac{y^2}{b^2} = 1$$

We shall show that this equation may be written in the form (1), after a translation of axes.

The fact that in our preceding development, $a = ke/(1 - e^2)$ suggests that we now let $k = [a(1 - e^2)]/e$, where e is the eccentricity of the given ellipse. (This is permissible, for since our ellipse is noncircular, $e \neq 0$.)

It follows that $a = ke/(1 - e^2)$, $a^2 = k^2 e^2/(1 - e^2)^2$.

Show that $b^2 = k^2 e^2/(1 - e^2)$.

Now if we translate our axis to the new origin $\left(-\dfrac{k}{1 - e^2}, 0\right)$, the equation (3) becomes:

$$(4) \qquad \frac{\left(\bar{x} - \dfrac{k}{(1 - e^2)}\right)^2}{k^2 e^2/(1 - e^2)^2} + \frac{\bar{y}^2}{k^2 e^2/(1 - e^2)} = 1$$

which is of the same form as (1).

Thus the given ellipse is the locus of points the ratio of whose distances to a certain point and a certain line is a positive real number $e < 1$.

Similarly, prove that any hyperbola has an equation of the form (2), *and therefore falls within the scope of our proposed new definition.*

Up until now we have defined no eccentricity for the parabola. The preceding theorem suggests that we define *the eccentricity of a parabola to be* 1; and that we define the line l to be a *directrix* of the ellipse and hyperbola also.

Considerations of symmetry show that actually the non-circular ellipse and the hyperbola each have *two* directrices.

As a final exercise, show that:

(i) The foci of an ellipse or a hyperbola are at a distance of ae from the center of each curve.

(ii) The directrices of an ellipse or a hyperbola are at a distance of a/e from the center of each curve.

We have now proved the following definition to be equivalent to our original definition:

Definition. In a given plane, let F be a point and l a line not containing F. Suppose e is a positive real number.

Then the set of all points in the given plane, the ratio of whose distances to F and l (in that order) is e, is called a *noncircular ellipse* (if $e < 1$), a *parabola* (if $e = 1$) and a *hyperbola* (if $e > 1$).

In each case, F is called a *focus*, e the *eccentricity* and l a *directrix* of the particular locus.

EXPONENTIAL AND LOGARITHMIC FUNCTIONS

11.1 INTRODUCTION

In earlier chapters we have often had occasion to write expressions of the form x^n, but rarely with values of n other than 2 or 3. (In the expression x^n, n, of course, is called an *exponent*.) In this chapter we shall consider exponents, and functions to which they lead.

Most of our statements concerning exponents will be made with little or no proof; a complete treatment of this material is left to later, more specialized courses in mathematics.

11.2 NATURAL NUMBER EXPONENTS

Suppose a is a complex number. (Our statements about a will then apply if a is a real number, since every real number is also a complex number.) Then if n is a nn, we define a^n to be a if $n = 1$, and to be the product of n factors, each equal to a, if $n > 1$. That is:

$$a^1 = a$$
$$a^2 = a \cdot a$$
$$a^3 = a \cdot a \cdot a, \text{ and so on}$$

If a, b are complex numbers and m, n are nn, it is not hard to see that the following familiar rules hold true as a consequence of the preceding definition:

(1) $\qquad\qquad a^m a^n = a^{m+n}$

(2) $\qquad\qquad (a^m)^n = a^{mn}$

(3) $$(ab)^m = a^m b^m$$

(4) $$\left(\frac{a}{b}\right)^m = \frac{a^m}{b^m} \quad (\text{where } b \neq 0)$$

(5a) $$\frac{a^m}{a^n} = a^{m-n} \quad (\text{where } a \neq 0 \text{ and } m > n)$$

(5b) $$\frac{a^m}{a^n} = \frac{1}{a^{n-m}} \quad (\text{where } a \neq 0 \text{ and } m < n)$$

11.3 INTEGER EXPONENTS

In simplifying the expression a^5/a^3, where a is a nonzero complex number, rule (5a) above permits us to proceed as follows:

$$\frac{a^5}{a^3} = a^{5-3} = a^2$$

But in simplifying the expression a^3/a^5, again for a nonzero complex number, rule (5a) does not apply, for in this case $m = 3$, $n = 5$, and the condition $m > n$ demanded by the rule is not satisfied.   That the condition $m > n$ is necessary in rule (5a) may be seen from the fact that otherwise we would be led to an exponent (namely $m - n$) which is *not* a nn, and the only exponents we have as yet defined are nn exponents.

It would seem, then, that it might be useful to extend our definition of exponents to include all integers, rather than just the nn; we shall find that rule (5a) suggests a reasonable definition for a^k, in case k is an integer other than a nn; i.e., in case $k = 0$ or k is a negative integer.

First, supposing that a is a nonzero complex number; we may consider the expression: a^2/a^2.   On the one hand we know: $a^2/a^2 = 1$.   On the other hand, *if rule (5a) did apply*, $a^2/a^2 = a^{2-2} = a^0$.   This suggests the following definition:

If a is a nonzero complex number, a^0 is defined to equal 1.

Again, supposing that a is a nonzero complex number, we may consider the expression: a^3/a^5.   On the one hand, we know (by rule (5b) above) that $a^3/a^5 = 1/a^2$.   On the other hand, *if rule (5a) did apply*, $a^3/a^5 = a^{-2}$. This suggests that we define $a^{-2} = 1/a^2$, and in general that we make the following definition:

If a is a nonzero complex number, and n is a nn, then a^{-n} is defined to equal $1/a^n$.

These definitions turn out to have been well-chosen.   For it may now be proved that under these definitions all of the rules (1)–(5b) continue to hold true, even when m, n are any *integers* (rather than just any nn), except that the expressions 0^0 and 0^{-n}, where n is a nn, continue to remain undefined.

As a matter of fact, the conditions $m > n$ and $m < n$ in rules (5a) and (5b), respectively, may be dropped now.

In addition, the following rule may now be proved in case a is a nonzero complex number and n is *any* integer:

(6) $$a^{-n} = \frac{1}{a^n}$$

11.4   RATIONAL EXPONENTS

Having enlarged our definition of exponent to apply not only to the set of all nn, but also to the more inclusive set of all integers, we now take the next natural step—that of extending our definition of exponent to the set of all rational numbers.

Again, it will be a rule which does not yet apply which will suggest a reasonable definition; in this case rule (2) above.

Suppose r is any rational number. Then r may be written in the form p/q, where q is a positive integer and p is an integer that may be positive, or negative, or zero. Suppose now that a is a *positive real number*. Then *if rule* (2) *did apply*:

$$(a^{p/q})^q = a^p$$

However, if a is positive, it easily follows that a^p is positive. In a manner similar to that in which we proved that 2 has a unique positive square root (see Section 4.15), it may be proved that if q is a nn, then any positive real number r has a unique positive qth root, denoted $\sqrt[q]{r}$, with the defining property that $(\sqrt[q]{r})^q = r$.

If $(a^{p/q})^q = a^p$, then $a^{p/q}$ must be a qth root of a^p. This suggests the following definition:

If a is a positive real number, p/q a rational number in which q is a positive integer, we define $a^{p/q}$ to equal $\sqrt[q]{a^p}$.

Since it may be proved that in this case: $\sqrt[q]{a^p} = (\sqrt[q]{a})^p$, we have, with the above conditions on a, p, q:

$$a^{p/q} = \sqrt[q]{a^p} = (\sqrt[q]{a})^p$$

A proof of the preceding statement follows:

If q is a nn, and x, y are positive real numbers, then to prove that $x = \sqrt[q]{y}$, it is sufficient to show that $x^q = y$.

Thus, to show that $(\sqrt[q]{a})^p = \sqrt[q]{a^p}$ (where a is a positive real number, q a nn, p an integer) it is sufficient to note that $(\sqrt[q]{a})^p$ and a^p are positive real numbers and to show that $[(\sqrt[q]{a})^p]^q = a^p$.

But $[(\sqrt[q]{a})^p]^q = (\sqrt[q]{a})^{pq} = (\sqrt[q]{a})^{qp} = [(\sqrt[q]{a})^q]^p = a^p$, which completes the proof.

(*Note.* Generally it is the form $(\sqrt[q]{a})^p$ which leads to a result most easily when evaluating $a^{p/q}$ for a particular value of a. For example: $16^{3/4} = (\sqrt[4]{16})^3 = 2^3 = 8$ is easier to carry through than $16^{3/4} = \sqrt[4]{16^3} = \sqrt[4]{4096} = 8$.)

Again our definition turns out to have been well chosen, for if a and b are any positive real numbers, and m, n any rational numbers, rules (1)–(6) continue to hold true.

It will be noted that although we have now extended our definition of exponent to include all rational numbers, we have lost something in that with this type of exponent our base a is restricted to being a positive real number, rather than any nonzero complex number. This restriction was forced upon us because at this point we have information at hand only about qth roots of positive real numbers. A study of the situation with respect to qth roots of complex numbers would be necessary before an extension of the present base to a complex number, or even to a negative real number, could be considered. Such a study is beyond the scope of this course, but is included in courses in "Functions of a Complex Variable."

In any case it turns out that an extension of the concept of rational exponents to apply even to negative real bases has some built-in deficiencies; for example, the important rule (3) above cannot be made to hold true (see Problem 3, Exercise 20).

11.5 REAL EXPONENTS

What shall we mean, now, by an expression like $2^{\sqrt{2}}$?

We approach this problem by means of approximations. We know that $\sqrt{2}$ lies between 1.4 and 1.5. Since 1.4 and 1.5 are rational numbers, our preceding section guarantees that $2^{1.4}$ and $2^{1.5}$ exist, and are real numbers. Any number between $2^{1.4}$ and $2^{1.5}$, for example $2^{1.4}$ itself, might therefore naturally serve as a first approximation to $2^{\sqrt{2}}$.

But $\sqrt{2}$ may be more narrowly pinched down between 1.41 and 1.42. A better approximation for $2^{\sqrt{2}}$ would therefore seem to be a number lying in the narrower range between $2^{1.41}$ and $2^{1.42}$, for example $2^{1.41}$ itself. And so on.

In fact it may be proved that this process "pinches down on" a unique real number which we define to be $2^{\sqrt{2}}$.

If a is any positive real number and r is any real number at all, we similarly define a^r by means of successive approximations.

The intuitive treatment sketched above may be rigorized by means of the following:

Theorem and Definition. Suppose $a \neq 1$ is a positive real number and r is any real number.

Let A be the set of all real numbers a^x, where x may be any positive *rational* number less than r.

Let B be the set of all real numbers a^y, where y may be any positive *rational* number greater than r.

Then there is a unique real number between A and B which we define to be a^r.

It is worth noting that this new definition is consistent with the old; that is to say, if r happens to be rational, the preceding definition of a^r leads to the same result as the definition of Section 11.4.

We complete the definition by defining: $1^r = 1$.

Once more, it turns out that rules (1)–(6) continue to hold true, this time for a, b any positive real numbers, and m, n any real numbers.

A function f is called *an exponential function with base a* if its mapping is given by the formula $f(x) = a^x$. (In this text, the base a, of course, is assumed to be a positive real number; and in order to avoid a trivial case, we shall further assume that $a \neq 1$.)

Unless otherwise noted, we shall understand that the domain intended for any exponential function is the set of all real numbers.

▶ **EXERCISE 61**

1. Sketch a representative portion of the graph of each of the following functions, and in each case state the range of the given function, and whether it is one-one or many-one:

(a) 2^x

(b) 3^x

(c) 4^x (Use some non-integral values of x, i.e., values other than integers in your table of values.)

(d) 8^x (Use some non-integral values of x in your table of values.)

(e) $(\frac{1}{2})^x$

(f) $(\frac{1}{3})^x$

(g) $(\frac{1}{4})^x$

(h) $(\frac{1}{8})^x$ } (Use some non-integral values of x in your table of values.)

(i) 2^{-x}

(j) 3^{-x}

2. Use your results in Problem 1 above to induce the answers to the following questions:

(a) If a is a real number such that $a > 1$, how may the graph of the function a^x be described? (Include statements as to range, asymptotes and intercepts.)

(b) If a is a positive real number such that $a < 1$, how may the graph of the function a^x be described?

(c) What may be said about the range of any exponential function a^x, as we have defined it? Will this function a^x be always one-one, always many-one, or sometimes one and sometimes the other?

(d) Describe the relation between the graph of a^x and the graph of a^{-x}.

3. Sketch a representative portion of the graph of each of the following functions, and in each case state the range of the given function, and whether it is one-one or many-one:

(a) $2 \cdot 2^x$ (b) $2 \cdot 2^{-x}$ (c) $-3 \cdot 2^x$

(d) 2^{x^2} [This means $2^{(x^2)}$] (e) 2^{-x^2} ("Bell" curve) (f) $2^x + 2^{-x}$

(g) $2^x - 2^{-x}$

4. Describe the relation between the graph of $c \cdot a^x$ and the graph of a^x, where c is a nonzero real number.

5. Suppose $f(x) = 2^x + 2^{-x}$, $g(x) = 2^x - 2^{-x}$. Find:

(a) $f(x) + g(x)$ (b) $f(x) - g(x)$ (c) $f(x) \cdot g(x)$

(d) $[f(x)]^2$ (e) $[g(x)]^2$ (f) $[f(x)]^2 + [g(x)]^2$

(g) $[f(x)]^2 - [g(x)]^2$

11.6 THE LOGARITHMIC FUNCTION WITH BASE a

(This section is based upon Section 2.6, "Inverse functions." The student is therefore advised to read that section before proceeding.)

The graph of the exponential function with base a indicates (and it may be rigorously proved) that this function is one-one and has a range that consists of all positive real numbers.

We abbreviate "the exponential function with base a" to "$\exp_a$" and summarize:

Just as we call the image which a function f assigns to x: $f(x)$, so we call the image which the function $\exp_a$ assigns to x: $\exp_a (x)$, read "exponent sub-a of x."

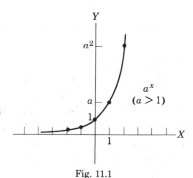

Fig. 11.1

But the definition given above for the mapping of $\exp_a$ tells us immediately:

(1) $$\exp_a(x) = a^x \qquad x \xrightarrow{\exp_a} a^x$$

For example: $$\exp_2(3) = 2^3 = 8 \qquad 3 \xrightarrow{\exp_2} 8$$

$$\exp_{10}(2) = 10^2 = 100 \qquad 2 \xrightarrow{\exp_{10}} 100$$

In fact, in most cases we dispense with the expression $\exp_a(x)$, using in its place its equal, a^x. However, we shall now find the notation $\exp_a$ useful in defining the "logarithmic function with base a."

Since the function $\exp_a$ is one-one, it must have an inverse (see Section 2.6) which we call the *logarithmic function with base a*, abbreviated: $\log_a$.

Since $\exp_a$ and $\log_a$ are each other's inverses, the statements (1) above are respectively equivalent to:

(2) $$\log_a(a^x) = x \qquad x \xleftarrow{\log_a} a^x$$

$$\log_2 8 = 3 \qquad 3 \xleftarrow{\log_2} 8$$

$$\log_{10} 100 = 2 \qquad 2 \xleftarrow{\log_{10}} 100$$

In fact, the statement $\exp_a(x) = N$ is equivalent to $\log_a N = x$; and since $\exp_a(x) = a^x$, we have the following important relation enabling us to transform exponential to logarithmic expressions, and vice versa:

> The following equations are equivalent:
> $$a^x = N; \ \log_a N = x$$

These equations may be thought of as saying that $\log_a N$ is equal to the (unique) *exponent* whose application to the base a results in the number N.

For example: Since $2^3 = 8$, i.e., since the exponent 3 applied to the *base* 2 results in the number 8, we may say $\log_2 8 = 3$.

And to find $\log_{10} 100$, we ask: What *exponent*, applied to the base 10, results in the number 100? The answer, of course, is 2. Therefore $\log_{10} 100 = 2$.

Now, remembering that $\log_a$ is the inverse of $\exp_a$, we see that the graph of $\log_a x$ must be as in Fig. 11.2.

In drawing the graph of $\log_a x$, we have made use of the information above to see that only positive x-values are involved, but that all real numbers will appear as y-values. Furthermore (p, q) is a point on the graph of $\exp_a$ if and only if (q, p) is a point on the graph of $\log_a$.

This may be interpreted to mean that the graphs of $\exp_a$ and $\log_a$ are simply each other's symmetric images with respect to the line whose equation is $y = x$ (as will of course be the case whenever we graph a pair of inverse functions; see page 264).

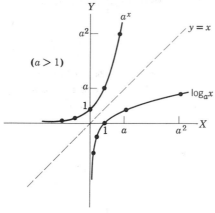

Fig. 11.2

Note that the function $\log_a$, being the inverse of a one-one function, must be a one-one function also.

▶ **EXERCISE 62**

1. Find:

(a) $\log_2 \left(\tfrac{1}{8}\right)$ (b) $\log_2 \left(\tfrac{1}{4}\right)$

(c) $\log_2 \left(\tfrac{1}{2}\right)$ (d) $\log_2 (1)$

(e) $\log_2 (2)$ (f) $\log_2 (4)$

(g) $\log_2 (8)$ (h) $\log_2 (0)$

(i) $\log_2 (-1)$ (j) $\log_{10} (0.001)$

(k) $\log_{10} (0.01)$ (l) $\log_{10} (0.1)$

(m) $\log_{10} (1)$ (n) $\log_{10} (10)$

(o) $\log_{10} (100)$ (p) $\log_{10} (1000)$

(q) $\log_{10} (0)$ (r) $\log_{10} (-1)$

2. Translate into logarithmic statements:

(a) $10^x = 5$ (b) $2^{10} = 1024$

(c) $10^{0.3010} \doteq 2$ (d) $2^{0.5000} \doteq 1.414$

3. Translate into exponential statements:

(a) $\log_{10} 3 \doteq .4771$ (b) $\log_{10} 5 \doteq .6990$

(c) $\log_{10} x = y$ (d) $\log_2 x = y$

4. Draw the graphs of each pair of functions on the same cc system:

(a) 2^x and $\log_2 x$ (b) 10^x and $\log_{10} x$

5. Induce a general description of the graph of the function $\log_a x$, where $a < 1$.

6. Draw the graphs of the following functions:

  (a) $3 \log_2 x$ (b) $0.1 \log_{10} x$

  (c) $\log_2 \left(\dfrac{x}{3} \right)$ (d) $\log_{10} (5x)$

7. Describe the graph of the function $\log_a x$, when $a < 1$.

8. Prove: $a^{\log_a w} = w$. *Hint:* Use the boxed statement on page 352.

9 Prove: $(\log_a b)(\log_b a) = 1$. *Hint:* Let $\log_a b = x$, $\log_b a = y$, so that $a^x = b$, $b^y = a$.

10. Prove: $\log_b N = \dfrac{\log_a N}{\log_a b}$.

11. What property of the function $\exp_a$ justifies our statement (on page 352) that the exponent whose application to the base a results in the number N is *unique*?

11.7 LOGARITHMIC COMPUTATION

Consider the table of values:

x	2^x
-3	$\frac{1}{8}$
-2	$\frac{1}{4}$
-1	$\frac{1}{2}$
0	1
1	2
2	4
3	8
4	16
5	32
6	64
7	128
8	256
9	512
10	1024

First of all we note that in this table of values, each number on the left is the $\log_2$ of the number on its right; for example: $\log_2 (\frac{1}{4}) = -2$.

Next, observe what happens when two numbers on the right are multiplied. For example, when we multiply 4 (whose $\log_2$ is 2) by 8 (whose $\log_2$ is 3), the result is 32 (whose $\log_2$ is 5).

In fact, the student may verify that whenever we multiply two numbers on the right, the corresponding numbers on the left, i.e., the logarithms, are added.

This may be used to reduce the labor involved in multiplying numbers on the right. For example, to multiply 16 by 32, we add their logarithms in the table above: $4 + 5 = 9$, and find the product $16 \cdot 32$ opposite 9: namely $16 \cdot 32 = 512$.

Our use of logarithms has converted a multiplication problem into an easier addition problem. Of course our miniature table will not permit us to do too much of this sort of thing, but we will shortly make use of a considerably more detailed table.

We should not be surprised to discover that (roughly speaking) multiplying numbers implies adding their logarithms; for logarithms may be thought of as exponents, and (again roughly speaking) when we multiply numbers with the same base, we add exponents.

We would expect, then, that to divide numbers (still roughly speaking) we should subtract exponents.

In the table above, for example, to divide 512 by 16, we find the difference of their corresponding logarithms: $9 - 4 = 5$; the result opposite 5 is 32, and indeed $512 \div 16 = 32$.

The following theorems now make precise what we have been saying.

Log Theorem 1. If p, q are positive real numbers, then:
$$\log_a (pq) = \log_a p + \log_a q$$
PROOF. Let $x = \log_a p$, $y = \log_a q$, $z = \log_a (pq)$
Then $a^x = p$, $a^y = q$, $a^z = pq$
$\therefore a^z = a^x \cdot a^y = a^{x+y}$

But since the exponential function with base a is one-one, $z = x + y$; i.e., $\log_a (pq) = \log_a p + \log_a q$, Q.E.D.

Log Theorem 2. If p, q are positive real numbers, then:
$$\log_a \left(\frac{p}{q}\right) = \log_a p - \log_a q$$
PROOF. Left as an exercise.

Two other theorems which also follow from the relations between logarithms and exponents, and which are useful in computation, are the following (proofs are left as exercises):

Log Theorem 3. If p is a positive real number and r is any real number whatever, then:
$$\log_a (p^r) = r \cdot \log_a p$$

Log Theorem 4. If p is a positive real number and n is a nn, then:
$$\log_a \sqrt[n]{p} = (\log_a p) \div n$$

(*Note.* Log Theorem 4 may be proved as a corollary of Log Theorem 3.)
Now we shall apply these log theorems to problems of computation.

In order to do so, we shall make use of a table of logarithms.   Actually, tables of logarithms are generally available only for the base $a = 10$, and for another base called "e"; the latter is a number which is approximately 2.7, and whose use in the calculus makes formulas more simply expressible.   (A reason we encountered before in explaining why *radian* measure is useful.)

From this point on we shall restrict ourselves, unless otherwise noted, to the base 10 in working with logarithms.   In fact, from now on we shall omit the base designation when we wish to indicate a logarithm to the base 10; i.e., log x will mean $\log_{10} x$.

In computing with the help of logarithms, our first task is to learn the use of the table.

The table we shall use actually gives logarithms of numbers between 1 and 10; the student may imagine a decimal point placed after the first digit of each entry in the column headed "N"; and to the right of "N," a second decimal place may be found.

For example, to find log 1.23, we run down the N column until we come to "12," and then we run across the page to the reading in the column headed "3."   There we discover the reading 0899.   Here a decimal point has actually been omitted, for obvious reasons.   All readings within the body of the table are to be understood as being prefixed by a decimal point. Finally, then:

$$\log 1.23 = .0899$$

But a word of caution: all values in the table, with the exception of one (which one?) are approximations, correct to four decimal places, and not exact.   It would be better to write $\log 1.23 \doteq .0899$, but the traditional usage will lead to no trouble if one keeps in mind that the equality here is only approximate.

Now what about numbers not between 1 and 10?   Their logarithms may easily be derived from the ones we have available, using the obvious facts that $\log 100 = 2$, $\log 1000 = 3$, $\log 0.1 = -1$, $\log 0.01 = -2$, etc.

For example:

$$
\begin{aligned}
\log 12.3 \ &= \log (10 \cdot 1.23) \\
&= \log 10 + \log 1.23 \text{ (by Log Theorem 1)} \\
&= 1 + .0899 \\
&= 1.0899 \\
\log 123 \ &= \log (100 \cdot 1.23) \\
&= \log 100 + \log 1.23 \\
&= 2 + .0899 \\
&= 2.0899 \\
\log 1230 \ &= \log (1000 \cdot 1.23)
\end{aligned}
$$

$$= \log 1000 + \log 1.23$$
$$= 3 + .0899$$
$$= 3.0899$$

$$\log 0.123 = \log \left(\frac{1.23}{10}\right)$$
$$= \log 1.23 - \log 10 \text{ (by Log Theorem 2)}$$
$$= .0899 - 1$$
$$= -.9101$$

We shall find, in what follows, that we rarely want to carry out the computation of a logarithm to an ultimate negative result, as in this last case. The reason is that such a value cannot be found in our table of logarithms, which contains only *positive* real numbers. Unless some good reason exists for doing otherwise, then, we shall stop short at:

$$\log 0.123 = .0899 - 1$$

A last example:

$$\log 0.0123 = \log \left(\frac{1.23}{100}\right)$$
$$= \log 1.23 - \log 100$$
$$= .0899 - 2$$

In general, we may write all logarithms in the form $k + m$, where k is an integer and m is a decimal between 0 and 1. k is called the *characteristic* of the logarithm, m the *mantissa*.

For example, log 1.23 has a characteristic of 0 and a mantissa equal to .0899; log 123 has a characteristic of 2 and a mantissa of .0899; log 0.123 has a characteristic of −1 and a mantissa of .0899.

It is easy to see that when decimal numbers differ only in the position of their decimal points, the logarithms of these numbers all have the same mantissa. We may find the mantissa of the logarithm of a decimal number, then, simply by disregarding the decimal point and using the table of logarithms (which might more accurately be called a table of mantissas).

A shortcut rule for finding the characteristic of the logarithm of a number in decimal form is easy to derive. From the examples given above one may see that the following rule holds:

To find the characteristic of the logarithm of a positive decimal: Place an arrow to the right of the first nonzero digit; count the number of digits from arrow to decimal point; +, if to the right and −, if to the left. The result is the characteristic of the logarithm of the positive decimal.

For example: the characteristic of log .0123 is −2. Therefore log
↑

.0123 = .0899 − 2; the characteristic of log 1230 is 3. Therefore log
↑
1230 = 3.0899.

Note that it would lead to an incorrect result to write a negative
characteristic immediately before the mantissa, as we may do in the case
of a positive characteristic. In the case of log 0.123, for example, this
would lead to the number −1.0899, whereas we have seen that −.9101
is correct. We shall therefore always write negative characteristics
following the mantissa.

Now what about finding something like log 12.34? There is no trouble
about the characteristic, which we know to be 1. The mantissa will be
log 1.234. Here we allow ourselves the luxury of linear interpolation,
since a very small section of the graph of log x approximates a straight line.
We find a value 0.4 of the way between log 1.23 and log 1.24; the result
is log 12.34 = 1.0913. We realize, however, that the result is only an
estimate, which in most cases works fairly well. It will work least well
where gaps in the table are largest (namely where?).

(The student will find it interesting to check the accuracy of some of
his interpolations with a five-place table, especially those in that part of
the table where gaps are largest.)

In finding something like log 12.347, there is no point in interpolating
.47 of the way between log 12.3 and log 12.4, since this would impute an
accuracy to the method of linear interpolation which it just does not have.
In cases like this (with our table) we would round off to four digits, and
find log 12.35 by interpolation.

Now we are ready to compute logarithmically.

Illustrative Example I:

To compute: (24.67) (0.0183)   {Let P represent this product}

SOLUTION. log 24.67 = 1.3922   *Note.* Set down characteris-
          ↑
          log 0.0183 = .2625 − 2   tics before looking up man-
          ↑   tissas

          log P = 1.6547 − 2 {by Log. Thm. 1}
                      = .6547 − 1

          ∴ P = .4516   .6547 is located between
                      ↑   .6542 and .6551 in table of
                                    mantissas; then we inter-
                                    polate between 451 and 452
                                    to find P. Finally, the deci-
                                    mal point in P is determined
                                    by the characteristic 1.

Illustrative Example 2:

To compute: $\dfrac{24.67}{0.0183}$ {Let Q represent this quotient}

SOLUTION. log 24.67 = 1.3922

         log 0.0183 = .2625 − 2

         log Q = 1.1297 + 2   {By Log Thm. 2}

                 = 3.1297

       ∴ Q = 1348
                 ↑

Illustrative Example 3:

To compute: $\dfrac{0.0183}{24.67}$ {Let Q represent this quotient}

SOLUTION. log 0.0183 = .2625 − 2

         log 24.67 = 1.3922

But here if we subtract as things stand, we will not immediately arrive at the mantissa we seek. The trouble is that the positive number to be subtracted is larger than the positive number from which it is to be subtracted. This may easily be remedied by expressing the characteristic −2 of log 0.0183 differently; 2 − 4, for example, will do:

        log 0.0183 = 2.2625 − 4

        log 24.67 = 1.3922

        log Q = .8703 − 4

          Q = .0007418
                ↑

Illustrative Example 4:

To compute: 2^{50}

SOLUTION. log 2 = 0.3010

        log 2^{50} = 50 log 2 = 15.0500 {By Log Thm. 3}

Counting off 15 places, however, would result in a number of awkward length. We therefore express the result as $10^{15} \cdot N$, where log N = .0500. Hence:

$$2^{50} = 1.122 \cdot 10^{15}$$

(This method may be justified as follows: If log 2^{50} = 15.0500, then $2^{50} = 10^{15.0500} = (10^{15})(10^{.0500}) = 10^{15} \cdot N$, where log N = .0500.)

Illustrative Example 5:

To compute: $\sqrt[3]{0.0183}$ {Let N represent this number}

        log 0.0183 = .2625 − 2 = 1.2625 − 3

(Here we have expressed the characteristic -2 as $1 - 3$, in order to make it possible to divide the negative part of the logarithm easily by 3)

$$\log N = \frac{1.2625 - 3}{3} = .4208 - 1 \quad \{\text{By Log Thm. 4}\}$$

$$\therefore \ N = .2635$$

Illustrative Example 6:

To compute: $N = \sqrt[3]{\dfrac{(1.23)(0.456)^2}{\sqrt[5]{0.987}}}$

SOLUTION:

$\log 1.23 \qquad = \quad .0899 \qquad\qquad \log 0.456 = .6590 - 1$

$\log (0.456)^2 \ = \ 1.3180 - 2$

$\qquad\qquad\qquad \overline{1.4079 - 2} = \log$ of numerator within cube root

$\log 0.987 \qquad = \ 4.9943 - 5$

$\log \sqrt[5]{0.987} \ = \quad .9989 - 1 = \log$ of denominator within cube root

$\qquad\qquad\qquad \left.\begin{array}{r} 1.4079 - 2 \\ .9989 - 1 \end{array}\right\}$ Subtract

$\qquad\qquad\qquad \overline{\quad .4090 - 1} = \log$ of expression within cube root.

$\log N \qquad = \dfrac{2.4090 - 3}{3} = .8030 - 1$

$\quad\ N \qquad = \quad .6353$

Illustrative Example 7:

Solve the "exponential" equation: $2^{0.4x} = 7$

SOLUTION.   Equivalent to the given equation is:

$\qquad\qquad \log 2^{0.4x} = \log 7$

or: $\qquad\quad 0.4x \log 2 = \log 7$

or: $\qquad\qquad\qquad x = \dfrac{\log 7}{0.4 \log 2} = \dfrac{.8451}{(0.4)(.3010)} = \dfrac{.8451}{.1204}$

Now if we wish we may complete the solution by long division, or by using logarithms again:

$$\begin{aligned} \log 0.8451 &= \ .9269 - 1 \\ \log 0.1204 &= \ .0806 - 1 \\ \log x \quad &= \ .8463 \\ x \quad &= \ 7.020 \end{aligned}$$

Illustrative Example 8:

Find: $\log_2 17$.

Solution: Let $x = \log_2 17$

$\qquad\qquad$ Then $2^x = 17$

Now proceed as in the preceding example.

(This method may be used to find logarithms to any base, when we have available a table of logarithms to a particular base, say the base 10. Note also: A short cut to the result is given by Problem 10 of the preceding exercise.)

▶ **EXERCISE 63**

1. Prove: (*a*) Log Theorem 2
          (*b*) Log Theorem 3
          (*c*) Log Theorem 4

2. Use the table on page 354 to compute:

(*a*) $16 \cdot 64$ (*b*) $32 \div 256$ (*c*) 4^5 (*d*) $\sqrt[10]{1024}$

3. Check the accuracy of the logarithmically computed results of Illustrative Examples 1, 2, and 3. If a result is inaccurate, how do you explain the inaccuracy?

4. Compute by means of logarithms:

(*a*) $(83.4)(.2176)$ (*b*) 2^{20}

(*c*) $0.162 \div 8735$ (*d*) 2^{40}

(*e*) $\sqrt{2}$ (*f*) 3^{10}

(*g*) $(3.142)(87.3)^2$ (*h*) $\sqrt[3]{5}$

(*i*) $\dfrac{(1.73)\,20^{.3}}{78.2}$ (*j*) $\sqrt{0.1}$

(*k*) $\dfrac{24.78\ \sqrt[3]{0.298}}{(12.46)^2}$ (*l*) $300(1.06)^{20}$

(*m*) $\sqrt[3]{\dfrac{17.6\ \sqrt{5}}{0.298}}$ (*n*) $2 \cdot 3.14\ \sqrt{\dfrac{5}{32}}$

(*o*) $\sqrt[3]{\dfrac{(-1.41)(89.76)}{(-24.7)^4}}$ (*Hint:* We cannot find the logarithms of negative numbers; but in cases like this we may determine the sign of the answer first, and then neglect all minus signs.)

5. Complete the solution of Illustrative Example 8.

6. Solve the following exponential equations:

(*a*) $2^x = 5$

(*b*) $3(2^x) = 10$

(*c*) $4(2^{0.5x}) = 25$

7. Find:

(*a*) $\log_2 10$

(*b*) $\log_2 3$

(*c*) $\log_3 2$

11.8 TRIGONOMETRIC LOGARITHMIC COMPUTATION

The tedious computation we have encountered in the solution of triangles may be considerably shortened by means of logarithms.

We indicate how this can be done by means of several examples.

Illustrative Example 1. (See Illustrative Example 1, page 193.)

Here we have: $h = 38 \tan 73°$

$$\log h = \log 38 + \log \tan 73°$$

It will not be necessary to find tan 73°, and *then* to find its logarithm, since our tables give log tan 73° directly:

$$\log 38 = 1.5798$$
$$\log \tan 73° = .5147$$
$$\log h = 2.0945$$
$$h = 124.3$$

Illustrative Example 2. (See illustrative example, page 271.)

Here: $$b = \frac{10 \sin 40° 40'}{\sin 51° 10'}$$

$$\left. \begin{array}{l} \log 10 = 1.0000 \\ \log \sin 40° 40' = 9.8140 - 10 \end{array} \right\} \text{ add}$$

$$\left. \begin{array}{l} 10.8140 - 10 \\ \log \sin 51° 10' = 9.8915 - 10 \end{array} \right\} \text{ subtract}$$

$$\log b = .9225$$
$$b = 8.366$$

We note that the law of cosines is not as well adapted as the law of sines to logarithmic computation, because the law of cosines involves the operations of addition and subtraction, which logarithms cannot make simpler. However when the numbers to be squared or multiplied in an application of the law of cosines are not easy to handle, logarithms may be helpful in computing these squares or products before they are added or subtracted.

▶ EXERCISE 64

Problem 5–15 of Exercise 31, and Problems 1–6, 8 of Exercise 49, may now be worked using logarithms.

11.9 THE BINOMIAL THEOREM

It may be verified, by successive multiplications, that if x, y are real (or even complex numbers), then:

$$(x + y)^1 = x + y$$
$$(x + y)^2 = x^2 + 2xy + y^2$$
$$(x + y)^3 = x^3 + 3x^2y + 3xy^2 + y^3$$
$$(x + y)^4 = x^4 + 4x^3y + 6x^2y^2 + 4xy^3 + y^4$$

One may induce that if n is any nn $(x, y$ as above), then:

(i) $(x + y)^n$ is equal to a sum [called the "binomial expansion" of $(x + y)^n$] of $n + 1$ terms of the form kx^uy^v, where k is a nn, and u, v are non-negative integers such that $u + v = n$.

From now on we shall assume that the terms of this binomial expansion are written so that the exponents of x occur, as above, in decreasing order.

(ii) In the binomial expansion of $(x + y)^n$, the first and last coefficients (i.e., the coefficients of x^n and y^n) are each 1; the coefficients form a symmetric array about the middle; the second coefficient, from either end, is n.

In fact, one may display the coefficients of successive expansions in the following interesting pattern, called the "Pascal triangle:"

```
      1   1

    1   2   1

  1   3   3   1

1   4   6   4   1
```

What is interesting about this pattern is that between the 1's which occur at the ends of a row, each number is the sum of the two numbers in the row above it between which it falls.

Thus, the successive coefficients in the expansion of $(F + S)^5$ are: 1, 5, 10, 10, 5, 1.   This information enables us to write:

$$(x + y)^5 = x^5 + 5x^4y + 10x^3y^2 + 10x^2y^3 + 5xy^4 + y^5$$

(iii) If ax^uy^v and $bx^{u-1}y^{v+1}$ are successive terms in the expansion of $(x + y)^n$, then:

$$b = \frac{au}{v + 1}$$

Thus, having found the coefficient of one term, one may find the coefficient of the next by multiplying the coefficient of the first of these terms by the exponent of x in that term, and dividing by one more than the exponent of y in that term.

The student should verify, in the examples given above, i.e., where $n = 1, 2, 3, 4, 5$, that this statement is true.

This process leads to the following formula:

$$(x + y)^n = x^n + nx^{n-1}y + \frac{n \cdot n - 1}{2}x^{n-2}y^2 +$$

$$\frac{n \cdot n - 1 \cdot n - 2}{2 \cdot 3}x^{n-3}y^3 + \cdots + y^n$$

The statement that this formula is true for all complex numbers x, y and all natural numbers n is known as the "binomial theorem."

A *proof* of the binomial theorem, by means of mathematical induction (see Section 4.17), follows:

Let S be the set of all nn for which the preceding formula is true. We prove that S contains all the nn by proving (i) and (ii) of the Principle of Mathematical Induction (page 102).

Proof of (i): That $1 \in S$ is trivial, since for $n = 1$ the preceding formula reduces to: $(x + y)^1 = x + y$.

Proof of (ii): Supposing $s \in S$, we show $s + 1 \in S$.

That is to say, we assume the preceding formula true for $n = s$, and prove that then it must be true for $n = s + 1$.

But a binomial expansion for $(x + y)^{s+1}$ may be derived from a binomial expansion for $(x + y)^s$ by multiplying the latter by $x + y$.

Clearly, the first term in this expansion of $(x + y)^{s+1}$ arises, in this multiplication, only from multiplying x by x^s, so that the first coefficient is 1, as we wish it to be.

Now for the other coefficients, we wish to prove that if $ax^u y^v$ and $bx^{u-1}y^{v+1}$ are successive terms in this expansion of $(x + y)^{s+1}$, then:

$$b = \frac{au}{v + 1}$$

But in our multiplication these terms arise only from multiplying the terms: $cx^u y^{v-1} + dx^{u-1}y^v + ex^{u-2}y^{v+1}$, in the expansion of $(x + y)^s$, by $x + y$. (If $v = 0$, omit the first term; if $u = 1$, omit the last. The student may complete the proof in these two special cases.) And in fact, upon multiplying we see that:

$$a = c + d, \qquad b = d + e$$

Also, from the inductive assumption, i.e., that our formula holds for $n = s$, we have:

$$d = \frac{cu}{v}, \qquad e = \frac{d(u - 1)}{v + 1}$$

Hence:

$$b = d + \frac{d(u - 1)}{v + 1} = \frac{dv + du}{v + 1} = \frac{cu + du}{v + 1} = \frac{(c + d)u}{v + 1} = \frac{au}{v + 1}, \text{ Q.E.D.}$$

Note on the preceding proof: Our proof utilizes the notation: x^{u-2} which, in case $x = 0$ and $u = 2$ becomes: 0^0. We have not yet defined 0^0; but if we define, at this point, $0^0 = 1$, the proof goes through. In fact, with this definition, we may push back the theorem we have just proved to include, for all complex numbers x and y the statement: $(x + y)^0 = 1$.

Illustrative Example I. We expand: $(2x - 3y)^4$

$$(2x - 3y)^4 = (2x)^4 + 4(2x)^3(-3y) + 6(2x)^2(-3y)^2 + 4(2x)(-3y)^3 + (-3y)^4 = 16x^4 - 96x^3y + 216x^2y^2 - 216xy^3 + 81y^4$$

The coefficients in this example may be derived from the Pascal triangle, or from the rule which derives each coefficient (after the first) from the preceding. In the latter case, because of the symmetric array of co-efficients, it is necessary to compute only the first three coefficients.

Note that in an expansion of the form $(x - y)^n$, the signs of the terms finally alternate.

An interesting and useful extension of the binomial theorem leads to certain approximation formulas. For example, suppose we attempt the following expansion, proceeding by our expansion rule:

(1) $(1 + x)^{\frac{1}{2}} = 1^{\frac{1}{2}} + \frac{1}{2}(1)^{-\frac{1}{2}}(x) + \frac{(\frac{1}{2})(-\frac{1}{2})}{2}(1)^{-\frac{3}{2}}(x)^2 + \cdots$

Now we know nothing of the truth of this statement, since we have proved the binomial theorem only for nn exponents. In fact, the statement is mcaningless, for the process never terminates and we have an infinite progression of terms on the right. But meaning may be given to this expansion, as the student will discover in later courses, when he encounters "infinite series." For the present, we state, without proof, that for certain values of x, in this case $-1 \leqslant x \leqslant 1$, the above equality is approximate if the expansion is terminated at any point, and the more terms we include in our sum on the right, the better the approximation.

For example:

$$(1 + x)^{\frac{1}{2}} \doteq 1 + \tfrac{1}{2}x - \tfrac{1}{8}x^2$$

is an approximation arrived at by terminating the expansion (1) above after three terms. Thus:

$$\sqrt{2} = (1 + 1)^{\frac{1}{2}} \doteq 1 + \frac{1}{2} - \frac{1}{8} = \frac{11}{8} \quad 1.4$$

$$\sqrt{10} \doteq \sqrt{(9)(1.11)} - 3(1 + 0.11)^{\frac{1}{2}} \doteq 3\left(1 + \frac{0.11}{2}\right) - 3(1.055) \doteq 3.16$$

In approximating $\sqrt{10}$ we used only two terms of our expansion. Three terms would have led to a better result.

▶ **EXERCISE 65**

1.   Extend the Pascal triangle to find the coefficients in the expansions of $(x + y)^6$ and $(x + y)^7$.

2.   Expand:

(a) $(a - b)^3$	(b) $(2a - b)^3$	(c) $(3a + 2b)^3$
(d) $(1 + x)^3$	(e) $(1 - x)^3$	(f) $(a - b)^4$
(g) $(2a + b)^4$	(h) $(3a - 2b)^4$	(i) $(1 + x)^4$
(j) $(1 - x)^4$	(k) $(a - b)^5$	(l) $(2a - b)^5$
(m) $(3a + 2b)^5$	(n) $(1 + x)^5$	(o) $(1 - x)^5$

3.   Approximate $(1.01)^{100}$ by using only the first four terms of the expansion of $(1 + 0.01)^{100}$. Why does this yield a feasible approximation?

4.   Find three-term polynomial approximations for:

(a) $\sqrt[3]{1 + x}$

(b) $\sqrt[3]{1-x}$

(c) $\dfrac{1}{\sqrt{1+x}}$

5. Use the results of Problem 4 above to approximate:

(a) $\sqrt[3]{1.1}$

(b) $\sqrt[3]{0.9}$

(c) $\dfrac{1}{\sqrt{1.1}}$

(d) $\sqrt[3]{10}$

6. The binomial theorem, as we have stated and proved it, implies that the coefficient k of $x^u y^v$ in the expansion of $(x + y)^n$ is given by:

$$k = \frac{(n)(n-1)\cdots(n-v+1)}{(1)\ \ (2)\ \ \ \cdots\ \ \ \ (v)}$$

We use the notation $v!$ (read "v factorial") to represent the product of all nn $\leqslant$ the nn v (cf. page 455).

Thus:

$$k = \frac{(n)(n-1)\cdots(n-v+1)}{v!}$$

Show, using the fact that $u + v = n$, that:

$$k = \frac{n!}{u!\,v!}$$

Use this fact to prove the symmetric property of the coefficients in the binomial expansion of $(x + y)^n$; i.e., that the coefficient of $x^u y^v$ is equal to the coefficient of $x^v y^u$.

CHAPTER 12

PARAMETRIC

EQUATIONS

On page 183 (Problem 2) we considered a situation involving a fly and an invisible man; t seconds after a certain moment, the fly was found to be at a point (x, y) of a certain coordinate plane, where x and y were given by the following formulas:

$$x = 3t$$
$$y = \tfrac{1}{2}t$$

Each real value of t, in this case, determines a point of the coordinate plane in question. For example, the value $t = 4$ determines the point $(12, 2)$. The set of all such points is called the graph of the given pair of equations.

In general, suppose that f and g are real-real functions. Then the pair of equations:

$$x = f(t)$$
$$y = g(t)$$

is called a pair of *parametric* equations, with *parameter t*. The graph of such a pair of parametric equations is defined to be the set of all points (x, y), where $x = f(t), y = g(t)$, and t belongs to the domains of both f and g.

To distinguish between parametric equations of a graph, and the equations $f(x, y) = g(x, y)$ whose graphs we have been considering, we shall call the latter *Cartesian* equations.

Now in the case of the parametric equations $x = 3t, y = \tfrac{1}{2}t$, we have already shown (page 183) that any point (x, y) satisfying these conditions also satisfies: $y = x/6$, so that each point of the graph of the parametric equations is also a point of the straight line whose equation is $y = x/6$.

It may also be shown that if all real values of t are used, then every point on the graph of $y = x/6$ is also on the graph of the parametric equations above.   Therefore the graph of the parametric equations is, in this case, exactly the same as the graph of the equation which results from the elimination of t algebraically from the pair of parametric equations.

However, if negative time is not allowed, then the graph of the parametric equations above is only the part of the line $y = x/6$ not in QIII, as indicated in Fig. 6.25.

It is not feasible in every case to eliminate the parameter from a given set of parametric equations.   We therefore often resort to our old stand-by, a table of values, in order to sketch the graph of a pair of parametric equations.   In this process, a *three*-column table of values is necessary. We *assign* values to t, *compute* associated values of x and y, and *plot* the points determined by corresponding values of x and y.

Unless otherwise noted, the domains of f and g, above, will be taken maximally; thus, if we are given, for example, that $f(t) = t + 1/t$, we shall assume that the domain of f consists of all real numbers except 0.

Illustrative Example 1.   We plot the graph G of the parametric equations:

$$x = t^2 - 4$$
$$y = t^3 - 4t$$

and we find a Cartesian equation for G.

Table of values and graph will be found in Fig. 12.1.

Note that the points of the graph are connected in an order determined by the order of the t's; i.e., the point associated with $t = -3$ is connected to the point associated with $t = -2$, which in turn is connected to the point associated with $t = -1$, etc.

This method of connecting points is applicable always when f and g above are polynomial functions, but the method must sometimes be modified in the case of rational or trigonometric functions.   In these cases certain real numbers may be missing from the domains of f and g, which causes the sequential connection of points to take place in intervals, rather than throughout the graph.

Now, as to a Cartesian equation for the graph G.

If (x, y) is a point of G, then there must exist a real number t such that:

$$y = t(t^2 - 4) = tx$$

Squaring:　　　　$y^2 = t^2x^2 = (x + 4)x^2 = x^3 + 4x^2$

i.e., each point of the graph satisfies the Cartesian equation: $y^2 = x^3 + 4x^2$.

Actually, $y^2 = x^3 + 4x^2$ *is* the Cartesian equation of G.   But to prove that it is, we must show further that every point (x, y) which satisfies this equation is in G:

Suppose x, y are real numbers such that $y^2 = x^3 + 4x^2$.   Then $y = x\sqrt{x + 4}$ or $y = -x\sqrt{x + 4}$.

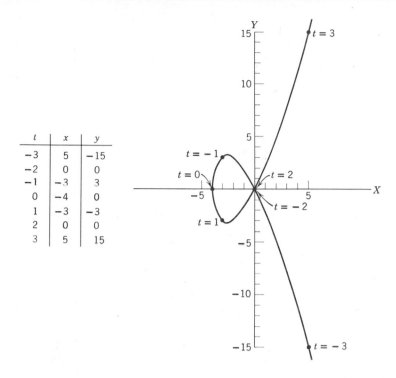

t	x	y
-3	5	-15
-2	0	0
-1	-3	3
0	-4	0
1	-3	-3
2	0	0
3	5	15

Fig. 12.1

Case 1. $y = x\sqrt{x+4}$. If $x = 0$, then $\sqrt{x+4}$ is the real number 2. If $x \neq 0$, then $\sqrt{x+4}$ is the real number y/x. Throughout this case, then, $\sqrt{x+4}$ is a real number, which we denote by t. We have then: $t = \sqrt{x+4}$, $t^2 = x + 4$, $x = t^2 - 4$, $y = (t^2 - 4)t = t^3 - 4t$, so that (x, y) satisfies the given parametric equations and is in G, Q.E.D.

Case 2. $y = -x\sqrt{x+4}$. As above, $-\sqrt{x+4}$ is a real number in this case, and we denote it by t. The rest of the proof is left as an exercise.

Illustrative Example 2. Parametric equations often arise naturally in certain physical situations, as in the case of the fly we discussed previously. Another important instance arises in the study of thrown objects (See, for example, Problem 5, page 185).

Parametric equations also arise naturally in many geometric situations. An important case is that of the circle:

Consider for example a circle C of radius r with center at the origin O of a ccd (or ccr) system.

Suppose $P = (x, y)$ is a point of C, and that ray OP has the label p in the given ccd (or ccr) system. Then by Lemma 1, page 237:

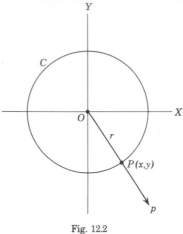

Fig. 12.2

$$(1) \qquad \begin{aligned} x &= r \cos p \\ y &= r \sin p \end{aligned}$$

In equations (1), we consider r as fixed and allow p to take on values equal to any real number of degrees (or radians). Every point (x, y) on C satisfies (1). Conversely, if (1) is satisfied by a point $P = (x, y)$, then:

$$d(O, P) = \sqrt{x^2 + y^2} = \sqrt{r^2 \cos^2 p + r^2 \sin^2 p} = \sqrt{r^2 (\cos^2 p + \sin^2 p)} = \sqrt{r^2} = r$$

i.e., P is on the given circle C.

The equations (1) are therefore parametric equations, with parameter p, for a circle with center O and radius r.

Illustrative Example 3. When a circle rolls on a straight line, the path traced by a point on that circle is called a *cycloid*. We find parametric equations for a cycloid.

Suppose that we have a circle of radius r, whose center is at the point $(0, r)$ on a ccr system, and that the point P is fixed on the circle, and at the moment is at the origin ($P_0 = O$).

Now suppose the circle rolls on the $+$ X-axis, to a new position as indicated in Fig. 12.3.

With the notation of the figure, we use the measure θ (in radians) of $\measuredangle PO'B$ as parameter, and we interpret the physical description of this situation to mean that the length of the heavily shaded arc PB is equal to the length of the line segment OB.

Now, to find the parametric equations (with parameter θ) of the path of P means, assuming $P = (x, y)$, to find equations for x in terms of θ, and for y in terms of θ.

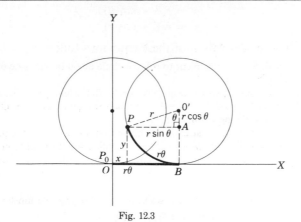

Fig. 12.3

First of all, we note that the length of the shaded arc PB is $r\theta$ (see Problem 6, Exercise 45). Therefore $OB = r\theta$. Also it is easy to show that $PA = r \sin \theta$ and $O'A = r \cos \theta$.

Now we see in the diagram that:

$$x = x_P = OB - PA = r\theta - r \sin \theta$$
$$y = y_P = O'B - O'A = r - r \cos \theta$$

Although we have leaned heavily upon a diagram in which P occupies a special position (e.g., $\measuredangle\ PO'B$ is acute), it may be proved that these actually are the parametric equations of the cycloid:

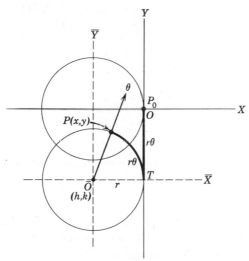

Fig. 12.4

(1)
$$x = r(\theta - \sin \theta)$$
$$y = r(1 - \cos \theta)$$

A more rigorous derivation of these equations follows:

This time we shall find it convenient to roll the circle down the left side of the Y-axis, starting at the origin (Fig. 12.4).

Suppose that the point P, which originally was at the origin, has reached the point (x, y), and that the center of the circle has reached the point $(h, k) = \bar{O}$. Translate the coordinate axes to the new origin (h, k).

Then we interpret the physical situation to mean that if one applies the proper label θ to ray $\bar{O}P$, then the length of arc which has been unrolled will turn out to be $r\theta$, i.e., that if T is the point of tangency at which the circle now meets the Y-axis, then OT is of length $r\theta$.

Thus: $h = -r$, $k = -r\theta$.

If in the new system, $P = (\bar{x}, \bar{y})$, then we have the following relationships:

$$\bar{x} = r \cos \theta, \bar{y} = r \sin \theta$$

(2)
$$\begin{cases} x = \bar{x} + h = r \cos \theta - r \\ y = \bar{y} + k = r \sin \theta - r\theta \end{cases}$$

Now the equations (2) are the equations of a cycloid generated by a circle rolling down the left side of the Y-axis.

To find the equation of a cycloid generated by a circle rolling along the right side of the X-axis, we need merely "reflect" our cycloid about the line $y = -x$. This can be done by replacing, in the equations (1), x by $-y$ and y by $-x$ (Fig. 12.5).

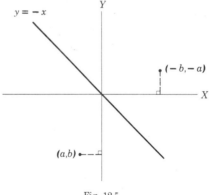

Fig. 12.5

The result is the set of equations (1), derived less rigorously above.

▶ **EXERCISE 66**

1. Plot the graphs of the following parametric equations as in Illustrative Example 1. Where feasible, eliminate the parameter to find the Cartesian equation of the graph.

(a) $x = t + 1, y = t^2$

(b) $x = 10 \cos p$, $y = 10 \sin p$.   (*Hint:* Let $p = 0°$, $30°$, $45°$, etc., up to $360°$.)

(c) $x = 10 \cos p$, $y = 5 \sin p$.   (*Hint:* to eliminate p, solve for $\cos p$, $\sin p$, square, and add.)

(d) $x = \sin p + \cos p$, $y = \sin p$

(e) $x = t + (1/t)$, $y = t - (1/t)$

(f) $x = 10 \sin u$, $y = 10 \sin 2u$

(g) $x = \sin^2 u$, $y = \cos^2 u$

(h) $x = \cos^3 u$, $y = \sin^3 u$

(i) $x = t^2$, $y = t^2$.   (The graph is *not* a whole straight line, even though eliminating t results in the equation $y = x$.   Why not?)

(j) $x = t + 1$, $y = t^2 - 1$

(k) $x = t^2 + 1$, $y = t^3 - t$

(l) $x = \dfrac{4}{t^2 + 1}$, $y = \dfrac{t^3 - t}{10}$

(m)   The equations (1) above.

2.   *Parametric equations for an ellipse.*   Suppose (x, y) is a point on the ellipse whose equation is: $\dfrac{x^2}{a^2} + \dfrac{y^2}{b^2} = 1$.   On a ccd (or ccr) system, locate the point $P = (x/a, y/b)$.   Suppose ray OP has the label θ in this system.

(a)   Show: $d(O, P) = 1$.

(b)   Show therefore that:

(1)
$$x = a \cos \theta$$
$$y = b \sin \theta$$

The equations (1) are actually parametric equations for an ellipse with semi-axes a and b.   For we have shown above that every point of the ellipse whose equation is $x^2/a^2 + y^2/b^2 = 1$ satisfies (1).   Conversely:

(c)   Show that if (x, y) is a point which satisfies (1), then (x, y) satisfies: $\dfrac{x^2}{a^2} + \dfrac{y^2}{b^2} = 1$.

3.   *Parametric equations for a hyperbola.*   Show that:
$$x = a \sec \theta$$
$$y = b \tan \theta$$

is a set of parametric equations for the hyperbola whose equation is:
$\dfrac{x^2}{a^2} - \dfrac{y^2}{b^2} = 1$.

Hint: In analogy with Problem 2 above, on a ccd or ccr system, let $P = (a/x, ay/bx)$.   Show then that $d(O, P) = 1$.   Let θ be a label for ray OP in this system; etc.

4.   *The hypocycloid.*   When a circle rolls upon the circumference of another circle,

and within it, the path traced by a fixed point on the rolling circle is called a *hypocycloid*. If the radius of the fixed circle is *n* times the radius of the rolling circle (where *n* is a nn), the hypocycloid is called a *hypocycloid of n cusps*.

We consider a hypocycloid with three cusps.

Suppose, then, that our smaller circle has a radius of *r*, our larger a radius of 3*r*. We choose a ccr system with origin at the center of the larger circle, and roll the smaller, with original point of tangency at (3*r*, 0), so that the point of tangency moves in a clockwise direction along the larger circle. We trace the path of *P* (Fig. 12.6).

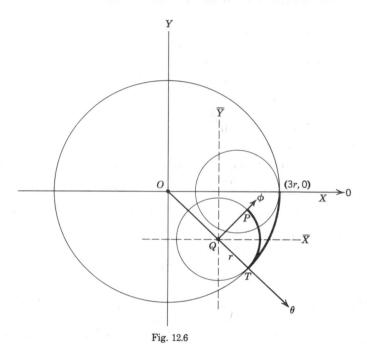

Fig. 12.6

Suppose that the center of the rolling circle has reached the point *Q*, the point of tangency has reached *T*, and that *P* has simultaneously reached the point (*x*, *y*). Translate the original ccr system to one with origin *Q*.

Now we interpret the physical situation as follows.

Among the labels of the ray *OT* and of the ray *QP* in their respective ccr systems, there are labels θ and ϕ respectively with the following properties: That the lengths of arc unrolled on the two circles may be expressed as $3r(0 - \theta)$ and $r(\phi - \theta)$, respectively, and are equal.

Show then that: $\phi = -2\theta$

If $P = (\bar{x}, \bar{y})$ in the new system, then:

$$\bar{x} = r \cos(-2\theta)$$
$$\bar{y} = r \sin(-2\theta)$$

Now show that the coordinates of Q are:

$$h = 2r \cos \theta$$
$$k = 2r \sin \theta$$

Hence that:

$$x = r \cos(-2\theta) + 2r \cos \theta$$
$$y = r \sin(-2\theta) + 2r \sin \theta$$

With the aid of trigonometric identities (*which*?), these equations may be transformed into the equivalent equations:

$$x = r(2 \cos \theta + \cos 2\theta)$$
$$y = r(2 \sin \theta - \sin 2\theta)$$

which are parametric equations for a hypocycloid of three cusps.

Now:

(*a*) Plot the graph of the set of parametric equations above, using any convenient value for r.

(*b*) Derive, as above, a set of parametric equations for a hypocycloid of four cusps. Show, using trigonometric identities, that these equations are equivalent to:

$$x = 4r \cos^3 \theta$$
$$y = 4r \sin^3 \theta$$

Show that these equations are equivalent to the Cartesian equation:

$$x^{2/3} + y^{2/3} = (4r)^{2/3}$$

(See the graphs of Problem 1(*h*) above and Problem 2(*f*) of Exercise 53.)

(*c*) What would a hypocycloid of two cusps be? That is, what path would be traced by a point on a circle of radius r rolling within a circle of radius $2r$?

(*d*) Find the Cartesian equation of the hypocycloid of three cusps whose parametric equations are given above.

5. *The epicycloid.* When a circle rolls upon the circumference of another circle, and outside it, the path traced by a fixed point on the rolling circle is called an *epicycloid*. If the radius of the fixed circle is n times the radius of the rolling circle, where n is a nn, the epicycloid is called an *epicycloid of n cusps*.

(*a*) Find parametric equations of an epicycloid generated by a point on a circle of radius r rolling on a circle of radius r.

Hint: Follow the method in the case of the hypocycloid; here arcs of lengths $r(0 - \theta)$ and $r[\pi - (\phi - \theta)]$ play roles analogous to those of lengths $3r(0 - \theta)$ and $r(\phi - \theta)$ in the example worked out above.

Show that the parametric equations for this epicycloid may be expressed:

$$x = r(2 \cos \theta - \cos 2\theta)$$
$$y = r(2 \sin \theta - \sin 2\theta)$$

(*b*) Choose a convenient value of r, and plot the graph of the epicycloid whose equations are given above.

6. A man stands on a ladder, one of whose ends rests on level ground, the other on a vertical wall. Show that if the ladder slips, the man travels along a path which is part of an ellipse whose semi-axes are the segments into which the man separates the ladder.

CHAPTER 13

POLAR

COORDINATES

13.1 INTRODUCTION

The student will recall that a Cartesian coordinate system in a plane is a system for identifying each point of that plane by means of an ordered pair of real numbers. It happens that there are other systems which serve the same purpose. Of particular importance is the *polar* coordinate system:

Suppose P is a point $\neq O$ in a ccd system, and that ray OP is labeled p (Fig. 13.1).

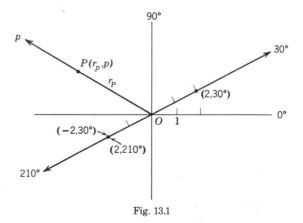

Fig. 13.1

Then given r_P (i.e., $d(O, P)$) and p, the point P is uniquely determined. For example, given that $p = 30°$, $r_P = 2$, we may locate the point P by first locating the unique ray labeled 30°, and then on that ray, the unique point P whose distance from the origin O is 2.

The ordered pair of numbers (r_P, p), then, may be used to identify P; (r_P and p are called the *polar* coordinates of the point P). The point P of the preceding paragraph may, for example, be labeled $(2, 30°)$.

If $P = O$, then one may identify P as the point for which $r_P = 0$ on *any* ray of the ccd system. That is to say, if k is any real number, then $(0, k°)$ are polar coordinates that identify the origin O.

Immediately we observe a distinction between Cartesian and polar coordinates: In Cartesian coordinates, each point has a unique label. This is not true in polar coordinates, where, for example, the point $(2, 30°)$ may also be labeled $(2, 390°)$, $(2, -330°)$, etc.

In fact, it is usual to introduce a convention that allows points to have different r_P values as well as different p values. What we have said so far has the consequence that r_P values are never negative. We shall now agree to allow negative r_P values, with this interpretation: When p and a negative value of r_P are given, then we shall mean that the point P lies on the ray that is the extension through O of the ray labeled p, at a distance of $|r_P|$ from O.

Thus, the point $(-2, 30°)$ is identical with the point $(2, 210°)$ (Fig. 13.1), and for any point $(a, b°)$ in polar coordinates, $(a, b°)$ and $(-a, b° + 180°)$ denote the same point.

It is customary in mathematics texts to use the letters "r" and "θ" to denote what we have called "r_P" and "p," respectively. We shall follow this practice. Thus, when we refer in polar coordinates to the point $P = (r, \theta)$, we shall mean that $r_P = r$, and $p = \theta$.

In polar coordinate systems, the origin is sometimes referred to as the *pole*, and the $0°$-ray as the *polar axis* of the system.

Note: a ccr system may also be used to define a polar coordinate system; in such a system, for example, the point' $(7, 11)$ would be that for which $r_P = 7$, $p = 11$ *radians*.

13.2 GRAPHS IN POLAR COORDINATES

Given an equation involving r or θ or both, the set of all points (r, θ) satisfying the equation is called the polar graph of the given equation.

Illustrative Example 1. We plot the graph of the equation: $r = 10 \cos \theta$ (Fig. 13.2).

Again, a table of values is our mainstay:

θ	0	30°	45°	60°	90°	120°	135°	150°	180°
r	10	8.7	7	5	0	-5	-7	-8.7	-10

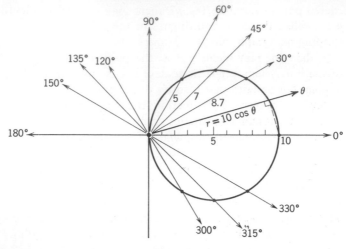

Fig. 13.2

(It will be found that the points of the graph obtained for $180° < \theta < 360°$ duplicate those found for $0° < \theta < 180°$; for example, the point $(210°, -8.7)$ is identical with $(30°, 8.7)$.

The graph appears to be a circle of diameter 10. That this is actually the case is suggested by the fact that an angle inscribed in a semi-circle is a right angle.

In fact, we shall prove in the next section that the graph of $r = 2k \cos \theta$ is a circle with center $(k, 0°)$ and radius k.

Illustrative Example 2. The graph of $r = 5$ is easily seen to consist of all points at a distance of 5 units from O, i.e., the graph of $r = 5$ is a circle of radius 5 with center at O.

In fact, for any real number k, the graph of $r = k$ is a circle with center O and radius $|k|$.

Illustrative Example 3. The graph of $\theta = 30°$ is easily seen to consist of all points on the line made up of the *two* rays labeled 30° and 210°, respectively; for each point $(c, 210°)$ may also be labeled $(-c, 30°)$, and therefore satisfies the equation $\theta = 30°$.

In fact, for any real number k, the graph of $\theta = k$ is a straight line through the origin.

▶ **EXERCISE 67**

1. Locate each of the following points in a polar coordinate system, and in each case identify the given point by two other labels. Choose labels with r's of opposite sign (if possible).

(a) (3, 30°)   (b) (0, 30°)   (c) (0, 0°)

(d) (4, 90°)   (e) (−4, 90°)   (f) (−3, 120°)

(g) (5, 700°)   (h) (−2, 0°)   (i) (−2, 270°)

2. Plot the graphs of:

(a) $r = 5$ (b) $r = -5$

(c) $r = \dfrac{5}{\sin \theta}$ (d) $r = \dfrac{5}{\cos \theta}$

(e) $\theta = 45°$ (f) $\theta = \pi$

(g) $r = 10 \sin \theta$ (h) $r = \dfrac{4}{2 + \cos \theta}$

(i) $r = \dfrac{4}{1 + \sin \theta}$ (j) $r = \dfrac{4}{1 + 2 \cos \theta}$

3. In each case, choose convenient nonzero values for a and b, and plot the graph of:

(a) $r = a \sin 2\theta$ (Four-leaved rose. *Hint:* $\theta = k \cdot 45°$, k any integer, are important.)

(b) $r = a \sin 3\theta$ (Three leaved rose. *Hint:* $\theta = k \cdot 30°$, k any integer are important.)

(c) $r = a \cos 2\theta$ (Four-leaved rose)

(d) $r = a \cos 3\theta$ (Three-leaved rose)

(e) $r = b + a \cos \theta$ [Limaçon; (if $|b| = |a|$, cardioid; choose values such that $|b| > |a|$; then values such that $|b| = |a|$; then values such that $|b| < |a|$. In the last, watch out for a loop in the graph!]

(f) $r^2 = a^2 \cos 2\theta$ (Lemniscate)

(g) $r^2 = a^2 \sin 2\theta$ (Lemniscate)

(h) $r = \dfrac{a}{\theta}$ (Hyperbolic spiral)

(i) $r = a\theta$ (Archimedean spiral)   Use radian measure

(j) $r^2 = \dfrac{a^2}{\theta}$ (Lituus or trumpet)

(k) $r = a \sec \theta + b$ [Conchoid; consider cases as in (e) above, including cases in which a, b are of opposite sign.]

4. *Conic Sections in polar coordinate systems.*

In this problem we consider a conic (i.e., a conic section) C with positive eccentricity e. The conic C (see Problem 2, Exercise 60) may then be considered to be the locus of points P in the plane of C, the ratio of whose distances to C's focus F and C's directrix l (which does not contain F) is e.

Let the distance from F to l be $k > 0$, and choose a ccd system whose origin is at F, and whose X-axis is perpendicular to l, so that the equation of l is $x = k$ (Fig. 13.3).

Then if P is a point of this ccd system, and P lies on a ray labeled θ_P, we have: The distance from P to F is r_P.

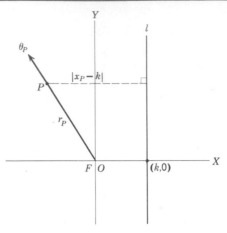

Fig. 13.3

The distance from P to l is $|x_P - k| = |r_P \cos \theta_P - k|$ (see boxed statement, page 179, and Lemma 1, page 237).

Therefore P lies on C if and only if:

(1)
$$\frac{r_P}{|r_P \cos \theta_P - k|} = e$$

i.e., the equation of C in polar coordinates is:

(2)
$$\frac{r}{|r \cos \theta - k|} = e$$

It may now be proved that (2) is equivalent to:

(3)
$$\frac{r}{k - r \cos \theta} = e$$

In order to prove that (2) is equivalent to (3), it is sufficient to show that every point P which satisfies (2) satisfies (3), and vice versa. We shall show the first part below; it will be left to the student to show that every point which satisfies (3) satisfies (2).

Suppose, then, that P is a point which satisfies (2), i.e., suppose that (1) is true. We consider two cases.

Case 1. $r_P \cos \theta_P - k < 0$. Then $|r_P \cos \theta_P - k| = -(r_P \cos \theta_P - k) = k - r_P \cos \theta_P$, so that there follows from (1):

(4)
$$\frac{r_P}{k - r_P \cos \theta_P} = e$$

but this means that P satisfies (3), Q.E.D.

Case 2. $r_P \cos \theta_P - k \geqslant 0$. Then $|r_P \cos \theta_P - k| = r_P \cos \theta_P - k$, so that there follows from (1):

(5)
$$\frac{r_P}{r_P \cos \theta_P - k} = e$$

Now show that $\cos (\theta_P + 180°) = -\cos \theta_P$, *hence that* $\cos \theta_P = -\cos (\theta_P + 180°)$. There then follows from (5):

(6)
$$\frac{r_P}{-r_P \cos (\theta_P + 180°) - k} = e$$

from which follows:

(7)
$$\frac{-r_P}{k - (-r_P)\cos(\theta_P + 180°)} = e$$

This means that the point whose coordinates are $(-r_P, \theta_P + 180°)$ satisfies (3).   But $(-r_P, \theta_P + 180°)$ are coordinates for P.   Therefore P satisfies (3), Q.E.D.

The student may now complete the proof that (2) *and* (3) *are equivalent equations by proving that every point P which satisfies* (3) *satisfies* (2).

Then proceed to solve (3) *for r, arriving at the following equation in polar coordinates for a conic section with eccentricity e:*

(8)
$$r = \frac{ek}{1 + e\cos\theta}$$

Similarly one may prove that the following are equations for conic sections with eccentricity e:

(9)
$$r = \frac{ek}{1 - e\cos\theta}$$

(10)
$$r = \frac{ek}{1 + e\sin\theta}$$

(11)
$$r = \frac{ek}{1 - e\sin\theta}$$

The directrices of (8), (9), (10), (11) have the equations $x = k$, $x = -k$, $y = k$, $y = -k$, respectively.

Identify and plot the graph of each of the following equations, and locate a directrix in each case:

(a) $r = \dfrac{4}{2 + 3\cos\theta}$ (*Hint:* $r = \dfrac{2}{1 + \frac{3}{2}\cos\theta}$. Comparing with (8) above, $e = \frac{3}{2}$, $ek = 2$; therefore $k = \dfrac{2}{e} = \frac{4}{3}$. Since $e > 1$, the graph is a hyperbola. The directrix is the line $x = \frac{4}{3}$. Make a table of values and plot.)

(b) $r = \dfrac{4}{3 - 2\cos\theta}$

(c) $r = \dfrac{1}{1 + \sin\theta}$

(d) $r = \dfrac{2}{1 - \sin\theta}$

13.3 CONVERSION FROM POLAR TO RECTANGULAR COORDINATES, AND VICE VERSA

Suppose that the point P on a ccd system is identified by the rectangular coordinates (x, y) and the polar coordinates (r, θ).

Then (as illustrated for a special case in Fig. 13.4):

(i) $x = r\cos\theta$

(ii) $y = r\sin\theta$

(iii) $\tan\theta = \dfrac{y}{x}$ (if $x \neq 0$)

(iv) $x^2 + y^2 = r^2$

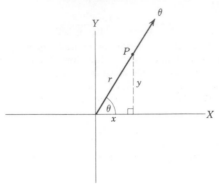

Fig. 13.4

[For $r \geqslant 0$ equations (i) and (ii) are true by Lemma 1 of Section 8.8; for $r < 0$, the proof of (i) and (ii) is left as an optional exercise; (iii) follows from the definition of $\tan \theta$; (iv) may be derived either by squaring and adding (i) and (ii), or from the formula for $d(O, P)$.]

These equations may be used:

(a)   To find polar coordinates of a point, given the rectangular co-ordinates of the point.

(b)   To find rectangular coordinates of a point, given the polar coordinates of the point.

(c)   To find the polar equation of a graph, given its rectangular equation.

(d)   To find the rectangular equation of a graph, given its polar equation.

Illustrative Example 1.   We find the rectangular coordinates of the point whose polar coordinates are $(-10, 60°)$.

Using (i) and (ii): $x = -10 \cos 60° = -5$
$$y = -10 \sin 60° = -5 \sqrt{3}$$

SOLUTION.   If $(r, \theta) = (-10, 60°)$, then $(x, y) = (-5, -5 \sqrt{3})$, uniquely.

Illustrative Example 2.   We find polar coordinates of the point whose rectangular coordinates are $(5, -5 \sqrt{3})$.

Clearly the given point is in QIV. Therefore, with positive r, $\tan \theta = y/x = -\sqrt{3}$ leads to $\theta = 300°$; from (iv), $r^2 = 25 + 75$, so that $r = 10$.

SOLUTION.   If $(x, y) = (5, -5 \sqrt{3})$, then $(r, \theta) = (10, 300°)$, but not, of course, uniquely; $(10, 660°)$ and $(-10, 120°)$ identify the same point.

Illustrative Example 3.   We convert the following polar equation to a Cartesian equation:

(1) $r = 2k \cos \theta$

From (i): $\cos \theta = \dfrac{x}{r}$; substituting into (1):

(2) $$r = 2k \cdot \frac{x}{r}, \text{ from which:}$$

(3) $$r^2 = 2kx$$

Now, using (iv), there follows from (3):

(4) $$x^2 + y^2 = 2kx$$

The required Cartesian equation is (4). The equations (4) and (1) are equivalent in this sense: they have the same graph. Any point whose polar coordinates satisfy (1) has Cartesian coordinates which satisfy (4), and vice-versa.

The substitution $\cos \theta = x/r$ is valid only if $r \neq 0$. Actually, we may check independently that the origin O satisfies both (1) and (4), and then note that the steps above guarantee that all *other* points which satisfy (1) satisfy (4), and vice versa.

Using the method of completing the square, (4) may be transformed into the equivalent equation:

(5) $$(x - k)^2 + y^2 = k^2$$

which we recognize as the equation of a circle whose center (in Cartesian coordinates) is $(k, 0)$ and whose radius is k.

We have proved, then, that the graph of the polar equation $r = 2k \cos \theta$ is a circle of radius k with center at $(k, 0°)$. (See Fig. 13.5.)

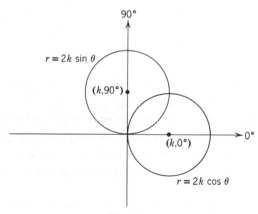

Fig. 13.5

Illustrative Example 4. We convert the following Cartesian equation to a polar equation:

(1) $$x^2 + (y - k)^2 = k^2$$

Clearly, (1) is equivalent to:

(2) $$x^2 + y^2 - 2ky = 0$$

Using (iv) and (ii) there follows from (2):

(3) $$r^2 - 2kr \sin \theta = 0$$

and dividing by r:

(4) $$r - 2k \sin \theta = 0, \text{ from which:}$$

(5) $$r = 2k \sin \theta$$

    Actually, factoring the left side of (3), we see that a point satisfies (3) either if $r = 0$, or if $r - 2k \sin \theta = 0$. The only point which satisfies $r = 0$ is the origin; but the origin happens to satisfy $r - 2k \sin \theta = 0$ also. The equation $r = 0$ is therefore redundant here, and may be discarded. Thus, in this case, no harm has been done by dividing both sides of an equation by r.

    We see, then, that $r = 2k \sin \theta$ is the polar equation of a circle whose radius is k and whose center is at $(0, k)$ in Cartesian coordinates, i.e., at $(k, 90°)$ in polar coordinates (Fig. 13.5).

▶ **EXERCISE 68**

    1. (a)–(i).   Find the Cartesian coordinates of each of the points whose polar coordinates are given in Problem 1 of the preceding exercise.

    2.   In each case find one pair of polar coordinates in which $r \geqslant 0$, and a different pair in which $r \leqslant 0$, to identify the point whose Cartesian coordinates are given.

(a) $(0, 0)$	(b) $(3, 0)$	(c) $(0, 3)$
(d) $(-3, 0)$	(e) $(0, -3)$	(f) $(2, 2)$
(g) $(-2, 2)$	(h) $(2, -2)$	(i) $(-2, -2)$
(j) $(1, \sqrt{3})$	(k) $(-1, \sqrt{3})$	(l) $(\sqrt{3}, -1)$
(m) $(-1, -\sqrt{3})$	(n) $(1, -\sqrt{3})$	(o) $(-\sqrt{3}, 1)$

    3. (a)–(j).   Transform each of the polar equations in Problem 2 (a)–(j) of the preceding exercise into an equivalent Cartesian equation.

    4. (a)–(g).   Transform each of the polar equations in Problem 3 (a)–(g) of the preceding exercise into an equivalent Cartesian equation.

    5. (a) Find the polar equations of the straight lines whose Cartesian equations are $x = a$ and $y = b$.

    (b) Plot the graph of the equation $r = 2a (\sin \theta + \cos \theta)$, and prove, by transforming the given equation into a Cartesian equation, that the graph is a circle.

    (c) Plot the graph of the equation $r = \dfrac{10}{\sin \theta + \cos \theta}$; identify the graph and prove that your identification is correct.

6. Suppose l is a line which passes through a point P whose polar coordinates are (a, α), where $a \geqslant 0$, and suppose l is perpendicular to the ray labeled α (Fig. 13.6).

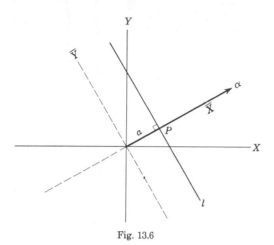

Fig. 13.6

(a) What is the equation of l in a new system derived from the original by rotating through an angle α?

(b) Using the equations of rotation of Problem 3, page 339, and the result of (a) above, show that the Cartesian equation of l in the original system is:

(1) $$x \cos \alpha + y \sin \alpha = a$$

If $O \neq P$, then there exists line segment $OP \perp l$, and this line segment of length a is called the *normal* to line l. If $O = P$, we say that the normal to line l is of length $a = 0$.

The equation (1) above is called the *normal form* of the equation of line l.

7. From the normal form of the equation of line l of Problem 6 above, derive the polar equation of l:

$$r \cos (\theta - \alpha) = a$$

Summarizing: The equation of a line l, perpendicular to a ray labeled α, at a distance of a from the origin, is:

(In Cartesian coordinates) $\qquad x \cos \alpha + y \sin \alpha = r$

(In polar coordinates) $\qquad r \cos (\theta - \alpha) = a$

8. Prove that equations (i) and (ii) of Section 13.3 hold for $r < 0$. [Hint: The point (r, θ) is identical with the point $(-r, \theta + 180°)$.]

P $_{ART}$ III ▶ INTRODUCTIONS TO THE CALCULUS AND PROBABILITY AND STATISTICS

14

INTRODUCTION TO
THE CALCULUS

14.1 THE GREEK CRISIS IN MATHEMATICS

In a world in which our faith in so many things is so often rudely shaken, mathematics has come to be revered as one of the last repositories of absolutely certain knowledge. To some extent this reputation is deserved; for there exists no field of knowledge and no area of thought that has been studied more extensively nor scrutinized more critically by greater or more penetrating minds. Moreover, the claim to infallibility which is made for mathematics is strengthened by the fact that the validity of mathematics in its applications to the problems of our daily lives and of the world about us has never been seriously challenged.

But it must be confessed that even mathematical knowledge falls short of the ideal of total certainty. Indeed, from the time of the Greeks, some twenty-five hundred years ago, right up to the present day, mathematics has had to struggle with baffling "paradoxes"—with results, that is to say, that are in conflict either with each other, or with intuition, or with experience. Early "crises," if they were resolved, were quickly followed by later ones; and this has become a characteristic pattern in the development of mathematics.

We have already discussed (in Section 3.3) the earliest of mathematical crises, precipitated by the remarkable probing intelligence of the Pythagorean mathematicians of the sixth century B.C.: The conflict between the proved irrationality of $\sqrt{2}$ and the strong intuitive feeling that one can number all the points of a scaled line using only rational numbers. Here, as often, the resolution of the conflict lies simply in the admission that there are cases in which our intuition is wrong.

Before another century had elapsed, the infant science of mathematics found itself faced with new difficulties, when Zeno brought forth the famous paradoxes which bear his name. Here, in somewhat edited form, is what he said:

Consider an arrow, and the space which it fills. Can the arrow move within that space? Obviously not—the arrow cannot move within the space that it exactly fills. Well then, consider some other portion of space. Can the arrow move there? This is preposterous—an arrow cannot do anything in a place where it fails to be. Well then, if the arrow cannot move where it is, and if even more certainly it cannot move where it is not, we must conclude that an arrow cannot move! But experience tells us that motion *is* possible. Something, quite obviously, is wrong.

Another paradox of Zeno is a fairly familiar one: Suppose I begin to cross a street, and proceed in the following way: First I walk half-way across. Then I walk half the remaining distance. Then I proceed to the midpoint of the distance which remains—and so on. Diagrammatically, with the first few successive positions numbered:

```
 .                    .        .   . .
|————————————————————————————————————|
1                     2        3   4 5
```

The question is: Will I ever reach the other side of the street? The answer seems to be *no*; for no matter how far I have gone, there will always be at least one more midpoint to cross. There is no last midpoint. My journey therefore, can never be completed.

But we all know that it *is* possible to cross a street. And in doing so, do we not first go halfway across? And then do we not go half the remaining distance? And in fact do we not go through all the steps of the preceding paragraph? Experience tells us we *can* cross a street. Logic seems to tell us we cannot.

The Greeks never were able to explain what was wrong with Zeno's reasoning. We, however, borrowing from much later thought, will soon be able to see where the trouble lies.

What, after all, is motion? We think of it usually as a state of being in different places *at different times*. We may describe the motion of a body in a given interval of time by telling where it is *at each instant* during its journey. Sometimes this is done by means of a formula. We learn in physics, for example, that a stone dropped from a height will fall about $16t^2$ ft in t seconds. Thus we know that in 1 second it will be at a point about 16 ft below its starting point, in 2 seconds 64 ft down from the starting point, and so on.

But what have we here but a function which assigns a point in space to each of a number of instants of time! Indeed, that fundamentally is all that any motion is. We make a formal statement, restricting ourselves, for the sake of clarity, to the motion of a point:

> The motion of a point, during an interval of time, is a function whose domain is the set of instants of time in that interval, and whose range is a set of points in space.

Now let us return to the two paradoxes we have described.

When we consider what motion actually is, the first of the paradoxes is easily disposed of. It is nonsense to speak of motion *in* one place or another. Motion consists of being in certain places at certain times—nothing more nor less than that. It is this correspondence between instants of time and points of space that constitutes motion. When an arrow is shot into the air, such a correspondence is set up—and logic and experience really do coincide.

The second paradox requires just a bit more in the way of explanation. Here the trouble seems to lie in the fact that we have, in some sense, too many midpoints to cross. Our subdivision of the line that stretches across the street has produced an infinite number of midpoints, and we feel it is impossible to cross all of them in a finite length of time.

But again our understanding of what motion is comes to the rescue. It is true that in crossing the street we must pass an infinite number of points. But just as the line stretching across the street contains an infinite number of points, so a time interval contains an infinite number of instants. Given an interval of time, we will have plenty of instants at our disposal, enough to take care of all the points. And in order to cross the street, it is only necessary that it be possible to set up a correspondence between the instants of time in some interval of time and the points of our path across the street.

For example, suppose the street is 40 ft wide, and we walk at a rate of 4 ft per second. Then the journey would take, of course, 10 seconds. Those 40 ft contain infinitely many of the midpoints Zeno wished to cross. But that 10-second interval contains just as many instants of time. For every midpoint there will correspond an instant, and in fact we can tell just which one, that is *when* any particular midpoint will be crossed. The diagram below illustrates the first few successive midpoints in this example, and the times to which they correspond:

Midpoint:	1	2	3	4	5	
Distance traversed:	20	30	35	37.5	38.75	(feet)
Instant of time:	5	7.5	8.75	9.375	9.6875	(seconds)

What the Greeks overlooked, then, in this paradox, is that it takes an interval of time to make a journey, and that although the journey requires traversing an infinite number of points, the interval of time will be able to furnish quite enough instants to take care of all the points.

14.2 THE SPEED AT 3:47

The indignant young lady asks a very interesting question. To understand its meaning clearly is to understand a great deal about motion and its concomitant concept, speed. Supposing that the answer to her question was: "720 miles per hour, dear," we shall make it our immediate goal to explain exactly what it means to be moving at a speed of 720 mph *at* 3:47.

"Punch—Ben Roth"

"And at what speed were you flying at exactly 3:47 this afternoon?"

Fig. 14.1

We begin by considering this simple case: Suppose I were to drive from Amherst to New York (a distance of 160 miles) in 4 hours. It is clear that this could be accomplished by driving 40 miles during each of the 4 hours, and we say that our *average speed* for the journey was 40 miles per hour. In fact we make the following definition:

> If a distance s is traveled in a positive time interval t, the *average speed v* for the journey is defined by the equation:
>
> $$\text{average speed} = \frac{s}{t}$$

For example, we know that the following formula describes the approximate distance s (in feet) traveled in t seconds by a falling body: $s = 16t^2$. We construct a table to show the average speed of a falling body during certain time intervals:

Total time elapsed:	1	2	3	4	5	(seconds)
Total distance traveled:	16	64	144	256	400	(feet)
Average speed for total fall:	16	32	48	64	80	(feet/second)
Average speed during last second of fall:	16	48	80	112	144	(feet/second)

Now when a body travels at a constant average speed, there is little difficulty in imagining what its speed at any instant of its journey should be considered to be. If we know, for example, that the average speed of an automobile, as computed between *any* two points of its journey between two towns, always came to 40 mph, then we would be inclined to say that its speed *at* any moment of its trip must have been 40 mph.

But the student will readily see that the above is a highly fanciful situation. For a car to maintain the same average speed between all pairs of points on a trip is a practical impossibility. A situation in which the average speed between points of a journey changes continually is the rule in nature, and constant average speeds the exception.

The point we have made is exemplified by the preceding table. The student will note that the average speed of a falling body in successive seconds is an increasing quantity. It can be shown, in fact, that the average speed a falling body attains in any time interval is never repeated in any later time interval, but that the average speed increases continually as time elapses.

Our problem first of all, then, is to decide what should be meant by speed *at* a given moment, when a body travels at average speeds which change with time. Problems involving changing quantities are typically the subject matter of the branch of mathematics known as "calculus," and the particular problem we have just mentioned was actually one of those which led Newton in England and Leibniz in Germany, about a hundred years before our Declaration of Independence was signed, to the independent invention of that part of calculus we call "the differential calculus."

Now returning to the problem of speed *at* a given moment (or "instantaneous speed"), we note that the computation of an *average* speed demands the existence of an *interval* of time, and that the interval of time cannot be zero in length; for in a time interval of 0 seconds nothing on earth, however jet-propelled, can travel any distance but 0 ft. An attempt to misapply our formula, which is defined only for $t > 0$, would only yield: average speed $= \frac{0}{0}$, which would fail, in any case, to give us a result.

Apparently, without an *interval* of time at our disposal, stretching from one instant *to* a later instant, it is impossible to have a *speed*. The man in our cartoon might, with a great deal of justice have said: "Why, at 3:47 I wasn't flying at *any* speed. Don't you know that in order to have speed one must have motion, and that motion involves more than just one instant of time? As a matter of fact, I believe I will say that *at* 3:47 I was standing quite still, just suspended motionless up there in the blue, and if you don't believe me try taking a picture of my plane with a really high-speed camera some afternoon *exactly* at 3:47, when you're suspecting me of the same thing again."

Let us give the young lady the last word:

"Don't be silly, darling—I've heard of Zeno too. As a matter of fact, while I watched your plane, quite a few instants of time slipped by, not just the one at 3:47, but all the instants between 3:47 and 3:47:05, five seconds later. And wow! Were you traveling! At 3:47 you buzzed our house; five seconds later you were disappearing over that hill, a mile down the road. Now five seconds is $\frac{5}{3600}$ of an hour. Your speed, in miles per hour, must have been: $\dfrac{1}{\frac{5}{3600}}$ or $\dfrac{3600}{5}$ or 720—and don't do it again."

At this point the reader may wish to enter the controversy with the objection that 720 mph is the average speed between 3:47 and 3:47:05, and still not the speed of the plane *at* 3:47. True, but an entering wedge into the concept of instantaneous speed has now been made.

Certainly, whatever we mean by the speed of a plane at 3:47, it is something that should not change very much in 5 seconds, and so the average speed of the plane (which we *are* able to compute) between 3:47 and 3:47:05 should afford at least an approximation to its instantaneous speed at 3:47.

But now two questions arise:

(i)   Why 5 seconds?

(ii)   How can we get a better approximation to what we mean by the speed *at* 3:47?

In answer, we observe that any "small" number of seconds will do for our purposes; or more precisely, that a smaller interval of time than 5 seconds would probably give a better approximation to what we mean by the speed at 3:47, and indeed that we may secure better and better approximations to the instantaneous speed we seek by choosing smaller and smaller intervals of time over which to compute average speeds.

We pause to apply these ideas to the case of a falling body. Suppose a stone is dropped from some height, and after a fall of 2 seconds, has not yet reached the ground. If we begin to count time from the moment the stone is dropped, i.e., if $s = 0$ when $t = 0$, what is the speed of the stone when $t = 2$; i.e., how fast is the stone falling at the end of two seconds of fall?

We first construct the following table, using the formula $s = 16t^2$.

Time (t):   2   2.1   2.01   2.001   2.0001   (seconds)
Distance fallen (s): 64 70.56 64.6416 64.064016 64.00640016 (feet)

Then from this table, we derive the following:

Length of time interval
past t = 2:   0.1   0.01   0.001   0.0001   (sec)
Distance fallen in time
interval: 6.56   0.6416   0.064016   0.00640016   (ft)
Average speed in time
interval: 65.6   64.16   64.016   64.0016   (ft/sec)

Now we note that as we choose shorter and shorter intervals of time, the computed average speeds seem to be heading toward, or approaching, the number 64.

It is this number 64 (ft/sec), which we define to be the instantaneous speed of the falling stone at t = 2.

For the moment we will content ourselves with this rough method of discovering instantaneous speeds. In the next section, however, we shall attempt to show more convincingly that the number "approached" by the average speeds in the preceding table is *exactly* 64 ft/sec, and not just some number near this value.

In conclusion, we state in the case of motion along a straight line, the general definition of instantaneous speed which has been implied by our discussion:

> Suppose that a body moves along a scaled line in such a way that at time t it is at a point s on the scaled line given by a formula: $s = f(t)$.
> Then the *instantaneous speed* of the body at a specific time $t = k$ is defined to be the speed which is approached by average speeds computed in intervals between $t = k$ and $t = k+h$, as h becomes smaller and smaller.

▶ **EXERCISE 69**

1. A stone falls for 5 seconds. Indicate, on a vertical scaled line, the position of the stone at each of the following instants: $t = 0, 1, 2, 3, 4, 5$.

(*Note:* The following problems refer to the stone of Problem 1; "*t*" is time measured in seconds.)

2. Find the speed at which the stone is moving:

(*a*)   at $t = 1$ (*b*)   at $t = 3$ (*c*)   at $t = 4$ (*d*)   at $t = 5$

3. (*a*)   How far has the stone fallen in 3 seconds?

(*b*)   How far has the stone fallen in 3.1 seconds?

(*c*)   How far has the stone fallen between $t = 3$ and $t = 3 + 0.1$?

(*d*)   How long is the time interval between $t = 3$ and $t = 3 + 0.1$?

(*e*)   What is the average speed of the stone between $t = 3$ and $t = 3.1$?

(In Problems 4 and 5 which follow, assume that h is positive.)

4. (*a*)   How far has the stone fallen in 1 second?

(*b*)   How far has the stone fallen in $1 + h$ seconds?

(*c*)   How far has the stone fallen between $t = 1$ and $t = 1 + h$?

(*d*)   How long is the time interval between $t = 1$ and $t = 1 + h$?

(*e*)   What is the average speed of the stone between $t = 1$ and $t = 1 + h$? (Express the answer as a polynomial in h.)

(*f*)   What real number does the expression of part (*e*) approach as h gets smaller and smaller?

5. (*a*)   How far has the stone fallen in k seconds?

(*b*)   How far has the stone fallen in $k + h$ seconds?

(*c*)   How far has the stone fallen between $t = k$ and $t = k + h$?

(*d*)   How long is the time interval between $t = k$ and $t = k + h$?

(*e*)   What is the average speed of the stone between $t = k$ and $t = k + h$? (Express the answer as a polynomial in h.)

(*f*)   What polynomial in k does the expression of part (*e*) approach as h gets smaller and smaller?

6. Another of Zeno's paradoxes is the so-called "Achilles and the Tortoise," in which Zeno "proves" that although Achilles is very fleet and a tortoise proverbially slow, if the tortoise is given a head start in a race, then Achilles will never be able to win. Here is how Zeno reasoned:

Let us call the initial positions of Achilles and the tortoise, 1 and *a*, respectively:

Achilles   1

Tortoise   *a*

Then before Achilles can catch up to the tortoise, he must reach the point *a* from which the tortoise started. By that time, of course, the tortoise has advanced to a point, *b*:

Achilles   1   2

Tortoise   *a*   *b*

Achilles, nothing daunted, keeps running. But before he can catch the tortoise, he must reach point *b*. The tortoise, though slow does not stand still, however. By the time Achilles reaches b, the tortoise will have advanced to c:

Achilles	1		2	3	
Tortoise			a	b c	

The argument may be continued indefinitely. Always, before Achilles can reach the tortoise, he must pass a point where the tortoise has recently been. And always by the time Achilles reaches that point, the tortoise has advanced a bit. Thus there will always be at least one such point left for Achilles to negotiate. Therefore Achilles can never catch the tortoise.

Now answer these questions:

(*a*) Suppose the tortoise has a head start of 495 ft, and that Achilles runs at a rate of 20 ft per second, and the tortoise at a rate of 1 ft in 5 seconds. Exactly how long will it take Achilles to overtake the tortoise?

(*b*) Where is the flaw in Zeno's "proof" that Achilles cannot catch the tortoise?

14.3 THE CONCEPT OF A LIMIT

In the preceding section we spoke of "approaching" the number 64. Speaking very roughly, a number that is thus approached is called a *limit*, in mathematics. The concept of a limit is one of the most important of all mathematical ideas. A major subdivision of mathematics, called "Analysis," devotes itself mainly to the study of mathematics involving limits and related ideas. Limits play a dominant role in calculus, which finds itself therefore classified as a part of Analysis.

In this section we shall further investigate the question of instantaneous speed, and in doing so we shall find it necessary to throw a little more light upon the idea of a limit.

We return to the problem of the falling stone; assuming the formulas we have previously given to be true, we may state:

In t seconds, a stone will fall: $16t^2$ feet

In $t + h$ seconds ($h > 0$), a stone will fall: $16(t + h)^2$ feet

Therefore, in the time interval between t and $t + h$ seconds, the stone will fall the following number of feet:

$$16(t + h)^2 - 16t^2 = 16[(t + h)^2 - t^2] = 16(2ht + h^2) = 16h(2t + h) \text{ ft}$$

The average speed of the stone between the times t and $t + h$ is therefore:

$$\frac{16h(2t + h)}{h} = 16(2t + h) \text{ ft per second, } \textit{for any positive time interval } h.$$

It is important to note that the result $16(2t + h)$ follows only if we assume that $h \neq 0$; for only if $h \neq 0$ may we cancel the h's in the preceding fraction.

This result enables us to answer Problems 3 (e), 4 (e), and 5 (e), above, very easily. In 3 (e), for example, $t = 3$ and $h = 0.1$. Substituting in the formula $16(2t + h)$, we find that the average speed in this case is $16(6.1)$ or 97.6 ft per second.

This formula for average speed may also be made to yield a general formula for the instantaneous speed at time t. For although the average speed is meaningless when $h = 0$, it is meaningful when h is very small, so long as h is not zero itself.

Let us consider what happens to the expression $16(2t + h)$ then, when h is very small. It seems reasonable to say that when h is very small, then $16(2t + h)$ is very close to $16 \cdot 2t$ or $32t$.

We conclude, then, that the number that is approached by the average speed $16(2t + h)$ as h becomes smaller and smaller is $32t$; and our definition of instantaneous speed now tells us that $32t$ must therefore be the instantaneous speed of the stone at time t. Again we may solve several of the preceding set of problems quite easily, using this formula. For example, the answer to Problem 2 (c) may now be seen to be $32 \cdot 4$, or 128 ft per second.

It happens very often in mathematics, as it happened just above, that we seek to find a number which is approached by some $f(u)$ as u becomes very small. In case f is a polynomial function, the problem is very easy; for whatever we mean by "very small" and "approach," we may agree that products and sums of very small numbers are still very small, so that the number approached by a polynomial in u may be determined simply by neglecting all terms involving u; this process, of course, amounts to nothing more than substituting 0 for u in the polynomial.

This number (if there is one) which is approached by a function $f(u)$ as u gets very small, is called the "limit" of $f(u)$ as u approaches 0. We shall use the letter "L" to denote the limit of a function of the particular letter h as h approaches zero.

Here are some examples of the way in which we shall use the symbol L:

   (i) $L(2 + h + h^2) = 2$

   (ii) $L(2 + h)(3 + h) = 6$

   (iii) $L(h) = 0$

   (iv) $L(7) = 7$

In the case of functions more complicated than polynomial functions, however, we soon discover that the problem of finding a limit is much more difficult.   For example, what would the limit, as h approaches zero, of the following function be?

$$f(h) = \frac{h}{2^h - 1}$$

Here a substitution of 0 for h leads to the well-known monster: $\frac{0}{0}$, or in other words, no answer at all.   The root of our trouble is that we need a more precise definition of what we mean by "very small" and by "approach," before a definition of "limit" which can be applied effectively to all functions can be made.   Such a general definition exists, of course, but it lies beyond the scope of this course.

We are now, however, in a position to restate our definitions of average and instantaneous speeds in somewhat better form.

Suppose, as before, that we consider a point that moves along a scaled line in such a way that at time t it is at a point on the scaled line given by a formula: $f(t)$. (Fig. 14.2.)

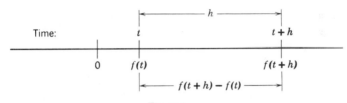

Fig. 14.2

Then in time $t + h$ it will be at a point: $f(t + h)$, and in the time interval between t and $t + h$, it will have traveled the distance $f(t + h) - f(t)$.

Following our preceding development, we would now be inclined to say that the average speed in this time interval is:

(1) $$\frac{f(t + h) - f(t)}{h}$$

But $f(t + h) - f(t)$ may be positive or negative, depending upon which way the point is moving on the scaled line; and h may also be taken as positive or negative, since one may consider the time interval between one instant and an earlier instant just as well as the time interval between one instant and a later instant.

Since we should like "speed" always to connote a non-negative quantity, we therefore say, in the case under discussion, that the average speed in the time interval between t and $t + h$ is:

$$\left| \frac{f(t + h) - f(t)}{h} \right|$$

and we shall call the expression (1) above the average *velocity* of the moving point in the time interval between t and $t + h$.

Actually, it is more useful to determine the velocity than to determine the speed of a moving point. For the velocity tells us both the speed and the *direction* of the motion. If the velocity is positive, then we know that the point is moving toward higher values on the scaled line as positive time elapses; and if the velocity is negative we know that the point is moving towards lower values on the scaled line as positive time elapses.

Now we define the *instantaneous velocity* of the moving point at time t to be:

$$v = L\left[\frac{f(t+h) - f(t)}{h}\right]$$

and the instantaneous *speed* at time t will be defined to be simply $|v|$.

For example, suppose that a bullet is fired straight upward from the ground, leaving the gun with a speed of 88 ft per second. Then in t seconds, if it were unaffected by gravity, it would *rise* to a height of $88t$ ft. But in t seconds, the force of gravity causes it to *fall* $16t^2$ ft. What actually happens, therefore, is that while it is in the air, at time t seconds after it is fired, its height above the ground is $88t - 16t^2$.

If we use a vertical scale with positive values upward and 0 at ground level, we may therefore say of the bullet:

Point reached at time t:

$$f(t) = 88t - 16t^2$$

Point reached at

time $t + h$:

$$f(t + h) = 88(t + h) - 16(t + h)^2$$
$$= 88t + 88h - 16t^2 - 32th - 16h^2$$

Distance traveled in time h
(or the negative of that
distance):

$$f(t + h) - f(t) = 88h - 32th - 16h^2$$

Average velocity:

$$\frac{f(t + h) - f(t)}{h} = 88 - 32t - 16h$$

Instantaneous velocity at time t:

$$v = L\left[\frac{f(t+h) - f(t)}{h}\right] = 88 - 32t \text{ (ft per second)}$$

When $t = 0$ seconds, this formula for v tells us that the bullet is traveling at a *speed* of 88 ft per second (upward, since v is a positive number in this case).

When $t = 1$ second, $v = 56$, i.e., the speed of the bullet is only 56 ft per second (upward). The falling off of speed is to be expected, however, since the force of gravity is slowing the bullet down.

When $t = 3$ seconds, $v = -8$ ft per second. This may be interpreted as a *speed* of 8 ft per second *downward*.

The bullet will be traveling upward when $v > 0$, i.e., when $88 - 32t > 0$, i.e., when $32t < 88$, i.e., when $t < 2\frac{3}{4}$ seconds.

The bullet will be traveling downward when $v < 0$, and as above, this may be shown to be when $t > 2\frac{3}{4}$ seconds.

At $t = 2\frac{3}{4}$, therefore, the bullet reaches its highest point. Since we know that at time t the bullet reaches the point $f(t) = 88t - 16t^2$, we may compute that the highest point reached by the bullet is

$$f\left(\frac{11}{4}\right) = 88 \cdot \frac{11}{4} - 16 \cdot \left(\frac{11}{4}\right)^2 - 121 \text{ ft}$$

The bullet is at ground level when $f(t) = 0$, i.e., when $88t - 16t^2 = 0$. Solving this equation:

$$t(88 - 16t) = 0$$
$$t = 0, 5\frac{1}{2}$$

Therefore the bullet takes $5\frac{1}{2}$ seconds to reach the ground after being fired. We see then that the time it takes to reach its highest point ($2\frac{3}{4}$ seconds) must be equal to the time it takes to fall from its highest point back to the ground; for $2\frac{3}{4}$ is exactly half of $5\frac{1}{2}$.

▶ **EXERCISE 70**

1. A point travels along a vertical scaled line (positive upward). Its position at time t is given by: $f(t) = t^2 - 11t + 10$.

(a) Draw a picture indicating the position of the point at times: $t = 0, 1, 2, 3, 4$.

(b) Find a formula for the speed at which the point is traveling at any time t.

(c) Use the formula to tell how fast the point is traveling at: $t = 0$, 1, 2, 3, 4.

(d) When will the point be traveling upward? When downward? When is the point at rest? When is it at point 0 on the scaled line?

2. A bullet is fired upward from the ground, leaving the gun with a speed of 96 ft per second.

Discuss the motion of the bullet as in the example of the preceding section; also, find the speed at which the bullet hits the ground when it falls. How does this compare with its speed when it left the gun?

3. Discuss the motion of a bullet fired *downward* from the top of a building 960 ft high, with an initial velocity of 96 ft per second.

4. A stone is dropped from the top of a building 400 ft high. How long does it take to reach the ground? How fast is it traveling when it reaches the ground?

5. The same as Problem 1, with $f(t) = t^2 + 10t$.

6. The same as Problem 1, with $f(t) = t^2 + t - 20$.

7. The Empire State Building is about 1000 ft high. How long does it take an object dropped from a height of 1024 ft to reach the ground? How fast is it traveling at the end of each second of its fall, and when it reaches the ground?

14.4 THE PROBLEM OF TANGENTS

Another problem to which mathematicians of the seventeenth century devoted a great deal of attention was that of drawing tangent lines to curves. We, in our mathematical education, have encountered the concept of a tangent line in connection with a particular curve, the circle. The student will recall that a tangent line to a circle was defined to be a straight line whose intersection with the circle consisted of exactly one point (Fig. 14.3).   (From which it followed that a tangent line to a circle with center O is a line perpendicular to a radius OP at P.)

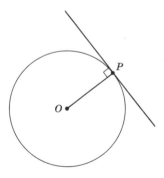

Fig. 14.3

But for most curves, in fact even for any arc of a circle, this definition will not do (Fig. 14.4).

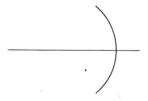

Fig. 14.4

We shall therefore frame a definition of a tangent line to a curve which applies more generally.

Let us suppose that we are given a curve C and a point P on the curve (Fig. 14.5), and that we are required to draw a line which shall be tangent to C at P.

Fig. 14.5

Suppose that in our first attempt to draw the required tangent line, we place a ruler down upon the paper so that it passes through P, but the ruler happens to intersect C in another point Q (Fig. 14.6).

Fig. 14.6

In most cases, the resulting line PQ would not seem to us to be tangent to C. However, whatever we mean by being "tangent," we would probably all agree that if point Q were very near point P, then the line PQ would come very close to being tangent to C (Fig. 14.7).

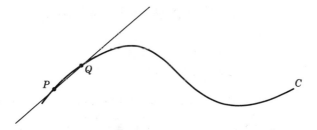

Fig. 14.7

We therefore devise the following physical experiment:

Drive a nail through a long thin rod, into the point P, so that the rod is free to pivot about the point P. Supposing that the rod intersects C

again at Q, snap a small ring about both the rod and the curve at Q. (One may imagine this done in Fig. 14.7.) Now slide the ring along the curve toward P. As the ring approaches P, the rod turns. *When the ring reaches P*, the rod will have turned to a position which it is reasonable to call a *tangent* position.

We shall use this idea in framing our definition of a tangent.

To make matters more precise, we shall assume that the curve C is drawn upon a coordinate system. A tangent line at the point P on the curve C will be determined as soon as we know its slope. The physical experiment we have just described leads us to make the following definition:

> Let C be a curve in a cc system, P a point on C. Let Q be another point on C. Suppose that the *slope* of line PQ approaches a limit m as Q approaches P along the curve C.
>
> Then a line through P with slope m is said to be a *tangent line* to the curve C.

An illustration will help to make this concept clear:

Suppose C is the curve called a parabola whose equation is $y = x^2$, and suppose we wish to draw a tangent line to C at the point $P(2, 4)$.

Now suppose Q is a point (different from P) on C, whose x-value differs from the x-value of P by h; more precisely, suppose:

$$x_Q = x_P + h = 2 + h, \text{ and } h \neq 0$$

(Note that in Fig. 14.8, Q happens to have been chosen so that $h < 0$.)

Since Q is on C, its coordinates must satisfy the equation of C. Therefore:

$$y_Q = x_Q{}^2 = (2 + h)^2 = 4 + 4h + h^2$$

The slope of line PQ, then, is:

$$\frac{y_Q - y_P}{x_Q - x_P} = \frac{4h + h^2}{h} = 4 + h$$

(Since $h \neq 0$, the cancellation of the factor h from the numerator and denominator of the preceding fraction is valid.)

Now we note that letting the point Q approach the point P along the parabola is equivalent to letting the number $h = x_Q - x_P$ approach the number 0. Therefore the limit that is approached by the slope of line PQ, as Q approaches P along C is: $L(4 + h)$, i.e., 4.

A tangent line T to the parabola C may therefore be drawn at the point (2, 4) by drawing a line with slope 4 through that point (Fig. 14.8).

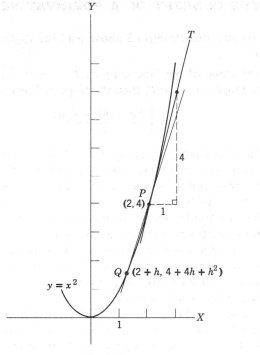

Fig. 14.8

▶ **EXERCISE 71**

1. Find the slope of the tangent line to the curve $y = x^2$ at each of the following points, and use this information to draw each tangent line:

(a) $(1, 1)$ (b) $(-1, 1)$ (c) $(-2, 4)$ (d) $(0, 0)$ (e) (a, a^2)

2. Draw the graph of the equation $y = x^2 + 5x - 6$. Then find the slope of the tangent line to this graph at each of the following points, and use this information to draw each tangent line:

(a) $(1, 0)$ (b) $(0, -6)$ (c) $(2, 8)$ (d) $(-6, 0)$
(e) the point whose x-value is a.

3. Suppose $y = f(x)$ is the equation of a curve C, and P is a point on C whose x-value is a. Then clearly $y_P = f(a)$, and P is the point $[a, f(a)]$.

(a) If Q is a point on C whose x-value is $a + h$, then Q is the point $(a + h, ?)$.

(b) Assuming $h \neq 0$, what expression represents the slope of line PQ?

(c) If a tangent line to the curve C at the point P exists, what expression represents the slope of that tangent line?

14.5 THE CONCEPT OF A "DERIVATIVE" FUNCTION

It was intended that Problem 3 above lead the student to the following conclusion:

If C is the graph of the function $f(x)$, $P = [a, f(a)]$ a point on C, and if l is a line tangent to C at P, then the slope of line l is:

$$L\left[\frac{f(a + h) - f(a)}{h}\right]$$

But we have encountered this expression before, in an entirely different context! It is (with the replacement of the letter "a" by the letter "t") exactly the expression at which we arrived in our search for a formula for instantaneous velocity (see Section 14.3).

From the situation involving tangent lines, and the situation involving instantaneous velocities, mathematicians have *abstracted* the idea of a "derivative" function, which they study independently. The results of that study are then applicable to problems involving tangent lines to curves, and to problems involving instantaneous speeds, and in fact to a great many other problems as well.

Before we define what is meant by a derivative function, we shall find it convenient to generalize the definition of an "interval" given on page 29. In what follows, we shall understand an *interval* of real numbers to mean a set of real numbers of one of the following four types:

(i) All real numbers between and including two different given real numbers a and b. (This is the type that we have already encountered, and that we have denoted $\{a \cdot\!\!-\!\!\cdot b\}$.)

(ii) All real numbers $\geqslant$ some given real number a.

(iii) All real numbers $\leqslant$ some given real number a.

(iv) All real numbers.

In the first three cases, a and b are called *endpoints* of their respective intervals.

When real numbers are associated with points on a scaled line, the four cases above are seen to represent, respectively:

(i) A line segment. (All points between two different given points on the line.)

(ii) A ray. (All points to the right of, and including, a given point on the line.)

(iii) A ray. (All points to the left of, and including, a given point on the line.)

(iv) The whole scaled line.

Now we are ready to make our definition of a derivative function:

Let f be a real-real function whose domain D is an interval of real numbers.

Let D' be the set of all elements x in D such that $L\left[\dfrac{f(x + h) - f(x)}{h}\right]$ exists.

Then the *derivative function of f*, denoted f', is a function with domain D' and mapping given by:

$$f'(x) = L\left[\frac{f(x + h) - f(x)}{h}\right]$$

NOTES.   (1)   The *derivative function* is often called simply the *derivative*. The process of finding a derivative is called *differentiation*.   For example, we say that when we differentiate x^2, the result is $2x$.

(2)   In the case of a polynomial function f (although we shall not prove this fact), $f'(x)$ exists for all real numbers x in the domain of D; that is to say, D' and D are the same.

Illustrative Example 1.   Let $f(x) = x^2$, and suppose the domain of f is $\{0 \longmapsto 3\}$.   Find f'.

SOLUTION.   Since f is a polynomial function, the domain of f' is $\{0 \longmapsto 3\}$ also.   As for the mapping of f':

$$f'(x) = L\left[\frac{f(x + h) - f(x)}{h}\right] = L\left[\frac{(x + h)^2 - x^2}{h}\right] = L\left[\frac{2hx + h^2}{h}\right]$$

$$= L[2x + h] = 2x$$

Illustrative Example 2.   Let $f(x) = x^2 - 3x + 2$, and suppose the domain of f is the set of all real numbers.   Find f'.

SOLUTION.   The domain of f' is the set of all real numbers.   In finding the mapping of f', we find it convenient to work out successively:

$f(x + h) = (x + h)^2 - 3(x + h) + 2 = x^2 + 2hx + h^2 - 3x - 3h + 2$

$f(x) \qquad = \qquad\qquad\qquad\quad x^2 \qquad\quad - 3x \qquad + 2$

$f(x + h) - f(x) = 2hx + h^2 - 3h$

$\dfrac{f(x + h) - f(x)}{h} = 2x + h - 3$

$f'(x) = L\left[\dfrac{f(x + h) - f(x)}{h}\right] = L[2x - h + 3] = 2x + 3$

Each of these results may now be interpreted in two important ways. For example, the result of Illustrative Example 1 above may be interpreted in the following two ways:

(i) If the position of a point on a scaled line at any time t between $t = 0$ and $t = 3$ is given by the formula $f(t) = t^2$, then the instantaneous velocity of that point at any time t between $t = 0$ and $t = 3$ is $f'(t) = 2t$.

Thus at $t = 1$ the point is at the position marked 1 on the scaled line, and its instantaneous velocity at that moment is 2 (units of distance per unit of time).

(ii) If G is the graph of the function $f(x) = x^2$, drawn between $x = 0$ and $x = 3$, and P is a point on G, then $f'(x_P) = 2x_P$ is the slope of the tangent line to G at P.

Thus, the slope of the tangent line to G at $(3, 9)$ is $f'(3)$, or 6.

It may now be explained that the branch of mathematics known as "differential calculus" is nothing more than a study of derivative functions, and their many applications to other branches of mathematics and to other sciences. These latter applications, although for a long time restricted primarily to physical sciences, have recently widened greatly in scope. At present it is a very rare branch of learning to which the differential calculus has not made some contribution.

▶ **EXERCISE 72**

In each of the following problems, the domain of f is to be the interval $\{0 \cdot\!\!-\!\!\cdot 5\}$. In each case, draw the graph of f, find f', and interpret your result for f' in two ways. Make use of one interpretation to draw the tangent to the graph at the point on the graph for which $x = 3$.

1. $f(x) = 0.5x^2$ 2. $f(x) = 3x$
3. $f(x) = 0.5x^2 + 3x$ 4. $f(x) = 0.5x^2 - 3x$
5. $f(x) = 5$ 6. $f(x) = 0.5x^2 - 3x + 5$
7. $f(x) = x$ 8. $f(x) = x + 5$
9. $f(x) = 3$ 10. $f(x) = 0.1x^3$

14.6 SHORT-CUTS IN FINDING DERIVATIVES

We *induce*, from the results of the preceding exercise, the following conclusions:

(i) If $f(x) = a$, where a is a real number, then $f'(x) = 0$.

(ii) If $f(x) = g(x) + h(x) + \cdots + j(x)$, and all these functions have derivatives, then $f'(x) = g'(x) + h'(x) + \cdots + j'(x)$.

(iii) If $f(x) = ax^n$, where a is a real number and n is a positive integer, then $f'(x) = nax^{n-1}$.

(iv) If $f(x) = ax$, where a is a real number, then $f'(x) = a$. [This is a corollary to (iii) above.]

Although we shall omit proofs here, these conclusions are all true, and extremely useful in finding derivatives of polynomial, and even other functions. For example, with their help Problem 6 of the preceding exercise may now be worked as follows:

$$f(x) = 0.5x^2 - 3x + 5$$
$$f'(x) = (2)(0.5)x^1 - (3) + (0) = x - 3$$

14.7   DERIVATIVES AND GRAPHS

Suppose P is a point on the graph G of a function $f(x)$, and that there is a line tangent to G at P. Then we know that $f'(x_P)$ is the slope of that tangent line. We know also that the tangent line will slant up to the right if its slope is positive, up to the left if its slope is negative, and that it will be horizontal if its slope is zero. Figure 14.9 illustrates various ways in which these possibilities may occur on a graph.

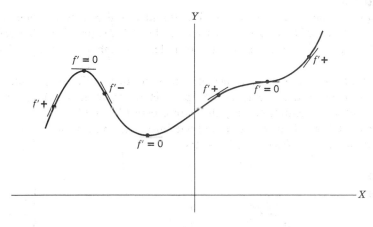

Fig. 14.9

We see, speaking intuitively, that as we go from left to right, the graph of a function will rise when its derivative is positive, fall when its derivative is negative, and "level off" when its derivative is zero.

We apply these statements now to the problem of drawing several graphs:

(i) $f(x) = x^2$. In this case $f'(x) = 2x$. Clearly, $f'(x)$ is negative when x is negative, zero when x is zero, and positive when x is positive. Going from left to right, then, the graph must fall until it reaches $x = 0$, level off at $x = 0$, and rise after $x = 0$. The student will note that this is consistent with our previous drawings of this graph.

(ii) $f(x) = 0.2x^3 + 0.3x^2 - 1.2x - 0.6$. Then $f'(x) = 0.6x^2 + 0.6x - 1.2$, or $f'(x) = 0.6(x - 1)(x + 2)$. Clearly $f'(x) = 0$ when $x = 1$ and when $x = -2$, so that the graph levels off at the points $(1, -1.3)$ and $(-2, 1.4)$.

The points $x = -2$ and $x = 1$ at which $f'(x) = 0$ separate the X-axis into three intervals. We investigate the sign of $f'(x)$ in each of these intervals:

$$\underset{-2}{\overset{\bullet}{\rule{3cm}{0.4pt}}}\underset{1}{\overset{\bullet}{\rule{3cm}{0.4pt}}}\rule{2cm}{0.4pt}$$

When $x < -2$, then $x - 1 < -3 < 0$, and $x + 2 < 0$, so that $f'(x)$ is the product of two negative factors, hence $f'(x)$ is positive. Therefore to the left of $x = -2$, as we go from left to right, the graph rises.

When $-2 < x < 1$, then $x + 2 > 0$ and $x - 1 < 0$. Therefore $f'(x)$ is the product of two factors of opposite sign, so that $f'(x)$ is negative. Therefore, between $x = -2$ and $x = 1$, as we go from left to right, the graph falls.

Finally, when $x > 1$, then $x - 1 > 0$ and $x + 2 > 3 > 0$. Here $f'(x)$ is the product of two positive factors, so that $f'(x)$ is positive. Therefore to the right of $x = 1$, as we go from left to right, the graph always rises.

Substituting a few more values of x into the formula for $f(x)$ would lead to a more accurate and extensive graph. Here, however, we shall content ourselves with computing only the Y-intercept $(0, -0.6)$.

Now, in Fig. 14.10, we use the above information in drawing the graph of $f(x) = 0.2x^3 + 0.3x^2 - 1.2x - 0.6$.

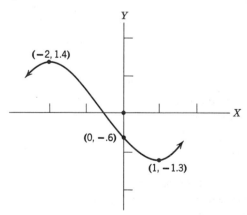

Fig. 14.10

▶ **EXERCISE 73**

1. For each $f(x)$ in the preceding exercise, find $f'(x)$ by means of a short-cut method.

2. In each of the following cases, find $f'(x)$ by means of a short-cut formula: $f(x) =$

(a) $3x^2 - 2x + 5$ (b) $5x^3 - 2x^2 + 1$
(c) $3 + 32x^2$ (d) $x^5 + 4x^3 - 2x + 15$
(e) $3 - 27x^4 + x$ (f) $3 + 10x + 2x^2$
(g) $2(x^2 - 1) - x^3$ (h) $4x^4 + 2x^3 - x^2 + 3x + 7$
(i) $(x - 3)(2x + 4)$ (j) $1 + 2x - 14x^3 + x^7$
(k) $1 - x - x^2 - x^3 - x^4 - x^5$ (l) $x^5 - 2x^2$
(m) $0.5x^2 + 0.4x^5 - 1 - x$ (n) $x + 1$

3. Making use of the derivative and several easily computed points, draw the graph of each of the following functions of x:

(a) $x^2 + 2x - 3$ (b) $2x^2 - 4$
(c) x^5 (d) $3x^2$
(e) $3x^2 - 2x$ (f) $3x^2 - 2x + 1$
(g) $x^3 - 12x + 1$ (h) x^3
(i) $x^4 - 2x^2 + 2$ (j) x^4
(k) $x^3 - x^2 - 5$ (l) $x^2(x - 3)$
(m) $x^4 - 2x^2$ (n) $x^3 - x^2 - x + 1$
(o) $x^{10} - 2x^5 + 2$

14.8 MAXIMUM AND MINIMUM PROBLEMS

Problems that involve the discovery of maximum or minimum values are among the most important encountered in applied mathematics. Here is an example of such a problem:

A farmer has 60 ft of fencing. He wishes to make a rectangular enclosure, using his fencing for three sides of the enclosure, and a long wall (over 60 ft in length) for the fourth.

What should be the dimensions of the enclosure, in order for it to be of maximum size (i.e., area)?

One might, as a first guess, try dividing the 60 ft equally among the three sides of fencing. In that case the area of the enclosure would be 400 square ft. But it is easily seen that we can do better—for the lengths 19, 19, 22 (feet) for these three sides would result in an area of 418 square ft.

What lengths, then, *would* give the greatest area?

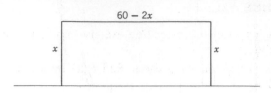

Fig. 14.11

Suppose we let x represent the length in feet of each of the equal sides of fencing. Then the other side of fencing must be $60 - 2x$, and if we denote the area of the square by y:

$$y = x(60 - 2x) = -2x^2 + 60x$$

We point out that the length of a side of fencing cannot be negative. Therefore

$$x \geqslant 0; \text{ and } 60 - 2x \geqslant 0, \text{ i.e., } 60 \geqslant 2x, \text{ i.e., } 30 \geqslant x$$

In summary: $0 \leqslant x \leqslant 30$.

Thus the problem may now be expressed as follows: To find a value of x, between 0 and 30, for which y is a maximum.

Or, if we think in graphical terms, it is to find the highest point on the graph of $y = -2x^2 + 60x$, where the graph is drawn over the interval $0 \leqslant x \leqslant 30$.

In fact the graph will help greatly in discovering an answer to our problem. (See Fig. 14.12.)

It appears from the graph that maximum area y will be attained when $x = 15$; hence, when $60 - 2x = 30$. Thus, the answer to the farmer's

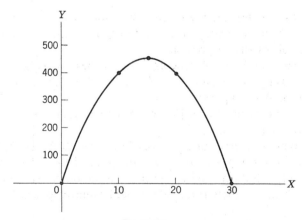

Fig. 14.12

problem is that the enclosure should be 15 ft wide and 30 ft long, and with these dimensions a maximum area of 450 square feet will be attained.

In the following problems the student will be expected to make use of a graph in searching for maximum or minimum values. This method, which often can yield only an approximate result, will later on be replaced by the more precise methods of differential calculus.

▶ **EXERCISE 74**

1. A wire whose length is 24 ft is to be bent into a rectangle. What should the length and width of the rectangle be in order for the area of the rectangle to be a maximum?

2. For a given perimeter p show that a square is the largest rectangle that can be constructed.

3. At the end of x seconds, a ball thrown upward with an initial velocity of 96 ft per second will be at a height y given by the formula: $y = 96x - 16x^2$. What is the maximum height reached by the ball?

4. An open rectangular tank with square base is to contain 750 cubic feet. If the base costs $6 per square foot and the sides cost $4 per square foot, find the dimensions which make the cost a minimum. (*Hint:* If the base is x units long and the height h, then $x^2h = 750$, or $h = 750/x^2$. The cost y of the box is given by $y = 6 \cdot x^2 + 4 \cdot 4xh = 6x^2 + (12000/x)$. Now draw a graph.)

5. A square sheet of tin whose edge is 12 inches long is to be made into an open box by cutting four equal squares from its corners and bending up the projecting portions thus formed. What should be the edge of each square removed if the volume of the box is to be a maximum?

6. If a positive real number is added to its reciprocal, what is the least possible result, and what positive real number produces this minimum result?

7. Find the minimum length of fencing required to go around three sides of a rectangular plot containing 200 square feet.

8. (*a*) A bus company is about to put into operation a bus which accommodates 30 passengers. It finds, after a survey, that if it charges $x for a trip, where $1 \leqslant x \leqslant 10$, then it can count on $5(10 - x)$ or more potential passengers for the trip. Assuming that the cost of the trip to the bus company is the same no matter how many passengers are carried, what should the bus company charge each passenger, in order to achieve a maximum income for the trip?

(*b*) What if the $5(10 - x)$ above were $10(10 - x)$?

14.9 DERIVATIVES AND EXTREMA

Problems involving "extrema" (i.e., maxima and minima) may often be handled very nicely by means of derivatives.

Consider, for example, the problem we discussed in the preceding section. The problem of maximizing the area of a certain enclosure reduced to finding the maximum value of the following function:

$$f(x) = -2x^2 + 60x \qquad [0 \leqslant x \leqslant 30]$$

In this case: $f'(x) = -4x + 60$.

Now, thinking of the problem graphically, we seek the highest point on the graph of $f(x) = -2x^2 + 60x$, between $x = 0$ and $x = 30$. It will therefore be useful to know when the graph is rising and when it is falling (as we move from left to right).

But (see Section 14.7) the graph rises when $f'(x)$ is positive and falls when $f'(x)$ is negative.

Therefore our graph rises when $-4x + 60 > 0$, i.e., when $60 > 4x$, or when $15 > x$, or when $x < 15$.

And our graph falls when $-4x + 60 < 0$, i.e., when $60 < 4x$, or when $15 < x$, or when $x > 15$.

Now unless our function behaves peculiarly at $x = 15$, since it rises to the left of $x = 15$ and since it falls to the right of $x = 15$, it must have a maximum value at $x = 15$.

(It may be proved that a peculiarity of the sort mentioned above can never occur with a polynomial function; and for a function that is the ratio of polynomial functions, i.e., for a rational function, it can occur at $x = a$ only if the denominator of the given function is zero at $x = a$.)

▶ EXERCISE 75

Note: The following formula, presented here without proof, will extend the range of problems which we can work by means of short-cut methods:

If $f(x) = a/x^n$, where a is any real number and n is any positive integer, then $f'(x) = -an/x^{n+1}$. (f and f' have the same domain: all real numbers except 0.)

For example, if $f(x) = \dfrac{7}{x^{11}}$, then $f'(x) = \dfrac{-77}{x^{12}}$.

1. Work the problems of the preceding exercise, being careful in each case to state the domain of the function involved, and using the derivative to locate extreme values.

2. In each of the problems of the exercise following Section 14.3 find, by a short-cut method, a formula for the speed at which the object is traveling at any time, t.

3. Show that the graph of $f(x) = 1/x^2$ is peculiar in that (as we go from left to right) it rises to the left of $x = 0$ and falls to the right of $x = 0$, but does not have a maximum value at $x = 0$.

4. In each of the following cases, find a polynomial function whose derivative is:

(a) $2x$ (b) $3x^2$ (c) $4x^3$
(d) x (e) x^2 (f) x^3
(g) 1 (h) 0 (i) $2x + 3x^2$
(j) $3x^2 - 4x^3$ (k) 2 (l) $3x$
(m) $2x^2$ (n) $x^2 - 3x + 1$ (o) $x + 1$

5. The same as Problem 3 above, for $f(x) = 1 - |x| + \tilde{x}$, where $\tilde{x}$ represents the greatest integer $< x$, and the domain of f is $\{-\frac{1}{2} \cdot\!-\!\cdot \frac{1}{2}\}$.

(Functions whose graphs are "broken" at a value of x are said to be *discontinuous* at that value (cf. (ii), page 282). For example, the functions of Problems 3 and 5 above are both discontinuous at $x = 0$.)

14.10 THE CONVERSE PROBLEM: INTEGRATION

The mathematician, faced with the process of differentiation, would inevitably wonder about the converse process. Instead of seeking the derivative of a given function, he might endeavor instead to find a function whose derivative is equal to the given function.

For example, the derivative of $3x^2$ is $6x$. But is there a function whose derivative is $3x^2$? It is not hard to see that in this case there is, namely the function x^3.

The process which reverses differentiation is called *integration*; and if one function is the derivative of another function, we say that the second is an *integral function* or an *integral* of the first.

Thus, since the derivative of $3x^2$ is $6x$, we may say that an integral of $6x$ is $3x^2$.

Definition. An *integral* of a given function is a function whose derivative is equal to the given function.

But note that an integral of a function is not unique. For example x^2, $x^2 + 1$, $x^2 - 1$, $x^2 + \pi$, etc., are all integrals of the function $2x$; that is to say, each has the derivative $2x$.

The process of integration turns out to be not only interesting from the mathematical point of view, but of great practical importance as well. The study of integration and its applications is called "the integral calculus;" it was investigated by Leibniz and Newton also. We shall examine several of the important applications of the integral calculus as soon as we have developed a little of the technique of integration.

First of all, we note that an integral of a polynomial function of the form ax^n is easily induced (see Problem 4, Exercise 75). Simply by differentiating the function $\dfrac{a}{n+1} x^{n+1}$, one may verify that it is an integral of the polynomial function ax^n; for if

$$f(x) = \frac{a}{n+1} x^{n+1}$$

then:
$$f'(x) = (n+1) \cdot \frac{a}{n+1} x^n = ax^n$$

For example, an integral of the function x^3 is $\frac{1}{4} x^4$.

Other integrals of x^3 are, of course, $\frac{1}{4} x^4 + 7$, $\frac{1}{4} x^4 - \sqrt{2}$, etc., since the real numbers added have derivatives of 0. For a large class of functions, other integrals may be derived in no other way. That is to say, given one integral of a function, any other integral of that function must differ from the first by only a real number. In this chapter, we shall consider only functions which behave in this way.

Since a sum or difference may be differentiated term by term, it is not hard to see that a similar fact is true for the reverse process of integration. We now summarize several of our preceding assertions about integration. *For the functions which we shall integrate:*

(i) An integral of the polynomial function ax^n is the function $\dfrac{a}{n+1} x^{n+1}$.

(ii) If $I(x)$ is one integral of the function $f(x)$, then the set of all integrals of $f(x)$ consist of all functions of the form $I(x) + r$, where r is a real number.

(iii) If the functions $f(x)$ and $g(x)$ have integrals, then an integral of the function $f(x) \pm g(x)$ is:

[an integral of $f(x) \pm$ an integral of $g(x)$]

Note that if $f(x) = a$, where a is a real number, then an integral of $f(x)$ is ax. We sometimes express this by saying that an integral of the real number a, *with respect to* x is ax.

Illustrative Example. Find all integrals of: $1 + 3x - 4x^2$.

SOLUTION. *An* integral of $1 + 3x - 4x^2$ is $1x + \frac{3}{2} x^2 - \frac{4}{3} x^3$, or $x + \frac{3}{2} x^2 - \frac{4}{3} x^3$.

Any function of the form $x + \frac{3}{2} x^2 - \frac{4}{3} x^3 + r$, where r is a real number, is an integral of $1 + 3x - 4x^2$, and there are no others.

▶ **EXERCISE 76**

1. Integrate (i.e., find all integrals of) the following functions.

(a) 0   (b) 1   (c) -1

(d) x (e) $-2x$ (f) $2 + 3x$

(g) $3 - 2x$ (h) $x - x^2$ (i) $3x^2 + 2x - 1$

(j) $4x^3 - 5x^4 + 1$ (k) $x^3 + x^2 - x + 1$ (l) $16t^2$

(m) $(x + 1)^2$ (n) $(2x + 1)^2$ (o) $(x + 1)(x - 1)$

2. An elementary practical application of the concept of an integral occurs in physical situations where the velocity of a particle moving along a scaled line is known, and one seeks information concerning the position of the particle.

For example, suppose it is known that the velocity of a particle moving along a scaled line is $2t$ at time t. Then if $f(t)$ represents the real number marking the position of the particle on the line at time t, $f(t)$ must be an integral of $2t$ [for the velocity is the derivative of $f(t)$].

Therefore $f(t) = t^2 + r$, where r is a real number.

To determine r, we need more information. Suppose we knew, in addition, that at time $t = 3$ the particle is at the point 7 on the scaled line. Then since: $f(t) = t^2 + r$

We have: $7 = 9 + r$

so that $r = -2$. Therefore the position of the particle at time t is: $f(t) = t^2 - 2$.

(a) If the velocity at time t of a particle moving along a scaled line is $32t$, and at $t = 0$ the particle is at the 0-point on the scaled line, find a formula $f(t)$ for the position of the particle at time t; find where the particle is at $t = 10$; draw a diagram to illustrate the position of the particle at times $t = 1, 2, 3, 4, 5$.

(b) The same as (a), but the velocity is $t - 1$, and at $t = 0$ the particle is at the point 4 on the scaled line.

14.11 THE PROBLEM OF AREA

An important application of the process of integration is to finding the areas of geometric figures. As an example, we shall find the area bounded by a parabolic arc and two straight line segments.

In particular, we shall compute the area bounded by the parabola $y = x^2$, the X-axis, and the line whose equation is $x = 3$. (Fig. 14.13.)

But in order to solve this problem, we shall find it convenient to solve even a more general problem: namely, to find a formula for the area

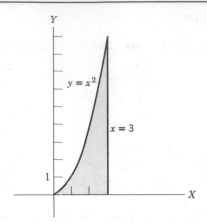

Fig. 14.13

bounded by the parabola $y = x^2$, the X-axis, and a vertical line with X-intercept x. (Fig. 14.14.)

We shall make several plausible assumptions. First of all, we shall assume that for each real value of x, a certain area A is bounded; that is to say, we assume that there is a function f such that $A = f(x)$.

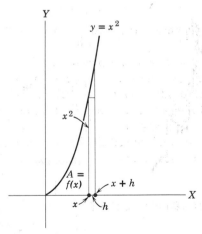

Fig. 14.14

Secondly, we assume that when $x = 0$, the area which is bounded by the three given boundaries is zero; i.e., we assume that $f(0) = 0$.

Now, assuming that x is positive (as in Fig. 14.14), suppose we draw a vertical line through the point $x + h$ on the X-axis, where h is a small positive number.

Then the area bounded by the new vertical line, the parabola, and the X-axis will be $f(x + h)$. The area of the strip between the original and new areas will be the difference of these areas, or $f(x + h) - f(x)$.

But if h is small, this strip will be very nearly a rectangle, with base h and height x^2. (Since the equation of the parabola is $y = x^2$, the ordinate that corresponds to an abscissa of x is x^2.) Therefore, for small h, the area of the strip is approximately hx^2.

Therefore we have (for small h):

$$f(x + h) - f(x) \doteq hx^2$$

so that:
$$\frac{f(x + h) - f(x)}{h} \doteq x^2$$

These are approximate equalities which would seem to improve as h grows smaller and smaller, i.e., as h approaches 0. For as h becomes smaller and smaller, it appears that the error made when we assumed that a certain strip of area was practically a rectangle, becomes less and less.

We may interpret this situation to mean that as h approaches 0, the quantity $\dfrac{f(x + h) - f(x)}{h}$ approaches the value x^2; i.e.:

$$L\left[\frac{f(x + h) - f(x)}{h}\right] = x^2$$

But:
$$L\left[\frac{f(x + h) - f(x)}{h}\right] = f'(x)$$

Therefore:
$$f'(x) = x^2$$

Integrating:
$$f(x) = \tfrac{1}{3} x^3 + r, \text{ where } r \text{ is a real number.}$$

Now we have stipulated above that $f(0) = 0$. By the preceding formula, $f(0) = r$. Therefore $r = 0$, and our formula for area becomes:

(1)
$$A = \tfrac{1}{3} x^3$$

The answer to our original problem, to find the area bounded by the parabola $y = x^2$, the X-axis, and the line $x = 3$ may now be given:

$$A = \tfrac{1}{3} \cdot 3^3 = 9 \text{ (square units)}$$

In fact, the formula (1) will now give us the area bounded by the parabola $y = x^2$, the X-axis, and any vertical line with non-negative abscissa x.

Just as in this special case, we may arrive at the following general principle:

Suppose that the curve $y = g(x)$ lies in the first quadrant and bounds, together with the X- and Y-axes, and a vertical line with abscissa x, an area (Fig. 14.15).

Then the area is equal to that integral of $g(x)$ which is 0 when $x = 0$.

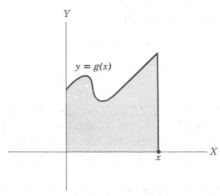

Fig. 14.15

Similarly, by means of the integral calculus one may find the areas of many more general plane figures (as for example the areas enclosed by circles and ellipses), as well as the surface areas and volumes of solids and the lengths of curves.

NOTE. It must be emphasized that the treatment of this chapter, and in particular that of the preceding section is highly intuitive. The advantage of this approach is that one arrives rather quickly at results which are both correct and powerful. It is typical of mathematics that results are often derived by rough-and-ready methods such as these. But to be *sure* that the results are correct, and even to be able to state quite clearly what is being said, a much more careful treatment is necessary. Such expositions exist, of course, but their length and detailed nature make them inappropriate in this introduction to the subject.

▶ **EXERCISE 77**

1. Find the area bounded by:

(a) The parabola $y = x^2$, the X-axis, and the line $x = 2$.

(b) The parabola $y = 3x^2$, the X-axis, and the line $x = 2$.

(c) The parabola $y = x^2$, the parabola $y = 3x^2$, and the line $x = 2$.

(d) The parabolas $y = x^2$ and $x = y^2$.

(e) The line $y = x$, the X-axis, and the line $x = 1$.

(*f*) The line $y = x$, the line $y = 2x$, and the line $x = 1$.

(*g*) The curve $y = x^3$, the X-axis and the line $x = 1$.

(*h*) The curves $y = x^2$ and $y = x^3$.

2. Prove that the curves $y = x^2$ and $x = y^2$ separate the square with vertices $(0, 0)$, $(0, 1)$, $(1, 0)$, $(1, 1)$ into three equal areas.

14.12   THE PROBLEM OF WORK

Climbing to the top of the Empire State building is hard work. But how much work? The physicist considers that work has been done when a force has been exerted over a certain distance, and measures the amount of the work by (roughly speaking) the product of the force and the distance.

The force that must be exerted to lift a 200-pound man from the ground is: 200 pounds. If that man were to climb the height of the Empire State building, a height of about 1000 feet, he would do 200×1000, or 200,000 *foot-pounds* of work.

But why the phrase "roughly speaking" above? Actually, it has to do with the possibility of forces that are variable. If a constant force is exerted over a distance, the rule given above for computing work is not rough, but quite precise. But just as velocities in nature are rarely constant, so with natural forces also.

Consider, for example, the force necessary to stretch a spring. Initially the force is small, but as we extend the spring, it resists further extension more and more forcibly. At each point of the spring's extension a different force is exerted; the greater the extension, the greater the force.

Problems involving quantities that change continually, as force does in the case of a spring being stretched, or as velocity does in the case of a falling body, are typically problems to which calculus applies. We have already seen how the calculus, both differential and integral, is useful in solving certain velocity problems. We shall now show how the problem of the work done by a variable force that moves in a straight line may be solved by means of the integral calculus.

We shall begin with this problem: Suppose a force of 5 pounds will stretch a spring 1 inch from its initial position. How much work will be done in stretching the spring 10 inches from its initial position?

In order to do this problem it is necessary to know that within certain limits of stretching (and we shall assume in this problem that we are not exceeding these limits), the force exerted at any point of the extension is proportional to the amount of extension.

That is to say, if an end of the spring is initially at a point 0 on a scaled line, and then is brought to a non-negative point x on that scaled line, then the force F being exerted on the spring at the moment when the moving end is at point x, is given by a formula:

$$F = kx$$

where k is a real number. (Fig. 14.16.)

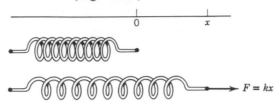

Fig. 14.16

Since we are given that $F = 5$ when $x = 1$, we have, in the case of this particular spring:

$$5 = k \cdot 1$$

so that $k = 5$.   Therefore, for the spring which is involved in our problem:

$$F = 5x$$

We will assume that the work w which is done in stretching the spring from its initial position to point x is a function of x; i.e., $w = f(x)$; and that no work is done when no stretching takes place, i.e., that $f(0) = 0$.

Now suppose we stretch the spring a small distance h farther than x, to the point $x + h$.

Then the work done in stretching the spring from point 0 to point $x + h$ is $f(x + h)$.   Since the work done in stretching the spring from 0 to x is $f(x)$, the work done in stretching the spring from x to $x + h$ would seem to be $f(x + h) - f(x)$.

Now we make the really crucial assumption that if h is small, then although the force on the spring changes between x and $x + h$, *it does not change very much*; so that no greater error is made by assuming that the force between x and $x + h$ is approximately what it was at x, namely $5x$. In that case, the work done in stretching the spring from x to $x + h$ would be the product of the constant force $5x$ by the distance h, namely $5xh$ (approximately).   Therefore, from this paragraph and the last, we have:

$$f(x + h) - f(x) \doteq 5xh$$

so that:

$$\frac{f(x + h) - f(x)}{h} \doteq 5x$$

These are approximate equalities which, as in the preceding case of areas, improve as h approaches 0; for the smaller h is, the less the force between x and $x + h$ will deviate from the force at x.

We may interpret this situation to mean that as h approaches 0, the quantity $\dfrac{f(x + h) - f(x)}{h}$ approaches $5x$; i.e.,

$$L\left[\frac{f(x + h) - f(x)}{h}\right] = 5x$$

But: $$L\left[\frac{f(x + h) - f(x)}{h}\right] = f'(x)$$

Therefore: $$f'(x) = 5x$$

Integrating: $$f(x) = \tfrac{5}{2}x^2 + r, \text{ where } r \text{ is a real number.}$$

We stipulated above that $f(0) = 0$. By the preceding formula, $f(0) = r$. Therefore $r = 0$, and our formula for work becomes:

(1) $$w = \tfrac{5}{2}x^2$$

To solve our original problem, then, if a force of 5 pounds stretches a spring 1 inch from its initial position, then the work done in stretching the spring 10 inches from its initial position will be:

$$w = \tfrac{5}{2}(10)^2 = 250 \text{ inch-pounds}$$

Just as in this special case, we may arrive at the following general principle:

Suppose that the force which is exerted at any point x of a given scaled line is $g(x)$.

Then the work done in exerting that force over the interval $\{0 \longrightarrow x\}$ is equal to that integral of $g(x)$ which is 0 when $x = 0$.

14.13 REMARKS ON THE CALCULUS

First of all, why so often the reference to "the" calculus? This is simply a matter of tradition. Before the time of Newton and Leibniz (and to some extent this holds true even today) a "calculus" meant a method of calculation. The "differential" and "integral" calculi of Newton and Leibniz were very special methods of calculation, sufficiently distinctive so that the combination of the two became known as *the* calculus.

Furthermore, no treatment of the calculus, not even one as brief as ours, would be complete without some consideration of the classical symbols of the calculus: Δ, d, and $\int$. These symbols are important not only because people have come to recognize their use as typifying the calculus, but also because they lend themselves to very fruitful intuitive manipulation, leading to results which more rigorous treatments have shown to be by and large correct.

The symbol Δ (the Greek letter "delta") is used to indicate a difference. If, for example, $x = 7$ is an original value of x, and $x = 11$ is a new value of x, we write $\Delta x = 4$ (read "delta x equals 4"), meaning that the difference between the new and old values of x is 4.

If now we consider the function $f(x) = 2x$, we see that when $x = 4$, $f(x) = 8$, and when $x = 7, f(x) = 14$. We say here that $\Delta f = 14 - 8 = 6$; or summarizing, we say that when $f(x) = x^2$ and $x = 7$ and $\Delta x = 4$, then $\Delta f = 6$.

More generally, if x is an original value, and $x + h$ is a new value in the domain of a function f, then $\Delta x = (x + h) - (x) = h$. Also, Δf is by definition the difference between the new and old functional values associated with x and $x + h$, i.e., $\Delta f = f(x + h) - f(x)$.

Thus our definition of the mapping of the derivative of f may be written:

$$f'(x) = L\left[\frac{f(x + h) - f(x)}{h}\right] = \lim_{\Delta x \to 0} \frac{\Delta f}{\Delta x}$$

where "$\lim_{\Delta x \to 0}$" means "the limit, as Δx approaches 0."

Now the traditional symbol for $\lim_{\Delta x \to 0} \frac{\Delta f}{\Delta x}$ is $\frac{df}{dx}$; speaking very roughly, as a mechanical procedure one "passes to a limit" by changing the "Δ's" to "d's."

Thus, that which we have written as $f'(x)$ may also be encountered in the literature as $\frac{df}{dx}$ (read "the derivative of f with respect to x," or "df over dx," or "df, dx.").

For example, if $f(x) = x^2$, then we may write $f'(x) = 2x$, or equally well, $\frac{df}{dx} = 2x$.

If we have given an equation $y = f(x)$, then we use Δy synonymously with Δf. For example, if $y = x^2$ and x changes from 5 to 3, then y changes from 25 to 16. In this case we say $\Delta x = -2$ and $\Delta y = -9$. Also, if $y = f(x)$, we use y' and $\frac{dy}{dx}$ synonymously with $f'(x)$. For example, if $y = x^2$, we write $y' = 2x$ or $\frac{dy}{dx} = 2x$ (read as in the case of $\frac{df}{dx}$).

Note that in this definition $\frac{dy}{dx}$ is *not* a fraction with numerator dy and denominator dx; $\frac{dy}{dx}$ *does not* mean: "dy divided by dx." It means, if

$y = f(x)$, simply $f'(x)$. It must nevertheless be confessed that a great many results that later on have turned out to be correct have resulted from thinking of $\dfrac{dy}{dx}$ in just this incorrect way.

Now we turn our attention to the symbol: $\int$.

We have made assumptions about the area under a curve which enabled us to compute such areas, but we have not yet actually defined that area. We shall now propose a definition.

Suppose g is a function defined on the interval $\{0 \longrightarrow x\}$, where $x \geqslant 0$, and that the graph G of $g(x)$ lies entirely above the X-axis.

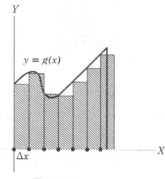

Fig. 14.17

Then if $x = 0$, we define the area under G to be 0. Otherwise, i.e., if $x > 0$, we proceed as follows.

Let Δx be any positive number $< x$. Beginning with 0, and stopping short of x, place as many points as possible on the interval $\{0 \longrightarrow x\}$ such that the distance from each to the next is Δx. At each such point a, erect an ordinate $f(a)$ (Fig. 14.17). Then intuitively, if Δx is small, the sum of the areas of the rectangles with sides equal to these ordinates and with bases Δx will approximate the area we seek. That is the sum of all $f(a)\,\Delta x$, where a is the x-value of any one of our division points, will be an approximation, which we shall denote $S_{\Delta x}$, to the area we seek.

It would seem that the smaller Δx, the better the approximation. We are therefore led to *define* the area under G (and over the X-axis), from 0 to x, as the limit (if it exists) of $S_{\Delta x}$, as Δx approaches 0; this limit is denoted: $\lim\limits_{\Delta x \to 0} S_{\Delta x}$.

It may now be proved, although we shall not do so here, that this definition is consistent with the assumptions we have already made about area, so that our preceding results about area still apply.

For example, let us consider again the question of the area under the curve $y = x^2$ from $x = 0$ to $x = 3$, which we investigated in Section 14.11.

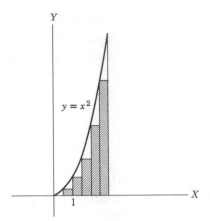

Fig. 14.18

We first choose $\Delta x = 0.5$ (Fig. 14.18). Then we construct the following table:

a	$f(a)$	$f(a) \cdot \Delta x$
0.0	0.00	0.000
0.5	0.25	0.125
1.0	1.00	0.500
1.5	2.25	1.125
2.0	4.00	2.000
2.5	6.25	3.125

$$S_{0.5} = 6.875 \text{ square units}$$

$S_{0.5}$ is an approximation to the area we seek, whose actual value we have already computed to be 9 square units. A better approximation to this area will be afforded by $S_{0.2}$, whose computation will be left as an exercise for the student.

The exact area being given by an integral of x^2, and approximate areas by sums of terms of the form $x^2 \Delta x$, the integral may be thought of as a sort of refined sum, the sum to which approximate sums tend as Δx approaches 0. The symbol "$\int$", an elongated "S" (for "sum") therefore was used to represent an integral in this way:

The integrals of x^2 are written:

$$\int x^2 \, dx$$

read "the integrals of x^2 with respect to x."

Thus we write:

$$\int x^2 \, dx = \frac{x^3}{3} + r$$

read: the integrals of x^2 with respect to x are $\frac{x^3}{3} + r$, where r is any real number; and similarly, more generally, for $\int f(x) \, dx$, where $f(x)$ is any function that has an integral.

▶ **EXERCISE 78**

1. Find the work done in stretching a spring two inches from its initial position if a force of one pound extends the spring:

(a) 1 inch   (b) 2 inches   (c) $\frac{1}{2}$ inch
(d) 0.1 inch   (e) a inches

2. Find the approximation $S_{0.2}$ to the area bounded by the parabola $y = x^2$, the X-axis, and the vertical line whose equation is $x = 3$. How close is this to the exact area? What value of Δx would lead to a better approximation?

3. (a)–(h) In each of the parts of Problem 1, Exercise 77, find the approximations $S_{0.5}$ and $S_{0.2}$ to the required area, and compare these approximations with the exact area.

4. Find:

(a) $\int x \, dx$ (b) $\int x^2 \, dx$ (c) $\int 2x \, dx$
(d) $\int -2x \, dx$ (e) $\int 3x \, dx$ (f) $\int -3x \, dx$
(g) $\int 1 \, dx$ (h) $\int (3x + 1) \, dx$ (i) $\int (3x - 1) \, dx$

5. Show how the work done by a force exerted over an interval along a scaled line may be defined as the limit of certain approximations, in a manner analogous to that by which we defined the area under a curve.

In each of parts (a)–(e) of Problem 1 above, find $S_{0.5}$ and $S_{0.2}$ where $S_{\Delta x}$ is defined for work in a manner similar to its earlier definition in the case of area.

15

15.1   INTRODUCTION

What do statisticians do?

Statisticians (or their assistants) collect "data." They telephone a thousand people, for example, to find out what television program they may be viewing at a certain time; they tabulate the examination grades of a class; they record the results of repeated measurements of the length of a given object; and so on and on.

Statisticians present data.   A page on which a thousand examination grades are listed in random order conveys little information.   The statistician groups and orders and visually charts his data so that important information about that data is more readily derived.   Tables and graphs of varied types are the tools of the statistician in this activity.

Statisticians operate on data.   Given a set of data, statisticians compute certain classical numbers that are useful in conveying information about the data.   The student is undoubtedly acquainted, for example, with the "average" of a set of grades, as a number which is in some fashion supposed to be typical of the collection of grades.   There are many more such descriptive numbers which the statistician associates with sets of data, and which in various ways characterize those sets.

Statisticians infer and predict.   This is of course their most important and at the same time their most hazardous function.   On the basis of telephone calls to a relatively small number of people, they come to a conclusion as to the *probable* number of people throughout the country who are tuned in on a given program at a given time.   On the basis of "public opinion" polls, they predict the results of an election in which very many more people will vote than were polled; on the basis of the lengths of time necessary to burn out 100 light bulbs of a certain brand, they will make statements concerning the longevity of all the bulbs of that brand.   The last case is clearly one in which the help of the statistician is necessary.   The manufacturer of light bulbs would not care to determine the longevity of each bulb by actual test any more than a manufacturer of chairs would like to determine the maximum weight each chair would support by measuring the exact weight under which each of his chairs collapsed.

Generally speaking, these are the activities of the statistician.   In terms of them one may distinguish a number of broad (and often overlapping) areas of the field of statistics.   *Sampling theory*, for example, considers especially the problem of choosing "representative" samples (how shall we choose the thousand people we poll in a television poll, or the 25 bulbs we burn out in a test of bulbs?) and the inferences one may draw from knowledge about a sample collection of data.   *Design theory* considers the problem of properly designing experiments so that a tentative hypothesis may be confirmed or rejected.   How many people should be inoculated with vaccine, how many not inoculated, in what geographical areas, when, etc., etc., in order that one may be fairly certain that the results indicate either an effective or an ineffective vaccine?   Clearly, if one person is inoculated and does not fall ill, that is insufficient evidence. His immunity may have been a case of *chance* and not due to the vaccine. Medicine and science in general lean heavily on the statistician for help in such questions.

The barest discussion of statistics inevitably introduces, as we have emphasized by italicizations above, the concepts of *probability* or *chance*. The inference or prediction of the statistician is typically not a statement of certainty, but only a statement that some event is more or less, or comparatively likely or probable.   We shall therefore find it eventually necessary, in our study of statistical inference, to examine certain rudiments of probability theory.

15.2 THE PRESENTATION OF DATA

Suppose that the following is a list of grades scored on an examination:

$$64, 77, 80, 61, 76, 82, 64, 80, 72, 90$$
$$65, 71, 85, 73, 67, 30, 53, 86, 80, 88$$

How shall we present this information in better fashion?   A first step might be to arrange the grades in order of size, indicating the number of times each grade occurs.   The number of times a grade occurs is called the *frequency* of that grade.   A table of the following sort is called a *frequency* table:

GRADE	FREQUENCY
30	1
53	1
61	1
64	2
65	1
67	1
71	1
72	1
73	1
76	1
77	1
80	3
82	1
85	1
86	1
88	1
90	1

20 = Total number of grades

In this array a number of facts fairly well hidden within the original listing come easily to light.   We now see, for example, that the lowest grade is 30, the highest 90, the difference between highest and lowest (called the *range* of the distribution) is 60, and the grade occurring most often (called the *mode* of the distribution) is 80.

The table above presents us with a set of ordered pairs, which may be graphed to arrive at a visual presentation of the data.   When the successive points of the graph are joined by straight line segments, the result is called a *frequency polygon*. (See Fig. 15.1.)

How many grades occurred that were less than or equal to 60?   An

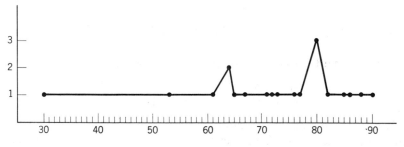

Fig. 15.1

examination of the table reveals that there were 2 such grades.   A question of this sort, however, is more easily answered if a *cumulative frequency* table is prepared.   We define the *cumulative frequency* of a grade to be the number of grades less than or equal to a given grade.   Another question that might arise is one of the sort: What percentage of the grades were less than or equal to 60?   The answer to this particular question is, of course, $\frac{2}{20}$, or 10%, or 0.1.   A *cumulative relative frequency* table is handy to have at hand to take care of questions of this type.   We define the *cumulative relative frequency* of a grade to be the percentage (usually expressed as a decimal) of grades less than or equal to a given grade.

GRADE	FREQUENCY	CUM. FREQUENCY	CUM. REL. FREQUENCY
30	1	1	0.05
53	1	2	0.10
61	1	3	0.15
64	2	5	0.25
65	1	6	0.30
67	1	7	0.35
71	1	8	0.40
72	1	9	0.45
73	1	10	0.50
76	1	11	0.55
77	1	12	0.60
80	3	15	0.75
82	1	16	0.80
85	1	17	0.85
86	1	18	0.90
88	1	19	0.95
90	1	20	1.00

(*Relative frequencies* may of course also be defined and computed, but we shall not find this concept particularly useful in our development.)

The data we have at hand still has the disadvantage of exhibiting many values sprawled over a large range.   A more compact presentation may be achieved by *grouping* the data into convenient non-overlapping "class intervals" whose union covers at least the range of the data.   Convenient intervals in the case we are considering are $20 - 30$, $30 - 40$, etc. Ambiguity arises with respect to the endpoints of these intervals.   In which interval, for example, should the grade 30 fall?   We shall resolve this ambiguity by agreeing that the interval $a - b$ shall include only numbers greater than a and less than or equal to b.   By this agreement, the grade 30 is to be counted as falling within the interval $20 - 30$.

CLASS INTERVALS	FREQUENCY	CUMULATIVE FREQUENCY	CUMULATIVE RELATIVE FREQUENCY
20–30	1	1	0.05
30–40	0	1	0.05
40–50	0	1	0.05
50–60	1	2	0.10
60–70	5	7	0.35
70–80	8	15	0.75
80–90	5	20	1.00

We note that the array of grouped data involves a loss of some detail; we know from the preceding table, for example, that there are 8 grades between 70 and 80, but we cannot tell from this table exactly what those grades are. Generally speaking, this loss of detail becomes less and less important as the mass of data becomes larger and larger.

The grouped data may now be displayed graphically by means of a *frequency histogram* (Fig. 15.2).

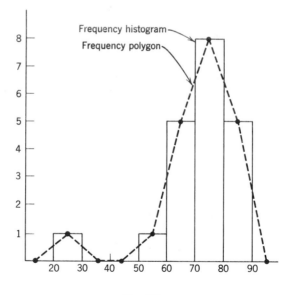

Fig. 15.2

A *frequency polygon* for the grouped data may be constructed by joining with line segments the midpoints of the upper sides of the successive rectangles in the histogram. It is customary, furthermore, to extend the class intervals far enough, on both left and right, so that the frequency polygon begins and ends on the horizontal axis (Fig. 15.2).

Similarly, a *cumulative* frequency diagram may be constructed for grouped data. In this case, however, the vertices of the polygon are the *upper right hand corners* of the successive rectangles, and the polygon begins, but obviously does not end, on the horizontal axis (Fig. 15.3).

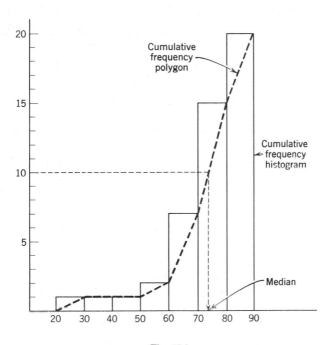

Fig. 15.3

▶ **EXERCISE 79**

Treat the following data as in the preceding section.

1. The grades scored by a class in an examination are: 75, 72, 92, 78, 65, 83, 56, 87, 72, 83, 72, 54.

2. A stone is dropped from the top of a building, and the time of descent determined by means of a stop-watch. The following times (in seconds) were recorded: 5.3, 5.4, 4.9, 5.0, 4.9, 5.1, 4.8, 5.1, 4.7.

3. Count the number of letters in each of the first 30 words of this chapter (beginning with the word "Statistics.")

4. Count the number of words in each of the first 20 sentences of this chapter.

5.   Toss 6 coins 25 times and record the number of heads occurring each time.

6.   A sample of 20 light bulbs of a certain brand burn for the following number of hours before burning out: 1010, 980, 860, 1300, 1280, 1410, 940, 720, 840, 970, 1120, 980, 1340, 1220, 990, 1130, 1100, 1040, 1120, 980.

7.   (*a*)   The scores posted by 15 winning basketball teams in a tournament were: 64, 78, 77, 74, 55, 51, 71, 62, 75, 67, 91, 94, 90, 73, 58.

(*b*)   The corresponding scores posted by the losing teams were: 62, 60, 67, 70, 45, 49, 68, 53, 52, 43, 47, 53, 54, 65, 56.

8.   Throw a single die 30 times and count the number of dots showing on the upper face each time.

9.   Throw a pair of dice 36 times and count the total of the number of dots showing on the upper faces each time.

10.   Explain the reason for the difference in the given techniques for drawing frequency polygons and cumulative frequency polygons for grouped data.

15.3   OPERATING ON DATA: MEASURES OF CENTRAL TENDENCY

In this section we shall consider numbers, called *descriptive statistics*, which are derived from sets of data, and which describe the sets from which they are derived in concise fashion.

The best known of these is commonly called the "average," but named by statisticians the *arithmetic mean* to distinguish it from other kinds of averages.   The arithmetic mean of *n* numbers is defined to be simply the sum of the numbers, divided by *n*.

Thus, the arithmetic mean of the grades of Section 15.2 is their sum 1444, divided by 20; i.e., 72.2.

The frequency table occasionally affords an appreciable short cut to this result.   To find the sum of certain numbers, one may multiply each of the *different* numbers given by its frequency of appearance, and then add the results.   (In the case of the data of Section 15.2, this does not help very much.   Why?)

Grouped data supplies even a shorter-cut to the result, although usually at the cost of accuracy.   We assume that all of the data falling within an interval fall at the midpoint of the interval.   This assumption is, of course, generally false; but with large masses of data, the errors it introduces often come close to cancelling each other out.

The work involved in computing the arithmetic mean of grouped data is illustrated in the following case, which uses the data of Section 15.2.

MIDPOINT OF CLASS INTERVAL	FREQUENCY	
x	f	xf
25	1	25
35	0	0
45	0	0
55	1	55
65	5	325
75	8	600
85	5	425
	20	1430

The arithmetic mean of the grouped data, then, is $\frac{1430}{20}$, or 71.5.

Note that we have used "x" to represent the set of midpoints of the class-intervals chosen in Section 15.2; "f" to represent the frequencies associated with each of these class intervals; and "xf" to represent the products of corresponding elements in (ordered) sets x and f.

We now introduce the notation "Σx" (read "Sigma x" or "summation x") to represent the sum of all the numbers in the column labeled "x."

Thus Σf, in our case, means the sum of all the frequencies, i.e., the total number of grades. In general, if there are n numbers in a set x, and f is defined as above, then:

$$n = \Sigma f$$

and if we define xf as above, then the arithmetic mean (which we denote $\bar{x}$) of the set of numbers x (for either the grouped or ungrouped case) may be given by the formulas:

$$\bar{x} = \frac{\Sigma xf}{\Sigma f} = \frac{\Sigma xf}{n}$$

The arithmetic mean, although the best known of "measures of central tendency," is not always as representative of the original data as we would wish it to be. A student, for example, whose grades in examinations are 90, 81, 0 would have a mean grade of 57. The single grade of 0 has had a catastrophic effect.

There is another type of average, called the *median*, which tends to minimize the effect of extreme values of the data. Assuming that a set of numbers has been written in order, we shall define the median to be either the middle number, if there is one, or the smaller of the two middle numbers, otherwise.

Thus, the median of the numbers 0, 81, 90 is 81; and the median of the numbers 1, 2, 3, 4 is 2.

The cumulative frequency table is useful in determining the median of a distribution, for the median may be equivalently defined as the first item of data which falls at or after a cumulative frequency of $n/2$ (or a cumulative relative frequency of 0.50).

Consulting the ungrouped cumulative frequency table of the preceding section, for example, we discover that the median of the given grades (corresponding to a cumulative frequency of 10, or to a cumulative relative frequency of 0.50) is 73.

In the case of grouped data, we interpolate between the right hand end-points of the class-intervals to find a number corresponding to a cumulative frequency of $n/2$ (or a cumulative relative frequency of 0.50), and define that number to be the median of the grouped distribution.

In the grouped cumulative frequency table of the preceding section, for example, a cumulative frequency of $n/2$ (i.e., 10) occurs between cumulative frequencies of 7 and 15, corresponding to class-intervals whose right hand endpoints are 70 and 80:

$$
\begin{array}{cc}
70 & 7 \\
\text{Median} & 10 \\
80 & 15
\end{array}
$$

$$\text{Median} = 70 + \tfrac{3}{8}(10) = 73.8$$

The median may also be determined graphically from the cumulative frequency polygon. The dotted lines in Fig. 15.3 indicate how the median may be found as that number on the horizontal azis which corresponds to a cumulative frequency of $n/2$ (or to a cumulative relative frequency of 0.50) on the vertical axis.

▶ **EXERCISE 80**

1–9. In Problems 1–9, Exercise 79, find the arithmetic mean and median for both the grouped and ungrouped data, and, in the case of the median of the grouped data, illustrate your result on the cumulative frequency polygon.

15.4 OPERATING ON DATA: PERCENTILES

The median of a set of data may be thought of as the first "datum" (i.e., element of data) below which half of the total number of data fall. The idea may be generalized:

Roughly speaking, the pth *percentile* of data is the first datum below which fall $p\%$ of the data. To phrase the definition more precisely, we consider the ungrouped and grouped cases separately.

In the case of ungrouped data, the pth percentile is the first datum at or after a cumulative relative frequency of $p/100$ [i.e., a cumulative frequency of $(p/100)\cdot n$].

In the case of grouped data, we use interpolation between right-hand endpoints of class-intervals to find a number corresponding to a cumulative relative frequency of $p/100$ [or a cumulative frequency of $(p/100)\cdot n$] and we define that number to be the pth percentile.

For example, in the case of the ungrouped data of Section 15.2, the seventieth percentile is the first grade which occurs at or after a cumulative frequency of $\frac{70}{100}\cdot 20 = 14$. That grade is 80.

We may interpret this result to mean that about 70% of the given set of grades arc less than or equal to the grade of 80; and by the same token, that about 30% of the grades are higher than 80. (Actually, what is the exact situation here?)

In the case of the grouped data of Section 15.2, the seventieth percentile may be computed by interpolation in the grouped cumulative frequency table; again we seek a grade corresponding to a cumulative frequency of $\frac{70}{100}\cdot 20 = 14$:

70	7
Seventieth percentile	14
80	15

Seventieth percentile $= 70 + \frac{7}{8}\cdot 10 = 78.8$.

Of course, the same result may be attained by interpolating in the cumulative *relative* frequency table:

Seventieth percentile $= 70 + \left(\frac{0.70 - 0.35}{0.75 - 0.35}\right) 10 = 78.8$.

In terms of percentiles, the median and certain other related concepts may be defined:

The *median* may be defined to be the 50th percentile.

The *first (or "lower") quartile* is defined to be the 25th percentile; the *second quartile* the 50th percentile; the *third (or "upper") quartile* the 75th percentile.

The *first decile* is defined to be the 10th percentile; the *second decile* the 20th *percentile*; etc.

Percentiles, quartiles and deciles for grouped data may be derived graphically from cumulative frequency polygons as in the case of medians.

Note: Students consulting other texts will probably find that definitions of medians, quartiles, etc., occasionally vary slightly from text to text.

▶ **EXERCISE 81**

1–9. In Problems 1–9, Exercise 79, find (for both grouped and ungrouped data) the lower and upper quartiles, the first and ninth deciles, and the 67th percentile. Interpret each result; illustrate by a graphical derivation of each result in the case of grouped data.

15.5 OPERATING ON DATA: MEASURES OF DISPERSION

In describing data, it is useful to give not only some measure of central tendency, i.e., some "average," but also some measure of the closeness with which the data clusters about this average.

One such measure of "dispersion" or "scatter" or "variability" is the *range*, which we have already defined (for ungrouped data) to be the difference between the smallest and largest data in the set. For grouped data, the range is defined to be the difference between the left-hand endpoint of the first class-interval and the right-hand endpoint of the last class-interval.

For example, the range of the grouped data in Section 15.2 is 70. This information is more meaningful when the actual boundaries of the range are given. It would be better to say: the grouped data in Section 15.2 has a range of 70, from 20 to 90.

The range, however, has several deficiencies as an indicator of scatter about the middle of the data. For one thing, it is affected only by the outermost data. A measure which supplements the range, and helps to repair this deficiency, is the *interquartile range*, defined (for both grouped and ungrouped data) to be the difference between the first and third quartiles.

For example, the interquartile range in the case of the ungrouped data of Section 15.2 is 16, from 64 to 80. This means that about half of all the grades in this distribution fall between 64 and 80.

But we still do not have a measure of dispersion that takes into account *all* values of the data. We proceed to develop such a measure of dispersion about the *mean*. (From now on we shall shorten "arithmetic mean" to "mean.")

If x_1 is an element of a set x whose mean is $\bar{x}$, we define the *deviation* of x_1 from the mean to be $x_1 - \bar{x}$.

For example, the deviation of the grade 80 from the mean 72.2 of the set of grades in Section 15.2 is 7.8; the deviation of the grade 30 in the same case is -42.2.

Now a measure of total dispersion might be attained by adding not the deviations (since then positive and negative deviations would tend to cancel each other out), but the absolute values of the deviations of all the data. For purposes of computation, however, it turns out that a more tractable non-negative quantity than the absolute value of the deviation is the square of the deviation.

Furthermore, to keep our measure from becoming too large a number, we shall seek an *average* rather than a total dispersion.

We therefore define the *variance* v of a set x of n numbers with mean $\bar{x}$ to be $1/n$th of the sum of the squares of the deviations from the mean of all the data. We write this symbolically:

$$v = \frac{\Sigma (x - \bar{x})^2}{n} = \frac{\Sigma (x - \bar{x})^2}{\Sigma f}$$

If the data has been arranged into a frequency table in which each element of x is written just once and associated with a frequency taken from a set of frequencies f, then the above formula may be more compactly expressed:

$$v = \frac{\Sigma (x - \bar{x})^2 f}{n} = \frac{\Sigma (x - \bar{x})^2 f}{\Sigma f}$$

If the set x is defined to be the set of midpoints of class intervals, then the above formula applies also to grouped data.

We illustrate by computing the variance first for the ungrouped, and then for the grouped data of Section 15.2.

In the case of the ungrouped data of Section 15.2:

$$(\bar{x} = 72.2)$$

x	f	$x - \bar{x}$	$(x - \bar{x})^2$	$(x - \bar{x})^2 f$
30	1	-42.2	1780.84	1780.84
53	1	-19.2	368.64	368.64
61	1	-11.2	125.44	125.44
64	2	-8.2	67.24	134.48
65	1	-7.2	51.84	51.84
67	1	-5.2	27.04	27.04
71	1	-1.2	1.44	1.44
72	1	$-.2$	.04	.04
73	1	.8	.64	.64
76	1	3.8	14.44	14.44
77	1	4.8	23.04	23.04
80	3	7.8	60.84	182.52
82	1	9.8	96.04	96.04
85	1	12.8	163.84	163.84
86	1	13.8	190.44	190.44
88	1	15.8	249.64	249.64
90	1	17.8	316.84	316.84
	20			3727.20

$$v = \frac{3727.20}{20} = 186.36$$

In the case of the grouped data of Section 15.2:

$$(\bar{x} = 71.5)$$

x	f	$x - \bar{x}$	$(x - \bar{x})^2$	$(x - \bar{x})^2 f$
25	1	−46.5	2162.25	2162.25
35	0			0.00
45	0			0.00
55	1	−16.5	272.25	272.25
65	5	−6.5	42.25	211.25
75	8	3.5	12.25	98.00
85	5	13.5	182.25	911.25
	20			3655.00

$$v = \frac{3655}{20} = 182.75$$

If the original data were, let us say, measurements in *inches*, then if we traced through the steps above we would discover that the variance would be expressed in terms of *square inches*. In order to arrive at a measure whose unit is the same as that of the original data, we define the *standard deviation s* to be the non-negative square root of the variance:

$$s = \sqrt{v}$$

In the case of the ungrouped data of Section 15.2, $s = \sqrt{186.36} = 13.7$. In the case of the grouped data of Section 15.2, $s = \sqrt{182.75} = 13.5$.

The standard deviation s has this important interpretation: Normally (we shall later throw further light on what we mean by "normally") one may expect to find about $\frac{2}{3}$ of all the data within s units of the mean; 95% within $2s$ units of the mean; and nearly all (about 99.7%) within $3s$ units of the mean.

Thus in the case of the ungrouped data of Section 15.2, we would expect to find about $\frac{2}{3} \cdot 20$, or about 13 elements of data between $72.2 - 13.7$ and $72.2 + 13.7$; i.e., between 58.5 and 85.9. (Actually there are 15 such elements.) We would expect to find about 95% of 20, or about 19 or 20 elements of data between $72.2 - 27.4$ and $72.2 + 27.4$, i.e., between 44.8 and 99.6. (Actually there are 19 such elements.) We would expect to find nearly all the data between $72.2 - 41.1$ and $72.2 + 41.1$., i.e., between 31.1 and 113.3. (Actually all but one element of data fall in this range.)

The same interpretation holds in the case of grouped data.

▶ EXERCISE 82

1–9. In Problems 1–9, Exercise 79, find and interpret the range, the interquartile range, and the standard deviation for both grouped and ungrouped data.   Compare your interpretation of the standard deviation with the actual situation.

15.6   THE SYMBOL Σ

Intuitively it seems plausible that increasing the grade of each student in a class by 5 points will raise the mean of the class by 5 points, and that doubling each grade will double the mean.   In this section we shall develop properties of the symbol Σ which help to prove these and similar facts.

First of all, whenever we use the symbol Σ, we shall assume in advance that we know the number of elements in the set to which the symbol applies.

Secondly, having specified that Σ applies to a set of say n elements, when we write Σc, where c is a real number, we shall mean the sum of n numbers, each of which is equal to c.   That is to say:

(1) $$\Sigma c = nc$$

Now suppose x is the ordered set of numbers: $(x_1, x_2, \cdots, x_n)$.   We have already defined:

$$\Sigma x = x_1 + x_2 + \cdots + x_n$$

If f is a real-real function and $x = (x_1, x_2, \cdots, x_n)$, we shall now define $f(x)$ to be the ordered set:

$$f(x) = (f(x_1), f(x_2), \cdots, f(x_n))$$

Thus, if $x = (x_1, x_2, \cdots, x_n)$, then:

$$x^2 = (x_1^2, x_2^2, \cdots, x_n^2),$$
$$2x = (2x_1, 2x_2, \cdots, 2x_n)$$
$$x + 2 = (x_1 + 2, x_2 + 2, \cdots, x_n + 2)$$

Supposing further that y is the ordered set of numbers $(y_1, y_2, \cdots, y_n)$, we define the ordered sets $x + y$ and xy as follows:

$$x + y = (x_1 + y_1, x_2 + y_2, \cdots, x_n + y_n)$$
$$xy = (x_1 y_1, x_2 y_2, \cdots, x_n y_n)$$

To take a particular case, suppose $x = (1, 2, 3, 4)$ and $y = (4, 3, 2, 1)$ then:

$$x^2 = (1, 4, 9, 16)$$
$$2x = (2, 4, 6, 8)$$
$$x + 2 = (3, 4, 5, 6)$$
$$x + y = (5, 5, 5, 5)$$
$$xy = (4, 6, 6, 4)$$

Now the following properties of the symbol Σ are easily proved:

(2) $$\Sigma(x + y) = \Sigma x + \Sigma y$$

(3) $$\Sigma cx = c\Sigma x, \text{ where } c \text{ is a real number}$$

Proof of (2):
$$\begin{aligned}
\Sigma(x + y) &= \Sigma(x_1 + y_1, x_2 + y_2, \cdots, x_n + y_n)\\
&= (x_1 + y_1) + (x_2 + y_2) + \cdots + (x_n + y_n)\\
&= (x_1 + x_2 + \cdots + x_n) + (y_1 + y_2 + \cdots + y_n)\\
&= \Sigma x + \Sigma y
\end{aligned}$$

[The proof of (3) is left as an exercise for the reader.]

Properties (2) and (3) are illustrated in the following table:

x	y	$x + y$	$7x$
1	4	5	7
2	3	5	14
3	2	5	21
4	1	5	28
$\Sigma x = 10$	$\Sigma y = 10$	$\Sigma(x + y) = 20$	$\Sigma 7x = 70$

Here we see that $\Sigma(x + y) = \Sigma x + \Sigma y$ and that $\Sigma 7x = 7\Sigma x$.

Now we apply these properties of the symbol Σ to a proof of the intuitively plausible facts stated in the first paragraph of this section.

Using a bar to indicate the mean of a set of numbers, and notation as above, these facts may be stated more generally:

(4) $$\overline{x + c} = \bar{x} + c$$

(5) $$\overline{cx} = c\bar{x}$$

Proof of (4):

$$\overline{x + c} = \frac{\Sigma(x + c)}{n} \quad \text{(by definition of "mean")}$$

$$= \frac{\Sigma x + \Sigma c}{n} \quad \text{(by (2) above)}$$

$$= \frac{\Sigma x + nc}{n} \quad \text{(by (1) above)}$$

$$= \frac{\Sigma x}{n} + \frac{nc}{n} \quad \text{(why?)}$$

$$= \bar{x} + c \quad \text{(by definition of mean and ...?)}$$

[The proof of (5) is left as an exercise for the reader.]

15.7 SHORT-CUTS

In this section we shall develop several methods which shorten the more tedious computations of Sections 15.3 and 15.5.

First we derive the following formula for the variance in the case of ungrouped data:

$$(6) \qquad\qquad v = \frac{\Sigma x^2 f}{n} - (\bar{x})^2$$

Proof of (6):

$$v = \frac{\Sigma(x - \bar{x})^2 f}{n}$$

$$= \frac{\Sigma(x^2 f - 2\bar{x}xf + \bar{x}^2 f)}{n}$$

$$= \frac{\Sigma x^2 f}{n} - \frac{\Sigma 2\bar{x}xf}{n} + \frac{\Sigma \bar{x}^2 f}{n} \qquad \text{(by (1) above)}$$

$$= \frac{\Sigma x^2 f}{n} - 2\bar{x}\frac{\Sigma xf}{n} + \bar{x}^2 \frac{\Sigma f}{n} \qquad \text{(by (3) above)}$$

$$= \frac{\Sigma x^2 f}{n} - 2\bar{x}(\bar{x}) + \bar{x}^2 \left(\frac{n}{n}\right) \qquad \text{(by definition of $\bar{x}$ and n)}$$

$$= \frac{\Sigma x^2 f}{n} - 2\bar{x}^2 + \bar{x}^2$$

$$= \frac{\Sigma x^2 f}{n} - (\bar{x})^2$$

Now we examine the effect of replacing the set x by the set $y = x + c$, where c is any real number. Supposing v_y represents the variance for the set y we have:

$$v_y = \frac{\Sigma(y - \bar{y})^2 f}{n}$$

But by (4), above, $\bar{y} = \overline{x + c} = \bar{x} + c$. Therefore:

$$v_y = \frac{\Sigma[x + c - (\bar{x} + c)]^2 f}{n} = \frac{\Sigma(x - \bar{x})^2 f}{n} = v$$

so that the variance is unchanged when we replace the set x by the set $x + c$, where c is any real number.

We illustrate by applying the formula (6), and the method of replacing x by $x + c$, to the computation of the variance in the case of the ungrouped data of Section 15.2.

It helps to choose a value of c which is the negative of some value at about the middle of the list of data. We choose the value $c = -72$.

Then $y = x - 72$, $\bar{y} = \bar{x} - 72 = 72.2 - 72 = 0.2$

Proceeding:

x	f	$y = x - 72$	y^2	y^2f
30	1	-42	1764	1764
53	1	-19	361	361
61	1	-11	121	121
64	2	-8	64	128
65	1	-7	49	49
67	1	-5	25	25
71	1	-1	1	1
72	1	0	0	0
73	1	1	1	1
76	1	4	16	16
77	1	5	25	25
80	3	8	64	192
82	1	10	100	100
85	1	13	169	169
86	1	14	196	196
88	1	16	256	256
90	1	18	324	324
	20			3728

$$v = v_y = \frac{\Sigma y^2 f}{n} - (\bar{y})^2 = \frac{3728}{20} - (0.2)^2 = 186.40 - 0.04 = 186.36, \quad \text{which}$$

agrees with the result of Section 15.5, and which has been arrived at somewhat more easily.

Now we turn our attention to a simplification of the processes of finding both the mean and the variance in the case of grouped data.

Again we make use of a transformation from a set x to a set y, but this time we examine the effect of the more general transformation: $y = bx + c$, where b and c are real numbers.

In the case of the mean:

$$\bar{y} = \overline{bx + c} = \overline{bx} + c \quad \text{[by (4) above]}$$
$$= b\bar{x} + c \quad \text{[by (5) above]}$$

Solving for $\bar{x}$: $\bar{x} = \dfrac{\bar{y} - c}{b}$.

In the case of the variance:

$$v_y = \frac{\Sigma(y - \bar{y})^2 f}{n} = \frac{\Sigma(bx + c - b\bar{x} - c)^2 f}{n}$$

$$= \frac{\Sigma(bx - b\bar{x})^2 f}{n}$$

$$= \frac{\Sigma b^2 (x - \bar{x})^2 f}{n}$$

$$= b^2 \frac{\Sigma(x - \bar{x})^2 f}{n}$$

$$= b^2 v$$

Therefore:
$$v = \frac{v_y}{b^2}$$

Summarizing: If x and y are ordered sets such that $y = bx + c$, then:

$$\bar{x} = \frac{\bar{y} - c}{b}$$

$$v = \frac{v_y}{b^2}$$

(where v is the variance of the set x and v_y is the variance of the set y.)

Now we apply the transformation $y = bx + c$ to the computation of the mean and variance in the case of the grouped data of Section 15.2. When the difference between successive x-values is a constant d, as it is in the case of grouped data, it will be found helpful to let $b = 1/d$.

In the case of the grouped data of Section 15.2, the difference between successive x-values is 10. We therefore let $b = \frac{1}{10} = 0.1$.

Then we let c be the negative of some value near the middle of the set bx. In our case, we choose $c = -5.5$:

x	f	$y = 0.1x - 5.5$	yf	$y^2 f$
25	1	-3	-3	9
35	0	-2	0	0
45	0	1	0	0
55	1	0	0	0
65	5	1	5	5
75	8	2	16	32
85	5	3	15	45
	20		33	91

$$\bar{y} = \frac{\Sigma yf}{n} = \frac{33}{20} = 1.65$$

$$v_y = \frac{\Sigma y^2 f}{n} - \bar{y}^2 = \frac{91}{20} - (1.65)^2 = 1.8275$$

$$\bar{x} = \frac{\bar{y} - c}{b} = \frac{1.65 + 5.5}{0.1} = 71.5$$

$$v = \frac{v_y}{b^2} = \frac{1.8275}{(0.1)^2} = 182.75$$

agreeing with our results in Sections 15.3 and 15.5.

▶ **EXERCISE 83**

1–9. In Problems 1–9 of Exercise 79, find the variance in the case of the ungrouped data, and the mean and the variance in the case of the grouped data, by the short-cut methods of the preceding section.

10. Prove formula (3) of Section 15.6.

11. Prove formula (5) of Section 15.6.

12. Prove that if x and y are ordered sets of n elements then $\overline{x + y} = \bar{x} + \bar{y}$. Illustrate this result by means of an example.

13. (a) The 9th grade at a certain school is subdivided into three classes of 15, 20, and 25 students each. Suppose that the average (mean) grade of students in these classes are, respectively, 85, 80, and 70. What is the average grade of all 9th grade students at this school?

(b) Prove that $\Sigma xf = \bar{x}n$, with notation as above. What has this to do with part (a)?

15.8 PROBABILITY

Further progress into the realm of statistics now requires that we develop something of the theory of probability.

Roughly speaking, the science of probability concerns itself with the description, by means of a number, of the "likelihood" of an event. We agree in advance that when an event is impossible we shall say that it has a probability of 0; that when an event is certain, we shall say that it has a probability of 1; and that the probability of *any* event shall be a number between 0 and 1, which by its proximity to 0 or 1 indicates the lesser or greater likelihood of the event.

Thus, if we toss a coin once, the probability that it will fall *both* heads and tails must be 0, since this event is impossible. And again by our agreement, the probability that it will *not* fall both heads and tails must be 1, since this event is certain.

But what probability shall we assign to the likelihood of the coin falling say *heads*? Assuming, as we shall, that the coin never falls and rests on its edge, and that the coin is uniformly weighted, it seems plausible to say that one of two events is certain to happen, and that they are equally likely. The two events are, of course, falling heads and falling tails. We therefore divide the probability 1, representing certainty, equally between these two events, and say that the probability of the coin's falling heads is $\frac{1}{2}$, and the probability of the coin's falling tails is $\frac{1}{2}$.

To put it a little differently, when we toss a coin, we assume that two equally likely events may occur, one which we call "tails" (T) and one which we call "heads" (H). The set of equally likely events $\{T, H\}$ constitutes what is called the *sample space* for this situation. Only 1 of the 2 elements of the sample space is H. Therefore we say that the probability of the coin's falling heads is the ratio of these two numbers: $\frac{1}{2}$.

Consider now the situation in which we roll a single die. Here any one of six numbers may turn up; we shall assume that the die is not "loaded," so that the numbers are equally likely. The sample space for this situation is therefore the set of numbers: $\{1, 2, 3, 4, 5, 6\}$.

What is the probability of rolling a "2?" Since only 1 of the 6 elements of the sample space is "2," the probability of rolling a "2" is $\frac{1}{6}$.

What is the probability of rolling an even number? Since 3 of the 6 elements of the sample space are even, the probability of rolling an even number is $\frac{3}{6}$, or $\frac{1}{2}$.

Now we shall try to phrase what we have been saying more generally and more precisely.

Every problem in probability involves a so-called *sample-space* of events that may occur. In this course we shall concern ourselves only with *finite* sample-spaces in which all elements are *equally likely*.

Now suppose we have a condition in mind that is satisfied by s of the n elements in the sample space. Then we *define* the probability that this condition is satisfied in the given situation to be: s/n.

Illustrative Example 1. Consider the case above in which we tossed a coin. Here the "condition" we had in mind was that the result of the toss should be H, which was satisfied by 1 of the 2 elements of the sample space $\{T, H\}$. Hence $s = 1$, $n = 2$, and the probability that the result of the toss is H is $\dfrac{s}{n} = \dfrac{1}{2}$.

Illustrative Example 2. In the case of rolling a die, which we considered above, the stipulated condition was that the result be an even number. This condition is satisfied by 3 of the 6 elements of the sample space $\{1, 2, 3, 4, 5, 6\}$. Hence $s = 3$, $n = 6$, and the probability of throwing an even number in rolling a die is $\dfrac{s}{n} = \dfrac{3}{6} = \dfrac{1}{2}$.

Illustrative Example 3. Suppose two checkers are drawn at random from a box containing two red checkers and one black checker.

Before asking, or answering any questions about this situation we shall construct the sample space involved. We shall find it convenient to denote the two red checkers R_1 and R_2, respectively, and the black checker B. Each drawing of two checkers is a two element subset of the set $\{R_1, R_2, B\}$.

The sample space is then:

$$\left\{\{R_1, R_2\}, \{R_1, B\}, \{R_2, B\}\right\}$$

Now we ask (and answer) the questions:

(a) What is the probability that both checkers are red? Answer: $\frac{1}{3}$.

(b) What is the probability that one checker is black? Answer: $\frac{2}{3}$.

(c) What is the probability that both checkers are black? Answer: $\frac{0}{3} = 0$ (i.e., this is impossible).

(d) What is the probability that at least one of the checkers is red? Answer: $\frac{3}{3} = 1$ (i.e., this is certain).

Illustrative Example 4. A box contains two red and one black checker. First one checker is drawn at random from the box (and not replaced), and then another is drawn.

(a) What is the sample space for this situation?

(b) What is the probability that the first checker drawn is red, and the second black?

(c) What is the probability that both checkers which are drawn are red?

(d) What is the probability that the first checker drawn is black and the second red?

Solutions:

(a) Here the order in which the checkers are drawn is in question, so that the possible draws must be listed as *ordered* pairs (see page 16). The sample space may be derived from that of the preceding example by listing the preceding draws in all possible orders:

$$\{(R_1, R_2), (R_2, R_1), (R_1, B), (B, R_1), (R_2, B), (B, R_2)\}$$

(b) This condition is satisfied by the elements: $(R_1, B), (R_2, B)$. Answer: $\frac{2}{6}$, or $\frac{1}{3}$.

(c) Answer: $\frac{2}{6}$, or $\frac{1}{3}$.

(d) Answer: $\frac{2}{6}$, or $\frac{1}{3}$.

▶ **EXERCISE 84**

1. A letter is drawn at random from the English alphabet. What is the probability that it is

(a) "a"?

(b) "b"?

(c) A vowel?

(d) Not a vowel?

(e) "π"?

2.   In throwing a die, what is the probability of throwing

(a)   A "six"?

(b)   A "seven"?

(c)   An odd number?

(d)   A number which is a perfect square?

(e)   An integer?

(f)   A rational number?

(g)   An irrational number?

(h)   A real number?

(i)   A number greater than $\sqrt{2}$?

3.   A playing card is chosen at random from a bridge deck.   What is the probability that it is

(a)   An ace?

(b)   A spade?

(c)   The ace of spades?

(d)   Not an ace?

(e)   Not a spade?

(f)   Not the ace of spades?

4.   Since there are (excluding the possibility of a leap year) 365 days of the year on which a person may be born, a student reasons that the probability that a person chosen at random has his birthday on July 4 is $\frac{1}{365}$.   What can you say about his reasoning?

5.   Suppose a *pair* of dice are rolled.   To distinguish between them, call one a first die and the other a second die.   Denote the result of a roll of the dice by an ordered pair in which the first element indicates the number showing on the first die and the second element indicates the number showing on the second die.   For example, we would write the ordered pair (2, 6) to indicate a roll in which the first die falls 2, the second 6.   In this case we would say that we had thrown an 8 (= 2 + 6) with the pair of dice.

(a)   Write the sample space showing all (36) possible rolls of a pair of dice.

(b)   Find the probability of throwing each of the following numbers in rolling a pair of dice: 1, 2, 3, 4, 5, 6, 7, 8, 9, 10, 11, 12, 13.

(c)   "On the next chuck, Charley yells 'money'!—meaning he finally makes his ten, although nobody sees it but him. . . . If Louie has any idea of asking Charley to let him see the dice in the hat . . . he does not speak about the matter . . .; nobody else says anything either, probably figuring Rusty Charley is not a guy who is apt to let anybody question his word. . . .

". . . Nobody as much as opens his face from the time we go in until we start out. . . . It is only just as we get to the door that anybody speaks, . . . 'Charley,' he says, 'do you make it the hard way?'

"Well, everybody laughs, and we go on out, but I never hear myself whether Charley makes his ten with a six and a four or with two fives—which is the hard way to make a ten with the dice— . . ." (Damon Runyon, *Blood Pressure.*)

Why is making a ten with two fives called the "hard" way?

6. Two coins are tossed.

(*a*) Denoting the result of a toss by an ordered pair in which the first element is *T* or *H* according as the first coin falls tails or heads, and similarly for the second element, write the sample space for this situation.

(*b*) What is the probability that both coins fall heads?

(*c*) What is the probability that the coins match?

(*d*) What is the probability that the coins do not match?

7. A coin is tossed three times.

(*a*) Denoting the possible results of the tosses by ordered triples, write the sample space for this situation.

(*b*) What is the probability that all three tosses are heads?

(*c*) What is the probability that the first toss is a head?

(*d*) Considering only those cases in which the first toss falls heads, what is the probability that the second toss falls heads? (Note that the number of elements in the sample space has been reduced in this part of the question.)

(*e*) Considering only those cases in which the first and second tosses fell heads, what is the probability that the third coin falls heads?

(*f*) Explain the statement that "a coin has no memory" in the light of (*d*) and (*e*) above. Also, tell what you think of the following strategy: A person betting on the toss of a coin decides to wait until 5 heads have fallen consecutively, and then to bet on tails, since he feels that after a long run of heads, tails are very likely.

8. Answer the questions of Illustrative Example 4 above, assuming that the first checker is put back into the box before the second checker is drawn.

15.9 CARTESIAN PRODUCTS

In many cases, writing out all the elements of a sample space is a tedious task, and in fact unnecessary; for often we are interested only in knowing *how many* elements the sample space contains. There are short cuts to this end which we shall consider in this and subsequent sections.

First of all, we pose this question:

Suppose A is the set of real numbers $\{1, 2, 3\}$, and B the set of real numbers $\{8, 9\}$. How many points in a Cartesian coordinate plane have an x-value chosen from A and a y-value chosen from B?

The answer is clearly: 6, as we may determine by actually writing down the set S of points in question: $S = \{(1, 8), (1, 9), (2, 8), (2, 9), (3, 8), (3, 9)\}$.

Because of this connection with the Cartesian coordinate plane, the set of ordered pairs S above is called the *Cartesian product* of the sets A and B above, and denoted $A \times B$.

In fact, we generalize the concept so that A and B may be any sets whatever:

Definition. If A and B are sets, the *Cartesian product* of A and B, denoted $A \times B$, is defined to be the set of all ordered pairs (a, b), where a is an element of A and b is an element of B.

(We previously called $A \times B$ simply a "product set." Exercise 2, Problems 13–16 should be read carefully at this point.)

For example, suppose A is the set of first names: $\{$Tom, Dick$\}$ and B the set of second names: $\{$Brown, Smith, Jones, Wilson$\}$. Then $A \times B$ is the following set of names. (We omit the usual parentheses and commas in this listing, since doing so leads to no ambiguity.):

Tom Brown	Dick Brown
Tom Smith	Dick Smith
Tom Jones	Dick Jones
Tom Wilson	Dick Wilson

We note that in each of the two cases above, the number of elements in $A \times B$ is the *product* of the number of elements in A and the number of elements in B. This is plausible. For in the case in which $A = \{1, 2, 3\}$, $B = \{8, 9\}$, each element of A may be combined with each of the 2 elements of B to produce 2 elements of the product set $A \times B$. Since there are 3 elements in A, there exist $3 \cdot 2 = 6$ elements in $A \times B$. Similarly, in the second case above, each first name leads to 4 whole names. Since there are 2 first names, there exist $2 \cdot 4 = 8$ elements in $A \times B$ in this case.

In fact, the following statement which we have induced from several cases, and which we have to some extent justified, may be rigorously proved (by using, for example, the principle of mathematical induction of Section 4.17).

Cardinal Principle of Product Sets. If A and B are sets of m and n elements, respectively, then the number of elements in the set $A \times B$ is mn.

Illustrative Example 1.   A tropical palace has 77 windows and 13 doors which are always open.   Every night a bird amuses itself by flying into the palace through a window and out through a door.   If the bird never takes the same route twice, for how many nights can it continue to play this game?

SOLUTION.   A route may be identified by means of an ordered pair, the first element identifying a window, the second a door; as, for example: (w_1, d_1) may be used to indicate the route in which the bird enters by a window labeled w_1 and leaves by a door labeled d_1.

The total number of such ordered pairs is, by the cardinal principle of product sets: $77 \cdot 13$, or 1001.

Therefore, the bird will be able to play its game for a thousand and one nights.

Illustrative Example 2.   In how many different ways may a pair of dice fall?

SOLUTION.   We have previously solved this problem by actually enumerating all possible ordered pairs in which each element is one of the six integers between 1 and 6.

By the cardinal principle of product sets, the number of such ordered pairs is $6 \cdot 6$, or 36.

Therefore a pair of dice may fall in 36 different ways.

Illustrative Example 3.   In how many different ways may a coin fall if it is tossed:

(*a*)   Once.
(*b*)   Twice.
(*c*)   Three times.
(*d*) n times.

SOLUTION.

(*a*)   A coin tossed once may fall in 2 different ways: heads (H), or tails (T).

(*b*)   The result of two tosses may be described by an ordered pair in which each of the two elements is one of the two elements: H, T.   Therefore a coin tossed twice may fall in $2 \cdot 2$, or 4 different ways.   [Since there are so few possible results in this case, we list them all: $(H, H), (H, T), (T, H), (T, T)$.]

(*c*)   The result of three tosses may be described by an "ordered triple" each of whose three elements is either H or T.   For example, (H, H, T) describes a sequence of three tosses in which the first two fall heads and the last tails.

The cardinal principle of product sets may be generalized to apply to cases of three or more sets in this way: *If sets A, B, C contain m, n, r elements, respectively, then the set of ordered triples A × B × C contains mnr elements; and similarly for cases involving more than three sets.*

To prove the generalized principle above, note that each ordered triple may be associated with an ordered pair whose first element is itself an ordered pair; for example, the ordered triple (a, b, c) may be made to correspond to the ordered pair whose first element is (a, b) and whose second element is c: $(a, b, c) \leftrightarrow [(a, b), c]$.

In other words, there are as many elements in $A \times B \times C$ as in $(A \times B) \times C$; but by the cardinal principle above, there are mn elements in $A \times B$, hence (again by the same principle) $(mn) \cdot r$ elements, or mnr elements in $(A \times B) \times C$. This proves the generalized principle in the case of three sets; and so on for more than three sets. The "and so on" argument may be rigorized by means of "mathematical induction."

Using the generalized cardinal principle of product sets, the number of ordered triples which may be written using the two letters T, H is $2 \cdot 2 \cdot 2$, or 2^3, or 8.

(d) 2^n.

▶ EXERCISE 85

1. In Connecticut, some automobile license plates consist simply of four letters. How many people (theoretically) may have these distinctive markers?

2. How many license plates of four symbols may be printed in which:

(a) The first two symbols are letters and the last two are digits?

(b) Each symbol is a digit?

(c) Each symbol is either a letter or a digit? (Assume that the letters "*O*" and "*I*" are indistinguishable from the digits "0" and "1" respectively.)

3. (a) A coin is tossed and a die is rolled. In how many ways may they fall? (i.e., how many elements are there in the sample space for this experiment?)

(b) What is the probability that the coin will fall heads and the die "2"?

(c) What is the probability that the coin will fall heads and the die an even number?

4. A die is rolled three times.

(a) How many elements are there in the sample space for this experiment?

(b) What is the probability of rolling exactly 3 sixes?

(c) What is the probability of rolling no sixes?

(d) What is the probability of rolling exactly 1 six?

(e) What is the probability of rolling exactly 2 sixes?

5.   Ten coins are tossed.

(*a*)   How many elements are there in the sample space for this experiment?

(*b*)   What is the probability that all the coins fall heads?

6.   A card is drawn at random from a bridge deck, replaced, and then a card is drawn again.

(*a*)   How many elements are there in the sample space for this experiment?

(*b*)   What is the probability that the ace of spades is drawn twice?

(*c*)   What is the probability that the ace of spades is drawn at least once?

(*d*)   What is the probability that the ace of spades is drawn exactly once?

(*e*)   What is the probability that the ace of spades is not drawn?

(*f*)   What is the probability that the same card is drawn twice?

(*g*)   What is the probability that both cards drawn are of the same suit? (i.e., both clubs, or both diamonds, or both hearts, or both spades.)

7.   (*a*)   A true-false test has five questions.   What is the probability that a student will score 100% purely by guessing?

(*b*)   What if the true-false test has 10 questions?

8.   (*a*)   How many integers less than 1000 can be written with the digits 0, 1, 2, 3?

(*b*)   How many of (*a*) are less than 334?

(*c*)   How many of (*a*) are even?

9.   A monkey pokes twice at the 26 lettered keys of a typewriter.   What is the probability that he will write the word "oh"?

15.10   PERMUTATIONS

Some Frenchmen like to eat their dinners not, as we do, by varying a forkful of this with a forkful of that, but by eating all of one item, and then all of another, and so on.

Let us suppose that each evening Pierre's dinner consists of meat (*M*) and potatoes (*P*).   To achieve variety, he wishes to consume these items in different orders on different evenings.   How many different orders are possible?

Clearly, not a great many; in fact, only 2, which we designate: *MP* and *PM*.

Now suppose that Pierre grows more prosperous, and adds a vegetable (*V*) to his dinner menu.   In how many different orders may he eat these *three* items?

Beginning with the vegetable, he may proceed to eat his meat and potatoes in either of the 2 orders previously determined. We arrive at the two possible orders: *VMP*, *VPM*.

But if 2 orders are possible beginning with *V*, then 2 orders must be possible beginning with *M*, and 2 orders must be possible beginning with *P*, making $3 \cdot 2$, or 6 possible orders in all:

VMP	*MPV*	*PVM*
VPM	*MVP*	*PMV*

Let us now add a salad (*S*) to Pierre's meal. In how many different ways will he be able to arrange the *four* items?

Beginning with the salad, he may proceed to eat the rest of the meal in any one of the 6 ways determined above. But if 6 orders are possible beginning with *S*, then 6 orders are possible beginning with *each* of the four items *S*, *M*, *P*, *V*, making $4 \cdot 6$, or $4 \cdot 3 \cdot 2$ or 24 orders in all:

SVMP	*MSVP*	*PMSV*	*VMSP*
SVPM	*MSPV*	*PMVS*	*VMPS*
SMPV	*MVSP*	*PSMV*	*VSMP*
SMVP	*MVPS*	*PSVM*	*VSPM*
SPVM	*MPVS*	*PVMS*	*VPMS*
SPMV	*MPSV*	*PVSM*	*VPSM*

Proceeding in this way, we conclude that 5 different items may be displayed in $5 \cdot 4 \cdot 3 \cdot 2$, or 120 orders, and so on.

Actually, we have been dealing with ordered sets of elements. Each ordered set of *n* different elements is called a *permutation* of the *n* different elements. What we have shown above is that there are 2 permutations possible with 2 elements, $3 \cdot 2$ with 3 elements, $4 \cdot 3 \cdot 2$ with 4 elements, and so on. In fact, the following may be proved to be true:

The number of permutations of a set of n different elements is:
$$(n)(n-1) \cdots (1).$$

(The last factor of 1 is included to allow for the possibility that we have a set containing only 1 element, in which case only 1 permutation is possible.)

The product $(n)(n-1) \cdots (1)$, where *n* is a natural number, is denoted *n*! (read "*n* factorial"). The exclamation point calls attention to the surprisingly large values attained by factorial expressions. For example:

$10! = 10 \cdot 9 \cdot 8 \cdot 7 \cdot 6 \cdot 5 \cdot 4 \cdot 3 \cdot 2 \cdot 1 = 3,628,800$

Illustrative Example 1. In how many ways may 3 books be placed next to each other on a shelf?

SOLUTION. The number of ordered triples which be formed with 3 different elements is: $3 \cdot 2 \cdot 1$, or 6.

Now we consider a variation on the theme of permutations. Suppose that we are asked to place 2 books on a shelf, but that we are given 3 books from which to choose the 2. In how many ways may this be done?

Again we attack the problem first by simple enumeration. If the given books are denoted a, b, c, then the following ordered pairs of different elements may be formed from these elements:

$$(a, b), (a, c), (b, a), (b, c), (c, a), (c, b)$$

Reasoning similar to that which we used just previously shows why there are 6 ways in which 2 books chosen from 3 may be arranged on a shelf. For if we place the book a first, then we may place either b or c second, making 2 possible arrangements beginning with a. If there are 2 arrangements beginning with the book a, then there must be 2 beginning with b and 2 beginning with c, or $3 \cdot 2$ arrangements in all. Each of these pairs of arrangements appears, of course, in our tabulation above.

Each ordered set of r different elements which constitute a subset of a set of n different elements, is called a *permutation of the n elements taken r at a time*. We shall denote the *number* of permutations of a set of n elements taken r at a time by the symbol $_nP_r$.

For example, we have determined above that $_3P_2 = 3 \cdot 2 = 6$.

A generalization of the reasoning by which we arrived at this result leads to this conclusion:

$$\overbrace{_nP_r = (n)(n-1) \cdots}^{r \text{ factors}}$$

Illustrative Example 2. Candidates for 3 different political offices are to be chosen from a list of 10 people. In how many ways may this be done?

SOLUTION. $\quad _{10}P_3 = \overbrace{10 \cdot 9 \cdot 8}^{3 \text{ factors}} = 720.$

▶ **EXERCISE 86**

1. Evaluate $n!$ for each integer value of n such that $1 \leqslant n \leqslant 10$.

2. How many different signals may be made with n flags arranged on a vertical staff if $n =$

     (a)   1   (b)   3   (c)   5   (d)   10   (e)   12

3. Suppose 12 flags are available. How many different signals may be made if each signal consists of the following number of flags arranged on a vertical staff:

     (a)   1   (b)   2   (c)   5   (d)   10   (e)   12

4.   How many different signals may be made by arranging flags on a vertical staff, if 6 flags are available?

5.   A "Scrabble" player has seven different letters before him, from which he wishes to form a word.   How many different arrangements of his letters may he consider, if the word is to consist of the following number of letters:

  (a) 1   (b) 2   (c) 3   (d) 4   (e) 5   (f) 6   (g) 7

6.   (a)   A "jotto" player has determined five different letters which he knows will, if properly arranged, form a word that his opponent has written down.   If he tries to discover the word by examining all possible arrangements of the five letters, how many arrangements may he have to consider?

   (b)   If the letters he has determined are a, e, m, s, t, what is the probability that a random arrangement of these letters will form an English word?

7.   Three letters are to be mailed and three mail-boxes are available in which to mail them.

   (a)   In how many ways may the letters be mailed if no box is to receive more than one letter?   (*Hint:* Call the letters: 1, 2, 3, and the mail-boxes: a, b, c, and use the ordered triple (c, a, b), for example, to represent a mailing in which letter 1 is dropped into box c, letter 2 into box a, and letter 3 into box b.)

   (b)   In how many ways may the letters be mailed if the restriction of (a) above is removed?

8.   Two secretaries leave an office for lunch.   One has 2 letters to mail and passes 3 mail-boxes on her way; the other has 3 letters and passes 2 mail-boxes.   Who may mail her letters in a greater variety of ways?   (See Problem 7 above.)

9.   In how many ways may 10 policemen be assigned to 2 beats? 2 policemen among 10 beats?   2 policemen among 10 beats, assuming that both cannot be assigned to the same beat?   (See Problem 7 above.)

10.   (a)   In how many ways may the letters v, w, x, y, z be arranged to form a nonsense word of five letters?

   (b)   In how many ways, if the first letter must be v?

   (c)   In how many ways, if the middle letter must be v?

   (d)   In how many ways, if the first letter must be v and the last z?

   (e)   How many five-letter nonsense words may be made with these letters if repetition of letters is allowed?

   (f)   How many nonsense words may be made with these letters if repetition is not allowed, but the word may have any number of letters?

11.　(a)　Five teams compete in a contest.　How many different rankings of the teams (assuming no ties) are possible at the end of the contest?

(b)　In how many different ways may a first and second prize be awarded in this contest?

(c)　Assuming the teams to be evenly matched, what is the probability that a given team will win first prize? second prize? one prize?

12.　The same as Problem 11 above, but with six, rather than five, teams competing.

13.　If two cards are dealt from a bridge deck, what is the probability that they will both be aces?

14.　(a)　$_nP_n = ?$

(b)　Replace the circled numbers in parentheses by correct expressions, in the order indicated by the circled numbers:

$$\overbrace{(r) \text{ factors}}\qquad\overbrace{(\textcircled{2}) \text{ factors}}$$
$$n! = \underbrace{(n)\,(n-1)\cdots(\textcircled{4})\,(\textcircled{3})\cdots(1)}_{(\textcircled{1})\text{ factors}}$$

(c)　Express $n!$ in terms of $_nP_r$ and $r!$

(d)　What is the "last" (i.e., the smallest) factor in the formula:

$$_nP_r = (n)\,(n-1)\cdots(\quad)$$

15.11　PERMUTATIONS WITH REPEATED ELEMENTS

There is a well-known story about a Texan returning home by train one day, who fell in with a boastful Easterner.　"All right," said the Texan, "this is my ranch we happen to be passing, and that is my herd of cattle. If you're as smart as you say you are, perhaps you can estimate the number of cattle in that herd?"　The Easterner glanced out the window and said: "1,684."　"Why that's *exactly* right," blurted the amazed Texan.　"How in the world did you do it?"　"It was easy," replied the Easterner.　"I just counted their feet and divided by 4."

In this section we shall find that a method like the Easterner's may actually be useful.

We know that the letters of the word "toe" may be arranged in 6 different ways, but what about the letters in the word "too"?

If the two "o's" were to be considered as different letters, say o_1 and o_2, then 6 arrangements would be possible:

(1)　　　$\begin{cases} to_1o_2,\ o_1to_2,\ o_1o_2t \\ to_2o_1,\ o_2to_1,\ o_2o_1t \end{cases}$

But since we are interested at the moment only in arrangements in which the two "o's" are not considered to be different, the 6 arrangements above yield only three in which we are interested:

(2) too, oto, oot

In fact, the second line of (1) above was derived from the first simply by interchanging o_1 and o_2 in each case.

The number of different ways in which the letters of the word "too" may be arranged may be derived, then, by dividing the 6 ways of (1) above by the number 2, which is the number of ways in which the letters o_1 and o_2 may be arranged.

Before generalizing, we consider two other cases.

In how many ways may the letters of the word "loll" be arranged?

If the three "l's" were different, we know that the answer to this problem would be $4 \cdot 3 \cdot 2 \cdot 1$, or 24. We group these 24 arrangements strategically:

$$(3) \quad \begin{cases} ol_1l_2l_3, & l_1ol_2l_3, & l_1l_2ol_3, & l_1l_2l_3o \\ ol_1l_3l_2, & l_1ol_3l_2, & l_1l_3ol_2, & l_1l_3l_2o \\ ol_2l_1l_3, & l_2ol_1l_3, & l_2l_1ol_3, & l_2l_1l_3o \\ ol_2l_3l_1, & l_2ol_3l_1, & l_2l_3ol_1, & l_2l_3l_1o \\ ol_3l_1l_2, & l_3ol_1l_2, & l_3l_1ol_2, & l_3l_1l_2o \\ ol_3l_2l_1, & l_3ol_2l_1, & l_3l_2ol_1, & l_3l_2l_1o \end{cases}$$

In fact, the last 5 lines of (3) above were derived by writing l_1, l_2, l_3 in all possible orders other than that of the first line, and leaving o in fixed position. There are, of course, 6 arrangements of l_1, l_2, l_3 that are possible, which accounts for the 6 lines of (3) above.

The 24 arrangements of (3) above may therefore be separated into $\frac{24}{6}$, or 4 groups [the columns of (3) above], such that each group leads (by dropping subscripts) to only one arrangement of the letters l, o, l, l, and such that all arrangements are thereby derived:

olll, loll, llol, lllo

The number of different ways in which the letters of the word "loll" may be arranged may be derived then, by dividing the 24 ways of (3) above by the number 6, which is the number of ways in which the letters l_1, l_2, l_3 may be arranged.

Finally, we consider the number of ways in which the letters of the word "hubbub" may be arranged.

Here each arrangement of the letters h, u, b, b, u, b, leads to 6 arrangements when the letters b, b, b are considered to be different, and *each* of these 6 yields 2 arrangements when the letters u, u are considered to be different. Thus, each arrangement of the letters h, u, b, b, u, b leads to $6 \cdot 2$ or 12 arrangements when these letters are considered to be 6 different letters. There are 6!, or 720 permutations of 6 different letters. There-fore they are $\frac{720}{12}$, or 60 possible ways of arranging the letters of the word "hubbub."

In general:

Suppose that in an ordered n-tuple, the elements which occur more often than once occur with multiplicity r, s, $\cdots$.

Then the number of permutations of the given n-tuple is given by the formula:

$$\frac{n!}{(r!)\,(s!)\cdots}$$

Note: Actually, we have so far defined only a permutation of a set of n *different* elements. More generally, a permutation may be defined as follows:

Given an ordered n-tuple, a permutation of the given ordered n-tuple is an ordered n-tuple whose elements are the same, and occur with the same multiplicity, as those of the given ordered n-tuple.

Illustrative Example. In how many ways may the letters of the word "Mississippi" be arranged?

SOLUTION. $\dfrac{11!}{4!\,4!\,2!} = \dfrac{11\cdot10\cdot9\cdot8\cdot7\cdot6\cdot5\cdot4\cdot3\cdot2}{4\cdot3\cdot2\cdot4\cdot3\cdot2\cdot2} = 34{,}650$

▶ **EXERCISE 87**

1. In how many ways may the letters of the following words be arranged?

(a) yoyo   (b) polo   (c) sissy
(d) scissors   (e) banana   (f) Massachusetts

2. How many linear patterns may be formed with

(a) 3 red checkers and 3 black checkers?
(b) 3 red checkers and 2 black checkers?
(c) 3 pennies, 2 dimes, and 1 nickel?

3. If 3 red checkers and 3 black checkers are arranged at random on a line, what is the probability that red and black will alternate?

4. How many baseball teams could be made using 9 players if:

(a) Any man can play any position?
(b) Jones can only pitch, but the others can play any position?
(c) Smith and Brown can only pitch or catch, but the others can play any position?

5. How many three letter arrangements of the letters of the word "troops" may be made? (*Hint:* consider three cases, according as to whether the three-letter word contains 0, 1 or 2 o's.

6. How many arrangements of 5 letters or less may be made with the letters of the word "speed"? (See Problem 5.)

7. How many arrangements of 5 letters or less may be made with the letters of the word "seeds"? (See Problem 5.)

8. If the letters of the word "loop" are arranged at random, what is the probability that they will spell an English word?

9. In how many ways may 4 people be seated around a table? (*Hint:* Suppose we write the ordered set (a, b, c, d) to mean that b sits to the right of a, c to the right of b, etc. Then the ordered sets (a, b, c, d), (b, c, d, a), (c, d, a, b), (d, a, b, c) all represent the same arrangement around a table. Every arrangement around the table leads to 4 arrangements in a line, and the number of arrangements around a table may be found by dividing the number of linear arrangements by 4.

10. In how many ways may 7 people be seated around a table? (See Problem 9.)

11. In how many ways may King Arthur and six of his knights be seated around the Round Table, if one of the seats is a throne upon which King Arthur must sit?

12. How many different patterns of wins and losses can a winning team post in a World Series contest between two baseball teams? (*Hint:* The Series is won as soon as one team wins 4 games. The Series may therefore be won in 4 or 5 or 6 or 7 games. The only pattern possible in a 4 game Series is (W, W, W, W), where W represents a win; etc.)

15.12 CHOICE (ORDERED)

The reasoning process that led to our formula for $_nP_r$ leads also to the following very general and very useful rule:

Suppose that a certain element of an ordered n-tuple may be chosen from a set of r elements, and that after that element has been chosen, another element of the ordered n-tuple may be chosen from a set of s elements; and so on.

Then the ordered n-tuple may be chosen in $(r)(s) \cdots$ ways.

In fact, the principles we have set down concerning the number of elements in a set of permutations or in a Cartesian product may be considered to be special cases of this rule; and the examples we have worked by these principles, and other examples of a more complicated nature, may be solved by means of this rule.

The student may find the following more intuitive phrasing of the rule helpful in applying it to particular situations:

Suppose that a first act may be performed in r ways; and that after the first has been performed, a second act may be performed in s ways; and so on.

Then the number of ways in which the first act, followed by the second, and so on, may be performed is given by the product:

$$(r)(s) \cdots$$

Illustrative Example I.   How many four-letter license plates are possible if the first and last letters are to be the same?

SOLUTION.   The first letter may be chosen in 26 ways.

After the first letter has been chosen, the last letter, since it must be the same as the first, must be chosen from a set containing only 1 element.

After these two choices have been made, the second letter may be chosen is 26 ways, and then the third letter may be chosen in 26 ways.

Therefore there are $26 \cdot 1 \cdot 26 \cdot 26$ four-letter license plates possible in which the first and last letters are the same.

In problems like the preceding, we find it convenient to write down a number of boxes to represent the places of the n-tuple in question, and then to fill in the appropriate boxes successively with the numbers $r, s, \cdots$ of the rule above.   For example, the following pattern may be constructed for the problem above:

| 26 | 26 | 26 | 1 |

and the product of the numbers entered is the solution to this problem.

Illustrative Example 2.   How many four-letter "words" (in the sequel we shall use "word" to mean any sequence of letters) which begin and end with a vowel may be formed from the letters a, e, i, p, q.

(*a*)   if no repetitions are allowed?

(*b*)   if repetitions are allowed?

SOLUTION.   (*a*)   We construct a pattern of four boxes to represent the four letters of the word to be formed:

| | | | |

Since the word is to begin with a vowel, the first letter may be chosen in 3 ways:

| 3 | | | |

Since the word must end with a vowel, and repetition of letters is not allowed, after the first place has been chosen only 2 letters remain from which to choose the letter in last place:

3			2

Having chosen first and last letters, thus using up two letters of the original five, 3 letters are left from which to choose the letter in second position:

3	3		2

Finally, 3 letters having been used, there remain 2 from which to choose the letter in third position:

3	3	2	2

The answer to (*a*) above, then, is: $3 \cdot 3 \cdot 2 \cdot 2$, or 36 words.

(*b*) If repetitions are allowed, we arrive at the following array:

3	5	5	3

so that 225 words may be formed in this case.

Illustrative Example 3. In how many ways may 3 girls and 3 boys stand in line, if boys and girls are to alternate?

SOLUTION 1. Clearly, there are 6 choices for first place. But after a choice for first place has been made, second place must be given to one of the 3 persons of sex opposite to that of the first choice.

Now a boy and a girl have been assigned, and 2 boys and 2 girls remain to be assigned. Third place must go to someone of sex opposite to that of the second choice; there are, therefore, 2 choices for third place; etc.:

6	3	2	2	1	1

The solution: 72 ways.

SOLUTION 2. If the line begins with a boy, the number of possible ways of forming a line in which boys and girls alternate is given by the product of the numbers in the following array:

3	3	2	2	1	1

Hence we see that there are 36 ways to form the line with a boy in first place. There must be an equal number with a girl in first place. There are, therefore, 36 + 36 or 72 different ways to form the line as required.

Illustrative Example 4. In how many ways may four bridge hands be dealt?

SOLUTION. The first hand may be dealt in $_{52}P_{13}$ ways. After that 39 cards are left, and the second hand may be dealt in $_{39}P_{13}$ ways, and so on. The four hands may be dealt in the following number of ways:

$$(1) \qquad\qquad (_{52}P_{13})(_{39}P_{13})(_{26}P_{13})(_{13}P_{13})$$

(Note that not all these hands are different. Some are the same hands dealt in different orders.)

We leave the computation of the number expressed in (1) above to the student with a great deal of time, or an adequate computing machine, at his disposal.

▶ **EXERCISE 88**

1. How many four-letter license plates may be issued in which:

(*a*) All the letters are the same?

(*b*) All the letters are different?

2. Using the English alphabet, how many "words" are there:

(*a*) Of 3 letters?

(*b*) Of 3 different letters?

(*c*) Of 3 letters, of which exactly two are the same?

(*Hint:* First find how many there are in which the *first* two are the same. How many other cases, in which there are as many possibilities as in this case, must be considered?)

3. A man who plans to drive from New York to Los Angeles and back, both by way of Chicago, finds 3 routes which he likes between New York and Chicago and 4 between Chicago and Los Angeles. He has a choice of how many routes going from New York to Los Angeles? How many for the round trip? How many for the round trip if the trip returning is to be totally different from the trip going? How many for the round trip if the trip returning is to be at least partially different from the trip going? How many for the round trip if the trip returning is to be partially but not totally different from the trip going?

4. How many linear patterns may be made with 3 red and 3 black checkers if the first and last checkers must be red?

5. A man has 3 jackets, 2 vests, and 4 pairs of trousers, all of which match. How many different costumes consisting of jacket, vest, and trousers does he have at his disposal?

6. In how many ways may:

(*a*) 3 billiard balls be dropped into 4 pockets?

(b)   4 billiard balls be dropped into 3 pockets?

(c)   3 billiard balls be dropped into 4 pockets, but not more than one in the same pocket?

7.   How many five-letter nonsense words may be made with the letters p, q, a, e, r if the middle letter is to be a vowel?

8.   How many even three-digit positive integers are there?   How many of them are less than 399?   How many of them are greater than 599?

9.   In how many ways may five people be seated on a straight bench, if two of them refuse to sit together?   In how many ways if two of them insist on sitting together?

10.   The same as Problem 9, but suppose that the bench is circular.

11.   Five couples for a square dance are to be chosen from a group consisting of 5 women and 5 men.   How many different sets of five couples may be chosen, if each couple is to consist of one man and one woman?

12.   Assuming that each seat has a window position and an aisle position, in how many ways may 5 men and 5 women be seated in 5 double seats on a train?   In how many ways if each double seat is to be occupied by one man and one woman?   In how many ways if the window seats are to be occupied by women?

13.   A test consists of three "sometimes-always-never" questions and three "true-false" questions.   What is the probability that a student will score 100% simply by guessing?   What is the probability that he will do equally well in a test consisting of ten "true-false" questions?

14.   The same as Problem 13, except that the student knows that no two consecutive answers are ever the same.

15.   How many different necklaces may be made with:

(a)   3 different beads?

(b)   5 different beads?

(c)   7 different beads?

16.   "Once upon a time a statistician made rapid calculations with graphs, slide rules, and simple arithmetic.   Then he announced that the chance of anyone picking the exact order of finish in either league was one in 40,400.   The chance of making the correct predictions in both leagues is one in 1,625,702,400.   Figures like that shake a fellow's confidence, and this soothsayer is beginning to doubt that he can do it."   (Arthur Daley, "Sports of the Times," *New York Times*, April 14, 1957.)

Show that one of Mr. Daley's figures is approximately, the other exactly, correct.   (The leagues to which he refers are the American and National baseball leagues, each containing eight teams.)

15.13 CHOICE (UNORDERED)

How many different committees of two people may be chosen from a group of three people?

This problem can easily be solved simply by setting down all of the possibilities in this case. If the set of three people is denoted $\{a, b, c\}$, the following committees of two may be formed:

$$(1) \qquad \{a, b\}, \{a, c\}, \{b, c\}$$

The answer to our problem, then, is: three committees.

Each of these 2-element subsets of the set of 3 elements $\{a, b, c\}$ is called a *combination of 3 things taken 2 at a time*. In general, an r-element subset of a set of n elements is called a *combination of n things taken r at a time*. The total possible number of combinations of n things taken r at a time, i.e., the number of r-element subsets of a set with n elements, is denoted $\binom{n}{r}$; what we have determined above may be expressed, then, in the following way:

$$\binom{3}{2} = 3$$

Note that combinations of r things differ from permutations of r things in that *order* is not at issue in the case of combinations. In fact, when order is taken into account, the combination $\{a, b\}$ leads to the permutations (a, b) and (b, a).

There is involved in the preceding statement a connection between combinations and permutations that will enable us to derive a formula for combinations from a known formula for permutations.

We know that the number of permutations taken 2 at a time of the 3 letters a, b, c is $3 \cdot 2$, or 6. In fact, these 6 permutations are:

$$(2) \qquad (a, b) \quad (a, c) \quad (b, c)$$
$$(b, a) \quad (c, a) \quad (c, b)$$

The 6 permutations of (2) above may be derived by writing each of the three sets of (1) above in all possible (namely 2) orders. In this case, there are *half* as many combinations as permutations.

Before generalizing, let us examine another case.

How many different committees of 3 people may be chosen from a group of 4 people?

If the set of 4 people is denoted $\{a, b, c, d\}$, the committees possible in this case may again easily be listed. (In fact, in both of the above cases, all we need do is omit one of the original set to form a committee as required):

$$(3) \qquad \{a, b, c\} \quad \{a, b, d\} \quad \{a, c, d\} \quad \{b, c, d\}$$

In this case, each combination of 3 elements gives rise to $3 \cdot 2 \cdot 1$, or 6 permutations of 3 elements. For example, the combination $\{a, b, c\}$ gives rise to the permutations:

$$(a, b, c), \quad (a, c, b), \quad (b, a, c), \quad (b, c, a), \quad (c, a, b), \quad (c, b, a)$$

Each combination in (3) above gives rise to 6 permutations. In this case, the number of combinations is *one-sixth* the number of permutations.

In general, each combination of r things gives rise to $r!$ permutations of the same elements; and the number of *combinations* of n things taken r at a time is $\dfrac{1}{r!}$ times the number of *permutations* of n things taken r at a time.

Or, in symbols:

$$\binom{n}{r} = \frac{{}_nP_r}{r!} = \frac{\overbrace{(n)(n-1)\cdots(\quad)}^{r \text{ factors}}}{(1)(2)\cdots(r)}$$

Illustrative Example 1. How many different three-card hands may be dealt from a bridge deck?

SOLUTION. $\binom{52}{3} = \dfrac{52 \cdot 51 \cdot 50}{1 \cdot 2 \cdot 3} = 22{,}100$

Note the difference between this example, and one like Illustrative Example 4 of the preceding section. Since the order in which the cards are dealt is immaterial so far as the final hand is concerned, we are dealing here with *combinations* rather than *permutations*.

Illustrative Example 2. Using the English alphabet, how many "words" of five letters may be formed, if exactly two of the letters are to be the same?

SOLUTION. First of all which two shall be the same? 2 places may be chosen out of 5 in $\binom{5}{2}$, or 10 ways.

After the choice has been made as to which two places shall be the same, the single letter that is to fill each of these places may be chosen in 26 ways.

There are left three places which may now be filled successively in 25, 24, and 23 ways.

The answer to the problem is therefore: $10 \cdot 26 \cdot 25 \cdot 24 \cdot 23$ ways.

[Compare this example with Problem 2(c) and the accompanying hint of the preceding exercise.]

Illustrative Example 3. What is the probability that a hand of 2 cards dealt from a bridge deck:

(a) will contain 2 red cards?

(b) will contain exactly one red card?

(c) will contain no red cards?

SOLUTION. (a) There are $\binom{52}{2} = \dfrac{52 \cdot 51}{1 \cdot 2}$ different hands of 2 cards which may be dealt from a deck of 52 cards.

Hands containing only red cards must be chosen from the 26 red cards of the deck. Therefore there are $\binom{26}{2} = \dfrac{26 \cdot 25}{1 \cdot 2}$ of the above hands of 2 cards which contain only red cards.

The probability, then, that a hand of 2 cards will contain only red cards is:

$$\frac{\binom{26}{2}}{\binom{52}{2}} = \frac{26 \cdot 25}{52 \cdot 51} = \frac{25}{102}$$

(b) A single red card may be chosen from the deck in $\binom{26}{1}$, or 26 ways. A single black card may then also be selected in 26 ways. One red and one black card may therefore be chosen in $26 \cdot 26$ ways. The required probability is therefore:

$$\frac{26 \cdot 26}{\binom{52}{2}} = \frac{26 \cdot 26}{26 \cdot 51} = \frac{26}{51}$$

(c) This hand must contain 2 black cards. The symmetry of the situation implies that the answer is the same as for part (a): $\frac{25}{102}$.

[Note that the probabilities in cases (a), (b), (c) add up to 1; this is to be expected, since it is *certain*, when two cards are dealt as described, that exactly one of the events (a), (b), (c) will occur.]

▶ **EXERCISE 89**

1. Evaluate:

(a) $\binom{5}{4}$ (b) $\binom{5}{1}$ (c) $\binom{7}{3}$ (d) $\binom{7}{4}$

(e) $\binom{8}{6}$ (f) $\binom{8}{2}$ (g) $\binom{n}{n}$ (h) $\binom{n}{0}$

(*Hint:* $\binom{n}{0}$ represents, given an *n*-element set, the number of subsets of that set which contain 0 elements. A set with 0 elements is called? How many such sets are there?)

2. From the results of Problem 1, one may induce that $\binom{n}{r} = \binom{n}{?}$.

3. (*a*) In how many ways may two apples be chosen from a box of eight apples?

(*b*) In how many ways may eight apples be divided equally among four people? (*Hint:* In how many ways may the first two apples be chosen? then the second two? etc.)

4. In how many ways may six people be separated into three equal groups? Into two equal groups? [See Problem 3(*b*) above.]

5. In how many ways may seven people be separated into a group of three people and a group of four people?

6. (*a*) In how many ways may five people be separated into a group of three people and a group of two people?

(*b*) In how many ways may a set of three people be chosen from a group of five people?

(*c*) In how many ways may a set of two people be chosen from a group of five people?

(*d*) How do you explain the interesting relationship among the answers to (*a*), (*b*), (*c*) above?

7. How many 3-element subsets does a set with 6 elements contain? How many 4-element subsets? How many 6-element subsets? How many null subsets?

8. How many subsets in all does a set with the following number of elements contain?

(*a*) 0   (*b*) 1   (*c*) 2   (*d*) 3   (*e*) 4   (*f*) *n*

9. Three musketeers arrive at an airport at the same time as three other people. All six want to board a plane which has only three available seats. They agree to decide who makes the trip by drawing straws.

(*a*) What is the probability that the three musketeers make the trip?

(*b*) What is the probability that Athos and Porthos go, but not Aramis?

(*c*) What is the probability that exactly two of the musketeers make the trip?

(*d*) What is the probability that exactly one of the musketeers makes the trip?

(*e*) What is the probability that none of the musketeers makes the trip?

10. The same as Problem 9, except that this time the three musketeers find themselves competing only with Cardinal Richelieu.

11. The same as Problem 10, except that Cardinal Richelieu says that even if he wins a seat he will give it up rather than ride with Athos.

12. In how many ways may 2 jackets, a vest, and 3 pairs of trousers be chosen from 3 jackets, 3 vests, and 6 pairs of trousers?

13. A committee consisting of two Russians, two Englishmen and two Irishmen is to be chosen from a group consisting of ten Russians, ten Englishmen and ten Irishmen. How many such committees are possible?

14. How many different two-card hands may be dealt from a bridge deck? How many different four-card hands?

15. What is the probability that a hand of two cards dealt from a bridge deck:

(a) will contain 2 spades?
(b) will contain exactly 1 spade?
(c) will contain no spades?
(d) will contain the ace of spades?

16. What is the probability that a hand of four cards dealt from a bridge deck will contain one card from each suit?

17. (a) Which is more likely, that all cards in a hand of four cards dealt from a bridge deck will be from different suits, or that they will all be from the same suit?

(b) What if only two cards are dealt?

18. Using the English alphabet, how many "words" of 4 letters may be formed if:

(a) all the letters are to be different?
(b) exactly 2 of the letters are to be the same?
(c) exactly 3 of the letters are to be the same?
(d) all the letters are to be the same?
(e) the first and last letters are to be the same?

19. (Compare this problem with Problem 8 above.) How many different amounts of money may be made with:

(a) a penny and a nickel?
(b) a penny, a nickel, and a dime?
(c) a penny, a nickel, a dime, and a quarter?
(d) a penny, a nickel, a dime, a quarter, and a half-dollar?
(e) a penny, a nickel, a dime, a quarter, a half-dollar, and a dollar?

20. In how many ways may a committee of 3 people be chosen from a group of 10 people? In how many ways if 2 of the 10 will only serve together? In how many ways if 2 of the 10 refuse to serve together?

21. (a) How many straight lines are determined by the vertices of a regular decagon?

(b) How many diagonals does a regular decagon have?

(c) How many diagonals does a regular n-sided polygon have? Verify for the cases $n = 3, 4, 5, 6$.

22. Show that:

(a) $\dbinom{n}{k} (n - k)! = \dfrac{n!}{k!}$ hence that $\dbinom{n}{k} = \dfrac{n!}{k! (n - k)!}$

(b) Suppose $n = r + s$. Show, using (a) above that:

$$\dbinom{n}{r} = \dfrac{n!}{r!\, s!}$$

$$\dbinom{n}{s} = \dfrac{n!}{s!\, r!}$$

hence that $\dbinom{n}{r} = \dbinom{n}{s}$

hence that $\dbinom{n}{r} = \dbinom{n}{n - r}$

(Compare with Problems 1, 2, and 6 above.)

23. Using the last formula proved in Problem 22 above, evaluate:

(a) $\dbinom{10}{9}$ (b) $\dbinom{20}{18}$ (c) $\dbinom{25}{21}$

(d) $\dbinom{50}{48}$ (e) $\dbinom{50}{49}$ (f) $\dbinom{50}{50}$

15.14 COMBINATIONS AND THE BINOMIAL THEOREM

(This section requires a prior consideration of the material of Section 11.9.)

An examination of the coefficient of $x^{n-r}y^r$ in the binomial expansion of $(x + y)^n$ on page 366 shows that this coefficient is nothing but our new friend $\dbinom{n}{r}$.

The elements of the "Pascal triangle" on page 363 are, then, the values of $\dbinom{n}{r}$. In fact, $\dbinom{n}{r}$ is the $(r + 1)$st entry in the n'th row of the Pascal triangle, as we have written it.

The fact that $\dbinom{n}{r} = \dbinom{n}{n - r}$ (see Problem 22, Exercise 89) now supplies a proof of our statement (see page 363) that the coefficients of a standard binomial expansion form a symmetric array about the middle of the expansion; for $\dbinom{n}{r}$ is the coefficient of $x^{n-r}y^r$, and $\dbinom{n}{n - r}$ is the coefficient of $x^r y^{n-r}$.

There is an intuitive explanation for the fact that the coefficient of $x^r y^{n-r}$ in the binomial expansion of $(x + y)^n$ is $\dbinom{n}{r}$: Consider, for example, the coefficient of $x^2 y^3$ in the expansion of $(x + y)^5 = (x + y)(x + y)(x + y)(x + y)(x + y)$. All the terms of this product may be arrived at by choosing either an x or a y (but not both) from each of the five factors $(x + y)$; for example, choosing an x from the first, a y from the second, and an x from each of the three remaining factors, one arrives at the term $xyxxx$, or x^4y. A term x^2y^3 arises in this multiplication by choosing x's from two of the five factors, and allowing the remaining factors to be y. But the two factors $(x + y)$ which are to supply x's may be chosen from among the five factors $(x + y)$ in $\binom{5}{2}$ ways; hence x^2y^3 occurs as a summand in the expansion of $(x + y)^5$, $\binom{5}{2}$ times, and when we add x^2y^3, $\binom{5}{2}$ times, the result is $\binom{5}{2}x^2y^3$. A general, and rigorous proof may be constructed along the lines of this intuitive argument.

If we let $x = 1$ and $y = 1$ in the binomial expansion of $(x + y)^n$, we arrive at the interesting result:

$$(1 + 1)^n = \binom{n}{0}(1)^n(1)^0 + \binom{n}{1}(1)^{n-1}(1)^1 + \binom{n}{2}(1)^{n-2}(1)^2 + \cdots$$

$$+ \binom{n}{n-1}(1)^1(1)^{n-1} + \binom{n}{n}(1)^0(1)^n$$

or: $\qquad 2^n = \binom{n}{0} + \binom{n}{1} + \cdots + \binom{n}{n}$

We have therefore proved that the number of subsets of a set with n elements (including the nullset as one subset), is 2^n (cf. Problem 10 of Exercise 2). If we exclude the nullset, then a set with n elements has $2^n - 1$ subsets. Another way of stating this result is: The number of combinations of n things taken any positive number at a time is $2^n - 1$.

This result has a direct application to problems such as Problem 19, Exercise 89.

▶ **EXERCISE**

1. In the binomial expansion of each of the following expressions, find the term in which the highest power of x or y is the given one:

(a) $(x + y)^7$; x^2 (b) $(x + y)^7$; x^5
(c) $(x + y)^{10}$; y^3 (d) $(x + y)^{10}$; y^7
(e) $(x - y)^{10}$; y^7 (f) $(x - 2y)^{10}$; x^8

(g) $(x - 2y)^{10}$; x^2 (h) $\left(x + \dfrac{1}{x}\right)^6$; x^0

(i) $\left(x - \dfrac{1}{x}\right)^5$; x (j) $\left(x - \dfrac{1}{x}\right)^{10}$; x^6

2. The construction of Pascal's triangle uses the following fact:

$$\binom{n}{r-1} + \binom{n}{r} = \binom{n+1}{r}$$

Prove that this equation is true. [*Hint:* Use the formula for $\binom{n}{k}$ in Problem 22(a) of Exercise 89, and the fact that $(m + 1)! = (m!)(m + 1)$.]

3. Prove $\binom{100}{0} + \binom{100}{2} + \cdots + \binom{100}{100} = \binom{100}{1} + \binom{100}{3} + \cdots + \binom{100}{99}$.

15.15 RELATED PROBABILITIES

We turn to an examination of the sample space for the experiment in which a coin is tossed 3 times, in order to induce a number of facts concerning the probabilities of certain related events:

$$\begin{Bmatrix} TTT, & TTH, & THT, & THH \\ HTT, & HTH, & HHT, & HHH \end{Bmatrix}$$

First of all we ask: What are the respective probabilities that 0, 1, 2, 3 heads appear in 3 tosses of a coin?

The subsets of the sample space and the probabilities associated with these four possibilities are:

0 heads:	$\{TTT\}$;	(probability $\frac{1}{8}$)
1 head:	$\{TTH, THT, HTT\}$;	(probability $\frac{3}{8}$)
2 heads:	$\{THH, HTH, HHT\}$;	(probability $\frac{3}{8}$)
3 heads:	$\{HHH\}$;	(probability $\frac{1}{8}$)

Note that these subsets are disjoint and exhaustive. (See page 17.)

Note also that the probabilities associated with these four possibilities have a sum of 1.

We shall call events *disjoint* if they are associated with disjoint subsets, and *exhaustive* if they are associated with exhaustive subsets of the sample space for these events.   Intuitively, events are disjoint if no two of them can happen simultaneously.   In three tosses of a coin, for example, one cannot achieve both exactly one head and exactly two heads.   These events are disjoint.   On the other hand, three tosses of a coin may simultaneously produce *at least one head* and *at least one tail*. (How?) These events are not disjoint.

Again intuitively, events are exhaustive if at least one of them must happen in the experiment with which they are associated.   Thus, in three tosses of a coin, at least one of the possibilities 0, 1, 2, 3, heads must occur; therefore these events form an exhaustive set.

Now the above discussion of the coin experiment suggests the following general rule:

The sum of the probabilities of a set of disjoint, exhaustive events is 1.

PROOF.   Let the set of disjoint, exhaustive events be associated with the set of disjoint, exhaustive subsets $A, B, C, \cdots$ of the sample space S. Suppose that the subsets $A, B, C, \cdots$ contain $a, b, c, \cdots$ elements, respectively, and that S contains s elements.   Then since the sets A, B, C are disjoint, and their union is S (cf. Problem 18, page 17):

$$a + b + c + \cdots \quad = s$$

Dividing through by s:

$$\frac{a}{s} + \frac{b}{s} + \frac{c}{s} + \cdots = 1$$

but the left-hand side of the above equation is the sum of the probabilities of the given set of events, so that our rule has now been proved to be true.

Now suppose we know the probability that an event E will occur. What is the probability that it will *not* occur? Suppose we call the event that it does not occur $\cancel{E}$. Then since an event cannot both occur and not occur, E and $\cancel{E}$ are disjoint. Also, since at least one of the two possibilities E, $\cancel{E}$ must occur, the events E, $\cancel{E}$ are exhaustive. Therefore the sum of their probabilities is 1. We therefore have, as a corollary to the above rule:

If p is the probability that an event will occur, then $1 - p$ is the probability that it will not occur.

Illustrative Example 1. If a coin is tossed three times, what is the probability that it will not happen that all three tosses fall tails?

SOLUTION. Since the probability that all three fall tails is $\frac{1}{8}$, the probability that this event does not happen is $1 - \frac{1}{8}$, or $\frac{7}{8}$.

Referring once more to the experiment of tossing a coin three times, we ask the question: What is the probability that either exactly 1 head or exactly 2 heads appear? The answer is clearly $\frac{6}{8}$, since exactly 1 or 2 heads appear in 6 of the 8 elements of the sample space. But note that $\frac{6}{8}$ is the sum of the probabilities of the events that exactly 1 head appears and that exactly 2 heads appear.

In fact in general:

If disjoint events have probability $p, q, \cdots$ of occurring, then the probability that at least one of the events will occur is: $p + q + \cdots$.

(The proof of this rule is omitted, since it is very much like the preceding proof.)

Illustrative Example 2. If a coin is tossed three times, what is the probability that at least 1 coin will fall heads?

SOLUTION. We shall use both of the two preceding rules in solving this problem.

First of all, by the preceding rule, the answer to the problem is $\frac{3}{8} + \frac{3}{8} + \frac{1}{8}$, or $\frac{7}{8}$.

Problems like this are often done more easily, however, by first finding the probability that the event in question will *not* happen. In our problem, if it does *not* happen that at least 1 coin falls heads, then all three must fall tails. The probability that all three fall tails is $\frac{1}{8}$. Therefore the probability that at least one coin falls heads is $1 - \frac{1}{8}$, or $\frac{7}{8}$.

15.16 INDEPENDENT AND DEPENDENT EVENTS

Suppose we toss an unbiased coin once; then the probability that it falls heads is $\frac{1}{2}$. Suppose, however, that the coin falls tails, and we toss it again. What is the probability that the second throw falls heads? Does the event that the first throw falls tails increase the probability that the second throw falls heads?

Let us examine the sample space for two throws of a coin: It is: $\{TT, TH, HT, HH\}$. If we are willing to admit that all of these possibilities are equally likely, then even after the first toss falls tails, the probability that the second falls heads is still only $\frac{1}{2}$. For there are two cases in which the first falls tails: TT and TH; and of these, there is exactly one case in which the second falls heads, namely TH. Even after the first toss falls tails, then, the probability that the second toss falls heads remains $\frac{1}{2}$; "the coin has no memory" (cf. Problem 7, Exercise 84).

When the probability that an event E occurs is unaffected by the occurrence or nonoccurrence of another event F, we say that the event E is *independent* of the event F. We have just observed that the event that a coin falls heads is independent of the event that it falls tails on a preceding throw.

We shall use the notation $P(E)$ to represent the probability of an event E, and $P(E \mid D)$ to represent the probability of an event E, given that an event D has occurred. Thus if E is the event "the second coin falls heads" and D the event "the first coin falls tails," we may write:

$$P(E) = \tfrac{1}{2}; \quad P(D) = \tfrac{1}{2}; \quad P(E \mid D) = \tfrac{1}{2}$$

Our definition of independence may now be more precisely phrased: *Event E is independent of event D if $P(E \mid D) = P(E)$.*

We are often interested in the probability that events E and D *both* occur. We denote this probability: $P(E \text{ and } D)$. With E and D as in the preceding example, $P(E \text{ and } D) = \frac{1}{4}$, for the events E and D both occur in exactly one of the four elements of the sample space for two throws of a coin.

We now derive a formula for $P(E \text{ and } D)$.

Suppose that event D contains d elements of a sample space of x elements (as for example, with D as above, $d = 1$ and $x = 2$), and that after D has occurred, E contains e elements of a sample space of y elements (as for example with D as above $d = 1$, $y = 2$). Then the sample space in which E and D may both occur is the Cartesian product of the sample spaces for E and D and contains xy elements; E and D both occur in de of these elements. Therefore:

$$P(E \text{ and } F) = \frac{de}{xy} = \frac{d}{x} \cdot \frac{e}{y}$$

But $\dfrac{d}{x} = P(D)$, and $\dfrac{e}{y} = P(E \mid D)$. Therefore:

$$P(E \text{ and } D) = P(D) \cdot P(E \mid D)$$

Illustrative Example. A card is drawn from a deck, and then another. What is the probability that:

(a) They are both spades, assuming that the first card is not replaced before the second is drawn?

(b) They are both spades, assuming that the first card is replaced and the deck shuffled before the second is drawn?

(c) They are of the same suit, assuming that the first card is not replaced before the second is drawn?

SOLUTION. (a) Let E be the event "the second card is a spade," D the event "the first card is a spade." $P(D) = \frac{13}{52} = \frac{1}{4}$; $P(E \mid D) = \frac{12}{51} = \frac{4}{17}$ (since after a spade has been drawn, there are 51 cards containing 12 spades from which to make the second choice). Therefore: $P(E \text{ and } D) = \frac{1}{4} \cdot \frac{4}{17} = \frac{1}{17}$.

(b) With E and D as above in (a), $P(D) = \frac{13}{52} = \frac{1}{4}$ as before, but in this case $P(E \mid D) = \frac{1}{4}$. Therefore $P(E \text{ and } D) = \frac{1}{16}$.

(c) Two cards will be of the same suit if they are both spades, or both diamonds, or both clubs, or both hearts. These are four disjoint events, so that the probability that at least one will occur is the sum of their respective probabilities of occurrence; but the four events are equally likely, so that the sum of the four probabilities is just four times the probability that any one of them will occur. We have found in (a) above that the probability that both cards are spades is $\frac{1}{17}$. Therefore the desired probability is $4 \cdot \frac{1}{17}$, or $\frac{4}{17}$.

▶ **EXERCISE 90**

1. A coin is tossed and a single die is rolled. What is the probability that:

(a) The coin falls heads?

(b) The coin does not fall heads?

(c) The die falls "6"?

(d) The die does not fall "6"?

(e) The coin falls heads and the die falls "6"?

(f) The coin falls heads and the die does not fall "6"?

2. A die is rolled twice. What is the probability that:

(a) The first roll falls "1"?

(b) The first roll does not fall "1"?

(c) The second roll falls an even number?

(*d*) The second roll does not fall an even number?

(*e*) The first roll falls "1" and the second roll falls an even number?

(*f*) The first roll falls "1" and the second roll falls an odd number?

3. A coin is tossed 10 times. What is the probability that there appear exactly:

(*a*) 0 tails? (*b*) 1 tail?

(*c*) 0 tails or 1 tail? (*d*) 2 or more tails?

(*e*) 8 or fewer heads?

4. A coin is tossed 8 times. What is the probability that there appear

(*a*) 0 heads? (*b*) 1 head?

(*c*) 2 heads? (*d*) 2 heads or fewer?

(*e*) 3 heads or more? (*f*) at most 5 tails?

5. A card is drawn from a bridge deck, and then another. Compute the probabilities of the following events, first assuming that the first card is not replaced, then that it is replaced before the second is drawn:

(*a*) Two aces. (*b*) An ace and a king. (*c*) No aces.

6. A baby has two sets of alphabet blocks to play with, each set containing each of the letters from A to Z just once. The baby chooses four blocks at random. What is the probability that he choses in succession the letters B, A, B, Y?

7. A box contains 3 red checkers and 4 black checkers. Three checkers are drawn in succession from the box. Compute the probabilities of the following events, first assuming that no checker is replaced after it is drawn, and then assuming that each checker is replaced before the next one is drawn:

(*a*) 3 red checkers.

(*b*) 3 black checkers.

(*c*) No red checkers.

(*d*) The first checker is red, the second black, and the third red.

(*e*) Only one of the checkers is red.

8. (*a*) Prove that if event E is independent of event D, then $P(E \text{ and } D) = P(E) \cdot P(D)$.

(*b*) Prove that independence of events is a symmetric relationship.

15.17 EMPIRICAL PROBABILITY

Sometimes a sample space or a probability is arrived at purely by mathematical computation (in which case we say that we are dealing with *a priori* probability), and sometimes by a physical experiment (in which case we say we are dealing with *empirical* probability). Empirical probability, as we shall soon see, forms a link between abstract probability theory and concrete statistical applications.

First of all, we offer some examples of both a priori and empirical probability. We have computed the a priori probability that a coin tossed twice falls heads both times to be $\frac{1}{4}$. Now if we conducted 100 experiments in which we tossed a coin twice and found that in 23 of these the coin fell heads twice, the empirical probability in this experiment, for the event that the coin fall heads twice, would be $\frac{23}{100}$.

When we determine the probability that a student chosen at random from a class will be a blonde, by actually counting the number of blondes and the number of students in the class and taking the ratio of the two; and when we assume that a baseball player's batting average represents the probability that he will get a hit in his next time at bat—we are once more dealing with empirical probability.

Illustrative Example I. Suppose that it has been determined by actual experiment that the probability that a certain coin fall heads is 0.8.

(*a*) If the coin is tossed twice, what is the probability that two heads appear?

(*b*) If the coin is tossed three times, what is the probability that at least one head appears?

(*c*) If the coin is tossed four times, what is the probability that the first two fall heads and the second two do not?

(*d*) If the coin is tossed four times, what is the probability that exactly two heads appear?

(*e*) If the coin is tossed four times, what is the probability that at least two heads appear?

SOLUTION. (*a*) The probability that a head appears the first time and a head appears the second time is (0.8)(0.8), or 0.64.

(*b*) Here it is easier to compute the probability that the event in question does not happen, and then to subtract that probability from 1.

If it does not happen that at least one head appears, then 0 heads appear, i.e., no toss falls heads. The probability that a toss does not fall heads is $1 - 0.8$, or 0.2. The probability that three successive tosses do not fall heads is (0.2)(0.2)(0.2), or 0.008. Therefore the required probability is $1 - 0.008$, or 0.992.

(*c*) The probability that these events occur in succession is (0.8)(0.8)(0.2)(0.2) = 0.0256.

(*d*) First we find the number of ways in which the two tosses which are to fall heads may be chosen. This is $\binom{4}{2}$. In each of these cases, the probability that the chosen two will fall heads and the other two will not is $(0.8)^2(0.2)^2$. Therefore the probability that exactly two will fall heads is $\binom{4}{2}(0.8)^2(0.2)^2$, or $(6)(0.0256)$, or 0.1536.

(*e*) At least two heads includes the cases exactly two heads, or exactly three heads, or exactly four heads.

We have already computed the probability of exactly two heads to be $\binom{4}{2}(0.8)^2(0.2)^2$.

The probability that a particular triple will fall heads, and the fourth not, is $(0.8)^3(0.2)$. A particular triple to fall heads may be chosen in $\binom{4}{3}$ ways. Therefore the probability that exactly three heads fall is $\binom{4}{3}(0.8)^3(0.2)$.

The probability that all four tosses fall heads may be computed directly as $(0.8)(0.8)(0.8)(0.8)$, or following the reasoning of the preceding cases as $\binom{4}{4}(0.8)^4(0.2)^0$, which comes to the same thing.

The probability that at least two heads appear is therefore:

$$\binom{4}{2}(0.8)^2(0.2)^2 + \binom{4}{3}(0.8)^3(0.2) + (0.8)^4$$
$$= 0.1536 + 0.4096 + 0.4096$$
$$= 0.9728$$

Illustrative Example 2. A baseball player has a batting average of .333 (which we approximate by the fraction $\frac{1}{3}$). Assuming that this represents the probability that he hits safely when he bats, what is the probability that he will garner at least one hit in three times at bat?

SOLUTION. (The answer "1" which suggests itself turns out to be wrong. It is *not* certain that this player will get a hit in 3 times at bat. The player, for example, might maintain his 0.333 average by hitting only in the last two of each set of six trips to the plate.)

We compute the probability of the negative of the required event, namely that he does not hit in each of three times at bat. This is $(\frac{2}{3})(\frac{2}{3})(\frac{2}{3}) = \frac{8}{27}$. Therefore the probability that he does hit at least once in 3 times at bat is $1 - \frac{8}{27}$, or $\frac{19}{27}$.

Illustrative Example 3. The following is a "mortality table" similar to those used by insurance companies in establishing their rates:

Age	I	20	40	60	80
No. living	100,000	95,000	88,000	68,000	18,000

What is the probability that a man of age 40 will live to age 60?

SOLUTION.   The required probability is $\frac{68}{88}$, or approximately 0.77.

▶ **EXERCISE 91**

1.   A coin is thrown 10,000 times and falls heads 6,000 times.

(a)   In this case, what is the empirical probability that the coin falls heads?   (Use this probability in the following examples.)

(b)   If the coin is thrown twice, what is the probability of the result HT? of the result TH? of throwing two heads? of throwing two tails? What is the sum of these probabilities?   Why?

(c)   If the coin is thrown three times, what is the probability of the result HTT? of throwing exactly one head? of throwing exactly two heads? of throwing three heads? of throwing no heads?

2.   The same as Problem 1, except that the coin falls heads 4,000 times.

3.   The probability that a certain coin falls heads is 0.1; the coin is tossed five times.   What is the probability that:

(a)   No heads appear   (b)   Exactly 1 head appears
(c)   Exactly 2 heads appear   (d)   Exactly 3 heads appear
(e)   Exactly 4 heads appear   (f)   Five heads appear
(g)   At least 1 head appears (h)   Three or more heads appear

4.   A baseball player has a batting average of 0.333.   What is the probability that he does not go hitless in four trips to the plate? in six trips?

5.   A baseball player has a batting average of 0.250.   What is the probability that he gets at least one hit in four times at bat? in five times?

6.   In a survey made in a certain freshman class, it was found that 90% of all students who passed mathematics passed physical education, 80% of all students who passed physical education passed mathematics, and 60% of the class passed both mathematics and physical education.

Interpreting these percentages as probabilities, and using the formula $P(E \text{ and } D) = P(D) \cdot P(E \mid D)$, what percentage of the class passed mathematics? what percentage passed physical education?

7.   It is reported that in a certain town, twice as many people own dogs as own cats, but 15% of all people who own dogs also own cats,

and 10% of all people who own cats also own dogs. Can this report be accurate? (See Problem 6.)

8. An anti-aircraft battery has been found to be 50% effective; i.e., the probability that it will shoot down a plane passing over it is 0.5. Suppose a plane must pass two such batteries in succession to reach a target. How effective will the two batteries be? (*Hint:* First find the probability that the plane is *not* shot down by the successive batteries.)

9. (*a*) If an anti-aircraft battery is 80% effective, what will be the effectiveness of three such batteries over which a plane must fly in succession? (See Problem 8.)

(*b*) What must the effectiveness of anti-aircraft battery be if two such batteries over which a plane must fly in succession are to have an effectiveness of 99%.

10. A certain finished product is assembled from three components. When components are inspected separately, it is found that about 1% of each are defective. Suppose only the finished product is inspected. What proportion may be expected to be defective? (*Hint:* First find the proportion *not* defective.)

11. Using the table of Illustrative Example 3 above:

(*a*) What is the probability that a 20-year old man will live for at least 20 years more?

(*b*) What is the probability that an infant 1 year old will attain the age of 80? 60? 40? 20?

(*c*) What is the probability that a 20-year old man will live until he is 40? 60? 80?

(*d*) What is the probability that a 40-year old man will die before he is 60? 80?

15.18 ODDS AND EXPECTATION

"Odds" are simply a popular way of expressing probability. They compare the probability that an event will occur with the probability that it will not. More precisely: If p is the probability of an event, then we say that the odds in favor of this event is the ratio $p : (1 - p)$, read: "p to $1 - p$."

(The ratio $p : (1 - p)$ is, of course, equal to the fraction $\dfrac{p}{1 - p}$.)

For example, if the probability of an event is $p = \frac{2}{3}$, then $1 - p = \frac{1}{3}$, and the odds in favor of this event are $\frac{2}{3} : \frac{1}{3}$, or $2 : 1$.

Conversely, if we are given the odds $r : s$ in favor of an event, we may determine the probability p of the event. For:

(1)
$$\frac{p}{1 - p} = \frac{r}{s}$$

Solving this equation for p we find:

(2)
$$p = \frac{r}{r + s}$$

For example, if the odds in favor of an event are $2:3$, then the probability of the event is $\frac{2}{5}$.

Odds are used to determine the amount of a "fair" wager. If the odds in favor of a certain event are $2:1$, for example, then a fair bet would be one in which a man betting $2 on the event would win $1 if the event occurs, and lose $2 if the event fails to occur.

To see why this is a fair bet, note that the odds of $2:1$ reflect the expectation that in a large number of trials of this event, the event will occur twice as often as it fails to occur. In 300 trials, for example, the event might be expected to occur 200 times, and to fail to occur 100 times. A man betting $2 at the above odds 300 times might be expected to win a total of $(200)(\$1)$, or $200, and lose a total of $(100)(\$2)$, or $200, and finally, therefore, to "break even." Neither "odds" nor "probability," however, *guarantee* that these expectations will be fulfilled. They only express likelihoods in which we can place more and more confidence with a larger and larger number of trials.

Allied to the concept of a fair wager is that of *mathematical expectation*:

Suppose $E_1, E_2, \cdots$ are disjoint, exhaustive events with probabilities $p_1, p_2, \cdots$, respectively. Suppose that the events $E_1, E_2, \cdots$ are associated respectively with amounts of money $m_1, m_2, \cdots$ (which may be rewards or losses when the associated event occurs, depending on whether the "m" involved is $+$ or $-$.) Then the *mathematical expectation* for this situation is defined to be:

$$m_1 p_1 + m_2 p_2 + \cdots$$

Thus, in the case of the bet we have just considered, the set of disjoint, exhaustive events is: E (the event in question occurs), and E' (the event in question does not occur). The probabilities of E, E' are $\frac{2}{3}, \frac{1}{3}$, respectively. The associated monetary rewards are $1, -2, respectively. The mathematical expectation in this case is $[(\frac{2}{3})(1) + (\frac{1}{3})(-2)]$, or $0.

In fact, we may *define* a bet to be fair if it results in a mathematical expectation of 0.

The mathematical expectation of a game may be thought of as the average amount which one may expect to win in the game. In a game with mathematical expectation $5, for example, one may expect to win

$500 in 100 games. Virtually all commercial gambling enterprises, of course, involve games with negative expectations (for the customer).

Illustrative Example I. In rolling a pair of dice, what are the odds in favor of a "2?"

SOLUTION. We have already (see Problem 5 of Exercise 84) computed the probability of this event to be $\frac{1}{36}$. The odds in favor of this event are therefore $\frac{1}{36} : (1 - \frac{1}{36})$, or $1:35$.

Illustrative Example 2. A person bets $5 at odds of $1:30$ that a roll of a pair of dice will show "2." What is his mathematical expectation?

SOLUTION. If he wins, he wins $150. If he loses, he loses $5. The probabilities of these two events are $\frac{1}{36}$, $\frac{35}{36}$, respectively. His mathematical expectation is therefore:

$$\$[(150)(\tfrac{1}{36}) + (-5)(\tfrac{35}{36})]$$

or about $-69\cent$. He may expect to lose an average of $69\cent$ per bet in a large number of these bets.

Illustrative Example 3. An insurance company finds from a mortality table that the probability that a certain man will live until the expiration of a short-term policy of $1000 is 0.99. Suppose the company feels that it needs a profit of $3 to cover expenses on this policy. What should the charge for the policy be?

SOLUTION. Let x dollars be the required charge. The expectation of the insurance company in this "game" is to be $3. If the insured lives, the insurance company "wins" x dollars. If the insured dies, the insurance company keeps x dollars and pays out $1000, a net gain of $(x - 1000)$ dollars. The probabilities of these two events are 0.99, 0.01, respectively. Therefore the expectation is:

(3) $$0.99x + 0.01(x - 1000) = 3$$

The solution of this equation is $x = 13$, so that the required charge is $13.

▶ **EXERCISE 92**

1. Using the results of Problem 5(*b*) of Exercise 84, find the odds in favor of rolling each of the numbers from 1 to 12 with a pair of dice.

2. ". . . the odds in any country in the world that a guy does not make a ten with a pair of dice before he rolls seven, is two to one." (Damon Runyon, *Blood Pressure*.)

Show that these odds are correct, using the following fact (which may be proved): The odds that one of two events occurs before another in successive trials of an experiment is the ratio of the probability of the first event to the probability of the second event.

3.   The odds that a certain horse will win a race are $9:1$.   What is the probability that the horse will win?

4.   (a)   Solve equation (2) above for p, to arrive at equation (1).

(b)   Solve equation (3) above, to show that $x = 13$.

5.   In a certain "numbers game," a person bets at odds of $600:1$ on three digits of his own choice.   If the digits he chooses are the last three digits (in the correct order) of the daily U.S. Treasury balance, as reported in the next day's newspapers, he wins.

(a)   What is the probability that he guesses the three digits, in their correct order?

(b)   If he bets $10, what is his expectation?

(c)   If he bets 10¢ a day, every day for a year, how much may he expect to win or lose?

6.   If the probability that a man dies before the expiration of a certain short-term policy is 0.05, and an insurance company charges $60 for a $1000 policy insuring the life of the man for that period, what part of the $60 may be considered to be for the purpose of paying expenses of running the company?   What may be considered to be the purpose of the remaining part of the $60 charge?

7.   If the probability that a man dies before the expiration of a certain short-term policy is 0.02, what should an insurance company charge for a policy insuring the life of that person for $1000 for that period, if expenses of $10 must be covered?

8.   Show that if the odds (to win) on two horses in a two-horse race are $5:3$ and $1:2$, then it is possible to place bets on the two horses in such a way as to be sure that the amount won will be greater than the amount lost.

9.   (a)   Suppose that the odds (to win) on two horses in a two-horse race are $a:b$ and $c:d$.   Prove that it is possible to place bets on the two horses in such a way as to be sure that the amount won will be greater than the amount lost, if and only if $ac < bd$.

(b)   Show that if the preceding odds are translated into probabilities, then the condition $bd > ac$ is equivalent to the condition that the sum of the probabilities is less than 1.

15.19   DECISION AND DESIGN

Statistics is more and more coming to be regarded as the science of making "wise decisions in the face of uncertainty."   In this section we shall examine statistical problems which illustrate this point of view.

Our main tool in the solution of the problems of decision which we shall propose, will be the following theorem (whose proof we shall omit):

Suppose that in one trial of an experiment, an event has an a priori probability p of occurrence. Then in n trials of the event, the mean number of occurrences of the event is given by the formula m = np, and the standard deviation for n trials is given by the formula s = $\sqrt{np(1-p)}$.

For example, suppose we consider the experiment of tossing a coin $n = 3$ times, and the event of showing heads, whose a priori probability in one toss is $p = \frac{1}{2}$. The sample space for this experiment is:

$$\{HHH, HHT, HTH, HTT, THH, THT, TTH, TTT\}$$

A frequency table for the number of heads appearing in elements of this sample space, and columns necessary to compute the mean $m = \bar{x}$ and the standard deviation s for this distribution follow:

NUMBER OF HEADS x	FREQUENCY f	xf	$x - \bar{x}$	$(x - \bar{x})^2 f$
0	1	0	−1.5	2.25
1	3	3	−0.5	0.75
2	3	6	0.5	0.75
3	1	3	1.5	2.25
	8	12		6.00

$$m = \bar{x} = \frac{12}{8} = 1.5$$

$$s = \sqrt{\frac{6}{8}} = \sqrt{0.75}$$

According to the formulas given above, $m = np = (3)(\frac{1}{2}) = 1.5$, and $s = \sqrt{np(1-p)} = \sqrt{(3)(\frac{1}{2})(\frac{1}{2})} = \sqrt{0.75}$. We see, then, that these formulas are correct, at least in the case we have just considered.

Now we attack a problem of decision:

Illustrative Example 1. A coin is tossed 100 times, and comes up heads 75 times. Decide whether or not the coin is "true," i.e., unweighted.

SOLUTION. We must understand first of all that it is quite possible for a perfectly true coin to fall heads 75 out of 100 tosses; in fact, if we had the patience and time to continue the experiment for a *very* long time, it is *almost certain* that we would even be able to make 100 tosses in which *all* the tosses fell heads.

In order to make a decision in cases like that of our problem, then, we are forced arbitrarily to choose some measure of likelihood beyond which we will not accept a result as being due simply to chance variation.

We recall (see page 440) that with a sufficiently numerous set of "normal" data, one may expect that only about 5% of the data will fall further than two standard deviations from the mean, and only about 0.3% will fall further than three standard deviations from the mean.

Our method, in this introductory treatment, will be crude, since, for one thing, we shall not look too carefully at what constitutes a "sufficiently numerous" n. It turns out, however, that for the values of n to which we shall apply the preceding principles, the results are fairly accurate.

Suppose we agree, as a practical matter, to consider a coin untrue if it produces an event which falls further than three standard deviations from the mean.

In the case of the coin of our illustrative example, $n = 100$, $p = \frac{1}{2}$, $m = np = 50$, $s = \sqrt{np(1 - p)} = \sqrt{(100)(\frac{1}{2})(\frac{1}{2})} = 5$. To be within 3 standard deviations of the mean, the number of heads would have to lie between $50 - 15$ and $50 + 15$, i.e., between 35 and 65; the given number of heads, 75, lies outside this interval. According to our arbitrary criterion of decision, this coin is untrue.

It is high time that we offered our promised explanation of what we mean by the term "normal," as applied to a set of data. Furthermore, our course is now nearly at an end; it would be well to re-examine once more the nature of mathematics, its connection with the material world, and how this last long chapter on statistics and probability fits into the general picture. Happily, the two are related: the question of "normality" in statistics touches upon the place which statistics holds in mathematics as a whole.

We have indicated earlier that although a great deal of mathematics has been suggested by material phenomena, there is also a considerable body of mathematics that has stemmed directly from the mathematician's imagination; in any case, whatever the source, pure mathematics is independent of the physical world. Pure mathematics consists of a set of axioms, from which the mathematician, using the rules of deductive logic, wrings consequences.

When a set of axioms "fits" a concrete situation, then we say that the set of axioms (and the consequences of these axioms) form a "mathematical model" for the concrete situation (cf. Section 6.1). Thus, the axioms of geometry form a mathematical model for the concrete world of strings and boxes and bridges, and so on.

But this "fitting" is always more or less approximate; for it depends on the senses of man, and the senses of man are notoriously inexact. What, for example, is the width of this page? The mathematical model called "Euclidean geometry" assumes that there is one and only one real number that expresses that width. To determine that unique real number is, however, as a practical matter quite impossible. The most accurate of measurements vary upon repetition.

The physicist and engineer, therefore, tend now to deal with *average* measurements, characterized by a *probability*, rather than a *certainty* of exactness. And just because of the inexactness with which mathematical models mirror the physical world, statistics and probability, which measure and deal with uncertainty, have within recent years begun to assume a tremendously important role in the applications of mathematics. The chemist or physicist, for example, is now likely to say not that if one does so and so, then such and such will happen, but if one does so and so, then *there is a probability of so much* that such and such will happen.

Now, to get back to the question of "normality."

We have built up an abstract, "a priori" theory of probability, which, as a matter of fact is a part of our theory of sets. When we analyze the events that may happen when a coin falls twice, let us say, we build up a a set of ordered pairs $\{HH, HT, TH, TT\}$, and actually this has nothing to do with a coin. Even a penniless beggar could work out the probabilities in this situation. We assume, however, that a "true" coin would, in some fashion, fit this analysis. What justification is there for our faith in the application of abstract probability theory to concrete problems? The answer is the same as that for geometry: it works, at least accurately enough for practical needs. It passes the "pragmatic" test.

In certain collections of data, there is a distribution of frequencies which resembles that of a coin tossing experiment. That is to say, there is a "middle" value which occurs with maximum frequency, and frequencies diminish as we move left or right of the middle value. (See the frequency polygons of Section 15.2.) Very roughly speaking, this is what we mean by a "normal" distribution. More precisely, it is a distribution to which the abstract probability theory we have developed and stated above applies (approximately, of course). We assume that a large number of tosses of a coin or rolls of a die or cards drawn from a pack will conform to this theory, and experience shows that our assumption works fairly well in practice. We assume that certain random collections of data, like the heights of all male students at X college, are "normal" also, and again experience has confirmed that our mathematical model is adequately faithful. But it is important to note that not *all* collections of data form normal distributions; for example, suppose we tabulated the *ages* of all male students at X college. Because of the drop-out in successive semesters, freshmen students predominate; the frequency polygon does not assume the symmetric bell-shape of the normal distribution.

We continue with further examples of statistical approaches to problems of decision.

Illustrative Example 2. A true-false test consists of 100 questions. Will a student be able to get as many as 60 right simply by guessing? How about 70?

SOLUTION. The probability that a student will guess the answer to a question correctly is $p = \frac{1}{2}$. The number of questions is $n = 100$; $m = np = 50$; $s = \sqrt{np(1-p)} = 5$.

If we accept only results further than two standard deviations from the mean as being unlikely to be attained by chance (we shall call this the "$2s$" criterion"), then getting as many as 60 right would be just barely possible by guessing, but getting as many as 70 right would not.

If we use a $3s$ criterion, then as many as 60 right would have to be regarded as being possible by pure chance, but as many as 70 would not; using the $3s$ criterion, $50 + 3s = 65$ is the "borderline" case.

In the case of small n, our statements about the percentage of data to be expected within 1, 2, and 3 standard deviations from the mean no longer hold. An alternative analysis is applied in the next example.

Illustrative Example 3. In a true-false test of 10 questions, can one get at least 6 right by guessing? 7? 8? 9? 10?

SOLUTION. The probability of getting exactly the following number right by guessing (see Illustrative Example 1(d), page 478), is:

6 right: $\dbinom{10}{6}\left(\dfrac{1}{2}\right)^6\left(\dfrac{1}{2}\right)^4 = \dbinom{10}{6}\left(\dfrac{1}{2}\right)^{10} = \dbinom{10}{4}\left(\dfrac{1}{2}\right)^{10} = \dfrac{210}{1024}$

7 right: $\dbinom{10}{7}\left(\dfrac{1}{2}\right)^7\left(\dfrac{1}{2}\right)^3 = \dbinom{10}{7}\left(\dfrac{1}{2}\right)^{10} = \dbinom{10}{3}\left(\dfrac{1}{2}\right)^{10} = \dfrac{120}{1024}$

8 right: $\dbinom{10}{8}\left(\dfrac{1}{2}\right)^8\left(\dfrac{1}{2}\right)^2 = \dbinom{10}{8}\left(\dfrac{1}{2}\right)^{10} = \dbinom{10}{2}\left(\dfrac{1}{2}\right)^{10} = \dfrac{45}{1024}$

9 right: $\dbinom{10}{9}\left(\dfrac{1}{2}\right)^9\left(\dfrac{1}{2}\right)^1 = \dbinom{10}{9}\left(\dfrac{1}{2}\right)^{10} = \dbinom{10}{1}\left(\dfrac{1}{2}\right)^{10} = \dfrac{10}{1024}$

10 right: $\dbinom{10}{10}\left(\dfrac{1}{2}\right)^{10}\left(\dfrac{1}{2}\right)^0 = \dbinom{10}{10}\left(\dfrac{1}{2}\right)^{10} = (1)\left(\dfrac{1}{2}\right)^{10} = \dfrac{1}{1024}$

Summing the appropriate probabilities, the probability of getting at least the following number right is:

$$\text{At least 6 right: } \frac{386}{1024} \doteq 0.377$$

$$\text{At least 7 right: } \frac{176}{1024} \doteq 0.172$$

At least 8 right: $\dfrac{56}{1024} \doteq 0.055$

At least 9 right: $\dfrac{11}{1024} \doteq 0.011$

All 10 right: $\dfrac{1}{1024} \doteq 0.001$

Assuming that an event with a probability of less than 0.06 (let us say) is unlikely to occur by chance, we decide that one may get as many as 7 right by guessing, but not 8 or more. (A 0.05 criterion here would correspond to the $2s$ criterion we used previously; see page 486.)

In fact the method of this example is sharper than our previous approach, and is applicable to the same problems. However, for large n the computations involved may be tedious. Fortunately, tables are available that greatly reduce the labor of computation by giving values of $\binom{n}{r}(p)^r(1 - p)^{1-r}$, and sums of these values, for a large number of values of n, r, and p.

Note that the expression $\binom{n}{r}p^r(1 - p)^{1-r}$ is one of the terms of the binomial expansion of $[p + (1 - p)]^n$. It is for this reason that what we have (loosely) called a "normal" distribution is often called a "binomial" distribution. We make this distinction however: although we have reserved the term "normal" to apply only to large n, binomial distributions exist for all positive integer values of n.

Illustrative Example 4. Tom claims that he has mysterious powers of extra-sensory perception (ESP). He does not claim to be infallible, but he says, for example, that he can tell significantly often in advance whether a coin will fall heads or tails. When pressed as to what he means by significantly often, he expresses the conviction that it is about 8 times out of 10. Design a fair test of his powers of ESP.

SOLUTION. Suppose we make the test involve 36 tosses of a coin. We would not be surprised at anyone's getting 18 right; that could easily happen by chance. We would demand that a person get more than 18 right before we would put any stock in his claim to ESP. The question is: how much more?

Tom, on the other hand, although he has laid claim to being able to guess right 0.8 of the time, would not abandon his claim if he guessed somewhat fewer than $(0.8)(36) \doteq 29$ on this particular test. Eight out of ten is his average feat, he says, and that figure may vary somewhat from test to test. Here the question is: How many fewer than 29 right will convince Tom that he is not particularly psychic?

Somewhere between 18 and 29 we must choose a number which will suit both the tester and Tom.

In this situation, $n = 36$.   If the guessing were purely random, $p = \frac{1}{2}$. Under this hypothesis, $m = np = 18$, $s = \sqrt{np(1 - p)} = 3$.   Using the $2s$ criterion, any number greater than $18 + 6 = 24$ right would be unusual, so that the tester feels that Tom must get at least 24 right to demonstrate that he has any ESP at all.

Under Tom's hypothesis, $n = 36$, $p = 0.8$, $m = 28.8$, $s = 2.4$.   Using the $2s$ criterion, any number fewer than $28.8 - 4.8 = 24$ right would be unlikely.   Tom agrees that if he gets fewer than 24 right, he will modify his claim.

The test we design, then, is this: A coin is tossed 36 times.   If Tom gets 24 or more right, we admit that Tom does have significant powers of ESP. If Tom gets fewer than 24 right we deny his claims.

It is purely fortuitous that in this example both hypotheses as to the value of p led to the same critical number: 24.   In fact with a smaller number of tosses, the two parties to the experiment might find themselves in conflict with regard to a fair critical number; with a larger number of tosses, as might be expected, agreement would be easier, and one might even expect to be able to use the more stringent $3s$ criterion.

It should be stressed that the result of any experiment of this sort cannot ever be considered to be quite conclusive.   There is always *some* possibility that real ability may not evidence itself, or that we may be led by chance to discover ability that does not actually exist.   Furthermore, it should be noted that we have here considered only a mathematical aspect of the problem of designing an experiment, and that very briefly.   There are, among others, mechanical and psychological aspects to be considered also.   There is a great deal more that can be said about such problems. In fact the field is one which, like all of mathematics, both pure and applied, is still very far from being a closed book.

▶ **EXERCISE 93**

1.   Verify the correctness of the formulas $m = np$ and $s = \sqrt{np(1 - p)}$ for the case of four tosses of a coin.

2.   In each of the following cases, the number of heads which a coin shows in a certain number of tosses is given.   Discuss the question of whether the coin is a properly balanced one.

(*a*)   60 heads in 100 tosses.

(*b*)   240 heads in 400 tosses.

3.   The same as Problem 2 above for the cases:

(*a*)   31 heads in 49 tosses.

(*b*)   62 heads in 100 tosses.

(*c*)   4 heads in 5 tosses.   (*Hint:* Use the technique of Illustrative Example 3.)

4.   Discuss the "normality" of the following sets of data:

(*a*)   The grades in an examination of 1000 students.

(*b*)   The grades in an examination of 30 students.

(*c*)   The grades in an examination of 10 students.

(*d*)   The heights of all voters in Boston.

(*e*)   The heights of all basketball players in the U.S.

(*f*)   The incomes in 1957 of all people in the U.S. who earned money in that year.

(*g*)   The incomes in 1957 of all people in the U.S. whose earnings exceeded $10,000 in that year.

5.   A pair of dice comes up 7 the following number of times in the following number of rolls.   Are the dice loaded?

(*a*)   25 times out of 80 rolls.

(*b*)   20 times out of 80 rolls.

(*c*)   15 times out of 80 rolls.

(*d*)   11 times out of 45 rolls.

(*e*)   14 times out of 45 rolls.

(*f*)   16 times out of 45 rolls.

(*g*)   4 times out of 4 rolls.   (*Hint:* Use the technique of Illustrative Example 3.)

6.   What would you say about a pair of dice which rolled "2" twice in succession?

7.   If a passing grade is 70%, will a student be likely to pass a true-false test of the following number of questions simply by guessing?

   (*a*)   81   (*b*)   64   (*c*)   49   (*d*)   36   (*e*)   25
(*f*)   5 (Use the technique of Illustrative Example 3.)

8.   If a passing grade is 60%, will a student be likely to pass an "always-sometimes-never" test of the following number of questions simply by guessing?

   (*a*)   100   (*b*)   50   (*c*)   25   (*d*)   5

9.   Suppose that p_1 represents the probability which Tom claims describes his ability to predict the fall of a coin.   Discuss the feasibility of designing a test of his claim which involves the following number of tosses, n, and if a test is feasible with this number, specify the test.

(*a*) $n = 25$, $p_1 = 0.7$ (*b*) $n = 36$, $p_1 = 0.7$

(*c*) $n = 64$, $p_1 = 0.7$ (*d*) $n = 100, p_1 = 0.7$

(*e*) $n = 144, p_1 = 0.7$ (*f*) $n = 25$, $p_1 = 0.8$

(*g*) $n = 100, p_1 = 0.8$

10.　In a certain large city 100 randomly chosen people are polled as to their preference between candidates A and B for a certain office. How many of these, in favor of candidate A, would convince you that he will probably win the election? (*Hint:* Suppose A's probability of winning were $\frac{1}{2}$. Then with $p = \frac{1}{2}$, $n = 100$, find numbers at 2 (or 3) standard deviations from the mean. More votes than these in favor of A in this sample would be very unlikely if A's actual probability of winning were only $\frac{1}{2}$, and even less likely if his probability of winning were $< \frac{1}{2}$.)

Note: The student should not be deluded by the ease with which this example can be worked out. Almost everyone, for example, has encountered at least one public opinion poll of notorious inaccuracy. A major difficulty, and one which we have not considered at all, is the selection of a truly random sample.

11.　The same as Problem 10 above, but 900 people are polled.

12.　Nine hundred randomly chosen people are telephoned at a certain hour and asked whether they are tuned in on "Uncle Jackie." How many answers in the affirmative would convince you that at least 10% of our population viewed "Uncle Jackie's" program that hour?

13.　Five per cent of a certain population has been succumbing to a certain virus. A new vaccine is tested on a random sample of 171 people, and it is found that only 4 of these (i.e., less than $2\frac{1}{2}\%$) succumb to the virus. Is the vaccine effective?

14.　It is found that of a randomly chosen sample of 100 "Glowell" light bulbs, 90% have a burning life of at least 1000 hours.

Show that it is likely that of a very large number of "Glowell" light bulbs, at least 80% will have burning lives of 1000 hours or more.

MATHEMATICAL
TABLES

N	0	1	2	3	4	5	6	7	8	9
10	0000	0043	0086	0128	0170	0212	0253	0294	0334	0374
11	0414	0453	0492	0531	0569	0607	0645	0682	0719	0755
12	0792	0828	0864	0899	0934	0969	1004	1038	1072	1106
13	1139	1173	1206	1239	1271	1303	1335	1367	1399	1430
14	1461	1492	1523	1553	1584	1614	1644	1673	1703	1732
15	1761	1790	1818	1847	1875	1903	1931	1959	1987	2014
16	2041	2068	2095	2122	2148	2175	2201	2227	2253	2279
17	2304	2330	2355	2380	2405	2430	2455	2480	2504	2529
18	2553	2577	2601	2625	2648	2672	2695	2718	2742	2765
19	2788	2810	2833	2856	2878	2900	2923	2945	2967	2989
20	3010	3032	3054	3075	3096	3118	3139	3160	3181	3201
21	3222	3243	3263	3284	3304	3324	3345	3365	3385	3404
22	3424	3444	3464	3483	3502	3522	3541	3560	3579	3598
23	3617	3636	3655	3674	3692	3711	3729	3747	3766	3784
24	3802	3820	3838	3856	3874	3892	3909	3927	3945	3962
25	3979	3997	4014	4031	4048	4065	4082	4099	4116	4133
26	4150	4166	4183	4200	4216	4232	4249	4265	4281	4298
27	4314	4330	4346	4362	4378	4393	4409	4425	4440	4456
28	4472	4487	4502	4518	4533	4548	4564	4579	4594	4609
29	4624	4639	4654	4669	4683	4698	4713	4728	4742	4757
30	4771	4786	4800	4814	4829	4843	4857	4871	4886	4900
31	4914	4928	4942	4955	4969	4983	4997	5011	5024	5038
32	5051	5065	5079	5092	5105	5119	5132	5145	5159	5172
33	5185	5198	5211	5224	5237	5250	5263	5276	5289	5302
34	5315	5328	5340	5353	5366	5378	5391	5403	5416	5428
35	5441	5453	5465	5478	5490	5502	5514	5527	5539	5551
36	5563	5575	5587	5599	5611	5623	5635	5647	5658	5670
37	5682	5694	5705	5717	5729	5740	5752	5763	5775	5786
38	5798	5809	5821	5832	5843	5855	5866	5877	5888	5899
39	5911	5922	5933	5944	5955	5966	5977	5988	5999	6010
40	6021	6031	6042	6053	6064	6075	6085	6096	6107	6117
41	6128	6138	6149	6160	6170	6180	6191	6201	6212	6222
42	6232	6243	6253	6263	6274	6284	6294	6304	6314	6325
43	6335	6345	6355	6365	6375	6385	6395	6405	6415	6425
44	6435	6444	6454	6464	6474	6484	6493	6503	6513	6522
45	6532	6542	6551	6561	6571	6580	6590	6599	6609	6618
46	6628	6637	6646	6656	6665	6675	6684	6693	6702	6712
47	6721	6730	6739	6749	6758	6767	6776	6785	6794	6803
48	6812	6821	6830	6839	6848	6857	6866	6875	6884	6893
49	6902	6911	6920	6928	6937	6946	6955	6964	6972	6981
50	6990	6998	7007	7016	7024	7033	7042	7050	7059	7067
51	7076	7084	7093	7101	7110	7118	7126	7135	7143	7152
52	7160	7168	7177	7185	7193	7202	7210	7218	7226	7235
53	7243	7251	7259	7267	7275	7284	7292	7300	7308	7316
54	7324	7332	7340	7348	7356	7364	7372	7380	7388	7396

From "College Algebra and Trigonometry," by F. H. Miller. Publisher: John Wiley and Sons (1945).

TABLE I. COMMON LOGARITHMS   495

N	0	1	2	3	4	5	6	7	8	9
55	7404	7412	7419	7427	7435	7443	7451	7459	7466	7474
56	7482	7490	7497	7505	7513	7520	7528	7536	7543	7551
57	7559	7566	7574	7582	7589	7597	7604	7612	7619	7627
58	7634	7642	7649	7657	7664	7672	7679	7686	7694	7701
59	7709	7716	7723	7731	7738	7745	7752	7760	7767	7774
60	7782	7789	7796	7803	7810	7818	7825	7832	7839	7846
61	7853	7860	7868	7875	7882	7889	7896	7903	7910	7917
62	7924	7931	7938	7945	7952	7959	7966	7973	7980	7987
63	7993	8000	8007	8014	8021	8028	8035	8041	8048	8055
64	8062	8069	8075	8082	8089	8096	8102	8109	8116	8122
65	8129	8136	8142	8149	8156	8162	8169	8176	8182	8189
66	8195	8202	8209	8215	8222	8228	8235	8241	8248	8254
67	8261	8267	8274	8280	8287	8293	8299	8306	8312	8319
68	8325	8331	8338	8344	8351	8357	8363	8370	8376	8382
69	8388	8395	8401	8407	8414	8420	8426	8432	8439	8445
70	8451	8457	8463	8470	8476	8482	8488	8494	8500	8506
71	8513	8519	8525	8531	8537	8543	8549	8555	8561	8567
72	8573	8579	8585	8591	8597	8603	8609	8615	8621	8627
73	8633	8639	8645	8651	8657	8663	8669	8675	8681	8686
74	8692	8698	8704	8710	8716	8722	8727	8733	8739	8745
75	8751	8756	8762	8768	8774	8779	8785	8791	8797	8802
76	8808	8814	8820	8825	8831	8837	8842	8848	8854	8859
77	8865	8871	8876	8882	8887	8893	8899	8904	8910	8915
78	8921	8927	8932	8938	8943	8949	8954	8960	8965	8971
79	8976	8982	8987	8993	8998	9004	9009	9015	9020	9025
80	9031	9036	9042	9047	9053	9058	9063	9069	9074	9079
81	9085	9090	9096	9101	9106	9112	9117	9122	9128	9133
82	9138	9143	9149	9154	9159	9165	9170	9175	9180	9186
83	9191	9196	9201	9206	9212	9217	9222	9227	9232	9238
84	9243	9248	9253	9258	9263	9269	9274	9279	9284	9289
85	9294	9299	9304	9309	9315	9320	9325	9330	9335	9340
86	9345	9350	9355	9360	9365	9370	9375	9380	9385	9390
87	9395	9400	9405	9410	9415	9420	9425	9430	9435	9440
88	9445	9450	9455	9460	9465	9469	9474	9479	9484	9489
89	9494	9499	9504	9509	9513	9518	9523	9528	9533	9538
90	9542	9547	9552	9557	9562	9566	9571	9576	9581	9586
91	9590	9595	9600	9605	9609	9614	9619	9624	9628	9633
92	9638	9643	9647	9652	9657	9661	9666	9671	9675	9680
93	9685	9689	9694	9699	9703	9708	9713	9717	9722	9727
94	9731	9736	9741	9745	9750	9754	9759	9763	9768	9773
95	9777	9782	9786	9791	9795	9800	9805	9809	9814	9818
96	9823	9827	9832	9836	9841	9845	9850	9854	9859	9863
97	9868	9872	9877	9881	9886	9890	9894	9899	9903	9908
98	9912	9917	9921	9926	9930	9934	9939	9943	9948	9952
99	9956	9961	9965	9969	9974	9978	9983	9987	9991	9996

[Characteristics of Logarithms omitted—determine by the usual rule from the value]

Radians	Degrees	Sine Value	Sine Log₁₀	Tangent Value	Tangent Log₁₀	Cotangent Value	Cotangent Log₁₀	Cosine Value	Cosine Log₁₀		
.0000	0° 00′	.0000	——	.0000	——			1.0000	.0000	90° 00′	1.5708
.0029	10	.0029	.4637	.0029	.4637	343.77	.5363	1.0000	.0000	50	1.5679
.0058	20	.0058	.7648	.0058	.7648	171.89	.2352	1.0000	.0000	40	1.5650
.0087	30	.0087	.9408	.0087	.9409	114.59	.0591	1.0000	.0000	30	1.5621
.0116	40	.0116	.0658	.0116	.0658	85.940	.9342	.9999	.0000	20	1.5592
.0145	50	.0145	.1627	.0145	.1627	68.750	.8373	.9999	.0000	10	1.5563
.0175	1° 00′	.0175	.2419	.0175	.2419	57.290	.7581	.9998	.9999	89° 00′	1.5533
.0204	10	.0204	.3088	.0204	.3089	49.104	.6911	.9998	.9999	50	1.5504
.0233	20	.0233	.3668	.0233	.3669	42.964	.6331	.9997	.9999	40	1.5475
.0262	30	.0262	.4179	.0262	.4181	38.188	.5819	.9997	.9999	30	1.5446
.0291	40	.0291	.4637	.0291	.4638	34.368	.5362	.9996	.9998	20	1.5417
.0320	50	.0320	.5050	.0320	.5053	31.242	.4947	.9995	.9998	10	1.5388
.0349	2° 00′	.0349	.5428	.0349	.5431	28.636	.4569	.9994	.9997	88° 00′	1.5359
.0378	10	.0378	.5776	.0378	.5779	26.432	.4221	.9993	.9997	50	1.5330
.0407	20	.0407	.6097	.0407	.6101	24.542	.3899	.9992	.9996	40	1.5301
.0436	30	.0436	.6397	.0437	.6401	22.904	.3599	.9990	.9996	30	1.5272
.0465	40	.0465	.6677	.0466	.6682	21.470	.3318	.9989	.9995	20	1.5243
.0495	50	.0494	.6940	.0495	.6945	20.206	.3055	.9988	.9995	10	1.5213
.0524	3° 00′	.0523	.7188	.0524	.7194	19.081	.2806	.9986	.9994	87° 00′	1.5184
.0553	10	.0552	.7423	.0553	.7429	18.075	.2571	.9985	.9993	50	1.5155
.0582	20	.0581	.7645	.0582	.7652	17.169	.2348	.9983	.9993	40	1.5126
.0611	30	.0610	.7857	.0612	.7865	16.350	.2135	.9981	.9992	30	1.5097
.0640	40	.0640	.8059	.0641	.8067	15.605	.1933	.9980	.9991	20	1.5068
.0669	50	.0669	.8251	.0670	.8261	14.924	.1739	.9978	.9990	10	1.5039
.0698	4° 00′	.0698	.8436	.0699	.8446	14.301	.1554	.9976	.9989	86° 00′	1.5010
.0727	10	.0727	.8613	.0729	.8624	13.727	.1376	.9974	.9989	50	1.4981
.0756	20	.0756	.8783	.0758	.8795	13.197	.1205	.9971	.9988	40	1.4952
.0785	30	.0785	.8946	.0787	.8960	12.706	.1040	.9969	.9987	30	1.4923
.0814	40	.0814	.9104	.0816	.9118	12.251	.0882	.9967	.9986	20	1.4893
.0844	50	.0843	.9256	.0846	.9272	11.826	.0728	.9964	.9985	10	1.4864
.0873	5° 00′	.0872	.9403	.0875	.9420	11.430	.0580	.9962	.9983	85° 00′	1.4835
.0902	10	.0901	.9545	.0904	.9563	11.059	.0437	.9959	.9982	50	1.4806
.0931	20	.0929	.9682	.0934	.9701	10.712	.0299	.9957	.9981	40	1.4777
.0960	30	.0958	.9816	.0963	.9836	10.385	.0164	.9954	.9980	30	1.4748
.0989	40	.0987	.9945	.0992	.9966	10.078	.0034	.9951	.9979	20	1.4719
.1018	50	.1016	.0070	.1022	.0093	9.7882	.9907	.9948	.9977	10	1.4690
.1047	6° 00′	.1045	.0192	.1051	.0216	9.5144	.9784	.9945	.9976	84° 00′	1.4661
.1076	10	.1074	.0311	.1080	.0336	9.2553	.9664	.9942	.9975	50	1.4632
.1105	20	.1103	.0426	.1110	.0453	9.0098	.9547	.9939	.9973	40	1.4603
.1134	30	.1132	.0539	.1139	.0567	8.7769	.9433	.9936	.9972	30	1.4573
.1164	40	.1161	.0648	.1169	.0678	8.5555	.9322	.9932	.9971	20	1.4544
.1193	50	.1190	.0755	.1198	.0786	8.3450	.9214	.9929	.9969	10	1.4515
.1222	7° 00′	.1219	.0859	.1228	.0891	8.1443	.9109	.9925	.9968	83° 00′	1.4486
.1251	10	.1248	.0961	.1257	.0995	7.9530	.9005	.9922	.9966	50	1.4457
.1280	20	.1276	.1060	.1287	.1096	7.7704	.8904	.9918	.9964	40	1.4428
.1309	30	.1305	.1157	.1317	.1194	7.5958	.8806	.9914	.9963	30	1.4399
.1338	40	.1334	.1252	.1346	.1291	7.4287	.8709	.9911	.9961	20	1.4370
.1367	50	.1363	.1345	.1376	.1385	7.2687	.8615	.9907	.9959	10	1.4341
.1396	8° 00′	.1392	.1436	.1405	.1478	7.1154	.8522	.9903	.9958	82° 00′	1.4312
.1425	10	.1421	.1525	.1435	.1569	6.9682	.8431	.9899	.9956	50	1.4283
.1454	20	.1449	.1612	.1465	.1658	6.8269	.8342	.9894	.9954	40	1.4254
.1484	30	.1478	.1697	.1495	.1745	6.6912	.8255	.9890	.9952	30	1.4224
.1513	40	.1507	.1781	.1524	.1831	6.5606	.8169	.9886	.9950	20	1.4195
.1542	50	.1536	.1863	.1554	.1915	6.4348	.8085	.9881	.9948	10	1.4166
.1571	9° 00′	.1564	.1943	.1584	.1997	6.3138	.8003	.9877	.9946	81° 00′	1.4137
		Value Log₁₀ Cosine		Value Log₁₀ Cotangent		Value Log₁₀ Tangent		Value Log₁₀ Sine		Degrees	Radians

From "Logarithmic and Trigonometric Tables," by Earle Raymond Hedrick. Reprinted by permission of The Macmillan Company, publishers.

TABLE II.   FOUR-PLACE TRIGONOMETRIC FUNCTIONS 497

[Characteristics of Logarithms omitted—determine by the usual rule from the value]

Radians	Degrees	Sine Value	Log₁₀	Tangent Value	Log₁₀	Cotangent Value	Log₁₀	Cosine Value	Log₁₀		
.1571	9° 00′	.1564	.1943	.1584	.1997	6.3138	.8003	.9877	.9946	81° 00′	1.4137
.1600	10	.1593	.2022	.1614	.2078	6.1970	.7922	.9872	.9944	50	1.4108
.1629	20	.1622	.2100	.1644	.2158	6.0844	.7842	.9868	.9942	40	1.4079
.1658	30	.1650	.2176	.1673	.2236	5.9758	.7764	.9863	.9940	30	1.4050
.1687	40	.1679	.2251	.1703	.2313	5.8708	.7687	.9858	.9938	20	1.4021
.1716	50	.1708	.2324	.1733	.2389	5.7694	.7611	.9853	.9936	10	1.3992
.1745	10° 00′	.1736	.2397	.1763	.2463	5.6713	.7537	.9848	.9934	80° 00′	1.3963
.1774	10	.1765	.2468	.1793	.2536	5.5764	.7464	.9843	.9931	50	1.3934
.1804	20	.1794	.2538	.1823	.2609	5.4845	.7391	.9838	.9929	40	1.3904
.1833	30	.1822	.2606	.1853	.2680	5.3955	.7320	.9833	.9927	30	1.3875
.1862	40	.1851	.2674	.1883	.2750	5.3093	.7250	.9827	.9924	20	1.3846
.1891	50	.1880	.2740	.1914	.2819	5.2257	.7181	.9822	.9922	10	1.3817
.1920	11° 00′	.1908	.2806	.1944	.2887	5.1446	.7113	.9816	.9919	79° 00′	1.3788
.1949	10	.1937	.2870	.1974	.2953	5.0658	.7047	.9811	.9917	50	1.3759
.1978	20	.1965	.2934	.2004	.3020	4.9894	.6980	.9805	.9914	40	1.3730
.2007	30	.1994	.2997	.2035	.3085	4.9152	.6915	.9799	.9912	30	1.3701
.2036	40	.2022	.3058	.2065	.3149	4.8430	.6851	.9793	.9909	20	1.3672
.2065	50	.2051	.3119	.2095	.3212	4.7729	.6788	.9787	.9907	10	1.3643
.2094	12° 00′	.2079	.3179	.2126	.3275	4.7046	.6725	.9781	.9904	78° 00′	1.3614
.2123	10	.2108	.3238	.2156	.3336	4.6382	.6664	.9775	.9901	50	1.3584
.2153	20	.2136	.3296	.2186	.3397	4.5736	.6603	.9769	.9899	40	1.3555
.2182	30	.2164	.3353	.2217	.3458	4.5107	.6542	.9763	.9896	30	1.3526
.2211	40	.2193	.3410	.2247	.3517	4.4494	.6483	.9757	.9893	20	1.3497
.2240	50	.2221	.3466	.2278	.3576	4.3897	.6424	.9750	.9890	10	1.3468
.2269	13° 00′	.2250	.3521	.2309	.3634	4.3315	.6366	.9744	.9887	77° 00′	1.3439
.2298	10	.2278	.3575	.2339	.3691	4.2747	.6309	.9737	.9884	50	1.3410
.2327	20	.2306	.3629	.2370	.3748	4.2193	.6252	.9730	.9881	40	1.3381
.2356	30	.2334	.3682	.2401	.3804	4.1653	.6196	.9724	.9878	30	1.3352
.2385	40	.2363	.3734	.2432	.3859	4.1126	.6141	.9717	.9875	20	1.3323
.2414	50	.2391	.3786	.2462	.3914	4.0611	.6086	.9710	.9872	10	1.3294
.2443	14° 00′	.2419	.3837	.2493	.3968	4.0108	.6032	.9703	.9869	76° 00′	1.3265
.2473	10	.2447	.3887	.2524	.4021	3.9617	.5979	.9696	.9866	50	1.3235
.2502	20	.2476	.3937	.2555	.4074	3.9136	.5926	.9689	.9863	40	1.3206
.2531	30	.2504	.3986	.2586	.4127	3.8667	.5873	.9681	.9859	30	1.3177
.2560	40	.2532	.4035	.2617	.4178	3.8208	.5822	.9674	.9856	20	1.3148
.2589	50	.2560	.4083	.2648	.4230	3.7760	.5770	.9667	.9853	10	1.3119
.2618	15° 00′	.2588	.4130	.2679	.4281	3.7321	.5719	.9659	.9849	75° 00′	1.3090
.2647	10	.2616	.4177	.2711	.4331	3.6891	.5669	.9652	.9846	50	1.3061
.2676	20	.2644	.4223	.2742	.4381	3.6470	.5619	.9644	.9843	40	1.3032
.2705	30	.2672	.4269	.2773	.4430	3.6059	.5570	.9636	.9839	30	1.3003
.2734	40	.2700	.4314	.2805	.4479	3.5656	.5521	.9628	.9836	20	1.2974
.2763	50	.2728	.4359	.2836	.4527	3.5261	.5473	.9621	.9832	10	1.2945
.2793	16° 00′	.2756	.4403	.2867	.4575	3.4874	.5425	.9613	.9828	74° 00′	1.2915
.2822	10	.2784	.4447	.2899	.4622	3.4495	.5378	.9605	.9825	50	1.2886
.2851	20	.2812	.4491	.2931	.4669	3.4124	.5331	.9596	.9821	40	1.2857
.2880	30	.2840	.4533	.2962	.4716	3.3759	.5284	.9588	.9817	30	1.2828
.2909	40	.2868	.4576	.2994	.4762	3.3402	.5238	.9580	.9814	20	1.2799
.2938	50	.2896	.4618	.3026	.4808	3.3052	.5192	.9572	.9810	10	1.2770
.2967	17° 00′	.2924	.4659	.3057	.4853	3.2709	.5147	.9563	.9806	73° 00′	1.2741
.2996	10	.2952	.4700	.3089	.4898	3.2371	.5102	.9555	.9802	50	1.2712
.3025	20	.2979	.4741	.3121	.4943	3.2041	.5057	.9546	.9798	40	1.2683
.3054	30	.3007	.4781	.3153	.4987	3.1716	.5013	.9537	.9794	30	1.2654
.3083	40	.3035	.4821	.3185	.5031	3.1397	.4969	.9528	.9790	20	1.2625
.3113	50	.3062	.4861	.3217	.5075	3.1084	.4925	.9520	.9786	10	1.2595
.3142	18° 00′	.3090	.4900	.3249	.5118	3.0777	.4882	.9511	.9782	72° 00′	1.2566
		Value Log₁₀ Cosine		Value Log₁₀ Cotangent		Value Log₁₀ Tangent		Value Log₁₀ Sine		Degrees	Radians

From "Logarithmic and Trigonometric Tables," by Earle Raymond Hedrick. Reprinted by permission of The Macmillan Company, publishers.

[Characteristics of Logarithms omitted—determine by the usual rule from the value]

Radians	Degrees	Sine Value	Sine Log10	Tangent Value	Tangent Log10	Cotangent Value	Cotangent Log10	Cosine Value	Cosine Log10	Degrees	Radians
.3142	18° 00′	.3090	.4900	.3249	.5118	3.0777	.4882	.9511	.9782	72° 00′	1.2566
.3171	10	.3118	.4939	.3281	.5161	3.0475	.4839	.9502	.9778	50	1.2537
.3200	20	.3145	.4977	.3314	.5203	3.0178	.4797	.9492	.9774	40	1.2508
.3229	30	.3173	.5015	.3346	.5245	2.9887	.4755	.9483	.9770	30	1.2479
.3258	40	.3201	.5052	.3378	.5287	2.9600	.4713	.9474	.9765	20	1.2450
.3287	50	.3228	.5090	.3411	.5329	2.9319	.4671	.9465	.9761	10	1.2421
.3316	19° 00′	.3256	.5126	.3443	.5370	2.9042	.4630	.9455	.9757	71° 00′	1.2392
.3345	10	.3283	.5163	.3476	.5411	2.8770	.4589	.9446	.9752	50	1.2363
.3374	20	.3311	.5199	.3508	.5451	2.8502	.4549	.9436	.9748	40	1.2334
.3403	30	.3338	.5235	.3541	.5491	2.8239	.4509	.9426	.9743	30	1.2305
.3432	40	.3365	.5270	.3574	.5531	2.7980	.4469	.9417	.9739	20	1.2275
.3462	50	.3393	.5306	.3607	.5571	2.7725	.4429	.9407	.9734	10	1.2246
.3491	20° 00′	.3420	.5341	.3640	.5611	2.7475	.4389	.9397	.9730	70° 00′	1.2217
.3520	10	.3448	.5375	.3673	.5650	2.7228	.4350	.9387	.9725	50	1.2188
.3549	20	.3475	.5409	.3706	.5689	2.6985	.4311	.9377	.9721	40	1.2159
.3578	30	.3502	.5443	.3739	.5727	2.6746	.4273	.9367	.9716	30	1.2130
.3607	40	.3529	.5477	.3772	.5766	2.6511	.4234	.9356	.9711	20	1.2101
.3636	50	.3557	.5510	.3805	.5804	2.6279	.4196	.9346	.9706	10	1.2072
.3665	21° 00′	.3584	.5543	.3839	.5842	2.6051	.4158	.9336	.9702	69° 00′	1.2043
.3694	10	.3611	.5576	.3872	.5879	2.5826	.4121	.9325	.9697	50	1.2014
.3723	20	.3638	.5609	.3906	.5917	2.5605	.4083	.9315	.9692	40	1.1985
.3752	30	.3665	.5641	.3939	.5954	2.5386	.4046	.9304	.9687	30	1.1956
.3782	40	.3692	.5673	.3973	.5991	2.5172	.4009	.9293	.9682	20	1.1926
.3811	50	.3719	.5704	.4006	.6028	2.4960	.3972	.9283	.9677	10	1.1897
.3840	22° 00′	.3746	.5736	.4040	.6064	2.4751	.3936	.9272	.9672	68° 00′	1.1868
.3869	10	.3773	.5767	.4074	.6100	2.4545	.3900	.9261	.9667	50	1.1839
.3898	20	.3800	.5798	.4108	.6136	2.4342	.3864	.9250	.9661	40	1.1810
.3927	30	.3827	.5828	.4142	.6172	2.4142	.3828	.9239	.9656	30	1.1781
.3956	40	.3854	.5859	.4176	.6208	2.3945	.3792	.9228	.9651	20	1.1752
.3985	50	.3881	.5889	.4210	.6243	2.3750	.3757	.9216	.9646	10	1.1723
.4014	23° 00′	.3907	.5919	.4245	.6279	2.3559	.3721	.9205	.9640	67° 00′	1.1694
.4043	10	.3934	.5948	.4279	.6314	2.3369	.3686	.9194	.9635	50	1.1665
.4072	20	.3961	.5978	.4314	.6348	2.3183	.3652	.9182	.9629	40	1.1636
.4102	30	.3987	.6007	.4348	.6383	2.2998	.3617	.9171	.9624	30	1.1606
.4131	40	.4014	.6036	.4383	.6417	2.2817	.3583	.9159	.9618	20	1.1577
.4160	50	.4041	.6065	.4417	.6452	2.2637	.3548	.9147	.9613	10	1.1548
.4189	24° 00′	.4067	.6093	.4452	.6486	2.2460	.3514	.9135	.9607	66° 00′	1.1519
.4218	10	.4094	.6121	.4487	.6520	2.2286	.3480	.9124	.9602	50	1.1490
.4247	20	.4120	.6149	.4522	.6553	2.2113	.3447	.9112	.9596	40	1.1461
.4276	30	.4147	.6177	.4557	.6587	2.1943	.3413	.9100	.9590	30	1.1432
.4305	40	.4173	.6205	.4592	.6620	2.1775	.3380	.9088	.9584	20	1.1403
.4334	50	.4200	.6232	.4628	.6654	2.1609	.3346	.9075	.9579	10	1.1374
.4363	25° 00′	.4226	.6259	.4663	.6687	2.1445	.3313	.9063	.9573	65° 00′	1.1345
.4392	10	.4253	.6286	.4699	.6720	2.1283	.3280	.9051	.9567	50	1.1316
.4422	20	.4279	.6313	.4734	.6752	2.1123	.3248	.9038	.9561	40	1.1286
.4451	30	.4305	.6340	.4770	.6785	2.0965	.3215	.9026	.9555	30	1.1257
.4480	40	.4331	.6366	.4806	.6817	2.0809	.3183	.9013	.9549	20	1.1228
.4509	50	.4358	.6392	.4841	.6850	2.0655	.3150	.9001	.9543	10	1.1199
.4538	26° 00′	.4384	.6418	.4877	.6882	2.0503	.3118	.8988	.9537	64° 00′	1.1170
.4567	10	.4410	.6444	.4913	.6914	2.0353	.3086	.8975	.9530	50	1.1141
.4596	20	.4436	.6470	.4950	.6946	2.0204	.3054	.8962	.9524	40	1.1112
.4625	30	.4462	.6495	.4986	.6977	2.0057	.3023	.8949	.9518	30	1.1083
.4654	40	.4488	.6521	.5022	.7009	1.9912	.2991	.8936	.9512	20	1.1054
.4683	50	.4514	.6546	.5059	.7040	1.9768	.2960	.8923	.9505	10	1.1025
.4712	27° 00′	.4540	.6570	.5095	.7072	1.9626	.2928	.8910	.9499	63° 00′	1.0996
		Value Log10 Cosine		Value Log10 Cotangent		Value Log10 Tangent		Value Log10 Sine		Degrees	Radians

From "Logarithmic and Trigonometric Tables," by Earle Raymond Hedrick. Reprinted by permission of The Macmillan Company, publishers.

TABLE II.   FOUR-PLACE TRIGONOMETRIC FUNCTIONS 499

[Characteristics of Logarithms omitted—determine by the usual rule from the value]

RADIANS	DEGREES	SINE Value	Log₁₀	TANGENT Value	Log₁₀	COTANGENT Value	Log₁₀	COSINE Value	Log₁₀		
.4712	27° 00'	.4540	.6570	.5095	.7072	1.9626	.2928	.8910	.9499	63° 00'	1.0996
.4741	10	.4566	.6595	.5132	.7103	1.9486	.2897	.8897	.9492	50	1.0966
.4771	20	.4592	.6620	.5169	.7134	1.9347	.2866	.8884	.9486	40	1.0937
.4800	30	.4617	.6644	.5206	.7165	1.9210	.2835	.8870	.9479	30	1.0908
.4829	40	.4643	.6668	.5243	.7196	1.9074	.2804	.8857	.9473	20	1.0879
.4858	50	.4669	.6692	.5280	.7226	1.8940	.2774	.8843	.9466	10	1.0850
.4887	28° 00'	.4695	.6716	.5317	.7257	1.8807	.2743	.8829	.9459	62° 00'	1.0821
.4916	10	.4720	.6740	.5354	.7287	1.8676	.2713	.8816	.9453	50	1.0792
.4945	20	.4746	.6763	.5392	.7317	1.8546	.2683	.8802	.9446	40	1.0763
.4974	30	.4772	.6787	.5430	.7348	1.8418	.2652	.8788	.9439	30	1.0734
.5003	40	.4797	.6810	.5467	.7378	1.8291	.2622	.8774	.9432	20	1.0705
.5032	50	.4823	.6833	.5505	.7408	1.8165	.2592	.8760	.9425	10	1.0676
.5061	29° 00'	.4848	.6856	.5543	.7438	1.8040	.2562	.8746	.9418	61° 00'	1.0647
.5091	10	.4874	.6878	.5581	.7467	1.7917	.2533	.8732	.9411	50	1.0617
.5120	20	.4899	.6901	.5619	.7497	1.7796	.2503	.8718	.9404	40	1.0588
.5149	30	.4924	.6923	.5658	.7526	1.7675	.2474	.8704	.9397	30	1.0559
.5178	40	.4950	.6946	.5696	.7556	1.7556	.2444	.8689	.9390	20	1.0530
.5207	50	.4975	.6968	.5735	.7585	1.7437	.2415	.8675	.9383	10	1.0501
.5236	30° 00'	.5000	.6990	.5774	.7614	1.7321	.2386	.8660	.9375	60° 00'	1.0472
.5265	10	.5025	.7012	.5812	.7644	1.7205	.2356	.8646	.9368	50	1.0443
.5294	20	.5050	.7033	.5851	.7673	1.7090	.2327	.8631	.9361	40	1.0414
.5323	30	.5075	.7055	.5890	.7701	1.6977	.2299	.8616	.9353	30	1.0385
.5352	40	.5100	.7076	.5930	.7730	1.6864	.2270	.8601	.9346	20	1.0356
.5381	50	.5125	.7097	.5969	.7759	1.6753	.2241	.8587	.9338	10	1.0327
.5411	31° 00'	.5150	.7118	.6009	.7788	1.6643	.2212	.8572	.9331	59° 00'	1.0297
.5440	10	.5175	.7139	.6048	.7816	1.6534	.2184	.8557	.9323	50	1.0268
.5469	20	.5200	.7160	.6088	.7845	1.6426	.2155	.8542	.9315	40	1.0239
.5498	30	.5225	.7181	.6128	.7873	1.6319	.2127	.8526	.9308	30	1.0210
.5527	40	.5250	.7201	.6168	.7902	1.6212	.2098	.8511	.9300	20	1.0181
.5556	50	.5275	.7222	.6208	.7930	1.6107	.2070	.8496	.9292	10	1.0152
.5585	32° 00'	.5299	.7242	.6249	.7958	1.6003	.2042	.8480	.9284	58° 00'	1.0123
.5614	10	.5324	.7262	.6289	.7986	1.5900	.2014	.8465	.9276	50	1.0094
.5643	20	.5348	.7282	.6330	.8014	1.5798	.1986	.8450	.9268	40	1.0065
.5672	30	.5373	.7302	.6371	.8042	1.5697	.1958	.8434	.9260	30	1.0036
.5701	40	.5398	.7322	.6412	.8070	1.5597	.1930	.8418	.9252	20	1.0007
.5730	50	.5422	.7342	.6453	.8097	1.5497	.1903	.8403	.9244	10	.9977
.5760	33° 00'	.5446	.7361	.6494	.8125	1.5399	.1875	.8387	.9236	57° 00'	.9948
.5789	10	.5471	.7380	.6536	.8153	1.5301	.1847	.8371	.9228	50	.9919
.5818	20	.5495	.7400	.6577	.8180	1.5204	.1820	.8355	.9219	40	.9890
.5847	30	.5519	.7419	.6619	.8208	1.5108	.1792	.8339	.9211	30	.9861
.5876	40	.5544	.7438	.6661	.8235	1.5013	.1765	.8323	.9203	20	.9832
.5905	50	.5568	.7457	.6703	.8263	1.4919	.1737	.8307	.9194	10	.9803
.5934	34° 00'	.5592	.7476	.6745	.8290	1.4826	.1710	.8290	.9186	56° 00'	.9774
.5963	10	.5616	.7494	.6787	.8317	1.4733	.1683	.8274	.9177	50	.9745
.5992	20	.5640	.7513	.6830	.8344	1.4641	.1656	.8258	.9169	40	.9716
.6021	30	.5664	.7531	.6873	.8371	1.4550	.1629	.8241	.9160	30	.9687
.6050	40	.5688	.7550	.6916	.8398	1.4460	.1602	.8225	.9151	20	.9657
.6080	50	.5712	.7568	.6959	.8425	1.4370	.1575	.8208	.9142	10	.9628
.6109	35° 00'	.5736	.7586	.7002	.8452	1.4281	.1548	.8192	.9134	55° 00'	.9599
.6138	10	.5760	.7604	.7046	.8479	1.4193	.1521	.8175	.9125	50	.9570
.6167	20	.5783	.7622	.7089	.8506	1.4106	.1494	.8158	.9116	40	.9541
.6196	30	.5807	.7640	.7133	.8533	1.4019	.1467	.8141	.9107	30	.9512
.6225	40	.5831	.7657	.7177	.8559	1.3934	.1441	.8124	.9098	20	.9483
.6254	50	.5854	.7675	.7221	.8586	1.3848	.1414	.8107	.9089	10	.9454
.6283	36° 00'	.5878	.7692	.7265	.8613	1.3764	.1387	.8090	.9080	54° 00'	.9425
		Value COSINE	Log₁₀	Value COTANGENT	Log₁₀	Value TANGENT	Log₁₀	Value SINE	Log₁₀	DEGREES	RADIANS

From "Logarithmic and Trigonometric Tables," by Earle Raymond Hedrick. Reprinted by permission of The Macmillan Company, publishers.

[Characteristics of Logarithms omitted—determine by the usual rule from the value]

RADIANS	DEGREES	SINE Value	Log₁₀	TANGENT Value	Log₁₀	COTANGENT Value	Log₁₀	COSINE Value	Log₁₀		
.6283	36° 00′	.5878	.7692	.7265	.8613	1.3764	.1387	.8090	.9080	54° 00′	.9425
.6312	10	.5901	.7710	.7310	.8639	1.3680	.1361	.8073	.9070	50	.9396
.6341	20	.5925	.7727	.7355	.8666	1.3597	.1334	.8056	.9061	40	.9367
.6370	30	.5948	.7744	.7400	.8692	1.3514	.1308	.8039	.9052	30	.9338
.6400	40	.5972	.7761	.7445	.8718	1.3432	.1282	.8021	.9042	20	.9308
.6429	50	.5995	.7778	.7490	.8745	1.3351	.1255	.8004	.9033	10	.9279
.6458	37° 00′	.6018	.7795	.7536	.8771	1.3270	.1229	.7986	.9023	53° 00′	.9250
.6487	10	.6041	.7811	.7581	.8797	1.3190	.1203	.7969	.9014	50	.9221
.6516	20	.6065	.7828	.7627	.8824	1.3111	.1176	.7951	.9004	40	.9192
.6545	30	.6088	.7844	.7673	.8850	1.3032	.1150	.7934	.8995	30	.9163
.6574	40	.6111	.7861	.7720	.8876	1.2954	.1124	.7916	.8985	20	.9134
.6603	50	.6134	.7877	.7766	.8902	1.2876	.1098	.7898	.8975	10	.9105
.6632	38° 00′	.6157	.7893	.7813	.8928	1.2799	.1072	.7880	.8965	52° 00′	.9076
.6661	10	.6180	.7910	.7860	.8954	1.2723	.1046	.7862	.8955	50	.9047
.6690	20	.6202	.7926	.7907	.8980	1.2647	.1020	.7844	.8945	40	.9018
.6720	30	.6225	.7941	.7954	.9006	1.2572	.0994	.7826	.8935	30	.8988
.6749	40	.6248	.7957	.8002	.9032	1.2497	.0968	.7808	.8925	20	.8959
.6778	50	.6271	.7973	.8050	.9058	1.2423	.0942	.7790	.8915	10	.8930
.6807	39° 00′	.6293	.7989	.8098	.9084	1.2349	.0916	.7771	.8905	51° 00′	.8901
.6836	10	.6316	.8004	.8146	.9110	1.2276	.0890	.7753	.8895	50	.8872
.6865	20	.6338	.8020	.8195	.9135	1.2203	.0865	.7735	.8884	40	.8843
.6894	30	.6361	.8035	.8243	.9161	1.2131	.0839	.7716	.8874	30	.8814
.6923	40	.6383	.8050	.8292	.9187	1.2059	.0813	.7698	.8864	20	.8785
.6952	50	.6406	.8066	.8342	.9212	1.1988	.0788	.7679	.8853	10	.8756
.6981	40° 00′	.6428	.8081	.8391	.9238	1.1918	.0762	.7660	.8843	50° 00′	.8727
.7010	10	.6450	.8096	.8441	.9264	1.1847	.0736	.7642	.8832	50	.8698
.7039	20	.6472	.8111	.8491	.9289	1.1778	.0711	.7623	.8821	40	.8668
.7069	30	.6494	.8125	.8541	.9315	1.1708	.0685	.7604	.8810	30	.8639
.7098	40	.6517	.8140	.8591	.9341	1.1640	.0659	.7585	.8800	20	.8610
.7127	50	.6539	.8155	.8642	.9366	1.1571	.0634	.7566	.8789	10	.8581
.7156	41° 00′	.6561	.8169	.8693	.9392	1.1504	.0608	.7547	.8778	49° 00′	.8552
.7185	10	.6583	.8184	.8744	.9417	1.1436	.0583	.7528	.8767	50	.8523
.7214	20	.6604	.8198	.8796	.9443	1.1369	.0557	.7509	.8756	40	.8494
.7243	30	.6626	.8213	.8847	.9468	1.1303	.0532	.7490	.8745	30	.8465
.7272	40	.6648	.8227	.8899	.9494	1.1237	.0506	.7470	.8733	20	.8436
.7301	50	.6670	.8241	.8952	.9519	1.1171	.0481	.7451	.8722	10	.8407
.7330	42° 00′	.6691	.8255	.9004	.9544	1.1106	.0456	.7431	.8711	48° 00′	.8378
.7359	10	.6713	.8269	.9057	.9570	1.1041	.0430	.7412	.8699	50	.8348
.7389	20	.6734	.8283	.9110	.9595	1.0977	.0405	.7392	.8688	40	.8319
.7418	30	.6756	.8297	.9163	.9621	1.0913	.0379	.7373	.8676	30	.8290
.7447	40	.6777	.8311	.9217	.9646	1.0850	.0354	.7353	.8665	20	.8261
.7476	50	.6799	.8324	.9271	.9671	1.0786	.0329	.7333	.8653	10	.8232
.7505	43° 00′	.6820	.8338	.9325	.9697	1.0724	.0303	.7314	.8641	47° 00′	.8203
.7534	10	.6841	.8351	.9380	.9722	1.0661	.0278	.7294	.8629	50	.8174
.7563	20	.6862	.8365	.9435	.9747	1.0599	.0253	.7274	.8618	40	.8145
.7592	30	.6884	.8378	.9490	.9772	1.0538	.0228	.7254	.8606	30	.8116
.7621	40	.6905	.8391	.9545	.9798	1.0477	.0202	.7234	.8594	20	.8087
.7650	50	.6926	.8405	.9601	.9823	1.0416	.0177	.7214	.8582	10	.8058
.7679	44° 00′	.6947	.8418	.9657	.9848	1.0355	.0152	.7193	.8569	46° 00′	.8029
.7709	10	.6967	.8431	.9713	.9874	1.0295	.0126	.7173	.8557	50	.7999
.7738	20	.6988	.8444	.9770	.9899	1.0235	.0101	.7153	.8545	40	.7970
.7767	30	.7009	.8457	.9827	.9924	1.0176	.0076	.7133	.8532	30	.7941
.7796	40	.7030	.8469	.9884	.9949	1.0117	.0051	.7112	.8520	20	.7912
.7825	50	.7050	.8482	.9942	.9975	1.0058	.0025	.7092	.8507	10	.7883
.7854	45° 00′	.7071	.8495	1.0000	.0000	1.0000	.0000	.7071	.8495	45° 00′	.7854
		Value COSINE	Log₁₀	Value COTANGENT	Log₁₀	Value TANGENT	Log₁₀	Value SINE	Log₁₀	DEGREES	RADIANS

SELECTED ANSWERS

Exercise 1, page 9

2. Yes; 6.
3. 6 one-to-one correspondences exist between the given sets.

Exercise 2, page 14

2. (b) $\{x, y\}, \{x\}, \{y\}, N$; 4.
4. (a) A nn a is said to be *even* if there exists a nn b such that $a = 2b$.
5. (c) For example, $24 = 2 \cdot 2 \cdot 2 \cdot 3$.
8. (a) T. (c) F. (e) F. (i) F.

Exercise 3, page 24

10. (a) Range: the set of all odd nn; the image of 3 is 5; the pre-image of 11 is 6; the function is one-one.
    (c) Range: the set of all nn that are 1 more than a perfect square; the image of 3 is 2; the pre-images of 2 are 1 and 3; the function is many-one, since there does exist an element of the range (2, for example) which has more than one pre-image.
    (e) Range: $\{1, 2, 3, 4, 5\}$; the image of 3 is 3; the pre-image of 4 is 4; the function is one-one.
    (g) Range: $\{16\}$; the image of 3 is 16; the pre-image of 16 is 3; the function is one-one.
11. (a) $f(x) = 5x$.

Exercise 4, page 27

2. (a) $f[g(3)] = 11$. (c) $f[g(x)] = 4x - 1$. (e) $f[g(5)] = 19$.
   (g) $g[h(3)] = 4$. (i) $g[h(x)] = 2x^2 - 8x + 10$. (k) $h[g(5)] = 65$.

Exercise 5, page 35

3. (a) $A \cup B = \{2 \cdots 7\}$. (c) $A \cap C = N$ (e) $A \cup N = A$.
   (f) $A \cap N = N$. (h) $B \cap D = \{3, 4, 5, 6, 7\}$.
13. (a) Range: $\{0 \cdots 9\}$; f is many-one.
    (c) Range: $\{-4 \cdots 3\}$; f is one-one.
    (e) Range: $\{-12 \cdots 9\}$; f is one-one.
    (h) Range: $\{7\}$; f is many-one.
    (l) Range: $\{-25 \cdots 6\}$; f is many-one.
    (n) Range: $\{0 \cdots 81\}$; f is many-one.
    (p) Range: $\{-7 \cdots 2\}$; f is many-one.
    (r) Range: $\{1 \cdots 6\}$; f is one-one.
15. (a) Range: $\{7, 11\}$; f is many-one.
    (c) Range: $\{10\} \cup \{0 \cdots 5\}$; f is many-one.

501

Exercise 6, page 44

7. (a) $8 \circ 2 = 14$; ○ is complete, closed, not comm., not assoc.
   (c) $8 \circ 2 = 17$; ○ is complete, closed, comm., not assoc.
   (f) $8 \circ 2 = 4$; ○ is not complete, not closed, not comm., not assoc.

Exercise 7, page 47

2. Subtraction.
5. (a) Yes; since $7 = 7/1$, and 7 and 1 are nn.

Exercise 8, page 51

2. $>$ is not reflexive, since it is not true for each real number a that $a > a$; $>$ is not symmetric, since it is not true that whenever $a > b$, then $b > a$; $>$ is transitive, since it is true that whenever $a > b$ and $b > c$, then $a > c$.
3. (a) Not reflexive, since it is not true that each American is his own father; not symmetric since it is not true that whenever a is the father of b, then b is the father of a; not transitive, since it is not true that whenever a is the father of b and b is the father of c, then a is the father of c; not an equivalence relation.

Exercise 9, page 58

2. (a) Hint: Construct a rectangle with sides of lengths a and $b+c$; a, b, c may be any *positive* real numbers.
3. (a) Construct (how?) a right triangle with hypotenuse of length 2 and an arm of length 1; then the other arm will be of length $\sqrt{3}$ (why?). Or proceed somewhat similarly, making use of the already constructed length of $\sqrt{2}$.

Exercise 10, page 68

2. (a) $\frac{1}{6} = 0.16666\cdots$.
10. For 0.77, columns 4, 5, 8 should be checked.

Exercise 18, page 113

3. Length: 150 gar; width: 24 gar.
5. $x = 1.6$.
6. (a) 7.   (c) $(1 \pm \sqrt{5})/2$.   (e) $\frac{1}{2}, -2$.
   (g) ± 1.   (i) $0, -1$.   (k) $(-1 \pm \sqrt{-3})/2$.

Exercise 19, page 119

2. (a) 1.7.   (c) 2.4.   (e) 2.8.   (g) 1.3.
   (i) 1.6.   (k) 1.8.   (m) 2.0.   (o) 7.5.
4. $x = 1.7$.   6. $x = 1.67$.
8. (a) 1.5.   (b) 1.52.   10. (a) -0.2.   (d) -0.25.

Exercise 20, page 125

1. (a) $0+0i$; real.   (c) $0+2i$; pure imaginary.
   (e) $-5 + (-12)i$; imaginary. (g) $4 + 0i$; real.
   (i) $6 + 0i$; real.   (k) $-1 + (-1)i$; imaginary.
   (m) $\frac{1}{2} + \frac{5}{2}i$; imaginary.
   (o) $\frac{14}{13} + \frac{8}{13}i$; imaginary.

5. (a) $7 + 0i$; real. (c) $[(1 \pm \sqrt{5})/2] + 0i$; real.
   (e) $\frac{1}{2} + 0i, -2 + 0i$; real.
   (g) $\pm 1 + 0i$; real. (i) $0 + 0i, -1 + 0i$, real.
   (k) $-\frac{1}{2} + (\pm \sqrt{3}/2)i$; imaginary.
6. (a) 2.44 (c) 3.16. (e) 3.88. (g) 4.48.
7. (c) $|2x|$. (e) -3. (g) $|x - 3|$. (i) $i|x - 3|$.

Exercise 21, page 130

1. (a) $x = \pm 2$. (c) $x = -2, 3$. (e) $x = 0, \frac{9}{4}$. (g) $x = 2, 3$.
   (i) $x = -\frac{1}{3}, -\frac{1}{2}$. (k) $x = 0$. (m) $x = 0$.
2. (a) $x = 4$. (c) $x = \frac{16}{9}$. (e) $x = 1$. (g) $x = \frac{4}{9}$.
   (i) No solution.

Exercise 22, page 135

1. (a) $x > 1$. (c) $x \geqslant -\frac{2}{5}$. (e) $-1 < x \leqslant 4$.
   (g) No solution. (i) $-2 < x \leqslant -1$.

Exercise 24, page 154

1. (a) $4\sqrt{2}$. (c) $4\sqrt{5}$. (e) 5. (g) 5.
   (i) 9. (k) 5. (m) 5.
2. (a) $2\sqrt{2}$. (c) $\sqrt{194}$.
3. (a) Isosceles; perimeter, $10\sqrt{2} + 2\sqrt{5}$.
   (c) Right; perimeter, $15 + 9\sqrt{5}$.
   (e) Equilateral; perimeter, 30.
4. (a) $(-2, 1)$ falls in QII; $(2, -3)$ falls in QIV.
   (c) $(6, 5)$ falls in QI.
   (e) $(0, 0)$ falls in no quadrant.

Exercise 25, page 160

1. $(2, -1)$.
4. (a) $(4, 7), (5, 8), (6, 9)$.
   (c) $(1\frac{2}{3}, -3\frac{1}{3}), (1, -4), (\frac{1}{3}, -4\frac{2}{3})$.
   (e) $(-3\frac{1}{3}, -4), (-3, -3\frac{1}{2}), (-2\frac{2}{3}, -3)$.
6. (a) $(-3, 4)$. (c) $(-1, 0)$. (e) $(-3, 10)$.
   (g) $(-1\frac{1}{2}, 2)$. (i) $(1\frac{1}{2}, \frac{1}{2})$.
7. (a) $(4, -9)$. (c) $(-1, 1)$.

Exercise 27, page 167

1. (a) $8x - 5y = 1$. (c) $x = y$. (e) $11x - 5y = 2$.
   (g) $5x + 8y + 19 = 0$. (i) $x + y = 7$.

Exercise 28, page 172

3. (a) $m = -3/5, b = 6$. (c) $m = -1, b = 0$.
   (e) $m = \sqrt{3}, b = -3$. (g) $m = -2, b = 7$.
   (i) $m = -2, b = 11$. (k) $m = -1, b = 5$.
4. (a) $y = 3x + 6$. (c) $2x - 3y = 12$.
   (e) $y - b = k(x - a)$. (g) $10x + 9y + 34 = 0$.

Exercise 29, page 177

3. (a) $(6, -3)$.   (c) No intersection.   (e) $(0, 2)$.
5. (a) $2x - 3y = -15$.   (c) $x = 1$.
     (e) $y = 2$.   (g) $x + y = 3$.

Exercise 30, page 184

3. Assuming a coordinate system with positive X- and Y-axes extending in the directions east and north respectively, the path of the plane would be in a north-easterly direction, at a speed of approximately 206 miles per hour, along a line with slope $1/4$.
4. With a coordinate system as above, the direction, approximate speed, and slope of the line which is the plane's path are:
     (b) Southwesterly; 206 mph; $1/4$.
     (d) Northeasterly; 206 mph; 4.
     (f) Southeasterly; 206 mph; -4.
     (h) Easterly; 250 mph; 0.

Exercise 31, page 195

5. (a) $BF = 100'$, $EF = 102'$, $F = 13°$.
     (c) $BF = 87'$, $EF = 231'$, $F = 67° 47'$.
     (e) $EB = 129'$, $EF = 161'$, $F = 52° 41'$.
     (g) $EB = 41'$, $EF = 63'$, $F = 40° 43'$.
     (i) $E = 72° 11'$, $EF = 59'$, $F = 17° 49'$.
     (k) $E = 13° 30'$, $EF = 129'$, $F = 76° 30'$.
7. 2109 ft.   9. $5° 43'$.   11. 1453 ft; 1469 ft.
13. 704 ft; 6923 ft.

Exercise 34, page 207

3. (c) $\sqrt{2}/2$.   (e) 1.   (g) -1.   (i) $-\frac{1}{2}$.   (k) -1.
     (m) 1.   (o) 1.   (q) $\frac{1}{2}$.   (s) $\sqrt{3}/2$.

Exercise 35, page 210

1. (a) 1; $y = x + 1$.   (c) 0; $y = 2$.
     (e) $1/\sqrt{3}$; $y\sqrt{3} - x = 5 + 7\sqrt{3}$.   (g) $-\sqrt{3}$; $y + x\sqrt{3} = 2 + 4\sqrt{3}$.
2. (a) $135°$.   (c) $0°$.   (e) $158° 12'$.   (g) $111° 48'$.

Exercise 36, page 214

1. (a) $120°$; 2.   (c) $180°$; 2.   (e) $90°$; 2.
     (g) $720°$; 5.   (i) $120°$; 2.

Exercise 37, page 219

2. (a). $\sin x$, $\sin 2x$ represent equally loud sounds, $\sin x + \sin 2x$ a sound louder than either; $\sin x$ and $\sin 2x$ represent sounds of the same pitch, $\sin 2x$ a sound of higher pitch. (In fact, an *octave* higher—sounds whose periods are in the ratio $2:1$ are said to be an *octave* apart.)

(c) Ranked from softest to loudest: $\sin 3x$, $2 \sin x$, $2 \sin x + \sin 3x$; the last two are of the same pitch, the first of higher pitch.

(e) Ranked from softest to loudest: $\sin 3x$, $2 \sin 2x$, $2 \sin 2x + \sin 3x$; this is also their ranking going from highest to lowest pitch.

Exercise 38, page 227

3. (a) $\frac{1}{2}\sqrt{3}, -\frac{1}{2}, -\sqrt{3}, -1/\sqrt{3}$.   (c) $\frac{1}{2}\sqrt{2}, -\frac{1}{2}\sqrt{2}, -1, -1$.

(e) $\frac{1}{2}, -\frac{1}{2}\sqrt{3}, -1/\sqrt{3}, -\sqrt{3}$.   (g) $-\frac{1}{2}\sqrt{3}, \frac{1}{2}, -\sqrt{3}, -1/\sqrt{3}$.

(k) $-0.3420, 0.9397, -0.3640, -2.7475$.

(m) $-0.7660, 0.6428, -1.1918, -0.8391$.

(o) $-0.3420, -0.9397, 0.3640, 2.7475$.

(q) $0.9848, 0.1736, 5.6713, 0.1763$.

(s) $-0.9848, 0.1736, 5.6713, -0.1763$.

(u) $0.3420, 0.9397, 0.3640, 2.7475$.

(w) $0, -1, 0$, nonexistent.

(y) $0.3420, -0.9397, -0.3640, -2.7475$.

Exercise 39, page 232

3. (a) $\sin x$.   (c) $\sin A$.   (e) 1.

(g) $\cot p + \tan p$.   (i) $|\csc x|$.

Exercise 40, page 236

1. $\sin p, \cos p, \tan p, \cot p, \sec p, \csc p$ are as follows:

(a) $-\frac{3}{5}; -\frac{4}{5}; \frac{3}{4}; \frac{4}{3}; -\frac{5}{4}; -\frac{5}{3}$.   (c) $\frac{3}{5}; \frac{4}{5}; \frac{3}{4}; \frac{4}{3}; \frac{5}{4}; \frac{5}{3}$.

(e) $\sqrt{3}/2, \frac{1}{2}, \sqrt{3}, 1/\sqrt{3}, 2, 2/\sqrt{3}$.

2. $\sin p, \cos p, \tan p, \cot p, \sec p, \csc p$ are as follows:

(a) $\frac{1}{2}, \sqrt{3}/2, 1/\sqrt{3}, \sqrt{3}, 2/\sqrt{3}, 2$.

(c) $-1/\sqrt{2}, -1/\sqrt{2}, 1, 1, -\sqrt{2}, -\sqrt{2}$.

(e) $-\frac{3}{5}, \frac{4}{5}, -\frac{3}{4}, -\frac{4}{3}, \frac{5}{4}, \frac{5}{3}$.

(g) $-\frac{1}{2}, -\sqrt{3}/2, 1/\sqrt{3}, \sqrt{3}, -2/\sqrt{3}, -2$.

(i) $1/\sqrt{2}, -1/\sqrt{2}, -1, -1, -\sqrt{2}, \sqrt{2}$.

(k) $\frac{3}{5}, -\frac{4}{5}, -\frac{3}{4}, -\frac{4}{3}, -\frac{5}{4}, \frac{5}{3}$.

3. (a) The ray labeled p must lie along either the positive or the negative Y-axis.

Exercise 41, page 240

1. The following are the sin, cos, tan, cot, sec, and csc of:

(a) $75°: (\sqrt{6} + \sqrt{2})/4; (\sqrt{6} - \sqrt{2})/4; 2 + \sqrt{3}; 2 - \sqrt{3}; \sqrt{6} + \sqrt{2}; \sqrt{6} - \sqrt{2}$.

(c) $105°: (\sqrt{6} + \sqrt{2})/4; (\sqrt{2} - \sqrt{6})/4; -(2 + \sqrt{3}); \sqrt{3} - 2; -(\sqrt{6} + \sqrt{2}); \sqrt{6} - \sqrt{2}$.

5. (a) $-\sin x$.   (c) $-\sin x$.   (e) $-\cos x$.   (g) $\cos x$.

(i) $-\cos x$.   (k) $-\cos x$.   (m) $-\sin x$.   (o) $\sin x + \cos x$.

(q) $\cos x - \sin x$.

7. (a) $\frac{1}{2}$.   (c) $\sqrt{3}/2$.   (e) 1.   (g) $-\frac{1}{2}$.

Exercise 42, page 243

1. (a) $\tan 2x = 2 \tan x/(1 - \tan^2 x)$.

(c) $\tan (180 - x) = -\tan x$.

(e) $\tan(45 + x) = (1 + \tan x)/(1 - \tan x)$.

(g) $\tan(90 + p) = -\cot p$.

2. For example, derive: $\cot(F + S) = (\cot F \cot S - 1)/(\cot F + \cot S)$.

4. (a) 1.

6. The following are the sin, cos, tan, cot, sec, and csc of:

(a) $p: \frac{3}{5}, -\frac{4}{5}, -\frac{3}{4}, -\frac{4}{3}, -\frac{5}{4}, \frac{5}{3}$.

(c) $p + q$: 1, 0, nonexistent, 0, nonexistent, 1.

7. (a) $p + q: \frac{33}{65}, -\frac{56}{65}, -\frac{33}{56}, -\frac{56}{33}, -\frac{65}{56}, \frac{65}{33}$.

Exercise 43, page 245

1. (a) 18° 26′.   (c) 71° 34′.   (e) 0°.

2. Angles P, Q, R are as follows:

(a) 36° 52′, 71° 34′, 71° 34′.   (c) 63° 26′, 90°, 26° 34′.

(e) 60°, 60°, 60°.

Exercise 44, page 246

1. (a) $\frac{1}{2}\sqrt{2 - \sqrt{2}}$.   (c) $\sqrt{2} - 1$.

3. (a) $\sin 4x = 4 \sin x \cos x (\cos^2 x - \sin^2 x)$.

5. The following are the sin, cos, tan, cot, sec, and csc of:

(a) $2x$: $5\sqrt{119}/72$, $-47/72$, $-5\sqrt{119}/47$, $-47/5\sqrt{119}$, $-72/47$, $72/5\sqrt{119}$.

$\frac{1}{2}x$: $\sqrt{42}/12$, $\sqrt{102}/12$, $\sqrt{7/17}$, $\sqrt{17/7}$, $12/\sqrt{102}$, $12/\sqrt{42}$.

(c) $2x$: 1, 0, nonexistent, nonexistent, 0, 1.

$\frac{1}{2}x$: $\frac{1}{2}\sqrt{2 + \sqrt{2}}$, $-\frac{1}{2}\sqrt{2 - \sqrt{2}}$, $-(1 + \sqrt{2})$, $1 - \sqrt{2}$, $-\sqrt{4 + 2\sqrt{2}}$, $\sqrt{4 - 2\sqrt{2}}$.

(e) $2x$: $-4\sqrt{2}/9$, $7/9$, $-4\sqrt{2}/7$, $-7/4\sqrt{2}$, $9/7$, $-9/4\sqrt{2}$.

$\frac{1}{2}x$: $(\sqrt{2} - 1)/\sqrt{6}$, $-(1 + \sqrt{2})/\sqrt{6}$, $2\sqrt{2} - 3$, $-2\sqrt{2} - 3$, $\sqrt{6} - 2\sqrt{3}$, $\sqrt{6} + 2\sqrt{3}$.

Exercise 45, page 251

1. (a) 57° 17′ 45″.   (b) 0.017453.

2. (a) $\pi/6$.   (c) $\pi/3$.   (e) $\pi/18$.   (g) $2\pi/9$.

(i) $7\pi/18$.   (k) $2\pi/3$.   (m) $5\pi/6$.   (o) $7\pi/6$.

(q) $4\pi/3$.   (s) $5\pi/3$.   (u) $11\pi/6$.   (w) 200π.

(y) $-35\pi/9$.

3. (a) 180°.   (c) 60°.   (e) 45°.   (g) 135°.   (i) 72°.

(k) 540°.   (m) 30°.   (o) $22\frac{1}{2}$°.   (q) $67\frac{1}{2}$°.   (s) $157\frac{1}{2}$°.

(u) 18°.   (w) 90°.   (y) 162°.

4. (a) 57° 18′.   (c) 171° 53′.   (e) 286° 29′.

(g) 11° 28′.   (i) 22° 55′.

6. (a) $s = 1.5''$.   (c) $s = (2\pi/3)''$.   (e) $\theta = \frac{1}{2}$ radian.

(g) $r = (20/3\pi)$ cms.

8. (a) $(\pi/30)$ radians per second.

9. (a) $(\pi/10)''$ per second.   (d) $30/\pi \doteq 9.5$ seconds.

Exercise 46, page 258

1. $\{\pi/6, 5\pi/6\} + 2k\pi$.
5. No solution.
9. $\{\pi/3, 2\pi/3\} + k\pi$.
13. $2k\pi$.
17. $\{90°, 36° 52'\} + k \cdot 360°$.
21. $\{0°, 63° 26'\} + k \cdot 180°$.
25. $(\pi/4) + (k\pi/2), \{\pi/12, 5\pi/12\} + k\pi$.
29. $\{7\pi/6, 11\pi/6\} + 2k\pi$.

3. $\{\pi/9, 5\pi/9\} + 2k\pi/3$.
7. $(\pi/8) + (k\pi/2)$.
11. No solution.
15. $\{0, \pi, 7\pi/6, 11\pi/6\} + 2k\pi$.
19. $2k\pi/3$.
23. $2k\pi, (\pi/2) + k\pi$.
27. $\{2\pi/3, 4\pi/3\} + 2k\pi$.
31. $k\pi/2$.

Exercise 47, page 260

The maximum ordinates and the abscissas at which they occur are respectively:

1. (a) $1; \frac{1}{2} + 2k$.   (c) $3; \frac{1}{4} + k$.
   (e) $4; k$.   (g) $2; \frac{1}{2} + 2k$.
2. (a) $1; (\pi/2) + 2\pi k \doteq 1.6 + 6.3k$.
   (c) $2; x \doteq 0.3 + 3.1k$.
3. (a) $1; 2k\pi$.   (c) $3; \frac{1}{2} + 2k$.   (e) $2; 2 + 4k$.

Exercise 48, page 267

2. (b) $-\pi/6$.   (d) $2\pi/3$.   (f) $-\pi/4$.   (h) $-\pi/3$.
   (j) $5\pi/6$.   (l) $3\pi/4$.   (n) $-\pi/2$.   (p) π.
   (r) $\pi/2$.   (t) $\pi/2$.
3. (b) $\{\pi + \text{Arcsin } 0.1, 2\pi - \text{Arcsin } 0.1\} + 2k\pi$.
   (d) $\{\pi \pm \text{Arccos } 0.1\} + 2k\pi$.
4. (b) $\frac{13}{14}$.

Exercise 49, page 271

1. $c = 2.339$.
2. (a) $C = 105°, a = 5.177, b = 7.321,$ area $= 18.30$.
   (c) $B = 15°, b = 2.988, c = 8.165,$ area $- 10.56$.
   (e) $C = 52° 4', a = 73.98, c = 177.4,$ area $= 6214$.
4. 700 ft, 412 ft; height $= 360$ ft.

Exercise 50, page 277

2. (a) $b = 13, A = 32° 12', C = 87° 48'$.
   (c) $a = 49, B = 16° 25', C = 103° 34'$.
   (e) $A = 41° 25', B = 55° 46', C = 82° 49'$.
4. Dad must exert a force of 95 lb. in the direction of a ray which makes angles of 106° 50' and 133° 10', respectively, with the rays which represent the given forces of 80 and 105 lb.
6. 6.3 in. and 8.0 in.
8. (a) $R = 4.8$.   (c) $F_2 = 3.8$.   (e) $\theta = 90°$.
   (g) $\theta = 0°$.   (i) $R = 2\sqrt{3}$.   (k) $F_2 = 0$ or 0.7.

Exercise 5I, page 286

2. (*a*) A constant polynomial of no degree, whose graph is a straight line, the *X*-axis.

(*e*) A second-degree, or quadratic, polynomial, whose graph only rises, both to the right and to the left of the origin. The graph is symmetric to the *Y*-axis, has one extremum (a minimum), and intercepts the axes only at the origin.

(*g*) A fourth-degree, or quartic, polynomial; the rest of our discussion is as for (*e*) above. How, then, do the graphs differ?

(*j*) The discussion in this case is exactly as in (*e*) above. How do the graphs differ?

(*l*) A third-degree, or cubic, polynomial whose graph only rises to the left and only falls to the right of the origin. The graph has 0 or 2 extrema (it turns out to be 0) and intercepts the axes only at the origin.

(*n*) A second-degree, or quadratic, polynomial whose graph eventually only rises on both right and left. It has one extremum (a minimum), no x-intercepts, and y-intercept 5.

(*p*) A third-degree, or cubic, polynomial whose graph eventually only rises on the right and falls on the left. The graph has 0 or 2 extrema (it turns out to be 2), an x-intercept between 2 and 3, and a y-intercept of -5.

(*r*) A cubic polynomial whose graph eventually only rises on the right and falls on the left. The graph has 0 or 2 extrema, and intercepts at the origin and $x = 3$.

(*t*) A cubic polynomial, whose graph eventually only rises on the right and falls on the left. The graph has 0 or 2 extrema, x-intercepts 2, -1, -3, and y-intercept -6.

Exercise 52, page 292

1. (*a*) Domain: All real numbers except 0; symmetric with respect to the origin; asymptotes: $x = 0$, $y = 0$.

(*d*) Domain: All real numbers except $x = 0$; symmetric with respect to the *Y*-axis; asymptotes: $x = 0$, $y = 0$.

(*f*) Domain: All real numbers except 1 and -1. Intercept: The origin; symmetric with respect to the origin; asymptotes: $x = \pm 1$, $y = 0$.

(*i*) Domain: All real numbers; y-intercept: 1; symmetric with respect to the *Y*-axis; asymptote: $y = 0$.

(*m*) Domain: All real numbers except 0; x-intercept: -1; asymptote: $x = 0$.

(*o*) Domain: All real numbers; x-intercepts: 1, -2; y-intercept: -2; asymptote: $y = \frac{1}{2}$.

(*r*) Domain: All real numbers except 1 and -1. Intercepts $x = -3$, $y = -3$; asymptotes: $x = \pm 1$, $y = 0$.

(*u*) Domain: All real numbers except -2; y-intercept: 2; asymptotes: $x = -2$, $y = x - 2$.

Exercise 53, page 298

1. (*a*) Intercepts: $x = 2$, $y = 2$; solutions for x and y: $x = (2 - y)/(1 + y)$, $y = (2 - x)/(1 + x)$; asymptotes: $y = -1$, $x = -1$.

(c) Intercepts: The origin, $x = -1$; symmetry with respect to the X-axis; solutions for x and y: $y = \pm\sqrt{x(x+1)}$, $x = (-1 \pm \sqrt{1+4y^2})/2$; excluded values: $-1 < x < 0$.

(f) Intercept: The origin; symmetry with respect to the X-axis; solution for y: $y = \pm x\sqrt{x/(4-x)}$; asymptote: $x = 4$; excluded values: $x < 0$, $x > 4$.

(h) Intercept: The origin; symmetry with respect to the X-axis; solutions for x and y: $y = \pm\sqrt{x/(x-2)}$, $x = 2y^2/(y^2-1) = 2 + [2/(y^2-1)]$; asymptotes: $x = 2$, $y = \pm 1$; excluded values: $0 < x < 2$.

(k) Intercept: The origin; symmetry with respect to the Y-axis; solutions for x and y: $x = \pm 4\sqrt{y/(y-2)}$, $y = 2x^2/(x^2-16)$; asymptotes: $y = 2$, $x = 4$, $x = -4$; excluded values: $0 < y < 2$.

Exercise 54, page 304

1. (a) $(x-1)^2 + (y-2)^2 = 9$.
   (c) $(x-1)^2 + (y+2)^2 = 9$.
   (e) $(x-3)^2 + (y-4)^2 = 25$.
   (g) $(x-3)^2 + (y+4)^2 = 25$.
   (i) $x^2 + y^2 = 49$.   (k) $x^2 + y^2 = 0$.
2. (a) Circle, center at the origin, radius 3.
   (c) "Point" circle: $(0, 0)$.
   (e) Equation equivalent to: $x^2 + y^2 = 25$.
   (g) Semicircle consisting of those points of the graph of $x^2 + y^2 = 25$ for which $y \geq 0$.
   (k) Circle, center $(2, 3)$, radius 5.
   (m) Circle, center $(-2, 3)$, radius 4.
   (o) Circle, center $(1, -5)$, radius 5.
   (q) Circle, center $(4, 4)$, radius $4\sqrt{2}$.
   (s) Circle, centre $(-3.5, -1.5)$, radius $3.5\sqrt{2}$.
   (u) Circle, center $(7.5, 2.5)$, radius 2.5.

Exercise 55, page 308

1. Equation, center, and radius are:
   (a) $x^2 + y^2 - 6x - 4y = 0$; $(3, 2)$; $\sqrt{13}$.
   (c) $x^2 + y^2 - 6x + 4 = 0$; $(3, 0)$; $\sqrt{5}$.
   (e) $x^2 + y^2 - 2x + 4y - 20 = 0$; $(1, -2)$; 5.
   (g) $3x^2 + 3y^2 - 4x - 14y - 4 = 0$; $(2/3, 7/3)$; $\sqrt{65}/3$.
2. (a) $(x+2)^2 + (y-1)^2 = 52$.
   (c) $(x-2)^2 + (y+3)^2 = 4$.
3. (a) $(1, -2)$; $(2, 1)$.   (c) $(3/2, \pm\sqrt{35}/2)$.
4. (a) $(x-h)^2 + (y-k)^2 = h^2 + k^2$.
   (c) $(x-h)^2 + (y-k)^2 = h^2$.
   (e) $x^2 + (y-k)^2 = r^2$.
   (g) $(x-h)^2 + y^2 = h^2$.

Exercise 56, page 316

1. Foci and eccentricity are:
   (a) $(0, \pm 4)$; 0.8.   (c) $(0, \pm 2\sqrt{3})$; $\sqrt{3}/2$.
   (e) $(\pm\sqrt{3}, 0)$; $\sqrt{3}/2$.   (g) $(\pm 1, 0)$; $\sqrt{2}/2$.

2. (a) $3x^2 + 4y^2 = 91$.   (c) $x^2 + y^2 = 25$.
3. $x^2 + 4y^2 = 16$; $4x^2 + y^2 = 16$.
5. $16x^2 + 25y^2 = 400$.   7. $e = 0.5$.

Exercise 57, page 322

1. The type of curve, foci, eccentricity [approximate, except in (a)], and asymptotes are:

   (a) Hyperbola; $(\pm 5, 0)$; 1.25; $y = \pm\frac{3}{4}x$.
   (c) Hyperbola; $(0, \pm 5)$; 1.67; $y = \pm\frac{3}{4}x$.
   (e) Ellipse; $(0, \pm 4\sqrt{3})$; 0.87.
   (g) Hyperbola; $(0, \pm 4\sqrt{5})$; 1.12; $y = \pm 2x$.
   (i) Hyperbola; $(\pm \sqrt{34}, 0)$; 1.94; $y = \pm\frac{5}{3}x$.
   (k) Hyperbola; $(\pm 2\sqrt{5}, 0)$; 2.24; $y = \pm 2x$.
   (m) Rectangular hyperbola; $(\pm 5\sqrt{2}, 0)$; 1.41; $y = \pm x$.
   (o) Rectangular hyperbola; $(6, 6), (-6, -6)$; 1.41; $x = 0, y = 0$.
   (p) Rectangular hyperbola; $(6, -6), (-6, 6)$; 1.41; $x = 0, y = 0$.
2. (a) $2y^2 - 3x^2 = 5$.   (c) $xy = 6$.
3. (a) $9x^2 - 16y^2 = 144$ or $9y^2 - 16x^2 = 144$.
   (c) $9x^2 - y^2 = 36$ or $y^2 - 9x^2 = 4$.

Exercise 58, page 326

1. (a) Parabola; symmetric to the Y-axis; y is never negative; $V = (0, 0)$;
       $F = (0, \frac{1}{4})$; directrix: $y = -\frac{1}{4}$.
   (d) Parabola; symmetric to the X-axis; x is never positive; $V = (0, 0)$;
       $F = (-\frac{1}{4}, 0)$; directrix: $x = \frac{1}{4}$.
   (f) Parabola; symmetric to the X-axis; x is never negative; $V = (0, 0)$;
       $F = (\frac{1}{12}, 0)$; directrix: $x = -\frac{1}{12}$.
   (i) Parabola; symmetric to the Y-axis; y is never negative; $V = (0, 0)$;
       $F = (0, 4)$; directrix: $y = -4$.
   (l) Parabola; symmetric to the Y-axis; y is never positive; $V = (0, 0)$;
       $F = (0, -4)$; directrix: $y = 4$.
2. (a) $12x = y^2$.   (c) $12x + y^2 = 0$.
   (e) $49 = 11x^2$, or $121x = 7y^2$.
3. (a) $(0, 0), (1, 1)$.   (c) $(0, 0), (1, 1)$.
   (e) $(-3, 9), (2, 4)$.

Exercise 59, page 334

1. The type of curve, and foci are:

   (a) Ellipse $(1 \pm \sqrt{3}, -2)$.   (c) Circle; $(1, -2)$.
   (e) Hyperbola; $(-4, 2), (6, 2)$.
   (g) Hyperbola; $(0, 0), (0, 10)$.
   (i) Parabola; $(2.5, -3)$.   (k) Parabola; $(2, 0)$.
   (m) Hyperbola; $(1 \pm 2\sqrt{13}, -2)$.
3. $3(x - 2)^2 + (y - 1)^2 = 12$.
5. $(x - 1)^2 - 3(y - 11)^2 = 12$.
7. $16(x + 1)^2 + 25(y + 1)^2 = 400$, or
   $25(x - 2)^2 + 9(y - 3)^2 = 225$.
9. $16(x - 1)^2 + 25(y - 3)^2 = 400$.

Exercise 61, page 350

1. (a) Range: All positive real numbers; function is one-one.

3. (d) Range: All real numbers ≥ 1; function is many-one.
   (f) Range: All real numbers ≥ 2; function is many-one.

5. (a) 2^{x+1}.   (c) $2^{2x} - 2^{-2x}$.
   (e) $2^{2x} + 2^{-2x} - 2$.   (g) 4.

Exercise 62, page 353

1. (a) -3.   (c) -1.   (e) 1.   (g) 3.
   (i) Nonexistent.   (k) -2.   (m) 0.   (o) 2.

2. (a) $x = \log_{10} 5$.   (c) $\log_{10} 2 \doteq 0.3010$.

3. (a) $10^{0.4771} \doteq 3$.   (c) $10^y = x$.

Exercise 63, page 389

4. (a) 18.15.   (c) 0.00001855.   (e) 1.414.
   (g) 23,940.   (i) 0.02723.   (k) 0.1066.
   (m) 5.092.   (o) -0.06979.

6. (a) $x = 2.322$.   (c) $x = 5.288$.

7. (a) $x = 3.322$.

Exercise 65, page 396

2. (a) $a^3 - 3a^2b + 3ab^2 - b^3$.
   (c) $27a^3 + 54a^2b + 36ab^2 + 8b^3$.
   (e) $1 - 3x + 3x^2 - x^3$.
   (g) $16a^4 + 32a^3b + 24a^2b^2 + 8ab^3 + b^4$.
   (i) $1 + 4x + 6x^2 + 4x^3 + x^4$.
   (k) $a^5 - 5a^4b + 10a^3b^2 - 10a^2b^3 + 5ab^4 - b^5$.
   (m) $243a^5 + 810a^4b + 1080a^3b^2 + 720a^2b^3 + 240ab^4 + 32b^5$.
   (o) $1 - 5x + 10x^2 - 10x^3 + 5x^4 - x^5$.

3 2.7.

Exercise 66, page 372

1. (a) $y = (x - 1)^2$.   (c) $x^2 + 4y^2 = 100$.
   (e) $x^2 - y^2 = 4$.   (g) $x + y = 1$.
   (k) $y^2 = (x - 1)(x - 2)^2$.

Exercise 68, page 384

1. (a) $(3\sqrt{3}/2, 3/2)$.   (c) $(0, 0)$.   (e) $(0, -4)$.
   (g) $(5 \cos 20°, -5 \sin 20°)$ (i) $(0, 2)$.

3. (a) $x^2 + y^2 = 25$.   (c) $y = 5$.   (e) $x = y$.
   (g) $x^2 + y^2 - 10y = 0$.   (i) $x^2 + 8y - 16 = 0$.

4. (a) $(x^2 + y^2)^3 = 4a^2x^2y^2$.
   (c) $(x^2 + y^2)^3 = a^2(x^2 - y^2)^2$.
   (e) $(x^2 + y^2 - ax)^2 = b^2(x^2 + y^2)$.
   (g) $(x^2 + y^2)^2 = 2a^2xy$.

Exercise 69, page 395

1. $s = 0, 16, 64, 144, 256, 400$ ft, respectively.
2. (a) 32 ft/sec.   (c) 128 ft/sec.
3. (e) 97.6 ft/sec.
4. (e) $(16h + 32)$ft/sec.
5. (e) $(16h + 32k)$ft/sec.

Exercise 70, page 401

1. (a) $s = 10, 0, -8, -14, -18$ (distance units), respectively.
   (b) speed $= |2t - 11|$ (distance units/time unit).
   (c) 11, 9, 7, 5, 3 (distance units/time unit), respectively.
   (d) Upward when $t > \frac{11}{2}$; downward when $t < \frac{11}{2}$; at rest at $t = \frac{11}{2}$; at $s = 0$ when $t = 1$ or 10.
2. Speed at which bullet hits ground: 96 ft/sec.
4. 5 seconds; 160 ft/sec.

Exercise 71, page 405

1. Slope $=$: (a) 2.   (c) -4.   (e) $2a$.
2. Slope $=$: (a) 7.   (c) 9.   (e) $2a + 5$.

Exercise 72, page 408

1. $f'(x) = x$; $f'(3) = 3$.   3. $f'(x) = x + 3$; $f'(3) = 6$.
5. $f'(x) = 0$; $f'(3) = 0$.   7. $f'(x) = 1$; $f'(3) = 1$.
9. $f'(x) = 0$; $f'(3) = 0$.

Exercise 73, page 411

2. (a) $6x - 2$.   (c) $64x$.   (e) $1 - 108x^3$.
   (g) $4x - 3x^2$.   (i) $4x - 2$.
   (k) $-1 - 2x - 3x^2 - 4x^3 - 5x^4$.   (m) $x + 2x^4 - 1$.

Exercise 74, page 413

1. Length $=$ width $= 6$ ft.   3. 144 ft.
5. 2 in.   7. 40 ft.

Exercise 75, page 414

2. Problem 2: Speed $= |96 - 32t|$; Problem 4: Speed $= 32t$; Problem 6: Speed $= |2t + 1|$.
4. Note: The following answers are not unique:
   (a) $x^2 + 7$.   (c) $x^4 + 11$.   (e) $(x^3/3) + \sqrt{2}$.
   (g) $x + \pi$.   (i) $x^2 + x^3$.   (k) $2x + 99$.
   (m) $\frac{2}{3}x^3$.   (o) $(x^2/2) + x$.

Exercise 76, page 417

1. Note: In the following, r may be replaced by any real number, to arrive at any one of the total set of answers:
   (a) r.   (c) $-x + r$.   (e) $-x^2 + r$.

(g) $3x - x^2 + r$.   (i) $x^3 + x^2 - x + r$.

(k) $\frac{1}{4}x^4 + \frac{1}{3}x^3 - \frac{1}{2}x^2 + x + r$.   (m) $\frac{1}{3}x^3 + x^2 + x + r$.

(o) $\frac{1}{3}x^3 - x + r$.

2. (a) $f(t) = 16t^2$; $f(10) = 1600$.

Exercise 77, page 420

1. (a) $\frac{8}{3}$.   (c) $\frac{16}{3}$.   (e) $\frac{1}{2}$.   (g) $\frac{1}{4}$.

Exercise 78, page 427

1. (a) 2 in. lb.   (c) 4 in. lb.   (e) $(2/a)$ in. lb.

3. $S_{0.5}$ and $S_{0.2}$ are respectively:

(a) 1.75; 2.28.   (c) 3.50; 4.56.

(e) 0.25; 0.4.   (g) 0.0625; 0.16.

4. (a) $(x^2/2) + r$.   (c) $x^2 + r$.

(e) $(\frac{3}{2})x^2 + r$.   (g) $x + r$.

(i) $(\frac{3}{2})x^2 - x + r$.

Exercise 79, page 433

1.

Grade	Frequency	Cumulative Frequency	Cumulative Relative Frequency
54	1	1	0.083
56	1	2	0.167
65	1	3	0.250
72	3	6	0.500
75	1	7	0.583
78	1	8	0.667
83	2	10	0.833
87	1	11	0.917
92	1	12	1.000

Class Intervals	Frequency	Cumulative Frequency	Cumulative Relative Frequency
50–60	2	2	0.167
60–70	1	3	0.250
70–80	5	8	0.667
80–90	3	11	0.917
90–100	1	12	1.000

3.

Letters	Frequency	Cumulative Frequency	Cumulative Relative Frequency
1	1	1	0.033
2	5	6	0.200
3	4	10	0.333
4	6	16	0.533
5	1	17	0.567

3.—*contd.*

Letters	Frequency	Cumulative Frequency	Cumulative Relative Frequency
6	1	18	0.600
7	3	21	0.700
8	1	22	0.733
9	1	23	0.767
10	3	26	0.867
11	1	27	0.900
12	1	28	0.933
13	2	30	1.000

Class Intervals	Frequency	Cumulative Frequency	Cumulative Relative Frequency
0–3	10	10	0.333
3–6	8	18	0.600
6–9	5	23	0.767
9–12	5	28	0.933
12–15	2	30	1.000

6.

Hours	Frequency	Cumulative Frequency	Cumulative Relative Frequency
720	1	1	0.050
840	1	2	0.100
860	1	3	0.150
940	1	4	0.200
970	1	5	0.250
980	3	8	0.400
990	1	9	0.450
1010	1	10	0.500
1040	1	11	0.550
1100	1	12	0.600
1120	2	14	0.700
1130	1	15	0.750
1220	1	16	0.800
1280	1	17	0.850
1300	1	18	0.900
1340	1	19	0.950
1410	1	20	1.000

Class Intervals	Frequency	Cumulative Frequency	Cumulative Relative Frequency
700–800	1	1	0.050
800–900	2	3	0.150
900–1000	6	9	0.450
1000–1100	3	12	0.600
1100–1200	3	15	0.750
1200–1300	3	18	0.900
1300–1400	1	19	0.950
1400–1500	1	20	1.000

7. (a)

Score	Frequency	Cumulative Frequency	Cumulative Relative Frequency
51	1	1	0.067
55	1	2	0.133
58	1	3	0.200
62	1	4	0.267
64	1	5	0.333
67	1	6	0.400
71	1	7	0.467
73	1	8	0.533
74	1	9	0.600
75	1	10	0.667
77	1	11	0.733
78	1	12	0.800
90	1	13	0.867
91	1	14	0.933
94	1	15	1.000

Class Intervals	Frequency	Cumulative Frequency	Cumulative Relative Frequency
50–60	3	3	0.200
60–70	3	6	0.400
70–80	6	12	0.800
80–90	1	13	0.867
90–100	2	15	1.000

Exercise 80, page 436

1. Ungrouped mean, 74.1; grouped mean, 75.0, ungrouped median, 72; grouped median, 76.0.

3. Ungrouped mean, 5.8; grouped mean, 5.6; ungrouped median, 4; grouped median, 4.9.

6. Ungrouped mean, 1066; grouped mean, 1065; ungrouped median, 1010; grouped median, 1033.

7. (a) Ungrouped mean, 72.0; grouped mean, 72.3; ungrouped median, 73; grouped median, 72.5.

Exercise 81, page 437

1. Ungrouped: 65; 83; 56; 87; 83.
   Grouped: 70.0; 83.3; 56.0; 89.3; 80.1.

3. Ungrouped: 3; 9; 2; 11; 7.
   Grouped: 2.2; 8.7; 0.9; 11.4; 7.3.

6. Ungrouped: 970; 1130; 840; 1300; 1120.
   Grouped: 933; 1200; 850; 1300; 1147.

7. (a) Ungrouped: 62; 78; 55; 91; 77.
       Grouped: 62.5; 78.8; 55.0; 92.5; 76.8.

Exercise 82, page 440

1. Ungrouped: 38; 18; 11.0.
   Grouped: 50; 13.3; 11.5.
3. Ungrouped: 12; 6; 3.7.
   Grouped: 15; 6.5; 3.8.
6. Ungrouped: 690; 160; 176.
   Grouped: 800; 267; 177.
7. (a) Ungrouped: 43; 16; 12.5.
   　　Grouped: 50; 16.3; 12.5.

Exercise 84, page 448

1. (a) $\frac{1}{26}$.   (c) $\frac{5}{26}$.   (e) 0.
2. (a) $\frac{1}{6}$.   (c) $\frac{1}{2}$.   (e) 1.   (g) 0.   (i) $\frac{5}{6}$.
3. (a) $\frac{1}{13}$.   (c) $\frac{1}{52}$.   (e) $\frac{3}{4}$.
6. (b) $\frac{1}{4}$.   (d) $\frac{1}{3}$.
7. (b) $\frac{1}{8}$.   (d) $\frac{1}{2}$.   (e) $\frac{1}{2}$.

Exercise 85, page 453

1. 456, 976.   2. (a) 67,600.   (c) 1,336,336.
3. (a) 12.   (c) $\frac{1}{4}$.
4. (a) 216.   (c) $\frac{125}{216}$.   (e) $\frac{5}{72}$.
5. (b) $\frac{1}{1024}$.
6. (b) $\frac{1}{2704}$.   (d) $\frac{51}{1352}$.   (f) $\frac{1}{52}$.
7. (a) $\frac{1}{32}$.   8. (a) 64.   (c) 32.

Exercise 86, page 456

2. (a) 1.   (c) 120.   (e) 479,001,600.
3. (a) 12.   (c) 95,040.   (e) 479,001,600.
5. (a) 7.   (c) 210.   (e) 2520.   (g) 5040.
7. (a) 6.   10. (a) 120.   (c) 24.   (e) 3125.
11. (a) 120.   (c) $\frac{1}{5}$; $\frac{1}{5}$; $\frac{2}{5}$.

Exercise 87, page 460

1. (a) 6.   (c) 20.   (e) 60.
2. (a) 20.   (c) 60.
4. (a) 362,880.   (c) 10,080.
6. 170.   8. $\frac{1}{4}$.   10. 720.

Exercise 88, page 464

1. (a) 26.   (b) 358,800   4. 4.
6. (a) 64.   (c) 24.   8. 450; 150; 200.
9. 72; 48.   11. 120.   13. $\frac{1}{216}$; $\frac{1}{1024}$.
15. (a) 1.   (c) 360.

Exercise 89, page 468

1. (a) 5.   (c) 35.   (e) 28.   (g) 1.
3. (a) 28.   5. 35.   7. 20; 15; 1; 1.
9. (a) $\frac{1}{20}$.   (c) $\frac{9}{20}$.   (e) $\frac{1}{20}$.
12. 180.   14. 1326; 270,725.
16. 2197/20,825, or approximately 0.1.
18. (a) 358,800.   (c) 2600.   (e) 17,576.
20. 120; 64; 112.

Exercise 90, page 476

1. (a) $\frac{1}{2}$.   (b) $\frac{1}{2}$.   (c) $\frac{1}{6}$.   (d) $\frac{5}{6}$.
    (e) $\frac{1}{12}$.   (f) $\frac{5}{12}$.
3. (a) $\frac{1}{1024}$.   (c) $\frac{11}{1024}$.   (e) $\frac{1013}{1024}$.
5. (a) $\frac{1}{221}$; $\frac{1}{169}$.   (c) $\frac{188}{221}$; $\frac{144}{169}$.
7. (a) $\frac{1}{35}$; $\frac{27}{343}$.   (c) $\frac{4}{35}$; $\frac{64}{343}$.
    (e) $\frac{18}{35}$; $\frac{144}{343}$.

Exercise 91, page 480

1. (a) 0.6   (b) 0.24; 0.24; 0.36; 0.16.
    (c) 0.096; 0.288; 0.432; 0.216; 0.064.
3. (a) 0.59049.   (c) 0.0729.   (e) 0.00045.   (g) 0.40951.
4. $\frac{65}{81} \doteq 0.802$; $\frac{665}{729} \doteq 0.912$.
6. $66\frac{2}{3}\%$; 75%.   8. 75%.   10. 2.9701%.

Exercise 92, page 483

1. The odds in favor of 1 are 0:1; of 2, 1:35; of 3, 1:17; of 4, 1:11; of 5, 1:8; of 6, 5:31; of 7, 1:5; of 8, 5:31; of 9, 1:8; of 10, 1:11; of 11, 1:17; of 12, 1:35.
3. $\frac{9}{10}$.   5. (a) 0.001.   (b) − $3.99.   (c) $14.56 (loss).
6. Expense money: $10.

Exercise 93, page 490

2. (a) Using either the 2s or the 3s criterion, the coin is true.
    (b) Using either the 2s. or the 3s criterion, the coin is untrue.
5. (a) Under either the 2s or the 3s criterion: Yes.
    (c) Under either the 2s or the 3s criterion: No.
    (e) Under the 2s criterion: Yes; under the 3s criterion: No.
    (g) The probability that this will happen is $\frac{1}{1296}$, which means that either under the 2s criterion ($\doteq 0.05$), or under the 3s criterion ($\doteq 0.003$), the dice must be considered to be loaded.
7. (a) Under either the 2s or the 3s criterion: No.
    (c) Under the 2s criterion: No; under the 3s criterion: Yes.
    (e) Under either the 2s or the 3s criterion: Yes.
9. (a) A test is not feasible in this case.
    (c) A test is not feasible in this case.

(e) A test is feasible in this case, under the $2s$ criterion. At least 85 right would demonstrate that Tom's claim is justified; fewer, and he would have to admit that it is not. Under the $3s$ criterion, a test is not feasible in this case.

12. Under the $2s$. criterion, at least 108; under the $3s$ criterion, at least 117.

INDEX

207522
CLG

510 ROSE

207522

DATE DUE

APR 10 '81		
AP 20 '87		

DEMCO